Ingo Berensmeyer
Author Fictions

Ingo Berensmeyer
Author Fictions

Narrative Representations of Literary Authorship since 1800

DE GRUYTER

ISBN 978-3-11-221501-2
e-ISBN (PDF) 978-3-11-105616-6
e-ISBN (EPUB) 978-3-11-105618-0

Library of Congress Control Number: 2023937346

Bibliographic information published by the Deutsche Nationalbibliothek
The Deutsche Nationalbibliothek lists this publication in the Deutsche Nationalbibliografie;
detailed bibliographic data are available on the internet at http://dnb.dnb.de.

© 2025 Walter de Gruyter GmbH, Berlin/Boston
This volume is text- and page-identical with the hardback published in 2023.
Cover image: Lesser Ury, *Frau am Schreibtisch*, 1898, Alte Nationalgalerie (Staatliche Museen zu Berlin – Preußischer Kulturbesitz)
Printing and binding: CPI books GmbH, Leck

www.degruyter.com

I have no more made my booke, then my booke hath made me.
– Montaigne

A writer who writes around the sentence "I am writing" fulfils the modern conception of authorship.
– Friedrich Kittler

Contents

Introduction: How Literature Makes Authors —— 1

Part I Literary Authorship in History and Theory

1 Towards a Literary History of Literary Authorship —— 19
   Combining Literary Sociology and Criticism —— 19
   Levels of Abstraction —— 26
   Reading Authorship Historically —— 31
   Authorship Today —— 45

2 Authors, Works, Audiences: Conceptual Foundations —— 53
   Authors and Narrators —— 53
   A Rhetorical Model —— 64
   Crossing the Gap —— 68
   Author, Work, Audience: An Interactional Loop —— 72

Part II Author-Making and Social Form in the Nineteenth Century

3 *Lost Illusions*: Balzac's Brutal Materialism —— 85

4 Compromise Formation in the English Literary *Bildungsroman* —— 99
   "The pursuit of literature": Bulwer-Lytton's *Ernest Maltravers* (1837) —— 102
   Taking to Authorship in Dickens's *David Copperfield* (1849–1850) and Thackeray's *Pendennis* (1848–1850) —— 103

5 The Novel of Allopoetic Deformation: Herman Melville's *Pierre* (1852) —— 115

6 "Sign it like a queen": Writing Female Authors in the Victorian Novel —— 127
   Charlotte Brontë, Rose Ellen Hendriks, Christina Rossetti —— 127
   A *Bildungsroman* in Verse: Elizabeth Barrett Browning's *Aurora Leigh* (1856) —— 133

"Lady Novelists" —— **137**
"Distorted Benthamism": Thomas Hardy's *The Hand of Ethelberta* (1876) and the Novels of Mary Braddon —— **140**

7 Starving in the Reading Room: Precarious Economies of Authorship in Late Victorian Fiction —— **153**
From 'We' to 'I': Anthony Trollope's *An Editor's Tales* (1870) —— **154**
"A trackless desert of print": George Gissing's *New Grub Street* (1891) —— **161**
"The off-chance of success": George Paston's *A Writer of Books* (1898) —— **170**

8 Curious Double Lives: Puzzles of Authorship in James, Kipling, and Beerbohm —— **173**
Henry James's Stories of the Literary Life —— **175**
Rudyard Kipling's Authorship Gothic —— **184**
Max Beerbohm's *Seven Men* (1919) —— **188**

Part III Modernist Author Fictions

9 The Ambivalence of Promise in Arthur Machen, E. M. Forster, and Henry Green —— **195**
Arthur Machen's *The Hill of Dreams* (1904) —— **198**
E. M. Forster's *The Longest Journey* (1907) —— **203**
Henry Green's *Blindness* (1926) —— **207**

10 "Do you seriously believe in literature?" Comic Turns from Aldous Huxley to Kingsley Amis —— **213**
"Humble Heroisms": Aldous Huxley's *Crome Yellow* (1921), Evelyn Waugh's *Vile Bodies* (1930) and *Scoop* (1938) —— **214**
"Hidden Souls": Authorial Celebrity in W. A. Darlington's *Wishes Limited* (1922) and William Caine's *The Author of "Trixie"* (1924) —— **218**
Author Hunting: N. O. Youman's *Best Seller* (1930), Anthony Powell's *What's Become of Waring* (1938), and Kingsley Amis's *I Like It Here* (1958) —— **224**

11 "Writing's a mug's game": Novels of Resentment and Regeneration in the 1930s and 1940s —— **233**
George Orwell's *Keep the Aspidistra Flying* (1936) —— **235**

"Everything that was literature has fallen from me": Samuel Beckett, Henry Miller, and Lawrence Durrell —— 240
Stevie Smith's *Novel on Yellow Paper* (1936) —— 245
"What an abominable occupation": Roland Camberton's *Scamp* (1950) —— 250

12 Working Women: Figurations of Female Authorship in Postwar Britain —— 255

The Feminine Point of View —— 255
Exorcism of the 'Lady Novelist': Elizabeth Taylor's *A View of the Harbour* (1947) and *Angel* (1957) —— 262
Meeting *The Cost of Living* (1956): Diana Gardner and Kathleen Farrell —— 265
Multiple Narrative Identities: Mary Renault's *The Friendly Young Ladies* (1944) —— 268
"A fine woman bashing away at a typewriter": Muriel Spark's *The Girls of Slender Means* (1963) —— 271

Part IV From Postmodernist Metafiction to Contemporary Autofiction

13 The Validity of Authorship: Postwar British Metafiction from Muriel Spark to William Golding —— 279

Beyond the Uncertainty Principle: Muriel Spark's *The Comforters* (1957) —— 282
"Telling the literal truth": Julian Mitchell's *The Undiscovered Country* (1968) —— 285
Fiction as a Tool of Knowledge: Iris Murdoch's *The Black Prince* (1973) —— 288
"Orpheus on the National Health": Russell Hoban's *Kleinzeit* (1974) —— 291
The 'Isness' of Reality: William Golding's *The Paper Men* (1984) —— 295

14 "The unreckoned consequences of art": Authorial Realism in Munro, Carver, Roth, and Moore —— 301

A Bad Smell in the House of Fiction: Alice Munro's "Material" (1973) —— 302
Raymond Carver's "Put Yourself in My Shoes" (1972) and "Intimacy" (1986) —— 306

"The rest was so much fiction": Philip Roth's *The Ghost Writer* (1979) —— **309**

"Tell them you're a walking blade": Lorrie Moore's "How to Become a Writer" (1982) —— **314**

15 Authorship Horror: Stephen King's *Misery* (1987) —— 319

16 The Tremor of Genre: Making and Unmaking Writers in Suspense Fiction —— 331

Authors as Detectives and Criminals: Patricia Highsmith's *The Tremor of Forgery* (1969) —— **332**

The Stolen Plot: John Colapinto's *About the Author* (2001) and Jean Hanff Korelitz's *The Plot* (2021) —— **335**

Romance Authorship: Colleen Hoover's *Verity* (2018) and the Dangers of Fiction —— **340**

Powerful Fictions of the Real: Chris Power's *A Lonely Man* (2021) and Hari Kunzru's *Red Pill* (2020) —— **342**

17 Economies of Authorship in Contemporary (Auto-)Fiction: Between Expressivism and Institutionalism —— 347

The Authenticity of Suffering: Dave Eggers's *A Heartbreaking Work of Staggering Genius* (2000) —— **350**

Bildungsroman Revisited: Sheila Heti's *How Should a Person Be?* (2012) and Lily King's *Writers & Lovers* (2020) —— **356**

Authorship and the (In)Authenticity of 'Race': Percival Everett's *Erasure* (2001) —— **363**

Forgery, Author Fiction, and the Canon: Arthur Phillips's *The Tragedy of Arthur* (2011) —— **366**

The Lives of Others: Rachel Cusk's *Outline* Trilogy (2014–2018) —— **370**

Conclusion —— 377

Appendix 1: An Incomplete List of Authorship Narratives, 1800–2022 —— 385

1800–1850 —— **385**
1851–1900 —— **385**
1901–1950 —— **389**
1951–2000 —— **392**
2001–2022 —— **398**

Appendix 2: Quantitative Survey, 1800–2022 —— 403

List of Illustrations and Tables —— 405

Glossary —— 407

Acknowledgements —— 409

References —— 411

Index —— 447

Introduction: How Literature Makes Authors

Charles Dickens, Patricia Highsmith, Thomas Hardy, Rachel Cusk, George Orwell, Iris Murdoch, and Stephen King make strange bedfellows, but there is one thing they all have in common: they have written novels about novelists. There are now so many of these that a reviewer in the *Guardian* (Hill 2022) called this a "moth-eaten [...] tradition" of "literary navel gazing", asking "who on earth wants to read another one?" Even Kurt Vonnegut, who referred to an even more intimate body part in his warning against excessive self-referentiality in literature,[1] is guilty as charged, having created the memorable Kilgore Trout, a writer of paperback science fiction novels whose fictional life extends across several of Vonnegut's works.

The persistence of self-referential representations of authorship in narrative fiction, however, is not only evidence of authors' ongoing interest in this topic. The success of those novels also bears witness to the fact that many readers share this fascination with fictional author figures. It is the more surprising, then, that this phenomenon has apparently never been comprehensively and systematically studied. The present book is an attempt to set this right. Its aim is to explore works of narrative fiction that feature writers as characters or narrators, and to suggest theoretical and historical perspectives on the representation of literary authorship in 'author fiction'.

Authors make literature, but literature also makes authors. This is what the elusive author Morelli in Julio Cortázar's 1963 novel *Hopscotch* calls "the strange self-creation of the author through his work" (Cortázar 2014, 405). Such self-creation through the work is made explicit in narrative texts that refer to and reflect on material facts and immaterial myths of authorship. By telling stories about invented authors, actual authors invite their audiences to reconsider the meanings and values of authorship, and of literature in general. Works of author fiction question or affirm prevailing notions of literary creation and production. They engage with existing ideas and practices of literary authorship, which are social and political as well as aesthetic. Moreover, writers of author fiction may be indulging in some magical thinking about changing their own position in the aesthetic and economic networks of the literary field.

In this book, I use the term 'author fictions' for the abstract concepts and performative expressions of literary authorship that can be realised historically with-

---

[1] In an interview for the *Paris Review* in 1977, he said: "I think it can be tremendously refreshing if a creator of literature has something on his mind other than the history of literature so far. Literature should not disappear up its own asshole, so to speak" (Vonnegut 2011, 42).

in the rhetorical conventions, social forms, and media infrastructures that govern the literary field at any given time. These are fictions in a general or philosophical sense. Works of author fiction (as a literary category) are concrete textual manifestations that draw on author fictions in the former sense, on abstract models, concepts, or figures of authorship (cf. Guttzeit 2017). Such works contribute to the generation, confirmation, intensification, modification, subversion, or transformation of these concepts – making literary history in the process.

Author characters in works of fiction, like Cortázar's Morelli, are often more than mere fictionalised stand-ins for their actual, flesh-and-blood authors. In writing about authors and authorship, writers do not simply write about themselves. They perform certain concepts of authorship by putting ideas into practice. They select from a range of possibilities and realise some of them while ignoring or rejecting others. And they expand (or at times contract) the possible positions of authors in literature and in wider cultural and social spaces. As authorships change over time, their dynamic and conflicting shifts are not merely registered but actively shaped and reshaped in such works. From the eighteenth century onwards, scenarios of authorship in narrative fiction have been crucial for establishing moments of literary modernity, creating occasions of reflexivity and friction in which new paradigms of literary creation and creativity could and did emerge. The present book unfolds a *literary* history of modern literary authorship, attentive to the interfaces between changing narrative forms and genres and emerging socio-economic formations and practices of authorship. Ranging from the Victorian *bildungsroman* to contemporary autofiction, my readings focus on the literary forms and rhetorical strategies actual authors use to negotiate the material (social) forms of authorship and changing notions of narrative authority in fiction.[2]

To get to the bottom of these processes and their dynamic interrelations, I adapt a set of tools from narrative theory and literary sociology, since author-making is a social as well as a textual process. The social reproduction of authorship takes place both inside and outside the literary text. In this respect, I follow Pierre Bourdieu's lead "to abolish the singularity of the 'creator' in favour of the relations which made the work intelligible, only better to rediscover it at the end of the task of reconstructing the space in which the author finds himself encompassed and included as a point" (1996, xvii). Some works make these relations more explicit by 'encompassing and including' authors as characters or narrators.

---

[2] In this, my book can be seen as a counterpart to Dorothee Birke's *Writing the Reader*, which investigates "the history of the novel [as] a history of shifting views of the value of novel reading" (2016, back cover). Similarly, I explore the history of narrative fiction as a history of changing ideas, values, and practices relating to authors, authorship, and literary creation.

It is in the novel, more than in any other literary genre, that the problem of literary authorship has been most fully reflected over the past three centuries. Lyric poetry rarely draws attention to the role of the poet as author or the processes of writing and publishing. Epic poems or, more recently, verse novels sometimes do.[3] In drama, the epic mode of introducing a narrator as a character on the stage is a special case, and there are few plays in which literary authorship is a major theme (Goethe's *Torquato Tasso* comes to mind, Pirandello's *Six Characters in Search of an Author*, or Tim Crouch's *The Author*). The 'authorship play' will have to wait for a different study. In narrative fiction, the often close, sometimes challenging alignment between characters, narrators, and their authors harbours an unwritten history of this aspect of literary form.[4]

After establishing a historical and theoretical foundation in part I, the book proceeds chronologically through three major historical periods: the Victorian age (part II), the late nineteenth to mid-twentieth century (part III), and the later twentieth to early twenty-first century (part IV). The large number of texts that could potentially have been included made some hard choices necessary.[5] The only legitimate apologies for my selection reside in the natural limitations of time and space, accompanied by the hope that these readings will be sufficiently representative while also opening a field for future studies.

A key inspiration for my work has been Mark McGurl's study of the emergence of institutional creative writing programmes, *The Program Era*, a best-practice example of the combination of literary criticism and sociology. McGurl introduces the term "autopoetics" to describe a cultural system that turns the "reflexive production of the 'modernist artist'" into a vital part of the modern artist's job (2009, 48). This coinage highlights the mutual implication of personal expression and institutional formation in the very idea and practice of creative writing. It combines *poetics* (the making of literature) with the concept of self-creation or self-perpetuation (*autopoiesis*) derived from biological systems theory (Maturana/Varela 1980 and 1988). Similarly, I describe "the strange self-creation" of authors "through [their] work" (Cortázar 2014, 405), as a process of *authorpoiesis*. By this I mean the reflexive-performative construction of a relational space in which

---

[3] I discuss Elizabeth Barrett Browning's *Aurora Leigh* in the context of the literary *bildungsroman* [→ ch. 6].
[4] Previous studies of 'author fiction' tend to focus on a more restricted historical or geographical field, such as Canada (Belleau 1980, Williams 1991) or Latin America (Kerr 1992) in the twentieth century, on contemporary literature (Savu 2009, Longolius 2016, Milne 2021), or on a particular genre like the *bildungsroman* (Buckley 1974, Jeffers 2005, Graham 2019) or the artist novel (Beebe 1964, Lewes 2006, Legleitner 2021).
[5] See appendix 1 for an inevitably incomplete list of titles.

(both fictional and real) authors find themselves "encompassed and included" (Bourdieu 1996, xvii).

'Self-creation' should be understood in the objective as well as subjective sense: it can involve forms of alienation, reification, and self-loss when an authorial persona is fashioned by the pressure of external forces. In these processes, authors as well as their works and their audiences are active, purposeful agents. Writers embark on becoming authors by using autopoetic strategies in their work, devising or suggesting an authorial self; when these strategies are successful, that is when the work is perceived by audiences as indeed 'authorpoietic', this transforms the writer into an author as the product or by-product of the work and its reception. Both processes, textual and social, depend on and stabilise one another. These processes are always at work in literature. Works of author fiction, however, are special cases that make these processes explicit in their content and often in their form. They are also, I will argue, performative: writing and reading such works contribute to the gradual emergence of new paradigms of authorship, new ways of understanding writers as authors.

After a long fallow period, narrative theory has recently been giving more attention to authorial agency as a constant of literary communication, and to seeing narrative as "ultimately not a structure but an action, a teller using resources of narrative to achieve a purpose in relation to an audience" (Phelan 2017, x; cf. Clark/Phelan 2020). Obviously, this has not ended critical debates about the form and extent to which authors are involved, implied, or implicated in narrative texts, about how they relate to elements of the storyworld, and how audiences respond to them. Yet Phelan and others (cf. Herman 2008, Birke/Köppe 2015b, Boyd 2017, Patron 2019 and 2021) have shifted the conversation in narrative theory towards a more realistic view of how actual authors create stories and how actual audiences engage with them.

Traditionally, narrative theory insists on the neat distinction between author and narrator, understanding the former as "a person" and the latter as "a method" (Tillotson 1959, 22). But their distinction, or rather the erasure of the author from the text, though theoretically useful, has never been a complete success. Almost inevitably, critics have felt compelled to reintroduce variants of the "implied author" as either "a construct formed by the reader" (Schmid 2013, par. 20) or "the ultimate source of narrative communication" (Phelan 2017, 156). The conceptual contortions around the "implied author" (cf. Booth 1983, Kindt/Müller 2006) are eloquent testimony to the critics' desire to have their cake and eat it: to exclude actual authors from the critical conversation, in the tradition of New Criticism's "intentional fallacy" (Wimsatt/Beardsley 1954), while at the same time bringing them back in whenever it suits them.

I propose that, ultimately, what audiences do with authors is more important than what authors do or whether their texts do or do not contain an 'implied author'. I will suggest that actual audiences view authors as neither *merely* textual constructs nor *merely* as real persons but rather like the duck-rabbit made famous by Ludwig Wittgenstein: as multistable figures, outside the work one moment, inside the next. Audiences' perceptions of these figures can cross the boundary between text and world from one aspect to the other and back again without ever resulting in a stable identity. Either aspect can be emphasised by writers or readers of texts, and each can become the figure to the other's ground.[6] Writerly and readerly activities negotiate this boundary between degrees of authorial presence and absence in works of fiction.[7]

The tools at our disposal to connect *and* separate authors from their fictions will be discussed in my reconstruction of narratological concepts like the 'authorial narrator' and the 'implied author' [→ ch. 2]. There, I also propose a new approach to the ontological boundary that separates actual and fictional entities when it comes to authors and narrators or characters. This duality of closeness and distance is essential to understanding the relationships between actual and fictional authors inside and outside narrative texts, and the ways in which audiences relate to them. I combine the terminological and theoretical resources of narratology and rhetorical reading with a diachronic perspective on the (social, economic, and literary) histories of forms of author-making.

Author-making, as I understand it, is a dynamic process between authors, texts, and audiences, perhaps best visualised as a loop (see fig. 1). Authors use literary devices, narrative and/or textual strategies and resources in their work to perform, confirm, or invalidate models of authorship; I call these strategies, with McGurl, 'autopoetic' to indicate their involvement in authorial self-making (*auto-* in the sense of 'self-directed'). Autopoetic strategies aim for authorpoietic effects. The work targets, addresses, and anticipates its audiences by means of

---

[6] On the duality of figure and ground in gestalt psychology, as developed by Edgar Rubin, see Iser 2006, 44–45. "During the process of perception", Iser explains, "we always select specific items from the mass of data available to our senses [...]. This assembly turns into a figure that is surrounded by the diffuse data which have, so to speak, ignored" (44). There is, then, a perceived figure and a perceived ground, and it is possible to switch between these but not to focus on both simultaneously. The duck/rabbit image is an example of this interchange.

[7] It would be necessary to consider in more detail than I can provide here the impact of what readers know about the actual author on how they construe that author's presence in the work. For instance, an audience's impression of Kipling's *Kim* as a realist novel, and their view of Kipling as a reliable authority on India, may be influenced by their knowledge about Kipling's Anglo-Indian background, and intensified if they correctly identify the Lahore Museum in the novel's first chapter as the workplace of Kipling's father.

what I call heteropoetic signals (hetero- in the sense of 'other-directed'), for example through adherence to (or deviations from) generic forms, narrative conventions, or stylistic decorum. Audiences will relate the work to their expectations and to established models, and they will draw aesthetic and ethical conclusions about the ideas of authorship that are explicitly or implicitly present in any given text. Writers can influence this process by means of auto- and heteropoetic strategies, but they cannot fully control it because author-making requires validation by actual audiences – audiences who are called upon to balance, in their reading, the boundaries between fiction and reality, possibly by means of what James Phelan calls "double-consciousness" (2017, 8) in their taking of different roles as narrative or authorial audiences (see Phelan 2017, 3–29).

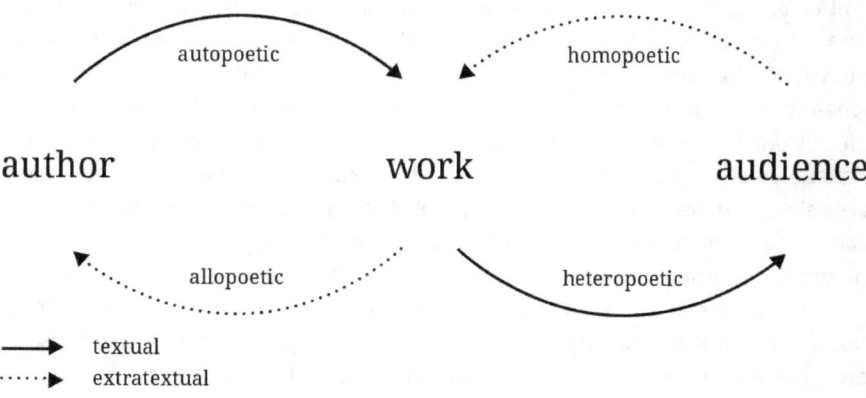

Fig. 1: The authorpoietic loop.

Audiences become attached to authors and their work, they become emotionally invested, and project their own author fiction(s) on the work. I call this audience engagement 'homopoetic'[8] (as in 'adapting or assimilating an object to one's own liking and/or likeness'). The resulting author persona is projected by an audience and thus necessarily resembles that audience's expectations and activities. Such projections need not go very far, but they can extend to the transformation of writ-

---

[8] 'Homoiopoetic' might be the more precise term, since it would more clearly indicate that this is about similarity rather than consubstantiality, but then religious battles have been fought over the difference an iota can make, and 'homopoetic' has the clear advantage of being easier to pronounce. All of these four vectors are 'poietic' as well as 'poetic' in that they refer to the making of objects and agential roles in connection with literature, inside as well as outside the textual dimensions of the work.

ers' houses into museums and tourist destinations, to the assimilation of an author's personal habits or attire, and – in the case of fan fiction – to a transition from consumption to production.

This dynamic then reflects back from the work and its audience reception upon its flesh-and-blood author in what I call 'allopoetic' effects (*allo-* in the sense of 'coming from outside and changing an object into something else'). These include the shaping of authors by existing literary forms, audience assignments of value and reputation, and what happens when authors become an audience in relation to their own creations. At times, a character's cultural presence eclipses that of its author, as in the case of Sherlock Holmes. Because he "feared that he would be known only as the detective's creator" (Edwards 2017), Arthur Conan Doyle tried (and failed) to kill Holmes. A witty variation on this is *Maigret's Memoirs* (1950), supposedly authored by inspector Jules Maigret, Georges Simenon's famous detective, in the French tradition of *auteur supposé* (cf. Jeandillou 2001). Here, Maigret sets the record straight on the errors Simenon committed in his "cheap publication[s]" (Simenon 2016, 16). He notes that, over the many years writing about the inspector, Simenon has "started walking, smoking a pipe, even talking like [his] Maigret" (39). In such cases, the process of creating the author through the work has truly come full circle.

The authorpoietic loop neither denies nor overstates authorial agency. Both actual authors and actual audiences share the work of negotiating the relations between author, text, and world. A performance of authorship (via the text) succeeds only if it is recognised and validated by an audience; only then can authorial performance become truly *performative* and achieve potentially transformative effects in the actual world – not only upon the actual author of the work in question, whose position in the literary field or the wider culture may change due to this performance-based recognition, but also upon concepts, practices, and paradigms of authorship more generally, and the meanings and functions of literature in society. This performativity of literary authorship is thoroughly social as well as textual; it involves authors and audiences as active agents in an ongoing conversation.

The result of this process is a dynamic relationship between author fictions, works of author fiction, actual authors, and audiences. As an alternative to the 'implied author' as the actual author's fictional representative in the work, the loop allows for a variety of the "middle ranges of literary agency" (Helle 2019, 113) between authorial presence and absence, proximity and distance from the text or work, to be achieved by means of different auto- and heteropoetic strategies. It also allows for readerly agency in the form of homo- and allopoetic effects: audiences apply their knowledge and imagination to construe an author persona based on textual and extratextual cues or clues, relating the work to its actual author and to what they know or think they know about this author, thus giving rise to yet another 'author fiction' that readers shape in their minds and that, at least in aggregate, will feed back not only on the work but on the work's actual author as well.

Moreover, I suggest that any work implies an author fiction – some idea of how *this* work's performance of authorship relates to or is informed by the set of historically available concepts of authorship. Some texts leave this relation unmarked; others will occasionally draw their readers' attention to auto- and heteropoetic effects; and yet others – the minority that is this book's key concern– will explicitly, deliberately, and systematically focus on processes of author-making in the text. Narratives that feature one or more (fictional) authors as central characters, or that place a strong emphasis on concepts and practices of authorship, fall into this category.[9]

There are, of course, also novels that include actual historical authors as characters, such as Thomas Mann's *Lotte in Weimar* (1939), Hermann Broch's *Death of Virgil* (1945), David Malouf's *An Imaginary Life* (1978), Jerome Charyn's *The Secret Life of Emily Dickinson* (2011) and Nuala O'Connor's *Miss Emily* (2015), David Lodge's *A Man of Parts* (2011), or Norah Vincent's *Adeline: A Novel of Virginia Woolf* (2015).[10] More rarely, novels feature other (living or dead) writers as characters, such as Daniel Kehlmann in Thomas Glavinic's *Das bin doch ich* (2007) or Gore Vidal as the focaliser of a section of John Boyne's *A Ladder to the Sky* (2018). I decided not to focus on such cases because these are names "one could talk about before one told any stories" (Kripke 2013, 82). In this, I adhere to Saul Kripke's theory of reference, according to which proper names are 'rigid designators' that refer to the same person in every possible world. Invented author characters, by contrast, are "abstract entit[ies]" (73) that exist only by virtue of the storytelling activities of their actual authors; their existence depends on the existence of the works of fiction that contain them. Hence, they allow more freedom to their creators but also force them to make strong choices related to their imaginative (re-)construction of the literary field within their fiction. In addition, I contend

---

9 I use the word 'fictional' here in the sense of 'existing in works of fiction'. Fictional entities exist by virtue of activities of fiction-making. But their existence is not fiction but fact; they are "abstract but quite real" (Kripke 2013, 78). Also, within the work of fiction, their reality is not in doubt, with few exceptions, such as Beerbohm's "Enoch Soames" and Spark's *The Comforters* (briefly mentioned in Kripke 2013, 74) [→ ch. 8, 13].
10 These are now often categorised as 'biofiction'; see Franssen/Hoenselaars 1999, Layne 2020, Lackey 2022. Malouf's *An Imaginary Life* reimagines the life of the Roman poet Ovid; see Boldrini 2012. The inclusion of actual authors in fictional works is not a modern phenomenon; Aristophanes' *The Frogs* (405 BCE) features a literary contest between the (deceased) playwrights Aeschylus and Euripides.

that, as in autofiction, the authenticity effect of the name shared by the actual author and a character or narrator is not as strong as one might think, and that, as in other works of fiction, capable readers will suspend their belief in the reality of the narrated world and enjoy the *frisson* of metalepsis as yet another aesthetic crossover effect.

To describe the writerly and readerly vectors of authorpoiesis even more precisely, I propose to conceptualise the relationship between actual authors and fictional entities (characters, narrators, even *auteurs supposés* like Simenon's Maigret) as a kind of propping or grafting. Similarly, John Frow (2021) has adapted the Freudian metaphor of *Anlehnung*, in English *anaclisis* (Freud 1953, 181), to rethink the relationship between author and writer, but it may equally serve to describe the relationship between actual authors and narrative resources such as narrators or characters. Freud used this "to describe the 'propping' of the infantile sexual instincts on certain bodily functions" (Frow 2021, 20). Analogously, we might say that abstract author fictions are anaclitically attached, in processes of writing and reading, to concrete textual phenomena or narrative resources. Thus, an 'authorial narrator', on the level of the work, could be used to stand in for (a version of) the actual author while still respecting the ontological barrier between reality and fiction. The author is anaclitically propped onto the narrator or character, as it were piggybacking on a narrative resource.

Taking the Freudian analogy further, the cognitive and emotional investment of audiences in fictional entities might be considered as a form of *cathexis* (*Besetzung*, 'attachment' or 'projection'). Authorial attachment works from actual authors towards their text (*autopoetic anaclisis*), readerly attachment from audiences towards their sense of how the work and its author relate to the world (*homopoetic cathexis*). The point of this terminology is not to imitate the finesses of Genettian structuralism but to reconstruct in greater detail the different aspects of the dynamic process that is author-making – the vectors of agency that connect actual and fictional, textual and extratextual, concrete and abstract entities – and to observe how these entities are produced through textual and social processes (see fig. 4 below).

This conceptual model is grounded in a historical trajectory ranging from the Romantic genius to contemporary autofiction. I begin in the early nineteenth century, when narrative fiction, and the novel in particular, develops into the form in which author fictions are predominantly negotiated, and in which the demands of the literary marketplace come to shape the narrative representation of authorship much more significantly than in earlier periods – a shift that Walter Benjamin recognised as one from storyteller to novelist and from the occasional administering of counsel or wisdom to the professional production of novels as entertainment (2006 [1936]). While this reduction cannot do justice to the actual complexity and variety of authorial roles, it is a useful shorthand for the transformation that occurs when, in the early nineteenth century, literary creation and production fall under the economic imperatives of industrialisation.

Thus, briefly and at the risk of caricature, I suggest that the history of author fictions in modernity can be mapped out as a trajectory from the Romantic idea of autonomy to a contemporary regime of visibility. Table 1 below shows successive authorship paradigms and emergent genres or modes of author fiction, offering a tabular summary of the major concepts and the generic or formal innovations with which they are predominantly correlated.

Table 1: Authorship paradigms and emergent genres or modes of 'author fiction'

Romanticism			
genius	autonomy	autobiographical epic	
Realism			
man/woman of letters	professionalism	literary *bildungsroman*	
Modernism			
artist	impersonality	artist novel	*Middlebrow fiction*
master of meaning		novel of resentment	
Postmodernism			
medium	intertextuality	metafiction	*Genre fiction*
witness	authenticity	magic realism	authorship crime,
		testimony	thriller, horror, romance ...
Contemporary			
creative person	visibility	autofiction	fan fiction
star			

In the major cultural transformation now known as 'Romanticism' (or as 'Romanticisms' in the plural),[11] self-expression and literary self-creation were promoted as a new standard in the arts. The poet's self became a topic worthy of representation, even at an epic scale. This development coincided with a new system of copyright legislation in which "artistic work [was] considered to be simultaneously a legal possession of the artist and the emanation of his personality" (Braudy 1997, 422–423). Personal artistic capital could, at least in theory, now be more easily transformed into economic capital. In the form of the *bildungsroman*, personal and artistic autonomy came to be toned down towards imperatives of professionalism, as

---

[11] Already in an address to the MLA by A. O. Lovejoy in 1923, first published in 1924 (see Lovejoy 2019 [1948]).

the natural genius was gradually replaced by the man or woman of letters. The nineteenth-century novel was the form in which authorpoietic processes and questions of narrative authority were primarily negotiated. Authors gained prestige through their integration into professional networks, adherence to the rules of the trade, and an ethos of literary craftsmanship. Romantic autonomy descended into more pragmatic forms of institutional self-realisation. The dialectic of authorial mastery and its ironic withdrawal established a working compromise, never entirely satisfactory, between artistic and social expansions and limitations. Yet, towards the end of the nineteenth century, as Bradley Deane succinctly points out, writers "discarded the roles of soul-baring Romantic poet or friendly mid-Victorian novelist in favor of a rhetoric of artistry designed to keep the artist's personality mysteriously enshrouded" (2003, 92).

Modernism departs from the realist paradigm by stressing the *distance* between artist and society in the *künstlerroman* or artist novel. This distance is at first more social (i.e., anti-bourgeois) than aesthetic, as when Henry James – who claimed the art of fiction as a "sacred office" (James 1984, 46) – rejects the "theory that a boy might be brought up to be a novelist as to any other trade" (1987, 9). In a notebook entry of 22 January 1879, James notes that Anthony Trollope "attempted to bring up [...] his own son on this principle, and the young man became a sheep-farmer in Australia" (ibid.). In late Victorian fiction, the conflict between art and the market is explored most comprehensively in George Gissing's novel *New Grub Street* (1891), where one of the characters rejects James's claims by asking "what on earth is there in typography to make everything it deals with sacred?" (Gissing 2016, 12) [→ ch. 7].

This distance between art and the market, artist and society is radicalised in the aesthetic ideal of impersonality from Flaubert to Joyce and T. S. Eliot. Paradoxically, this authorial non-presence *within* the work coincides with an ever-increasing mass media celebrity status of authors *outside* their works – an irony that has not been lost on cultural critics (Glass 2004, 5–8). God-like in their art, authors were the stuff of human-interest stories in the papers.

This paradigm of impersonality is then further radicalised in postmodernism, when the 'death of the author' yields the strongest possible concept of authorless textuality and intertextuality: Julia Kristeva's and Roland Barthes's vision of the text as "a tissue of quotations", "a multi-dimensional space in which a variety of writings, none of them original, blend and clash" (Barthes 1977, 146). At about the same time, however, and in stark contrast to this formation, we see the rise of witness literature (cf. Engdahl 2002, Craps 2012), predicated on an ideal of personal authenticity: authors make themselves or are made into representatives of particular, often marginalised social communities, traumatic experiences, or 'identities' in the combative sense of identity politics. Instead of dissolving into boundless textuality, authors whose personal experience matches their writing become anchor points for a privileged notion of (authenticated) authenticity.

As we approach the present, struggles between institutionalist and expressivist modalities of making literature and of making authors continue, but they do so in an even more diversified and centrifugal, even dissociated literary field (cf. Hartling 2009). The boundaries between literary fiction and genre fiction are shifting as literary fiction is increasingly commercialised. Recent turns towards literary nonfiction, literary genre fiction, and autofiction tend to de-emphasise the specialness of the author's social position and to stress their ordinariness and relatability. Writers have become – to quote the title of Sally Rooney's 2018 novel – *Normal People*, because the idea of the creative individual has now taken hold of society at large. The expressive and creative self, invented in the Romantic period as energised by what Charles Taylor called "a new poietic power, that of the creative imagination" (Taylor 1992, 198), has turned from an exception – the artist as psychologically divergent from the rest – into a 'new normal'. The "creative ethos" (Florida 2003, 21), according to Andreas Reckwitz (2012), has been expanded into a social norm for the economy and society at large, a "creative economy" (Brouillette 2014).

If authorship has now been normalised to a large extent as merely another instance of a socially ubiquitous demand to be creative, distinction needs to come, more than ever before, from audiences and their response to what authors have to offer them; and authors are called upon to use all the means of social media at their, or their agents' and publisher's, disposal to gain audience attention. This can also be established and maintained by political activism or by encouraging audiences to 'read' an author as the representative of a particular (group) identity. For certain kinds of bestseller success in the age of TikTok, audience attachment can take precedence over even the lowest standards of literary quality.

Today, the boundaries between authors and their texts have again become more permeable, more fluid – a partial reprise but not a simple repetition of the Romantic paradigm. Instead of autonomy or impersonality, let alone boundless intertextuality, authors now strive for, or are pushed towards, visibility, in a few cases even hypervisibility. Instead of emphasising their social or temperamental distinction from non-authors, the aim is to establish a connection with the audience, to come across as 'relatable'. Author characters in contemporary fiction, from Dave Eggers's *A Heartbreaking Work of Staggering Genius* (2000) to Lily King's *Writers & Lovers* (2020), are concurrently normalised; they are presented as not very different from non-authors in that they struggle with personal problems, everyday vicissitudes or triumphs, doubting their vocation or trying not to come across as 'special', arrogant, or crazy. No wonder that Karl Ove Knausgård's epoch-making behemoth of Norwegian autofiction (2009 to 2011), running to some three and a half thousand pages, is simply, if somewhat controversially, titled *Min Kamp* (*My Struggle*).

In some cases, narrative genres themselves develop into sites in which the connections and boundaries between literary and social forms are negotiated and contested, as they are in the author-*bildungsroman* and *künstlerroman*. Initially, those boundaries concern conflicts between Romantic and Realist concepts of authorship, the genius vs. the man or woman of letters; later, between the author as artist and those who regard writing as a craft or trade, as in the 'dignity of literature' debate [→ ch. 4] and the controversy between Henry James and first Anthony Trollope, then Walter Besant [→ ch. 7, 8]; and later still, in modernism, in the struggle about demarcations of taste that has become famous as the "battle of the brows" (Brown/Grover 2012), between those writers proud of what Graham Greene called "the exclusiveness of unsuccess" (2019, 122) bestowed by a minority of readers, and the authors of middlebrow fiction, who sought the acclaim of a mass audience.

In all these struggles, narratives that deal with the topic of authorship are compelled to show their hand. They may be novels of resentment, in the tradition of George Gissing's *New Grub Street* (1891) [→ ch. 7] or novels of regeneration [→ ch. 11], like Henry Miller's *Tropic of Cancer* (1934) or Lawrence Durrell's *The Black Book* (1938). These novels of the 1930s translate their authors' anger at conventional fiction, at what Durrell called "the ancient tinned salad of the subsidised novel" (Durrell 1968, 751) into a stimulus for revitalisation, even in personal and physical terms: "Books should be built of one's tissue or not at all" (Durrell 1977, 121). Disputes over the validity of authorship and the relevance of literature in society continue in the postwar literary world [→ ch. 13], in the tripartite division that David Lodge identified between the 'realists', the 'fabulists' and the 'nonfictionists' (1986, 18–19), as they do today.

Such narratives performatively reflect on the functions and values of literary authorship – as when Dickens, in *David Copperfield* (1849–50), presents authorship as a source of professional respectability, social esteem, and cultural capital, in a self-confirming performance of the generic core of the *bildungsroman* [→ ch. 4]; or when Stephen King, in *Misery* (1987), bemoans the lack of prestige accorded to the writer of popular mysteries, in a performance of authorship that seeks to subvert the all too neat separation between 'high' and 'low', 'literary' and 'genre fiction' [→ ch. 15]; or when Alice Munro, in her short story "Material" (1973), exposes the pretentiousness of a certain kind of late modernist male authorship by presenting and undermining it from a female perspective [→ ch. 14].

In these narrative texts, there is a wide spectrum of similarity and distance between the actual author and fictional author characters. They can be fictions of wish-fulfilment: in *Hadrian the Seventh* (1904), the destitute Frederick Rolfe, better known as 'Baron Corvo', imagines an alternative life for himself in which his alter ego, George Rose, is elected Pope (cf. Symons 1979). More often, they are fictions of disappointment and resignation. Quite frequently, invented authors are set against their actual authors' ideas and ideals or suffer a worse fate than the actual authors wish upon themselves. These are what Hugh Kenner called "shadow selves" (Kenner 1976, 178–179), protagonists who share some biographical facts with their authors but contradict others: Joyce's Stephen, Nabokov's Sebastian Knight and Pnin, Orwell's Gordon Comstock [→ ch. 11]. Yet others constitute radical departures or counterlives: 'Philip Roth' in Roth's *The Counterlife* (1986), Roland Baines in Ian McEwan's *Lessons* (2022).[12]

A history of the infrastructures and institutions of authorship as represented in literature cannot afford to ignore other mechanisms of inclusion or exclusion in the literary field, most notably biases of gender but also of race and class. The marginalisation of female authorship is one such zone in which, despite several decades of feminist research, more work needs to be done. It was easier for women, apparently, to access literary authorship compared to other professions in the nineteenth century. Female authorship has been shown to have been more widespread than previously assumed, especially in the field of periodicals, where many contributors remained anonymous (Onslow 2000, Easley 2004 and 2018, Peterson 2009). Nevertheless, a recent quantitative study shows that the number of women authors of fiction declined significantly in proportion to men between c. 1850 and 1970 (Underwood/Bamman/Lee 2018), confirming the thesis that women were by and large 'edged out' of the literary field (Tuchman/Fortin 2012) by their male competitors. Women writers were regularly denounced as 'scribbling women' or 'lady novelists' producing work of little value in large quantities. Their fictional reflections on authors and authorship are thus of special interest and prime importance to this study. Each part of this book includes readings of texts by women, with chapters dedicated to female authorship in the Victorian period [→ ch. 6] and the mid-twentieth century [→ ch. 12]. Class-based social factors play a role in many of my readings, particularly for the nineteenth and early twentieth century, when social status is the conceptual foundation of the *bildungsroman* [→ ch. 4, 7, 11]. Yet another crucial aspect of authorial self-making is race, which,

---

12 Roland Baines has a lot in common with McEwan, but he ends up as a failed poet and bar piano player instead of "Britain's most successful literary novelist" (Harvey 2022, 17) – whereas his first wife does a Robert Lowell on him, abandoning him and their young child to pursue a stellar literary career, arguably subverting still prevalent gender stereotypes about the genius who sacrifices life for art. –Fictional author characters almost always match their actual author's gender; see fig. 7 in appendix 2 for a quantitative survey of matching and non-matching genders in works of author fiction.

though not as central to this book, is going to be considered in a reading of Percival Everett's *Erasure* [→ ch. 17].

Having traced the duck-rabbit duality of authors from the nineteenth century to the present, this book concludes with a chapter on economies of authorship in novels by Dave Eggers, Sheila Heti, Rachel Cusk, and others that explore tensions between individual expression and institutional constraints [→ ch. 17]. Historically, it seems that works of author fiction are particularly prevalent in transitional periods of crisis and transformation in the literary field. Based on the list compiled for this study [→ appendix 1], the number of such works reaches its two major peaks in the 1890s and the 2000s [→ fig. 5 in appendix 2] , both decades that witness upheavals in the world of publishing – respectively, the end of the three-volume novel and the rise of commercial fiction as mass entertainment in the *fin de siècle*, and the digital transformations of publishing, self-publishing, and the book trade at the start of the new millennium. Such situations of crisis and change pose challenges to authors' professional self-understanding, which are then reflected and refracted in works of author fiction.

Authors make literature, and literature makes authors, then, in precisely this dual sense: by unfolding authorship paradigms and the tensions that reside within them into fictional scenarios, writers perform "the strange self-creation" of authors through their work (Cortázar 2014, 405). On the other hand, through institutional processes, "the relations which [make] the work intelligible" (Bourdieu 1996, xvii), and the recognition mechanisms of the literary field, which transform writings into works, authors are socially produced as unique and singular creators. Audiences attach emotional energy to them. These processes are universally relevant for literature; but they are more intensely scrutinised in novels and stories that have authorship as their topic and feature authors (and, very often, readers) as characters. Such works of author fiction, I argue, take an analytic interest in observing how authors are made, and they experiment with new ways of authorial (self-)creation. They take us closer to the "reflexive-performative matrix" (McGurl 2009, 366) of literature, the source of its variety of forms as well as its social and political power.

Part I Literary Authorship in History and Theory

> 'Tis to create, and in creating live
> A being more intense, that we endow
> With form our fancy, gaining as we give
> The life we imagine [...].
>
> — Byron

1 Towards a Literary History of Literary Authorship

Combining Literary Sociology and Criticism

While there are many established and competing protocols for analysing and interpreting texts and studying readers' responses, the discipline has tended to neglect the creation and production of literature as objects of inquiry. If these aspects become thematic at all, it is in the fields of textual editing and genetic criticism, or in studies of author-publisher relations. Compared to the aspects of production (book history, literary sociology) and reception (hermeneutics, reader response theory, cognitive literary studies), there has been much less research on the aspects surrounding the *creation* of literary works. Unless it took the author out of the equation entirely, literary studies has been vacillating between positions that saw the author as the *destination* or the *point of departure* of textual interpretation.

Methods of textual interpretation that seek to focus meaning in the text's author include psychoanalytic literary theory, which associates artistic creation with the artists' personal wish-fulfilment (Freud 1959), their ailments, neuroses, or unconscious desires. In some famous examples, psychoanalytic theorists pathologised the creative act, as in Freud's reading of *Hamlet* as a manifestation of Shakespeare's Oedipus complex, or in Marie Bonaparte's study of Poe.[13] Locating the source of creativity in the author's unconscious, psychoanalytic criticism reinforced the Romantic myth of the artist as a distinct personality type, the creative individual or 'genius' who deviates from the bourgeois norms of society (Reckwitz 2012, 81–84). It also continued an older tradition of biographical criticism that connects authors' lives to their works in a self-reinforcing cycle. In England, this tradition begins with Aubrey's *Brief Lives* in the seventeenth century and is continued in Johnson's *Lives of the Poets* and many subsequent literary histories and biographies.

Projects of reconstructing an author's intentions, including unintended intentions, or of "understand[ing] a writer better than he understood himself" (Bollnow

---

[13] "I am not thinking of Shakespeare's conscious intention, but believe, rather, that a real event stimulated the poet to his representation, in that his unconscious understood the unconscious of his hero" (Freud 1985, 272; cf. Birke/Butter 2020). Bonaparte's study of Poe (1971) was first published in French in 1933.

1979, 16),[14] ran parallel to the rise of formalist reading strategies within an ahistoricist "pure aesthetic" (Bourdieu 1996, 285). Hermeneutic approaches further removed authors from scrutiny by fixing them as points of origin within the firmament of a tradition that was normatively defined, as in Matthew Arnold's generous universalist phrase, "the best that has been thought and said in the world" (1993 [1864], 37), less generously reducible to what was being taught in British public schools at the time. Canonical authors, in this view, are depersonalised geniuses who share the essential attribute of being part of a select group within a tradition that, by virtue of its greatness, has propelled itself beyond history. The New Critics famously denounced attempts to locate textual meaning in an author's mind as the "intentional fallacy" (Wimsatt/Beardsley 1954). For most professional critics trained in these traditions, the author cannot be the destination of textual interpretation. If it shows up at all in their writings, the "authorial instance" does so merely as a "zero point of discourse", a generative source that remains inaccessible to knowledge (Iser 2013, 122).

To take the author as a point of departure can mean several things. In poststructuralism, it led to an exploration of the "author function" (Foucault 1977) as an important element in the formation of discourses as orders of knowledge and power. Provoked by Foucault's intervention and by Barthes's proclamation of the "death of the author" (Barthes 1977), scholars and critics thought and fought harder about the connections between writers as historical agents and the interpretation of 'their' texts. Instead of being "the unique master of meaning" (Chartier 1994, 28), the author's textual agency comes into view as "dependent" on historical and social forces (Stougaard-Nielsen 2019, 284), his or her textual agency limited by institutional possibilities and constraints. Poststructuralism, far from being the last gasp of authorship in literary theory, thus gave a new life to authorship research.[15]

French scholars played a leading role also in the field of literary sociology, most prominently Pierre Bourdieu (1996; cf. Joch/Wolf 2005, Martin 2010).[16] Liter-

---

[14] As a principle of interpretation, the phrase "to understand the author better than he understood himself" derives from Wilhelm Dilthey (1996, 255); for discussion, see also Berensmeyer 2020b and Guillory 2022, 384–385.
[15] See, among others, Burke 1992, Chamarat/Goulet 1996, Jannidis et al. 1999, Brunn 2001, Irwin 2002, Bennett 2005. That this new life also extends to literary works 'post theory' is argued in Sayers 2021.
[16] Others, less well known in the Anglophone world, include Paul Bénichou (1996), Jean-Benoît Puech (1982), Alain Viala (1985), Jérôme Meizoz (2007, 2011, 2016), José-Luis Diaz (2007, 2011), and Dominique Maingueneau (2004, 2016). Cf. Kiparski 2018 for a brief survey of French-language theories of literary authorship after Barthes and Foucault. Maingueneau's discourse-theoretical concept of 'literary space' as a 'paratopia' (2004) and Meizoz's concept of literary 'postures' (2007) can both be considered as developments of the Bourdieuan notion of authors' "position-taking" (1996,

ary sociology has explored the emergence and institutional stabilisation of the literary field in modernity, and the rise of the profession of the author, as a permanent conflict between aesthetic and economic demands (Bourdieu 1996, Childress 2017, Sapiro/Rabot 2017, Amlinger 2021; cf. also Saunders 1964). In doing so, it has gradually moved away from earlier, deterministic views that saw art as a mere expression or reflection of social reality, towards a more nuanced, dynamic understanding of art and its institutions as shaping forces *within* society. Among other impulses, social systems theory (Luhmann 2000), actor-network theory (Latour 2005), and empirical social research have, each in their own way, contributed to the interdisciplinary formation of a 'new institutionalism' in literary studies, which recognises that "any act of writing is both enabled and constrained by specific institutional bonds" (Scherr/Nünning 2020, 232), and which conceives of authorship as an "assemblage of resources" (Puskar 2019, 442) including people, practices, and texts rather than merely a single individual or an abstract textual function. Such models of distributed agency have become widespread in recent approaches to media history (Drucker 2014). Moreover, studies of the material book and the history of publishing have led to a more complex understanding of historical practices of literary authorship (Sutherland 1976, Finkelstein 2002, Kirschenbaum 2016, Fuchs 2021).[17]

Over the past two decades, numerous research groups as well as individual scholars have made authorship studies into a vibrant subfield of literary and cultural studies.[18] Though concerned with merely a single agency in the "communications circuit" (Darnton 1982; Adams/Barker 2006), authorship studies require interdisciplinary exchanges between book history, textual scholarship, economics, and legal studies, among others. Authorship, in the words of Rebecca Braun, is "not ex-

---

231) in the literary field. Diaz (2007) investigates the rise of imaginary author models in Romanticism as an aesthetic process. In the German reception of Bourdieu, studies have focused on the 'staging' of authorship in literary texts and the public sphere (Künzel/Schönert 2007, Grimm/Schärf 2008, Jürgensen/Kaiser 2011, John-Wenndorf 2014, Kyora 2014). In a Genettian vein, Jean-Benoît Puech (1982) develops a typology of imaginary authors in literature; he is also the author of the novel *La bibliothèque d'un amateur* (1979), which features fictional authors and their books. For the French tradition of *auteurs supposés* and literary 'trickery' (*supercherie*), which is outside the scope of this book, see Jeandillou 2001, Ferguson 2018.

17 In German literary studies, interest in media and their impact on authorship was fuelled by Friedrich Kittler's *Discourse Networks* (1990), stimulating research into historical practices of authorship and copyright (Bosse 2014), authorship and literary form (Wirth 2008), the 'scene of writing' (Campe 1991), and those aspects of literary creation and production that result in an author's works or *oeuvre* (Martus 2007, Spoerhase 2018). For surveys, see Detering (2002), Schaffrick/Willand (2014), and Wetzel (2022).

18 See the bibliography in Berensmeyer/Buelens/Demoor 2019, 444–457.

hausted by the writers who first set pen to paper" but "repeatedly modulated by the many different ways in which the bridge between responsibility for the literary world of the text and the various iterations of the real world that surround it is crossed by different people at different times" (Braun 2020a, 4). Such ties can range from the contribution of a particular writing implement (as part of an authorial 'actor-network') to the shaping of texts by editors and other agents in the publishing process. This perspective calls for a revision of earlier views of the history of literary authorship as a pattern of 'rise and fall' (Gross 1973). Authorship thus comes into view as a set of performative cultural practices which cannot be sufficiently grasped from structuralist or intentionalist positions and should not be presented as residing in a single human agency (cf. Berensmeyer/Buelens/Demoor 2012 and 2019).

Connections, crossings, and modulations between text and world have also come into view from the perspective of the 'new formalism' (cf. Levinson 2007; Theile/Tredennick 2013), which investigates the mutual implications of literary and social or political forms (Levine 2015). One of the most influential studies of this kind, which combines social, institutional, and literary history, has been Mark McGurl's *The Program Era* (2009). Taking up the conflict between aesthetics and economics that marks the literary field, McGurl shows how creative writing programmes in the twentieth century tamed the radical aesthetic impulses of literary modernism, transforming and institutionalising them into a teachable "craft" (McGurl 2009, 409). In McGurl's analysis, texts are marked by the institutional contexts in which they have been written, but they are also documents that intervene in these contexts. Institutions and texts are "nested in [a] larger reflexive-performative matrix" (2009, 366). For literature and literary studies, this means that the aesthetic domain is never completely autonomous. On the contrary, its type or degree of autonomy is the result of institutional processes that, for the most part, tend to remain invisible in the literary text (cf. Amlinger 2021, 673).

In a similar vein, Clayton Childress points out that novels, though they appear to readers as "complete and finished products", are in fact "hodgepodges of experiences, chance encounters, enacted suggestions, demands, enthusiastic support, doubt, and compromises within and across fields and their transitions" (2017, 188–189). It is this complex interplay of enabling and constraining institutions and literary texts that becomes the centre of attention for a literary criticism interested in the creation and production of texts. It would then be the task of literary studies to make these institutional conditions visible again, to re-present in an analysis of the text the (hidden) "reflexive-performative matrix" (McGurl 2009, 366) that has brought the text into the world.

In reassessing the role of the author in the creation of literature, the goal cannot be to revive mystifications of the "zero point of discourse" (Iser 2013, 122) or to reinstate the author as a "master of meaning" (Chartier 1994, 28). The author (as a social role, a professional identity) is part of the institutional infrastructure of literature – neither its origin nor its endpoint but *one* node in a complex network of activities, identities, and tasks that must come together to make literature – to write a poem, perform a play, or publish a novel. This identity, like others, is socially produced – a disposition that can be inhabited, a *habitus* in Bourdieu's sense (1996, 214), or a social role that is acquired. Today, authors still embody a privileged position in relation to 'their' texts. Modern copyright laws ensure their ownership and control over their works (Rose 1993, Bosse 2014); the author's name, next to the title, is the most important "paratext" of a book (Genette 1997, 37–54). Authors win prizes. Residual forms of mystification continue to shape the public image of authors as somehow special and to be admired, even though their economic reality is often precarious (Childress 2017, Amlinger 2021).

If an author's name, pseudonym, or tag such as 'the author of *Waverley*' are already a part of the work, so is the author's persona or reputation, or any additional knowledge about the person or persons who are 'behind' the work but outside the text. Genette asserts that "using a pseudonym is already somewhat like a work. If you can change your name, you can write" (1997, 54). Authors, in writing, create themselves as well as, and by means of, creating a work, even though they may merely consider themselves as "a by- or waste-product of the work" (McCarthy 2016, 2). To do so, however, they depend on other agents within the literary field and the "communications circuit" (Darnton 1982; Adams/Barker 2006), and on the attention of an audience. Authors are thus also a "by-product" of such attention, and of the contingencies of recognition. Their success or failure within an "economy of attention" (Franck 2018) may have everything or nothing to do with themselves or their work. They depend on the rules and conventions of the literary field, the hierarchies and categories of publishers, booksellers, reviewers, and other participants who collaborate and compete over the "consecration" (Bourdieu 1993, 112) of authors.[19]

Literary forms and traditions are part of these conventions. At different times in history, authors could achieve recognition for following rules and emulating the

---

[19] In this book, I retain the Bourdieuan designation of the 'literary field' without clinging to Bourdieu's theory, particularly concerning the static separation between literary texts and a given social reality. Alternatives like 'literary space' ("*espace littéraire*", Maingueneau 2004, 70; Diaz 2007, 4), 'system', or 'complex' are tempting but unwieldy, at least in English, where the term 'fields', with or without its Bourdieuan context, is well understood as denoting "social arenas of focused attention and habituated action" (Childress 2017, 8).

forms of the ancients, or they could be prized for their originality and rule-breaking in creating new forms. At times, even the revival of a form that had been considered 'done' could be viewed as particularly innovative – like alliterative verse in Middle English poetry, the sonnet in Romanticism, or the verse novel today. Forms and the prestige accorded to them are an important part of the horizon of expectations within which authors situate their work and against which their work will be perceived and valued. In an economy of literary forms, an author's reputation or value will also be associated with the value of a genre, where 'value' should be understood both in terms of economic profit and/or aesthetic appreciation. Ideally, the image of an author and their work match according to these values, which are in conflict but not always irreconcilable in practice.

When the author's personality takes on a media presence of its own, there is an increasing tension between the "fervent desire for recognition" and an "abhorrence of the notion that one's self is for sale" (Ryan 2016, 18). There is a conflict between "the fame of ostentation and the fame of evasion" (Braudy 1997, 392). Too much recognition of the wrong kind can be damaging for a writer's reputation, yet too little or no recognition is even worse. With growing numbers of titles published each year for a shrinking number of readers, the overall attention available for individual authors has been dwindling. *Winner Take Nothing*, the title of Hemingway's 1933 collection of stories, was prophetic in this sense, although of course it assumes that there still is a competition to be won (cf. Braudy 1997, 546), just as Shelley, when he spoke of poets as "unacknowledged legislators", implied that they should be "famously unacknowledged" (Braudy 1997, 430), not simply obscure – an idea better summed up by Graham Greene (1955) as *Loser Takes All*.

Only occasionally do we see a migration of authors between publishing categories. When this happens, it tends to be easier to move from the aesthetic to the economic pole than vice versa. It is much more difficult for a successful author of popular thrillers to be recognised as *also* a 'serious' writer (the case of Stephen King) than it is for an established author of literary fiction to be recognised as *also* a writer of crime fiction (the case of John Banville).[20] The market, apparently, is more forgiving in this respect than the gatekeepers of literary consecration. Yet it seems that literary fiction has increasingly become more welcoming to elements of genre fiction. This is not merely an aesthetic effect of postmodernism's dissolution of boundaries between 'high' and 'low' forms but also an effect of economic

---

[20] Having published a number of detective novels under the *nom de plume* 'Benjamin Black' to distinguish these books from his 'literary' novels, Banville complicated the picture when he abandoned the pseudonym for *Snow* (2020).

constraints and possibilities envisaged by 'literary' authors and publishers, placing bets on the added value of 'genre' features [→ ch. 16]. Good writing, moreover, has never been limited to any such category: parts of the penny dreadful *The String of Pearls* (1846–1847) are as good as anything in Dickens, and the laconic style of Lee Child, author of the Jack Reacher novels, has received praise from authors and critics alike (Martin 2015 and 2019).

To understand publishers' and booksellers' categories and literary genres as institutional infrastructures allows us to see them as resources for the creation of new works. Rather than merely measuring their "individual talent" against literary "tradition" (Eliot 1928) or wrestling with the ghosts of their forebears in a psychological struggle (Bloom 1973), authors engage with conventions of language, form, and genre in a series of recursive loops between their own writing and what Raymond Williams called the "force" of "literary form". "When I hear people talk about literature", Williams wrote in 1980, "describing what so-and-so did with that form – how did he handle the short novel? – I often think we should reverse the question and ask, how did the short novel handle him" (2001, 216). Williams locates some agency in "the actual and available forms of writing": "what is being written, while not separate from [the writer], is not only him either, and of course this other force is literary form" (ibid.). On a yet more basic level, the agency of authors is limited by "the logic of a language" (Frow 2021, 18) that enables certain choices and disables others (cf. Lodge 2002). Authors make choices (or have these choices made for them by editors and other audiences) based on existing forms and expectations, and this interaction between authors, forms, and audiences structures the dynamics of the literary field.

The resources of form are closely aligned with available technical and technological media (Berensmeyer 2022) as well as with institutions and social networks such as literary coteries, the court, the theatre, the patronage system, the book trade and the literary market, regimes of formal or informal censorship, book reviewing, libraries, reading groups, book tours, websites, universities, creative writing programmes, and other institutional infrastructures that contribute to the making of literature as well as of authors. The institutional infrastructures – social, economic, and material – within which both authors and texts are produced will only rarely be made visible in the texts themselves, but their reflection is a regular feature of texts that, directly or indirectly, in form as well as subject matter, address these conditions of creation and production.

Levels of Abstraction

Authorship is not a monolithic entity. Though there have been authors for thousands of years, the concept of authorship is malleable and variable – which comes as no surprise given its institutional historicity. It makes sense, therefore, to distinguish between *acts* and *concepts* of authorship. Authorial acts can be broken down into minimal elements, such as the building blocks of authorship proposed by Harold Love as "authemes": "a set of linked activities [...] which are sometimes performed by a single person but will often be performed collaboratively or by several persons in succession" (2002, 39). Besides "executive authorship", where a text's author is also its writer, i.e., the efficient cause of the text's existence, Love identifies the authorial acts of "precursory", "declarative", and "revisionary authorship" (2002, 39–49).[21] This model allows us to think of authorship also as a result of attributions by others. It no longer takes the author to be the central controlling instance hovering over the text but breaks down authorship into "a set of [...] activities" (ibid., 39) – editing, correcting, revising, printing, etc. – located on a scale between the autonomous solitary genius and the anonymous hive mind. Love's authemes allow a more precise focus on empirical acts of authorship independent from exaggerated theoretical claims about the discursive power (or powerlessness) of authors.

In order to contextualise and historicise these activities, we can identify superordinate *concepts* of authorship in which they are embedded, and which give them meaning. If authemes define what authors *do*, author concepts describe what authors *are* or what they are supposed to be. These descriptions, which circulate in a society, mediate between individual "physical *act[s]* of writing creatively, and the more general *practice* of writing creatively" (Childress 2017, 20), which is informed by social interactions and conventions. These concepts are subject to change, but they tend to remain fairly stable over long periods of time. They can be part of dominant, residual, or emergent cultural formations (Williams 1977, 121–127), and the more interesting historical periods tend to be those in which one concept gradually comes to supersede an earlier formation. These concepts include, for example, the idea of the poet as a divinely inspired seer (*poeta vates*), as a learned person writing

---

[21] Precursory authorship is marked by a significant contribution from a previous writer which is integrated into a new work. If the author is a 'maker', an 'artifex' who writes alone or in collaboration with others, this constitutes executive authorship. The third category, declarative authorship, applies if the author is responsible for the work without having written it (as in the case of the King James Bible or celebrity autobiographies). Finally, revisionary authorship takes place when a work is revised by an executive author or somebody else, such as an editor or censor (Love 2002, 40–49).

within a tradition (*poeta doctus*), as a 'maker' who pursues literature as a craft (*poeta faber*), the notion of the author as teacher (*praeceptor populi*), and the genius, whose authority is based on an aesthetics of originality and autonomy.

In their turn, acts and practices of writing are involved in social conventions, frames, or scripts that ascribe meaning to social actions (e. g., 'creative individualism' or 'autonomy of art'). Following Peter Lamarque, these frames or scripts can be grouped into three prevalent and competing *models* of authorship: *contextualism*, the view that a work is always connected with its author as a historical person and "essentially embedded in the historical context of its creation" (Lamarque 2009, 84); *institutionalism*, which understands literature as defined by practices, roles, norms, and conventions; and *expressivism*, which regards the work as an expression of its author's intention, state of mind, or personality. The third of these models, expressivism, is the foundation of the Romantic theory of authorship (Bennett 2006) and can be most clearly mapped onto a concept: the idea of the free and independent genius who expresses him- or herself without any external constraints.

In an earlier publication (Berensmeyer/Buelens/Demoor 2012), my co-authors and I proposed a taxonomy of author concepts on a scale from strong heteronomy (the writer as merely a textual function, a compiler) to strong autonomy (the genius who rules over the work and its meaning). Such a taxonomy helps to identify actual historical performances of authorship – that is, actualisations of author concepts within literary texts or peritexts – as belonging to a particular position on a scale. Here, I revise this approach for the sake of what I consider a more accurate model. Like all models, it simplifies reality and reduces the actual complexity of historically available positions. However, it will at times prove useful to indicate the types of fictional authors imagined in the texts I analyse, and it is with this heuristic function in mind that I adapt it here (see table 2). The concepts of autonomy and heteronomy in this table refer to ideas associated with authors as persons and with practices of authorship, not to ideas associated with works of literature or literature in general. They need to be distinguished from historical manifestations that assert the autonomy of literature independent of the person of the author, as in modernism and postmodernism. The modern idea of the autonomy of *literature*, as opposed to the autonomy of authors, departs from a Romantic model of authorial expression and replaces it with an institutionally and contextually based model that, in its extreme form, "sees literature as pure linguistic artifact" (Lamarque 2009, 85) and the author as "only a medium and not a personality" (Eliot 1928, 56). Literary autonomy thus presupposes a weakening of authorial autonomy, in fact a paradigm change towards a new author concept.

Table 2: Taxonomy of author concepts[22]

	authorial heteronomy	authorial autonomy
weak to moderate	author as storyteller / mediator INSTITUTIONALISM *Premodernity, Classicism*	author as creator of works CONTEXTUALISM, INSTITUTIONALISM *Modernism*
strong	author as medium CONTEXTUALISM *Postmodernism*	author as master of meaning EXPRESSIVISM *Romanticism*

These conceptual frameworks should not be regarded as historically static. Revivals of earlier concepts are always possible, especially in authorial self-conceptions – consider the example of Vladimir Nabokov, who presented the strongest possible model of authorial sovereignty at a time when critics had long sought to deny the idea of strong individual authorship (Tammi 1985, 100). There are good reasons to consider the Romantic paradigm as a continuous strand or resource within modernity (Reinfandt 2003). The Romantic and modernist conceptions of literature are conflicting positions, but they could and did coexist. The period terms in table 2, then, are merely intended as examples to show when a particular concept was dominant. The history of authorship is not one of radical ruptures but one of gradual, often slow and contradictory shifts. Even the premodern type of author, the storyteller or mediator whose predominant purpose "is to assert known and publicly acknowledged ideals" (Weimann 1988, 435; cf. Helle 2019, 113–114; Benjamin 2006), can be and has been revived in modernity for various purposes.[23]

Arranged on a scale (table 3), this model allows us to associate author concepts with a range of possible positions between the extreme poles of strong autonomy and strong heteronomy, or between expressivism and contextualism:

---

22 Adapted from Berensmeyer/Buelens/Demoor 2012, 14.
23 Weimann's example of this type of authorship is the epic poet who expresses a communal "shared property" (1988, 434), but this heteronomous paradigm of folklore authorship (cf. Jakobson/Bogatyrëv 1982) is active in many later periods and cultures as well, including (for instance) late twentieth-century Northern Ireland, where there was "a sense of the poet as exemplifying the values of [a] community" and "an insistence that the poet can mediate the truths already inherent in the community to the community" (Kirkland 1996, 153).

Table 3: Scale of authorship concepts

strong autonomy ↔	weak autonomy ↔ weak heteronomy	↔ strong heteronomy
expressivism	institutionalism	contextualism
Romanticism	Modernism	Postmodernism
genius	*doctus* *faber*	*vates*
master	creator	medium

This model pays due attention to the "middle ranges of literary agency", which are all too easily lost sight of when we focus on the extremes of "the author as either creative God or passive scribe" (Helle 2019, 113). Sophus Helle rightly points out that this middle ground is far from homogeneous but "a shifting and dynamic frame of investigation" (ibid., 115). In the model proposed here, strong autonomy designates the position of the author as an independent creator and ruler over the work and its meaning, an original genius and "master of meaning" (Chartier 1994, 28) who creates out of his or her own self (expressivism) and creates himself in the process of creating the work. Weak autonomy still defines the author as a creator but in a less assertive fashion that acknowledges extraneous influences and material constraints. At this point, authorship will also typically appear in forms of collegial cooperation, in networks, coteries, workshops, and other forms of collaborative or collective authorship (institutionalism). Weak heteronomy refers to the author as a producer of text who has a certain degree of freedom but is no longer thought to be independent. This is a writer whose principal goal is not self-expression but the expression of the ideas of others; this will typically be a 'hack' or a ghost-writer who performs acts of executive authorship but is not the declarative author of the published work.

Finally, an extreme version of the contextualist model implies an even more heteronomous concept of authorship, denoting the author as a scribe who takes dictation, a compiler of prior material, or an author inspired by, for example, a divine source or the Freudian unconscious (cf. Berensmeyer/Buelens/Demoor 2012, 14). Strong concepts of inspiration imply "that poetic creation is outside the conscious control of the artist" (Lamarque 2009, 96), turning them into the very opposite of the concept of authorship as (self-)expression, i.e., into the author as "only a medium" (Eliot 1928, 56). William Blake, to give just one example, claimed to have written one of his long poems "from Immediate Dictation twelve or sometimes twenty or thirty lines at a time without Premeditation & even against my Will", noting that as a result of this experience "an immense Poem Exists which seems to be the Labour of a long Life all producd [sic] without Labour or Study" (Blake 1988, 729).²⁴

In this typology of authorship concepts, varieties of institutionalism steer a middle course, understanding authorship as neither entirely based in authors as individuals nor entirely in their environment but in the social institutions and conventions that enable and constrain the creation, production, and reception of literature (cf. Lamarque 2009, 111).

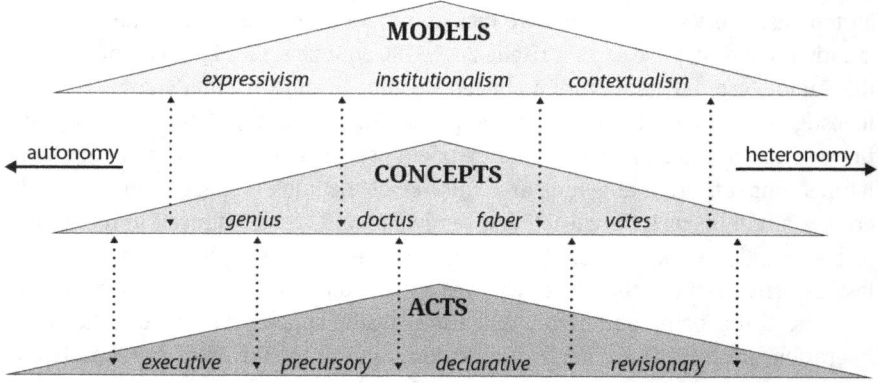

Fig. 2: Acts, concepts, and models of literary authorship.

As we examine the history of authorship concepts and models in modernity, the 'author fictions' in which they are paradigmatically condensed, and the literary texts in which they are expressed, we will see more clearly that the literary history of literary authorship is best characterised not as a parade of changing paradigms but as a gradual unfolding of interlocking paradoxes – irresolvable conflicts between mutually opposing orientations. These orientations do not follow a teleological sequence but move about in the space of possibilities marked by the extremes of expressivism, institutionalism and contextualism. Authors and audiences establish and redraw the boundaries between the free creative expression of 'authentic' experience, the rules of craft, profession or trade, and the values, inhibitions, and opportunities of tradition (cf. McGurl 2009, 23), as well as conflicts between aesthetic and economic values. Tracing the historical processes of author-making in

---

24 Letter to Thomas Butts (Blake's London patron), 25 April 1803. The unnamed poem in question has been variously identified as *Jerusalem*, *Milton*, or *The Four Zoas*. In a letter to Butts dated 6 July of the same year, Blake refers to his writerly role as that of "the Secretary", while "the Authors are in Eternity" (Blake 1988, 730).

modernity (in its duality of social as well as textual dynamics), there emerges a sequence of guiding paradoxes that structure these processes. This sequence includes, among others, the polar oppositions of the genius and the hack; the professional and the amateur; the modernist celebrant of impersonality and the feted personality (frequently embodied in the same person); the 'dead' postmodernist author as medium of an authorless textuality and the author as representative of a particular experience of class, gender, and ethnicity; and, finally, the hypervisible celebrity author and the author who embodies the routinisation of creativity.

Reading Authorship Historically

Works of literature contain implicit or explicit information about their origins, their "matrix" (McGurl 2009, 366). They do so because they are actualisations of historical possibilities: they present a selection from a range of concepts, but they select and actualise *these* instead of other concepts, in response to specific questions or problems of their time. The task of interpretation, then, is to identify the problems or questions to which the text is a response. Analysing novels and stories that explicitly stage and comment upon acts and concepts of authorship is one possible way of investigating the literary history of literary authorship, as a constant intersection and interplay between practices, concepts, and texts.

This is not the place to unfold a complete history, but a closer look at a few crucial historical turning points will help me to make my point.[25] "Explicit statements of authorship" go back at least to c. 2300 BCE, to the Sumerian high priestess Enheduanna, "the first author in world history who can be associated with a surviving literary work" (Foster 2019, 13). Authors' names have been recorded and preserved for many reasons, and many archaic and classical Greek authors identified themselves, at least indirectly, to mark their authorship of a text (Scodel 2019). In classical Roman literature, poets like Catullus and Ovid achieve a degree of complexity in playing with their authorial *personae* that rivals modern notions of autofiction (Badura/Möller 2019, 72–73). The emperor Augustus founded public libraries that "contained busts and medallions of the great writers" in what Leo Braudy terms "the first hall of fame" (1997, 119). Authors like Virgil and Horace became models to be imitated, teaching later generations of writers "how to write and how to comport themselves as writers" (117). For probably the first time in history,

---

[25] For more detailed discussions of some aspects of this history, see chapters 2–14 in Berensmeyer/Buelens/Demoor 2019.

writers could achieve the kind of fame (or "symbolic singularity", 27) that was previously limited to gods and emperors (118–121).

Since the *Confessions* of Augustine, autobiography has been a special case of self-naming and self-performance in a literary work (Lejeune 1975), insisting on a connection, even an identity between the instance of narration and the text's actual author. In confessional writing, the dominant model of authorship is self-expression, but its early forms are tempered by an institutionalist emphasis on norms and practices of self-fashioning. In many cases, they split the autodiegetic narrator into a past and a present self (e.g., Augustine before and after his conversion; Petrarch's distinction between a youthful lover and a penitent object of shame in the *Canzoniere*), into an experiencing and a narrating subject. Dante's *Divine Comedy* (before 1320) contains a younger, less experienced version of its mature and assertive author figure, distinguishing between the poet who writes the account and the young man whom Virgil guides through hell and into purgatory (Braudy 1997, 233–238). Chaucer similarly appears as a character in many of his works, most famously in *The House of Fame* and *The Canterbury Tales*, but when he does so, unlike Dante, he casts doubt on his authority. Whether these self-parodies spring from genuine doubt or are mere tropes of modesty, in the tradition of the autopoetic strategy of *captatio benevolentiae*, is difficult to say with any certainty.

The same is true for Thomas More's *Utopia* (1516), in which More and his circle of humanist friends are given walk-on parts. More's Latin name 'Morus', moreover, means 'foolish', thus ironically calling the author's reliability into question. Shakespeare features a couple of author characters in his plays, most memorably the poet Cinna in *Julius Caesar*, who is mistaken for one of Caesar's assassins and killed by a mob, and the poet John Gower, who is enlisted as the narrator of *Pericles*; but it is in the "sugred Sonnets among his priuate friends" (Meres 1598, sig. Oo1^v–Oo2^r) that a poet-character appears who may resemble the historical Shakespeare in many ways, and whose drama in a love triangle or even quartet has given rise to endless (biographical) speculation, even though he does not name himself in the poems. In the mid-seventeenth century, Margaret Cavendish (possibly inspired by *Utopia*) includes a version of herself as a character in her proto-science fiction novel *The Blazing World* (1666), at a time when writers begin to be more assertive about seeking individual fame through their works (Berensmeyer 2020a, 104–114).

In the eighteenth century, many observers register a crucial change in the world of literature, brought about by the sheer number of authors "posting with ardour [...] to the press" (Johnson in Keen 2014, 218). This leads Samuel Johnson, in 1753, to name his time "the age of authors" (ibid.). In addition to quantity, there is greater social diversity among writers in mid-eighteenth-century print culture as "men of all degrees of ability, of every kind of education, of every profession and employment" compete for attention in print (ibid.). Similarly, in eighteenth-century Germany, access to authorship expands the republic of letters into a socially diverse community, which excites opposition.[26] Complaints about the surfeit of authors and the superabundance of print become commonplace in the eighteenth century and the Romantic period: as one complaint among many puts it, "every insignificant emmet who crawls upon the face of the earth has thought proper to blot paper, and be the hero of an useless tale" ('Dionysius' 1806, 23). The singular, original author is threatened by the plural "swarm of imitators": "an author no sooner produces something *original*, and admirable, into the world, but a swarm of imitators copy his grains of sentiment and language at second-hand, with equal absurdity and impropriety, as the chambermaid the airs and elegancies of her lady's dress and manners" (ibid.).

In this competition, authors, critics, and reviewers (often the same individuals in different roles) stake their claims to separating the wheat from the chaff, the geniuses from the "swarm of imitators".[27] Some authors make this competition explicit in their works, as does Swift in *The Battle of the Books* (1704) and Pope in *The Dunciad* (first version 1728). Literature itself, in these texts, is a battleground in the fight over inclusion and exclusion from the literary field and from the master texts of an emerging national culture. In criticising and condemning their peers and competitors, Swift and Pope (to name only two) assert their own original authorship and their authority over the field. In these texts, as in many of the influential essays in Addison and Steele's *Spectator*, the aesthetic, social, and political aspects of criticism are merged. If the good writers are ladies, the imitators can only be chambermaids or worse (cf. 'Dionysius' 1806, 23). The rise of (all kinds of) authors is due to a vast expansion of the market for books, especially in the second half of the eighteenth century, which coincides with the first major expansion of the reading public (Saunders 1964, Altick 1998, St Clair 2004).

At the low end of the scale are the hacks – authors for hire, whose chief place of residence, Grub Street, becomes the eponym of a precarious and devalued authorship and the semi-industrial production of texts for print. The discourse of Grub Street establishes the 'distressed poet' as a commonplace of eighteenth-cen-

---

[26] Fuchs quotes the complaint, dated 1795, of a reviewer on finding "a chimney-sweep, several teachers, a tobacco manufacturer, a church-warden, and a gardener" included in a dictionary of learned authors (2021, 9); he also mentions the low-born, often self-taught author characters that populate the novels of Jean Paul (1763–1825).
[27] This dichotomy continues in popular music: "Imitators steal me blind", Bob Dylan sings in "Idiot Wind" (*Blood on the Tracks*, 1975), and Stormzy tells detractors and epigones to "shut up" (*Gang Signs & Prayer*, 2017).

tury literary culture. This topos combines a sense of the cultural aspirations of poetry with a critical view of the poet's economic reality – a reality frequently marked by poverty, as the professionalisation of literature and the competition among poets in the literary marketplace transformed a writer's life into a career characterised by radical insecurity (cf. Schellenberg 2019). In the history of authorship, this period marks an important turning away from traditional concepts and models of patronage, of writing as an élite pastime, or other forms of "social authorship" (Ezell 1999) not intended for commercial gain or wide distribution. Print comes to be the dominant medium of authorpoiesis. The Grub Street garret develops into a spatial metonymy for the self-exploitation of an artistically autonomous but economically heteronomous writer, as famously visualised in Spitzweg's painting of *The Poor Poet* (1839).

Grub Street is not merely a place but the name of a key mode of literary production, a mode in which a modern sense of print authorship emerges. Book history and historical media studies have explored this configuration as a shifting and changing network of writers, printer-publishers, readers, and critics engaged in textual production as a form of labour (e.g., Klancher 1987, St Clair 2004), in what Clifford Siskin called "the work of writing" (1998). In these emerging institutional practices, authors develop a professional sense of their craft. As part of this dynamic environment, Grub Street is a "literatory" (Saunders/Hunter 1991), a laboratory in which writers and printers experiment with new forms under new conditions of production and reception. As the stereotypical embodiment of hack writing, Grub Street has come to denote a form of literary labour that is the very opposite of gentlemanly or respectable authorship as practised by the likes of Pope and Swift.

An exclusive focus on the two opposing figures of the genius and the hack, however, obscures the actual diversity of possible authorial positions in the eighteenth century. Authors assume a wide range of roles, in some cases changing places or taking up multiple positions at the same time while performing different authemes or concepts. The hack could be a genius forced to exploit his creativity for bread. Samuel Johnson and others looked down upon Grub Street hacks as "drudges of the pen, the manufacturers of literature, who have set up for authors" (Johnson 2020 [1751], 351). Yet "some of them enjoyed a good reputation, were respectably middle-class, and worked with leading publishers" (Berensmeyer 2022, 95). In 1758, James Ralph's pamphlet *The Case of Authors by Profession or Trade, Stated* initiated a wider debate about the business and professional respectability of authors, provoking the 'gentlemen authors' of the age.[28]

---

[28] For a more detailed analysis of this constellation, based on the eighteenth-century authorship

The familiar genre of authorship satires tends to escalate such conflicts and should not be read as documentary evidence. Nevertheless, they shed light on conditions of their own production and, like other works of author fiction, perform their own self-analysis by focusing on the material, institutional conditions of author-making and text production. In "The Brain-Sucker" (Oswald 1787), the young author's individual genius is harnessed to the mechanised, alienated and alienating conditions of modern production, which separates workers from the fruits of their labour. Complaints about servitude are ubiquitous in eighteenth-century authorship satires, which regularly figure authors as slaves to booksellers.[29] In the it-narrative "Adventures of a Pen" (1806), the pen that tells its own story is at first proud to be owned by an author but then quickly disappointed: "of all my bad situations, this was the most displeasing to me; for I was at once the packhorse of the public and the slave of the press, the hireling of booksellers and the drudge of letters" ('Dionysius' 1806, 277). Here, responsibility for literary composition is shifted from the author to the pen, from human being to mechanical object (cf. Hatton 2020, 69). The pen is autonomous since "long use in the hands of authors has habituated it to a form of writing that it can now carry out on its own" (Hatton 2020, 74). Yet the shift from author to instrument works both ways, as the pen's autonomy is sublated to the heteronomy of writing as a "slave of the press" and a "drudge of letters". Mechanical, uncreative text work turns into a metonymy for the alienated position of the author in the marketplace, who is not that different from a prostitute.

As patronage declines, fame becomes the reward of the writer alone, no longer to be shared with the patron. The writer now becomes "a member of [...] a 'republic of letters' that understands writing as a tool of class power for itself rather than for others" and that aligns itself with an idea of serving a "national culture" (Braudy 1997, 362–363). Fuelled by this increased self-confidence and an incipient professionalisation of authorship, as seen in Ralph's *The Case of Authors*, the driving force of literary ambition in the eighteenth century is reputation in the present, within the community of writers, and hope for fame in posterity. This double aspect initiates the duality of the modern economy of literature between the imperatives of art (fame, posterity) and the market (reputation, later economic success in the present).

---

satire "The Brain-Sucker: Or, the Distress of Authorship" (1787), see Berensmeyer/Guttzeit/Jameson 2015 and Berensmeyer 2014.

29 Elfenbein 2020 refers to Charles Churchill's poem "The Author" (1763) and Archibald Campbell's dialogue *The Sale of Authors* (1767) in this context (283–284), noting the Romantic transformation of the author from "slave to the market" to "hero of literature" (286).

In a short span of time between the end of the eighteenth and the first two decades of the nineteenth century, authors' private and personal lives became central to their public status and inseparable from their artistic achievements. Older religious views of divine inspiration came to be secularised in the figure of the genius. Those figures were themselves the sole source of their own creative inspiration. The genius thus achieved an autonomy and independence from literary and social models that was potentially scandalous but also generated vast amounts of previously unheard-of public attention. Byron embodied this Romantic concept of the author as genius, becoming the "first hero-victim" of "literary celebrity" (Braudy 1997, 408). Byron's name even became an eponym for the kind of hero (or anti-hero) that was often featured in his works. In his poem *Childe Harold's Pilgrimage* (1812–1818), "an autobiographical journey into and through a deep personal malaise which [he] represents as a symbol of the condition of Europe" (McGann 2008, 1026), Byron figures himself as 'Childe Harold' (the original manuscript makes the connection even more explicit by naming him 'Childe Burun'), even though he strenuously denied the identification in the 1812 preface: "It has been suggested […] that in this fictitious character […] I may incur the suspicion of having intended some real personage: this I beg leave, once for all, to disclaim" (Byron 2008, 19). At the beginning of canto III, however, 'Harold' invokes Byron's daughter Ada, making the identification between the "real personage" and his "fictitious character" almost inevitable. He also comments, in a key passage of the poem (III.6), on the act of poetic self-creation (2008, 105):

> 'Tis to create, and in creating live
> A being more intense, that we endow
> With form our fancy, gaining as we give
> The life we imagine, even as I do now.

Here, the process of writing creatively gives "form" to the "fancy", not only as something external to the writer, but as an increase and intensification of the author's "life" and "being" through the very act of literary creation. Literary writing thus has a double function: it brings forth a work (like the poem *Childe Harold's Pilgrimage*) and it also creates, enables, or at least intensifies that work's author's "being".[30]

---

[30] The passage is even more complex since it not only refers to writing but *also* to Byron's fathering of Ada, superimposing literary and sexual 'creation' and thus adding yet another layer to the imbrication of life and work, fiction and fact in *Childe Harold's Pilgrimage:* "What am I? Nothing; but not so art thou, / Soul of my thought! with whom I traverse earth, / Invisible but gazing, as

Earlier historical figurations partly anticipated this paradigm (Shakespeare, in the sonnets, comes close to articulating it at times), but it was only around 1800 that self-expression and literary self-creation came to be celebrated as a positive value in the arts. The poet's own self could now be presented with impunity, even at an epic scale. In *The Prelude*, Wordsworth's "felt experience" was at the centre of what Geoffrey Hartman has called "a new attitude toward consciousness" (1975, 125), making the poet's "inner life" worthy of poetic exploration and representation "without the artifice of a fictional or displaced perspective" (127). In its focus on the poet's self-formation, "*The Prelude* is a *Bildungsroman* that takes the child from solipsism to society and from his unconsciously apocalyptic mind [...] to a sense of realities" (132). Whereas Byron played with an array of masks and several discontinuous layers of self-revelation, Wordsworth in *The Prelude* presented the process of subjective self-discovery and self-creation as a form of organic growth, in a poetic autobiography. Both shared a heightened sense of 'the poet', whom they celebrate as endowed with a special kind of sensibility. Genius was now a state of "being", "more intense" than that of ordinary citizens (Byron 2008, 105).

This development coincided with a new system of copyright legislation in which "artistic work [was] considered to be simultaneously a legal possession of the artist and the emanation of his personality" (Braudy 1997, 422–423, cf. Woodmansee 1984). In this system, it was now possible, at least in theory, to transform personal artistic capital into economic capital, adding a pecuniary sense to Byron's "gaining" through poetic creation.

Conversely, to be difficult and neglected could come to be seen as an index of genius, a mark of distinction for the true artist. The reputation/fame binary was accompanied by a split between the (despised, ephemeral) "public" and the (more abstract, lasting, and worthy) "people" identified as the target audience of the 'genuine' writer (Braudy 1997, 428–430).[31] Against the ephemeral embrace of a shallow public, poets posited as a more desirable model the (famously) unacknowledged artist's struggle "against a hostile or indifferent society" (Braudy 1997, 485) and their "belief in *fame later*" (490, emphasis original).

For many writers and thinkers throughout the nineteenth century, the act of creation remained "inseparable from self-creation" (Braudy 1997, 427). At about the same time as Byron, Mary Shelley pursues this idea in *Frankenstein* (1818), a

---

I glow / Mix'd with thy spirit, blended with thy birth, / And feeling still with thee in my crush'd feelings' dearth" (106).

31 Braudy cites Wordsworth's 1815 preface to his collected poems, where Wordsworth's distinguishes between "a local acclamation, or a transitory outcry" and a more lasting fame; the first kind of attention he identifies with "the PUBLIC", the second with "the PEOPLE" (qtd. in Braudy 1997, 428).

novel about a creator and his creation who remain profoundly connected even though the former desperately tries to separate himself from the latter, his 'work', which turns out to have a subjectivity of its own and cannot therefore be controlled. As a creator, Victor Frankenstein displays "the symptoms of severe melancholia" that were associated with "the dark side of artistic creativity" (Groom 2019, xxxii). We might take this as an incentive to read *Frankenstein* as an allegory of literary creation and the relationship between author and work. Once it is in the world, the artist's "Being" (the word actually used for the creature in the novel)[32] takes on an independent life beyond the artist's control, even though it remains connected with its creator – an aspect of paternity that Byron's poem, in the guise of Childe Harold, prefers to ignore.

Through reading other works of literature, the Being in Shelley's novel humanises himself and thus gains further independence from his creator, in a text that is itself a 'Frankentext', a patchwork of documents and interlocking unreliable narratives, which replace the 'organic' view of self-formation and self-expression with a sense of fragmentation and loss.[33] Although not explicitly about literary authorship, *Frankenstein* is one of the very first gothic counterpoints to the more optimistic, Goethean strain of authorial self-creation that came to dominate the English *bildungsroman*, while that tradition in turn, from Bulwer-Lytton to Dickens and Thackeray, illustrates the tempering of more radical and, as Shelley shows, precarious, unstable Romantic notions of autonomy by means of social compromise and the author's self-formation as a literary professional. As we will see in later chapters of this book, gothic fantasies of the monstrosity and horror of (literary) creation, from Herman Melville to Rudyard Kipling to Stephen King, throw a persistent, darkly brilliant shadow on the forms and formations of author-making [→ ch. 5, 8, 15].

Why does the nineteenth-century novel become the form in which authorpoietic processes and questions of narrative authority are primarily being negotiated? If we remind ourselves of Georg Lukács and his greatly influential, if somewhat difficult *Theory of the Novel* (1914–15), a possible answer might lie in the way

---

32 Cf. Groom 2019, xi, who points out that "the Being" is also the word used by Percy Shelley c. 1817 to describe this character; see ibid., 199–200.

33 For a more detailed reading of *Frankenstein* as a figuration of authorship and of the "potential fragmentation of the authorial subject" (285), see Guttzeit 2018, 282–285. It would be interesting to compare this to Carlyle's *Sartor Resartus* (1833–1834), in which authorship is similarly figured as a patchwork of scraps and rags, but in a satirical and not in a Gothic vein. Authorship and Gothic doubling also feature in other Gothic novels of the Romantic era such as Charles Brockden Brown's *Wieland* (1798; cf. Hesford 1982/1983, Scheiding 2018) and James Hogg's *Private Memoirs and Confessions of a Justified Sinner* (1824; cf. Davison 2008).

that the novel, more than other literary forms, is based on a problematic attitude to its own form. Lukács presents novelistic creation as a double reflection, first of "the actual nature of [the form-giving] process", which then "in turn becomes an object for reflection" (2000, 202). In *Frankenstein*, we can see this doubly reflexive irony at work in the self-positioning of the novel's actual author, Mary Shelley, in relation to the scientist-creator-author within the novel, and her autopoetic strategies of literary form. In its dismembered and re-membered narrative, Shelley's novel comes to reflect "the actual nature" of that (highly 'unnatural') form- and life-giving process as not at all 'organic' growth but messy patchwork. Ironically, thus, Shelley draws an implicit analogy between her own authorship and Victor Frankenstein's monstrous act of giving life to a hybrid body out of dead body parts.

According to Lukács, the author – "the subject, as observer and creator" – "is compelled by irony to apply its recognition of the world to itself and to treat itself, like its own creatures, as a free object of free irony" (197). Irony is the structural principle that makes this double reflection possible, while the narrator functions as its main narrative resource. It is the author's stand-in that, as it were, gives a concrete (objective) shape to what would otherwise remain merely "subjective or postulative" (202).[34] In other words, the distinction between author and narrator can thus be redescribed as a distinction between enunciation and the enounced (Easthope 1983, 30–47) or between first- and second-order observation. What Lukács means by irony, I think, is a form of second-order observation. The first-order observer (the narrator) observes objects in the (fictional) world, whereas the second-order observer (the author) observes other observers observing. While the narrator is manifested in direct textual utterances, the second-order observation resides on a higher level within the composition of the text and its "aesthetic materiality" (Hühn 1995, 1: 15).[35] This materiality of textual composition is the synthesis of narrative, poetic, or dramatic resources into a work in which the author is doubly reflected, as is Mary Shelley in *Frankenstein*.

The distinction between narrator and author as a distinction between first- and second-order observation can be further explained by pointing to its manifestation in the novels of Jane Austen. Here, free indirect discourse serves not only to represent a character's consciousness but to maintain a variable distance between character and narrator, or indeed between character and author as well as between narrator and author – an author whose power of (second-order) observation relies on her crisp impersonality, indeed on the erasure of any hint at her per-

---

[34] For the German text of these quotations, see Lukács 1971, 65, 73–74.
[35] My translation. I owe the idea of understanding textual composition as second-order observation to Hühn's history of English poetry (1995), who in turn derives his terminology from discourse theory (Easthope 1983) and Luhmannian systems theory.

sonal social position from the narrative. As D. A. Miller has argued, the authorial aloofness achieved by this "truly out-of-body voice, so stirringly free of what it abhorred as 'particularity' or 'singularity' that it seemed to come from no enunciator at all" (Miller 2003, 1), is what grants Austen "narrative authority" and a kind of freedom from the social limitations of her "authorial self" (ibid.), partly anticipating if not yet programmatically implementing a Flaubertian authorial policy of non-intervention in narrative affairs.[36]

The objectified, apparently omniscient narrator, whose ironic distance to the characters and their limitations is Austen's most powerful instrument of observation, depends on a second-order point of view that is free of any limitations, social or cognitive, and that can only be established on the level of textual composition as a fiction of independence and wisdom. This authorial second-order observation is manifested in the irony that extends to the narrator itself (or herself?), for example in the famous first sententious sentence of *Pride and Prejudice:* "It is a truth universally acknowledged ..." – a statement and a sentiment whose negation is to be supplied by the audience, encouraged not by the narrator directly but by the higher-order enunciation on the level of textual composition.

As Romantic autonomy descends into more pragmatic forms of institutional self-realisation, the contradiction between "free irony" and its "compell[ing]" force (Lukács 2000, 197) becomes a structuring factor that regulates the relationship between author, narrator, and characters, as well as between objective and subjective modes of literary worldmaking. The dialectic of authorial mastery and its ironic withdrawal into forms of reification establishes a working compromise, never entirely satisfactory, between artistic and social expansions and limitations.

In the wake of Lukács, both Benjamin and Adorno indicated further impulses towards a historicisation of the novel and its main narrative mode, realism, in connection with the historical development of the narrator figure, also in relation to actual authors. Benjamin did so in his article "The Storyteller" in 1936, Adorno mainly in an essay on "The Position of the Narrator in the Contemporary Novel" from 1954. Both saw the development of narration in the modern novel as a decline. For Benjamin, the art of storytelling was dying. Modernity had shattered the (oral) tale and its sense of purpose for a community and replaced it with the mass production of stories in the modern novel. The authors and narrators of industrially produced fiction were only a poor substitute for the old kind of storyteller. Only rarely could the isolated reader grasp something meaningful – a Kermodean "sense of an ending" (Kermode 2000) – from the "dry material" of nov-

---

36 On the question of narrators in Austen, see also Quinn 2007, Boyd 2017 [→ ch. 2]; on her social position, cf. Downie 2006.

els (Benjamin 2006, 373). Adorno, writing in the early 1950s, saw the breakdown of conventional realism as a response to the destruction of the bourgeois social order in the two world wars. While capitalism continued to produce illusions about the true nature of society, antirealist fiction responded to this by disrupting illusion. What Adorno described as a post-Flaubertian type of reflection was, he argued, "taking a stand [...] against the lie of representation, actually against the narrator himself" (2019, 56). The "destruction of form", the fusion of commentary with action (in Proust), the "ironic gesture" that unmasks the "unreality" of what the author was creating (in Mann), all this (56) made modernist novels into "negative epics" (57).

There is no need to subscribe to the rigours of Hegelian or Marxist theory, nor to share the Frankfurt School's lofty cultural pessimism, to view this association of literary and social form, and of narrators and authors, as a promising departure, a road not taken in the structuralist and poststructuralist schools of narrative theory. To connect types of narrator and styles of narration with changing experiences of subjectivity and practices of authorship and publishing might yet prove fruitful for a 'diachronic narratology' (cf. Fludernik 2003) interested in the history of narrative forms. Not, however, in a rigid alignment between formal codes and political programmes. One Marxist theorist, Franco Moretti, interprets the "multiplicity of viewpoints" of the modern novel as "typical of [...] the democratic ethos itself" (2000, 124); whereas another, Fredric Jameson, can see in the "multiple narrative shifts" (2006, 212) of modernist fiction nothing more than a "reprogramming of individuals to the 'freedom' [note the scare quotes] and equality of sheer market equivalence" (2006, 210). An all too rigorous mapping of literary techniques onto large-scale social, political, and economic forms, such as – in Jameson's writing – (a particular interpretation of) the history of capitalism, does not strike me as particularly inspiring. Connections between historical formations and literary forms need to be carefully scaled to avoid theoretical grandstanding on the one hand and New Historicist anecdotalism on the other.

Moreover, the history of novelistic form does not correspond to a straight line of development but is characterised by ruptures and, at times, sudden throwbacks to allegedly obsolete forms. For instance, while many writers still cherish the multiple viewpoints that are possible in the novel as a means towards narrative empathy or a "democratic ethos" of plurality (Moretti 2000, 124), others imagine a return to either more subjective or more objective modes of narration. In proposing her idea of a "tender narrator" (2019, 21), Olga Tokarczuk may have been suggesting an alternative to the current fashion of – sometimes quite raw – autofiction with its increasingly particularised and idiosyncratic points of view.³⁷ Similar to contemporary novelists toying with omniscient narrators (Dawson 2013), she envisages a return to a suprapersonal narrator that can "encompass the perspective of each of the characters, as well as [have] the capacity to step beyond the horizon of each of them" (Tokarczuk 2019, 21). Her own example of such a narrator is that of the book of Genesis. This idea recalls Émile Benveniste's definition of the voice of "historical enunciation" (1966, 241), based on the grammatical third person as not a person at all but "the verbal form whose function it is to express the *non-person*" (1966, 228). Benveniste identified this as the voice of (ancient) historiography, in which "[t]he events are given as they happen and as they appear on the horizon of the story/history [*histoire*]" so that "the events seem to tell themselves" without a narrator (241).³⁸ This 'absent' third person as the voice of historical or fictional narration is a tempting alternative to ideas of a person-like or personified narrator posited as the voice of a narrative text, or to the shortcut of assuming that voice to be the actual author's.

The oldest occurrences of this impersonal form of narration, besides the Old Testament, are ancient myths and wisdom texts, where "[c]ommenting and narrating are not disjointed from one another; rather, one comments while narrating" (Weinrich 1964, 183, trans. in Moretti 2000, 124). Yet, the modern novel thrives on irony, on "the split between story and comment" (Moretti 2000, 124), making such non-personal narrative effects either impossible or undesirable. The zero focalisation of Hemingway's "The Killers" or some late texts by Beckett are rare examples, but they are not exactly 'tender'. There have been several attempts to write serious modern fiction without irony, as for example Thomas Mann's *Joseph* novel, but Mann's suprapersonal voice and his "haut-bourgeois composure" were already anathema to other modernist writers like Joyce, who "rejected precisely the all-encompassing voice that had made [Conrad's] *Youth* and [Mann's] *Tonio Kröger* possible" (ibid., 235) and, for Joyce, impossible.

Yet, the "depersonalization of the text, the laundering of authorial intervention" (Jameson 2006, 209) was crucial to the development of the modernist novel. From Flaubert to Conrad and beyond, novelists employed different formal strategies in a "search for [...] narrative presence" (Jameson 2006, 211). What these

---

37 I would like to thank Joanna Rostek for pointing me to Tokarczuk's Nobel lecture.
38 My translation. In the original: "la '3ᵉ personne' n'est pas une 'personne'; c'est même la forme verbale qui a pour fonction d'exprimer la *non-personne*" (228). "Les évenement sont poses comme ils se sont produits à mesure qu'ils apparaissent à l'horizon de l'histoire. Personne ne parle ici; les événements semblent se raconteur eux-mêmes" (241). These quotations come, respectively, from Benveniste's essays "Structure des relations de personne dans le verbe" (1946) and "Les relations de temps dans le verbe français" (1959).

have in common is a radicalisation of point of view that deprivileges the author's position and presence in the narrative, aiming for an impression of impersonality and impartiality, even indifference. They "refine", as Joyce's Stephen puts it, the artist "out of existence" (Joyce 2000, 181), wishing to present, in Virginia Woolf's term, "moments of being" (Woolf 1985) instead of panoramic views of society as in *Middlemarch*. In what David Trotter called "their insistence that consciousness should be represented from within rather than without" (1993, 3), these modernists avoid intrusive or overt narration as much as possible, favouring free indirect discourse or interior monologue to (quoting Woolf again) "record the atoms as they fall upon the mind" (2008, 9).

Paradoxically, the removal of the author from the work coincides with an ever-increasing mass media presence and celebrity status of authors *outside* their works (Glass 2004, 5–8). Many tales by Henry James explore this contradiction, as does Evelyn Waugh's novel *Vile Bodies* (1930) for the generation of the 'Bright Young Things' in the late 1920s.

While the biographical association between author and work was a commonplace in nineteenth-century literary life and literary criticism, it was also increasingly regarded as aesthetically and morally problematic. Authors at the end of the nineteenth century strove to conceal rather than reveal their personalities; as Oscar Wilde put it in his preface to *The Picture of Dorian Gray:* "To reveal art and conceal the artist is art's aim" (Wilde 1994, 17). At times, as in Wilde's own case, this concealment served to whet public curiosity and to increase the writer's celebrity. Impersonality became a modernist creed also to counter this excessive prying into the private lives of authors. Flaubert and others removed the author's position from the text, "refin[ing it] out of existence", as Joyce's Stephen puts it in *A Portrait of the Artist as a Young Man* (Joyce 2000, 181). In doing so, they assume a God-like authority over the text: "[a]n author in his book must be like God in the universe, present everywhere and visible nowhere" (Flaubert 1980, 204, trans. in Abrams 1991, 23).[39] As Joyce's Stephen puts it: "The artist, like the God of the creation, remains within or behind or beyond or above his handiwork, invisible, refined out of existence, indifferent, paring his fingernails" (2000, 181).

The history of literary authorship is structured by paradoxes of freedom and limitations, God-like indifference and all-too-human cravings, and conflicts between expressivism and institutionalism, a conflict that takes us to the interfaces between literary and social forms. Thus, the concept of genius arose when author-

---

[39] In the original: "L'auteur, dans son œuvre, doit être comme Dieu dans l'univers, présent partout, et visible nulle part" (letter to Louise Colet, 9 Dec. 1852, Flaubert 1980, 204). Flaubert varied the same idea in several later letters; see Berensmeyer 2000, 51.

ship was first perceived as a mass phenomenon, asserting a sense of the author's singularity exactly at a time when that singularity was at risk of being drowned out in a cacophony of publications (Haynes 2005). But this is of course not its only causal link or historical correlation; political and social connections also suggest themselves. For instance, artistic autonomy took hold as a concept at a time when individual human rights gained prevalence after the American and French revolutions. The realist novel explored conflicts between individual freedom and social pressures, in France in the form of irreconcilable and often deadly confrontations against the backdrop of political divisions and further revolutions (*The Red and the Black, Sentimental Education, Bel-Ami*). In Britain – where a proper revolution did not happen – it did so in the form of what Chesterton would later call "the Victorian compromise" between individual and society and between the upper and middle classes (1946, 21). The modernist creed of impersonality was promoted by authors and critics just as 'personality' was becoming all the rage in popular journalism, and authors who wished to be seen as artists sought to protect themselves from the taint of mass audiences. From the 1950s onwards, journals like the *Paris Review* regularly published author interviews, attracting attention to authors' personalities and thus contributing to the cultural demise of the ideal of impersonality (cf. Dawson 2012, 104).[40]

Later, in the last third of the twentieth century, the authorial subject came to be reinstated as a position of 'strategic essentialism' (cf. Spivak 1996, 214) in feminist and postcolonial theory, scotching earlier late modernist and poststructuralist attempts to dissolve authorship into pure intertextuality (itself a radicalisation of modernist impersonality). In a partial reprise of premodern forms of authorship as a form of cultural mediation, the person of the author was no longer considered an autonomous creator but the representative of a particular identity or social positionality in identity politics. Hailed as a witness in struggles over equal rights and social visibility, the author's authority derived from authentic experience. Authors on display, in real or virtual spaces (public readings, interviews, literature festivals, etc.) gained a new importance as visible "symbolic markers" to which audiences developed an affective attachment (cf. Reckwitz 2012, 245). Under the label of 'diversity', differences based on authors' (group) identities gained relevance also in publishing and reviewing – creating new pressures and paradoxes for authors whose aesthetic principles do not match with their (actual or attributed) 'identity'. In Percival Everett's *Erasure* (2001), for example, public demand for racialised representations of 'authentic' Blackness clashes with an author's personal

---

40 Cf. Glass 2004 and Micevska 2021, who show that the fascination with celebrity authors was already a factor in modernism.

sense of who he wants to be as a writer. His attempt to satirise dominant representations of race backfires, however, and he is trapped in a cycle of critical awards and financial rewards, effectively 'made' into the kind of author that the media and the public want him to be [→ ch. 17]. Here, the autopoetic desire for freedom of expression is curbed by the allopoetic force of institutional expectations and limitations.

Authorship Today

The conflict between the economic and aesthetic values of literature is now frequently represented in the form of literary autofiction: autobiographical fiction that often refers to its authors' daily lives, known or unknown biographical facts, and the writing and publication of their works. By making the author not only the subject but the *subject matter* of its narrative, autofiction shares the key defining features of autobiography. Blurring the distinction between the author-function and the author-subject as a character, however, leads to the creation of a hybrid of fact and fiction as poles between which the narrative can oscillate, leaving it to the audience to refer the author-as-character back to the text's actual author or to treat the "real personage" as a "fictitious character" (Byron 2008, 19; cf. Kreknin 2014, 179).

Moreover, autofiction frequently stages conflicts of norms and goals between the values of art and commerce. The writing of literary fiction thus becomes part of its own marketing, asserting its cultural value by comparing itself to other forms. In claiming a factual foundation in real life, autofiction satisfies a widespread "reality hunger" (Shields 2010), or rather a dissatisfaction with 'mere' fiction. The popularity of memoirs and literary nonfiction confirms this trend. The author as character, as narrator, and as the (real) person who wrote the book, are finally merged – or at least these fictions (strive to) produce the impression that this is the case. The author as an individual, a real person, guarantees the authenticity and sincerity of autofiction by adhering to the "autobiographical pact" between author and reader (Lejeune 1975) that also underwrites the category of witness literature. On the other hand, authors and readers can appeal to the licence of *fiction* to deny the strict identity of character and 'real personage', leaving their precise relationship in abeyance.

Like singer-songwriters or other performers of popular music, autofictionists promise authenticity on at least two different levels: that of the performer and the audience. Yet this authenticity depends on acts of authentication. Understood as performances, autofictions and memoirs "articulate on [the author's] behalf 'this is what it's like to be me'", thereby establishing what musicologist Allan F. Moore calls "authenticity of expression" (Moore 2012, 269). Yet, again, successful authentication depends on an audience's willingness to play along, and their sense of being willing and able to share the author's experience (Moore, ibid., calls this "authenticity of experience", meaning "this is what it is like to be you").[41]

Autofiction and its aesthetics of relatability is one example of the persistence of "subject-centric authorship models" (Maitra 2020, 116) in contemporary literature. However, these still dominant practices of personal, or personalised, literary authorship are challenged by the digital revolution. A more in-depth assessment of these new challenges is beyond the scope of this book. One would think that mass authorship, self-publishing (Laquintano 2016), and easy access to text-sharing platforms online ought to have eroded the appeal of the individual author in favour of a nameless, authorless textuality as envisaged by Barthes. However, the opposite is the case. Obscurity is a worse fate than piracy (cf. Childress 2017, 45). Even though acts of authorship and publication have today become easier than ever, in the form of digital self-publishing, the "democratization of authorship" promised by web-based publishing and distribution platforms (Maitra 2020, 118) turns out to be accompanied by new, platform-specific economic constraints on the freedom of writers, with algorithms and aggregated data about user behaviour (formerly known as 'reading') taking over the function of editors or publishers in the production of literary 'content' (Hartling 2009, Laquintano 2016, McGurl 2016, van der Weel 2019).

This new regime also expands an already vast shadow economy of 'independent' authorship and encourages forms of self-exploitation. In contrast to this new kind of Grub Street (or Amazon Grub River) the traditional book world continues to operate with the gatekeeping functions of literary agencies, editors, publishers, prizes, and so on, that manage processes of selection and status allocation. It is these authors who tend to be better known and favoured by social media followers, even though the general attention paid to books and reading in a panoply of media and entertainment options has been dwindling. The successful transition of authors from the fan fiction and self-publishing scene into the domain of trade publishing has been rare – E. L. James's *Fifty Shades of Grey* and Colleen Hoover being the most spectacular cases so far (van der Weel 2019, 218–219) [→ ch. 16].

An even bigger challenge comes from sophisticated models of machine-learning, neural networks, and data analysis which can generate literary texts that resemble texts written by human authors. The rise of artificial creativity, based on artificial intelligence (AI), exerts pressure on traditional concepts of (human) authorship in aesthetic and legal terms (cf. Bridy 2016, Fletcher 2021, Gervais

---

41 Thanks to Christoph Reinfandt for pointing me to Moore's work on authenticity.

2020).⁴² Like the use of computers and word processing software (Kirschenbaum 2016), AI is used increasingly as an assistive technology – with human authors still, as it were, in the driver's seat. At the time of writing, AI programmes like Sudowrite, based on OpenAI's language model GPT, are being used by some writers of genre fiction to increase their output by automating parts of the writing process. Since audiences of genre fiction tend to demand the same product in endless serial variation, lack of originality is not a problem in this field (Dzieza 2020). As has been the case in the past, technological, legal, social, and institutional changes will require a rethinking and retooling of central concepts and practices of authorship as agency, ownership, and accountability (cf. Rose 1993, Woodmansee/Jaszi 1994, Sapiro 2011).

A perspective on institutions as both enabling and constraining the creation and production of literature will not lead to a neat distinction between 'myths' and 'facts' of authorship, as suggested in the title of Linda Peterson's *Myths of Authorship and Facts of the Victorian Market*. The "models and myths of the author", those accounts that authors give of themselves to explain or justify their work, are not merely "as important for understanding the struggles [in the literary field] as are the market pressures and possibilities in which they worked" (Peterson 2009, 10). They have a crucial impact on the very workings of the literary field and the wider culture. Moreover, author concepts as I understand them are not merely "authorial self-constructions" (ibid.) but are equally shaped by what audiences – readers, editors, publishers, and others – expect of writers, and they are an expression of available ideas, norms, and values.

In modernity, such concepts become increasingly complex, carrying economic and social as well as aesthetic connotations and distinctions. They tend to attract theorists to binary oppositions (between art and commerce, suffering and service, artist and professional, etc.), but these are rarely mutually exclusive or as neatly drawn as these theories suggest. Even an all-out artist like Henry James acted with professional *nous* and commercial savviness, fully *au fait* with the demands of the book market though not always fortunate in the realisation of his economic intentions (Chung 2019).

More recently, the conglomeration of large publishing corporations has made literary fiction, at least occasionally, highly profitable (Thompson 2012, Brouillette 2014), disproving claims of a binary division between literary and commercial value, or between symbolic and economic credit (Bourdieu 1993, 46–48). The reality of the literary field is thus "not so clearly delineated as [Bourdieu's] theoretical

---

42 As part of the early history of AI authorship, Bridy mentions the Datatron, programmed in 1956 to "compose Tin Pan Alley songs" (2016, 395) at the rate of 4,000 an hour.

models assume" but marked by "complexities and confusions" (Peterson 2009, 54). The starkly dualistic "economic world inverted" that Bourdieu identifies as characteristic of the modern literary field, in which "the artist cannot triumph on the symbolic terrain except by losing on the economic terrain [...] and vice versa" (Bourdieu 1996, 83), is an abstraction that may be occasionally true but is not universally applicable. In nineteenth-century Britain, George Eliot is only one case in point: a novelist who found both economic and symbolic success. Towards the end of the century, the distinction between art and commerce becomes more acute, with some writers like Robert Louis Stevenson worrying about their popularity as a danger to their reputation;[43] but this is not a permanent phenomenon. In most cases, the distinction between literary reputation and commercial success or failure is less clear-cut.

To give just one brief example: Maurice Bendrix, the writer-narrator of Graham Greene's *The End of the Affair* (1951), reflects on his standing in the literary field before being interviewed by a journalist: "Patronizingly in the end he would place me – probably a little above Maugham because Maugham is popular and I have not yet committed that crime – not yet, but although I retain a little of the exclusiveness of unsuccess, the little reviews, like wise detectives, can scent it on its way" (Greene 2019, 122). Here the "crime" is popularity, which the "little reviews" in their role as gatekeepers of literature-as-art are said to punish with disdain. So far, so Bourdieu. But Greene's novels *were* popular as well as 'literary', so this sentence can also be read, and perhaps better understood, not as a diagnosis of the literary field of the mid-twentieth century but as a dig against the very notion of "detectives" of literature (given that the real detectives in this novel are not drawn in an entirely sympathetic light), against being 'patronized' and 'placed', and also against his older rival W. Somerset Maugham, whose works covered much the same territory as Greene's but who did not share his Catholic faith. Not too much should be made of just a single sentence, but such meta-reflections within a narrative often do contain more than mere intrafictional representation or a depiction of the state of the literary field.

Among Bourdieu's many useful insights is the notion of the literary field as "the site" where "a struggle over the definition of writer" and related terms is being played out (1996, 224). Terms like 'author' or 'writer' are not defined from the outset, but their "legitimate definition" is subject to debate, negotiation, and conflict; poems, plays, and narrative texts themselves take part in this negotiation. The field is always under construction, and what is at stake are the "boundaries

---

[43] "There must be something wrong in me, or I would not be popular" (Stevenson to Edmund Gosse, qtd. in Margree 2016, 367).

[...] (between genres and disciplines, or between modes of production inside the same genre) and, therefore, hierarchies" that order the field (225). Yet these hierarchies are never uncontested, never permanent, with the exception of those very few authors, long dead and buried, who constitute the "core canon" (Grabes 2008, 317) or "hypercanon" (Damrosch 2006) of literary classics. Publishers, booksellers, and critics are not the only contributors here; authors and their works have a crucial share in this ongoing boundary work.

From the nineteenth century onwards, authorial self-constructions and constructions by others have become a significant element in literature, with writers and their personalities increasingly moving into the focus of readers' and marketers' attention. Some narrative genres, like the literary *bildungsroman* and the *künstlerroman* or artist novel, developed into central sites of conflict in which these paradigms were negotiated and contested. In Dickens's *David Copperfield*, for example [→ ch. 4], the novel provides not only a model of subjectivity (cf. Poovey 1988) or retrospective autopoetic self-formation, as presented to an audience, but also an instance of "the subject position of the novelist" as "hailed" by a mass audience (Deane 2003, 56) – a combination of autopoetic signals and allopoetic effects that reflects back on the individual person and public role of the work's author.

In modernity, under the "imperative of permanent innovation" (Reckwitz 2012, 11), the self-description of the artist becomes "a large part of the [artist's] job" (McGurl 2009, 48), something to be performed inside as well as outside the text, in interviews, public readings, and later on dedicated author websites and social media platforms that present curated author images. In the age of social media, visibility and reach supersede earlier paradigms of authorial success. Especially for literary fiction (as opposed to genre fiction), "name-economy authors" (Childress 2017, 42) have become important selling points. In residual form, the Romantic identification of author and work continues when readers ask for 'the new Zadie Smith' rather than the book's title. Audiences' emotional attachments are increasingly important in a world of shrinking readerships and mass publishing, where attention is a scarce resource (cf. Franck 2018, Felski 2020). In a globalised world where publishing is dominated by the Big Five (Thompson 2012), less visible authors who have not yet made a name for themselves now stand a better chance of being promoted by smaller independent publishers who have gained a reputation for innovative literary fiction, and thus bestow credibility on new writers included in their list.[44] An exception to this 'name economy' is genre fiction, where

---

[44] Consider the recent critical and commercial successes of independent publishers in Britain: Lucy Ellmann's *Ducks, Newburyport* (2019), published by Galley Beggar Press, won the Goldsmiths

readers tend, for the most part, to be less interested in authors than in a particular type of story.

Public attention is still directed towards individual authors, while authors hanker for public recognition and the revenue that this (rarely enough, alas) brings their way. Without intending to appear cynical, one might suggest that some authors use political activism or other forms of public commitment as leverage for their literature, or – perhaps now even more often – vice versa. Though this is nothing new (Dickens immediately springs to mind), the opportunities for doing so have multiplied. Authors who have hundreds of thousands of followers on social media enjoy – if that is the word – an unprecedented degree of influence. The historical tension between the modernist author and the marketplace of celebrity (cf. Glass 2004, 27) has, in the twenty-first century, given way to more flexible, transient, or even "dissociated" (Hartling 2009, 10) constellations between authorial invisibility and extreme forms of publicity or hypervisibility.[45]

Author fictions do not merely reflect or repeat, in the mode of fiction, an existing set of social roles and places, but they contribute actively to the transformation of the reality of which they are a part. Certain genres and plot patterns gain traction and attraction in the literary field because they allow the right questions to be formulated. They serve as autopoetic problem-solving strategies for challenges in the relations between subject matter and form, for the ways in which the subject position of the author can be objectified as an instance, however 'impersonal' or 'absent', that inhabits the "split between narration and comment" (Moretti 2000, 124).

For authors, the creation of author characters poses not only a particular attraction but also a problem: to invite or to avoid the identification of the character with the actual author, and to conflate or separate the voice of the narrator and the voice of the author.[46] This formal challenge, which persists through various forms of narration (first-person, third-person, even second-person narration) and focalisation (from external to zero), has led to a wide variety of solutions. It is, however, not merely a formal challenge. Because of its self-reflexive subject matter, author fiction poses a challenge to the author's social position in the struggle for recognition. In this sense, the alignment between actual and fictional author can invite uncomfortable parallels between art and life, or it can be used to

---

Prize and was shortlisted for the Booker; Fitzcarraldo, the English publisher of Annie Ernaux, suddenly had a Nobel Prize winner on their list in 2022.
45 On authorship, celebrity, and publicity, see also Moran 2000, Lilti 2014, Franssen/Honings 2016, Braun/Spiers 2016, Braun 2020b.
46 It has also led to difficulties in coming to terms with these issues in literary theory and criticism; see the next chapter.

deal with these parallels in the mode of fiction, to reflect or project "how to become what you are" (Nietzsche 2007). The projection of the author's image as something that the real author can then hope to inhabit in real life is certainly one of these autopoetic strategies. As such, this becomes a kind of self-fulfilling prophecy related to the writer's social or artistic ambitions. An alternative strategy is the projection of a negative "shadow self" (Kenner 1976, 178–179) that embodies what the author has not become or does not wish to become.[47] While this can also apply to novels without author characters, it tends to be made explicit in the many literary *bildungsromans* and autobiographical novels of the nineteenth to twenty-first centuries.

While the genres of the *bildungsroman* and *künstlerroman* had their heyday around 1900, changing social, economic, and cultural circumstances in the twentieth and twenty-first century continue to exert pressure on author concepts, which is why their negotiation is still ongoing, predominantly in the novel. While I do not think that what I call the 'author fiction' constitutes a distinct, coherent subgenre of narrative fiction, I do believe that it presents a persistent problem constellation in literary history, a constellation that brings together available, historically variable author concepts with the empirical, biographical subjects of actual authors and the fictional authors they create as characters in narrative texts (as performative expressions of author concepts). Works of author fiction actualise a selection of available author positions and perform a concrete instance or token of a type that is an abstract configuration of (imaginary) possibilities. Moreover, this constellation also feeds on and intervenes in current practices and conventions of relating individual and social perspectives on discursive expression and authority, ranging from the premodern conception of the author as a communicator of commonly accepted knowledge and wisdom to the most egregious instances of confessionalism and voyeurism. Author narratives thus engage with claims to narrative authority and with changing concepts of the function and value of literature and literary fiction.

The next chapter will address the conceptual foundations of author fictions and author fiction. To conceptualise the relations between author, work, and audience that regulate the field of possibilities for author fiction, I engage with narra-

---

[47] Cf., in the context of a discussion of French-Canadian author novels, this remark by Falardeau: "L'écrivain des romans, dont les affirmations souvent résonnent comme celles du 'je' à peine travesti du romancier lui-même, incarne l'ambition la plus résolue d'émancipation sociale" (2016, 319). See also Belleau 1980 for a distinction between three major types of author novels as novels of code, of language, and of writing; however, such a typology, even if meant to denote ideal types in a Weberian sense, is too static to grasp the full range of possibilities in author fictions. Anglo-Canadian artist-novels are discussed in Williams 1991.

tive theory and revisit the distinction between author and narrator. I also present a more detailed model of the 'authorpoietic loop' and a workable solution to the thorny problem of the boundaries between actual and non-actual (fictional) entities in literature.

2 Authors, Works, Audiences: Conceptual Foundations

Authors and Narrators

The terms 'writer' and 'author' are often used synonymously, but not every act of writing constitutes an act of authorship. The term 'author' commonly describes "a weightier figure with legal rights and social standing, a producer of texts deemed to have value" (Lamarque 2009, 106). There can be writing without authorship, though not (at least not in the full sense) authorship without writing or without the assumption of having written a text, or rather of having completed a 'work' – a text transformed into a valuable object (in an aesthetic or economic sense, or both) through the agency of what Foucault called "the author-function" (Foucault 1977; cf. Lamarque 2009, 108–111), i.e., "a principle of textual coherence" that "has the force of [...] a consolidated belief reinforced by a complex social apparatus" (Frow 2021, 8). H. Porter Abbott refers to the self-writing of the author within the work, more specifically within the autograph manuscript, as a kind of "autography" (Abbott 1996); yet such acts of self-writing are not autonomous but embedded in material practices in which the self is written: a dialectical exchange between personal circumstances, available forms, and institutional conditions of creation and production. The most common type of text in which this reflection takes place is narrative fiction.

The second and equally important distinction to be addressed in this context is that between author and narrator. Ever since this distinction had become entrenched in narrative theory, there have been only hesitant attempts at considering the possibility of connections between actual authors – sometimes referred to as "flesh-and-blood authors" (Phelan 2017, 205) and narrators. Treating authors and narrators as identical or equivalent is frowned upon as an undue contamination of ontological domains, and in many ways rightly so, or at least for good reasons (for example, the modern claim of literary autonomy). "The 'narrator'", wrote Kathleen Tillotson in the late 1950s, at a time when this distinction was just coming to be firmly established, "is a method rather than a person; indeed the 'narrator' never is the author as man; much confusion has arisen from the identification, and much conscious art has been overlooked" (1959, 22).

But their distinction, or rather the erasure of the author from the text, though theoretically useful, has never been a complete success. Almost inevitably, critics have reintroduced variants of the (implied) author as, for example, "a construct formed by the reader" (Schmid 2013, par. 20), a "controlling intelligence" that presides over the text (Lamarque 2009, 102, citing Lyas 1983), "an anthropomorphic centre for a narrative" (Dawson 2012, 105), a "streamlined version of the actual author" (Phelan 2018, 8) or "the ultimate somebody who tells" (ibid., 10), "the ultimate source of narrative communication" (Phelan 2017, 156).[48] Some overarching "authorial level" (Schmid 2013, par. 25) seems to be required to mediate between the semantic and pragmatic aspects of textual communication and to resolve their (potential or actual) contradictions. Yet, if the concept of the implied author was introduced to safeguard semantic/pragmatic coherence, it clearly does not always cut the mustard. For example, in *The Brothers Karamazov*, some critics have felt it necessary to postulate two implied Dostoevskys, one affirming God and one criticising God (ibid., par. 23). Clearly, something's got to give. Here, the concept of the implied author has obviously failed its coherence-inducing purpose, and nothing should keep us from applying Occam's razor or Phelan's shaver. If the ambiguity about God is indeed part of the work, why not ascribe it to the one (and singular) Dostoevsky as "the ultimate somebody" (Phelan 2018, 10) who put it there, and leave it for audiences to resolve it or to let it stand?

In some cases, as in unreliable or deficient narration, the desire may be overwhelming to protect authors from their narrators (Nabokov, for example, from Humbert Humbert), or narrators from their authors (Charles Marlow from Joseph Conrad, perhaps), or to shield a work of fiction from the documented opinions of its author – Kipling, Céline, or Pound spring to mind. This seems to have been one of the main reasons for Booth to introduce the concept of the implied author in the first place. The distinction between author and narrator is useful for, among other things, establishing "unreliable narration, a type of narratorial report in which the inferential pathway to the author is particularly mediated or oblique" (Herman 2008, 242). This is clearly desirable when that text is potentially controversial, because then the author cannot be blamed for the narrator's or characters' opinions and actions: as Christoph Bode explains, "you can't accuse an *impersonal entity* of something that is a matter of reproach only in a *person*" (2011, 136, emphasis original).

But one should question whether the implied author construct 1) really achieves these purposes and 2) whether these purposes could not be achieved more easily and straightforwardly by other means. Yet, more recently, authors themselves have been muddying the waters by writing autofiction, novels that blur

---

[48] The distinction between implied and actual authors can verge on theological subtlety. See also Nünning 1997, Kindt/Müller 2006. Phelan 2011 offers a spirited defence of the implied author in the light of rhetorical theory, but he vacillates between using and not using the epithet 'implied'. Surely, the *ultimate* source of narrative communication is the actual author, not a construct that only exists in the audience's mind.

the (already contested) lines between fiction and autobiography, and that thrive on the confusion and conflation of authorial and narratorial dynamics. This return of the author in literary fiction challenges established scholarly practice – always a sure sign that this practice is ripe for revision (cf. Burgelin/Grell/Roche 2010, Dix 2018, Wagner-Egelhaaf 2012, Womble 2018). Especially so as the distinction between authors and narrators is also hotly contested in the debate between 'optional' and 'pan-narrator theorists' (cf. Patron 2021) – those who argue that every narrative includes a narrator and those who do not distinguish "between narrative-making and narrative-telling" (Currie 2010, 65).

The distinction between author and narrator, having been stabilised in structuralist theory and firmly implemented in narrative studies, certainly has merit as a powerful tool for readers, scholars, and students alike that allows for a neat separation between the domains of fiction and the actual world. The existence of narrators depends on the fictional works that feature them, whereas that of authors does not. Authors have a life independent of their works; narrators do not. There is thus a clear ontological, and not merely epistemological, hierarchical distinction between the two. They are "in no way to be confused" (Barthes 1982, 282) because they inhabit mutually exclusive ontological domains.

This distinction chimes with standard models of literary communication that separate what happens *within* a text – the (fictional) world of characters, narrators, and, depending on the terminology that is used, the *implied* author – from whatever lies *outside* the text, in the (real) world of actual authors and audiences. The latter includes the person or persons who wrote the text, as either a living or dead, known or unknown, named or anonymous entity. In narrative fiction, the mode of being of the intratextual entities is fictional, or at least fictionalised: the real London and the London in Dickens's novels resemble each other, but they are not identical, just as "[a] map is not the territory it represents" (Korzybski 1958, 58). Extratextual entities like actual writers and readers, just like the real London, have a life of their own beyond the confines of the text.

Yet, even though this distinction is both rational and apparently useful, its introduction to literary studies has been comparatively recent. Earlier periods did not insist on it, to say the least.[49] It has also come under renewed scrutiny

---

49 For Plato, for instance, the crucial distinction in epic poetry is not between author and narrator but between author and character, or between "pure narrative" [ἀπλῆ διήγησις] and "representation" [μίμησις] (*Republic* 393d). Taking the *Iliad* as his example, Plato's Socrates explains that "Homer starts by speaking in his own voice and doesn't try to lead us astray by pretending that anyone else is the speaker [...]. Next, however, he speaks in Chryses' voice and tries his very hardest to make us believe that it isn't Homer who is speaking, but the old priest. And the same method of composition is employed throughout nearly all his narrative of events in Troy and Ithaca and in

by the above-mentioned 'optional-narrator theorists' (Patron 2021), who question whether every narrative requires a narrator other than the author. Moreover, empirical observation shows that, when it comes to authors, there appears to be a common temptation to connect the person of the author to the text he or she has created, in ways that either attempt to bridge the ontological gap between reality and representation or seek to give reasons why that gap needs to be minded. Do authors form a special class of extratextual beings? Is the real Charles Dickens somehow still present inside his novels, despite being dead for more than 150 years?

Such questions are of course much older than modern literary theory. Already in sixteenth-century France, Montaigne noted the consubstantiality of book and author: "I have no more made my booke, then my booke hath made me" (Montaigne 1915, 2: 392). Others, by contrast, sought ways to separate authors from their work. Nathaniel Hawthorne, in the preface to *Mosses from an Old Manse* (1846), warned readers not to identify the author who signed himself 'Hawthorne' with the real person: "So far as I am a man of really individual attributes I veil my face" (Hawthorne 1982, 1147; cf. Thompson 1993, 17–18). In 1877, the Victorian critic Edward Dowden sought to distinguish the real George Eliot from "that second self who writes her books" (qtd. in Tillotson 1959, 22; cf. Iser 1974, 103).

In these quotations, writing has not yet been isolated from narration. That distinction only gradually emerges in the nineteenth and early twentieth century. It hovers, as yet unformulated, over Lubbock's *The Craft of Fiction* (1921). Stanzel reports that "it began to become accepted around the end of the 1950s" (1984, 13). The major structuralists all insist on it: "the (material) author of a narrative is in no way to be confused with the narrator of that narrative", writes Barthes (1982, 282). Chatman concurs: "[i]t is a fundamental convention to ignore the author, but not the narrator" (1978, 33), adding that "the speaker is not the author, but the 'author' (quotation marks of 'as if'), or better the 'author'-narrator, one of several possible kinds" (148). As Genette explains,

> the narrator of *Père Goriot* "is" not Balzac, even if here and there he expresses Balzac's opinions, for this author-narrator is someone who "knows" the Vauquer boardinghouse, its landlady and its lodgers, whereas all Balzac himself does is imagine them; and in this sense, of course, the narrating situation of a fictional account is *never* reduced to its situation of writing. (1983, 214, emphasis original)

---

the *Odyssey* in general" (393a–b; Plato 1993, 88–89). Notably, even though Plato goes on to disapprove of representational narrative, the dialogue in which this is discussed features Socrates as a first-person narrator: "Yesterday I went down to the Piraeus with Glaucon [...]" (327a). Greek text as in Perseus Digital Library (http://www.perseus.tufts.edu/hopper/).

Likewise, the 'narratee', the instance who is being addressed by a narrator, is said not to "merge a priori with the reader (even an implied reader) any more than the narrator necessarily merges with the author" (ibid., 259).[50] In the standard view, authors cannot help but invent fictional narrators, no matter whether they consciously decide to do so or not (cf. Birke/Köppe 2015a, 9).

An example will take us deeper into the philosophical foundations of this ontological divide. Dickens the man is connected to *Little Dorrit* through his being the real-life origin – the author – of this particular novel, and that is why his name is on the cover and title page of many (one would hope: all) editions of the novel. But this only matters for the liminal level of the paratext, the threshold that allows readers to cross over from the external into the internal dimension of the text (Genette 1997). Otherwise, authors of course matter for many real-world purposes from copyright to catalogues, publishing, marketing, and other public-facing functions. But it is the *name* rather than the actual *person* that matters for most of these purposes, and where the actual person of the author makes an appearance, as in interviews, public readings, or on social media, it is the author as (public) author rather than private individual that audiences get to meet – however approachable or 'folksy' authors might appear.

Inside the world of *Little Dorrit*, Dickens the man has no place, even though his views on various topics may be represented in that novel, by chance or by design. The author-narrator of *Little Dorrit* may be identical to the Dickens who previously told the story of *Hard Times*; there may or may not be a continuity between the living writer and the narrator inside the novels. In any case, that narrator within the novels is *a textual function*, activated or made manifest whenever the text is read. The author we (imagine to) encounter within the work is a function of that work, not – how could he be? – physically identical to the real author who, besides being the novelist who went on to write *A Tale of Two Cities* and other works, was many other things: son, husband, father, lover, journalist, antislavery activist, philanthropist, Anglican Protestant, and so on. As "a man of really individual attributes" (Hawthorne 1982, 1147), he may or may not have shared the opinions that could be attributed to him on the basis of his writings; he may express different opinions from one text to another.

For many theorists, this textual function that stands in, within the text, for the intentional acts of the flesh-and-blood author outside it, is the "implied author", understood as one or more "versions" of the actual author (Booth 1983, 71 and pas-

---

50 Cf. Birke/Köppe 2015b. For a historical survey and critical discussion of narrator concepts, see Patron 2009 and 2019.

sim) or as "the governing consciousness of the work as a whole, the source of the norms embodied in the work" (Rimmon-Kenan 2002, 87–88). But this concept is at least as disputed as the notion of authorial intention.[51] It is so disputed because, at the point where textual production and reception meet, there is an unavoidable asymmetry. Actual authors have no control over how audiences will receive their work. If the implied author must be constructed by the audience, how can it be a version of the actual author? Actual readers infer an abstract 'image of the author'[52] from textual signals, an image that serves several useful purposes – among others, to resolve contradictions or deficiencies in the text by referring to a "governing consciousness of the work as a whole". But this "implied author" obviously must be inferred during or after the reading process. Though it may seem to be a stand-in for the author in the *text*, it exists only in the reader's *mind*. To lump it with the actual author would therefore be a fallacy of misplaced concreteness.

Wolf Schmid posits an "abstract author" as a "reconstruction, by the reader, based on the creative acts that have produced the work", which he argues is "necessary because it objectivizes the narrator and the narration" (2010, 218, cf. 48–50). Yet, in effect, this makes the implied author another "fictional character" in a work (Lamarque 2009, 109), albeit one that would be seen to have a certain privilege over all the other characters because it serves as the work's "controlling intelligence" (ibid., 102, citing Lyas 1983). Some theorists have even multiplied these entities further, adding an "arranger" to "designate a figure or a presence that can be identified neither with the author nor his narrators, but that [in *Ulysses*] exercises an increasing degree of overt control over increasingly challenging materials" (Hayman 1982, 84). Many find the concept of the implied author and the multiplication of 'controlling intelligences' in a text superfluous (e.g., Juhl 1980, Nünning 1993, Nünning 1997, Kindt/Müller 2006). David Herman has suggested to relocate the intentionality attributed to the implied author in "more general processes of folkpsychological reasoning" that are involved in narratives and their reception (2008, 257).

Optional-narrator theorists insist that we do not need to posit any additional entities, and that in Jane Austen's novels, it is Jane Austen whose words we encounter, not the words of a fictional narrator (see, e.g., Kania 2005, Köppe/Stühring 2011, Boyd 2017, Patron 2021). As Gregory Currie states: "There is no distinction that should or can be made between authors and narrators, for there is no distinction to be made between narrative-making and narrative-telling" (2010, 65). Similarly,

---

[51] For more on this dispute, see Phelan 2005, 38–48, Nünning 1997 and 2005a; also see Herman 2008 for a thoughtful assessment of different kinds of intentionalism and anti-intentionalism in literary studies.
[52] In Russian Formalism: *obraz avtora* (Vinogradov 1930).

Richard Walsh has argued that "[e]xtradiegetic heterodiegetic narrators (that is, 'impersonal' and 'authorial' narrators), who cannot be represented without thereby being rendered homodiegetic or intradiegetic, are in no way distinguishable from authors" (2007, 84). Aspects of a narrative that are relevant to interpreting that narrative can be understood, according to this view, "without assuming that they are attributable to a narrator" (Birke/Köppe 2015a, 7), or indeed to an implied author as a stand-in for the actual one.

Occam's razor is a useful tool. But shaving off the implied author does not solve the problem of understanding the relations between actual authors and the fictional entities (narrators, characters) in their works. Optional-narrator theory does not resolve the issue of relating the Jane Austen outside the novels to the one we are supposed to get to know inside them. Even if one were to argue that it 'is' Austen who tells the story of *Pride and Prejudice*, the Austen who tells that story is at best tangentially aligned with Jane Austen as a historical flesh-and-blood person.[53] For one, obviously, that person died in 1817. Audiences may imagine hearing her voice when they read the novel – this association of a text to a human intentional agent appears to be a deep-seated human disposition (cf. Eibl 2013) –, but the author's voice in such cases cannot be anything but a metaphor.

A possible solution to this quandary is to view a third-person 'omniscient' or 'authorial' narrator as a resource activated by "a contextual assumption that allows us to read fiction as a mode of authorial discourse distinct from other public authorial statements" (Dawson 2015, 96). In this view, audiences know, based on context and conventions, when authors are speaking in their own voice and when they are using language in the mode of fiction. But this does not solve problems or ambiguities of attribution that may occur *within* fiction, when inferences about the actual author need to be made, e.g., in the case of errors, deficient or 'unnatural' narration, use of irony, or conflicts of values.[54]

Invariably, such reflections return to the fundamental question 'who is speaking?' Whose voice do audiences hear or imagine they can hear when reading a fictional narrative? For Genette, "the 'person' of the narrator" is always present in a narrative (independent of the narrative situation) because, "like every subject of an enunciating in his enunciated statement", "the narrator can be in his narrative

---

53 Bakhtin similarly holds that authors are "tangential" to "the chronotopes represented in [their] work" (1981, 254; cf. 256). Clearly not a pan-narrator narratologist, Bakhtin also holds that authors can "deliver the story directly from [themselves] as the author pure and simple (in direct authorial discourse)" "without utilizing any intermediary", but that they do so in the mode of fiction, in the mode of an "*as if*" (256). Cf. also Uspensky 1973, who frequently employs the terms 'author' and 'narrator' as synonyms (e.g., 11, 58–59).
54 More on these cases below. Cf. Skov Nielsen 2010 on authors and 'unnatural' narration.

[...] *only* in the 'first person'" (Genette 1983, 244). Although the voice of this type of narrator-persona "must not be confused with the author's" (Birke 2015, 99) in the classical narratologies of Genette and Stanzel, Stanzel nonetheless refers to it as the 'authorial narrative situation' (*auktoriale Erzählsituation*), which in his typology of narrative situations is the first major type besides the 'first-person' and the 'figural narrative situation'. This narrator, Stanzel writes, "seems to be identical with the author at first sight" but is in fact "an independent entity which has been created by the author in the same manner as the novel's characters". Its purpose is to act as an agent of mediation (*Mittelsmann*) between the fictional world and the real world, and its principal mode of narration is the report (Stanzel 1987, 16).

Stanzel's description of the authorial narrative situation is not too far from Lubbock's, who speaks of the "omniscient author" (1926, 115) and of an author who "becomes a personal entity" in the novel when, like Thackeray, "so far from trying to conceal himself, [he] comes forward and attracts attention" (114). All the weight of the problem of the author/narrator distinction rests on the verb "becomes" in this sentence. Lubbock later specifies that readers tend to get so spell-bound by scenic narration that they forget about "the presence of the minstrel" (i.e., the author) and that it is only when "the spell is weakened" that they are "recalled from the scene to the *mere* author" (251, my emphasis). For Lubbock, apparently, scenic or "pictorial" narration (255) requires a narrator, whereas report or "direct assertion" in a novel (251) can be identified as the author's. Other typical modes, according to Stanzel, include the commentary on what is being narrated, which can extend to a meta-commentary on the act of commenting (Stanzel 1987, 19–20). "In the role of the authorial narrator, the author fictionalises and dramatises his narrative function", Stanzel explains further (18).[55] Elsewhere, he specifies that "the authorial narrator [...] is, within certain limits, an independent character who has been created by the author (just as the other characters of the novel have been) and with whose own peculiar personality the reader and critic are confronted" (1984, 13).

The phenomenon is familiar enough, but if the narrator is indeed, like other characters, merely a part of the fictional world, Stanzel ought to have avoided the word 'authorial' and thus severed the link between author and narrator for good. If the narrator is a character "within certain limits" (that remain unspecified), 'personal narrator' might have worked as a term for this persona, but it would have invited confusion with the figural narrative situation. Stanzel himself in fact at one point uses the term *persönlicher Erzähler* ('personal narrator') as a

---

55 My translation. In the German original: "In der Rolle des auktorialen Erzählers fiktiviert und dramatisiert der Autor seine Erzählfunktion".

synonym (1987, 20; cf. Lubbock's "personal entity", 1926, 114). He also cites Thomas Mann's description of the meta-commentary in *Joseph and his Brothers* as "not the words of the author but of the work itself" (Mann 1990, 656)[56] – adding yet another possible category besides author and narrator, the 'work' as having a voice of its own. That, as far as I am aware, is a road not taken by any narratologist since; Mann himself quickly links his comment on 'authorial' meta-commentary to irony (656), as does Stanzel (cf. 1987, 20).

The work that speaks, rather than an author or narrator – this could be a proposition worth pursuing. Kathleen Tillotson mentions the example, not often noted by narratologists, of the Edwardian novelist William De Morgan, in whose novels the narrator "generally speaks not as 'I' or 'we', but by personifying 'the story'", which, moreover, "is not omniscient" but functions as "the nameless muse of Narrative" (1959, 31). Such a narrator one might be tempted to call 'operal' to indicate that it stands for the voice of the work (*opus*) or of narrative per se, in De Morgan's and Tillotson's sense. An operal narrator would come closest to Benveniste's idea of an impersonal form of enunciation in which events tell themselves without a narrator (1966, 241, 287). We can identify some authors striving for such a degree of objectivity (cf. Tokarczuk 2019), but in most cases, at least in modern narrative literature, some form of commentary on events will be inevitable.

Contrary to the rhetorical tradition, which links communicative action to intentional agents, the anti-intentionalist position (for example, New Criticism, French poststructuralism, American deconstruction) would seek to sever the connections between author and text even more radically. At its most extreme, this position denies the idea that language can be used to communicate meaningfully and effectively. But the underlying problem of relating an utterance to its origin and finding meaning in this relationship is much older. The emphasis on language as an active agent in literary texts, from Julia Kristeva (1980) to David Lodge (2002), was an attempt to find a new solution to this problem. Language is notoriously slippery, polysemic, ambiguous. Modern literature and literary studies have thrived on these qualities, which are a major constituent of the pleasure and enjoyment to be had in reading. The novel speaks in many voices, according to Bakhtin even in several distinct languages (*heteroglossia* or "the social diversity of speech types", Bakhtin 1981, 263).

Yet, even if the novel is a prime example of 'many-voiced' discourse, the question of polysemy is more fundamental, extending to all texts, written or spoken. The greater need to interpret written texts, compared to direct, dialogic speech,

---

[56] My translation. In the original: "nicht die Rede des Autors, sondern die des Werkes selbst".

has been debated since the days of Socrates and Plato. Socrates already invokes the writer as an absent "father" unable to help his "offspring" (the text) when difficulties of understanding arise (*Phaedrus* 275d–e, in Plato 2002, 70). Even among anti-intentionalists, the author is frequently called upon as a last resort, for example as a historical anchor of the text to preclude anachronisms in interpretation (cf. Berensmeyer 2020b). Furthermore, the radical anti-intentionalist stance ignores the fact that, despite the indisputable slipperiness of language, linguistic communication undeniably *works* – if it did not, humanity would have invented something better by now. So why should literary language be doomed to fail in its communicative purpose? Why not allow real authors to communicate with real audiences by means of language and texts? If this is possible in history, philosophy, or in literary criticism (even of the variety that disputes the knowability of intentions), why should it not be possible in literature?

Some theorists have revisited the ontological boundary between author and narrator by paying renewed attention to the concept of narrative voice. Feminist narratology in particular has drawn attention to the ways in which narrative authority has traditionally been associated with an authorial narrator identified as male, and on subsequent struggles by women writers to achieve an authoritative voice of their own outside this male tradition (Lanser 1992; cf. Birke 2015). Susan Lanser focused on how the "authorial voice" is given "a privileged status among narrative forms" by inviting readers "to equate the narrator with the author and the narratee with themselves" (1992, 16). She coined the term "authoriality" to refer to "'extrarepresentational' acts" like "reflections, judgments, generalizations about the world 'beyond' the fiction" but also "comments on the narrative process, allusions to other writers and texts" (16–17). In doing so, she brought together typical features of 'authorial narration' – Lubbock's "direct assertion" (1926, 251), Stanzel's report, commentary, and meta-commentary (1987, 16, 19–20) – with features of authority or power that are frequently ascribed to authors. Authorial narration conveys such authority precisely because of its link to the process of writing and the author's power or control over the text, as well as to common cultural and social associations of discursive authority related to this idea of control.

Developing this idea further, Dorothee Birke suggests reconceptualising "'authorial narration' as a process or rhetorical strategy which, in various ways, foregrounds the logic of the text's production […] enacting a rhetorical stance the actual author assumes towards its readership" (2015, 102). Rather than viewing authorial authority as monolithic, she proposes that we read such extrarepresentational acts as "a bid for establishing authority claims" (103). Authors who make such claims in an excessive manner may be seen as protesting too much, and this may actually weaken their authority by inviting "the possibility of contradiction" (104) and exacerbating rather than solving "the problem of authorial control" (104). She concludes:

> One of the central functions of extrarepresentational acts – in particular, those of the metadiscursive kind – is to negotiate the status of fictional narrative and its authors at a particular time. Authority claims that are put forward – other than claims to narrative authority – cannot be taken as straight-forward assessments of a truth but should be read as rhetorical strategies employed in the service of such negotiations. (110–111)

Narrative voice, even an 'authorial' narrative voice, thus appears much less authoritative and incontestable than its name makes it sound. Its relative strength or weakness as a rhetorical strategy depends on various historical contextual factors like "general notions about the expertise of novel writers, and the potential of fictional representations" (Birke 2015, 104). Thinking about narrative authority opens up a field of study interested in the connections between actual authors, texts, and actual audiences. It is the reading public that accepts or refuses such claims of authority, which are made in narrative texts but also in the paratexts that seek to establish or confirm an author's discursive authority (Dawson 2012, 110), all of this in connection with historical norms and values that regulate how authors and audiences conceive literary authorship.

As Lanser and others have noted, such historical norms and values have had a strong impact upon traditional views of authorship and discursive authority in relation to gender differences.[57] Well into the twentieth century, female authorship remained marked as the exception to a largely male norm that wielded discursive authority and power. Other social markers of class and ethnic identity functioned in similar ways as mechanisms of exclusion and stratification in the literary field. Birke is right to say that we should not regard the authority of male authors "as a monolithic foil" but that "authorial voice *in general*" is "an act of rhetorical positioning" and anything but "an unproblematic expression of control over a text's meaning and the functions it is supposed to fulfil" (Birke 2016, 45). Yet, marginalised groups are at a particular disadvantage in this respect and thus need to find their own solutions to the lack of social recognition and discursive authority. These solutions typically involve the use of rhetorical resources such as 'minor' literary forms, popular genres, sincerity, irony, or subversiveness.[58] The inclusion of an author character within the work may be one such autopoetic strategy.

---

[57] See Warhol 1989. For a collection of essays on gendered notions of authorship and creativity see Zwierlein 2010.
[58] On the idea of 'minor literature', see Deleuze/Guattari 1986. As a genre, the essay has also been hailed as "giving a voice to minority groups" (Flothow/Oppholzer 2017, xi); this might explain its attractiveness as a resource in recent author novels and autofiction. Thanks to Daniel Schneider

A Rhetorical Model

Unless we wish to assign this role to the implied author, as discussed above, "the ultimate source of narrative", or indeed textual, "communication" (Phelan 2017, 156) is usually understood to be the text's actual, flesh-and-blood author, the person who wrote or otherwise created the text. This author – assuming a single author for the sake of simplicity –, using the resources of language and the cultural techniques of writing, created an immaterial *work* that is materially presented in a *text*, i.e., a sequence of words or other symbols. This text can be edited, published, and distributed in multiple *documents* (e.g., in the material form of a printed book or a recording), and it is in this format that it reaches an *audience*, usually readers or listeners. The audience, in reading or otherwise processing the text, works its way through the text and beyond it to a cognitive semantic representation of the work, and possibly beyond that to an idea of the work's author. In cases where a greater degree of precision is required, we might want to refer to that audience's version of the work as work$_2$ to distinguish it from the author's creation, work$_1$, and from further iterations.

As audience members process the text and experience the work, they respond to it in multiple ways. In this process, deficiencies in the document, such as misprints or other errors, can and will in most cases be corrected by means of readerly inference. Many textual errors or inconsistencies in a work are usually passed over by audiences without too much friction, at least when such flaws do not detract too much from audiences' sense-making efforts and enjoyment of the work or infringe too many literary conventions.[59]

The concept of the *work*, despite its residually idealistic implications, is necessary as an abstract counterpart to the concrete and material text. Authors write texts, but what they create in the process of writing is a work (a mental representation laid down in textual form). Texts are multiple whereas a work is usually singular. A text can come in different editions; a defective text does not impair the work – unless it is the only surviving copy. A work can exist in several different versions (Marlowe's *Doctor Faustus* A and B, Henry James's original and revised

---

for pointing this out to me. Connections between the genre of the 'personal essay' and historical forms of subject formation are explored by Emre 2022.

[59] Debates about such problems go at least as far back as the discussion of "probable impossibilities" in Aristotle's *Poetics* (2013, 50). James Phelan has explained the toleration of "breaks in the probability code" (2017, 49) in a narrative as "instances in which the logic of author-audience relationships trumps the logic of event sequence or of telling situations" (2017, 4; see ibid., 32–59). Such things have also been discussed in the context of so-called 'unnatural narratives'; see Richardson 2015, Alber 2016, Alber/Heinze 2011.

Daisy Miller) but these versions are versions of the same work. Audiences read texts, but they actualise works in their minds.

In fig. 3, I propose a modification of Phelan's ARA chart (authors, resources, audiences; see Phelan 2018, 7) of constants in literary communication, adding what I think is a useful and necessary distinction between 'text' and 'work'.

Author ↔ Work ↔ Text (Document) ↔ Audience
↕
Resources

Fig. 3: Constants in literary communication.

The author's intention in creating the work will have been successful if and when audiences imaginatively reconstruct that work to a sufficient extent, or to an extent necessary to fulfil the text's communicative purpose. There is some circularity in this argument that is regrettable but, I think, unavoidable. To put it another way, work$_2$ has been successfully actualised if and only if an audience has processed the text (according to the resources of language, of grammar, etc.) in such a way that a sufficient approximation of work$_1$ has been realised. Now it is obviously difficult to say what level of approximation will be sufficient, and this may very well differ from one work to the next based on the resources of genre, style, metaphors, ambiguities, and the like that need to be processed. Reading *Ulysses* obviously differs in this respect from reading a Jack Reacher novel, and the pleasures to be had in doing either are of a very different kind. Yet, in most cases, it will not be asking too much of readers to expect them to actualise an adequate amount from the possible range of meanings provided in the text. Many details in a work are left to the audience's imagination – hence the famous gaps or indeterminacies of reader response theory (Iser 1974, 1978) – and even many details that *are* specified in a text may be misconstrued or forgotten without harming audience enjoyment or impairing an adequate construal of the work.

As Wolfgang Iser has shown, reading is a co-creative process, but the acts of creation involved take place at different times: first work$_1$, then work$_2$ – or rather work$_n$ (as many as there are readers of the text). Together, in each new actualisation, these form the unity of the work as a whole (which, since it has no definite material form, can live on indefinitely as long as there are audiences interested in it). Reading is not merely a reconstruction of something given, nor is it pre-formatted by the dictates of 'reading communities' (Fish 1982). The work emerges from the choices made (or not made) by its author, consciously or unconsciously, unintended mistakes included (such as when Keats falsely attributes the discovery of the Pacific Ocean to Cortez rather than Balboa). It is made manifest in a text and becomes accessible to audiences through documents like printed books, magazines, or audiobooks. The audience's cognitive processing of textual information from a document results in a mental representation of the work. What emerges from this process is a work that is made up of all its resources but that, as a perceived whole, is more than the sum of its resources, and also more (and different) from what its author may have intended before or during the process of creation.

In a work of fiction, authors can present a vision of the world that is not necessarily their own vision as flesh-and-blood individuals. Neither does the harmonising of deficiencies or errors require an implied author to preserve the work's unity of intention or effect. Keeping work and text as separate categories enables us to distinguish between the pragmatic (ontological) and semantic (epistemological) aspects of literary communication. Author, text (document), and audience are individually necessary and jointly sufficient components of the pragmatic aspect – of the "worldliness" (Said 1983, 35) or "worldedness" (Hayot 2012, 25–26) – of literary communication. They have an actual physical existence. The semantic aspect encompasses the work that is encoded in and decoded from the text. The work harbours all those features that Phelan calls 'resources', an open list of more or less indispensable variables including narrator(s), characters, genre, style, arrangement, ambiguities, intertextual references, and other elements that "the teller can deploy in order to connect with the audience" (Phelan 2018, 7). Moreover, what distinguishes the work, in all its iterations from 1 to n, is that it and everything it contains is fictional in the sense that it exists only in the mind, a figment of authors' and audiences' imaginations that depends on the existence of the work, whereas the text, and the documents that contain the text, as well as authors and audiences, exist in the actual world in a material form and are in that sense 'real'.[60]

A possible solution to the quandary of actual and imagined authors and their textual representations resides in the conventions of fictionality. The words of a text that constitute the work were written by an author, but they are not intended as statements made by the author personally, like other "public authorial statements" (Dawson 2015, 96) in interviews etc. They are made in the mode of fiction,

---

[60] These terms may not satisfy some, who might object that the works I talk about here are nevertheless real, in the sense that *Hamlet* is a real work, which moreover includes an extract from the fictional work *The Murder of Gonzago*, and so on. I am aware of this difficulty, but I think the difference between works and texts as one of fiction vs. reality is a good enough shorthand to express my meaning. In this sense, Hamlet is a fictional character, whereas Gonzago is a fictional fictional character. Cf. also Kripke 2013: "The entities which one calls 'real entities' are the ones one could talk about before one told any stories. When one imitates this and tells stories, then one has fictional entities of the same kind. Then fictional fictional entities arrive, when a story itself talks about stories. And so on *ad infinitum* [...]" (82).

of an 'as if' (cf. Bakhtin 1981, 256). A familiar view defines fiction by its independence from questions of (factual) truth: "the poet, he nothing affirms, and therefore never lieth" (Sidney 1973, 102). This kind of storytelling involves, if not a Coleridgean suspension of disbelief, a mutual agreement of make-believe: "tellers and listeners (or writers and readers)" must agree "that the story told merely looks as if it conveyed information about matters of fact" (Birke/Köppe 2015a, 4). Of course, nothing prevents the storyteller from *also* providing truthful and accurate factual information, but that would be rather irrelevant to the story *qua* fictional narrative.

For rhetorical narratologists, fictionality is one of the resources of narrative that can be activated in storytelling (Phelan 2018, 7). Instead of viewing fictionality as a necessary requirement for this conventional understanding of authorial discourse in narrative, one might point to the conventions of storytelling as sufficient for a contextual distinction between authors and narrators. In this sense, I use the terms 'fiction' and 'fictionality' rather loosely as a means to distinguish the non-actual entities that appear in works of literature (including narratives designated as nonfiction) from the actual entities we encounter in the world.

Speech act theorists, inspired by Philip Sidney, hold that speech acts in a story do not permit inferences about the actual author's beliefs (Birke/Köppe 2015a, 4, citing Lamarque/Olsen 1994, 45–46), although in the real world such inferences happen quite frequently. Audiences rightly or wrongly make such inferences about authors' personal beliefs or qualities all the time, for example when they infer Jane Austen's perceptiveness, Tolstoy's pacifism, or Philip Roth's puckishness from their works. The separation between the actual and the non-actual (or fictional) clearly is not impermeable. As a contextual convention, however, it has been socially and culturally useful, because it places an "aesthetic screen" (Morton 2007, 35) between the (fictional) storyworld and the (actual) world of authors and audiences. This convention creates a protective shield for the author, in a moral and also a legal sense, although this shield is neither impenetrable nor universal, as censorship, libel cases, or the *fatwa* against Salman Rushdie demonstrate (Ross 2019). Fictionality emphasises or increases the distance between actual authors and their alleged narrative presence in their works. The conventions of fictionality mandate that an author's presence within a narrative (no matter how this is defined exactly or perceived by audiences) must not be confused with the actual author. To do so would be to commit a "category mistake" (Birke/Köppe 2015a, 6).

If we assume that narrators are fictional beings, nothing forces us to conclude that the narrators in Jane Austen's novels are all unmarried women or members of the lower gentry like Austen herself (cf. Miller 2003, Downie 2006, Quinn 2007), or indeed that they simply *are* Jane Austen (Boyd 2017). An author's real-life identity need not match the authorial voice inside the narrative. Even if there is a personalised and intrusive heterodiegetic narrator N (of the Thackeray type) who identifies himself in the story by the same name as the author A whose name is stated on the book's cover, there is no need to assume that this fictional 'A' is identical to the A who wrote the novel. Some autodiegetic narrators share a name with their author: Marcel is the first name of the narrator of the *Recherche* as well as that of its flesh-and-blood author. Autofiction explicitly encourages readers to identify the narrator with the real author, warts and all, and thus to do away with fictionality altogether.

Nothing about this is new. The association between an actual author outside the text and a character inside the text who shares the actual author's name has been frequently played out in literary history to varying degrees of complexity. (I have pointed to the examples of Dante and Chaucer in ch. 1.) Many narrative texts imply an affinity or closeness, if not an absolute identity, between their actual authors and their narrators. In some texts, "the fictionalizing of the authorial self" (Thompson 1993, 2) is so prominent that "the relationship between [an author's] real and fictive selves" becomes "thematic": "at once a disguise [...] and a manifestation of [their] most intimate concerns", the "writer's identity" becomes "the organizing principle or conceptual center of [their] work" (Dryden 1977, 11). Examples would be author-foregrounding authors like Cervantes, Defoe, or Hawthorne. Cervantes parades several layers of authorial mediation in *Don Quixote*; Defoe pretends to have edited rather than authored works like *Robinson Crusoe*; Hawthorne constantly manipulates the author/narrator boundary (cf. Thompson 1993, 17–18). But these are all nonetheless fictions, distinct from their authors. Although some texts invite us to identify their narrator with the author, most narrative theorists would place an emphasis on the word 'fiction' in 'autofiction' – precisely because the ontological boundary between narrative fiction and reality cannot be entirely dissolved.

Combining rhetorical poetics with the concept of fictionality, I suggest the revised model of communication, now built around what I call the ontological gap or boundary between actual and non-actual entities, or reality and fiction for short. This should help to illustrate the fact that this divide is not limiting so much as it is productive of attempts to cross to the other side.

Crossing the Gap

The binary model of literary communication that I have been discussing at some length, which separates reality from fiction, text from world, inside from outside, certainly has many benefits. It harmonises neatly with a modern (Western) notion of the freedom of art, because it serves to disengage the actual author as a real person from the persona inside the work that, in its role as the narrator of a story, or as the voice of the work, most closely resembles the function of the writer outside the text but need not be in any way identical to the actual speaking position of the writer.

Unless they constitute an injury to the rights of other living persons, an author's words in a literary text are protected in many countries by laws pertaining to freedom of speech (which also applies to non-literary texts) and freedom of art: in the latter context, the work, and the words that constitute the work, are *autonomous* and *autotelic*.[61] Unlike everyday communication, they enjoy the protection of the aesthetic. If you disapprove of Humbert Humbert, you can fault Nabokov, but only on artistic grounds; you cannot blame him personally or take him to court for fictional child abuse. Here the ontological gap functions as a moral and legal boundary. The shift of accountability away from authors is part of the historical trajectory of establishing literature as an autonomous discourse, a discourse that can freely entertain all kinds of controversial propositions. This autonomy of literature as an institution endowed with "the right to say everything and [...] the right of everything to be said" (Bourdieu 1996, 91) is a hard-earned privilege, granted to literature only after protracted struggles from the early modern period until today, and it may in fact, like Habermas's modernity, be an unfinished project (cf. Habermas 1997).

In the early 1990s, both Bourdieu and Derrida emphasised freedom as a foundational condition of literature. "What we call literature", Derrida asserted, "implies that license is given to the writer to say everything he [sic] wants to or everything he can, while remaining shielded, safe from all censorship, be it religious or political" (1992, 17). But, as Lukács and his successors of the Frankfurt School knew, this is not a universal law but a far from irreversible historical achievement tethered to a specific socio-historical constellation. Licenses can be revoked. In recent years, forms of political, state-organised suppression and censorship have returned in many countries, while in many democratic countries self-described progressive movements have been developing more informal forms of intolerance towards the freedom of fiction. For some, it is no longer acceptable if authors write about 'identities', cultures, or experiences outside of their own personal corner of the world. Slogans like 'cultural appropriation' indicate an intolerance towards artistic freedom, more precisely, towards the freedom to write about whatever or whomever

---

61 Historically, this autonomy of literary fiction was part of the "logic of modernism" (Hilliard 2021, 63, following Bourdieu 1996), but it was never absolute; libel and obscenity laws continue to limit the freedom of literary expression, making little or no distinction "between fact and fiction, but between utterances that could be construed as broadly political, and those which were frivolous or meretricious" (Hilliard 2021, 73). Cf. Latham 2009, Grüttemeier 2016, Ross 2019.

one likes to write about. The special achievement and privilege of fiction – the freedom to inhabit other minds, other bodies than one's own, to explore other possibilities of living– appears to have become suspect (Smith 2019). The right to tell "everything [one] wants to or […] can" (Derrida 1992, 17) has come under scrutiny, as in the example of Jeanine Cummins's 2020 novel *American Dirt* and its largely scandalous reception as an insult to Latinx writers. In a culture where "placements and positionings on various levels of literary communication" (Griem 2021, 73), including not only the work itself but also its marketing and reviewing, matter to the extent they currently do, it is doubtful whether a novel like William Styron's *The Confessions of Nat Turner* (1967), a white author's novel inhabiting a Black perspective, could be awarded a Pulitzer Prize today. Whether Nabokov's *Lolita* (1955) – controversial then as now – would still be published, even by the likes of the Olympia Press, is an open question.

In this cultural climate, irony has also come under pressure and is often no longer understood or appreciated. Faced with increasing competition from other media and an alleged cultural saturation of the inauthentic, many authors from the 1990s onwards felt the need to return to seriousness and sincerity (Wallace 1993). Literary nonfiction, which had been a niche interest, now sold exceedingly well and was praised by critics (e.g., Thomas Kenneally's *Schindler's Ark*, 1982, and Erik Larson's *The Devil in the White City*, 2003).[62] After the exhaustion of postmodernist metafiction at the end of the Cold War (suggestively linked by Grausam 2011), there was a renewed appetite for the real, a 'hunger' even (Shields 2010). Literature was increasingly regarded as a privileged form of witnessing, injecting the concept of authorship with renewed moral imperatives of virtue and social or political commitment (cf. Aryan 2020, 186). The notion of 'witness literature' as a truthful engagement with traumatic experiences gained traction globally after the end of the Cold War, particularly in postcolonial contexts (Engdahl 2002, Craps 2012). After many turns of the screw of Lukácsian reflection, writers and critics were drawn to new forms of subjectivity, sincerity, and authenticity, not only with regard to content but to their own speaking position or positionality in a world increasingly aware of the cultural and social power of differences and/ as distinctions, a world of identity politics.

To put it bluntly, authors from the mid-twentieth century onwards jettison impersonality for visibility. They leave the modernist ivory tower behind to find their readers among the members of specific communities, particular audiences (and,

---

[62] I am certainly oversimplifying at this point; one would have to consider in more detail the connections between the novel and the New Journalism in the US of the 1960s and 1970s, e.g., Hunter S. Thompson, Joan Didion, Tom Wolfe, Norman Mailer, and others (cf. Hollowell 1977).

more rarely, to establish a wider appeal to more or larger groups). They establish a rapport with their audiences that makes them stand out and achieve visibility as authentic members of a certain group, both in terms of Moore's "authenticity of expression" and "authenticity of experience" (2012, 269). Their individual but representative experience helps that community (often a marginalised one) to gain collective visibility. This kind of authorial authenticity is thus a two-way process that depends not merely on the person or position of the author but on the perception of the audience. The authenticity of the author needs to be ratified, authenticated by audiences as relevant to their experience. Authors as witnesses lend visibility to otherwise hidden experiences or communities, testifying to the truth of a lived reality – with dire consequences if that trust is betrayed, for instance in cases where the author's alleged identity turns out to be false. In the social and economic logic of the contemporary literary scene, only some "star authors" (Moran 2000) transcend the diversification of the market and achieve a condition of hypervisibility.

Among the expressions of such an "aesthetic of trust" (Hassan 2003) is the rise of autofiction and the memoir, as well as a growing impatience with 'mere' fiction. If the clichéd advice to 'write what you know' is applied as a formula of legitimation, interpreting knowledge more narrowly as personal experience, it turns into the imperative to 'write *only* what you have yourself experienced or witnessed with your own eyes'. Moreover, it invites audiences to infer a much stronger link between the actual author and the narrative than is usually the case in fiction, similar to the 'autobiographical pact' (Lejeune 1975). When this link is severed, as in cases of autobiographical fraud, the author is unmasked as a false witness, one who has abused the audience's trust. Whether the 'new sincerity' (cf. Voelz 2016) is genuinely detrimental to the audience's tolerance for fiction in general, as some authors have claimed (e.g., Smith 2019), would be difficult to prove. Yet there has undoubtedly been a sea-change in what many readers expect from authors as not only purveyors of fiction but as messengers for progressive causes (e.g., Jonathan Safran Foer as a campaigner against animal cruelty), and a trend towards a greater identification of author and work. In this cultural re-alignment of reality and fiction, irony returns with a vengeance, as when the author of the first biography of Philip Roth in 2021 was dropped by his publisher and his agency because of alleged sexual misconduct. One cannot help feeling that this would have made a perfect scenario for yet another Roth novel.

The models of narrative theory may erect and defend an ontological barrier between fiction and reality, but there will always be attempts by authors and audiences to tear it down again. The distinction between author and narrator, like the autonomy of literary fiction, took a long time to evolve. As renewed arguments about its tenability demonstrate, it is a precarious distinction, liable to breakdowns, crises, and moral panics. Periods of high overall tolerance for the fictionality of fiction appear to alternate with less open-minded periods. Yet in literature, too, the boundaries are often blurred: in literary biographies and autobiographies, in some examples of metafiction, in confessional writing, witness literature, and autofiction. The ontological gap, apparently, has a pulse that quivers with the tension between fiction and reality. If the gap cannot be overcome, perhaps it can be at least temporarily crossed?

Author, Work, Audience: An Interactional Loop

In the real world, we can observe such crossings all the time. Audiences almost inevitably establish connections between authors and the fictional content of their works – narrators, characters, events, ethical and political orientations expressed or implied in the work. According to classical literary theories, especially the New Criticism but also many varieties of structuralism, authors' individual attributes – genders, classes, ethnicities, religious and sexual orientations, etc. – should not play any role in our reading of their works, because texts are to be considered as artefacts, 'well-wrought urns', independently of their context of creation and production (cf. Wimsatt/Beardsley 1954). The objectified concept of the text in these theories also calls for a neutral, affectless, apparently objective reading position that is equally devoid of personal characteristics or attitudes, irrespective of the actual diversity of audiences. While this had clear advantages for pedagogy as well as for the development of literary theory, since it demanded close attention to the text, its component parts or structures, and their intrinsic functionality, it was also reductive in its deliberate exclusion of authorial and audience input in the making and understanding of literary texts.

While this position never became popular with extramural audiences, it is also no longer self-evident within the walls of academia. On the contrary, it has come to be identified with antiquated notions of (white, male) academic privilege and, frankly, ignorance. Historicist and Marxist practices of literary criticism rely on knowledge about authors' social affiliations and their place in history. Feminist, postcolonial, and queer studies crucially depend on the alignment between authors and their work, as do all theories and reading strategies that adhere to a version of 'strategic essentialism' (cf. Spivak 1996, 214). They need to know or to reconstruct an author's positionality in a mesh of intersectional differences. Hence the person of the author has been resurrected and returned to literary criticism with a vengeance: as an entity, as a standpoint, as a carrier of a certain combination of features that legitimise specific forms of expression and vitiate others. In critical practice, there is a persistent "desire to read literatures by authors from marginalized or oppressed groups as representative experiences" and thus to assume an autobiographical referent that is expressed in the text (Elfenbein 2020, 281). For these critics, the link between author and work, and between work and world, is indeed essential.

If this link is broken, audiences who are invested in the concept of "authenticity of experience" (Moore 2012, 269) cannot but feel betrayed. There are many cases of authors who have duped their audiences, and sometimes even their publishers, by assuming an identity that was radically different from their own. This is not only the case in nonfiction genres like the memoir, which naturally places a high premium on authenticity. Even in the field of fiction, the public sometimes expects congruity between the author's person and the world of the work. For example, in 1987, Virago Press published *Down the Road, Worlds Away*, a collection of stories mainly about young Asian women by 38-year-old author Rahila Khan. This alleged Asian British woman writer and mother of two was soon unmasked as the Anglican vicar Toby Forward from Brighton. In such cases of a glaring mismatch between the alleged and actual identity of an author, the public rightly feels deceived. Forward's defence that he had merely availed himself of artistic license was unsuccessful (Mullan 2007, 114–118). In this case, the writing was not perceived as mere fiction but "as a lens on a marginalized identity" (Elfenbein 2020, 282). As long as they were by Rahila Khan, the stories could be regarded as authentic, based on personal experience. When they turned out to have been written by a white male vicar, however, they lost any claims to such authenticity and authority. They infringed an unwritten moral code of authorship that applies not only to nonfiction but also to fiction, at least when that fiction makes claims of probability and applicability to real-life events or social conditions.

In such cases, we see the rhetorical purpose of the work break down. We also see how a disappointed audience turns away from the fictionality of the stories and demands retribution from the stories' actual author. In situations like this, the alignment between author and work connects them firmly and anchors them in the real world. Possibly, audiences' acceptance of fictional narrative depends to some extent on this alignment, and on the confidence that they are not being duped. If that is the case, one could say that an author's license to tell stories in the mode of fiction depends on the audience's trust that they are not being deceived about this meta- or paratextual level of authorship outside the fiction. This is one reason why audiences care about who the author is, and why deceptions or hoaxes tend to receive so much attention.[63]

---

[63] A more recent instance is the hunt for the true identity of 'Elena Ferrante'. Here, too, readers desire the narrative to be legitimised and authenticated by the author's identity. Cf. Emre 2019.

A related question of authorial agency or involvement in the text, across the ontological gap between reality and fiction, concerns the presence of errors or blunders – not misprints or other flaws in textual transmission, but genuine mistakes, errors of judgement or errors of fact. Should they be attributed to the author or the narrator? In the first case, we have Homer nodding; in the second, we take it that the error was deliberately planted by the author. In the latter view, we would have to argue that Shakespeare *wanted* Bohemia to have a seacoast, Thackeray *wanted* us to be confused about the age of Laura Bell in *Pendennis* (cf. Sutherland 2006, 1–27), and Keats *wanted* us to think it was Cortez and not Balboa who first spotted the Pacific Ocean (cf. McAlpine 2020). As James Joyce – or rather, Stephen Dedalus (the quotation is frequently attributed to Joyce without respecting the ontological gap) – proclaimed: "A man of genius makes no mistakes. His errors are volitional and are the portals of discovery" (Joyce 1987, 156). In such cases, audiences need to make a critical judgement about the kind of genius they are confronted with, and in so doing cross the ontological boundary between the fiction, or the world projected by the text, and the authorial context of its making.

We are faced with a different but related problem when information about the actual author's life and opinions damages their reputation and leads audiences to reconsider their enjoyment of this author's works. Here, then, the author's faults are not necessarily visible in the text, as they are in the case of certain errors, but they come to reside in the person of the author outside the text, often *a posteriori*, as a result of an audience's superior knowledge about that author. This, too, is an inevitable alignment between author and work. For some readers, for example, Philip Larkin's posthumously published views on foreigners and women damaged their appreciation of his poems. There may be gradations to such damage, possibly depending on the kind of work or genre the author was working in. Knowledge of Patricia Highsmith's antisemitism may be less detrimental to audiences' enjoyment of her crime novels than the same knowledge about Roald Dahl would be to that of his children's books.[64] Highsmith's novels explore morally dubious situations and amoral characters, so there is a fitting alignment between author and fiction that is missing in Dahl, even though that does not make Highsmith's racism any less distasteful. Similar, even more notorious cases concern Ezra Pound and Louis-Ferdinand Céline, among others.

This raises interesting questions about the moral aspects of authors' lives and their works; should they be considered distinct – eclipsing the author and privileg-

---

[64] In Dahl's case, the situation is complicated by the knowledge that "[m]ost of [his] longer books [...] were in effect co-authored by Stephen Roxburgh at Farrar, Straus and Giroux", after 1981, and by other editors before then (letter by Jeremy Treglown, *TLS*, March 3, 2023, and cf. Treglown 1994).

ing the aesthetic aspects of the work – or inseparable (cf. Sapiro 2020)? Moreover, the moralist approach often involves changing ideas of what is considered reprehensible. Not in the examples of Céline, Dahl, and Highsmith, whose views were as abominable during their lifetimes as they are now. But some ideas or forms of behaviour that are now anathema were acceptable in the past, and vice versa. Oscar Wilde, for instance, condemned for his sexuality by laws valid during his lifetime, is today just as likely to be fêted as a figurehead of LGBTQ+ pride as for his literary achievements. That said, evidence of his sexual abuse of underage boys might well come to undermine the image of Wilde as a martyr (Bucknell 2021), and possibly harm his literary reputation as well.

Conversely, where the work displays positive qualities like wisdom, compassion, or sincerity, it is difficult to view these qualities as entirely disconnected from the actual author's personality, which is then often assumed to possess these qualities "at least on that occasion" (Lamarque 2009, 104). In reading or teaching literature, audiences can try to exclude any external information, to sever any link between text and world, and to ignore any such knowledge that might come their way – but experience shows that this is not how reading works in real life. Audiences have always been interested in authors ('always', in this case, meaning at least since the eighteenth century, and probably much earlier) and in the connections between 'life and work'. As Philip Roth reminds us, "art is life too" (2017, 133). Complete disconnection between work, author, and world, in the sense of an absolute autonomy of art, is a chimera. There will always be ethical, social, political, economic, legal, and other concerns that persistently connect texts to their authors and thus to the world outside the fiction. The boundaries between fiction and reality are not absolute; authors and audiences are constantly engaged in 'boundary work' that establishes, maintains and at times transcends the ontological gap between author and text.

I propose that the authorial and audience-related aspects of this ontological boundary work can be modelled as a series of vectors, comprising textual and extratextual actions and feedback effects. This 'authorpoietic loop' (fig. 4), I suggest, allows a more precise and dynamic conceptualisation of the interactions between authors, works and audiences, as well as between abstract concepts and concrete textual phenomena.

With the top left vector arrow, the author attaches him- or herself to the work in what I term, following a suggestion from John Frow, *anaclisis* (Freud 1953, 181; cf. Frow 2021). By means of autopoetic strategies or signals, textual entities and narrative resources are invested with an authorial stamp of presence. The work takes its identity from the author, whose authorial identity in turn is formed by the work, as embodied in one or more texts (including paratexts). These "texts bear […] marks that betray the assumptions of the creator" (Hutcheon 2013, 108–109).

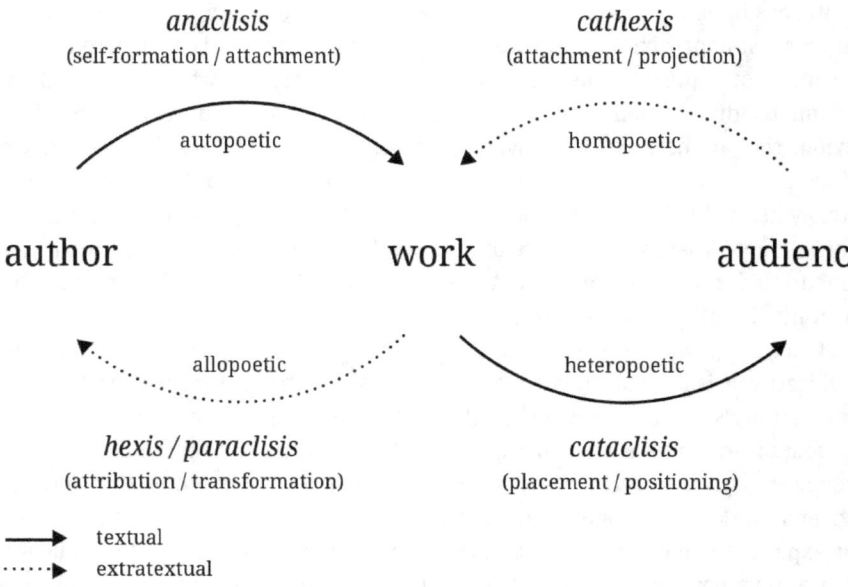

Fig. 4: The interactional loop between author, work, and audience.

This conceptualisation of authorial presence in the work as a form of attachment or grafting might also help to account for the relationship between the mimetic and thematic aspects of fictional character, for example: to allow us to see more clearly how a particular fictional character relates not only to the work's actual author but also to more general ideas of what people whom this character resembles are like or could or should be like. In this sense, then, *anaclisis* is not only autopoetic (geared towards authorial self-understanding and self-creation) but also heteropoetic, working outwards from the text, anticipating an audience's perspective, and conveying to the audience certain ideas or meanings about the ways in which fictional entities relate to the real world.

The heteropoetic dimension of literary communication intends to situate or articulate an audience in relation to the work and its author, anticipating what Peter J. Rabinowitz has called an "authorial audience" (1976, 126), one that is asked to share, as much as possible, the author's knowledge and values, as opposed to the "narrative audience" that, in the words of Jim Phelan, "takes on the beliefs and values that the narrator ascribes to it, and in most cases responds to the characters and events as if they were real" (1996, 93). This placement or positioning of an audience within the work I call, in analogy to anaclisis, *cataclisis*. In Greek, that word can literally mean the placement of a guest at the dinner table. Like a dinner guest, the reader is invited by the author-as-host, invoking welcome metaphors of hospitality but also more contentious associations of parasitism (cf. Miller 1977).

Ana- and *cataclisis* describe auto- and heteropoetic processes of attachment and placement that proceed from author to work and from work to audience. Yet, the other direction is at least equally important. Authorial attachment works from actual authors towards their text; readerly attachment works from audiences towards the work and back towards themselves and their sense of how both work and author relate to the world. Using another Freudian metaphor, I refer to the cognitive, affective, and ethical engagement of audiences with fictional entities as *cathexis* (*Besetzung* as 'attachment' or 'projection'). I call this vector 'homopoetic' to emphasise the aspects of assimilation and appropriation that occur when audiences relate to works and construe an image of the author based on the work (and other paratextual information) in the light of conventions and expectations.[65] Value judgements by audiences on this basis will then reflect back upon the author, leading to forms of recognition such as financial and/or critical success, awards and honours, cultural capital, social prestige. This shaping of actual authors based on audience reception I call the 'allopoetic' vector; here, the author is at the receiving end of the dynamic relationship and is changed through the process of audience interaction with the work and its creator.

Allopoetic effects can be further distinguished into forms of audience attribution that confirm rather than transform how actual authors would like to be perceived (in cases where there is a match between auto- and allopoetics); for this, I suggest using the word *hexis*, which, similar to Bourdieu's concept of *habitus* and sometimes used by him as a synonym, indicates a fusion of personal attributes and socially ascribed attributions. For the more transformative effects of allopoiesis, my suggestion would be *paraclisis* – an attachment that changes its object into something or someone else. *Paraclisis* is a neologism derived from the Greek verb *paraklíno*, 'to bend, turn aside or make something go astray'.

Once more, in a terminological nutshell:[66]

- *anaclisis:* authorial self-formation and attachment to the work via autopoetic textual signals;
- *cataclisis:* textual 'placement', anticipation or positioning of an audience in relation to work and author via heteropoetic textual signals;

---

65 As I state in the introduction to this book, 'homoiopoetic' might be the preferred term because this vector is about assimilation rather than sameness, but I opted for 'homopoetic' for the sake of simplicity and symmetry.
66 See also the glossary for a more detailed survey of the terminology introduced in this book.

- *cathexis:* audience's homopoetic assimilation of the work and projection of an author image based on auto- and heteropoetic signals, audience expectations, and conventions;
- *hexis:* the attribution of an aptitude, quality, ability, or prestige etc., which authors acquire by means of audience responses; the allopoetic formation of an author by the work and its reception (beyond the author's control); this is
- *paraclisis:* deviation, transformation, or deformation when the work changes its author in unwelcome ways.

The auto- and heteropoetic vectors are primarily textual, having their place inside the work in the form of textual or rhetorical strategies directed towards achieving certain purposes with an audience. The homo- and allopoetic vectors are primarily located in the world outside the text or work, and they are in that sense 'extratextual'; however, this does not mean that they do not involve textual communication – they very often do. Yet, whereas the former are primarily intentional strategies, the latter are better described as outcomes or effects that can *potentially* be the result of these strategies (given the right felicity conditions of literary communication) but that can also diverge widely from whatever authors may have intended for their work or for themselves. All of these vectors, finally, are 'poietic' as well as 'poetic' in the sense that they are involved in the making of agential roles in the literary and wider social fields as well as in the creation, production and reception of works of literature.

This dynamic and interactive model of authorship proceeds from the key assumption that the connections between authors, works and audiences, like those between actual and fictional entities, are not usually simple, uniform, or straightforward. What Thompson has called the "inscribed author-figure trope" (1993, 19) that we find in many narrative texts can be understood not only as an (autopoetic-anaclitic) representation of that text's actual author, but more productively as a token of a particular type of "authorial construct" or, in my terminology, an 'author fiction' that is expressed in the form of a "figured literary self" in the text (ibid., 20). It becomes thematic as well as mimetic, and thus is involved in discursive formations and conventions that are valid in the world outside the narrative text.

Moreover, these connections are mediated by institutions in the literary field and by tacit or explicit rules of genre and literary form that shape how literary authorship functions within the field and how it is perceived by audiences. The fictional author can assume one or several such roles in a narrative, in relation to the availability and valorisation of these roles in the literary field and in society at large. Likewise, there are many different forms and genres in which stories about fictional authors can be told. The challenge is to find meaningful connections between social and literary forms without imposing a top-down analytic or theoretical grid: to describe the "reflexive-performative matrix" (McGurl 2009, 366) of works of literature, in which social scripts and cultural conventions, negotiations of authorial authority, and affective alignments with the audience are propped onto and merged with literary forms. For such processes, the history of representations of authorship in narrative fiction provides a paradigmatic example.

These connections between author, work and audience are even stronger and arguably more relevant in the case of forms of autobiographical life-writing in which author and narrator are assumed to be identical, and in which the acts of narration and writing shape the author as well as the text. A powerful early example of this is Olaudah Equiano's *Interesting Narrative* (1789), a foundational text for subsequent slave narratives and "the most detailed narrative of the slave trade that survives from the captive perspective" (O'Malley 2014, 32). Equiano, a former slave, presents the act of writing his book as an achievement of personal sovereignty and autonomous subjecthood; his book, one could say with Montaigne, has made him as much as he has made the book. Among the many autopoetic strategies in this narrative is Equiano's plain style, signalling his humility as a writer, and the episode of the slain chicken in which he asserts his inability to tell lies. He also employs heteropoetic strategies, for example stylistic elements of gothic and sentimental fiction that would have been familiar to eighteenth-century audiences. The authenticity and credibility of his narrative thus not only derives from his presentation of an eyewitness account – even though this might include "eyewitness testimony to the experiences of others" (ibid., 34) – but is also an effect of literary techniques that associate the actual horrors of the Middle Passage and the slave trade with the sublime aesthetics of the gothic novel.[67] These strategies articulate Equiano's authorial audience as receptive to those effects in order to win them over for the cause of abolition.

In self-declared fiction, the link between actual authors and fictional narrators or characters is obviously less direct and more tenuous. Yet novels that feature writers as characters, and sometimes as protagonists, also invite their audiences to establish possible connections or associations across the ontological boundary, and to read these characters not only as mimetic (as revealing who they are in and for themselves) but also as thematic (as a representation of a more general category of persons, in this case of writers or authors). In this, I follow Susan Lanser, who argues that the representation of authorship in a literary text "(re)produces" within the fiction "the structural and functional situation of author-

---

[67] Thanks to Philipp Schweighauser for reminding me of this in his talk "A Self-Made Slave: Cultural Techniques in Olaudah Equiano's *Interesting Narrative*" at the *SANAS* conference in Fribourg in November 2022. On authenticity and fiction in Equiano, see also Kelleter 2004, Carretta 2005, O'Malley 2014, Hanley 2018.

ship" in the world outside the text (Lanser 1992, 16). Yet Lanser's vacillation between production and reproduction is telling in this context, as she appears to underestimate the productive, performative feedback between fiction and reality. As Dorothee Birke explains in a comment on Lanser, such representations should be understood "as parts of a performance of authorship" or as expressing "a rhetorical stance" (2016, 43) – yet not only on the part of authors but also on the part of audiences, in a dynamic cycle of transactions or interactions. What I mean by 'performances' in this context not only includes the actions of an author but also the interventions of other agents: the ways in which authors not only make themselves in certain ways through writing and publishing (*anaclisis*) but also how they are in a sense *made* by institutions, other texts and authors, genres, audiences across multiple fields (*hexis* or *paraclisis*).

I assume that all writing involves some degree and form of performative reflection of authorial "position-takings" (Bourdieu 1996, 231), "postures" (Meizoz 2007, 2011), or "performances" of authorship (Berensmeyer/Buelens/Demoor 2012), some more explicit and self-aware, others more covert to the point of invisibility.[68] Writing and publishing are performative acts in the strongest possible sense, bringing forth its author(s) along with the text for audiences to appraise. Audiences in turn shape how actual authors are perceived and thus made into public figures, prompting further iterations of the authorpoietic process. What Italo Calvino has called "self-realization on paper" (Calvino 1998, 96) should be seen as a dynamic and interactive process between authors, works and audiences: the reflexive-performative construction of a relational space in which (both fictional and real) authors find themselves "encompassed and included" (Bourdieu 1996, xvii).

The interactional loop between authors, works, and audiences is intended as a model of how authors and audiences are positioned in relation to a work that is itself not a static object but a dynamic process. Here representation *is* performance that creates and modifies its own conditions of production and reception, within the limits imposed by the literary field and other cultural and social systems. Bour-

---

[68] Meizoz's concept of *posture auctoriale*, perhaps best translated as 'authorial positioning', emphasises the author as an active agent but retains the sense of an interactive, dynamic co-construction that takes place within texts and outside them among multiple participants (cf. Meizoz 2011, 83). It has been criticised for privileging the author over other participants (e.g., readers) and not clarifying which textual or non-textual information should be relevant to the reconstruction of a posture (Stiénon 2008, Saint-Amand/Vrydaghs 2011). The Ghent approach of a "performativity theory of authorship" (Berensmeyer/Buelens/Demoor 2012, 7–12) is less author-centric, based on speech act theory and the concept of performativity as developed in cultural studies. For further elaborations of the notions of performance, rhetoric, and figuration, see Guttzeit 2017. Also helpful in this context is Guttzeit's contrast between a "performative" and a "theoretical rhetoric of authorship" (2017, 31–32).

dieu's case study of Flaubert's *Sentimental Education* (Bourdieu 1996, 1–43) provides a model for analytic readings that combine literary and social structures, but I would argue, with Phelan, that Bourdieu underestimates the interpersonal, textual, and readerly dynamics involved in these relations, as well as the agency of literary resources like genres and forms (Phelan 2018, 13). Bourdieu's view is too deterministic in its construction of economic and artistic success as polar opposites. Moreover, some texts reflect on the processes of their own creation, production, and reception more explicitly than others, making this performative representation an integral part of the work and to some extent analysing themselves in the process – an analysis that the close reader will seek to trace and bring to the fore. The interactional model I propose here is obviously an abstraction, reduced to three sites of agency (author, work, audience), each of which can harbour a plurality of actual agents. It could be expanded to include further processes of translation between the fields of creation, production, and reception (Childress 2017) and specify further agents in the "communications circuit" (Darnton 1982; Adams/Barker 2006).

The model shows how 'authorpoiesis' or author-making can be understood as a dynamic process that combines social and textual dimensions, including the mainly text-based auto- and heteropoetic strategies that authors (as well as editors and publishers) use to situate and to communicate with audiences via a work (*cataclisis*), and the predominantly non-textual homo-and allopoetic effects that reflect back from audiences' responses to the work (*cathexis*) upon that work's author, confirming (*hexis*) or transforming (*paraclisis*) the author's authorial self. A performance of authorship can only be considered complete if it is recognised and judged by an audience; only then can authorial performance become truly *performative* and have potentially transformative effects in the actual world – not only upon the actual author of the work in question, whose position in the literary field or the wider culture may change due to this performance-based recognition, but upon concepts, practices and paradigms of authorship more generally, and the meanings and functions of literature in society. This performativity of literary authorship through its several interconnected stages is therefore social as well as textual; its place is outside as well as inside the text; and it involves both authors and audiences as active agents in an ongoing conversation.

The alignment between a work's actual author and its fictional author characters can vary considerably, ranging from a high degree of closeness or even assumed identity in the case of autobiographies or autofiction to various degrees of dissimilarity, distance or contrastiveness. Writing about authors and authorship can be a form of authorial wish-fulfilment, but it can also be an apotropaic or cautionary gesture of avoidance or evasion. It can be a retrospective idealisation (as in the case of *David Copperfield*) or an anticipatory move towards self-realisation.

More important than the connection between actual author and fictional author-character is the reflexive-performative manipulation within these narratives of the conceptual and practical paradigms of literary authorship. In the following readings and historical case studies of author fictions, my principal aim has been not to subject a selection of texts to a previously established set of paradigms but to assemble a significant long-term corpus of novels and stories and to extract from that corpus a new view of the literary history of literary authorship – a bottom-up, not a top-down approach of explication. This is also why, in the following parts of this book, I rely for the most part on close reading to tease out the implications of those narratives for the history of authorship concepts and practices from the early nineteenth century to the present.

Part II Author-Making and Social Form in the Nineteenth Century

I heard some time ago, that Anthony Trollope had a theory that a boy might be brought up to be a novelist as to any other trade. He brought up – or attempted to bring up – his own son on this principle, and the young man became a sheep-farmer in Australia.

– Henry James, *Notebooks*, Jan. 22, 1879

3 *Lost Illusions*: Balzac's Brutal Materialism

Throughout the nineteenth century, author fictions engage with the formation of the author's professional identity, increasingly depicted as a conflict between the individual writer's aspirations and the commercial demands of the market. We first see the concept of genius descend from its Romantic heights to the middle depths of social formation and adaptation to the demands of society and the market in the rise of the literary *bildungsroman*, following the enthusiastic international reception of Goethe's *Wilhelm Meister* (1795–96); subsequently, we see a shift of genre towards the *künstlerroman* or artist novel, which insists on the artist's isolation and alienation from society. In complex ways, this development is associated with the gradual erosion of nineteenth-century novelistic realism. The decline of the author-*bildungsroman* is accompanied by the rise of fantastic, gothic tropes that resist integration into a realist paradigm of novelistic representation. Moreover, the authority of the narrator and author vis à vis the narrated world is cast into doubt as "the traditional burden of authorial representativeness" (Weimann 1988, 442) becomes less and less convincing. One, if not the only, explanation for this paradigm shift from autonomy to impersonality can be found in the conditions of industrialised mass production of novels (and their authors) throughout the nineteenth century.

One of the first European novels to address the material pressures of the literary marketplace is Balzac's *Lost Illusions* (*Illusions perdues*, 1837–1843), one of the masterpieces of the massive narrative project that is Balzac's *Comédie Humaine*. Its historical importance for the development of nineteenth-century author fiction is undeniable. It intervenes in a literary conversation about the changing economic conditions of literary production and professional authorship that takes place in other European countries beyond France. Though *Illusions perdues* was not translated into English until the end of the nineteenth century, Balzac had many admirers in England, including Thackeray, Wilkie Collins, and the Brownings, who would read him in French (cf. Lesser 2012). Thackeray's *Pendennis*, for example [→ ch. 4], is difficult to imagine without this model.

In *Lost Illusions*, the novel comes to terms with its own physical, material, and social foundations. From Lukács (1972) onwards, critics have noted how Balzacian realism engages with a capitalist world characterised by economic dynamism and social mobility. Balzac's characters tend to be sucked in by a maelstrom of events that hurries them along as the plot moves relentlessly forward. Often, as in the case of Lucien Chardon / de Rubempré, this movement involves spectacular transformations and bizarre reversals of fortune, and the dynamics of the story propel the protagonist beyond the confines of the plot and into its continuation in another novel. Lucien, who is about to commit suicide towards the end of *Lost Illusions*, is picked up at the last minute by the Abbé Herrera (who turns out to be the master criminal Jacques Collin / Vautrin) and given a new lease of life in *A Harlot High and Low* (*Splendeurs et misères des courtisanes*, 1838–1847).

The loose ends and weak endings of Balzac's novels are a precondition for the serial narration that is their hallmark (cf. Moretti 1988, 124), but they also represent the sense of endless possibilities in a dynamic world that, in the plot, is best represented by contingent events, accidents and coincidences. This unstoppable sense of movement is symptomatic of a society in the fast lane, characterised by competition, opportunities and risk-taking. What has often been pointed out is the apparent discrepancy between the melodramatic events of the story and the gnomic wisdom of the narrative discourse, which only *seems* to counteract the headlong dash of the story but is actually propelled along with it and becomes ironic, presenting merely the pretence of a superordinate moral authority that is actually no longer compelling or that seems misplaced (Brooks 1976, Prendergast 1978).

Narrative 'wisdom', pronounced by an all-seeing, all-knowing, all-understanding and all-forgiving narrator, is thus merely another commodity in the world of commodity capitalism that is post-restoration France. These moral *sententiae* have turned into hollow, increasingly cheap conventions. If they present 'common opinion' on 'normality' – i.e., on "what is both 'widespread' and 'commendable'" (Moretti 1988, 292 n. 6) – a *doxa* enshrined in "prevailing normative codes" (Moretti 2000, 96) – their cheapness leads to a rift in the comfort they may offer the reader. Instead of a narrative synthesis by means of "persuasive and all-inclusive wisdom", they encourage a more "complex, ambiguous and ironic manner" of reading (ibid.).

The Balzacian narrator, then, while still going through the motions of omniscience, of being the voice of common sense, has actually lost his authority as an instance of narrative truth. Instead of achieving a totalising synthesis of multiple points of view, which would confirm his narrative authority, his general observations and extrareferential statements do not amount to more than a series of incoherent assertions or "plain tripe" (Auerbach 2003, 478).[69]

---

[69] Fredric Jameson argues that "[o]mniscience [...] is the least-significant thing about such authorial intervention", suggesting instead that it is "the aftereffect of the closure of classical *récit*, in which the events are over and done with before their narrative begins", and a "symbolic[ ] attempt to restore the coordinates of a face-to-face storytelling institution which has been effectively disintegrated by the printed book and even more definitively by the commodification of literature and culture" (Jameson 2006, 140–141). He regards "the Balzacian narrative apparatus", particularly Balzac's descriptions, as a form of "authorial wish-fulfillment, [...] of symbolic satisfaction in which

While this is true for many novels in the *Comédie*, it is particularly acute in *Lost Illusions*, the one novel in which Balzac directly addresses the material conditions of literature and literary authorship in the early nineteenth century. What is the connection between the theme of this novel – the disillusionment about the Romantic idea of literature as free creative expression, or about the idea of freedom *tout court* – and the position of its narrator in relation to the story? *Lost Illusions* presents a diagnosis of the literary field in the early nineteenth century, where literary authorship has become merely one commodity among others. As Lukács remarked, it shows how literature, and thus the human spirit, fall under the spell of capitalism (1972, 351). But even its way of showing this, i.e., the relationship between 'authorial' narrator and narration, is affected by the institutional changes that are its subject matter: "This material extension of the theme – the capitalisation of literature from paper-making to lyric sentiment – determines [...] the artistic form of the composition" (352).

Lost Illusions "offers a trenchant portrait of the postrevolutionary book trade" in France (Haynes 2010, 1), where "the traditional printer-bookseller" was replaced by the "new figure" of "the publisher (*éditeur*) [...] who specialized in commissioning, financing, and coordinating the creation, production, and marketing of books by others" (ibid., 8–9). It describes the world of publishing as brutally materialistic, as a marketplace where "printed matter is manufactured and distributed by capitalist enterprises, subject to the laws of supply and demand" (ibid., 2). This is a world in which books will be cheaper not only in their price but also in their material and literary quality. Thanks to more cost-effective ways of making paper pulp out of "vegetable substances" (Balzac 2004, 515), books can become ephemeral products, disposable commodities.

"What a shame it is", exclaims the young printer David Séchard, "that our era cannot make books which will last!" (Balzac 2004, 112). He is talking about the quality of paper, but the novel extends this lament to the quality of literature, the debasement of which is illustrated by the cautionary tale of David's best friend, Lucien. Lucien's stellar rise and fall as the author, journalist, and celebrity Lucien de Rubempré is the arc that keeps the novel's plot inexorably moving forward. Lucien's real name Chardon ("thistle") also denotes the very same organic matter that David uses as his raw material for pulp ("nettles and thistles", 515), thus emphasizing the connection between the two friends (cf. Pasco 2016, 214). Lucien Chardon / de Rubempré is an efficient social climber, but he will remain a weed in the liter-

---

the working distinction between biographical subject, Implied Author, reader, and characters is virtually effaced" (141). Cf. also Pfeiffer 2021, who takes a more sanguine view of the 'abdication' of narrative authority in Balzac as an experiment that corresponds to the flexible forms of modern economies (76).

ary field. He is a man without qualities, whose superficial handsomeness makes him attractive to others (and thus lubricates his movement up the greasy pole) but conceals an emptiness inside; Balzac's narrator compares him to sculptures of Apollo or "the Indian Bacchus" (Balzac 2004, 26), but he also keenly stresses some aspects of Lucien's appearance as 'feminine' (e. g., ibid.; repeated in d'Arthez's letter to Eve, 510), possibly hinting at non-heterosexual tendencies. Be that as it may, these aspects are a sign of Lucien's weak constitution, which makes him unfit, in the view of some of his journalist friends, for the struggle that, as we will see, defines the life of an author: "You are of slight and slender build, you'll lose the battle", as one of them tells him (469).

Lucien has talent but is no genius. He has "an ardent thirst for literary glory" (23) but clearly lacks the stamina or substance required to leave a lasting mark on the literary scene. His weed-like opportunism briefly turns him into a "fashionable commodity" (Moretti 2000, 134), first in the provincial town of Angoulême (traditionally a centre of French papermaking) and then in Paris (always the centre of modernity for Balzac, and for the nineteenth century in general) until the city sucks him dry and spits him out again after eighteen months. When he returns home, he has wasted his talent and his family's money, causing his sister Eve and her husband, his best friend, David to spiral into debt and contributing to David's failure as an inventor.

In the early chapters, Balzac emphasises David's and Lucien's youthful romantic reading of Romantic literature, contrasting their enthusiasm for the poetry of André Chénier with the harsh reality of their poverty (2004, 28–29). Lucien enters the salon of Louise de Nègrepelisse, Mme de Bargeton, but his social ambitions and his attempt to drop his father's bourgeois name for the aristocratic surname of his mother make him an object of ridicule in provincial society. Louise, "infatuated with the Byron of Angoulême" (80), elopes with him to Paris, but once there, she immediately realises her mistake, and he immediately despises her provincial appearance and decides to make it in Paris without her assistance.

In the provinces, poetry – even though it is only dimly understood and, when recited, has a rather soporific effect – still commands respect. In Mme de Bargeton's salon, the bishop of Angoulême utters these familiar commonplaces:

> We cannot show too much respect to those noble minds whom God has endowed with a beam of His own light. Indeed, poetry is a sacred thing. Poetry involves suffering. How many nights of silence have paid for the stanzas you admire! Pay a tribute of love to the poet who almost always leads an unhappy life and for whom God no doubt reserves a place in Heaven among his prophets. (95)

Noble, divine light, a poet's corner in Heaven: poetry is "sacred" – *chose sainte* (Balzac 2013, 167) – and deserves veneration, in this (by now rather old-fashioned) view, because it is in touch with a higher world, is not yet a fully secularised activity but one that is committed to higher ideas and ideals. The bishop does not quite say exactly why "poetry involves suffering" and why the poet's life should be "unhappy" – is he merely referring to intellectual sufferings, the agonies of creativity, as the "many nights of silence" may lead us to assume, or is he – or Balzac through him – foreshadowing the more prosaic and material aspects of the poor poet's suffering? The narrator here keeps his counsel; it is Lucien who responds to the bishop, gratefully accepting the compliment and adding some more clichés to his commonplaces:

> No one knows the grief we [poets] suffer or the toil we endure. A miner has less labour winning the gold from his mine than we have in wresting our imagery from the entrails of this most obdurate language of ours. [...] Must [the poet] not have felt all there is to feel in order to give expression to it? And if one feels keenly, is not that suffering? Therefore poetry is only born after arduous journeys through the vast regions of thought and society. Are they not immortal, the works to which we owe those creations whose life becomes more authentic than that of people who have really lived – Richardson's Clarissa, Chénier's Camille, [...] Walter Scott's Rebecca and the Don Quixote of Cervantes? (Balzac 2004, 95–96)

Here Lucien is also subtly correcting the bishop: it is not waiting for divine inspiration but steady *toil* and *labour* that define the creative process. The works that result from this are the result of hard graft, as the French original makes even clearer in speaking not of immortal *oeuvres* but *travaux* (Balzac 2013, 168). The poet is not a priest but a miner, a worker in the mine of language – a much more secular image, and one that foreshadows the novel's obsession with capitalism and the *auri sacra fames*. Here, however, this metaphor is not yet a commercial one but reserved for the 'gold' of linguistic expression and the "world of ideas" (Balzac 2004, 96). Lucien also echoes the Romantic notion of the poet as a representative of humanity via his privileged sensibility, his *feeling* "all there is to feel in order to give expression to it" – a human, humane and social rather than divine legitimation of poetic activity; and he ends on a note of literary rather than religious *immortality,* conferred on author and work by the public ("we") who admire the authenticity of literary characters, a sense of authenticity that surpasses that of actual historical persons. The goal, then, for Lucien, is clear: he wants his future work – and his (mother's maiden) name to become as "immortal" as those of Richardson, Scott, and Cervantes. He is young, so he still has time – indeed, as the narrator wisely asserts, time is the only resource at his disposal: "time is the sole capital of people whose future depends on their intelligence" (102).[70] But this

---

70 "[L]e temps est le seul capital des gens qui n'ont que leur intelligence pour fortune" (Balzac

capital, as it turns out, will soon be frittered away in the expensive life of the city, which costs time as well as money.

These are the initial illusions about the literary life that Lucien is about to lose; some almost immediately after this conversation, when his recital in the salon falls on deaf ears; others later in Paris, where he soon learns that literature has irrevocably been transformed into a business, swept up like everything else in the common dynamic of market values and universal competition. His formation, in this novel of formation, is a deformation of the high-minded ideals he sets out with. He soon learns, for instance, that publishers have no patience for speculations about immortality – they need to make a tangible profit quickly, and they are unwilling to make an investment in unknown authors. "I'm a speculator in literature", says one of them, Dauriat, "I'm not here to be a springboard for future reputations, but to make money for myself and provide some for the celebrities", i.e., those who already have made a "name" for themselves (273; cf. 354). "You only invest your time, while I have to lay out two thousand francs", another publisher, Doguereau, coldly advises Lucien (206) – but then again, even the young ultimately run out of time: as he learns from his friend Lousteau, "if you reckon to live on what your poetry brings in, you have time to die half a dozen deaths before you make your name" (244). The budding writer also learns that publishers have their own language, a "commercial jargon" (202) that defines books by their saleability. The first booksellers he accosts laugh in his face at the mention of poetry: "'Poetry! [...] Who do you take us for?'" (ibid.). "To these publishers books were like cotton bonnets to haberdashers, a commodity to be bought cheap and sold dear" (ibid.) Here Lucien finds himself confronted "by the brutally materialistic aspect that literature could assume" (ibid.). It is this aspect, *brutal et matériel* (Balzac 2013, 286), that governs the remainder of Lucien's literary experiences in Paris.

Lucien's ambitions are manifested in a volume of sonnets, *Les Marguerites*, and a historical novel, *The Archer of Charles the Ninth*. He sets out like a conquistador – the narrator ironically refers to him on his departure as "this Fernando Cortez of literature" (Balzac 2004, 147) – and he quickly achieves success in the literary world, though only by sacrificing his principles and becoming a mercenary journalist in the mushrooming print periodical market of the early 1820s. In Paris, the provincial "great man in embryo" (413) – *grand homme en herbe* (Balzac 2013, 517) soon adapts to the cynicism of the age and replaces a desire for lasting fame with a desire for wealth and power. Already in his first letter from Paris to his sister in Angoulême, he declares: "Unknown talent alone is subject to the vexations of

---

2013, 175). Modern sociology concurs: "Time is the only resource freely available to those at the bottom of society" (Sennett 1999, 16).

poverty; once writers have made their name they grow rich. I shall be rich" (Balzac 2004, 191). He makes friends, at first with a group of similarly ambitious writers and artists known as the Cénacle, and later with a shadier group of hacks and journalists who will hasten his meteoric rise but also contribute to his downfall. Among the Cénacle, Lucien's chief counterpart is d'Arthez – the model of a committed and serious writer, both poor and hard-working, and the only author in the novel (besides Balzac) who is ultimately going to 'make it' and leave a lasting imprint on the literary scene. In one of his (not infrequent) prolepses, the narrator tells us that d'Arthez is "today one of the most illustrious writers of our time" (211). In conversation with Lucien, d'Arthez adds a fourth definition of literature to the ones we have already encountered in this novel: literature as ordeal, a kind of evolutionary struggle for survival:

> 'It costs a lot,' said Daniel in his gentle voice, 'to become a great man. The works of genius are watered with its tears. Talent is a living organism whose infancy, like that of all creatures, is liable to malady. Society rejects defective talent as Nature sweeps away weak or misshapen creatures. Whoever wishes to rise above the common level must be prepared for a great struggle and recoil before no obstacle. A great writer is just simply a martyr whom the stake cannot kill. [...] If you are doing fine work, what does an initial setback matter?['] (211)

The writer's suffering, and, with it, the value of literature, has now been redefined at least four times in *Lost Illusions:*
1) as a sacred office, a struggle to receive divine inspiration, rewarded by heavenly immortality (as imagined by the bishop of Angoulême);
2) as emotional work, a struggle to achieve an emotional authenticity that will be rewarded by a secular kind of immortality (as outlined by Lucien);
3) as a competition among fellow writers, a proto-Darwinian struggle for the 'survival of the fittest' and a sacrifice of present happiness for, again, a secular kind of immortality (as outlined by d'Arthez in the words *un martyr qui ne mourra pas*, 2013, 296); and
4) as a business defined by bookseller-publishers intent on buying cheap and selling dear, the "brutally materialistic aspect" of literature (2004, 202).

Later in the novel, the liberal journalist Claude Vignon, according to whom literary genius is primarily a form of illness, adds a fifth definition:

> Genius is a terrible malady. In every writer's heart is a monster which devours all feelings like a tapeworm the moment they are born. Which will prevail, the malady over the man, or the man over the malady? One must certainly be a great man to keep the balance between genius and character. As talent increases the heart dries up. Short of being a colossus, short of having the shoulders of Hercules, one remains either without heart or without talent. You are of slight and slender build, you'll lose the battle. (2004, 468–469)

This somewhat muddled pronouncement outlines a heroic view of the literary struggle, which is here completely internalised and psychologised, situated in the "writer's heart", where it is played out as an inner struggle for supremacy between "genius" or "talent" on the one hand and "character" or "heart" on the other. Only the strong survive this struggle – and it is no longer a question of immortality vs. oblivion but purely one of personally conquering the "malady" without any long-term hope for the more distant future beyond death.

D'Arthez's definition, we can assume, is the one that comes closest to Balzac's own ideas about authorship. Lukács refers to this character as a "self-portrait" of Balzac (1972, 354). Moreover, the company of the Cénacle and its idea of mutual support is a recurrent element of the *Comédie*, and we may assume that this is one of Balzac's extrareferential claims to something like the dignity of literature, notwithstanding all the lost illusions about art that are this novel's great theme. But despite the prolepsis that informs us about d'Arthez's future success, these are not the final words on the matter. Any success, in Balzac's world, is short-lived and difficult to define as such. What is striking here is that the model of competition, presented by d'Arthez, is also valid for the different models of literature presented in this novel: they stand for different (if occasionally overlapping) value systems in conflict and competition with each other, all of which demand to be heard and demand the same degree of legitimacy. The narrator himself flexibly adopts any or none of these concepts as it suits him – as when he returns to the bishop's idea of the "splendid sacerdotal function" of the poet (Balzac 2004, 481) – wisely suspending his judgement in supreme irony. In a world like that of the *Comédie Humaine*, where competition has become the be-all and end-all of society – and the key mechanism of a new kind of plot (cf. Moretti 2000, 147) –, literature and ideas about literature are just as subject to this universal principle of capitalism as everything else. Juggling these conflicting value systems is Lucien, an empty vessel waiting to be filled by ideas, none of which he will ever sincerely embrace.[71] Back in Angoulême, he was merely parroting Romantic clichés of poetic expressivism. Now he learns to embrace an institutionalist understanding of the literary life or the literary field, and he attempts a strategic approach to plan his success. But he remains naïve: "Lord forgive him! He's just a child", exclaims one of his friends in the Cénacle (Balzac 2004, 230). He becomes an opportunist and gives up the struggle for achieving anything of lasting value.

---

[71] As Moretti observes, Lucien does not "possess[] features which are meaningful in and of themselves [...] but [...] none whatsoever, and this emptiness, this transparency allow us to perceive the great game of social 'backgrounds' played out through him" (2000, 157). He is, in other words, one of literature's first 'men without qualities'.

Lucien begins to make use of his newfound connections mainly as leverage to increase his reputation. The narrator commends him for networking in this manner, because: "In Paris, [...] luck only comes to people who move around a great deal: the number of relationships increases the chances of success in every sphere, and moreover luck is on the side of the big battalions" (198). Competition is thus not harmful but *productive*, as entrepreneurial capitalism is productive. Success can, to some extent, be arranged (cf. 230), can be manufactured. As fellow hack Lousteau tells him, "the key to success in literature is not to work oneself, but to exploit others' work. [...] [T]he more mediocre a man is, the sooner he arrives at success" (249). The true power in the literary field is in the periodical press, in the *feuilleton*. "Dame Reputation" is "almost always a crowned prostitute" (248), and Lucien just cannot afford to "wait for the day when your creation will spring to life once more – resurrected by whom, when and how?" (250–251), because "*Time and bride wait for no man*" (251, emphasis original). "Today", Lousteau continues, "in order to succeed, one needs to be in with such people [famous or influential men who may prove useful]. It's all a matter of chance, you see. The most dangerous thing is to churn out wit all alone in a corner" (277). It is to the journals, then, that Lucien takes his talent – he leaves his literary and artistic friends behind and becomes a hack who writes whatever he is paid for, no matter by whom.

These mostly satirical parts of *Lost Illusions*, perhaps unsurprisingly, did not go down too well with Balzac's contemporaries. They present the world of journalism as equally competitive and embroiled in all kinds of nepotism and corruption. Anything and anyone can be bought, everything has a price: "fame costs twelve thousand francs in reviews and three thousand francs in dinners" (275) "Everything is taxed, everything is sold, everything is manufactured, even success" (387). Articles are written to suit the journal's current agenda rather than express the writer's genuine opinion: "Everything is bilateral in the domain of thought", explains the journalist Blondet, who tells Julien about the need to "have mettle enough to see everything from two points of view" (372).

Making easy money and finding sexual fulfilment with the actress Coralie, whose love for Lucien is genuine but who ultimately pays for this with her life, Lucien soon falls prey to the temptations of the city and gives up any pretences to hard literary work:

> Hard work! ... Does it not spell death to temperaments avid for enjoyment? Hence the readiness of writers to sink into a *dolce far niente* attitude, take to good cheer and the luxurious delights of the life lived by actresses and women of easy virtue. Lucien felt an irresistible longing to continue the frantic life of the last two days. [...] Seeing himself lionized and envied, the poet felt self-assured; he sparkled with wit and became the Lucien de Rubempré who for a few months was to be a shining light in the literary and artistic world. (326–327)

His facility for journalism destroys any serious efforts of writing. In one article, he castigates literary Romanticism from the point of view of Enlightenment reason and political liberalism, in another journal he comes out in favour of royalism and Romanticism. He is then publicly ridiculed by some of his former allies; the acting career of Coralie is ruined by (paid) negative reviews and disturbances; Lucien borrows money, loses it at the gambling table; he even forges David's signature and swindles his best friend out of much needed funds. Having written a harsh critique of d'Arthez's book (in order, as he thinks, to save Coralie), he is challenged to a duel by another member of the Cénacle and wounded in the chest; after nursing him back to health, Coralie falls ill and dies. Adding insult to injury, the novel then shows us the devastated and destitute Lucien having to write comic drinking songs to pay for Coralie's funeral, enacting a topos of Romantic literature as he prostitutes himself for a sacred cause – similar to Coralie's faithful servant Bérénice, who *actually* prostitutes herself (cf. Noiray 2013, 937). His novel is published but "under an eccentric title" and without "the slightest success" (Balzac 2004, 465).

Only a few years later, the narrator tells us, the "intrinsic worth" of this novel will be recognised (465) – but it will be too late. Instead, some of his former friends publish a sonnet in mockery of Lucien's (as yet unprinted) sonnet sequence. These sonnets, some of which are included in the novel (composed by poet friends of Balzac, including Théophile Gautier), are yet another example of the key mode of competition in *Lost Illusions*, as the sequence stages a comparison and contest between different flowers: the field daisy, the marguerite, the camellia, the tulip etc. The sonnet that satirizes Lucien's literary and social ambitions fittingly features the thistle, thus picking on the meaning of Lucien's real name, Chardon, as denoting a "vulgar" weed, and implying the coarseness of his origins (438). At the end of his tether, the upstart thistle has no other choice but to leave Paris and return home, dejected and, additionally, emotionally distanced from his family (whom he now disdains from the viewpoint of a Parisian bohémien as "bourgeois", 587).

Meanwhile, back in Angoulême, Lucien's friend and brother-in-law David Séchard has been busy trying to make his fortune by inventing a new method for manufacturing "cheap paper" (490). He is the character most closely associated with the technological and industrial aspect of printing and, hence, the mediation of literature and other kinds of books. The novel in fact opens with a reflection on technological progress in the print industry, where wooden presses are being replaced by "ravenous machines" like the British "Stanhope press" (3). Their hunger, increased by the rise of the periodical press, demands an ever-growing supply of paper, and the search for a cheaper method of papermaking dominates the third part of the novel, "An Inventor's Tribulations". It describes how the struggling young printer David Séchard actually succeeds in implementing his invention, but how he is robbed of its fruits by a number of antagonists – including his main competitors, the Cointet brothers – and through the negligence of family members like his stingy father and Lucien, who embezzles his money in ignorance of David's and Eve's true financial situation. David, who dreams of becoming for the paper industry "what Jacquard [the inventor of the mechanical loom] was in the weaving industry" (515), is another main character in this novel to be disillusioned (yet another, of course, being Lucien's first patron and lover, Mme de Bargeton).

Though briefly fêted as a published author in his hometown, Lucien is deeply embarrassed by his failure and decides to commit suicide but is then swept up by the criminal mastermind Vautrin, disguised as a Spanish priest, who gives him money to pay his debts and takes him back to Paris. As a minor character remarks, Lucien is "not a poet" but "a serial novel" (665) – to be continued in Balzac's *Splendeurs et misères des courtisanes* (1839–1847). Once he arrives there, Lucien has achieved some of his social ambitions – his name is now officially de Rubempré – but he has "so completely abandoned all thought of literary fame, that he was insensible to the success of his novel, reissued under its real title [...], and to the stir made by his collection of sonnets [...], sold out by Dauriat in a week. 'It is posthumous success,' he replied with a laugh to Mademoiselle des Touches when she complimented him" (Balzac 1970, 76). His days as a penniless writer are over, and now his life – and the novel in which his story continues – increasingly assumes the sensational, lurid features and the speed of the serial novel, the popular form of *roman feuilleton* mastered by Dumas and Sue; this is the format in which Balzac published the later parts of *Splendeurs et misères* (cf. Balzac 1973, 740).

If disillusionment is the key theme of *Lost Illusions*, that disillusionment does not yet affect the novel's belief in storytelling per se or cast a general doubt on the form of the novel or the ability of the narrator to stay in control of the story. And yet, the subject matter of literary authorship as an increasingly debased spiritual activity in a world of commerce cannot but have a somewhat corrosive effect on the machinery of narrative itself, and in particular on the relationship between author, narrator and story. Balzac's "peculiar passivity" and "absolute relativism" (Sennett 2002, 160) usually encourage a distance between the narrator as detached observer and the various 'molecules' of the narrated world, but here the detachment cannot be as absolute as usual. The narrator's role changes from that of detached observer to (at least intermittently) committed satirist. The anger of his attacks against rapacious publishers and corrupt journalists is real, and it is this intrusion of reality into the fiction that Balzac's contemporaries resented as a fouling of his (and their) own nest. It is also, arguably, the major point in which this novel fails to be entirely convincing. By its own diagnosis, a univocal and coherent overarching perspective, a meta-point of view from which to classify or to evaluate the different models of literature that are being negotiated in this novel, can no longer exist. The novel evokes the various notions of literature as spiritual or divine activity; as emotional work; as competition; as a business; or as a form of illness. However, the novel fails to unite this contradictory multiplicity of functions into a coherent whole. They are conflicting perspectives on the relationship between a 'spiritual activity' and its material, social, economic, and institutional underpinnings.

The novel itself or its authorial narrator does not decide which of these models is the true one, or even the one that best represents literature; if he has a discursive preference for the model represented in the novel by d'Arthez, he makes no effort in the story to sponsor this model in particular – quite the opposite! The point is that for Balzac there is no longer a single true paradigm for literature in the modern world but a spectrum of conflicting orientations. And this loss of stability is also a gain because it allows for a new sense of dynamism – suddenly, trying to be a writer can make for an interesting story – because there are no longer any fixed rules or roles for how to be or to become a writer, there are now many different alternative segments in the literary field that aspiring writers can decide to compete in. What makes a writer or a 'poet'? No one in the novel can still give a clear answer to this question. And this is a boon to the novelist whose work thrives on the conflict between alternatives. Absolute relativism – also for the narrator, whose position is no longer absolute but has now also turned into something relative, like everything else.

Hence, the narrator's loss of ultimate authority (always imminent in Balzac but here quite palpable) is connected with the author's loss of illusions about the authority of literature more generally in postrevolutionary France, where literature is no longer a stable institution. Wisdom turns to irony because of the loss of a stable point of view on what literature principally *is* or who or what it *is for.* But: on the other hand, irony as the new mode of presenting social reality or realities, plural, in the bourgeois novel is not only loss but gain: loss of 'wisdom' (but whose, and for whom or for what purpose? – as soon as this question can be formed, wisdom is no longer an attractive proposition) but gain of openness, flexibility, provisional orientations, and a new narrative dynamic in which the narrator's *doxa* gets swept up and carried away by the flow of narration. An older (eighteenth-century) kind of moralistic narrator is still being evoked, but he has no chance to survive in this new world, where the finality of synthesis is abandoned for the sake of ever new and transitory compromises. Irony is corrosive of established orders and old certainties, but it is also enabling – ultimately investing the authorial narrator with new powers. It is thus, as Moretti observed, *"from within ironic representation"* that "the necessity of a stable viewpoint" is produced (2000, 98, emphasis original).

Lost Illusions is a 'novel about paper in all its conditions' (cf. Noiray 2013, 13). Paper is being manufactured, written on, printed on, sent as letters, or sold as journals or books – even chewed and swallowed, as in the bizarre story Carlos Herrera tells Lucien about the secretary of the Swedish minister, who ends up being condemned to death for having eaten a treaty between Russia and Sweden (Balzac 2004, 637–638). It connects papermaking to author-making and associates the physical ingestion of paper with the consumption of literature and of authors. It alerts its readers to the fact that, early in the nineteenth century, the age of disposable reading matter has begun. Authors themselves are under threat of becoming disposable commodities in an increasingly economised literary marketplace. In this awareness and the clarity with which it is expressed, Balzac anticipates Gissing's *New Grub Street* 1891 by half a century, while his English contemporaries – as we will see in the next chapter – still dream of a workable compromise between literary and social forms of professional authorship.

4 Compromise Formation in the English Literary *Bildungsroman*

In England as well as in France, the struggles of writers become part of the genre of the literary *bildungsroman* (cf. Howe 1930, Salmon 2013). The grounds for this are laid by Thomas Carlyle, who translates Goethe's *Wilhelm Meister's Apprenticeship* (1795–96) into English in 1824, and whose *Sartor Resartus* (1836) is itself a meta-literary reflection on creative labour. Several such 'art novels' or 'artist apprentice' novels (cf. Beebe 1964) are written in England in the 1830s and 1840s, including Benjamin Disraeli's *Contarini Fleming* (1832), Edward Bulwer-Lytton's *Ernest Maltravers* (1837), and G. H. Lewes's *Ranthorpe* (1847). As these novels explore, in Disraeli's phrase, "the development, and formation of the poetic character" (1878, v), they represent literary institutions and infrastructures of their time with varying attention to detail. More importantly, they question the indeterminate social status of authors in English society, especially in relation to the aristocracy. As "member[s] of the great aristocracy of intellect", authors "yearned for recognition and fellowship in the great aristocracy of birth" (Lewes 1847, 93), but as that aristocracy "is no longer the power which it was formerly [...] both Rank and Wealth must [now] bend the knee" to "Intelligence" (ibid.).

Rank, Wealth, Intelligence – one senses an antagonism of powerful conflicting entities or principles that does not allow for synthesis and is therefore "predispos[ed] to compromise" (Moretti 2000, 10). And what is compromise if not "the novel's most celebrated theme" (ibid., 9), or what is the novel, especially the *bildungsroman*, if not a "symbolic form" (10) with the "capacity to mediate and compromise – to teach us how to 'live with' disturbing phenomena" (160)? Richard Salmon concurs: "At its most prescriptive, the *Bildungsroman* has been defined as a form of autobiographical narrative which should end in a compromise between the desires of the individual and the normative values of existing society" (2012, 91).

The literary *bildungsroman* is the genre in which these conflicting principles are negotiated most acutely, taking into account that the writer's place in society lacks and requires legitimation. One way of achieving this was by success and admiration. "I felt", writes Contarini Fleming, "that nothing but decided success could justify a person in my position to be an author" (Disraeli 1878, 170); while Lewes in *Ranthorpe*, a novel that shows how a "poor attorney's clerk" becomes "an honoured author" (Lewes 1847, 306), asks: "Who occupies the foremost position in the world's eye – the lord or the admired author?" (93) But what about authors who aim high but remain struggling below, industrious but poor? To what extent should society, should the state support these authors? The writer's "dignity in intellectual rank" (95), as opposed to or mediated by social status, is much debated in the late

1840s in novels and newspapers, culminating in the "dignity of literature" controversy of 1850. Ultimately, these novels reflect, directly or indirectly, on the form of the realist novel as a "compromise formation" (Moretti 2000, xiii, 245).

As authorship was increasingly understood as a profession in Victorian Britain, authors were concerned about the social meaning of their "collective identity" (Salmon 2013, 210) in distinction to other professions, trades, or forms of wage-labour (cf. Waithe/White 2018). Many writers, male and female, were anxious to avoid "the taint of trade" (Peterson 2009, 2) and wanted to be seen as members of a superior profession. Coleridge, in his *Biographia Literaria* (1817), advises aspiring authors *"never* [to] *pursue literature as a trade"* (qtd. in Cross 1988, 90, emphasis original). As this sense of a professional group identity was still in the process of formation and organisation, writers were intent on finding a compromise between art and the market, between their commercial activity in the publishing world and what George Eliot, echoing Carlyle, called "the sacredness of the writer's art".[72] The term 'man of letters', which in the early nineteenth century designated the amateur writer, gradually came to be "nearly synonymous with the concept of a professional author" (Peterson 2009, 3), aided by a vast expansion of print culture and a massive increase in the periodical press (cf. Gross 1973). It was soon (in 1863) joined by the term 'woman of letters', a professional identity that was even more contested than that of her male counterpart (Peterson 2009, 4 and passim).

In addition to the middle- and upper-class novels of literary apprenticeship, there is a strand of working-class literary *bildungsromans*, including Thomas Miller's *Godfrey Malvern* (1842–43) and Charles Kingsley's *Alton Locke* (1850), whose writer-heroes experience social inequality as a barrier to their intellectual aspirations, and are consequently stunted in their development (Salmon 2013, 135–173; Abraham 2016). Thomas Miller promises (and delivers) a disillusioning behind-the-scenes investigation of the literary life: "Authorship looks pretty enough in perspective – so does the scenery of a theatre; but let the beholder once step behind the scenes, and all the enchantment is gone" (Miller 1844, 88–89, qtd. in Abraham 2016, 33).

The need to earn money compels Miller's hero to forgo his true ambitions and to work as a hack, echoing eighteenth-century authorship satires like "The Brain-Sucker" as well as anticipating the torments of Gissing's *New Grub Street* at the end of the nineteenth century. Like many other Victorian narratives of authorship,

---

[72] *Westminster Review* 66.130, Oct. 1856, 460; qtd. in Stang 1959, 45. Carlyle himself echoes earlier Romantic ideas, particularly Fichte's, when, in *On Heroes, Hero-Worship, and the Heroic in History* (1841), he claims that "[i]n the true Literary Man there is thus ever, acknowledged or not by the world, a sacredness: he is the light of the world, the world's Priest: – guiding it, like a sacred Pillar of Fire, in its dark pilgrimage through the waste of Time" (Carlyle 1986, 237).

Godfrey Malvern "demystifies the hero as man of letters" (Abraham 2016, 35). In Miller's case, the hero is redeemed at the end through that most conventional of Victorian novelistic solutions, a stroke of good fortune: he finds out that "he is in fact the disinherited heir of an estate" (ibid., 37) and can thus leave his worries behind. Important later examples of this working-class strand of author fictions include Jack London's *Martin Eden* (1909), in which the hero, a former sailor, finds himself incapable of enjoying the success and fame he achieves as a writer after a long struggle. He feels alienated from his public image; as his "inner self" turns "against the outer self", and as "[n]either the focus on money nor on professional craft" is any help in this conflict, the only solution for Martin Eden is to commit suicide (Braudy 1997, 534–535).

With different outcomes, these author-*bildungsromans* reflect on the conditions of literary and/as personal and, above all, social success or failure. Their author characters are, for the most part, anaclitic 'versions' of their actual authors, who articulate their positioning in relation to audiences by means of auto- and heteropoetic strategies, in a reflexive performance or performative reflexion that can often be read as a self-fulfilling prophecy. Contarini Fleming, Ernest Maltravers, Godfrey Malvern – they all embody their authors' ambitions to "justify a person [...] to be an author" (Disraeli 1878, 170) and to make authorship into a respectable profession.

The formation of authors is a topic that runs through nineteenth-century literature, in several distinct strands marked by gender and class but also by different actualisations of several author concepts. John Stuart Mill deplored "the trading author" as one who, for "pecuniary gain", would aim "to write down to the level of his readers", instead of seeking "to provide [...] that good and wholesome food for the wants of the mind, for which the competition of the mere trading market affords in general so indifferent a substitute" (Mill 1859, 1: 31; cf. Knights 1978, 154–158). When Anthony Trollope, in his *Autobiography* (1883), dared to compare novel-writing to shoemaking, he was posthumously accused of "confusing art with trade" (Sutherland 1976, 149) and betraying the more elevated (and thoroughly class-based) aspirations associated with literature (Aguirre 2002).

From 1884 onwards, the Society of Authors, founded by Walter Besant, sought to further the professional interests of writers along the lines already suggested earlier in the century by Bulwer, Dickens, and others, but these (increasingly successful) attempts at professionalisation also caused ambivalent reactions from authors who opposed the idea of writing as a craft or as mechanised production and cultivated an image of writers as artists, as Henry James did in "The Art of Fiction" (1884), written in response to a lecture by Besant with the same title (cf. Salmon 2013, 219). In a note from 1879, James makes fun of the idea, which he attributes to Trollope, that one could "be brought up to be a novelist as to any other trade" (James 1987, 9), deliberately using the less respectable term 'trade' as a slur against Trollope and against what was perceived as an insult to the profession. The questions whether novel-writing was an art or a craft, and whether novelists were born or trained, would come to dominate novels and stories about the making of literature and of authors in the later decades of the nineteenth century.

"The pursuit of literature": Bulwer-Lytton's *Ernest Maltravers* (1837)

Although it has since fallen into oblivion, Edward Bulwer-Lytton's literary *bildungsroman Ernest Maltravers* enjoyed widespread popularity throughout the nineteenth century. It was adapted into a film twice in the early twentieth century, and it was the first European novel to be translated into Japanese in 1879 (Keene 2023). Bulwer was inspired by Goethe (cf. "Preface to the Edition of 1840" in Bulwer 1893, x), as were Disraeli and Lewes. Like many a *bildungsroman* hero, Ernest Maltravers is an *homme moyen sensuel*, "neither a majestic demi-god nor a fascinating demon" but "a man with the weaknesses derived from humanity, [...] not often obstinate in error, more often irresolute in virtue; [...] influenced by the circumstances to which he yet struggles to be superior, and changing in character with the changes of time and fate" (Bulwer, "A Word to the Reader" [1837] in Bulwer 1893, vii–viii).

Thackeray, in the *History of Pendennis* (1848–1850), similarly introduces his protagonist "not [...] as a hero or a model, only as a lad, who, in the midst of a thousand vanities and weaknesses, has as yet some generous impulses, and is not altogether dishonest" (Thackeray 1994, 237, ch. 19); this passage prepares the more famous final sentence of the novel, in which the narrator bids farewell "to Arthur Pendennis, with all his faults and shortcomings, who does not claim to be a hero, but only a man and a brother" (977, ch. 75).[73] The same sentiment is echoed, even more famously, at the beginning of *David Copperfield* (1849–1850): "Whether I shall turn out to be the hero of my own life [...] these pages must show" (Dickens 1985, 49, ch. 1). The heroes of Victorian *bildungsromans* tend to be unheroic and somewhat unstable persons who need to carve out a place for themselves in the "complicated system" of society (Disraeli 1985, 349). Yet, their instability also renders them plausible as realist characters rather than types.

---

[73] The phrase "a man and a brother" is borrowed from the discourse of abolition, arguably presenting Pendennis as "a slave of sorts, in bondage to the conventionalities of life" (Fisher 2002, 95).

In his 1840 preface, Bulwer writes about "the great and obvious difficulty of representing an author living in our own times", and he notes with some amusement that readers apparently "confound[ed] the author *in* the book with the author *of* the book" (1893, xi, emphasis original). This, too, was to become a commonplace of the literary *bildungsroman* and later author fictions. In chapter two, Bulwer's hero begins writing following an urge of intellectual exertion and knowing his own mind (154–155). When Ernest becomes a published author, Bulwer comments that "Ernest Maltravers had lost the happy rights of the private individual: he had given himself to the public; he had surrendered his name to men's tongues, and was a thing that all had a right to praise, to blame, to scrutinize, to spy" (1893, 259). But his hero's work is a success, followed eighteen months later by a "second work" (262). As in *David Copperfield* a decade later, we learn nothing about the titles or contents of Ernest's books: "Of the character of his works it will be enough to say that, whatever their faults, they were original, – they were his own" (272). They make him a public figure. Ernest is now "an author in fashion", enjoying "momentary celebrity" (271). Bulwer uses this occasion to comment at length on the mechanics of authorship, advising aspiring authors against publishing in periodicals before they have become famous (261–262) and on the different attitude of a writer's colleagues towards a second as opposed to a first book: "envy wakens, malice begins" (262). In conversation, Ernest's friend De Montaigne advises against writing for money, while Ernest assures him that "the pursuit of literature is a pursuit apart from the ordinary objects of life" (266), clearly placing Intellect above Wealth and Rank.

Bulwer also comments on the "terrible disconnection between the author and the man" (517): when the book is published, the author's circumstances and feelings have changed, and this time-lag between writing and publication prevents the writer from enjoying "the pomp and parade of authorship" (517). Bulwer's novel has some interest in the life of "writing men" (154), but this interest in the life of the writer is mainly idealistic and abstract; apart from some general remarks on envy and celebrity, it depicts the writer's life as an inner struggle only. It does not mention the literary market, critics, or reviewers, and the technicalities of publication or negotiations with publishers are absent from the novel, quite in contrast to the darker template provided by Balzac's *Lost Illusions*.

Taking to Authorship in Dickens's *David Copperfield* (1849–1850) and Thackeray's *Pendennis* (1848–1850)

In *David Copperfield*, by contrast, the young writer's struggles are predominantly social. While Mary Poovey has argued that David's psychological and social development depends on an idealised (and ideologised) view of gender and class differences (Poovey 1988, 89–125), recent critics tend to read the novel rather "as an earnest attempt to work out the complications of the author's relationship to labor and the market" (Willson 2017, 195 fn. 7); these include Jennifer Ruth (2006), Richard Salmon (2013), and Matthew Titolo (2003). The novel's position on authorial labour, the literary profession, and literary productivity has come under increasing scrutiny as critics explore the fundamental tension, in *David Copperfield*, between the sheer material heft of a very long and complex text (the result of an author's laborious work) and the novel's fantasy of "transcending" the realities of literary production by means of imagination and pleasure (Willson 2017, 198). Thus, David's gift of imagination enables him to connect with lower-class characters, reflecting "Dickens's investment in depicting the imaginative capacity as something that transcends class boundaries more than it asserts status" (ibid., 207). The novel sketches David's literary development in parallel to Dickens's own, from "Boz-like amateur vagrancy" (208) as he lounges in the streets of London towards a novelist in full control of his powers. A key element of this learning process, which the novel explores, is David's coming to terms with the exigencies of the literary market, his key achievement of a compromise between the desire for freedom and the alienation of literary labour (cf. ibid., 209, 211). Though it is not clear at what point in the novel's gestation Dickens decided to make David a novelist (cf. Flynn 2010, 170), he took until the twelfth number to tell his readers of David's idea to become a newspaper reporter, and until number 14 (chapter 43) to make him declare "I have taken [...] to authorship" (Dickens 1985, 692).

There is a heavy irony in the fact that Dickens presents the novel as David's "personal history", which David "never meant to be published on any account", as the title page of the serial informs its readers (Dickens 1985, n. p.), contradicting David's explicit wishes that his "manuscript is intended for no eyes but [his]" (671, ch. 42). In contrast to the editorial fictions of the eighteenth century, Dickens does not even pretend not to be the author of this novel. The cover "actually brands the novel as a quintessentially Dickensian product" (Willson 2017, 213). The tension between David's writing only for himself and Dickens's writing for a large audience, like the tension between the free-ranging literary imagination and the commodification of literature in the marketplace, is not dissolved but rather confirmed by the novel's humorous, ironic packaging. As Andrew Willson has argued, *David Copperfield* is Dickens's way of addressing his own ambivalence about creativity and productivity, pleasure and work, "pure aesthetic value" and "market value" (215). The novel is his attempt "to bridge [the] divide between economic distance and market participation" (214). Like Carlyle, Dickens extolled the value of work, particularly for the middle classes, but he struggled with the idea of writing as a form of labour, as an ordinary kind of profession, and – like his fellow writers

– with the social status of an author. *David Copperfield* offers, in other words, an uneasy compromise between the private pleasures of writing and the public pressures of the literary marketplace.

Dickens at this time was very concerned about the plight of professional writers, insisting that literature was not merely a trade or profession but a 'calling', which merited dignity and honour over and beyond the market forces of supply and demand. In Lewes's terms, Dickens also placed Intellect above Wealth and Rank. In the context of the 'dignity of literature' debate that was raging while both *David Copperfield* and *Pendennis* were being written and published, Dickens supported the idea of insurance policies and a pension fund for writers, as well as founding a Guild of Literature and Art, which materialised in 1854 (Hack 1999; Salmon 2013, 119–127). In the eyes of his contemporary and rival, Thackeray, however, Dickens's shame about the market was a mere sham. Thackeray saw more harm than good in the idea of public institutions sponsoring authors, as the Royal Literary Fund had been doing since 1790.[74]

Instead of keeping mediocre authors from starvation, Thackeray thought it would be better to professionalise the arts as part of a wider social trend to promote professional careers in mid-Victorian England (cf. Reader 1966, Ruth 2006, Salmon 2013). In a letter to the *Morning Chronicle* of 12 January 1850, Thackeray writes: "I believe that the social estimation of the man of letters is as good as it deserves to be, and as good as that of any other professional man" (1945–1946, 2: 636). The trend towards recognising literary work as a form of mental labour was an important step away from Romantic ideas of genius, a "process by which the 'poet' [was] converted to the function of 'wage-labour' within modern society" (Salmon 2013, 102–103, quoting Marx), but it was attended by unresolved contradictions, mainly pertaining to authors' insecure social position and the ambiguous status of literary works as products of non-alienated labour *and* as commodities in a market. Calls for a stronger regulation of the market and a more powerful institutional organisation of authors go further back to the early 1830s, when Bulwer suggested the foundation of a "Literary Union" (Salmon 2013, 74).

In *The History of Pendennis,* serialised at the same time as *David Copperfield*, Thackeray indirectly engages in this debate by caricaturing London's literary world as seedy, self-serving, and rarely capable of 'dignity'. He skewers predatory publishers as well as meretricious hacks, but he also presents authors – especially his protagonist, the aptly named Pendennis – as hard-working, self-doubting, and rarely valued professionals. If they fail to compete, they have themselves to blame. Though himself writing for money, Thackeray the gentleman regarded Dickens as

---

74 On the early history of the Royal Literary Fund, see Cross 1988, 8–37.

his social inferior and a snob; their rivalry was informed by their unequal social status as well as by literary and commercial envy. Contemporary readers and reviewers compared *Pendennis* and *Copperfield* as works emerging "in dialogue or competition" (Flynn 2010, 152), and read them as rival operations engaging with the dignity of literature and the social status of authors. Yet both also took the genre of the *bildungsroman* in a British direction, away from German and French models, combining their heroes' experiences of disillusionment with visions of compromise between rivalling social classes.[75] For Dickens, the chief agents of this compromise were the middle and lower classes; for Thackeray, bourgeois and high society. Both novels display symptoms of the social stratification of the literary field; both present an anxious negotiation of "the legitimacy of literary work" (Flynn 2010, 182) and of the contradictions between art and the market in mid-Victorian Britain.

Dickens's treatment of authorship as a serious and dignified profession in *David Copperfield*, and his hero's emphasis on the middle-class virtues of self-discipline ("my perseverance", "patient and continuous energy", "punctuality, order, and diligence", "determination", etc. [Dickens 1985, 671, ch. 42]), can certainly be read as reactions to the satire of *Pendennis* and Thackeray's less dignified view of the trade (cf. Flynn 2010, Cheadle 2017). More than any other Victorian novel, *David Copperfield* has been identified with a post-Romantic view of authorship as a "model of disciplined mental labour" (Salmon 2013, 111). Dickens, as Salmon observes, "seeks to invest the role" of the "professional author" with "moral authority" (118), and he does so by representing David's personal development in retrospect in a way that resembles Wordsworth's *The Prelude* (posthumously published in 1850; cf. Salmon 2013, 118).[76] Dickens's project was one of ennobling the author's profession and of giving it "credibility, admirableness, and influence", as Susan Ryan defines those qualities that invest authors with "(perceived) good character" and "moral authority" (2016, 5). The "good character" of David Copperfield as a literary character thus transcends the boundaries of fiction to cast a positive light on its real author, Charles Dickens, both individually and as a member of the class of authors, making them more respectable by improving their moral reputation. As Salmon also notes, "*David Copperfield* may well be the first novel

---

[75] Whereas a few earlier critics have argued that *Pendennis* and even *David Copperfield* should not be considered as belonging to the genre of the *bildungsroman* (see Salmon 2013, 242 n. 67), their focus on personal development and the formation of character is evident – even in *Pendennis*, a novel whose narrator explicitly opposes the idea of development (see below).

[76] For a related discussion of the "complex interrelations between moral authority [...] and various aspects of self-presentation, marketing, and reception" in mid-nineteenth-century American literature, see Ryan 2016.

in which authorship is presented as the unequivocal summit of the hero's worldly and spiritual aspirations, rather than as a provisional stage in more diffuse schemes of personal development or social ambition" (2013, 121), which precisely sums up its depiction in *Pendennis* by contrast.

Crucially, for this "narrative of self-authorization" to succeed, David has to remain the only professional author in the novel, while "all the other potential candidates" turn out to be in one way or another unfit for the task (Salmon 2013, 128). Moreover, David's character and his direct address of the narratee or the reader can be read as contributing to "Victorian representations of novelists as sympathetic, intimate, and friendly" (Deane 2003, xiii), an image of the author as the (individual) reader's friend that Bradley Deane has identified as emerging with Dickens from the *Pickwick Papers* onwards. According to Deane, this "rhetoric of literary production" served to veil the economic realities of the mass market that "created 'Dickens'" (2003, 57). *David Copperfield*, in this view, is a novel that not only provides a model of subjectivity for its readers (cf. Poovey 1988, 89) but also a model for "the subject position of the novelist" as "hailed" by a mass audience (Deane 2003, 56) – an authorpoietic fiction *par excellence*.

David's hard-earned integration as a member of the middle class and his commitment to the literary profession is in stark contrast to Pen's somewhat more accidental rise in status, who at the end becomes "Arthur Pendennis, Esq." (Thackeray 1994, 976), a Member of Parliament, whose literary "reputation" is no longer relevant for his social status, only a small "prize[]" in the "lottery" of life (977) compared to his other achievements. In this and many other respects, David Copperfield is as unlike Arthur Pendennis as possible. Where David strives to be earnest, diligent, and industrious, Arthur (aptly nicknamed 'Pen') is a bohemian amateur who first neglects his studies at Oxbridge (a blend of Oxford and Cambridge, coined by Thackeray) and then neglects his duties as a young lawyer while pursuing literature as a potentially profitable hobby. His first "symptoms" of the literary bug, a "violent efflux of versification", are noticed favourably by his uncle, Major Pendennis (ibid., 182, ch. 16). The worldly-wise major recommends literature as a career, or rather as an opportunity to a career *beyond* literature:

> My object, Arthur, is to make a man of you – to see you well placed in the world, as becomes one of your name and my own, sir. You have got yourself a little reputation by your literary talents, which I am very far from undervaluing, though in my time, begad, poetry and genius and that sort of thing were devilish disreputable. There was poor Byron, for instance, who ruined himself, and contracted the worst habits by living with poets and newspaper writers, and people of that kind. But the times are changed now – there's a run upon literature – clever fellows get into the best houses in town, begad! (Thackeray 1994, 464, ch. 36)

Major Pendennis outlines a historical shift in the "reputation" of writers from the Romantic to the Victorian era; now, as he claims, literature is very much in demand and has become a door-opener to the higher echelons of society. Though Major Pendennis casts some doubt on his literary education in the next sentence by misattributing a line from Pope to Shakespeare, Pen follows his own inclination and his uncle's advice. His friend and mentor George Warrington encourages him in the idea that writing means easy money, but it is for Pen (and Thackeray) less of a noble calling than a potentially profitable pastime.

As the Major's remark about "the best houses in town" suggests, literature in *Pendennis* is an institution of social advancement, and literary life a hotbed of snobbery. Pen's semi-autobiographical first novel, *Leaves from the Life-Book of Walter Lorraine* (Thackeray 1994, 519, ch. 41), "written under the influence of his youthful embarrassments, amatory and pecuniary" (517), is a *bildungsroman* within a *bildungsroman*, inspired by German literature (ibid.). As a book, *Walter Lorraine* is believed by its author to be "not very good" but also not much worse than "most books of the kind that had the run of circulating libraries and the career of the season" (521). These "darling greasy volumes" are "devoured" by their readers (608, ch. 47); they are material commodities, meant to be consumed, not preserved for eternity. Commerce is key; thus, his publishers have requested that Pen promote his characters in rank to make the novel sell more copies: "The young duke was only a young baron when the novel was first written; his false friend the viscount was a simple commoner, and so on with all the characters of the story" (513) – a witty allusion to the fashionable silver-fork novel and the social pretensions of writers, publishers, and readers in the early Victorian period.

The "commodified status" extends from the commodity to the producer of that commodity: the author who sells not only his labour but also himself, in part or entire, to the "publishing industry" (Salmon 2013, 91). The mercenary qualities of writers are discussed by Pen's friend Warrington in a disillusioned manner: "All poets are humbugs, all literary men are humbugs; directly a man begins to sell his feelings for money he's a humbug" (Thackeray 1994, 520). Pen's riposte that "Shakespeare was a man who wrote for money" (ibid.) shuts Warrington up; nevertheless, the conflict between authorial sincerity and dishonesty remains the elephant in the room. Writing for the *Pall Mall Gazette*, Pen becomes "a literary hack, naturally fast in pace, and brilliant in action" (606, ch. 47). The other hacks whom he meets in London, including an editor named – what else? – Mr Hack, are for the most part vicious (and funny) caricatures of the literary profession. These often come in pairs, as do the exploitative publishers Bacon and Bungay, or the Irishmen Hoolan and Doolan. An exception is the tragicomic (and rather Dickensian) Captain Shandon, a drunk who edits a magazine while in debtor's prison. Many of these characters are recognisably based on actual figures of literary London, such as the publishers Richard Bentley and Henry Colburn (Flynn 2010, 157). Their cynical practices are bitterly satirised, culminating in ch. 34, "A Dinner in the Row" (i.e., Paternoster Row, at that time the heart of London's publishing industry), which John Sutherland has described as "unusually bad-tempered" (1994, 1041 n. 440).

Other writers, most notably Dickens's friend George Forster, accused Thackeray of fouling his own nest (cf. Flynn 2010, 159). In consequence, when he returned to writing after a hiatus due to serious illness, Thackeray abandoned the more extreme forms of literary satire that had dominated the previous numbers and made Pen and Warrington more dedicated and serious in their work as journalists. Yet he was ultimately, as Flynn also argues, less interested in writing about writing than in writing about class – Pendennis is all about snobbery, and only partly about literary snobbery (162). As with Balzac, the arts in Pendennis are not distinct or protected from the social world, they are deeply implicated in it, and the business of literature is just like other businesses: a competition for resources and profits, with no room for idealism but with a lot of room for envy and resentment. Nevertheless, unlike Lost Illusions, Pendennis's realistic, if somewhat cynical, portrayal of London's literary bohemia does not end on that diagnosis but allows for some redeeming features in the characters of Warrington and Pen. Pen, above all, is no Lucien Chardon, and his trajectory in the second half of the novel is very different from that of Balzac's young poet. Indeed, Sarah Rose Cole has argued that Thackeray "reworked Balzac's Lost Illusions" in Pendennis, "transforming Balzac's narrative of revolutionary dislocation into a self-consciously British narrative of peaceful change" (2007, par. 3), a narrative with a happy ending.[77]

For Flynn, Thackeray's key concern was to reconcile the tension between the middle and upper, not lower, classes, quite in contrast to Dickens (cf. 2010, 186 n. 12). Unlike Dickens's David, Thackeray's Pen can abandon his literary labours on becoming a gentleman, pursuing a life of leisure, and in the same movement support Thackeray's "claim to realism" contra Dickens (Flynn 2010, 177). Yet, pace Flynn, that claim is not easily identified with the upper class per se, but with a flexible social elite composed of bourgeois and aristocratic members, a 'class' with permeable and shifting boundaries. As a gentleman, Pen – like Thackeray – belongs to a social category that "allows a collaboration – even a merger – between the bourgeois and aristocratic ruling classes" (Cole 2007, par. 14) – in other words, a compromise. Whereas, for David, the "task" of writing (Dickens 1985, 950, ch. 64) is motivated

---

77 There is no proof that Thackeray knew Lost Illusions, as Cole also notes (2007, par. 8), but it is highly likely; he does mention numerous other novels by Balzac, and there are many similarities between Lost Illusions and Pendennis (cf. Salmon 2013, 238 n. 24).

from within, profoundly connected with the (personal and social) identity that he grows into, Pen grows out of it and outgrows writing as a temporary stage in his formation.[78] In contrast to Balzac's disillusioned view of society, Thackeray constructs for his hero a "private ethical realm that marks the British realist tradition" (Cole 2007, par. 20), but it is one that leads him into the heart of the British political system: the House of Commons – not out of any commitment to one party or another but more as a complex symbol of public duty, personal advancement, and the value of political compromise. "Compromise" is a key word in *Pendennis*, for example when Pen contemplates entering Parliament, "not car[ing] much what side he took, as there was falsehood and truth on every side. And on this and on other matters he thought he would compromise with his conscience" (Thackeray 1994, 817, ch. 62; cf. 801–802, ch. 61).[79]

Compromise, and the word "compromise", occur at several instances in the novel in connection with situations of conflict, twice in connection with a potential duel, twice in connection with politics and religion, and twice in connection with the ethics of personal life.[80] In each case, compromise is coded as beneficial or at least value-neutral. If we compare this to *David Copperfield*, we get a very different picture. Occurring six times in the novel, the word "compromise" is used apparently less systematically and more ironically, for instance in reference to the mourning weeds of Mrs Heep (Dickens 1985, 313, ch. 17), Mrs Crupp's cooking (471, ch. 28), and Betsey Trotwood's dislike of the name 'Peggotty' (558, ch. 34). It is then associated with the despicable and insincere Uriah Heep, who is described as having "a sulky, hurried, defeated air of compromise" (642, ch. 39). In ch. 42, David remarks on Heep's "twisting" "all the mingled possibilities of innocence and com-

---

[78] Notwithstanding the fact that Thackeray used Pendennis as an authorial mask in his later novels *The Newcomes* and *The Adventures of Philip* (cf. Tillotson 1963, 50, 56).

[79] The same phrase ("compromise with his/her conscience") occurs in *A Shabby Genteel Story* (Thackeray 1993, 78, ch. 6). It is not attested in any work by Dickens. Thackeray was associated with ideas of compromise and of having "no convictions" early on, by Carlyle ("Thackeray had no convictions, after all, except that a man ought to be a gentleman, and ought not to be a snob"; qtd. in Henkle 1980, 97), and in literary criticism since Wells 1929, who applies Chesterton's idea of a Victorian compromise between middle and upper classes (see below) to Thackeray.

[80] In ch. 6, Smirke's refusal to fight with Pen over the Fotheringay's reputation is described as a "compromise" (1994, 70). In ch. 27, Pen resolves to "compromise and forget his wrath, and make his peace with the Frenchman", the Chevalier de Juillet, whom he has mistaken for a chef (337). In both episodes, a duel is avoided. In ch. 61, Pen describes the Church of England as "a compromise" achieved by "an Act of Parliament" (802). In conversation with Blanche Amory in ch. 64, Pen even refers, though in the form of a question, to "all life" as "a compromise", and Blanche suggests the same about Pen's upcoming marriage (836). – The word "compromise" in the sense of 'damage one's reputation' also occurs in the same chapter (828).

promise" (674), a phrase in which the two concepts are apparently posited as opposites, and 'compromise' is used in the sense of reputational damage; but the phrase itself reads somewhat like a badly mingled or twisted linguistic compromise. In ch. 45, David talks to the Doctor about Uriah Heep "without any other compromise of the truth than a little softening of [Heep's] coarseness" (727), implying that he told a few white lies and that he deplores this "compromise" as insincerity. Every single compromise in *David Copperfield* which is named as such is a bad compromise or a compromising deed.

Whereas Thackeray tends to depict compromise as unavoidable and necessary for human happiness, even at times as a force for the good (when it serves to avoid violence, for example), Dickens appears to regard it as demeaning and, literally, compromising, an abject condition of moral defeat that David is eager to overcome. In contrast to David's earnest adherence to Carlyle's gospel of work and his striving for honesty and sincerity, Pen achieves, through compromise, the relaxed attitude of detachment and nonchalance that, for Thackeray and many of his Victorian readers, defined a country gentleman. Thackeray's novel introduces a greater degree of detachment, and potential for ironic distance, already in its third-person narration; whereas Dickens pretends to present David's "personal history" as written by himself, Thackeray explains that his "narrative is taken from Pen's own confessions" (1994, 234) but – crucially – not presented in Pen's own voice.

Moreover, Thackeray's is a strange sort of *bildungsroman* as his narrator professes not to believe in development as a genuine change to the person: "We alter very little", he proclaims, in the "voyage of life". And he goes on to say: "When we talk of this man or that woman being no longer the same person whom we remember in youth, and remark (of course to deplore) changes in our friends, we don't, perhaps, calculate that circumstance only brings out the latent defect or quality, and does not create it" (766–767, ch. 59). In this philosophy, the individual is essentially "alone", "alone in the midst of the crowd" (767). A similar statement is made much earlier in the novel, in ch. 16: "How lonely we are in the world! [...] you and I are but a pair of infinite isolations, with some fellow-islands a little more or less near to us" (183–184). In this sceptical, pessimistic, anti-Donnean, and politically conservative view of society as consisting of monadic, isolated islands, Thackeray denies the possibility of change as well as of connection as a binding, unifying force (which Dickens maintains, if only as a principle of hope).

Compromise here can thus not mean much more than the individual's accommodation to other people's expectations, not a recipe for social reform and more permeable class boundaries; it will always remain subject to the "wicked but" of "reflection", which is "the sceptic's familiar", as Pen explains to his future wife Laura (916, ch. 71). Pen is, as Fitzjames Stephens recognised in 1855, "the irresolute, half-ashamed, sceptical hero, conscious of his own weakness, conscious of his own ignorance [...] not very bad, nor very good, nor very anything"; and George Saintsbury in 1908 observed that "Pen, if anybody in modern fiction, is *l'homme sensuel moyen*" (both qtd. in Tillotson 1963, 240, emphasis original). If *Pendennis* can be called a *bildungsroman*, it is one that does not believe in the Goethean idea of organic development. If it believes in anything, it believes in compromise as a positive social force.

The word 'compromise' as a noun is fairly rare in nineteenth-century British texts, but its use increases steadily from 1810 onwards, reaching a peak in 1866.[81] Moreover, in the course of the nineteenth century, the term 'compromise' seems to perform a semantic shift: originally meaning a joint agreement or settlement between two or more parties, and later a "coming to terms [...] by concessions", the *Oxford English Dictionary* attests a new meaning and function in 1833 with its use as an attributive noun, "defining a thing intermediate between two others or possessing an accommodating combination of characteristics". From 1848 onwards, 'compromise' can also mean "a settlement of debts" (*OED*). In English fiction, there are two peaks in 1849 and 1852, at the time of *Pendennis* and *Copperfield*, and another one at the end of the 1850s, the time of Meredith's *Ordeal of Richard Feverel* (though here the compromise count is zero) and Eliot's *Adam Bede* (also none).[82] There are no compromises at all in *Jane Eyre*, and a mere three in *Middlemarch*. As Moretti has argued, following Lukács, the nineteenth-century novel is itself a form of compromise (Moretti 2000, viii), a form that possesses "an accommodating combination of characteristics" (*OED*) and is thus capable of combining social and aesthetic dimensions of form (cf. Levine 2015). In the Victorian social problem novel of 1840s and 50s, where one would expect to encounter the word more often, there is only one "unsatisfactory compromise" in *North and South* (Gaskell 2005, 145; vol. 1, ch. 20), three in *Mary Barton*, none at all in *Alton Locke* or *Hard Times*, but a key passage in Disraeli's *Sybil* in which the heroine realises "that the world was a more complicated system than she had preconceived", and finds out "to her surprise [...] that human affairs, even in an age of revolution, are the subject of compromise; and that the essence of compromise is littleness" (Disraeli 1985, 349).

Little or otherwise, satisfactory or not, compromise is an essential Victorian response to social complexity. For the individual, the word assumes the sense of resigned acceptance of what life has to offer, or of the sacrifice of principles for the sake of contentment. "A happy life means prudent compromise", as Lord

---

81 Google Books Ngram Viewer, corpus of British English (2019).
82 Google Books Ngram Viewer, corpus of English Fiction (2019). According to the same corpus, compromises in fiction tend to be good ones in the early 1800s but bad ones after 1856.

Howe admonishes the poet in *Aurora Leigh* (bk. 5, l. 922; Barrett Browning 2018 [1856], 330), a sentiment echoed by the author-protagonist's friend Biffen in Gissing's *New Grub Street:* "The art of living is the art of compromise" (Gissing 2016 [1891], 391).

Compromise, and the avoidance of being compromised, are both features of the "Victorian compromise" (Chesterton 1946, 21), as is a constant kind of boundary work that explores "the limits of compromise" (Morley 1877, 34). The intellectual high point in this Victorian debate is John Morley's book-length essay *On Compromise* (1874, 2nd ed. 1877), a sustained philosophical and political critique of "the practice of the various arts of accommodation, economy, management, conformity, or compromise" (1877, 1), and an exploration of the point where compromise ends and hypocrisy begins (cf. ibid., 39).

Thackeray uses the word 'compromise' some fifty times across his entire work, Dickens more than a hundred times, in various meanings. In whatever denotative or connotative sense the word was being used, its increasing presence perhaps tells us something about the Victorian mindset. In any case, it became a keyword to describe the Victorian age almost as soon as that age had run its course. Ever since G. K. Chesterton coined the expression 'Victorian compromise' in 1913,[83] it has become a catch-all phrase to describe the uneasy social, political, religious, and aesthetic situation of Victorian Britain, from the survival of the "romantic imagination" to Catholic emancipation (Clausen 1993, 385).[84] It looks as if we find compromise, for better or worse, wherever we look in the Victorian period: "the Victorian age", as Moretti succinctly states, "was [...] a time of *compromise*, much more than contrast" (2013, 6). The *bildungsroman* as the period's key "symbolic form" (Moretti 2000, 10) is at the heart of this cultural negotiation of a complicated social and moral system, and one of many Victorian compromises is the complicat-

---

83 In his book *The Victorian Age in Literature,* Chesterton first uses the expression to describe "the fundamental fact of Early Victorian history", namely "the decision of the middle classes to employ their new wealth in backing up a sort of aristocratical compromise, and not (like the middle class in the French Revolution) insisting on a clean sweep and a clear democratic programme" (Chesterton 1946, 21); then he employs it to address the gap between Victorian social theory and practice, something he describes Dickens as attacking (52); next, he uses it to explain the aesthetic of the Victorian novel as a "working [...] compromise about what should happen behind the scenes and what on the stage" (63). In the book's final chapter, Chesterton attributes "the break-up of the compromise" (125) in the late Victorian period to its "glaring deficiencies" (148). He does not mention Morley at all.
84 More recently, the legal historian Lawrence Friedman (2007, 4 and passim) added the double standard to this list of increasing length, describing as "the Victorian compromise" the moral hypocrisy that tolerated some immorality in private, as long as public respectability remained intact.

ed notion of the "professional writer" (cf. Salmon 2013, 93) that the author-*bildungsroman* explores.

In their different attitudes towards compromise, Dickens and Thackeray reveal their era's contradictory approach towards the resolution of irresolvable social and aesthetic conflicts, such as those between industrial progress and social injustice, and between moral theory and social practice. In their major *bildungsromans*, they reveal both the inevitability and the unease associated with the "Victorian compromise" on several levels, both of content and form. They explore the aesthetics of literary realism in what amounts to an aesthetics of compromise, even in the "narrative opportunism" (Sutherland 1976, 103) of serialised fiction and its notoriously loose plotting. Their heroes, too, are 'compromise formations': both David and Pendennis are, each in their own way, social climbers; yet it takes but little exaggeration to say that this is associated with shame and guilt in Dickens (even more so in *Great Expectations*) but not in Thackeray, who rather applauds his Pen's canniness and ability to rise through compromise (making compromises with his conscience without entirely compromising himself). The fact that both heroes are writers and to some extent youthful self-portraits of their authors adds an important reflexive-performative, authorpoietic dimension to this. Thackeray, more than Dickens, connects his hero's literary to his personal development at key points in the novel, yet he also takes care to present these connections as rather accidental. Dickens is silent about the specifics of literary life and does not tell his readers what exactly David writes (apart, of course, from the "personal history" that is the book they are reading) but is keen to emphasise how integral David's writing is to his personal identity. Both present the figure of the author as a compromise formation, fraught with social and ethical contradictions between art and the marketplace, moral commitment and economic constraints, auto- and allopoetic forces, which characterise the novel of authorial formation as a genre.

David Copperfield, at the end, *is* a writer in the most emphatic sense of being; Arthur Pendennis is about to enter politics as someone with a literary reputation, which is not at all the same thing. Yet, whether they liked the word 'compromise' or not, both Dickens and Thackeray allowed their heroes to find a liveable compromise, and in this they are typical of the British strand of the European *bildungsroman*. Whereas Balzac's Lucien determines to end his life by suicide, both Dickens's David and Thackeray's Pen are allowed to succeed and prosper, each in their own way, and to accommodate the insecure social status of Intellect in a 'complicated' society dominated by Wealth and Rank.

5 The Novel of Allopoetic Deformation: Herman Melville's *Pierre* (1852)

The nineteenth-century realist novel is justly praised for its astonishing multiplicity of different characters, voices, and values. Its immensely varied population corresponds to a more differentiated, more democratic society. However, this multiplicity can only be brought into a meaningful arrangement and prevented from disintegration if the narrator functions as a superordinate observer and, as it were, 'stage-manager' of what is being represented. The narrator formerly known as omniscient or 'authorial', but better described as heterodiegetic, must keep his or her distance from the represented world for that world to remain amenable to representation in the novel form. As a formal principle of coherence, the narrator must be strengthened lest the heteroglossic "social diversity of speech types" (Bakhtin 1981, 263) overwhelm the novel.

The strengthening of the narrator, it seems, and the narrator's subsequent aloofness, even coldness towards the characters is the price to be paid for differentiation, variety, and flexibility on the level of story and plot. The narrator's elevated position vis à vis the narrated world, and often vis à vis the form of narration itself, becomes almost inevitably ironic. The obverse of a more democratic inclusiveness in the novel, it seems, is a greater degree of authority and control for the narrator – an uneasy compromise, as we have seen in the novels of Balzac, Dickens, and Thackeray.

Early in the nineteenth century, Balzac's narrator confines himself to the occasional gnomic remark and otherwise remains a more or less purely functional, perfunctory instance of narration. Other novels feature more personalised narrators who mingle with their characters: they happen to meet as tourists in Wiemar (Thackeray, *Vanity Fair*) or they are close friends (Pushkin, *Eugene Onegin*). But even Thackeray's satirical narrator, who introduces himself as a puppet-master, is still a long way away from the all-encompassing irony of Thomas Mann, whose narrators enjoy complete mastery over their material. Later adepts of this kind of formal aestheticism include Nabokov, who famously claimed to lord it over his characters with a God-like, autocratic omnipotence (Tammi 1985, 100).

Auerbach claims that nineteenth-century realism preserved the idea of the author as having "knowledge of an objective truth" and thus remaining "the final and governing authority" of narrative (2003, 536). He acknowledges that already in the (later) nineteenth century there were narrative texts that "undertook to give us an extremely subjective, individualistic, and often eccentrically aberrant impression of reality" (536). These texts, however, differ fundamentally, and in principle, from those of modernism, which according to Auerbach are not merely subjective but based on the consciousnesses of a "multiplicity of persons" (536).[85] Auerbach sees this change from realism to modernism as a shift of narrative authority, from claims to an objective truth (and the writer's ability to represent this in narrative) to a concept of truth as subjective, partial, and limited, and from an ambition to represent a totality towards the isolation of moments of experience. These moments only attain meaning and validity for the individual. Meaning, no longer objectively given, needs to be extracted time and again from the unceasing flow of individual experiences and shaped into a meaningful form by each person individually. The same task of synthesising a worldview out of discrete and conflicting data now falls to the reader of modernist literature (cf. 2003, 549; 1994, 510).

In other words: the synthesis of a "cosmic worldview" is no longer or not always created for the reader by the author or the narrator but must be created by the reader via "interpretive synthesis" out of "overlapping, complementing, and contradict[ory]" textual data (Auerbach 2003, 549). Writing in the 1940s, Auerbach clearly still clings to the possibility of such a synthesis, even though achieving it has become more difficult. His harsh judgement of *Ulysses* results from what he regards as the impossibility of synthesis in Joyce's novel, i.e., the negation of a total meaning or central intention. This, Auerbach feels, is a deliberate act of destruction and an affront to nothing less than "culture and civilization" (2003, 551; 1994, 513). In contrast, he recognises in the loving attention to everyday details in *To the Lighthouse* a life-affirming vision that is universal, no longer tied to any particular cultural framework. Woolf's novel, in his view, is a beacon of a more unified and simplified global culture (2003, 552).

By implication, we can see that, for Auerbach, although authors are less tangibly present in modernist literature via a central narrative voice as "the final and governing authority" (536), they are still thought to be responsible for the text, and they are praised or rebuked for their text's epistemological (in-)adequacy, its relationship to reality, or the possibility of finding out (a) truth about reality. Authors may withdraw from their texts, become invisible or inaudible, but they cannot disappear completely or cut themselves off entirely from what they have written (cf. Guttzeit 2021 on the trope of the invisible author). Through their activities of "selection and emphasis and tone", authors remain "subliminal" guiding instances in narratives even though they are "technically 'invisible'" (Tillotson 1959, 12).

But as Auerbach's own example, Balzac, shows, already in the early nineteenth century the relationship between author, narrator, and narrative is more complicated than Auerbach is willing to accept. It is wrong to see in Balzac merely "the writer as narrator of objective facts" (2003, 534). Auerbach's own analysis of

---

85 In the German original: "Vielheit der Subjekte" (1994, 498).

a passage from *Père Goriot* makes clear how Balzac mixes different rhetorical strategies, styles, and metaphorical comparisons in order to create a sense of the demonic in his description of Madame Vauquer (2003, 468–472) – an approach that can hardly be circumscribed as an adherence to "objective facts". This is the 'Romantic' in the phrase "Romantic realism", which later critics applied to Balzac (Fanger 1967), an element of imagination within realism (Warning 1999), or even the "melodramatic imagination" itself (Brooks 1976). In fact, the notion of reality already becomes so unstable in Balzac that the narrator is hard put to keep up with the speed of change, and this contributes to the discrediting of his moralistic impulses, which hardly serve as points of rest in the narrative but succumb to the overall sense of melodrama and the forward gallop of the suspense plot. The staccato of successive events sweeps away any attempt at narrative control, let alone any sense of a "final and governing authority" (Auerbach 2003, 536). Of course, this is an effect of Balzac's prose, of his organisation of the narrative, but if we accept the narrator as a fiction or as part of the fiction of the *Comédie*, then that narrator may *claim* to possess moral authority or wisdom, may *attempt* to gain an overarching supreme viewpoint, but his authority is ultimately undermined by the instability of the narrated world. As the mundane turns into the realm of adventure, the very notion of an overarching and stable perspective on reality is attenuated by the incalculable dynamic of the flow of capital. Towards the end of *Lost Illusions*, the master criminal's Machiavellian philosophy offers a more convincing and memorable moral commentary on the world of this novel than all the narrator's gnomic pronouncements combined (cf. Moretti 1988, 292 n. 5).

Similar conflicts between narrators and the narrated world in other nineteenth-century novels are not difficult to find. Setting aside technical authorial incompetence – a factor that cannot be ignored in a literary form that was attempted by so many writers from all walks of life (see Sutherland 2006, 159–172) –, we can assume that such conflicts are not accidental but a part of these novels' intentional structure and strategies. As we saw in the previous chapter, such conflicts or tensions become formative elements in the British author-*bildungsroman*, as authors' simultaneous attempts at self-management, control of their material, and maintaining ethical principles are confronted with the potentially compromising challenges of a social world that exacts compromise solutions.

In some mid-nineteenth-century novels, as for instance in many by Anthony Trollope, the narrator is an avuncular presence guiding and occasionally cajoling the 'gentle reader'. Yet, in others the relationship between the narrator and the storyworld is less harmonious, in fact conflict-ridden. In Eliot's *Middlemarch* (1871–72) or in Meredith's *The Ordeal of Richard Feverel* (1859), authorial narration almost constantly undermines the values and perspectives of the characters. As J. Hillis Miller has shown (1975), the terminologies that Eliot's narrator employs in organising the world of *Middlemarch* fail to converge and instead turn into incongruous metaphors. Out of this incongruity arises a tension between the fictionality of the story and the fictitiousness of the narrator's explanatory perspectives, illustrating the precarious position of this authorial narrator. If the authority of the narrator, his or her ability to harmonise different viewpoints, is in doubt, there are several solutions. One solution is the aestheticist option, placing style above sincerity (cf. Wilde 1994, 406) – the route that leads into literary modernism, towards Mann and Joyce. The other is a more or less undisturbed continuation of realist conventions in twentieth-century middlebrow fiction. Yet another option – already present in the earlier epistolary novel – is the multiplication of narrators and texts within the novel, by incorporating different kinds of documents (*The Woman in White*, *Dracula*) or by having (unreliable) storytellers within the story (*Heart of Darkness*, *The Turn of the Screw*), thus subtly but indisputably redistributing the problem of narrative authority throughout the text. Yet another is the introduction of even more limited personal narrators or focalisers (*What Maisie Knew*), confining the events of the story to what one character or a small group of characters can perceive and/or tell (*Esther Waters*).

In such instances, the authorial audience can and must distinguish between the narrator's presentation of the story and the superior vantage point provided by the author as the composer or framer of the text's segmentivity. However, particularly in cases of author fiction where the second-order observation provided by the author (i.e., by the composition of the text) clashes with the first-order observations provided by the narrator and/or by an author-character, there is a disturbance in the integrative flow of the authorpoietic process from autopoetic authorial *anaclisis* to heteropoetic *cataclisis* and homopoetic audience *cathexis* and back to a confirmatory appreciation of the author. In such cases, the alignment between author and character, however ironic it may have been in its construction (as it certainly is in *Pendennis*), breaks down and disintegrates. At its most extreme, the result is a novel not of formation but of de-formation, a novel that focuses not on authorial success but on failure. These novels provide worst-case scenarios of allopoetic *paraclisis* in which authors are first made and then abandoned, ending in self-destruction: a perfect example of this being Jack London's *Martin Eden*.

We tend to assume that such novels come to the fore only towards the end of the nineteenth century, but one of the earliest examples, Herman Melville's *Pierre; or, The Ambiguities* (1852), dates from the early 1850s and is thus a contemporary of *David Copperfield*. To contextualise this novel, we need to take a brief look at the phenomenon of celebrity authorship as it developed in a transatlantic perspective in the nineteenth century.

The decline of the Romantic conception of the author as a Carlylean "man of letters as hero" or an Emersonian "representative man" is evident in the US as well as in Britain (Knights 1978, 99; Braudy 1997, 445–449). Instead, transatlantic print publications, journals, and lecture tours help to create authors as celebrities, at the mercy of their audiences' interests and attention. Moreover, commercial literary publishing in the nineteenth century is not interested in 'making' authors, i.e., in establishing or maintaining the reputations of "name-economy authors" (Childress 2017, 42), but relies to a large part on reprinting, recycling, or recombining existing texts, and on providing cheap reading matter in popular genres (later called genre fiction, pulp fiction, or formula fiction) where authors' names, at least at first, are unimportant (McGill 2003).

Celebrity authorship is a mere shadow of the heroic authorship envisaged by Carlyle. It does not emerge from the author's own heroic efforts (to make a name for himself, to overcome the resistance of established public taste towards the novelty of his work) but is a result of publishers' marketing ploys, which, if successful, present the author's personality as a product. It is not the quality of the writing that gains a reputation but the author as a commodity, a fictitious image. Complaints about this inflation of literature through widespread practices of 'puffing' and 'log-rolling' are legion around mid-century. "The most 'popular,' the most 'successful' writers among us, (for a brief period, at least) are, ninety-nine times out of a hundred, persons of mere address, perseverance, effrontery – in a word, busy-bodies, toadies, quacks", Poe writes in 1846, their "ephemeral 'reputations'" – note the scare quotes –"manufactured" by "favourable notices written or caused to be written by interested parties" ("The Literati of New York City", in Poe 1984, 1118). The alternative – commercial fiction – is equally unheroic but even more destructive of the author's authority, because in this case the authors have merely their productivity to sell, with little to no control over the product, whose form and content are largely dictated by the expectations that dominate the market at the time of publication. The question here is obviously not: "Is it art?" but: "Will it sell?"

At least from the 1850s onwards, there is a heightened awareness of the (possible and actual) tensions between the public and private dimensions of literary authorship. This tension is evident, for instance, in Herman Melville's relationship with his publishers and critics, and vice versa. Many of Melville's contemporaries – like the critics Edwin Percy Whipple and William Alfred Jones – refused to accept the distinction between a writer's public and private persona. As André Kaenel explains, "[a]ll texts were thought to bear the mark of their authors, to be the visible emanations of a consciousness which critics invariably viewed as unified and coherent" (1992, 54). In the eyes of these critics, "authors were necessarily 'present' in their writings in the guise of a fictional persona reconstructible from the act of reading" (60).⁸⁶ Poe, in an article on Margaret Fuller, notes the perfect congruence between "her personal character and her printed book" (1984, 1179), and concludes: "The supposition that the book of an author is a thing apart from the author's self, is, I think, ill-founded" (1178).

At the time, this congruence between 'self' and 'book' was often understood as a correspondence of aesthetic and moral qualities. Melville rebelled against this identification and the concurrent tendency to judge literary works according to moral values. Instead of conforming to the requirements of the marketplace, he withdrew from them. In "Hawthorne and His Mosses" (1850), Melville expressed the desire to sever the connection between authors and their books: "Would that all excellent books were foundlings, without father or mother, so that it might be, we could glorify them, without including their ostensible authors" (Melville 2014, 123). He appears to have seen the marketing of author images as the beginning of an industrialised levelling of authorial individuality, a degradation of the unique (Romantic) creative subject. For example, he refuses to submit a photograph of himself to his publisher Evert Duykinck for a magazine whose editorship he was about to assume. In his letter to Duykinck of 12 Feb. 1851, Melville writes: "The fact is, almost everybody is having his 'mug' engraved nowadays; so that this test of distinction is getting to be reversed; and therefore, to see one's 'mug' in a magazine, is presumptive evidence that he's a nobody. [...] I respectfully decline being *oblivionated* by a Daguerreotype [sic]" (qtd. in Parker 1996, 816). In *Pierre*, similarly, the narrator asserts that the daguerreotype "instead of immortalizing a genius [...] now only *dayalized* a dunce" (Melville 1996, 253), and that "when every body has his portrait published, true distinction lies in not having yours published at all" (ibid., 254).

Similar "stances of evasion" (Kaenel 1992, 63) are explored in Melville's novel *Pierre, or The Ambiguities* (1852). Here, there is no longer a common bond between narrator and reader, but a gap of distrust that no one can hope to bridge. The authorial narrator gradually unmasks himself as a 'confidence man' or trickster, abandoning residual conventions of politeness or agreement between author and reader. The place of the 'gentle reader' as the narratee is taken over by a Baudelairean *hypocrite lecteur*. Especially in the second half of *Pierre*, probably written while he was reading the first negative reviews of *Moby-Dick*, Melville destroys the Romantic myth of authorship as original composition in having his hero produce writing that is both spontaneous and immature, written for short-lived fame merely to supply the printing press. Perhaps with a satirical nod towards Carlyle's *Sar-*

---

86 Kaenel 1992 refers in this context to Edwin Percy Whipple's *Lectures on Subjects Connected with Literature and Life* (Boston 1850) and Alfred William Jones's 1857 essay "Literary Egotism".

tor Resartus and its 'philosophy of clothes', Pierre's first publishers, Wonder and Wen, are former tailors who produce books as a way of recycling the waste of their tailoring business "with an economical view of working up in books, the linen and cotton shreds of the cutter's counter" (Melville 1996, 246).

Pierre's publishers want to market his authorial personality at a moment when this is not yet fully formed. His signature keeps changing, as does his outward appearance:

> Applications for autographs showered in upon him; but in sometimes humorously gratifying the more urgent requests of these singular people Pierre could not feel but a pang of regret, that owing to the very youthful and quite unformed character of his handwriting, his signature did not possess that inflexible uniformity, which – for mere prudential reasons, if nothing more – should always mark the hand of illustrious men. [...] Alas! posterity would be sure to conclude that they were forgeries all. (252–253)

Pierre, like Melville himself at this stage in his career, rejects media publicity. He refuses to be photographed. Melville was keenly aware of the effects of publicity, as he was also finding it difficult to reshape his own public image from an author of popular tropical adventures (*Typee, Omoo, Mardi*) to a serious writer of literary fiction.

Later in *Pierre*, Melville stresses the industrial aspects of nineteenth-century authorship by making his author-hero try to sell his novel to the publishing company of Steel, Flint, and Asbestos. Pierre writes out of economic necessity, "born of unwillingness and the bill of the baker" (258), as Melville himself had done in writing potboilers like *Redburn* and *White-Jacket*. His writing is "in the way of a mere business transaction" (260). Authorship here is no longer a means of fulfilment but a form of self-exploitation and self-destruction, as it already is in Balzac's *Lost Illusions*, but now even more drastically envisaged in metaphors of auto-vampirism, self-digestion, and Promethean punishment. The pen is compared to "the beak of the vulture in his hand" (305). Far from a male symbol of textual and/as sexual control and domination, the pen becomes a weapon of self-destruction and self-castration. Pierre the writer emasculates Pierre the man. The gendered aspects of nineteenth-century authorship are heavily inscribed in *Pierre*, which differs from Melville's other novels in its allusions to the genre conventions of gothic fiction and its covertly and sometimes overtly erotic charge of mystery and horror.

A certain "anxiety of authorship" (Gilbert/Gubar 2000, 49) can also be sensed in Melville's dedication of this novel "To Greylock's Most Excellent Majesty". "In old times", he writes, "authors were proud of the privilege of dedicating their works to Majesty" (Melville 1996, n.p. [1]). Royal patronage, however, does not exist in postcolonial America, where authors have to work for a living; Melville dedicates his book to a mountain in the Berkshires, displacing the grandeur of majesty from social to natural forces, and possibly projecting his own masculine authorial power onto the mountain through images of tumescence and insemination: Melville praises the (masculine) mountain's "Imperial Purple Majesty (royal-born: Porphyrogenitus)" and notes that he has received "his most bounteous and unstinted fertilizations" (ibid.).

The author of *Moby-Dick*, whose white whale is one of the most unmistakably phallic images in the Western canon, here genders himself as feminine and receives his inspiration not from the female Muse but from a thoroughly masculine mountain that is implored to "benignantly incline his hoary crown" (ibid.). It is unclear how much of this is intended as self-parody and self-deprecation. The ambiguities in the dedication foreshadow the ambiguities that fill the pages of this novel, *Pierre; or, the Ambiguities*, which was to be Melville's greatest commercial failure. One of its ambiguities is the double-gendered nature of authorship as both an act of insemination and a form of male pregnancy (receiving "fertilizations"), thus completing the subversion of the traditional imagery of the female Muse.

In the process of writing, Pierre loses not only his sense of identity but also his sense of masculinity: "Now he began to feel that in him, the thews of a Titan were forestallingly cut by the scissors of Fate" (1996, 339). The result, for Pierre, is the most intense loneliness and existential despair, aggravated by the fact that in the end he can no longer even believe in the mystery that is at the basis of his relationship with his half-sister Isabel, discrediting it as mere fiction. He aimlessly walks through New York City like Poe's man of the crowd (1840), as if eager to convince himself of being human by rubbing against other people. At this point, he has become a stranger to himself as well as others. Like Bartleby, Pierre at the end is a figure of futile but irrepressible resistance to social conformity. Writing has sucked him dry and left him an empty shell, "a doorless and shutterless house for the four loosened winds of heaven to howl through" (1996, 339–340).

The inability to achieve an authentic autobiographical self in writing, under the pressure of institutional and commercial forces in the literary marketplace, is the main theme of Melville's *Pierre*. The novel envisages Pierre's trajectory as a tragedy infused with elements of gothic fiction and the *bildungsroman*. Ambiguity is this novel's keyword, but not in the Empsonian sense of something having more than one meaning, but in the etymological sense of *ambigere*, 'to wander about, to waver, to dispute'. The word 'ambiguous' is used excessively in the text and applied to various objects, including nature, love, death, fairies, Pierre's father's portrait, his mother's views on the portrait, a smile, Pierre's relationship with Isabel and his cousin Glen Stanley, and so on,[87] and it is later applied in reflexive passages to the "procession of events" recounted in the novel, so that "the ambiguities which hemmed [Pierre] in" (1996, 337) also become legible as the ambiguities from which the novel as form can no longer free itself. The character's and the narrative's progression become allegories of one another. Moreover, the character of Pierre and the physical book that lends him a fictional existence for the individual reader converge at the end: "Here, then, is the untimely, timely end; – Life's last chapter well stitched into the middle! Nor book, nor author of the book, hath any sequel, though each hath its last lettering! – It is ambiguous still" (360). Timely for the novel form, untimely for Pierre, end and ending are ambiguously joined together. The format of the novel exacts an ending, but it is not the conventional ending of the *bildungsroman* but of a tragedy that leaves all four main characters dead.

Pierre, who had been forced to write sequels for his work in progress that fit to what was already at the printer's, literally 'loses the plot', as does the novel that features him as its central character. The form of the *bildungsroman*, reliant on the idea of a subject that is in the process of self-formation and self-fulfilment, breaks down under the pressure of depicting the subject's de-formation. Ambiguities, understood as an excess of meaning in an overdetermined world, affect Pierre's ability to move and act in the world. He gets caught up in 'mystery', another central category in this novel that describes incessantly shifting relationships. Pierre, the rock, is petrified and rendered immobile by 'mystery', a sense that the meanings of the world have become impenetrable. He is increasingly unknowable to others as well as himself, and there is no Christ in sight who would seek to build his church upon him. On the other hand, stone, a symbol of supposedly solid reality, is liquefied and dissolved in 'imaginings', just as the "perfect marble form" (60) of Pierre's father is dissolved in the portraits painted of him and turns into merely "a certain imagined ghost of that same imagined image" (83).

If the mind in *Pierre* is presented as "roam[ing] up and down in the ever-elastic regions of evanescent invention" and as creating "multitudinous shapes [...] out of the incessant dissolvings of its own prior creations" (82), this recursive process of dissolution and creation is reflected in the novel through its narrator's mocking attitude towards literary conventions. The intrusive authorial narrator ("I write precisely as I please", 244) incessantly dissolves what he creates, so that construction and destruction become coterminous in *Pierre*. This destructive attitude extends to the material texts and other physical objects in the novel: letters, paintings, poems. Pierre's printed poems are used to light cigars. The portrait is burned.

---

87 Cf. Melville 1996, 13, 29, 52, 54, 71, 80, 82, 83, 84, 85, 87, 151, 181, 196–197, 220, 224, 262, 337, 351, 360.

So is his former fiancé Lucy's letter. The pamphlet by Plotinus Plinlimmon that Pierre picks up en route to New York City is sewn into a coat. Part of a sonnet manuscript is turned into a brooch but then partly dissolves in the rain (cf. 263). Letters from Glen Stanley and from Pierre's publishers are stuffed into the pistols that Pierre uses to shoot Glen.

Many critics have either loathed *Pierre* or preferred to ignore it. If it is indeed made of "milk" rather than "salt water", as Melville claimed in a letter to Sophia Hawthorne,[88] extending the feminine quality of the text, the milk turns sour when the novel is two thirds completed. The authorial narrator seems to develop a distaste for his subject matter, his protagonist, and himself. Narratorial irony gives way to an uncomfortable blend of sarcasm, cynicism, and self-pity. It is only in book XVII that we learn that Pierre is himself an author of poetry and fiction, and we are given extracts from his writings, which are belittled by the narrator. The tone of the novel changes from here on, as we are given to understand that Pierre's attempts at authorship are at least in part to blame for his overall failure. In other words, *Pierre* is the very opposite of *David Copperfield*. The novel enacts this failure of Pierre as a novelist while reflecting on Melville's own disappointment, and it replicates these themes in its form by subverting the central idea of the *bildungsroman:* the idea of harmonising the interests of the individual and society. Instead of achieving a liveable compromise, the melancholy hero turns into a *solitaire* who revolts against the world, an American Hamlet and later a Timon, while the narrative turns erratic, inconsistent, and rhetorically overblown. Moreover, its narrator insists on the unknowability of its central character: "All's o'er, and ye know him not!" (362).

A similar conclusion is reached by the elderly lawyer at the end of "Bartleby, the Scrivener" (1853), who is forced to admit his moral, rational, and experiential defeat when confronted with the inscrutable scrivener who, by 'preferring not to', effectively withdraws not only from the work of writing that he has been hired to do but from all human contact. The lawyer's Dickensian tolerance of the foibles of his other employees, nicknamed 'Turkey' and 'Nippers', is frustrated by the sheer intransigence of Bartleby's refusal to engage. Arguably, the story continues the concern with writing from *Pierre* but shifts it from the literary to the legal terrain, where writing is not merely representational but directly functional and socially effective (the lawyer is a Master in Chancery whose work involves transactions of property). Its legal setting and its absurdity may well have been inspired by

---

88 "But, My Dear Lady, I shall not again send you a bowl of salt water. The next chalice I shall commend, will be a rural bowl of milk" (8 Jan. 1852, Melville 1993, 219). The "bowl of salt water" refers to *Moby-Dick*.

Dickens's *Bleak House*, which was published in serial form from March 1852 onwards. Bartleby's erratic behaviour completely undermines the lawyer's authority and capacity for action, and the lawyer's helplessness culminates in the exclamation "Ah Bartleby! Ah humanity!" (Melville 2002, 34).

As many readers have pointed out, "Bartleby" is more than an allegory of its author's personal evasiveness. For Gilles Deleuze, Bartleby's resistance opens up a zone of ambiguity that makes action impossible (1998). For Giorgio Agamben, Bartleby becomes a figure of "pure, absolute potentiality" (1999, 254), the embodiment of a realm of possibilities that is impossible to translate into reality by means of will or decisiveness. Yet, in the lawyer-narrator, Bartleby wakes a powerful strain of "melancholy" and "gloom", an emotional response that prepares his final exclamation (Melville 2002, 17). Bartleby's potentiality may be pure, but it nevertheless triggers powerful consequences in others. The despair of the narrator at Pierre's final unknowability is mirrored by the lawyer's despair at understanding Bartleby's utter strangeness.[89]

Pierre and Bartleby may well be the most alienated of all nineteenth-century literary 'heroes'. In both *Pierre* and "Bartleby", Melville effectively transforms the Romantic author's autonomous subjectivity into a proto-modernist obscurity. "Bartleby" even invokes a Dickensian multiplicity of eccentric characters, only to deny its narrator any overarching, controlling, or consoling perspective that could make sense of Bartleby's intransigence, let alone sublate his eccentricity within a superior "cosmic worldview" (Auerbach 2003, 549). Instead, the narrator is left puzzled and in despair. The protagonist of *Pierre* becomes similarly intransparent and unreadable (to himself, to the other characters, and to the reader), a black box of inscrutable motivations. Thus, the novel turns into an anti-*bildungsroman*, a novel of *de*formation that undermines Romantic, Goethean ideas of development and organic growth by confronting them with the harsh realities of industrial society and the vagaries of human psychology. *Pierre; or, the Ambiguities* is one of the earliest examples of a "novel of resentment" (Bergonzi 1976, 20), prefiguring later realist novels of the literary life such as *New Grub Street* and *Keep the Aspidistra Flying* [→ ch. 7, 11], while also anticipating some of the gothic and fantastic strands in later nineteenth-century author fictions. While Dickens and Thackeray are still envisaging forms of social compromise and integration for their literary heroes [→ ch. 4], for Melville the lonely writer's psychological and physical disintegration is a more realistic possibility within the economic structures of nineteenth-century capitalism. Here, almost as soon as it had been estab-

---

[89] For a more detailed reading of "Bartleby", see Berensmeyer/Spies 2011.

lished, the integrative power of the *bildungsroman* has already vanished, and we are left with a horrific vision of allopoetic authorial dysmorphia.

The author-*bildungsroman* and anti-*bildungsroman* with their generally male-dominated tradition is undeniably an important strand of nineteenth-century literature. However, it is only part of the story. There is also a long-neglected line of female authors exploring literary authorship at the same time, as well as an even more obscure set of male responses that likewise explore the possibilities and constraints of female authorship in narrative fiction. Both these strands are the topic of the next chapter.

6 "Sign it like a queen": Writing Female Authors in the Victorian Novel

Charlotte Brontë, Rose Ellen Hendriks, Christina Rossetti

Feminist scholars have taught us to see that female authorship, for a long time, used to be the exception to a norm defined as masculine (Gilbert/Gubar 2000). This marginal position makes it useful for questioning the centre from the periphery and for deconstructing the hierarchy of values implied in this confrontation, ranging from the eighteenth-century expansion of print culture, via the genre of the nineteenth-century *bildungsroman*, to modernist questionings of the value of female authorship in the "battle of the brows" (Brown/Grover 2012) and the increasingly industrialised world of modern publishing [→ ch. 11, 12]. Recent research has come to view earlier feminist interpretations of the (lack of) integration of women writers into the literary field with scepticism, arguing that many Victorian women writers were indeed capable of a "conscious construction of [their] public identity and literary career" (Peterson 2009, 229 n. 32). Narratives of exclusion or marginalisation have been revised by more complex accounts that emphasise the agency of women as professional authors in the nineteenth century, particularly in the vastly increasing market of periodicals that offered publishing opportunities to women writers, often anonymously (cf. Onslow 2000, Easley 2004 and 2018, Peterson 2009).

Census records from nineteenth-century Britain "show a steady increase in the number of women listed as writers, authors, or authoresses" (Easley 2018, 41), rising from 29 in 1841 to 1,140 in 1881 (ibid.). Indeed, as Easley notes, many middle-class women would not have revealed their profession in a census, so the actual figures are probably much higher (ibid.). Employing a nautical metaphor, Anthony Trollope asserts in 1870 that "the port of literature is open to women" and that "a female captain can steer her vessel with much hope of success" (Trollope 1995, 217). Nevertheless, the texts discussed in this chapter leave little doubt that dominant social expectations and economic arrangements had 'female captains' at a significant disadvantage compared to their male peers when it came to asserting themselves confidently as professional authors. Many men and women in the Victorian age, and sometimes far beyond that period, viewed women writers as "a disruption of the literary field" (Peterson 2009, 30) – even though, by the end of the nineteenth century, the Society of Authors accepted them as members (51).

When not publishing under their own name, women tended (and still tend) to choose male or gender-neutral pseudonyms ('George Eliot', 'Currer Bell',

'Lucas Malet'), whereas men almost always opt for a same-sex pseudonym (Jung 2017). Use of initials as in 'J. K. Rowling' is a similar strategy to make an author's name gender-neutral. Male authors with female pseudonyms are rare (cf. Mullan 2007, 127–128). Exceptions include Thomas Sedgewick Whalley, who in 1781 published his moralistic poem, *The Fatal Kiss*, as written by "A Beautiful but Unfortunate Young Lady" (Behrendt 2011, 10); the Victorian essayist John Skelton, who published some of his work under the pseudonym 'Shirley' (Mullan 2007, 129); and an epistolary novel by Swinburne disguised as 'Mrs Horace Manners' (ibid., 130). Grant Allen published one of his novels, *The Type-Writer Girl* (1897) under the moniker 'Olive P. Rayner', and the Scottish writer William Sharp (1855–1905) is better known by his pseudonym 'Fiona Macleod' (Mullan 2007, 131–137). Arnold Bennett, as editor of the women's magazine *Woman* in the 1890s, published articles under the name of 'Gwendolen' (Gross 1973, 233). 'Lindsay Anderson', the pen-name of the "obscure nautical novelist Alexander Christie (1841–95)" is at best "vaguely female" (Sutherland 2006, 168). In the 1950s, Laurence Meynell wrote fiction for girls under the pseudonym 'Valerie Baxter' (Morse 2004), including the novelised advice book *Jane: Young Author* (Baxter 1958). Philip Larkin, as an Oxford undergraduate, wrote several works, including the slightly naughty girls' school novella *Trouble at Willow Gables*, in the female persona of 'Brunette Coleman', an assumed identity that apparently stimulated his creativity; but these texts were only published posthumously, and not under the Coleman moniker (Larkin 2002).

In one episode of the classic BBC sitcom *Blackadder* ("Ink and Incapability", 1987) the butler Edmund hopes to publish his autobiographical novel under the female pseudonym "Gertrude Perkins" to sell more copies, assuming that all women authors of Regency Britain are in fact men in disguise, with the exception of James Boswell, whom he takes to be the only living female writer in England. There is a similar example in Henry James's tale "The Death of the Lion" (1894), in which the author 'Guy Walsingham' turns out to be a woman, and the person writing bad fiction under the pen-name of 'Dora Forbes' is a bald man with "a big red moustache" who wears "showy knickerbockers" (James 1999, 2: 159). As the narrator remarks to an interlocutor in the story, "in the age we live in one gets lost among the genders and the pronouns" (ibid., 2: 155).

Apart from the texts discussed in more detail below, Victorian examples of novels by women that focus on authors as characters include Charlotte Yonge's *The Clever Woman of the Family* (1865), Charlotte Riddell's *A Struggle for Fame* (1883), Eliza Lynn Linton's *The Autobiography of Christopher Kirkland* (1885), and Mary Cholmondeley's *Red Pottage* (1899). Notable among novels about women authors written by men, besides Hardy's *A Pair of Blue Eyes* and *The Hand of Ethel-*

berta (discussed below), is James Payn's *The Heir of the Ages* (1886), about a former governess who writes under the male pseudonym 'John Javelin' (see Law 2012).[90]

In earlier centuries, Margaret Cavendish included a fictional version of herself as an author in her novel *The Blazing World* (1666) (cf. Berensmeyer 2020a, 104– 114); a similar case can be found, almost a century later, in Elizabeth Justice's autobiographical novel *Amelia, or the Distress'd Wife* (1751). As Dorothee Birke points out, Justice's novel is ambivalent about female authorship, wavering between assertions of a woman's "enterprising spirit and assertiveness" on the one hand and "protestations […] of Amelia's reluctance to expose herself to the public eye" (Birke, forthcoming). French readers could point to Félicité de Genlis's *La femme auteur* of 1802 as an earlier novel about female authorship. In late eighteenth-century America, several of Susanna Rowson's novels feature "fictional female writers" (Henderson 2017, 150). In novels such as *The Inquisitor* (1793) and *Trials of the Human Heart* (1795), Rowson explores the possibilities and constraints of female authors, who are "more often faced with opposition than success" (Henderson 2017, 151) and "often retreat into silence" (ibid., 166).

The literary *bildungsroman* or novel of literary apprenticeship of the first half of the nineteenth century was clearly gendered masculine. This was certainly not due to a lack of female novelists. In John Sutherland's sample of 878 Victorian novelists, 312 are women (2006, 168). There is no simple answer to the question why women writers by and large refrained from imagining themselves or their peers as authors in fiction. Scholars in feminist narrative studies have paid significant attention to the representation of women in fiction, to changing plot patterns, or certain types of female characters such as single women, but there has not been much systematic study of how women writers represented their own activities, their own roles as authors in fiction.[91] When they come close to doing so, as in Charlotte Lennox's *The Female Quixote* (1752), they appear to avoid the topic as much or as soon as possible: Arabella, Lennox's protagonist, is cured of her vivid literary imagination at the end and chooses marriage instead of authorship. This would set a strong trend in the "development of the woman of letters as a conceptual category" (Peterson 2009, 9), namely a central conflict between the woman

---

90 Bassett (2020) lists 103 Victorian novels between 1841 and 1900 that have authors as characters; in many of these cases, however, the author character is not central to the plot. *A Struggle for Fame* and *Red Pottage* are discussed in detail in Peterson 2009, 151–170 and 207–223.

91 See, for example – in addition to the classics of feminist literary criticism by Gilbert and Gubar (1988–1994) or Showalter (1972) – DuPlessis 1985, Hanson 2000, Sterry 2017. Miller 2003 goes so far as to claim that the absence of a biographical equivalent of the 'real' Jane Austen within her novels is a precondition for her style.

writer's "domestic femininity" and her "professional status" (Salmon 2013, 174). This conflict was renegotiated over and over again, as the female author- *bildungsroman* and *künstlerroman* of the late nineteenth and early twentieth centuries not only focused on the heroine's development and self-assertion as an artist, but also had to contend with gendered stereotypes of femininity, not least with the question whether a literary career could be reconciled with the duties of marriage (cf. Abel/Hirsch/Langland. 1983, Lazzaro-Weis 1990, Maier 2007).

Charlotte Brontë's *Jane Eyre* (1847), often considered the first female *bildungsroman* in England,[92] and one of the first texts to advertise itself as an 'autobiography', does not depict the development of a professional woman author, yet it can arguably be read as "the *Bildungsroman* of a professional writer *manqué*" (Salmon 2013, 177; cf. Marcus 1995). After all, Jane tells her audience in her own words about her life up until ten years after her marriage to Rochester – in the famous words "Reader, I married him" (Brontë 1985, 474). By that time, Jane has grown into a woman writer to tell the story of her own life. She addresses the reader directly – as will David Copperfield a year later –, but she does not disclose whether (and it seems rather unlikely that) she has any further literary ambitions beyond this narrative. Some of Brontë's imitators in the form of fictional autobiography more explicitly introduce their heroine as an aspiring author, thus adding an additional complication to the novel's marriage plot.[93]

Published in the same year, Rose Ellen Hendriks's *The Young Authoress* traces the life of its heroine, Rosalie de Rochequillon, from orphaned girl to successful writer, apparently with some autobiographical touches. In contrast to *Jane Eyre*, however, this novel is narrated in the third person. In addition to the distinction between narrator and character-focaliser, there is an overt distinction in the novel between narrator and author. The narrator, in one passage, even refers directly to Hendriks when naming Rosalie's favourite authors: Rosalie "seemed always in a wild, fluttering ecstasy of literary hopes and fears – always talking of Dickens, or Bulwer, or Rose Ellen Hendriks" (Hendriks 1847, 3: 207). The narrative audience must believe that the narrator does not know that he or she is in fact *inside* a work of Rose Ellen Hendriks, whereas the authorial audience will perform a double-take and recognise this intrusion of the actual author's name in the narrator's story as a *mise-en-abyme*, a conflation of ontological domains.

---

[92] This is contested, as is the relevance of the *bildungsroman* genre for novels of female development; cf. Rowe 1983, Salmon 2019, 68–69; see Fraiman 1993 for an interpretation of earlier novels by and about women in this context (Burney's *Evelina* and Austen's *Pride and Prejudice*).

[93] See Hobbs 2019 for a discussion of Julia Addison's *Evelyn Lascelles* (1855) and Barrett Browning's *Aurora Leigh* in this context.

Hendriks's overt, an almost aggressive act of self-promotion, is in stark contrast with the Victorian stereotype of feminine modesty and reticence. At the end of the novel, Rosalie marries, and the narrator comments:

> She began her career as a genius, and found that, after all, she was but a woman.... [S]he began, as many a creature of genius does, relying upon the strength and reputation of her own talents, and ended by the wisest of all reparation for her mistake – namely, acknowledging that man has the superior power of guiding the talents of youth, and that none will do so, as willingly, gently, and efficaciously as he to whom she pledges her faith. (1847, 3: 291)

Here the narrator reports Rosalie's feelings about the contrast between being an artist and being a woman, and he or she aligns the character's views with that of received social wisdom ("acknowledging that ..."). The passage invites comparison with the first sentence of *Pride and Prejudice* ("It is a truth universally acknowledged ..."), yet here there is no apparent irony to the acknowledgement, and the mood is one of resigned acceptance of "the superior power". Although matrimony will not make Rosalie give up writing, the novel clearly states the "central dilemma" and tension between the constricted personal, domestic life of a woman and her public professional status as a writer in the Victorian period (Salmon 2013, 178). This tension is the key to narrative progression in many subsequent texts by women, both fictional and nonfictional.[94]

This is not quite the "anxiety of authorship" diagnosed by Gilbert and Gubar in *The Madwoman in the Attic* (2000, 48–49), but it does represent a conflict of roles that male authors rarely, if ever, experience. The status of author is available to women, yet boundaries of gender as well as class need to be stretched, if not overcome, in attaining and maintaining it. Compared to its male counterpart, female authorship requires additional efforts of legitimation and (self-)authorisation, because "the female writer's battle for self-creation involves her in a revisionary process", as Gilbert and Gubar have argued: "In order to define herself as an author she must redefine the terms of her socialization" (2000, 49), and in doing so she will necessarily challenge, revise, or complicate, if not entirely abandon or reject, the generic conventions, in particular the linear developmental trajectory, of the (masculine) *bildungsroman*. On the other hand, the "thematic and formal treatment of authorship" in more or less autobiographical writing by women also opens up new possibilities of engaging "with discourses of both popular fiction and women's rights reform", as Katherine Hobbs has argued (2019, 701).

---

[94] Cf. Salmon 2013, 174–209 for a reading of *Aurora Leigh* along these lines, in connection with Harriet Martineau's *Autobiography* (1877) and Gaskell's *Life of Charlotte Brontë* (1879).

Christina Rossetti's *Maude*, written in 1850 when its author was herself still young (nineteen) but only published posthumously in 1897, is such a female *bildungsroman manqué*, also discussed by Gilbert and Gubar in their classic study. It outlines the arrested development of a woman poet, whose chief failing is "that when she had written a good poem, she felt it to be good", as Rossetti's brother William Michael noted in editing the text (W. M. Rossetti 1897, 4). The text presents some of Rossetti's poems integrated into the narrative, as part of the "writing-book" (Rossetti 1897, 9) of the story's protagonist, the fifteen-year-old Maude Foster. Maude herself diagnoses her major fault as "putting [herself] forward and displaying her verses", and the narrator concurs in calling this "vanity" (72). At a birthday party, Maude, her cousins Mary and Agnes, and other guests compose *bout-rimés* sonnets as a party game. Maude envies her cousins, who "live in the country, and are exactly what [they] appear, and never wish for what [they] do not possess", confessing herself to be "sick of display and poetry and acting" (38). A year later, Agnes and Mary visit Maude in London. They perceive her to have grown "more delicate" and "very thin", connecting this to her "still writ[ing] verses" (44). At a social visit, Maude is introduced to the nieces of her mother's friend, Mrs Strawdy. The narrator expresses pity for Maude's increasing discontent with their superficial and boring conversation, even more so when she is asked to recite some of "her verses" (60), which she "coldly" refuses (61). On Christmas Eve, Maude has written a new poem, and her cousin Agnes thinks she has "overtired" herself in the process (65). The last section introduces the dispersal of the friends as they move into adulthood: one gets married, another becomes a nun. An accident leaves Maude "sofa-ridden" and in pain (89). She does not recover. After her death, her cousin Agnes follows her wishes and places Maude's "locked book" on her coffin when she is buried, "with all its records of folly, sin, vanity, and, she humbly trusted, of true penitence also" (116); she burns Maude's other papers, preserving only very few for Maude's mother and copying three for herself.

Rossetti's short narrative of stunted author-making ends with the young woman poet's death and the suppression of her work, which is never going to be available "for general perusal" (116).[95] Maude's self-doubts and self-reproaches, strongly motivated by religious scruples, are encouraged by her (all-female) friends and family. Writing verses is seen as a female accomplishment, albeit as one that should never be done to excess; according to this view, it is by no means to be taken seriously as a vocation or career for a young woman. If pursued to excess,

---

[95] The burial of Maude's manuscript book anticipates Rossetti's brother Dante Gabriel's burial of his poems with his late wife Elizabeth Siddal in 1862; this coincidence has been much commented on. In stark contrast to *Maude*, Dante Gabriel Rossetti had the poems exhumed in 1869 (cf. Gilbert/Gubar 2000, 692 n. 40).

it is regarded as unhealthy. Perhaps the most interesting episode is when Maude refuses to recite her verses in public, because her diffidence shows the seriousness of her vocation. But for Maude herself, under the influence of her environment, her ambition to be a poet turns into a source of shame. Her death seals her self-abnegation (cf. Gilbert/Gubar 2000, 545–554; Linley 1999). Yet, in including her own poems in this story of a failing woman poet, Christina Rossetti nevertheless enacts the text's central paradox of combining self-denial with self-affirmation and authorial self-creation. The lethal paraclisis of her author-character on the level of narrative progression can thus be set against the autopoetic and heteropoetic strategies of self-affirmation that Rossetti employs on the second-order, authorial level of composition. In depicting a female poet as a frail misfit or outsider, a victim of the shallowness of the society around her, Rossetti as author may in fact be cataclitically preparing her target audience for a greater willingness to accept a serious, professional woman poet. In including her own poems as Maude's in the narrative, she employs a similar metaleptic device as Hendriks in *The Young Authoress*, but the contrast could not be greater. The autopoetic positioning of the poems as by turns Maude's and Rossetti's is not brazen self-promotion but an act of reflexive-performative empowerment.

A *Bildungsroman* in Verse: Elizabeth Barrett Browning's *Aurora Leigh* (1856)

What would a successful and serious woman poet's career look like in a Victorian *bildungsroman?* It would be a constant struggle between 'love' and 'work', or 'love' and 'fame', as it is in Elizabeth Barrett Browning's verse novel *Aurora Leigh* (1856), a key example of the mid-Victorian female *bildungsroman* that has numerous connections to the social-problem novels of that era.[96] Written only a few years after Rossetti's *Maude*, *Aurora Leigh* is a much more ambitious and mature work that presents the successful integration of the conflicting demands on a woman artist. The eponymous young writer-protagonist is not a direct autobiographical stand-in for Barrett Browning herself but a fictional projection of several of her (and the period's) key concerns and fascinations, from the 'woman question' to poor relief and the social mission of art. Composed between 1853 and 1856, this "novel-poem" in nine books was intended by its author to be "completely modern […], running

---

96 So numerous in fact that it is surprising to find that *Aurora Leigh* is not mentioned even once in Josephine Guy's essential discussion of the genre in Guy 1996. – Quotations from the poem, giving book and line numbers, refer to Barrett Browning 2018.

into the midst of our conventions, [...] meeting face to face and without mask, the Humanity of the age."[97] Aurora Leigh, orphaned at age thirteen, grows up in her aunt's house in close proximity to the country estate of her second cousin, Romney Leigh. She educates herself through reading books, feels transformed by poetry, and begins to pursue a career as a poet, moving to London as a single woman after her aunt's death.

Deeply religious, Aurora believes in the mission of poets as "the only truth-tellers, now left to God, – / The only speakers of essential truth, / Opposed to relative, comparative, / And temporal truths" (1: 857–860). In her twenties, she experiences the disillusionment typical of *bildungsroman* heroes: though she is successful, and is lionised by society, she is dissatisfied with the immaturity of her own work, and she is forced to write for money to keep her name in print and to support her own art financially.

> I had to live, that therefore I might work,
> And, being but poor, I was constrained, for life,
> To work with one hand for the booksellers,
> While working with the other for myself
> And art. [...]
> ....
> In England, no one lives by verse that lives;
> (3: 301–307)

Editors and critics want her merely to repeat what she has already done, rather than write something new and original. But, for Aurora, the problem is not only that of art as a "vocation" (2: 454) that is rarely acknowledged as "serious work" (2: 458) but also the conflict she feels between being an artist and a woman. Increasingly, she realises that she is sacrificing her life for her art, and she strives towards a reconciliation of these roles. The price for art, i.e., for an intensified vision of "life upon the larger scale", appears to be suffering and hard work (4: 1150). Her most important interlocutor in these matters is her cousin Romney, whose socialist projects for the benefit of humanity in the abstract lead him to neglect those who are close to him. Aurora longs for "the approbation of a man" (5: 63). She labours to produce a great work, but the price is loneliness. In a key passage, she explains to Romney that "fame" and "love" are not coterminous, and that "the love of all / [...] / Is but a small thing to the love of one" (5: 478–480):

---

[97] Letter to Robert Browning, 27 Feb. 1845, in Barrett Browning 2018, 99. – On *Aurora Leigh* as autobiography, see Peterson 1999, 109–145, and Laporte 2013.

> You bid a hungry child be satisfied
> With a heritage of many corn-fields; nay,
> He says he's hungry, — he would rather have
> That little barley-cake you keep from him
> While reckoning up his harvests. So with us;
> (Here, Romney, too, we fail to generalise!)
> We're hungry.
>
> (5: 481–87)

In Richard Salmon's reading (2013, 182–183), the key to this passage is the replacement of the classical notion of fame as a medium of bourgeois recognition by the suspicion that the pursuit of fame may be no more than the symptom of an emptiness inside: "hunger". Aurora, being a woman, cannot simply share the "masculine vocation plot" (188), which remains largely inaccessible to women. As a "printing woman", she has "lost her place" in society – meaning the domestic sphere, "[t]he sweet safe corner of the household fire / Behind the heads of children" (5: 804–806) – without carving out a new place for herself. She is unwilling to make a "prudent compromise" (5: 922) and accept a wealthy husband, because the status as a wife would imply the sacrifice of her "artist-dream" (5: 968).

Aurora finds companionship in Italy with Marian Erle, a 'fallen woman', but staying in Florence (the former home of her English father and Italian mother) threatens to stifle her creativity: "I did not write, nor read, nor even think" (7: 1305). The stasis, or sterility, possibly induced by returning to a country identified with Aurora's mother – and thus lacking contact with a creative principle identified as male (cf. Gilbert/Gubar 2000, 60) – is interrupted by a visit from Romney, now blind and cured of his superficial materialism. United with Romney at the end, Aurora concludes that "Art is much, but love is more" (9: 656); she had "exalt[ed] / The artist's instinct in [her] at the cost / Of putting down the woman's" (9: 645–647). They plan to work together for a better future for humanity, but by reaching people's individual souls rather than through "programmes" or "systems" (9: 865–866).

There is no better mid-Victorian text to illustrate "the contradictions between [...] vocation and [...] gender" that threaten to "lead to complete self-destruction" (Gilbert/Gubar 2000, 70) for women artists in the nineteenth century. Significantly, the female literary *bildungsroman*, compared to its dominant male cousin, is fractured by additional complications because of the conventional social roles of women and the dominant psycho-cultural imaginary associated with femininity. For women artists, the desire for both personal and professional fulfilment is presented as bound to be frustrated – unless they also find "love". It is here that *Aurora Leigh* does not so much rebel against normative expectations but attempt to fulfil them, even overfulfil them in showing Aurora as *not* a madwoman or a freak but as a perfectly acceptable and respectable female member of society, as if responding to Southey's notorious 1837 letter to Charlotte Brontë, in which he saw fit to tell her that "[l]iterature cannot be the business of a woman's life, and it ought not to be".[98] At least in *Aurora Leigh*, the *dénouement* of this female version of the vocation plot looks exactly like a compromise, even a very reasonable compromise[99] – yet it is essential for the poem not to present it as such but as a genuine solution to the central dilemma, a sublation of thesis and antithesis into a new synthesis.

While Barrett Browning's verse novel is more attentive to the social contexts of the artist's maturation, compared to Wordsworth's long "autobiographical poem" about the "growth of a poet's mind", *The Prelude*,[100] it remains focused on an individual biographical process of becoming that, finally, succeeds both in stilling the 'hunger' for fame and the hunger for love. Aurora can fulfil her youthful ambition of earning the "royal" name of 'poet' and "to sign it like a queen" (1: 934– 935) only when she acknowledges her love for Romney, a kind of broken secular king to her religious poet-queen, and unite her Platonic idealism (cf. 5: 762 et seq., 834 et seq.) to his reformed and purified version of materialism in a new synthesis that transcends the perceived shortcomings of Christian socialism. It does this, quite conventionally, by ending with a marriage, a marriage that not only unites Aurora and Romney but also serves to defuse the masculine 'other' and to absorb it, now substantially weakened and reduced, into the feminine self. Like Jane Eyre's Rochester,[101] Romney, Aurora's antithesis throughout the text, is symbolically blinded, thus requiring her guidance. Romney's disability can be read as a "narrative prosthesis" (Mitchell/Snyder 2001) for Aurora's empowerment, serving the same narrative purpose as Rochester's blindness does for Jane Eyre. Romney re-

---

98 Robert Southey to Charlotte Brontë, 12 March 1837, https://www.bl.uk/collection-items/letter-from-robert-southey-to-charlotte-bronte-12-march-1837. Apparently, discouraging hopeful novices against authorship was something of a systematic strategy of Southey's to protect his status in the profession (Cross 1988, 90).
99 Cf. Gilbert/Gubar 2000: "[*Aurora Leigh* embodies] the most reasonable compromise between assertion and submission that a sane and worldly woman poet could achieve in the nineteenth century" (575).
100 The 1850 edition of *The Prelude* carries the subtitle *or Growth of a Poet's Mind* and the generic label "an autobiographical poem" (Wordsworth 1850).
101 The parallel, also noted by George Eliot in her review of *Aurora Leigh* in *The Westminster Review* in January 1857, is acknowledged by Barrett Browning in a letter to Anna Jameson, 26 Dec. 1856, in which she clarifies that Romney, in contrast to Rochester, is not physically disfigured but that his blindness is the result of "a great shock on the nerves", and that it has a symbolic significance: "For it was necessary, I thought, to the bringing-out of my thought, that Romney should be mulcted of his natural sight" (Barrett Browning 2018, 552).

nounces his socialist ideals after the burning of the family estate, Leigh Hall, and exchanges them for a different idea of radical utopian renewal that he shares with Aurora but that remains, at best, vaguely sketched at the end (cf. 9: 941–949).

"Lady Novelists"

The Victorian author-*bildungsroman* is a paradigmatic example of the "reflexive-performative matrix" (McGurl 2009, 366) of author-making that combines literary and social forms, using autopoetic and heteropoetic strategies of authorial self-making and audience articulation. To male authors, this type of *bildungsroman* afforded a form, or a formula, for representing their own formation as authors, their *hexis* both as individuals and as members of society with a definite professional status. In this form, they could celebrate the (male) author as a hero overcoming individual and social obstacles, even if their heroes sometimes – often – behave less than heroically.[102] They could also signal to their audiences that this is what it meant to become an author, and thus justify their own choices and present themselves at least indirectly in an equally heroic light. Performatively, this could contribute to the very stabilisation of an authorial self that these novelists strove towards; fiction could help bring about what they desired for themselves.

By contrast, women told different stories in the same form, stories fractured by an array of difficulties and dilemmas, which may be summed up in the phrase "anxiety of authorship" (Gilbert/Gubar 2000, 48–49) but are perhaps better characterised as an anxiety about the place of women in society and the value of their work. In this respect, Aurora's exclamation echoes down the ages: "This hurts most, this ... that, after all, we are paid / The worth of our work, perhaps" (1: 464–465).[103] A woman writer as heroine becomes imaginable, but her professional position and status is seen as problematic. This is not only because of the gender ideology of separate spheres, and a lack of female precursors, but also because of a dominant prejudice against women's "literary fecundity" (Thackeray 1993 [1841], 304), their overproduction of what was seen as low-quality popular trash. Hawthorne's invective of 1855 against the "d—d mob of scribbling

---

[102] On nineteenth-century authorship and ideas (and performances) of the heroic, see also Leypoldt 2016.
[103] On women's work in *Aurora Leigh*, see also Lackey 2012, Wallace 1997. It should be noted, *pace* Gilbert and Gubar, that "anxiety of authorship" also pertained to male authors in the nineteenth century and beyond, who worried about their professional status and the literary or cultural value of their work, including a masculine anxiety about genres like the gothic that were perceived as feminine or "feminising" (cf. Margree 2016, 372) [→ ch. 5].

women" (1987, 304) was merely the tip of the iceberg in this respect. In the 1850s, fiction by women was frequently denounced as a waste of time (more usefully spent on "weightier" matters) or even as a "threat to the moral good of society" (Connor 2018, 145). Sharon Connor cites the 1859 essay "False Morality of Lady Novelists" by W. R. Greg, who describes women's novels as "light literature" which is "effective by reason of its very lightness: it spreads, penetrates and permeates, where weightier matter would lie merely on the outside of the mind".[104] She also points out, however, that much of this criticism was specifically directed at younger, unmarried women authors, whereas novels by older married women were not seen as a danger to society. Even women writers like George Eliot sought to distance themselves from the "silly novels by lady novelists" (1990 [1856]), which filled the circulating libraries but gave female authors a bad name in the literary field.

For this bad name, Thackeray gives a spirited early example in his satirical sketch "The Fashionable Authoress" (1841), in which he mocks the boundless creativity of the fictional woman writer Lady Fanny Flummery, explaining that women "possess[] vastly greater capabilities" of writing than men: "while a man is painfully labouring over a letter of two sides, a lady will produce a dozen pages, crossed, dashed, and so beautifully neat and close, as to be well-nigh invisible" (Thackeray 1993, 304). Like the mythical horse Pegasus, her writing "runs so fast that it often leaves all sense behind it; and there it goes on, on, scribble, scribble, scribble, never flagging until it arrives at that fair winning-post on which is written 'Finis', or 'The End'; and shows that the course, whether it be of novel, annual, poem, or what not, is complete" (ibid.). What is more, Thackeray denies the existence of the word "authoress": "*Auctor*, madam, is the word" (305). He even envisages a "Golden Age" (311) when there will be no more "writeresses" (306): "No more fiddle-faddle novels! no more namby-pamby poetry! no more fribble 'Blossoms of Loveliness'!" (311).

The professionalisation of literary authorship, and its reflection in the novel, were to a large extent propagated by men, whereas women writers were increasingly stigmatised as embodying the opposite of professionalism: dilettantism. Once a privilege of the nobility, dilettantism received a bad name in the bourgeois nineteenth century, which privileged serious work over the pleasures of amateurism (cf. Hibbitt 2006). We have observed the residual form of the literary amateur in *Pendennis* and its bourgeois condemnation in *David Copperfield*.

The woman writer, professional or not, became an object of ridicule in realist English fiction. Perhaps the best-known example is Lady Carbury in Anthony Trol-

---

[104] *National Review* 15, Jan. 1859, 144–167, here: 144 (qtd. in Connor 2018, 145).

lope's *The Way We Live Now* (1874–75), a baronet's widow who tries to support her family by writing fiction and who does not shy away from actively pursuing editors to 'puff' her work in progress, a compendium on *Criminal Queens* (Trollope 1994, 7, 11, ch. 1). Trollope had originally intended her to be the central character of *The Way We Live Now* before its focus shifted to "the great French swindler" Melmotte (Mullen/Munson 1996, 532). "A woman devoted to Literature, always spelling the word with a big L" (Trollope 1994, 7), Lady Carbury is prolific, pretentious, and dishonest. Yet she is not, after all, more dishonest than the editors and other members of the literary profession she is dealing with; in this respect, Trollope's satire is not gender-specific but of a piece with Thackeray's *Pendennis*. It is part of the novel's wider satire on the era's rampant materialism. The novel's focus quickly shifts away from literary life to Lady Carbury's family troubles, and to even less tangible fictions than literary ones, such as "paper instead of actual money" or, even less substantially, "an exchange of words" as the basis of shady financial schemes (Trollope 1994, 346, ch. 45). Only towards the end, six months having passed in the novel, does the reader learn that "Messrs Leadham and Loiter" have published "Lady Carbury's great historical work on the Criminal Queens of the World" (678, ch. 89), and that she is now busy on a novel – not because "she had any special tale to tell" but "because Mr Loiter had told her that upon the whole novels did better than anything else" (679). In depicting the author as a market participant who tries to fulfil expectations and cater to popular demand, Trollope does not single out women writers as culprits in the economisation of the literary field but shows Lady Carbury as a shrewd agent in a thoroughly professionalised business – in which Trollope was himself a capable participant, as his *Autobiography* (written in 1875–76, published posthumously in 1883) revealed, no matter how critical the narrator pretends to be of the machinations of the literary world. However, having completed her first novel, *The Wheel of Fortune*, Lady Carbury finds out that "[i]t is so very hard to get paid for what one does" (756, ch. 99), and in her marrying the editor of the *Breakfast Table* there is an implication that she will give up her literary career.[105]

---

[105] Other portrayals of women writer characters in Trollope include the short stories "Mrs. Brumby", "Josephine de Montmorenci", and "Mary Gresley", collected in *An Editor's Tales* (1870) [→ ch. 7]. Women poets are satirised in Trollope's *He Knew He Was Right* (1869) and in *The Three Clerks* (1857), where the name Ugolina Neverbend says all one needs to know about this minor character (cf. Mullen and Munson 1996, 547, 549–550). For a critical discussion of the women characters in *An Editor's Tales*, see Wilkes 2017; for a reading of these tales in relation to *The Way We Live Now*, see Garcia-Fernandez 2017; for a (rare) transatlantic view of Trollope's professionalism in relation to Edith Wharton's, see Bex 2016, 513–514.

An anecdote about Trollope is the source for Henry James's short story "Greville Fane" (1892), at whose centre is a recently deceased prolific celebrity author of popular fiction, a Mrs Stormer, who published under the pseudonym "Greville Fane". The narrator, tasked with writing her obituary, visits her home, where he sees, among other literary paraphernalia, her writing table, which he describes as "the battered and blotted accessory to innumerable literary lapses" (James 1996a, 218). Like other stereotypical 'lady novelists' of nineteenth-century fiction, Mrs Stormer, according to the narrator, "could invent stories by the yard, but she couldn't write a page of English" (220) and knew nothing of life (222). Like Trollope himself (see James 1987, 9), James has her try to "train up" her son Leolin to be a novelist also (1996a, 222). However, nothing comes of her son's literary efforts, he only wastes the money she spends on him and ends up as her salaried research assistant (233). The narrator remarks that this story about her life contained more interest than any of the stories she ever wrote (219).

Compared to earlier narratives about female authorship, from Thackeray to Trollope, James's later tale shows the hardening of a stereotype of female authorship into an all too easy formula, immediately recognisable with only a few strokes of the pen and not in need of further elaboration. A few keywords suffice to characterise and dismiss the 'lady novelist': the pretentious pseudonym, the blots and lapses, the writing of potboilers instead of literary art; also, as in Trollope, the quick shift of focus from her writing to her family troubles, as defining the more appropriate feminine sphere of concern.

Yet there are exceptions to this stereotype of women writers as perpetuated by male (as well as some female) authors in the Victorian period. Thomas Hardy, for one, bristles against the cliché of the 'silly' lady novelist at least twice in his fiction. In both cases, the woman writer ends up a lady by marriage, but she certainly does not begin life in such an exalted condition.

"Distorted Benthamism": Thomas Hardy's *The Hand of Ethelberta* (1876) and the Novels of Mary Braddon

"I am not 'silly'!" Elfride Swancourt exclaims "indignantly" (Hardy 2005, 149) when she finds herself so designated in Harry Knight's review of her first novel, the medieval romance *The Court of Kellyon Castle*, published under the pseudonym 'Ernest Field' (134). Elfride's literary activities have been tolerated by her father, the upwardly mobile vicar of Endelstow; indeed, she often writes his sermons for him (30–31). Her novel-writing has been actively encouraged by her new stepmother: "All ladies do that sort of thing now", the wealthy widow Troyton tells her; "not for profit, you know, but as a guarantee of mental respectability to their future husbands" (125). Female authorship, in Hardy's *A Pair of Blue Eyes* (1872–1873), thus has a decidedly social function within the marriage market. Elfride's novel, a weak imitation of Scott's medieval romances, is entirely unoriginal and unfashionable; but it is, as her stepmother – a shrewd critic in her own right, it seems – also tells her, "good enough to be bad in an ordinary literary manner" (149). Along with the financial capital acquired by her father through his recent marriage, the cultural capital of her authorship gains Elfride the attention of Harry Knight, the third of her suitors in a slowly escalating line that will lead her to her final, and fatal, marriage to Lord Luxellian.[106]

After her initial foray into literature, Elfride – and the novel in which she lives – loses interest in her writing. There is certainly enough real-life incident, including the famous cliff-hanging scene in which Elfride takes off her clothes to save her lover's life, to make her, and the reader, forget about this aspect of the narrative. But the character of the woman writer did not cease to fire Hardy's imagination. Only three years later, he was to revisit it in *The Hand of Ethelberta* (1876). One of Hardy's least well-beloved novels (the other contender being *A Laodicean*, written four years later), *The Hand of Ethelberta* was his sixth, written and published after his first major success, *Far from the Madding Crowd* (1874), allowed him to focus on writing full-time. J. Hillis Miller's judgement represents the critical consensus in dismissing it simply as "that strange novel" (1970, 208). It is indeed highly unusual because of its – for Hardy – strange genre, a comedy of manners, and for being set in the upper echelons of London society. Neither is Hardy's forte. It reads, for the most part, as if he had been trying to write a mediocre Trollope novel, along the lines of *Ralph the Heir* (1871) or *Lady Anna* (1874). Certainly, not every bad novel is a self-conscious parody of bad novels that merits closer scrutiny, but this is, after all, bad Hardy, and in fact it turns out to deserve to be better known, if only for its strong female heroine and its far from muddled treatment of Victorian literary celebrity. But it is also notable for its heroine, a "successful schemer", who is stronger than most of Hardy's other central characters (ibid.). Beneath the surface of social satire, the novel contains an important layer of literary self-reflection and an allegory of Hardy's view of the possibilities and constraints of authorship.

First published serially in the *Cornhill* magazine from July 1875 to May 1876, *The Hand of Ethelberta* is a "pastiche" of many styles and genres and can be read as a parody of "the conventions of the popular periodical romance"

---

[106] The first versions of the text imply what Hardy makes explicit in the 1912 version, that her death at the end is due to a miscarriage (cf. Hardy 2005, 379 and editor's note on p. 427).

(Dolin 1997a, xxi).[107] As such, it hovers uneasily between the generic patterns of the *bildungsroman* and a somewhat risqué erotic comedy (cf. ibid.). The *Cornhill*'s editor, Leslie Stephen, made Hardy tone down the novel's eroticism in some places, in accordance with his conception of the *Cornhill* as a middle-class family magazine. Yet his interventions were fewer than in Hardy's previous novel, *Far from the Madding Crowd*, which had also first appeared in the *Cornhill* (Dolin 1997b, 408). By the time of writing *Ethelberta*, Hardy knew what was expected of him; and yet he decided to "make a plunge in a new and untried direction" which "had nothing whatever in common with anything he had written before" (Hardy 2011, 135). In the *Life* – Hardy's biography, whose declarative author is his second wife Florence Emily Hardy but which was at least partly ghost-written by Hardy himself – he shows himself to have been aware of the risk to his "reputation" and its "pecuniary value" of taking this step but avers that "he had not the slightest intention of writing for ever about sheepfarming, as the reading public was apparently expecting him to do, and as, in fact, they presently resented his not doing" (ibid.). He also implies that he was responding to criticism "that novel-writing was coming to a pretty pass, the author of *Lorna Doone* having avowed himself a market-gardener, and the author of *Far from the Madding Crowd* having been discovered to be a house-decorator (!)" (ibid.).[108] It is no surprise, then, that the novel he wrote next should have been all about overcoming class barriers and doing so with the help of literature.

Ethelberta, the novel's heroine, is a butler's daughter and former governess who eloped with and married her employer's son, a young aristocrat who died – "a minor [...] in his father's lifetime" (Hardy 1997, 283) – a few weeks into the marriage. With the help of her mother-in-law, Lady Petherwin, Ethelberta has managed to keep her lowly origins a secret by living abroad. Now the young widow returns to England as Mrs Petherwin and gains some celebrity with the publication of a collection of lyric poems titled *Metres by Me*.[109] After Lady Petherwin's death, Berta inherits a furnished house in London, but she needs to earn money to support her nine siblings, some of whom are employed as her servants.

---

[107] To provide some context, it might be useful to know that, in the *Cornhill*, *The Hand of Ethelberta* was preceded by Anne Thackeray Ritchie's domestic novel *Miss Angel* and succeeded by Eliza Lynn Linton's sensation novel *The Atonement of Leam Dundas*. The novel was published simultaneously in the *New York Times*. See Dolin 1997b for a history of the text.
[108] Hardy had trained and worked as an architect, which is also the profession of Elfride's unhappy second suitor, Stephen Smith, in *A Pair of Blue Eyes*.
[109] Hardy changed the title to *Metres by E* in the 1877 edition and subsequently. I have used the Penguin edition (Hardy 1997), which is based on the first volume edition, published by Smith, Elder and Co. in two volumes in 1876.

Berta decides to capitalise on her literary talents and to perform as a public storyteller, a scheme that works well for a while but fails to promise lasting success when its novelty wears off. The marriage market remains her best bet for an economically secure future. Numerous complications ensue when she tries to find a rich husband but also one she can at least respect. She is pursued by an old flame, the impoverished musician and composer Christopher Julian, for whom she has genuine feelings that, however, she needs to suppress to move upwards in society. Her younger sister Picotee, who works as a pupil teacher, also falls in love with him. His rivals for Berta's affections are the painter Eustace Ladywell (several names in the novel evoke the spirit of Restoration comedy), the notorious misogynist Alfred Neigh, and the sexagenarian viscount Mountclere. Berta has her hands full to prevent her suitors from knowing about her humble beginnings; in particular, she is forced to ignore her father, Mr Chickerel, when he waits on her at a party at his employer's, Lord Doncastle's, house.

Consulting a treatise on ethics by John Stuart Mill, Berta makes what she thinks is a rational decision to accept Lord Mountclere's proposal and to assume the "*rôle*" of his bride (Hardy 1997, 289, emphasis original). From a romantic, she has become a "*pseudo*-utilitarian" (ibid., emphasis original). The narrator rhetorically asks, in what might be an affirmation or a parodic critique of the novel's realism: "Was there ever such a transformation effected before by the action of a hard environment?" (ibid.) Yet her aristocratic husband-to-be is not quite as solid as he seems; like his showy country house, Lychworth Court, he is less than meets the eye. At his house, she gives a storytelling performance in which she dresses up her own story as fiction. Surprisingly, however, Mountclere reveals that he had already known about her secret and that he does not mind at all. "Modern developments", he declares, "have shaken up the classes like peas in a hopper" (300–301). She marries him against her family's objections, who have heard rumours about him, and his brother's, who fears for his inheritance. Through her industriousness, she saves the viscount from impending bankruptcy; she also reforms his morals and his diet, sending a French mistress packing and limiting his alcohol consumption "to three glasses of wine per day" (399). Two and a half years after the marriage, she runs the estate, "lives mostly in the library", and "is writing an epic poem" (404). She takes care of her family, while her old flame Christopher Julian weds her sister Picotee.

It is tempting to draw a connection between Hardy's own situation as an emerging novelist in the 1870s and his heroine's plight as a literary performer, and – unbeknownst to most of her audience – a performer who draws on her own life story for a narrative performance in the climactic scene in chapter 40. Hardy's discomfort with class and his (related) difficulty in finding an appropriate literary style are the bread and butter of Hardy studies (cf. Hartley 2016, 82–85). In

The Hand of Ethelberta, class-passing is an obvious theme, and Hardy's experiments with style result in an uneasy mix of semi-serious, often bathetic quotations from Shakespeare and the Romantic poets on the one hand, and imitations of Daniel Defoe's prose style on the other. Berta also embodies Hardy's duality of being a poet and a novelist – even though she prefers to call herself a "Novel-teller" (Hardy 1997, 122) and to perform her story-telling in front of a live audience, in what may be an allusion to Dickens's highly successful public readings (cf. Andrews 2006).

The novel has been discussed as, to some extent, a secret expression of Hardy's private concerns (Gittings 1975, 204–210). Peter Widdowson, for example, identified Ethelberta as an ironic, secret self-portrait of Hardy, an author without a private income, who in this novel satirises the stifling aspects of circulating libraries and monthly periodicals and "self-consciously re-present[s]" his own position (Widdowson 1989, 159) of being forced, in Tim Dolin's words, to "work[] the literary marketplace as Ethelberta works the marriage market" (1997a, xxvii). There are certainly parallels between author and character, yet the self-portrait is at best an "oblique" one (Roberts 1994, 90). The witty female adventurer, who might have sprung from a sensation novel (cf. Radford 2011), is not simply Hardy in drag. The 'hand' of Ethelberta may, after all, refer both to the writing hand and to the hand given in marriage (Dolin 1997a. xxiv). Yet the associations go further, for instance in references to the working class as "the hard-handed order" (Hardy 1997, 209) or the hand of a card-player – she "has played her cards adroitly", as Lord Mountclere's brother admits (366) – or a puppeteer (cf. Radford 2011, 4). There is also the hand Ethelberta raises to hit her husband with (Hardy 1997, 393). Hands are important at several points in the text, culminating in the scene towards the end when husband and wife swap hands in a trick worthy of a Restoration comedy (394). Like the novel itself, its hands will not be confined to a single meaning or purpose. What kind of hand, one may ask, was Hardy playing here?

If the novel is a satire about class, as critics have also argued, which class or classes are being satirised? Was Hardy taking aim at the declining aristocracy, or the *arrivistes* of the middle or lower class, like Ethelberta herself, or the narrow-minded servants and labourers who profit from but resent her schemes? Against the widespread view that the target in *Ethelberta* are the upper classes, Robert Schweik has claimed that Hardy distributes his ridicule quite evenly across all social strata in the novel and is "non-judgmental" in his "acceptance of enterprise and calculation" as motivating forces of his characters, a spirit that sets this book "distinctly apart from his other novels" (Schweik 2002, 240). In this view, the upper classes are not simply depicted as oppressing or destroying individuals of lower rank; on the contrary, Hardy is hard at work on a kind of "Victorian compromise" (Chesterton 1946, 21) of his own that shows how "class barriers […] are highly permeable by the acquisition of wealth" (Schweik 2002, 246). This, too, however, may be a result of Hardy's adoption of the sensational romance form, in which – as in *Lady Audley's Secret* (1862)– female upward mobility is of the essence, and in which class barriers are depicted as much more fluid than they would have been in real life, following a plot pattern that is at least as old as *Pamela.* In this concrete case, the daughter of a servant marries not just one aristocrat but two, consecutively. But Hardy complicates this by making Berta marry once for love and the second time against her own heart, and he endows her with enough of a heart to regret the consequences of her self-sacrifice. The "compromise" (Hardy 1997, 395) that she finds in her arrangement with Mountclere, born of rational calculation, comes at the price of emotional emptiness. The clichéd romance ending here receives a twist of the realist's knife that turns comedy into biting satire, not merely against the upper classes but against the class system as such. Despite her overcoming of society's barriers, Berta's victory is a Pyrrhic one, "tinged with a bitterness of spirit against herself" (Hardy 1997, 282). This is more familiar Hardy territory.

The character of Ethelberta raises pertinent questions about Hardy's conception of literary authorship, and of female authorship in particular.[110] It would be premature to dismiss her as a mere dilettante, even though she does not develop into a professional writer. Her literary performances allow her to achieve an economic position from which she can again afford to be an amateur without having to make sacrifices in her chosen genre. Her progress from lyric to epic follows the Virgilian *rota*, and it is left to the reader to construe whether this is intended as praise of Berta's ingenuity or as a jibe against female literary ambition. When Picotee tells Christopher that her sister is now writing "an epic poem, and employs [her sister] Emmeline as her reader", Christopher's astonished response – "Dear me" (404) – may refer to either or both of these facts, but his views are as limited as those of all the other characters in the novel, including the narrator's. For what it's worth, Hardy himself wrote an epic drama, *The Dynasts*, some years later.

As his protagonist rises from humble Berta Chickerel to viscountess Mountclere, Hardy portrays social identity as a performance, ratified and sanctioned by conventions, somewhat in the manner of Thackeray's *Vanity Fair* (or, in fact, Trollope's *The Way We Live Now*, published just a year earlier). With Becky Sharp, Ethelberta has many things in common, despite her far less disreputable character. The reader's limited view of her is programmatically declared at the outset: she is "one of those people who are known, as one may say, by subscription:

---

[110] Among feminist readings of *Ethelberta*, see Boumelha 1993 and Davies 1993. Davies, for example, believes "that [in *The Hand of Ethelberta*] Hardy deliberately attempts to undermine and therefore go beyond the constraints of traditional patriarchal ideology" (123).

everybody knows a little, till she is astonishingly well known altogether; but nobody knows her entirely" (79). This is obviously true for the reader of the serial narrative, who has no alternative but to get to know the character "by subscription" to the *Cornhill*. Berta is thus presented at several points in the text as a self-conscious product of literary artifice, motivated by desire for success and yet hollow at the core, as the romance form most likely appeared to Hardy as the author of a self-parodic novel. Moreover, Berta is free to invent and reinvent herself, having considerably more freedom than other Victorian women because of her status as a widow and a literary celebrity. Authorship provides her with the means of self-authorship and self-authorisation, as it were – but only up to a point, when it seems wiser to adopt the more conventional compromise of marrying up.

Literature, then, appears as a medium of freedom in this novel, of imagination and self-creation, but as a medium whose freedom is soon constrained by external pressures of form on the performer, both social and in relation to the literary form of romance and the conventions of serial narration in a family periodical. The character of Ethelberta thus becomes legible as an allegory of the uncomfortable authorial position of Hardy as a creator of a self-conscious literary hybrid between romance and realism, a novel that strains the reader's credulity as it stretches the formal conventions of the genre almost beyond their load-bearing capacity. In this self-professed hollowness of conventions, the novel is more Meredith than Trollope.[111] Hardy, in other words, does not mock his heroine but the normative literary conventions of depicting women in fiction, and thus "draws the reader's attention [...] to his own deliberate parody of th[ose] convention[s]" (Davies 1993, 124).

The social mobility that is possible in the romance form, however, also rings hollow in Hardy's implicit realistic assessment that the rigours of the reality principle (here: Berta's "*pseudo*-utilitarianism" or "distorted Benthamism" [1997, 289, emphasis original]) will always win against the pleasures of the pleasure principle – her "Bohemianism" (278) or "soft and playful Romanticism" (289). "English society", the narrator comments at the crucial point of her decision to marry again, "appeared a gloomy concretion enough to abide in" (282–283). On the one hand, the narrator and many of the characters applaud Berta's ingenuity and "self-command" (120). At the end, it is she who saves Lord Mountclere's estate after marrying him, and her newly acquired wealth and status allow her to pursue her literary ambitions in a more serious vein. Yet the "bitterness of spirit" (282) that results from her "mak[ing] a virtue of a necessity" (395) rather than following her

---

[111] Cf. Pfeiffer 1981 on the self-trivialisation of narrative and the "systematic disjunction between narrative technique and the potentiality of human life" in Meredith's novels (140).

heart mars her success and introduces a discordant note to the ending of Hardy's self-proclaimed "comedy" (Hardy 1997, n. p.).

The Hand of Ethelberta is less remarkable, then, for its parallels with its empirical author than for the way it addresses, from within the form of middlebrow serial fiction, the social contexts of literary production in the second half of the nineteenth century: as dominated by a popular culture of fast-paced literary celebrity, and by an industrialised production of self-performing authors, who rise or fall at the mercy of the literary marketplace. Its "generic instability" (Radford 2011, 5) is less a symptom of Hardy's failure but a wholesale programmatic and systematic dismantling of the form of serialised romance in a family magazine, with its economic and social underpinnings of "saleable originality" (Hardy 1997, 210), its false pieties and its mechanical melodrama. Like Hardy in the *Cornhill*, Ethelberta has some power to tell whatever stories she likes, but she has no final say in the shape that her own story is going to take. Both make a display of themselves, and both try, with disputable success, to "compromise matters" and "make a virtue of a necessity" (395).

As a society poet and self-performer, Ethelberta may to some extent be intended as an object of ridicule, but this is muted by the self-conscious parallels between author and character, and by further, more admirable aspects of her character. For one, she escapes censure as a woman who makes use of her talents to achieve a better place in society. Hardy's narrator shows genuine admiration for her ability to escape from the standard images of Victorian "household womankind" (Hardy 1997, 240). In becoming a writer, she "adopts the role of the family provider, replacing her father in the domestic hierarchy" (Davies 1993, 125–126). She is presented as a complex, sophisticated woman who is shown to be given to "deep thinking" and to possess a "hermit spirit" (Hardy 1997, 168).

Which other Victorian heroine chooses marriage only after consulting Mill's *Utilitarianism* and "an old treatise on Casuistry" (288)? By giving her an intellectual and literary bent, Hardy moves Berta into quite a different sphere compared to even the most unusual and emancipated of Victorian heroines. The modernity of *The Hand of Ethelberta* lies in its presentation of a woman writer not as an oddity, madwoman or freak but as a respectable, intelligent, and hard-headed person, whom the reader is invited to admire, at least to some extent. The novel's comedy is not at her expense. In fact, Hardy invests her with a seriousness that makes the comedy founder, as he registers a clear discomfort with her decisions and their costs, in a way that at least resembles the plight of Dorothea Brooke in *Middlemarch* and anticipates the conundrum of Isabel Archer in James's *The Portrait of a Lady* (1881).

Hence the unease that many readers and critics have felt about this novel's "generic instability" (Radford 2011, 5). Its comedy soon turns sour, and like the solid veneer of Lychworth Court the novel reveals the brittle bricks of a more Hardyesque tragedy underneath. It is, as the narrator puts it a typical architectural metaphor that reflects Hardy's first profession as well as his interest in self-consciously constructed narrative surfaces that conceal the truth, "a stone mask worn by a brick face" (Hardy 1997, 296). Berta's moral trajectory from writing "emotional poetry" to agreeing "to marry for the good of her family" is described as a change "from soft and playful Romanticism to distorted Benthamism" (289), but it is left deliberately open, and for the reader to decide, whether this "moral incline" is "upward or down" (ibid.). The conclusion of the marriage plot is presented self-consciously as a cliché but also as "a bitterly ironic version of the bourgeois myth" as presented, for example, in *Pride and Prejudice* (Radford 2011, 12), with the "elderly Viscount Mountclere" as "a grotesque parody of the dashing Darcy" (13). In the final analysis, the novel remains ambivalent and conflicted about its heroine's successes and sacrifices, registering both Hardy's discomfort with the romance form and his discontent with the economic and social aspects of literary life in late Victorian England.

Celebrity, and the discrepancy between an author's public persona and their real-life identity, were much-discussed topics in the 1860s and 1870s. A key instance of this is the case of George Eliot. After the publication and international success of *Adam Bede* (1859), the true identity of its author, named 'George Eliot' on the title page, was still a secret, and a convenient secret for the publishing house of Blackwood, because sales would certainly suffer if the public found out that it had been written by Marian Evans, "the woman famous for taking someone else's husband" (Hughes 2001, 207). Crisis loomed when another contender turned up, one Joseph Liggins from Nuneaton, who for reasons not entirely clear found supporters who claimed that he was the real author of *Scenes of Clerical Life* (1857) and *Adam Bede*. The Leweses first found this amusing and even helpful for preserving the secret of the 'George Eliot' pseudonym, but it soon stopped being funny. The impostor's supporters even circulated a fake manuscript to prove his authorship. Letters to the *Times* by George Eliot, endorsed by John Blackwood, did nothing to alleviate the situation. Some contemporaries even assumed that 'George Eliot' herself had planned the scandal "to boost the sales of her books" (Hughes 2001, 209). It took months for the rumours and other allegations of plagiarism to die down, and Marian Evans found her reputation tarnished when her identity was revealed. For her contemporaries, it was hard to accept that a woman could have written *Adam Bede*, even more "the self-educated daughter of a Warwickshire land agent", and one whose private life as the unmarried partner of G. H. Lewes was "considered scandalous" (Hirsch 2003, 15). Eliot's narrative persona henceforth remained "complexly gendered" (Easley 1996, 145). Linda K. Hughes has demonstrated how the topic of authorship, and the literary marketplace, pervade *Middlemarch* (1871–

1872), beginning with the "thwarted authorship" of Casaubon to Lydgate's somewhat more successful pursuit of writing that results in a treatise on gout (Hughes 2005, 158), with Rosamond functioning "as a trope for those pressures exerted on authors that could subvert idealized conceptions of their role" (ibid. 159–160), i. e., economic and domestic pressures.

If, according to Hughes, Eliot used the character of Rosamond to veil the commercial pressures on her own writing (2005, 177), others had fewer scruples in acknowledging the material aspects and benefits of literary publishing. In her variation of Flaubert's *Madame Bovary*, *The Doctor's Wife* (1864), Mary Elizabeth Braddon, "the queen of the mid Victorian literary marketplace" (Beller 2016, 245) includes the character of Sigismund Smith, a successful and entirely unashamed author of popular sensation novels who is depicted in a positive light. Braddon's novel has been read as an engagement, in fiction, with her own status as a prolific and popular writer who exemplified a new shift towards literary mass production. Braddon "presents readers as consumers, and Smith as a successful producer of marketable wares" (Conary 2014, 429). Through the character of Smith, who recurs in Braddon's *The Lady's Mile* (1866) as 'Smythe', thus signalling upward mobility, she indirectly reflects her own position as a bestselling author whose works are enjoyed by many, even if they are not granted the acclaim of literary value: "If a man can't have a niche in the Walhalla, isn't it something to have his name in big letters in the play-bills on the boulevard?", he asks (Braddon 2008, 48). In other words, Smith/Smythe is perfectly willing to exchange ephemeral celebrity for any kind of lasting literary fame.

Isabel Gilbert, the Madame Bovary character in the novel, has her head turned by respectable fiction, works like *Adam Bede*; had she read sensation novels, Braddon implies, she would merely have been harmlessly entertained, with no negative consequences (which, in any case, this being an English variation on Flaubert, are nowhere near as drastic as in the French original). Cast in a realist mode, *The Doctor's Wife* also contrasts two modes of writing: Smith's industrial, mechanical production of novels as opposed to the Romantic model of writing as self-expression and self-consolation, represented in the novel by the poet Roland Lansdell, Isabel's would-be seducer (Beller 2016, 250–252). As Beller argues, "[i]n the symbolic discourse on authorship in *The Doctor's Wife*, older (more idealistic) modes are superseded by newer (perhaps less honourable) models of literary production" (253).

In contrast to earlier readings of the novel, Dorothee Birke sums up the more recent critical trend of seeing the character of Sigismund Smith as "sympathetic"; "his representation", she argues, "serves to criticize orthodoxies about the degenerative effect of writing and reading for entertainment" (Birke 2016, 161) and to reflect on "the evaluative stratifications in the established literary system" (166). Commercial fiction may be "less honourable" (Beller 2016, 253) but in *The Doctor's*

Wife it is depicted as less dangerous than the serious literary fiction that leads the doctor's wife astray.

A later novel by Braddon, *One Thing Needful* (1886), depicts a female novelist who "finds her vocation as a writer and publishes a highbrow novel to extensive critical acclaim" (Beller 2016, 260 n. 46; see Mattacks 2009). By that time, serious literary fiction is no longer an exclusively male domain, but this fictional woman writer's name, Stella Boldwood, still resonates with the unlikelihood of the scenario. In their negotiation of the predicaments of authorship and gender in the Victorian age, these author novels remain entangled in a complex web of critical and social hierarchies of values, and conflicts between the spheres of privacy and publicity as well as between commercial and more artistic forms of literary writing. Braddon's Stella Boldwood at the end settles for marriage, and she "undercut[s]" her "originality" in having her novel published anonymously (Mattacks 2009, 228). But perhaps she has merely realised, as have Elfride Swancourt and her stepmother, that publishing a novel may have more than an exclusively literary or exclusively commercial purpose; it can also be done as a symbolic gesture, "as a guarantee of mental respectability" (Hardy 2005, 125), a means to improve the author's position in the marriage market.

By contrast, Ethelberta's literary ambition, like Hardy's, is too great to be content with a position like that of Sigismund Smith, or with the anonymity chosen by Stella Boldwood or Elfride Swancourt. Hardy, in *The Hand of Ethelberta*, shows the Romantic paradigm and the "distorted Benthamism" of popular fiction (1997, 289) vying for supremacy within a *single* author persona. If these characters, from Aurora Leigh in the 1850s to Berta Chickerel / Ethelberta Petherwin in the 1870s, suffer from an "anxiety of authorship" (Gilbert/Gubar 2000, 49), they overcome this anxiety as they carve out a niche for themselves in life as well as in literature. They become, in Milton's words, "[a]uthors to themselves" (*Paradise Lost* 3: 122, in Milton 1957, 261) as well as to their works, bringing forth a new social and literary identity. However, they illustrate different possible conditions and outcomes of female author-making as forms of self-making in the mid-nineteenth century. Aurora Leigh can only truly fulfil her "artist-dream" (Barrett Browning 2018, 5: 968) after accepting her love of Romney as part of her feminine nature and uniting with a substantially weakened version of her masculine counterpart. Barrett Browning is keen to present this marriage as not a compromise but a fusion of "art" and "love" (9: 656), and of the male and female components that she regards as necessary for a mature and serious artist, whose work must be socially useful as well as beautiful. Hardy, who has no truck with such high-minded Romanticism, presents Berta's marriage more cynically as the material and utilitarian precondition for her self-realisation as a writer. She first needs to acquire wealth and status by tying the knot so that she can become independent –whether she loves her husband is completely irrelevant. The Victorian compromise has come a long way.

In the mode of fiction, *Aurora Leigh* and *The Hand of Ethelberta* present female author-making in the mid-Victorian era as a complex negotiation of conflicting values: love and art, dilettantism and professionalism, economic necessity and personal freedom, utility and beauty. They show women authors as self-creators who lose at least as much as they gain in this process, unlike the male heroes of most Victorian *bildungsromans*. Mary Braddon and George Eliot, by contrast, illustrate different yet related Victorian responses to female success in the business of literature. Both had a keen business sense as well as talent, which they used for opposite ends of the literary spectrum – commercial entertainment on the one hand, serious literature (yet with an equally strong commercial appeal) on the other. The one embraced her success, the other struggled with it; both also showed a sense of detachment from their own work, as if the public persona created by their books took on an independent life of its own. For George Eliot, self-realisation in the work carried the risk of petrifying an authorial image in the audience's imagination, locking the author into a rut of convention, egged on by the Rosamonds of this world. Art or love? Art or the market, or possibly both? These questions will *not* be answered in even more desperate ways as we approach the end of the Victorian age.

7 Starving in the Reading Room: Precarious Economies of Authorship in Late Victorian Fiction

Towards the end of the nineteenth century, literary production entered what John Sutherland has called an "exhausting cycle" of "rapid production, low reward, disincentive for the artist to write at [their] best and the early extinction of whatever talent [they] had" (1976, 46). The "massification of literature", powered by technological progress and significantly increased literacy rates, created new "opportunities for authors", but it also challenged the cultural values associated with books as essentially different from other commodities, and with authorship as different from other professions (Margree 2016, 362; cf. Brantlinger 1998, Leypoldt 2016 and 2021). After a long and difficult process of professionalisation earlier in the century, authors now saw themselves becoming "interchangeable and expendable" (Thompson 2019, 318). More books and more texts were produced than audiences could possibly care for; most authors' earnings dwindled as literary "supply outstripped demand", and authorship was turned into a "prototype of the gig economy" (ibid.).

Only a tiny minority of writers could boast of a commercial and critical success like George Eliot's, whose books almost single-handedly kept the Blackwoods in business in the 1890s, outsold only by their Educational Series and Scottish Hymnals (Finkelstein 2002, 162–163). In the late nineteenth century, there is no single or unified economy of authorship but a diversified and stratified set of different markets and different media, ranging from the three-volume novel to the popular magazine. This economic and social predicament – precarity, for short – results in a long list of late Victorian realist and anti-romantic narratives that address the contradictions of the literary profession, of which George Gissing's *New Grub Street* (1891) is only the most famous example. In this chapter, I place Gissing's diagnosis of "the wretchedness and the pettiness of authorial existence" (Sutherland 1995, xiv) next to Anthony Trollope's *An Editor's Tales*, published twenty years earlier, which display a similarly anti-romantic, if not quite as pessimistic, view of the realities of the literary life, and I briefly compare *New Grub Street* with George Paston's (i.e., Emily Symonds's) less well-known and more optimistic depiction of the economies of 1890s authorship in her novel *A Writer of Books* (1898).

From 'We' to 'I': Anthony Trollope's *An Editor's Tales* (1870)

An early example of the post-Thackerayan literary *bildungsroman* turned cautionary tale of literary failure is Anthony Trollope's short story "The Adventures of Fred Pickering", originally titled "The Misfortunes of Fred Pickering" when first published in the *Argosy* in September 1866. Trollope's charitable work for the Royal Literary Fund inspired this tale of authorial adventures/misfortunes, which ultimately derive from a young man overestimating his professional opportunities in the literary market. Unwilling to become a lawyer like his father, Fred Pickering aims for "a literary career", hoping "to make literature his profession" (Trollope 1995, 38). Yet he is inexperienced and has no connections among the London literati. Worse, he has severed his ties to his father and is soon without means. Even worse, he has unwisely gotten married, and a child is on the way. Towards the end, after all his literary ventures have failed to earn him any money, he is forced to return to Manchester like a "prodigal son" (54) and to take up work as an attorney's clerk.

Young Pickering's trajectory is one of heroic ambition curtailed by reality. He thinks of literature as "a high vocation" (42) but he lacks practical and professional sense. Working industriously "in the reading-room at the Museum" (45), i.e., the British Museum – a key location for the narratives discussed in this chapter –, he produces critical essays on Milton that no one wants to buy, and a pastoral poem inspired by his honeymoon in the Lake District, which does not sell either. An index he compiles for a publisher is refused because he fails to stick to the rules of indexing. In the guise of the established writer Wickham Webb, Trollope provides free advice to budding authors: Webb explains to Pickering "that literature is the hardest profession in the world" (45) and that "all who make literature a profession should begin with independent means" (47).

Trollope here rehearses a rhetoric of authorship that is thoroughly characterised by understanding literature as a profession or a trade, comparing it to other walks of life. In literature, unlike other professions, the novice cannot rely on financial support, so that the economic risks of taking up this profession are much higher than in other fields (in this case, the law). If the novice is not "a genius", he "must be [...] a journeyman" (53). Later, he can belong to either of two groups: those "who have learned to work in accordance with the directions of others" (47), mostly in journalism, and "those who do their work independently" (48). In this story, the genius idea is only briefly evoked only to be rejected. The story's protagonist has to learn that literature is not only hard work, but rarely "of a remunerative nature" (40). Above all, he learns that becoming an author means to acquire a professional identity by practice, an identity that needs to be confirmed by other members of the profession –by the acceptance of fellow writers, editors, and publishers. If the "journeyman" does not play by their rules, does not heed their advice, or does not behave professionally, he will end up a failure.

Between October 1869 and May 1870, Trollope pursued this topic in a series of six short stories published in *St Paul's*, a short-lived literary magazine whose editorship he had taken on. They were collected in volume form under the title *An Editor's Tales*, published by Alexander Strahan in 1870. These stories are told by the genial figure of a literary editor, who is approached by hopeful entrants into the literary profession. Fittingly, they are narrated in the first person plural, in "the editorial we" (Trollope 1995, 75), and the narrator doubts, in the first of these stories, "The Turkish Bath", "whether the story could be told at all in any other form" (ibid.). In this tale, the editor is cornered in a public bath by an Irishman, who persuades him to consider an article for publication. The piece of course turns out to be unpublishable, as does a second one on the Church of England that is "unintelligible, absurd, and farcical" (91). The benevolent editor takes pity on the poor man and his family. He assists him with some money and the free advice to "turn [his] hand to some other occupation" (89). When he visits the author at home, however, he finds that the Irishman is not at all living in poverty but that his wife earns good money as "head day nurse at Saint Patrick's Hospital" (93). The man turns out to be "mad" (94), suffering from the delusion of being a great writer, filling his desk with manuscripts and "treating all the world around him with the effusions of his terribly fertile pen" (94). Once again, in this story, Trollope carefully draws a dividing line between acceptable and inacceptable ways of pursuing a literary career, between professionalism and amateurism. The amateur, in this case, is not even talented but simply "mad", as his own wife calls him. For this delusion of genius, there is apparently no cure. The focus of the story, however, is on the editor's professionalism and his chief responsibility to his readers in his function as a gatekeeper. This role clashes with his human instincts of benevolence and charity. Professionalism, Trollope shows, consists in the ability to distinguish between private inclinations and professional duties.

This professional view of literary production is also tested in "Mary Gresley" (1869), in which the editor is tempted by the personal charms of a young woman, whom he successfully convinces that she will have to undergo a lengthy "apprenticeship of ten years" (Trollope 1995, 110) if she is ever to achieve "fame or fortune" as a writer (105). The professional ethos implies that she should not give away her work for free, because "money payment for work done is the best and most honest test of success" (110). Here, Trollope shows the continuity of his ideas that shocked readers when his *Autobiography* was posthumously published, in which he broke the taboo of giving detailed information on his earnings from literature and dared to compare the writing of novels to the making of shoes. In this case, though young

Mary Gresley shows some genuine "literary merit" (115), she does not pursue a career in literature because she has made a promise to her dying husband, a curate, to "make no more attempt at novel writing" (114) out of religious and moral reasons. In this case, the editor feels that there has been a genuine loss to literature.

In the next story, "Josephine de Montmorenci" (1869), Trollope notes that an editor must reject "four-fifths" of the manuscripts he receives, and that there is no gender bias in this selection: "It is equally so with the works of one sex as with those of the other" (Trollope 1995, 121). In this story, an editor named Brown encounters a good-looking female "aspirant" (121) to the literary profession, but he finds her novel a mixture of good and bad – it is a novel, and he needs one, but it is also full of "metaphysical twaddle" (122). Should he help her to edit the novel for publication or should he rather not take the risk? The editor first insists on seeing the author in person, but he is misled by appearances. The pretty young lady who visits him is not the real author but merely her sister-in-law; when he finally meets the true author, he learns that her real name is not Josephine de Montmorenci but Maryanne Puffle – the implication being that this is not a name that would sell books. Moreover, Maryanne Puffle suffers from a physical disability, which provides even more reason for her belief "that genius should not show itself publicly" (130). Brown's desire to "see the author" (130), intended as a trust-building exercise between editor and writer, is doubly frustrated; first, when the appearance of the pretty young lady does not match his mental image of the author of *Not so Black as He's Painted:* "There should be more of stature [...] with dark hair, and piercing eyes. The colour of the dress should be black, with perhaps yellow trimmings" (128); and a second time, when he needs to correct his prejudices yet again, even more drastically, on meeting the real Mrs Puffle. The editor has turned the author into an image, based on the text of the novel and the author's importunate letters, as if that author were a literary character invented by the editor.

In this act of inventing a suitable physical appearance for the author, the editor draws on racialised and sexualised categories such as skin tone and blushing:

> For such an adventure the appropriate colour of the skin would be, – we will not say sallow exactly, – but running a little that way. The beauty should be just toned by sadness; and the blood, as it comes and goes, should show itself, not in blushes, but in the mellow, changing lines of the brunette. (128)

The story invests authorial invisibility with a strong undercurrent of male scopophilia, fed by erotic desires. The act of seeing the real author can then only result in disillusionment, as expectations are bound to be frustrated. Conversely, the story implies that the 'right' sort of physical appearance and the 'right' sort of name that suits a particular kind of novel will help sell the book. In a time characterised by an oversupply of authors, the idea "that genius should not show itself publicly" (130) can only be considered quaint. If the editor is partly tricked into assisting this author with getting published, we are made to understand that this is his own fault in not always acting professionally. The editor has blurred the lines between authorship and editorship in giving his author a fictional, imaginative identity – a process resembling Virginia Woolf's description of the novelist's transformation of people into characters in "Mr. Bennett and Mrs. Brown" (1924). In doing so, the editor in Trollope's story has allowed his professional interests to take a back seat to his private fascination for a beautiful woman with a French name, a woman who turns out not to exist – one more reason for Trollope, in this story, to make his own editor persona invisible behind the veil of 'Mr Brown'.[112]

Professionalism, or the lack thereof, is also the topic of "The Panjandrum" (1870), which details the early failure of a literary magazine because its group of editors cannot agree on anything. This failure is signalled early on by the breakdown of the "editorial we" that is quickly "split [...] into parties" as early as the story's fourth sentence, so that the narrator then continues in the first person singular (Trollope 1995, 136). Most painfully for the narrator, his fellow editors cannot agree to include novels or prose fiction of any kind in their magazine: "Novels were not then, as now, held to be absolutely essential for the success of a magazine" (146). All his pleading even for the inclusion of a short story is in vain, and at the end he gives up. The 'we' has fully disintegrated into an 'I' as opposed to 'them': "I myself had become so small among them that my voice would have had no weight" (171). Yet the story, besides recording this failure (likely based on a similar venture of Trollope's in 1840–41), also depicts the working of the novelist's imagination, his building "wondrous castles in the air" (163) based on spontaneous experiences and observations of people around him.

The editor's professional patience is tested in "Mrs. Brumby" (1870) by an overbearing but untalented woman writer, who is remarkable for her perseverance and impertinence in her attempts to secure publication in the editor's magazine. Here, the editorial we remains firm "against [a] strong-minded female intruder[]" (Trollope 1995, 221), even after she threatens the proprietors of the magazine with legal action and is able to win a financial settlement. In this story, the editor's sympathies are with Mrs Brumby's henpecked husband, an army lieutenant whose respectable status serves as a shield to her wickedness.

---

112 See Sutherland's note in Trollope 1995, 584–585 for a brief discussion of the potential biographical context of this story, including the intriguing parallel between 'Maryanne Puffle' and Marian Evans alias George Eliot.

In "The Spotted Dog" (1870), one of Trollope's best shorter fictions, as he also remarks in his *Autobiography* (Trollope 1996, 214), the editor is confronted with the appalling fate of an impoverished gentleman scholar, Julius Mackenzie, who has been deprived of his class status through a series of misfortunes and wrong turns, descending into alcoholism and destitution. One last time, Mackenzie tries to raise himself through literary work, with the editor's help: he is hired to compile an index to a scholarly work on *The Metres of the Greek Dramatists*. But, though the work progresses, it is frustrated by his wife, who destroys the manuscript in a gin-fuelled fit of rage. Mackenzie, at his wit's end, commits suicide. The story is remarkable in its unsparing depiction of a slum tenement, but also as a tale about the lowest end of literary life: the "tragedy" (Trollope 1995, 206) of Mackenzie also involves his descent from gentlemanly scholarship to writing cheap "prose fiction" (187) "at the rate of sixpence for a page of manuscript containing two hundred and fifty words" (186). He has become a wage slave "on the staff of two or three of the 'Penny Dreadfuls'" (174), a content provider for the lowest kind of literary entertainment. The respectable middle-class editor professes not even to have been aware of this kind of publication, but he is immediately concerned about its potentially damaging influence on the lower classes: "We had not even known of the existence of these papers; – and yet there they were, going forth into the hands of hundreds of thousands of readers, all of whom were being, more or less, instructed in their modes of life and manner of thinking by the stories which were thus brought before them" (185).

Mackenzie himself, in conversation with the editor, tells him that he has been working at these publications for "seven hours a day" and that he "hate[s] the very words" he has been writing (178). Trollope does not explicitly link this kind of literature to alcohol and alcoholism, but there is at least an indirect parallel in the story between the consumption and addiction to large quantities of cheap booze and the consumption of cheap sensational fiction, which degrades both its authors and its readers. The story draws a contrast between respectable and disreputable forms of prose fiction and authorship, as it does between legitimate and illegitimate places and habits of drinking (the pub named the Spotted Dog vs. the slum tenement). These contrasts also carry connotations of class and anxieties of social decline and degeneration.

Taken together, *An Editor's Tales* sketch a realist portrayal of literary life in mid-Victorian England, at a period when magazines have become the most important venues for literary production and consumption. They attest to the increasing professionalism of literary production in showing how editors go about their business and how they negotiate with authors. They also do this by focusing on situations of crisis or breakdown in an editor's dealing with his clients. They register the hierarchical distinctions and divisions that have developed within the literary market between quality magazines like the *Cornhill* at one end and cheap 'penny dreadfuls' at the other. Literary success and failure now come in many forms, and these stories also record the many different ways of getting by which lie somewhere in between success and failure.

From a narrative perspective, these stories are notable for their use of the editorial we: a form intended to convey authority and respectability is injected with irony and subjected to critique. In some of the stories, as in "Mrs. Brumby", the form can barely be maintained; in others, like "The Panjandrum", it breaks down completely. The communal first person plural is quickly unmasked as concealing merely a single individual, whose authority and discursive power turns out to be limited and curtailed by his colleagues (as in "The Panjandrum") or who proves to be an unreliable judge of others (as in "The Turkish Bath" and, even more, in "Josephine de Montmorenci"). The 'we' hovers between an impersonal narrative authority and a personalised 'I' that can claim to speak merely for itself – resulting in "a narrative mode that is inherently contradictory and semantically unstable" (Garcia-Fernandez 2017, 468). In using this "convoluted convention" only to "destroy" it (ibid., 470), Trollope casts doubt on the authority and reliability of that alleged Victorian staple of narration, the 'omniscient narrator' [→ ch. 2].

An Editor's Tales include the narrator as an embodied character whose intradiegetic presence makes itself felt, even though he tries to keep aloof from the other characters (cf. Garcia-Fernandez 2017 on the lack of a physical description). In this case, the close autobiographical proximity between the editor-narrator and the actual author of these stories, Anthony Trollope, adds an additional layer of complexity and potential confusion, which these tales inherit from Dickens and Thackeray, among others. They deconstruct the generic formula of the literary *bildungsroman* by refracting some of its key elements and transforming them into short fictions whose key modality, despite the occasional humour and light touch, is one of crisis and, at best, tenuous survival in straitened economic and social circumstances. It is a development of Victorian realist fiction, propelled by the periodical press, that exerts pressure on the *bildungsroman*'s too tidy and teleological trajectory of the literary career. They respond to the increasing professionalisation and stratification of literature in the nineteenth century by illustrating how diverse, how flexible, unstable, and risky literary careers had become. It was increasingly difficult to determine what success or failure really meant in this commercial environment. Was popularity, were high sales (always) indicative of success, or could they also be understood as a form of failure, given that high sales could be understood as damaging an author's critical reputation?

In the late nineteenth century, we see a distinct division of the literary field into what Bourdieu has called "an economic world inverted": popular mass-market authorship is split off from the kind of authorship that is marked by low sales but a high reputation among the author's fellow professionals. According to Bourdieu, "the artist cannot triumph on the symbolic terrain except by losing on the economic terrain [...] and vice versa" (1996, 83). Although this overstates the case, especially for nineteenth-century Britain, where both economic and symbolic success were possible at least for some (including George Eliot), it is surely true to say that the distinction between literature as art and literature as commerce becomes more acute towards the end of the Victorian period.

While this happened earlier for poetry, it certainly happened for the novel at this time, which splits up into three segments: the 'art novel', which enjoys the greatest prestige but sells few copies; the popular mass-market novel, which sells a lot of copies but has no aesthetic value; and something in between that will later be called the 'middlebrow novel', identified by Henry James in 1895 as "the middling good" (James 1999, 2: 245), perhaps best summed up by Rachel Cusk in her novel *Kudos* [→ ch. 17] as a cultural product that reproduces the "connotations" of great literature without "making [...] demands and inflicting [...] pain" on its readers (Cusk 2019, 40). The tripartite division of the literary field in the modernist period has been widely noted as a "battle of the brows" (Brown/Grover 2012, Macdonald/Singer 2015), in which authors identified as 'middlebrow' are under particular attack as "pamper[ing] the taste of the worst category of the reading public – not those who revel in detective yarns [...] but those who buy the worst banalities"; as the eponymous author in Nabokov's *The Real Life of Sebastian Knight* (1941) expounds in a letter to one of his publishers, such writers "travel second-class with a third-class ticket" (Nabokov 1996, 42).

Yet, travel as they might, towards the end of the nineteenth century authors increasingly began to worry about this axiological conundrum of quality, success, and popularity. As Robert Louis Stevenson wrote to Edmund Gosse: "There must be something wrong in me, or I would not be popular" (qtd. in Margree 2016, 367). Those who professed to produce art rather than serve popular demand risked starvation; but those who catered to a popular audience risked being denounced as "novelist-merchant[s]" (qtd. in ibid., 378). "The common kind of success", remarks the failing writer Edwin Reardon in Gissing's *New Grub Street*, "is never due to literary merit" (Gissing 2016, 48). Popular success, even celebrity, within a mass market were attainable for authors at the *fin de siècle*, but they now had a negative impact on the author's cultural status, on the respect of professional colleagues, in a way that Dickens and his contemporaries would not have understood. This stratification of the literary field is clearly mapped onto class differences, particularly in England, where its boundaries are heavily fought over in the early twentieth century. Upwardly mobile middle-class readers would not want to be seen with a book that would make them look less respectable. Thus, social norms and distinctions of class and gender intersect with literary values in struggles over the definition of the literary field [→ ch. 11 and 12 for more on the 'middlebrow' debate].

"A trackless desert of print": George Gissing's *New Grub Street* (1891)

Many authors at the end of the nineteenth century anticipate Bourdieu's main ideas about the segmentation of the literary field. Henry James, in many of his stories from the 1890s, draws the same line between artistic merit and economic success, the latter being, as the narrator of "The Next Time" (1895) asserts, "a mere distributor's, a mere hawker's word", referring to the sale of books as if they were "like potatoes or beer" (James 1999, 2: 243) [→ ch. 8]. "Success without a long and heartbreaking struggle would be almost proof positive that her work was only destined for an ephemeral popularity", notes the narrator of *A Writer of Books* (Paston 1999 [1898], 19–20). Some, like the best-selling and prolific novelist Guy Boothby, professed to revel in such popularity (while showing some doubts in their fiction; cf. Margree 2016); others, like Robert Louis Stevenson, at least occasionally experienced an anxiety of popular authorship. Others, yet again, turned their suffering or their cynicism about what William Dean Howells, in 1893, called "the hungriest profession" (Howells 1893, 433) into "metanarratives of authorship" (Margree 2016, 384). Howells himself published such a novel about an adolescent novelist who comes to New York to pursue a literary career: *The World of Chance* (1893), a send-up of the publishing world that came out in the same year as his better-known essay "The Man of Letters as a Man of Business" (see Dennis 1980). The most prominent examples of late nineteenth-century novels that address the economics of authorship are Knut Hamsun's *Hunger* (*Sult*, 1890; first translated into English by George Egerton in 1899) and George Gissing's *New Grub Street* (1891).

Whereas Hamsun's proto-modernist *künstlerroman* zooms in on the anxiety of a solitary writer, impoverished, isolated, and starving, whose failure emphasises the unbridgeable gulf between art and the market (Pulkki 2018), *New Grub Street* branches out to tell a more complex story about a group of characters who are involved in the literary life and respond to its antinomies in different ways, thus embodying distinct concepts and situations of authorship.[113] The events of the novel unfold from 1882 to 1886, and its author-characters explore several possible positions in the literary field of late nineteenth-century London. To keep himself afloat, Gissing wrote and published about a novel per year, next to writing for periodicals,

---

113 See Harputlu Shah 2019 for a direct comparison between these two novels.

and *New Grub Street* portrays several professional writers who need to adapt to publishers' demands and the expectations of a popular audience in a thronged commercial marketplace for literature, at the risk of sinking if they refuse to do so. Gissing revives the eighteenth-century notion of 'Grub Street' as a term for low-paid subsistence writing. He emphasises how the new conditions of the marketplace have exacerbated the living conditions of an already impoverished literary underclass, whose "normative affirmation of the development of a professional self has demonstrably dwindled" since the mid-nineteenth century (Salmon 2013, 220). Jasper Milvain, the novel's most adaptive, flexible, and morally unprincipled writer, no longer refers to authorship as a "profession" (which would imply a distinct vocational identity and status) but as a "trade" or a "business" (Gissing 2016, 10, 12).

At this time, the publishing of novels was still dominated by the three-decker format, introduced by Walter Scott's publisher Archibald Constable in the 1810s. The market for these books, apparently named after "the three decks of guns" on "large warships" (Colclough 2019, 256), was mainly in the circulating libraries such as Mudie's or W. H. Smith's (Bassett 2010, 74–76). But profits were dwindling, until the triple-decker format was finally abandoned by most publishers from 1894 onwards and replaced by a cheaper, more commercially viable one-volume format (Menke 2019, 93–111). In Ella Hepworth Dixon's *Story of a Modern Woman* (1894), for example, the "imminent obsolescence" of the three-volume novel is announced when the author-heroine herself cannot fathom a meaningful distribution of her planned novel's events across the conventional format (Menke 2013, 217). *New Grub Street*, though still published – like Gissing's later titles – in the old-fashioned way, depicts a world in which the staid appearance of "the old three-decker" (Kipling 2015 [1894], 472, l. 8) belies the grim reality of the literary economy that its creators suffer.

Jasper Milvain has realised that literature has become not merely "a trade" and "a business" (Gissing 2016, 8, 12) but one that, like other businesses, is dominated by the question of supply and demand. He knows his limits: he is neither a genius, nor is he skilled to produce mere "trash" for the "multitude" (13). Instead, he aims for a middle ground: "I shall write for the upper middle-class of intellect, the people who like to feel that what they are reading has some special cleverness, but who can't distinguish between stones and paste" (13). Gissing (through the voice of Milvain) here identifies the phenomenon of 'middlebrow' writing, which satisfies a demand for intelligent reading matter without being too challenging for a certain class of readers. Jasper explicitly denies the 'sacredness' of literature as art, so forcefully asserted by Henry James in his rejoinder to Walter Besant in 1884 ("The Art of Fiction") as the writer's "sacred office" (James 1984, 46): "what on earth is there in typography to make everything it deals with sacred?"

(Gissing 2016, 12), Jasper asks; since not everyone "can be a George Eliot", most authors would have to do with "work[ing] methodically" to produce "good, coarse, marketable stuff for the world's vulgar" (12). It is craft, not art, let alone the "divine afflatus" (12), that is the key to economically sustainable, successful authorship.

In "the modern Grub Street" (Gissing 2016, 17), authorship is no longer a professional path that writers follow almost by accident, as they did in authorship novels around 1850 such as *David Copperfield* and *Pendennis*. Once chosen, the business of literature condemns them to a life in "the valley of the shadow of books" (15, 32), as Jasper repeatedly quips in a parody of Psalm 23 (where the shadow is the shadow of death) – a life, moreover, in which hard work, even overwork, does not guarantee the financial well-being required for matrimony and middle-class domestic happiness. The narrator picks up this phrase at a later point in the novel (167), in a passage focalised through Marian Yule, though Jasper has not uttered it in her presence. As the literary market is oversaturated, conventional arguments about the social benefits of literature no longer convince. When Jasper, perhaps in jest, suggests that literature "helps to spread civilisation" (21), the idea is ridiculed by John Yule, a producer of paper:

> Do you call it civilising men to make them weak, flabby creatures, with ruined eyes and dyspeptic stomachs? Who is it that reads most of the stuff that's poured out daily by the ton from the printing-press? Just the men and women who ought to spend their leisure hours in open-air exercise; the people who earn their bread by sedentary pursuits, and who need to *live* as soon as they are free from the desk or the counter, not to moon over small print. (22)

Though nowhere near as central to the plot of *New Grub Street* as David Séchard is to Balzac's *Lost Illusions* [→ ch. 3], the papermaker in Gissing's novel is important because he adds an even more materialistic perspective than Jasper's, who despite his careerism still thinks about literature in terms of ideas rather than merely "small print" that keeps people away from 'living'. In this radical assertion, literature has become life-denying, a force of death for both its producers and its recipients. Cheap paper is the material basis without which "the rise of mass publishing" would not be possible (Menke 2018, 68). Paper is now produced much faster than the content that is meant to fill it (ibid., 74).[114] And yet, even this can still be a subject for literature, as the novel itself demonstrates. In a metafictional nod to the novel we are reading, Jasper considers he might "make a good thing of writing against writing. It should be my literary specialty to rail against literature" (Gissing

---

[114] See Menke 2018 for a detailed reading of this aspect of the novel, and the interesting suggestion that in its background story of the Yule family there lies "a mini-*Buddenbrooks* of the paper industry" (71). Cf. also Birch 2018, 198.

2016, 23). This is not to say that Jasper Milvain is a self-portrait of Gissing; rather, like Hardy's Ethelberta, and like most of the other characters in *New Grub Street*, he is an expression of, and engagement with, a particular historical paradigm of authorship. Gissing in fact disperses features that describe his own professional and personal situation across several characters in the novel. In the mode of fiction, he achieves a superordinate point of view, a second-order observation on the business side of literature.

The main counterweight to Jasper Milvain is Edwin Reardon, seven years his senior (and thus very close to Gissing's own age when he wrote the novel). Reardon has been married for two years and is the father of a small child. His "miseries" (50, 51) stem mainly from his inability to reconcile his artistic ambitions with the necessities of making enough money by writing to maintain a middle-class household. Unable or unwilling to give up what his wife calls his "morbid conscientiousness" (44) and produce less than mediocre work, Reardon suffers from writer's block. He cannot envisage the prospect of beginning another three-volume novel: "The three volumes lie before me like an interminable desert", he tells his wife (44); but he also refuses to "do a short story of a kind that's likely to be popular" (49). "I might perhaps manage a novel in two volumes, instead of three" (49). Without money and a network of literary friends, long-term success in the "trade" (46) is virtually impossible. In the character of Reardon, Gissing explores the conflict between a "literary career" (26) and marriage: Reardon is unwilling to compromise his artistic ideals for his family's material well-being, but he is also ashamed of his shortcomings as the family's male breadwinner – a feeling that is exacerbated by his wife Amy, who calls his behaviour "unmanly" (45).[115] Like Hardy and Wells, Gissing here explores "the pitfalls of marriage for the ambitious male" (Bergonzi 1976, 18).

Reardon toils away at his next novel as financial pressures mount. When he finishes the third volume in a white heat, he has no energy left to think of a better title than the name of its central character, *Margaret Home*. "Already, with the penning of the last word, all its scenes, personages, dialogues had slipped away into oblivion; he knew and cared nothing more about them" (Gissing 2016, 132). Gissing shows the impersonal nature of ephemeral literary creation also in Reardon's submission of the manuscript to his publishers; when he goes to deliver it to "that member of the firm with whom he had previously had personal relations" (133), he finds him out of town and leaves the manuscript with someone else in the office. This deprives him of an opportunity to borrow some much-needed money; in-

---

[115] In contrast to Knox 2014, I do think that Reardon "finds his masculinity imperiled by literary labour" (95); so do the other bachelors in *New Grub Street* who, for economic reasons, are unable to get married.

stead, he visits an acquaintance, Carter, who lends him five pounds. In asking for a loan, Reardon feels "like an automaton. It seemed to him that he turned screws and pressed levers for the utterance of his next words" (134). Later, he feels like "a machine for earning so much money a week" (312). In Reardon's sense of alienation, Gissing portrays the mechanised nature of literary creation and production, as well as the economic, money-based nature of social relationships: "Blessed money! root of all good, until the world invent some saner economy" (137).[116]

Since literature has become a trade, monetary value trumps "literary value" (161). For authors, the monetary value of their work often barely sustains their livelihood; for publishers, sales are based on advertising, and without the successful bestseller it would not be possible to pay for advertisements of other books in their catalogue. This is illustrated with the example of 'Miss Wilkes' and the publisher Jedwood, based on Mary Braddon and her publisher and later husband, John Maxwell (145, 475).

Reardon, the emotional and psychological centre of the novel, is surrounded by a set of other writer characters, including the opportunist Milvain, but also Biffen, Whelpdale, and Sykes. Struggling authors all, each of them occupies a different position in the literary field. Harold Biffen is the self-proclaimed "realist" (299) who wishes to outdo Zola in depicting life as it really is among the lower classes, among what he calls "the decently ignoble" (187). So poor that he must pawn his coat and other possessions repeatedly, and "reduce[] his meals to the minimum" (378), he is undeterred by the prospect of writing a novel along naturalist lines, a novel about the boredom of everyday life that will bore its readers. He almost sacrifices his life in rescuing the completed manuscript from a fire that destroys his flat. The result, *Mr Bailey, Grocer*, fails despite Jasper's attempts to promote it; it will not sell because of the Darwinian "struggle for existence among books" (404; cf. 430–31). Hopelessly in love with Amy Reardon, and seeing no further purpose in life, Biffen commits suicide.

The unsuccessful novelist Whelpdale, whose novel has been "refused on all hands" (131), gets a second wind as a "literary adviser" (146) to would-be authors, on the model of a literary agent. This is ridiculed by Jasper and deplored by Reardon (146). Whelpdale's next literary project is an "author's Guide" (192). He assures his friends that these "sell splendidly" (192), as indeed his will (241). Gissing here satirises the vogue for such literary advice books (e.g., Edgar Foster's *How to Write a Novel*, 1887) that have the side effect of entrenching popular subject matters and plot patterns, for instance "to write about the wealthy middle class" (192).

---

[116] On alienation in *New Grub Street*, see also Selig 1970. Gissing's anti-capitalist animus is echoed later in Orwell's *Keep the Aspidistra Flying* [→ ch. 11].

This, apparently, is sound business advice, because, as another literary acquaintance of Reardon's explains, working-class readers do not like "stories that treat of their own world" (336) and demand escapism. Later, Whelpdale is en route to another likely success with a popular magazine to be called *Chit-Chat* (407), targeting "the quarter-educated" whose "attention can't sustain itself beyond two inches" of print (407–408) and who "constitute a very large class indeed" (425).[117] He is set to become a wealthy man and marries one of Jasper Milvain's sisters. His success is a "reward" for his "ingenuity and perseverance", the obverse of Reardon's and Biffen's "unpractical" attitude and "logical" failure, as Jasper asserts (450).

At the lowest end of the literary scale is the poor alcoholic Sykes, a semi-Dickensian caricature not only by name. Reardon and Biffen meet Sykes in a public reading-room above a circulating library, which has "a chamber for the use of those who desired to write", next to the lavatory (334). Sykes is busy writing his "autobiography for the 'Shropshire Weekly Herald'", titled "Through the Wilds of Literary London" (335). This is another metafictional hint at the subject matter of *New Grub Street* itself: "Most people will take it for fiction", Sykes asserts, adding: "I wish I had inventive power enough to write fiction anything like it" (336). Indirectly, Sykes supports Gissing's claims for a realistic depiction of London's literary life and its "nether world" (301). It is Sykes, also, who explains the literary preferences of working-class readers to Biffen and Reardon.

The alignment between literature and class is analysed with great clarity and bitterness in *New Grub Street*. "Society", Reardon exclaims at one point in one of the most Zolaesque statements of the novel, "is as blind and brutal as fate" (176). While working-class readers aspire to improve their lot, at least in fiction, it is almost impossible for lower-class writers of fiction to do so in real life by means of writing and publishing. Writers who aspire to a middle-class income from literature (defined as "three or four hundred a year", 333) require sufficient capital, both financial and social, to establish themselves on the literary marketplace – a wisdom already stated with similar candour by Trollope in "The Adventures of Fred Pickering" in 1866: "all who make literature a profession should begin with independent means" (Trollope 1995, 47). If that capital – money and connections – is lacking, respectable success and a reputation will be hard to come by. "*You have to become famous before you can secure the attention which would give fame*", as Jasper explains this crucial paradox (Gissing 2016, 342, emphasis original). This is impossible without a network of connections, and that network is impossible to achieve without money. Money is "a great fortifier of self-respect" if it is there (278) but a destroyer of self-

---

[117] On *Chit-Chat* and its real-life model, George Newnes's popular magazine *Tit-Bits*, see Menke 2019, 81–92.

respect if it is lacking. As Jasper puts it: "Want of money makes me the inferior of the people I talk with, though I might be superior to them in most things" (292). Those who possess it "live a better and fuller life" (370).[118]

If society is fate, people are "prisoner[s] of fate" (366): in this respect, Gissing provides a model of key concerns in late Victorian serious fiction that is aligned with current notions of naturalism (Thomas Hardy obviously springs to mind). Concerns about money, class, and marriage dominate the novel, and they dominate the self-fashioning of its characters. One way in which Gissing illustrates this, with a sly nod at Balzac's *Cousin Pons* (318), is by means of the inheritance plot and its intersection with the Married Women's Property Act of 1882. Both Amy and Marian Yule gain in "self-respect" after their inheritance, but in Marian's case this is crushed when the firm of Turberville & Co. fails, and she suddenly finds herself "weaker than she had thought" (366). Money as a provider of stability and social status has immediate consequences for its owners, sustaining them in their self-determination. Poverty, on the other hand, brings more than financial ruin.

Reardon, unwilling and perhaps unable to make compromises with popular taste and to play by the new rules dictated by literary journalism and "the world's labour-market" (377), learns the hard way what slow but steady failure in the business of authorship feels like. His situation is made worse by his being married to a woman who expects him to succeed and provide for her. The strain on the marriage between Reardon and Amy is the main thematic strand of *New Grub Street* next to the topic of authorship. Unable to divorce, they agree to separate. Amy takes their small son and moves back to her mother; Reardon relocates from Bloomsbury to cheaper lodgings in Islington. Amy's situation is considerably improved when she inherits a substantial sum from an uncle, but the marriage is already too broken to allow for a reconciliation: "No amount of wealth could undo the ruin caused by poverty" (331). Only after their son dies from diphtheria, fate appears to bring them closer again, but Reardon already has a high fever and dies soon after. On Jasper's prompting, his novels are reissued and favourably received. He becomes Reardon's executor also in marrying his widow, having cynically abandoned his earlier love interest, Marian Yule, for the wealthy Amy.

Amy, an astute reader, professes to dislike novels as all the same "silly nonsense" about romantic love (318). Fortified by money, she educates herself on the serious journalism of "the solid periodicals" (320), which fashion her into "a typical woman of the new time" (320), or in other words, a New Woman *avant la lettre*. Her remarriage to Milvain, the successful journalist, appears as the logical

---

118 Earlier economic readings of *New Grub Street* include Vernon 1984, James 2003, Severn 2010, and McPherson 2017.

complement of her reading preferences (cf. Knox 2014, 102–103 n. 27). Jasper's "dreamy bliss" (Gissing 2016, 457) ends the novel, but his achievements, like Whelpdale's, ring hollow, and in his case cynicism in love has disqualified him from deserving such a happy ending.

New Grub Street astutely describes the tragedy of literary production in a socially and economically stratified literary market. As a novel, it is a curious artifact: "a financially successful work of serious fiction that describes a world where poverty inevitably awaits the writers of serious fiction" (Taft 2011, 363). Its tragic heroes, Reardon and Biffen, are allowed to preserve their dignity because of the sacrifices they are willing to make for their literary ideals. They "find solace" in a view of literature as a form of art and in their worship of a "Golden Age of literature", represented in the novel by Greece, the land of Reardon's dreams (Knox 2014, 106). At the opposite end are those careerists, like Milvain and Whelpdale, who have no ideals to lose and no scruples to consider in pursuing their materialistic goals. Another position, only briefly hinted at, is the popular woman novelist à la Braddon whose income subsidises an entire publishing firm (Gissing 2016, 145). In between are those characters, like Marian Yule, who become mere victims of the literary profession, performing machine-like literary work for others that destroys any creative impulse they might otherwise enjoy. The only literary position that is not represented in this system is Gissing's own, as Taft observes: someone who finds a successful compromise between commercial fiction and literary realism (Taft 2011, 363–364). As in the case of Jane Austen, his keen observations depend on eliding his own observer position from the narrative: heterodiegesis by erasure (cf. Miller 2003).

Gissing's style, far from the austere novelties of Zolaesque naturalism, allows for some very conventional Victorian narrative features, including the sensational element of Biffen's rescuing his manuscript from a burning building and even the direct address of the reader at the beginning of chapter 31 (Gissing 2016, 377; cf. Taft 2011, 371–372) – although it is hard to say if such features were intended to be read as "enthusiastic" endorsements of realism (Taft 2011, 372) or as self-conscious parodies of such hallowed conventions.[119]

---

[119] For Gissing's own views on the concept and practice of literary realism, see his 1895 essay "The Place of Realism in Fiction", in which he takes a stand against the "popular understanding" of the term "realistic" as a synonym for "painful or revolting", and inveighs against the naturalists' claims for "objectivity" and a "science of fiction", in favour of the artist's personal "sincerity" and "spirit of truthfulness" (Gissing 1978, 84–86). – French readers compared Gissing to Zola and Maupassant; on Gissing and French realism, see Birch 2018, 190.

In an early chapter of the novel, Marian, the daughter and assistant of yet another writer and editor, Alfred Yule, ponders the overproduction of print matter while working in the Reading Room at the British Museum:

> She kept asking herself what was the use and purpose of such a life as she was condemned to lead. When already there was more good literature in the world than any mortal could cope with in his lifetime, here was she exhausting herself in the manufacture of printed stuff which no one even pretended to be more than a commodity for the day's market. What unspeakable folly! To write – was not that the joy and the privilege of one who had an urgent message for the world? Her father, she knew well, had no such message; he had abandoned all thought of original production, and only wrote about writing. She herself would throw away her pen with joy but for the need of earning money. And all these people about her, what aim had they save to make new books out of those already existing, that yet newer books might in turn be made out of theirs? This huge library, growing into unwieldiness, threatening to become a trackless desert of print – how intolerably it weighed upon her spirit! (Gissing 2016, 95)

Here, the literary profession has descended to "the manufacture of printed stuff", in which "new books" are made "out of those already existing", in an endless production cycle that no longer generates literary innovation but merely the eternal recurrence of the same. The passage culminates in Marian's vision of a "trackless desert of print". She even imagines an inventor like Edison developing a "Literary Machine" that would work like a blender: "Only to throw in a given number of old books, and have them reduced, blended, modernised into a single one for today's consumption" (96). What need for authors when their work could as easily be accomplished by machines? The idea of having literature produced by machines is much older, of course; Swift included it in *Gulliver's Travels*, and Carlyle already grumbled in 1829 "that books are not only printed, but, in a great measure, written and sold, by machinery" (1986, 66). But it achieves new urgency towards the *fin de siècle*, in the age of many technological media innovations.

As the fog seeps into the Reading Room, in a reprise of Dickens's famous opening of *Bleak House* (possibly to show literary recycling *in actu*), Marian imagines the library turning into a prison-house of literature: "the book-lined circumference of the room would be but a featureless prison-limit" (Gissing 2016, 96). Like Marian, most of the other writers in *New Grub Street* are prisoners of the literary market as well as "prisoner[s] of fate", i.e., of society (366). The professionalisation of literature, so eagerly desired in earlier decades, has turned into a dead end, as the possibilities for survival in the "business" (12) are severely limited. Moreover, as Bernard Bergonzi argued, "all natural human relations are affected by the claims of 'literature', which forms a thin disguise for basic economic pressures, since literature is itself no more than a commodity" (Bergonzi 1976, 15). The commodification of literature has led to an almost complete reification, in Lukács's term, of human relationships.

The novel's "echoing subplots" offer "a *combinatoire* of the objective variants still possible in [an] increasingly closed universe" (Jameson 2006, 183). Gissing's characters are, as it were, "submitted to experiments in a controlled environment" (ibid., 184). But what is the outcome of these experiments? Is this metaliterary novel merely a personal expression of authorial disillusionment, "a novel of resentment" (Bergonzi 1976, 20), or is it more ambivalent or even more positive in its evaluation of the conventions of late Victorian fiction and its assessment of the "business" of literature (Gissing 2016, 12)?

As to the novel's portrayal of the literary world in the 1880s, or in 1890 when Gissing wrote it, one may doubt its accuracy or completeness. Gissing paints a dire picture of the future of literature, but his insistent miserabilism and declinism need to be balanced by more optimistic assessments of the situation, both in contemporary periodicals and other novels, which regarded the combined expansion of literacy and print "as a source of limitless opportunities for success" (Stetz 2015, 12). Gissing paints a realistic, if also very pessimistic, picture of "the thoroughly mechanical, depersonalized routines of literary production" in the late Victorian era (Salmon 2013, 219). His pessimism was quickly transformed into a melodramatic formula, as in Marie Corelli's *The Sorrows of Satan* (1895, see Menke 2019, 114–126), or countered by more upbeat representations of the literary world.

"The off-chance of success": George Paston's *A Writer of Books* (1898)

Gissing's scene in the British Museum's Reading Room is echoed but also substantially revised in *A Writer of Books* by 'George Paston' (i.e., Emily Morse Symonds, 1860–1936). In this novel from 1898, the budding author Cosima Chudleigh first enters "the gloomy building" "with feelings of awe and reverence": "When she had passed through the swinging-doors into the great circle of the Reading Room, she stood still for a moment to gaze with enraptured eyes upon the book-lined walls, and to sniff once again the familiar odour of ancient tomes" (Paston 1999, 29). Like Marian Yule, twenty-three-year-old Cosima Chudleigh is overwhelmed by "the ever-increasing burden of books" around her (32), but she is far from despondent. She is a hopeful "newcomer" to the literary institutions of London (31), "the very centre, the holy of holies, of the book-world" (19), but she has already "served more than a seven years' apprenticeship to her profession" (31) and is unfazed by the initial difficulties she faces.

Symonds also echoes Gissing's metaphor of the library as a prison, but she does so ironically, giving the word to Cosima's helpful guide, Miss Nevill: "Bless me, I'm letting you into all the secrets of the prison-house" (31).[120] For Cosima, the principal challenge is not the professionalisation of authorship but its "masculine bias" (Stetz 1999, vi), and her task – and the novel's purpose – is to liberate her from this "prison-house". As she launches her literary career, she is forced to "measure herself against a standard of 'experience' tailored to men" (Stetz 1999, xiii). *A Writer of Books* relativises Gissing's pessimism by depicting a New Woman (and a New Man) as achieving success despite the odds that Gissing presented, and despite the biases in the industry that put women writers at a disadvantage. Symonds combines her critique of the literary and the marriage market when she has Cosima recollect laconically "that literature, like marriage, was a lottery" (Paston 1999, 75). Yet, from this insight into the contingencies of life and literature, Cosima draws some strength. Indeed, knowing what the odds of success are inspires her with some hope: "even for her, there was just the off-chance of success" (ibid.). And the novel proves her right – to some extent; she fails miserably in her choice of a husband, whom she leaves at the end of the novel after finding out that he has been unfaithful. Yet, on the literary side of the "lottery", she is allowed a moderate success in publishing several novels and successively realising her own ideals rather than catering to popular taste.

Being a published author also gives her a perspective of freedom and independence beyond the domestic sphere, and the hope of writing a "masterpiece" offers her a road into a self-defined life beyond marriage (Paston 1999, 258). In allowing this author to achieve her aims, the novel combines a realistic assessment of the literary field (where "the average life of the average novel was three months at most", 92) with a wish-fulfilling fantasy of 'making it' as a professional woman writer in the literary field – a recurrent theme in New Woman fiction of the 1880s and 1890s (cf. Knox 2014, 116). It was to be, however, Symonds's last novel before she turned to writing nonfiction (Flint 2004).

From *An Editor's Tales* to *New Grub Street* and *A Writer of Books*, late Victorian realists depict literary life as stratified by codes of class and gender that need constant attention and negotiation. They question the conditions of literary success and the causes of failure, breaking up the post-Goethean solidity of the literary apprenticeship plot into a kaleidoscope of more individualised and less predictable trajectories. Their characters' destinies alternate between forms of critical or popular recognition, various kinds of personal or literary failure, and mere muddling through to make ends meet. These plots of formation, deformation, or

---

120 On the Reading Room and women, see Hoberman 2002.

stagnation correspond to a variety of narrative situations and types of focalisation, in which conventional forms of narration and familiar resources of narrative authority, from the occasional revival of the intrusive authorial narrator in Gissing to the fragile editorial we in Trollope, are tested for their relative stability or, rather, instability. Such straining at the leash of conventional forms is of course not limited to metaliterary narratives such as the ones discussed here, but the fact that it occurs in, and is correlated with, stories of the literary life adds another reflexive-performative dimension to it. In the final analysis, these stories about authors and editors test the limits of realist narration and probe the modes of mediation of narrative fiction, its own conditions of possibility as a literary and social form.

Close to the *fin de siècle* and in the first decade of the twentieth century, the conditions of economic and aesthetic instability, both on the level of story and the level of discourse, are explored further in tales by Henry James and Rudyard Kipling, and in novels by E. M. Forster and Arthur Machen [→ ch. 8, 9]. As the narrative resources of realism come to be viewed as exhausted, authorial identities are split up even further, moving beyond the social aspects and multiple authorial roles of realist 'author fictions' towards psychological and psychopathological dimensions of writers' (split) personalities. In the process, representations of writers and writing in late Victorian and Edwardian fiction are invested with non-realist formal resources such as the gothic, the grotesque, and the fantastic. In the early twentieth century, the novel of resentment in the realist tradition of Gissing is continued by Orwell and others [→ ch. 11]. The *künstlerroman* is firmly entrenched in high modernist fiction, while the miseries of authorship are increasingly depicted in comic and satirical ways.

Authors have been returning to Gissing's *New Grub Street*, consciously or not, as a realist model of the pathologies of literary life, and this tradition has never quite disappeared, as more recent stories by Alice Munro and Raymond Carver [→ ch. 14] but also contemporary novels like *Kudos* by Rachel Cusk (2018) and *Writers & Lovers* by Lily King (2020) demonstrate [→ ch. 17]. At the end of the nineteenth century, the Romantic paradigm of solitary and successful authorship has been thoroughly discredited, a development that had already been anticipated by Balzac in the 1830s and Melville in the 1850s. The tenuous compromise between author and society that could be attempted in the literary *bildungsroman* came to nothing when the overproduction of novels, and of *bildungsromans*, returned authors to the material and economic challenges of making a living, and a life, in writing and publishing.

In the next part of this book, we will see how the material and spiritual conflicts between art and life play out in modernist author fictions, and how the *bildungsroman* genre is further dis- and reassembled in new forms beyond a realist framework.

8 Curious Double Lives: Puzzles of Authorship in James, Kipling, and Beerbohm

"It is a curious double life that I lead when once my people and their surroundings have taken form in my imagination", notes Jean Dacre, the woman novelist and autodiegetic narrator of Eliza Tabor's *Diary of a Novelist* (1871, 5). She also wonders "how the story of my own life would seem to me if I were to put it down now, just as it happens, and read it over again in twenty or thirty years' time" (7).

Writing exteriorises the writer's self. It creates an autodiegetic "double" (Tabor 1871, 314) by splitting the self into an experiencing and a writing 'I', as is also the case in *David Copperfield*. It creates a tension between life as reality and life as possibility. When she has finished a novel, Dacre the diarist records waking up "each morning to a blank, such as loved and loving guests leave behind them" (286). Considering "the cheque" she has received for her manuscript as a "tangible residuum" of her creative work, she returns to the topic of the imaginative writer's split personality: "What a bundle of contradictions one's nature is! Myself gets puzzled with myself sometimes, to decide which is the real Me [sic], and which is the other one" (289). She concludes that there must be – at least – two Jean Dacres and "wonder[s] [...] how they manage to get along with one another at all" (291). The "duality within" (ibid.) is expressed as a union of opposites, somewhat like 'sense' and 'sensibility' (the "dreaming Jean" vs. "the sensible one", 292). Similarly, the fictional authors in Henry James's stories often feel dissociated from their work; for example, when they refer to the experience of receiving a new book of theirs as "seeing one's self 'just out'" ("The Middle Years", James 1999, 2: 103) but then note that they have "forgotten what [their] book was about" (ibid., 105) – an experience they share with the luckless Edwin Reardon in Gissing's *New Grub Street*.

In the last three decades of the nineteenth century, we find this "strange alienation" (James 1999, 2: 105), duality, or split personality of authors increasingly enacted in works that subvert or transgress the conventions of the literary *bildungsroman*, venturing into darker territories of the gothic and the fantastic. As the relationship between art and life is turned more and more into a matter of public concern in the 1880s and 1890s, culminating in the trial of Oscar Wilde, authors are irresistibly drawn to the ambiguities and contradictions of this relationship. Writers, whose private lives are at risk of being exposed to public scrutiny, address the boundaries between their private and public roles in their work, just as they debate the purpose of literature in an era of mass production, commodification, and a perceived decline of cultural standards. In the 1880s and 1890s, aestheticism – with its war-cry of 'art for art's sake' – develops into a serious rival of literary realism and naturalism, whose 'scientific' aspirations tend to be combined with a sense of the moral or social purpose of literature, in particular the novel.

Without unduly reifying these terms, one can perhaps say that both strands participate in the emergence of literary modernism, widely defined, as a cluster of attempts to salvage the exclusiveness of serious literary writing as distinct from mass-market forms of entertainment and genre fiction. The duality of art and life, negotiated in many *fin de siècle* texts, is thus itself double: the dual nature of authors (as private and public figures) is mapped onto the dual nature of literature itself as belonging to the sphere of art or of life, as serving either the lofty principles of artistic form (aestheticism) or the equally lofty ideals of social utility (realism, naturalism). The autopoetic self-expression and self-projection of authors who are involved, even if only in a marginal capacity, with the aestheticist movement, frequently takes the form of the *roman à clef* that allows both sides of this duality their due. The author-making force of such artful narratives is attested by Oscar Wilde's *The Picture of Dorian Gray* (1891) as much as, if not more so, by Frederick Rolfe's *Hadrian the Seventh* (1904), the self-styled Baron Corvo's most successful and brazen act of literary self-imagination (cf. Symons 1979, 173–174). Here, the playful joy of artistic self-invention hardens into eccentricity and paranoia.

In Henry James's stories of the literary life, these contrasts are played out in the form of ambiguous narratives and their often ironic or downright comic treatments of the topic. They are usually told from the point of view of an outside observer, often a naive admirer. But humour, irony, ambiguity are literary strategies that enable James to explore serious concerns about the development of literature and the public/private lives of authors without descending into sentimental mystifications of authorship or pessimistic clamouring about its lack of public (or even private) appreciation.[121] They allow him to address questions of aesthetics that are obviously close to his heart, as his reflections in the essays and prefaces demonstrate; yet they are also characterised by a darkening tone that James shares with Gissing (on the part of the realists) and with Wilde, Stevenson, Kipling, Beerbohm and other authors more closely associated with the gothic revival. In this chapter, I will read James's stories of the literary (double) life next to gothic and fantastic authorship tales by Kipling and Beerbohm as transitional texts between literary realism and modernist impressionism.

---

[121] The classic study of James's professional authorship sums up his attitude to the marketplace and fame as a "calculated attempt to avoid both the din of commercialism and the silence of oblivion" (Anesko 1986, 11). Cf. Culver 1984. Chung 2019 goes much further in asserting that James combined the ideals of literary art with a canny awareness of the commercial world of liberal capitalism. I would like to thank Gert Buelens for pointing this out to me.

Henry James's Stories of the Literary Life

Many of James's tales about writers are concerned with the antagonisms and insecurities that characterise the literary profession at the end of the nineteenth century: conflicts between art and life but also between art and commerce, established authors and novices, literature and journalism, and between fame and celebrity. In most of these stories, a cruel fate awaits the author or authors at their centre, or their closest friends and supporters, a fate often related to one or more errors of judgement. Many are blinded by what they think is love, or at least admiration, but what is more often based in their own egotism. For example, in "Greville Fane" (1892), a writer of popular fiction fails to realise that her son, whom she wanted to train to the profession, has all the while been wasting her money. In "The Coxon Fund" (1894), a group of people give substantial sums to support an unworthy writer who will never produce anything of note: "The very day he found himself able to publish he wholly ceased to produce" (James 1999, 2: 220). In "The Aspern Papers" (1888), a prying biographer is almost willing to marry a woman he does not desire only to get access to a cache of letters by the dead American poet he idolizes.[122] In "The Figure in the Carpet" (1896), a literary critic similarly considers marrying his friend's widow to find out the secret, the "general intention" behind the works of a novelist they admire (James 1999, 2: 333, 338).

James's key narrative technique, the marginal narrator or reflector, is the perfect vehicle for observations from the margins of the literary world: emerging authors, young journalists and critics, hopeful novices and hungry biographers offer a plausible point of view on the insecurities of authorship, on careers fulfilled or never properly begun, on the never ceasing but forever unrealised hope for "The Next Time" (1895), on success that may be just around the corner, on illusions built up and lost. The other central technique is the indirectness of these narratives; frequently sketchy despite their length, they sometimes withhold crucial information and force readers to find their own orientation in the story, often in negation of the narrator's norms, by reading against the grain and paying attention to the story's indeterminacies.[123]

In terms of genre, this technique of calculated indirectness and the ironic perspective on the narrator constitute a departure from the harmonising pull of the *bildungsroman*. Whereas the *bildungsroman* was concerned with achieving a compromise between centrifugal social forces, the Jamesian tale reveals their irrecon-

---

[122] On authors' letters in James, see Stougaard-Nielsen 2012. On "The Aspern Papers", see also Hochman 1996.
[123] Cf. Wolfgang Iser's reading of "The Figure in the Carpet" in Iser 1978, 3–10.

cilable contradictions. Whereas a novel like *David Copperfield* seeks to bridge the widening gap between narration and experience, James's tales of literary authorship trace the continuing process of their disintegration under the conditions of modernity.

James's earliest story about the literary life is "The Author of 'Beltraffio'" (1884).[124] In this tale, the English author Mark Ambient, understood to be a proponent of the "gospel of art" (James 1999, 1: 729), is visited at his home in Surrey by a twenty-five-year-old American admirer, the story's nameless narrator, who describes himself as "a young American of an aesthetic turn" (731), and whose aestheticist preferences indeed shape his presentation of everyone he meets and everything he sees during his visit. For instance, he is fixated on external beauty and compares people to paintings (744, 763); he reads "literary allusions" into the landscape he walks through (753). The visitor is a fan, in whose eyes Mark Ambient is "a happy combination" of "an English gentleman and a man of genius" (731) who can do no wrong and whose modest house in the country appears to the visitor to be "a palace of art" (732). For the young American, there can be no distinction between Ambient the man and Ambient the artist; both are "delightful" (738).

In a manner that is very typical of James's stories, the narrator's perceptions are gradually revealed to be faulty, and the style of the narrative offers indications of unreliable narration, encouraging readers to come to their own conclusions beyond what is explicitly stated in the tale. Signals of unreliability in the story include the familiar special pleading, as in the phrase "All I can say is that I acted in perfect good faith" (765). Gradually, the visitor learns of the deep-seated disagreement and distrust between Ambient and his wife, whose name is Beatrice but who has nothing in common with Dante's idealised vision of that name. Mrs Ambient disapproves of her husband's literary work on moral grounds, based on her Christian values; she thinks that "a work of art ought to have a 'purpose'" (752), and she fears her husband's influence on their seven-year-old son. According to his "artistic temperament" (758), the narrator compares the boy, whom he knows only by his nickname, Dolcino, to "an angel", but also "an orphan, or a changeling" (735) and, strikingly, he anticipates the boy's death when he first sees him: "there is a kind of charm which is like a death-warrant" (735).

In his conversations with the author, Mrs Ambient, and the author's sister Gwendolen, the narrator gradually constructs a different view of Ambient's marital situation, casting him in the role of the suffering artist tied to a 'Philistine' wife

---

[124] Quotations from the tales refer not to James's later revisions, in which he sometimes drastically changed the text, but to editions based on their first publications. "The Author of 'Beltraffio'" first appeared in the *English Illustrated Magazine* in June 1884.

(cf. 759: "if she had a passion at all, it would be that of Philistinism"), and he shapes his story into a story about the conflict of 'art' and 'life': "for him, too, life was a struggle, as it has been for many other men of genius" (750). This is shown in heavily gendered terms as a conflict and contrast between the male homosocial bonding of artists and art lovers – expressed as tactile at several key moments in the tale – and the protection of social conventions, conformity, and "propriety" (759) that is identified with femininity, keen on preventing the men from touching each other. Regretfully, the narrator remarks that he "never touched Dolcino" (767), as the boy is carried away by his mother. In this misogynist framework, art is masculine, a field of 'mastery' (cf. 747: "the school in which he was master"), while life is feminine, personified as "She" by Mark Ambient (755), and its purpose is to be used as "literary material" (756), to be "resolve[d] [...] into a literary form" (747). The narrator's attempt to reconcile the "disagreement" (765) between husband and wife only brings about the tragic *dénouement*. The boy dies of diphtheria in his mother's care (as does little Willie in *New Grub Street*), apparently because she refuses to have him treated. She has decided to "let him die" (773) to preserve his purity "from ever being touched" (774) by the immorality of her husband's novels – a decision brought on, apparently, by the narrator's urging her to read the manuscript of her husband's work in progress.

The story's gruesome ending can be interpreted in several different ways, similar to the death of young Miles in *The Turn of the Screw* (1898).[125] Yet, there are sufficient indications in the story that James, far from endorsing the aestheticist creed of Ambient and his American admirer, intends audiences to decode the narrator's version of events as distorted by a vision of art that is anything but true to life, a view that places beauty above life and is therefore sterile and in fact lethal. The narrator values the artificial more highly than the natural. His tendency to reduce human beings to static images leads him to pronounce that the boy "was more exquisitely beautiful in death than he had been in life" (775). The narrator is, in a sense, revealed as the real author of "The Author of 'Beltraffio'", because the tale is presented in his voice and through his jaded vision.[126] The reader is left with

---

[125] James himself twice refers to the ending as "gruesome" in his notebooks (1987, 25–26). The story is based on an anecdote about the marriage of John Addington Symonds, told to James by Edmund Gosse (ibid.). Different approaches to the story are briefly summed up in Álvarez 2008.
[126] On this kind of Jamesian narrator, cf. Álvarez 2008: "At times they can even be seen to take over the role of the great writers themselves whose tribulations they are supposed to relate" (321). Álvarez also observes that, as these narrators "attract[] more and more attention", there is a "gradual diminishing of the protagonist's narrative presence" in the story (321). Cf. also Kraver 2001 for a reading of "The Author of 'Beltraffio'" that focuses on the narrator "as author of the events – both figuratively and literally" (40). On James and aestheticism, cf. Izzo/O'Hara 2006.

the impression that the self-centred narrator has learned nothing from the events he has witnessed or believes to have witnessed. Nor has he revised any of his preconceptions, which is particularly disconcerting as his version of Dolcino's death is based on a second unreliable witness, Gwendolen Ambient. Instead, he forces whatever may have actually occurred into a literary form that, on the surface, exactly corresponds to his received ideas about art. And yet, while he is telling it, his story unmasks itself as that of a callous, ignorant, attention-seeking aesthete lacking in empathy.

James's artistic treatment of his own aesthetic ideas transcends the mere discursive contrast between effete aestheticism and Philistine morality, which is the nucleus of this story in his notebooks (James 1987, 25). By means of his "usual narrator-observer" (ibid. 195), James injects the tale with narrative unreliability and effects a "weakening of traditional narrative authority" (Álvarez 2008, 322). Instead of the conventional realist author-narrator, whose authority is often described, not entirely accurately, as 'omniscient' but who, whether intrusive or not, generally serves as a reliable guide to the fictional world, James sheds doubt on his first-person narrators' accuracy and reliability as he limits their powers of perception and understanding, making it impossible for the reader to determine whether the events in the story "have been *correctly* perceived, assessed, and presented" (ibid.). James is not the first to do this, of course, as any reader of Poe, Hawthorne, and other earlier writers will know. But it is significant that James uses this technique of "massive dissonance" (ibid. 323) with perhaps the greatest possible *éclat* in his tales about authors, thus casting a spell of ambiguity over the stories that infects their subject matter and their central questions: what is the purpose and status of authors in modernity? How can they achieve and maintain artistic integrity? Can they still establish a meaningful communication with their readers and the wider public, and if so, how?

James engaged with these and similar questions throughout his oeuvre, from *Roderick Hudson* (1875) to *The Sacred Fount* (1901), but it is in the shorter stories that he arguably found the most convincing form for this engagement. In refracting the problem of authorship through the very aesthetic of narrative form, he transposes a discursive discussion into a literary puzzle, an enigmatic 'secret' woven into his texts as is the famous "Figure in the Carpet" in the story of that title (1896). The fact that he wrote so many metaliterary stories that work in this way attests to the importance of these questions, at least for him, but also in the literary culture around him – as we will see in some stories by Kipling and Beerbohm that follow a similar recipe.

Whereas "The Author of 'Beltraffio'" ends in a cruel death, a more subtle kind of cruelty is the point of "The Lesson of the Master" (1888), concealed in the advice given by a respected author to a younger colleague, whom he urges not to marry and have children but to sacrifice everything to his art. This story is an elegant variation on the theme of art vs. life that was at the core of "The Author of 'Beltraffio'" and "The Aspern Papers". But here the conflict shifts from the husband and wife (or, as in "The Aspern Papers" and "The Figure in the Carpet", the prospect of marriage for mercenary reasons) to the fraught relationship between an established writer – "the head of the profession" (James 1999, 1: 1001–1002) – and his younger admirer.

Outwardly, the writer Henry St George is "an honourable image of success, of the material rewards and the social credit of literature" (James 1999, 1: 991), but he confesses to the young Paul Overt that he has merely been coasting for years instead of writing the masterpieces worthy of his inflated renown. However, when his wife dies, he quickly marries again – marries the beautiful woman with whom Paul had fallen in love, and whom he had renounced to focus solely on his writing. Paul has no way of knowing if Henry's advice had been well-intentioned or deceitful. The duplicity of the master's lesson is accentuated by the frequent, echoing repetition of Paul's unanswerable questions: "'Was it a plan – was it a plan?' Sometimes he cried to himself, breathless, 'Am I a dupe – am I a dupe?' [...] He didn't know what he had expected – he only knew what he hadn't. It wasn't this – it wasn't this" (1: 1020).

Life-lessons in resignation, resentment or disappointment lie in store for many of James's protagonists. Yet one of the most pervasive themes in these tales of authorship is destructive celebrity, the kind of success that damages an author's hopes for lasting recognition as a serious artist.[127] Without implying a strictly biographical reading, this was clearly a topic that nagged the Master, since he suffered a number of critical and commercial failures (most famously, of course, as a playwright). His own criticism returns to the conflict between art and commerce again and again: to the maintenance of aesthetic and critical standards in the face of "the uncompromising swarm of authors" to be read and reviewed (James 1984, 99; from "The Science of Criticism", 1891), and to the "sacred office" (ibid., 46) of the serious writer in contrast to those who produce and consume novels like puddings (44) or as "an exercise in skipping" (48) rather than attempting "to represent life" (46, 47; all from "The Art of Fiction", 1884). Already his early review of Trollope's *The Belton Estate* (1866) shows his critical coordinate system fully established; he does not mince words when it comes to attacking a commercially successful work that he regards as an artistic failure (James 1984, 1322–1326).

---

[127] James's tales about artists and authors can certainly be read as stories about "human interaction" more generally (Wirth-Nesher 1984, 126), but my interest here is in their precise negotiation of the field of literature, authorship, and celebrity.

"The Death of the Lion" (1894), written (like "The Coxon Fund" and "The Next Time") for *The Yellow Book*, is the cruel story of an author and his work destroyed by the effects of celebrity. This was very much on James's mind at the time; in a notebook entry of February 3 of that year, he condemned "the ravenous autograph-hunters, lion-hunters, exploiters of publicity" (James 1987, 86). In the story, the fifth novel of fifty-year-old writer Neil Paraday becomes a smash hit, aided by international newspaper coverage that turns the author into "a national glory" overnight (James 1999, 2: 133). Unfortunately, he is now lionised and fêted to such an extent that his writing suffers, as he is forced to give his attention to worthless admirers whose only intention is to bask in the sunshine of his celebrity. No one is genuinely interested in his books; worse, one of his admirers manages to displace the unfinished manuscript of Paraday's new novel. On a society outing, the author catches a cold and dies soon after, unaware of the fact that his priceless final literary effort has been lost and will never be published. As his name perhaps suggests, Paraday will be an author 'for a day' only, not for eternity – an ephemeral celebrity without a chance of lasting fame.[128]

The same theme is varied in "The Next Time" (1895), where the author Ralph Limbert is an artist to such an extent that he is incapable of writing badly even when he tries. Motivated by economic necessity, having to support a wife and three children, he desperately aims for a novel that will "lay[] waste the circulating libraries" (James 1999, 2: 260). Yet he is destined for higher literary honours rather than mere ephemeral success. His is a story of perverse "hope of a market" (254) that is disappointed every time because Limbert just cannot "cultivate the market" (243), he "*can't* temporise" (250, emphasis original), "can't be vulgar for trying" (254). He is incapable of achieving the right kind of balance for a middlebrow audience, "the mediocrity that attaches, that endears" (245). The story contains one of James's most bitter indictments of "the age of trash triumphant" (224), in which a kind of Gresham's law of literature applies, so that writing that is truly "original" and "exquisite" (236) is driven out by poor imitations, by "the middling good" (245). Limbert's work is too fine; it will never sell because it suffers from what the narrator with mordant irony refers to as "the taint of literature" (234).

"John Delavoy" (1898) tackles the relationship between authors and their audience from yet another angle. In this story, a critic is at first delighted to have persuaded the editor of a "celebrated" periodical (James 1996b, 3) to commission an article on the recently deceased author John Delavoy, whom the critic admires

---

[128] See DaRosa 1997 for a more detailed reading of this story, including the astute (Bourdieuan) observation that "'The Death of the Lion' shifts its attention from the question of how authors create meaning to the question of how authors are produced [...]" within a field of cultural production (846).

as "a great man", a "wonderful writer" and an "immense novelist" (2). However, on reading the article, the editor turns it down, claiming it will damage the journal's circulation because it is too explicit "about the relations of the sexes" (19). Yet, as the critic points out, he has only been giving a statement of the "essence" of Delavoy's "very topic" (19). The true reason for the editor's refusal, the critic surmises, is that there is a chance of securing a more "personal" memoir from Delavoy's sister, and that the editor (and his subscribers) prefer the personal angle to the literary – the more so, in this case, because Delavoy throughout his life kept his private life secret and concentrated only on "his work, the most unadvertised, unreported, uninterviewed, unphotographed, uncriticised of all originals" (3).[129] The editor's most valuable prize, however, is a pencil portrait that he reproduces in his magazine, against the express wishes of the author's sister, boosting the journal's circulation by "a tremendous jump" (35). The critic's protests only serve to advertise it even more. His only consolation, in a fine irony related to the topic of "the relations of the sexes", is that he, and not the editor, who had been his rival in this regard, secures the affections of Delavoy's sister. The story thus, in its plot, turns into the exact equivalent of "the nice familiar chat about the sweet home-life" (32) that the critic so disparages. Here, the private, domestic, and erotic have become intermingled with the literary to such an extent that they dominate the narrative. Ironically, the reader learns nothing of substance about the work of John Delavoy from the story – not even, as in many other tales by James about authors, the title of one of his novels – beyond the bare fact (applicable certainly to almost any novel) that it deals with relationships between men and women.

Finally, the newspaper manufacture of celebrity is depicted from a more humorous angle in the longer tale "The Papers" (1903). This focuses on a couple of young journalists who serve the celebrity industry. A key metaphor that resonates throughout this story, as a comparison to the activities of the press, is the feeding of wild animals in the zoo (e.g., 1999, 2: 825, 865). The desire of people to become or remain famous, and of journalists and readers of the yellow press to feed and be fed by what they take to be 'news' about the famous, is shown to lead to well-nigh disastrous consequences. Interestingly, this convinces the story's journalists to give up their job and perhaps try what they call "littery" authorship instead (881).

In many of these tales, James addresses how the public images of authors, whose private lives become the focus of public attention, threaten to dispel interest in their work and replace it by a prurient, prying curiosity and a penchant for 'home stories': "anecdotes, glimpses, gossip, chat" ("John Delavoy", James 1996b,

---

129 The novelist Dencombe in "The Middle Years" [→ ch. 9] likewise prides himself "on having never answered the photographers" (James 1999, 2: 111).

22–23). Criticism that appreciates their literary work is displaced by human interest stories in what the narrator of "John Delavoy" ambiguously calls the "intellectual economy" (6) of even the more upmarket periodical press. This process not only shifts the focus of attention from the work to the author; it actually causes, or at least emphasises, a split between an author's work and life. It thus creates or accentuates conflicting images of the author and multiple identities that are difficult to reconcile within a single image. This conflict of identities can be represented in the tales as a conflict, within the author's persona, between different social roles (writer, lover, husband, professional or amorous rival) – a panoply resembling, perhaps not entirely accidentally, the roles evoked in Shakespeare's sonnets –, between different ideas of what constitutes literary success or failure, and between different kinds of literary reputation (prehumous vs. posthumous recognition, short-term celebrity vs. long-term fame).[130]

In some of James's stories, this tension between different images of an author's persona is dramatised in the form of a ghost story. It can be based on the theme of the unlived life or alternative life, as suggested most explicitly, and to some extent autobiographically, in the late tale "The Jolly Corner" (1908), in which an elderly expatriate returns to his former family home in New York City and confronts the ghost of the life he might have lived had he not left for Europe.[131] In "The Real Right Thing" (1899), the young critic and journalist George Withermore is hired by a deceased author's widow to write her husband's biography. While working among the author's papers in his former study, the young man can sense the presence of "his master", i.e., the dead writer he admires so much (James 1999, 2: 545). The "connection" (547) even seems to materialise into a "personal presence" (548), one however that he feels unable to look at directly:

> There were moments, for instance, when, as he bent over his papers, the light breath of his dead host was as distinctly in his hair as his own elbows were on the table before him. There were moments when, had he been able to look up, the other side of the table would have shown him his companion as vividly as the shaded lamplight showed him his page. (549)

---

[130] One story which I cannot discuss here for reasons of space is "The Birthplace" (1903), which also deals with the public manufacture of an author's posthumous image, in this case an author who can only be Shakespeare. The couple of caretakers who end up doubting the value of their job resembles the role of the journalists in "The Papers", which dates from the same year.
[131] James's most famous story about the unlived life is "The Beast in the Jungle" (1903). While that tale is characterised by retrospective remorse about a road not taken, "The Jolly Corner" ends on a note of retrospective self-justification.

However, as he continues working on the biography, Withermore slowly begins to perceive this presence no longer as a benign and helpful fatherly being. As papers are mysteriously misplaced, Withermore realises that his subject might be actively interfering with his efforts to complete the book. It seems as if the ghost of Ashton Doyne is dead set on preventing anyone from writing his biography: "He's there to *save* his Life. He's there to be let alone", as Withermore explains to his employer, Mrs Doyne (554, emphasis original). When the ghost also appears to Mrs Doyne, she is so terrified that she immediately gives up on the idea of a biography, an idea that had been motivated, in any case, more by self-interest than by any genuine regard for her husband's achievement (544). The story relishes the ambiguity of the word 'life' as denoting existence, being alive, and the written record of that life in the form of a biographical account. The author's continuing ghostly existence beyond his physical death militates against any attempt to fix his life into such a settled representation. He helps his wife and her assistant to do "the real right thing" instead of merely the right thing. Ashton Doyne does not want a biography, he wants his work to stand alone and speak for itself.

In "The Private Life" (1892), James produces yet another story of transgression and violation that contains a gothic element. Here, he also shows that what is violated is first constituted by the act of transgression itself: privacy "is always already subject to 'knowledge'" (Salmon 1997, 89). The first-person narrator of the story, himself a writer of fiction, wants to find the true, private self of the celebrated author Clare Vawdrey. Vawdrey's literary profundity, however, is contrasted to the shallowness of his public persona. While on holiday in Switzerland, the narrator finds out that the famous author is in fact two separate persons: Vawdrey public is superficial and sociable, while Vawdrey private hides in his room to write. The private self is the 'true' writer, alone in a darkened room, producing great works of art.

The author's duality is contrasted with the condition of Lord Mellifont, who apparently does not exist outside of company. He cannot be seen alone; his privacy cannot be violated because his publicity precludes exposure. Mellifont is mere display; the writer, however, needs to have two personae, two identities, one for society and one for privacy – suggesting that these two aspects cannot otherwise be brought into a meaningful, functional correlation: "One goes out, the other stays at home. One is the genius, the other's the bourgeois, and it's only the bourgeois whom we personally know" (James 1999, 2: 22).[132] The genius and the bourgeois;

---

[132] In his notebooks, James refers to "The Private Life" as based on "the little conceit of the private identity of a personage suggested by F. L., and that of a personage suggested by R. B." (James 1987, 60). Leon Edel identifies the first as Frederic Leighton, the second as Robert Browning, whose "conventional" and "middle-class" (Edel 1962, 3: 277) personality had made James wonder how

the private and the public – the two roles and their respective domains, which the Victorian literary *bildungsroman* tried so hard to reconcile, have finally parted ways.

Rudyard Kipling's Authorship Gothic

The splitting of authorial personae, either temporal in the ruptures (rather than development) experienced by a single author character, or spatial in the division of labour among several characters, also dominates the stories of Rudyard Kipling that deal with authorship.[133] Already in the early story "The Dream of Duncan Parrenness" (1884), Kipling presents the price of a young writer's entrance into adulthood as a loss – of his "trust in man", "faith in women", and his "boy's soul and conscience" (Kipling 1987, 137). In this story, the young writer's double is his older self, whom he meets in a dream; it ends on a note of further disillusionment as the "gift" left behind by the double is merely "a little piece of dry bread" (138).

The encounter with prior or subsequent instances of an authorial self is also thematic in "The Finest Story in the World" (1891), where Kipling inverts the Jamesian constellation of an older author and his younger admirer by making the older writer narrate the story. The older writer gets to know a young clerk with literary aspirations, Charlie Mears. Lacking both education and experience, Charlie is a good storyteller but a writer of "horrible sentences" (1994, 261). They come to an agreement that the narrator should write the tale, "The Story of a Ship" (261), based on Charlie's telling, but the narrator wonders about Charlie's sources of knowledge and inspiration for a historically accurate story of "a Greek galley-slave, as told by himself" (267). As the narrator remarks to Charlie, "I can't imagine your imagining it" (263). Charlie appears to have "real" knowledge of ancient ships: "It's as real as anything to me until I try to write it down", he tells the narrator (265). This 'reality effect', it turns out, is a result of Charlie's involun-

---

someone so unremarkable could have written such great poetry. Edel also notes that the story can equally be read as an autobiographical "fantasy about [James] himself" (ibid.), in relation to his unfulfilled ambition to succeed as a playwright. On James and Browning, see also McDonell 2015. For a deconstructive reading of "The Private Life", see Walton 1992. On authors as ghosts in James and Beerbohm, see also Bugliani 2022.

133 Only some of these are relevant to my concerns here. For a full survey of references to authors and writing in Kipling's works, see Stewart 1988, who concludes that most of the fictional writers portrayed by Kipling are caricatures that their author dislikes (276–277), and that they display contradictory attitudes about the origins of literary creativity.

tary memory of his previous lives. He can even reproduce a piece of graffito in "extremely corrupt Greek", which the narrator has authenticated by an expert at the British Museum (267). The more experienced author recognises the literary potential of his source:

> He would supply me – here I capered among the dumb gods of Egypt and laughed in their battered faces – with material to make my tale sure – so sure that the world would hail it as an impudent and vamped fiction. And I – I alone would know that it was absolutely and literally true. I – I alone held this jewel to my hand for the cutting and polishing. Therefore I danced again among the gods of the Egyptian court, till a policeman saw me and took steps in my direction. (267)

The policeman's admonishing presence, which curbs the author's exuberance, perhaps serves as a reminder of the – to say the least – unusual origins of his "material", a stolen "jewel", while his vain egotism is underlined by the doubling of the phrase "I – I alone", ironically undercut by the doubling (and possibly splitting) of the "I".

As Charlie Mears's present life is invaded by memories of his "past lives" (268), introducing a temporal rupture in his identity, the narrating author's professional identity is at least compromised by his use of (someone else's) real-life material rather than his own imagination. He becomes an exploiter of somebody else's past that he wants to market as fiction. He is more interested in taking possession of this story than in the mystery of its origins (cf. Jullien 2020, 846). Charlie, however, angers the narrator by reading too much English poetry, which threatens to corrupt the purity of his recollections.

As a medium, Charlie is a channel distorted by noise: "The plastic mind of the bank-clerk had been overlaid, coloured, and distorted by that which he had read, and the result as delivered was a confused tangle of other voices most like the mutter and hum through a City telephone in the busiest part of the day" (Kipling 1994, 269). Other previous lives join this tangle: Charlie, it turns out, was also part of a Viking expedition to America "in the ninth or tenth century" (274). The author worries about getting the stories properly disentangled from the "maddening jumble" of Charlie's narration (275), and he also worries increasingly about the consequences that might ensue when the world learns the truth about the transmigration of souls (276–277). He discusses Hindu beliefs in reincarnation with a Bengali acquaintance, who tells him that the first kiss from a woman that Charlie receives and returns will erase his memories of past lives. The intensity of love in *this* life makes the memories of other lives disappear. This is indeed what happens, and the door to the past is closed forever.

Kipling's narrator realises that the material he has been able to record from Charlie's recollections is not as promising as he had hoped, as they include only glimpses of the past rather than a coherent narrative: "I saw that the tale might indeed be written, but would be nothing more than a faked, false-varnished, sham-rusted piece of Wardour Street work at the end" (285–286), referring to shops that sell counterfeit antique furniture. The story, if it were written, would remain indistinguishable from other historical fiction, despite its foundation in actual memories of past lives. This can be read as a comment on the nature of fiction, and hence as a cautionary tale about the wrong kind of literary ambition in producing historical realism without the 'varnish' of art. The uncanny element in literary authorship, as described in this story, is that it *always* comes from a source outside of the author's self and beyond his control.

The uncanny doubling of a writer being invaded by something or someone from the past is taken to yet another level in Kipling's "'Wireless'" (1902). Here, an experiment with radio waves turns a young chemist's assistant into a conduit for the ghost of John Keats. On a winter evening, the narrator visits his friend, a chemist, as the chemist's nephew, an electrician, is just about to conduct the experiment. The narrator is fascinated to learn about "Hertzian waves" and "induction" (Kipling 1994, 562). While they are waiting and drinking alcoholic beverages concocted from the chemist's stock, the narrator's attention wanders to the young chemist's assistant, Mr Shaynor, who exhibits symptoms of tuberculosis. Shaynor is briefly taken for a walk by a beautiful young woman named Fanny Brand, around the nearby church of St. Agnes. Later, after trying a couple of the narrator's cocktails, Shaynor falls into a kind of trance and begins to write poetry. In fact, what he writes is largely identical to parts of Keats's poem *The Eve of St. Agnes*. But he is not rewriting the poem from memory but literally re-*creating* it. He stops now and then, writes parts of it first in prose and then in verse, and in between seeks inspiration in an advertisement that shows a picture of a woman. The narrator is astonished, the more so as he later hears from Shaynor that the young man has never read anything by Keats. The similarities with Keats are, however, striking: like Keats, Shaynor is a chemist by profession, suffers from consumption, and his girlfriend's name is Fanny Brand, echoing the name of Fanny Brawne. Something must have happened in analogy to the electrical induction of the radio waves, by means of which signals from a great distance have been transmitted – signals from a temporal rather than spatial distance: Shaynor has been turned into a receiver (his head, while writing, is described as "moving machine-like", 565). Charlie Mears in "The Finest Story in the World" was compared to a "surcharged phonograph" and a "City telephone" (267, 269); Shaynor is a radio receiver.

The similarities between Keats and Shaynor appear to the narrator "logical and inevitable", as a technological and scientific fact "[a]s inevitable as induction" (566): "If he hasn't [read Keats], it's the identical bacillus, or Hertzian wave of tuberculosis, *plus* Fanny Brand and the professional status which, in conjunction with the mainstream of subconscious thought common to all mankind, has thrown up temporarily and induced Keats" (567, emphasis original). But Shaynor is not only a receiver; he is even capable of improving on Keats's poem (568). It is therefore only logical that, when he and the narrator discuss spiritualism, Shaynor retorts that "mediums are all impostors" and are only in it "for the money they can make" (573). He, in other words, is no impostor but has indeed been invaded by an author from the past.[134]

Kipling himself was critical of spiritualism and automatic writing, not least because of his troubled sister Trix, who dabbled in crystal gazing and other spiritualist practices (Lycett 1999, 478). Yet, he shared a fascination for the unexplored sources of literary inspiration, writing in a letter to Rider Haggard in 1918: "We are only telephone wires" (Kipling 1965, 100), echoing the earlier reference to the telephone in "The Finest Story in the World". In "'Wireless'", the action at a distance enabled by Marconi's "Hertzian waves" (Kipling 1994, 562) serves as a metaphor for the obscure sources of creativity, presenting inspiration as induction: "something coming through from somewhere" (565). Did Shaynor's revival of Keats come from the subconscious or was it due to social and personal factors that accidentally resemble the life circumstances of a great poet from the past? The story leaves this open, but it registers an anxiety about the limits of creativity that resembles Gissing's, if in a different literary mode (gothic instead of realist). The potential for literary innovation appears to be exhausted, and authors are compelled to repeat, remix, and reproduce their forebears. Kipling here anticipates a Bloomian "anxiety of influence" (Bloom 1973). The integrity of the authorial self is compromised by these signals from the past. Even the narrator himself has a sensation of dissociation for a while: "my own soul most dispassionately considered my own soul" (Kipling 1994, 566), until he reassuringly reports: "I found myself one person again" (567).

As critics have noted, Kipling not only explores in this story the technological possibility of being "in two places at the same time" (Kern 2019, 147) but also "the power of writing itself" (Grimes 2011, 32). Yet he only does so with the irony that this power has spun out of control. The story questions, in a more radical fashion than "The Finest Story in the World", how these new technologies will affect an

---

[134] Kipling's story anticipates not only the *donnée* of Borges's "Pierre Menard" (1939), in which a modern author rewrites *Don Quixote* word for word, independently of the original, but also, even more uncannily, the opinion of Judge Learned Hand in *Sheldon v. Metro-Goldwyn Pictures* (81 F.2d 49, 54 [2d Cir. 1936]): "if by some magic a man who had never known it were to compose anew Keats's 'Ode on a Grecian Urn', he would be an 'author,' and, if he copyrighted it, others may not copy that poem, though they might of course copy Keats's" (qtd. in Saint-Amour 2003, 7; cf. Frow 2021, 15).

older media constellation of authorship, writing, and selfhood. The narrator's limited understanding of events also places this story in the context of modernist impressionism, "situating the wireless at the origin of the impressionist subject" (Fielding 2015, 27) and shattering the narrator's belief in "objectivity, reliability, and authority" (29) as what was thought of as knowledge is transformed into (not more than) consciousness (cf. 33). The new technologies of connection do not lead towards a utopia of universal connectivity (cf. Trotter 2020) but to horrifying experiences of mental, physical, and social dissociation. The curious multiple lives and split identities of these writer characters give the lie to teleological narratives of development, coming of age, or reaching maturity. Instead, they are formed into enigmatic puzzles in which temporal and spatial boundaries are transgressed and in which performances of literary authorship are attenuated in an echoing hall of mirrors.

Max Beerbohm's *Seven Men* (1919)

Max Beerbohm's fictional writers, in the stories collected in *Seven Men* (1919), "Enoch Soames" and "Hilary Maltby and Stephen Braxton", are similarly ghostly presences. The stories are self-consciously retrospective, looking back on the literary culture of the 1890s as an already distant decade. They have been aptly described as "mock-memoirs", imitations of "nonfictions written about authors whose lives were quasi-fictions designed to be written about" (Maner 1991, 139). The first-person narrator of "Enoch Soames", as in the other stories collected in this volume, is a version of Beerbohm himself. Each of the five stories is named after one man, except for the two names that make up the title of "Hilary Maltby and Stephen Braxton"; Max Beerbohm is the seventh man indicated in the volume's title.

At the beginning of "Enoch Soames" (the volume's first story), Beerbohm relishes his memories of the fashionable artists and ideas of the 1890s, Whistler and Sickert, Beardsley, the Bodley Head, the *mot juste* (Beerbohm 1922, 4–6). He remembers being introduced to Enoch Soames, a young writer "unsuccessfully" (6) striving to be as immediately recognisable a figure as Oscar Wilde, who is not named, but whose *Picture of Dorian Gray* clearly influenced Beerbohm's story. Like Dorian Gray, Soames has his portrait painted, and the portrait is said to have "'existed' so much more than he" (21), who is described as a "dim", indistinct "shade" (10, 22). If Soames is a perfect parody of the pretensions of the English aesthetes of the *fin de siècle*, down to the pitch-perfect titles of his two books, *Negations* and *Fungoids*, he is also a version of Beerbohm's own youthful involvement with the *Yellow Book* and what it stood for, and as such is not drawn without sympathy. For this minor artist, who describes himself as a "Catholic Diabolist" (14), posthumous recognition means everything, and must do so because his writings fail to make "a stir" (18) in the present. Beerbohm admires Soames's uncompromising belief in his art, or rather he feels somewhat ashamed of having, for his own part, given in to the lures of journalism and become "a – slight but definite – 'personality'" (22). Here as elsewhere in his work, Beerbohm "mock[s] his own involvement with" journalism and "mass publication" (Maner 1991, 134) At these points in the story, Soames can be interpreted as the narrator's double, or more precisely as the real Beerbohm's fictional other, the artist who pursues his course of seeking eternal fame in spite of present neglect and who refuses the minor "gloss" (Beerbohm 1922, 22) of mere transitory celebrity, as Beerbohm says he did. In 1897, he meets Soames again in a fashionable Soho restaurant, in the company of a foreign-looking gentleman, who turns out to be the Devil. In a variation on the Faustian pact, the Devil grants Soames the ability to travel a hundred years into the future to see how famous he will be in 1997, and what impact he will have had on literature. He expects to be vindicated when he will see, in the Reading Room of the British Museum, "the pages and pages in the catalogue: 'SOAMES, ENOCH' endlessly – endless editions, commentaries, prolegomena, biographies" (27, emphasis original). He is willing to pay the price of eternal damnation for an afternoon of reading what future authors and critics will have to say about him.

With the help of the Devil's "Supernatural Power" (31), Soames is magicked off to 1997. When he returns, he tells Beerbohm of his inevitable disappointment at not finding his name in the *Dictionary of National Biography*, and merely being mentioned in "T. K. Nupton's book" about "Inglish Littracher 1890–1900", published in 1992, as an "immajnari karrakter" in a story by one Max Beerbohm (39). In the future, all spelling except for proper names will be phonetic. The production of literature will be "auganized az a departmnt of publik servis" (ibid.), so writers will be paid by the state and no longer need to worry about posterity. Beerbohm's vision of a uniformed and numbered population is proto-Orwellian also in this respect. Soames is offended that Beerbohm will make him a character in a story. As the Devil pushes him out the door, Soames pleads to Beerbohm to "*try* to make them know that I did exist" (43, emphasis original).

After his disappearance, Soames is quickly and "utterly forgotten before any one, so far as I am aware, noticed that he was no longer hanging around" (45). He is punished for his vanity, but the story's focus lies less on the cautionary tale it tells than on the predicament of the absolute, the autonomous artist having to write and live in the present *as if* he was or could be certain of attaining eternal fame. Beerbohm, who cuts a modest figure in his own story, is at the end of it "furious" when the Devil just passes him by on a Paris street: "To be cut – deliberately cut – by *him!*" (48, emphasis original). Even the Devil's recognition is, after all, recognition.

In "Hilary Maltby and Stephen Braxton" (1919), Beerbohm produces a version of the author ghost story. Maltby and Braxton are authors of short-lived first novels in 1895, plausibly titled (again with Beerbohm's characteristic flair for pseudo-bibliography) *Ariel in Mayfair* and *A Faun on the Cotswolds*. Their second novels are both unsuccessful, and they are quickly forgotten. While their success lasts, however, they are locked in a fierce rivalry for social attention. When Maltby is invited to a party by the Duchess of Hertfordshire at her country estate, he manages to convince her not to invite Braxton as well, whom she similarly admires; but Braxton takes revenge by appearing to Maltby as a ghost, like a manifestation of his bad conscience. Before dinner, Maltby cuts his cheek while shaving in front of a mirror in which he has seen Braxton's reflection. At dinner, he briefly sees the other one "scowling at [him] from behind the opposite diners" (Beerbohm 1922, 76), making him spill soup over his shirt-front. In his bedroom, he finds he has to spend the night lying next to the sleeping ghost of his competitor. On the next day, Braxton's sudden appearance causes Maltby to crash his bicycle into that of Lady Rodfitten, just as Maltby had been dreaming about dedicating to her the sequel to his *Ariel* novel, *Ariel Returns to Mayfair*. The Duchess invites him to church, where he is tripped up by Braxton yet again. When Maltby is finally seated in his pew, Braxton walks down the aisle and then seats himself "slowly and fully" on Maltby, who tells this part of the story in retrospect to Beerbohm when meeting him in Lucca seventeen years later:

> What befell me was not mere ghastly contact with the intangible. It was inclusion, envelopment, eclipse. What Braxton sat down on was not I, but the seat of the pew; and what he sat back against was not my face and chest, but the back of the pew. I didn't realise this at the moment. All I knew was a sudden black blotting-out of all things; an infinite and impenetrable darkness. I dimly conjectured that I was dead. What was wrong with me, in point of fact, was that my eyes, with the rest of me, were inside Braxton. You remember what a great hulking fellow Braxton was. I calculate that as we sat there my eyes were just beneath the roof of his mouth. Horrible! (96)

In this scene, the grotesque physicality of Maltby's being "inside Braxton" underlines their unity as doubles of each other, while adding a touch of body humour to the "William Wilson"-style plot of the story. As critics have noted, "Beerbohm exploits not the horror but the comedy of the *doppelgänger*" (Maner 1991, 135). Maltby tries to flee but is pursued by the ghost of Braxton, until he reaches the railway station and returns to London. He leaves England the next morning after having burnt the manuscript to the *Ariel* sequel. At the story's ending, he reveals to Beerbohm that he is now married to an Italian aristocrat, having swapped his snobbish admiration for the English aristocracy (certainly a target of Beerbohm's humour here) for Italy, telling Beerbohm that his wife is "a lineal descendant [...] of the Emperor Hadrian" (Beerbohm 1922, 104).[135]

Maltby's marriage to an Italian Contessa – his way of raising himself above the vulgar crowd – is the opposite of bourgeois striving for recognition by means of work and merit, the opposite also of striving for artistic recognition. This is a perfect symbolic expression of Beerbohm's shift away from the beginnings of a literary career, from a narrative of formation, to a story of endings and of arrested development. Beerbohm's stories, written during and shortly after the Great War, already display the results of a radical conceptual and aesthetic change in fictions of authorship. We have seen this shift prepared in some of James's stories and in Kipling's, where Charlie Mears gives up his literary ambitions at the end, and Shaynor is merely a conduit for an external creative force. These, like Beerbohm's "Enoch Soames", are stories that "succeed [...] by fictionalising failure" (Jullien 2020, 856). "Failure", as Beerbohm's narrator muses in that story, "has always a certain dignity" (Beerbohm 1922, 22).

The supernatural element in these gothic tales of authorship supports the impression that late nineteenth- and early twentieth-century fiction about writers and literature increasingly seeks to transcend or subvert the dominant realist paradigm in favour of the fantastic. Moreover, following the model of James's "The Private Life", later modernist stories about authorial *doppelgängers* are frequently cast in a comic or satirical mode. In Aldous Huxley's "The Farcical History of Richard Greenow" (1920), for example, a writer's body is inhabited by two personalities, one male and one female; the female *persona* is "an increasingly aggressive female novelist and war propagandist named Pearl Bellairs" (Sheets 1993, 197).[136]

The irruption of the fantastic into these author fictions can, on the one hand, be attributed to a more general trend towards the supernatural in late Victorian literature (the gothic revival that also brings forth *The Picture of Dorian Gray, Dracula, The Beetle,* and *The Strange Case,* among many others). On the other hand, it can be read as an indication that the mimetic representation of the topic of authorship has reached its limit. As the bourgeois value system and ideas of personal development come under intense pressure in the later nineteenth century, the gener-

---

135 A later story by Beerbohm, "Felix Argallo and Walter Ledgett" (1927) was interpolated into new editions of the book from 1950 onwards, which was then re-titled *Seven Men and Two Others*. This is another story about a pair of authors, which I cannot discuss here for reasons of space (but see Maner 1991 for the view that they are again "copies of one another", 138). Cf. also Bugliani 2022.
136 See ch. 10 for a more detailed discussion of comic treatments of literary authorship in the interwar years.

ic resources of the *bildungsroman* have been exhausted. Literary authorship is now less amenable to being narrated as a story of individual growth and accommodation of self to society. As the rise of the *künstlerroman* shows, the literary focus shifts towards the isolated artist in conflict with society, as in *Hunger*, or the group of artists demoralised by the commercialisation of literature, as in *New Grub Street*. The "Victorian compromise" (Chesterton 1946, 21) apparently is no longer a convincing social, economic, and literary model for understanding and conceptualising authorship. James's tales, and to some extent Kipling's as well, show what can still be done with the residual forms of these genres. They represent an atrophied form of the author's narrative: condensed into a short story instead of a novel, reduced to a moment in time or a momentary crisis. They stage the breakdown of the classical model of the *bildungsroman* in sometimes realistic, sometimes fantastic variations. Authors' artistic or commercial achievements and their personal lives drift apart, and these stories address the resulting chasm that opens up between life and art.

The *doppelgänger* stories of James and Beerbohm, in their uncanny though humorous exploitation of a conventional gothic motif, radicalise the "doubleness" of nineteenth-century literary authorship that was seen to inhere in "the ambiguous commerce of making public a private act of feeling" (Braudy 1997, 484), while also registering an increasing unease with the demands of artistic originality at a time when mass authorship stifled innovation and encouraged mass-produced imitations of the kind that Beerbohm invents in *Seven Men*. They begin as originals but end as copies. For James, and in a different way for Kipling, these stories harbour a sense of insecurity and anxiety about their authors' status as artists and the sources of their creativity. Beerbohm, however, from the perspective of a self-consciously 'lesser' writer, relishes his talents as an imitator and parodist of other authors' styles in his more explicitly metaliterary stories. With a dominant focus on works that fail to be written or that remain unpublished, on 'promising' authors who give up, go mad, or die, and on style as a resource not of originality but of endless imitability, we have finally entered the modernist paradigm of author fiction.

Part III Modernist Author Fictions

> I am a writing machine.
> – Henry Miller

9 The Ambivalence of Promise in Arthur Machen, E. M. Forster, and Henry Green

Henry James's story "The Middle Years" (1893) introduces a new paradigm into narratives of authorship. Like many of the other tales by James, discussed in the previous chapter, it circles around the topic of an author's reputation, during his life and beyond; but it also introduces a new angle, a new variation on that topic. Though "The Middle Years" repeats the constellation of the older author and the young male admirer, there is a decisive formal difference: Dencombe, the author character, is not observed from the outside but is himself the central reflector figure whose consciousness is being represented. Indeed, his enjoyment of observing others from a distance and imagining stories for them is shown to be a key element of his literary creativity. Dencombe has just published a new novel in one volume, called (like James's own unfinished autobiography) *The Middle Years*, but his pleasure in receiving an early copy of the book is reduced by the awareness that it may be his last completed work. Though his age is never stated, he is most likely himself in or beyond "the middle years", and he is severely ill. Convalescing in Bournemouth, he muses that, for him, "[t]he infinite of life had gone" (James 1999, 2: 103). He feels "the sense of ebbing time, of shrinking opportunity" (105). Even worse, he feels that he has let himself down in his writing life, that he has not fulfilled his promise: "He had not done all that he should ever do, and yet he had not done what he wanted" (105). He longs for "an extension", a reprieve (106). When he meets Doctor Hugh, his young admirer, Dencombe's regrets for his unlived life are gradually replaced by a new hope for a continuation. In nursing him, Doctor Hugh even sacrifices the prospect of inheriting the wealth of the Countess who has hired him to stay with her at Bournemouth.

There is more than a hint of homoeroticism in the relationship between Hugh and Dencombe. Dencombe's opinions of the Countess and her female companion, Miss Vernham, are coloured by misogyny, and the narrator towards the end describes Hugh's voice as having "the ring of a marriage-bell" (123). But it is too late: Dencombe's illness proves fatal. As a writer and as a man, he has only the one lifetime, "his first and only chance" (123). On his deathbed, he utters his artistic creed, lines that are among the best-known quotations from Henry James: "We work in the dark – we do what we can – we give what we have. Our doubt is our passion and our passion is our task. The rest is the madness of art" (123). These lines recall the Victorian 'gospel of work', mixed with the aestheticists' gospel of art, but they also echo – deliberately or not – verses spoken by Romney in Barrett Browning's *Aurora Leigh:* "[...] let us be content, in work / To do the thing we can, and not presume / To fret because it's little" (8: 732–734). Dencombe's famous lines are perhaps less to be read as an authorial statement or creed by James himself than as a performance by Dencombe, who is trying to justify his life's achievement, to assuage his sense of failure, and to impress – or at least not disappoint – young Doctor Hugh (whose name may connote that he is, possibly, Dencombe's ideal 'you').[137] As a statement of what constitutes an artist's life it does not, after all, amount to much more than a curious blend of aestheticist clichés ("passion", "madness of art") and the Victorian work ethic ("do what we can", "task"). Reading the story closely, one finds that these phrases do not fully match Dencombe's actual artistic practice: earlier, the narrator had asserted that in fact Dencombe's key virtue was nothing like "madness" or "passion" at all but mere "diligence" (James 1999, 2: 106).

Dencombe, the sick and dying author who has given his life for his art and yet failed to fulfil his promise, at least according to his own standards, in some respects anticipates by almost twenty years another equally famous and equally middle-aged fictional author. Like Dencombe, Gustav von Aschenbach in Thomas Mann's *Death in Venice* (1912) is a widower who likes to observe other travellers on holiday and, during his trip to Venice, singles out a young male. Yet the object of his homoerotic desire is much younger than in James's story, and death comes to him after a short illness that is symbolically linked to his infatuation with Tadzio. Both tales share the focus on an older male writer and his death, made even more prominent in the title of Mann's novella. Something, apparently, has changed from the mid-nineteenth to the late nineteenth and early twentieth century, from the Middle Years to the moment of Death, something more than merely a new fashion for 'decadence' around 1900. In contrast to the novel of literary apprenticeship around 1850, literature is now apparently less interested in the self-fashioning of a young author but in the waning of an older author's powers. Possibly, as Robert Weimann opines, this is the way in which literary writing can represent "the erosion of representativeness itself", in the "loss of social integration and bourgeois respectability" of the artist figure (1988, 439).

James's story already contains an analysis *in nuce* of this shift of focus from the beginning of a literary career to its end. For the profession of authorship, the language of development has now proven less and less appropriate. The discourse of formation, of *Bildung* that we have seen at work in the literary *bildungsroman* of the mid-nineteenth century and its subsequent variations has reached a plateau and has come to feel 'done'. By the 1890s, it has exhausted its potential. For Dencombe, art and life are in conflict; thus, to describe the one in terms of the other, as developing in tandem with each other, has become an impossibility:

---

[137] This pun is also recognised, although interpreted differently, by Oates 1996, 262.

"His development had been abnormally slow, almost grotesquely gradual. He had been hindered and retarded by experience, and for long periods had only groped his way. It had taken too much of his life to produce too little of his art" (James 1999, 2: 106). Life and literature are at loggerheads: we have reached the era of stunted growth, of arrested development, of the "enemies of promise" (Connolly 2008 [1938]). There are many modernist author characters who share the merciless self-analysis of James's Dencombe: "Only to-day, at last, had he begun to *see*, so that what he had hitherto done was a movement without a direction. He had ripened too late and was so clumsily constituted that he had to teach himself by mistakes" (James 1999, 2: 116, emphasis original). Stagnation and decline are more likely to be represented in modernist author narratives than any sense of growth or progress. The end is not experienced as a culmination but as a disappointment: as the moment when "Comes the blind *Fury* with th'abhorred shears, / And slits the thin-spun life" (Milton, *Lycidas* ll. 75–76, in Milton 1957, 122).

Too early or too late, the artist is no longer synchronous with his time; he also, often, finds himself in the wrong place. Joyce's Dublin; Mann's Lübeck; Hamsun's Kristiania; Machen's London, Forster's Sawston – the list could be continued almost *ad infinitum.* Temporal and spatial dislocation, movement without direction: thus also Stephen Dedalus, possibly the most roundly 'developed' artist character in the modernist *künstlerroman* and chief inheritor of the decadent aesthetic attitude, proud advocate of a pseudo-religion of art, escapes provincial Ireland at the end of *A Portrait of the Artist as a Young Man* (1916) – only to return a few years later, in *Ulysses* (1922), with his wings clipped, his intellectual and artistic ambitions humbled, caught up in a similar state of paralysis as the characters in Joyce's *Dubliners* (1914). The only direction of his movement has been circular, in Henry James's words "hindered and retarded by experience" (James 1999, 2: 106).[138] Experience, a key term of the discourse of formation, of *Bildung*, both in the sense of *Erfahrung* and *Erlebnis*, has lost its innocence. It is now no longer a factor that enables writers to pursue authorship as a profession but a set of clogs that slows their progress and halts their development. A number of English novels of the early twentieth century explore this situation further. In some cases, the budding artist is hamstrung by a symbolic illness or physical disability: lameness in *The*

---

138 Unless we take Stephen to be the author of *Ulysses* and *Ulysses* to be his metafictional *künstlerroman* (as proposed by McBride 2001), the only literary composition we see him engage in is the "Parable of the Plums" in ch. 7 (Joyce 1987, 119–123) – a story that would not look out of place in *Dubliners* and that confuses his listeners. His relationship with Bloom may indicate an end to Stephen's self-centredness and creative impotence, but the promise of a great work remains unrealised unless we take *Ulysses* to be that work. – Thanks to Georgina Nugent for sharing her thoughts on the "Parable of the Plums" with me.

Longest Journey (1907), a club foot in *Of Human Bondage* (1915), tuberculosis in *The Magic Mountain* (1924), blindness in *Blindness* (1926).

The modernist focus thus comes to be placed on the "enemies of promise", as in the title of Cyril Connolly's critical study and memoir of 1938. Connolly has often been condemned, not only by feminists, for the statement "that there is no more sombre enemy of good art than the pram in the hall" (Connolly 2008, 116), but his critique of the enabling and disabling conditions of literature goes much further. Connolly identifies "health, sex, and money" as "sources of creative happiness" (135), and their lack as conditions of discontent and failure. This is in stark contrast to the decadent and also the Jamesian models of authorship, with their emphasis on the artist's suffering, weakness, and isolation. In this respect, Connolly's study signals an anti-modernist stance. Yet Connolly, at least implicitly, shares a sense that the conventional form of the novel of development has reached an impasse, and that the promise of youth is no longer a promising theme for literature: "Whom the gods wish to destroy they first call promising" is a famous sentence from his book (109); another is "promise is the capacity for letting people down" (260). Connolly likewise has his doubts about ideas and concepts like "talent" and the Aristotelian idea of *entelecheia:* "'If it's in you it's bound to come out' is a wish-fulfilment. More often it stays in and goes bad" (116).

There were earlier signs that the literary *bildungsroman* in its traditional form had exhausted its possibilities. For example, consider the hero of Arnold Bennett's first novel, *A Man from the North* (1898), written in the mid-1890s. Richard Larch is the usual young man coming to London from the North with literary ambitions that are soon frustrated. A "study of drab, unremarkable lives" (Lucas 1974, 19), of sexual frustration and the psychology of the suburbs, the novel is written in the mode of Gissing, or even of Harold Biffen, the extreme naturalist in Gissing's *New Grub Street.* The hero's "downward curve from would-be writer to ex-non-writer" (ibid., 22) ends with his giving up on the idea of literature as his vocation. Instead of the model of author formation established in the *bildungsroman*, the "novel about not writing a novel" (Gross 1973, 233) begins to take precedence in the literary field. In *The Truth about an Author,* a bold autobiography published anonymously in 1898, Bennett further deconstructed any residual romantic ideas that late nineteenth-century readers might still have been entertaining about authorship (cf. ibid., 234).

Arthur Machen's *The Hill of Dreams* (1904)

One of the least known and yet most sustained indications of this exhaustion of the trope of the budding author was written at the height of literary 'decadence', in the

1890s. Arthur Machen wrote his first novel *The Hill of Dreams* between 1896 and 1897, but it was only published for the first time in serial form in 1904 and then as a book in 1907. Machen is now known mainly for his 'weird' tales of horror, like "The Great God Pan" (1894). Yet *The Hill of Dreams*, though written in a highly stylised prose redolent of 1890s aestheticism, offers a fascinating combination of realistic and fantastic elements. It may well be one of the most radical examples of the (anti-)*künstlerroman* in English and as such deserves to be better known. At the outset, it tells a story in the tradition of the novel of formation, based on Machen's own early life: Lucian Taylor, a rector's son in rural Wales, develops literary aspirations. He buys a copy of De Quincey's *Confessions of an English Opium-Eater* and starts writing verse; but in his "pathetic ignorance of the trade" he has only the vaguest of ideas how to proceed with "the career of literature" (Machen 2019, 30). From book reviews and publishers' catalogues, he learns that the books that sell are works of "[h]armless amusement" (33) such as "sporting novels" (32), and that the wider world does not care for literary art. At the age of twenty-three, he sends a manuscript to a publisher and receives a rejection; yet not much later he finds out that a substantial part of his work has been stolen and inserted into somebody else's published novel. He feels that it is fruitless to do anything against this blatant plagiarism, since he considers his work as too "'degenerate', *decadent*" (43, emphasis original) for the popular fiction market. A small inheritance enables him to move to London to pursue a career as a writer.

Lucian is an artist who cuts himself off from society. He rebels against "the plain English view", traced back to Thackeray's *Pendennis*, that "novel-writing" was "an agreeable way of making money, a useful appendage to the cultivation of dukes" (58). His ambition is to pursue art, not money. What the novel describes as his "fury of literature" (58) is almost a kind of disability, isolating him from other people and enforcing long periods of solitude and desolation in a London garret. His "nights of toil" are "holy" to him (49). He has neo-Pagan mystical experiences in which his imagination, even his sense of self and of bodily and spatial boundaries, are overwhelmed by sensuous impressions, to the extent that these experiences appear more real to him than actual reality. He keeps returning to a traumatic but formative, occult childhood experience that occurred in the Roman ruins of his hometown, Caermaen, which blends a sense of "mad panic terror" and "strange exultation" (24). This is the ur-scene of his life as a writer. He is so deeply involved in these fantasies that he loses interest in a real girl from his village, Annie, preferring to idealise her into a symbol of femininity and engaging in ritual acts of self-torture.

Writing is described in *The Hill of Dreams* in great detail as a physical and intensely personal activity. At one point, Lucian "copie[s] and recopie[s]" a "manuscript nine times" before writing it out on vellum, making his own books and his own ink and illuminating his own manuscript like a medieval "monk in the scriptorium" (2019, 60). His own handwriting, we learn, is otherwise "both ugly and illegible" (61). When he inflicts pain on himself by lying on a bed of thorns, he likewise "view[s] the marks" on his skin "with pride" (63), as if they were a kind of writing on the body (cf. Boyiopoulos 2017). He is thus both monk and martyr. Yet he has left behind any conventional practices of modern-day Christianity, which he despises as mere pretence and hypocrisy.

For Lucian, both writing and self-inflicted pain are ways of escaping from the limitations of ordinary reality. From "books of modern occultism" he has learned that "[t]he adept [...] could annihilate the world around him and pass into another sphere" (Machen 2019, 72). His visions and daydreams become increasingly elaborate. The novel's *pièce de résistance* arrives when Lucian's imagination returns the ancient Roman city of Isca Silurum to vibrant and colourful life (75–89). These pages, which amount almost to a historical novel in miniature, would possibly have reminded contemporaries of Pater's Roman novel *Marius the Epicurean* (1885), while Lucian's aesthetic and poetic ideas recall those expressed by Pater in the conclusion to his *Renaissance* (1873). Like Pater, Lucian "saw the true gold into which the beggarly matter of existence may be transmuted by spagyric art; a succession of delicious moments, all the rare flavours of life concentrated, purged of their lees, and preserved in a beautiful vessel" (81). Lucian's objective in all this is decidedly anti-modern: "he was gradually levelling to the dust the squalid kraals of modern times, and rebuilding the splendid and golden city of Siluria" (75), a town that exists principally for his own "delight" (75). He revels in his synaesthetic sensory experiences; like Jean des Esseintes of Huysmans's *À rebours* (*Against Nature*, 1884), he "continually searched for new and exquisite experiences" (78). Literature, for him, is part of this "sensuous art" (83), "independent of thought" (84) and clearly to be kept separate from "ethics" (85): "the sensuous art of causing exquisite impressions by means of words" is the aim (84).[139]

Machen here makes Lucian a mouthpiece for a highly typical 1890s aesthetic credo. But he shows how this leads his protagonist further and further into isolation. Lucian ceases to believe in "the actual, material life" (91) around him, and he loses himself in his dreams and fantastic visions of a different life, a higher "truth" (91) that lies beyond the senses, in his mind only. He studies the works of Poe, De Quincey, Coleridge, Hawthorne, and other writers to refine his own style. He also suffers torments of insecurity about his art, which he regards as "proof of his vocation" (108). Not knowing anybody in London, his life becomes increasingly desolate. His only refuge "from that dreary contemplation of the white paper and the

---

[139] On Machen and Pater, see Villa 1988.

idle pen" (108) are some aimless walks around Bloomsbury during the day, and occasional excursions further North or West into the London suburbs. He despises the ugliness of the modern city, but he also invests it with occult power: "It was a town as great as Babylon, terrible as Rome, marvellous as Lost Atlantis [...] All London was one grey temple of an awful rite [...]; the rocky avenues became the camp and fortalice of some half-human, malignant race" (115–116).[140]

As these passages show, Lucian increasingly loses control over his fantasies, which at this point, in a moment of lucidity, he is still aware are delusions: "He knew that he deluded himself with imagination" (116). He feels cut off from the rest of humanity, comparing himself to Keats in his isolation (117): the artist who is despised or, worse, unacknowledged by society.[141] After his father dies, he also senses that he no longer has a home in the country to return to. He is increasingly desperate about his future, feeling a strong sense that he is not gifted enough to ever fulfil his lofty ideals about literature – like James's Dencombe, but in a far more extreme manner, he deplores the "vast gulf that yawned between the conception and the work" (134–135), and he lives through "agonising nights when the pen seemed an awkward and outlandish instrument" (145). His sense of desolation and alienation, expressed repeatedly throughout the last chapters of the novel, is complete and unbreakable.

Lucian seems to reach a turning point when he manages to finish and publish a "little tale", which even becomes "a moderate success" (152). Yet it is too late: slowly but surely, his phantasms have overwhelmed the vestiges of reason, and he descends into madness. His perceptions of the city turn increasingly shrill (cf. 141–142). He is no longer able to tell what is real and what is imagined: "Truth and the dream were so mingled that now he could not divide one from the other" (153). He is overwhelmed by a phantasmagoria centred around a female figure that he calls the Amber Venus and with whom he has half-willing, half-unwilling sexual intercourse during a witches' sabbath. Following this, he blacks out: "And then a vast silence overwhelmed him" (155).

Up to this point, the novel has closely followed Lucian's consciousness. Now, a surprise ending reveals that Lucian is dead, and the narrative is now focalised through an unnamed woman (like the Amber Venus, her hair is described as "bronze", 155) and a man named Joe, who discover Lucian's body, still seated at his desk. From their conversation, the reader learns that Lucian has been taking a drug, most likely opium, from a now "empty bottle of dark blue glass" (156).

---

140 The depiction of London is by far the most frequently covered aspect in critical discussions of *The Hill of Dreams*; see Caleb 2010, Wargen 2010, Boyiopoulos 2013, Mantrant 2013, Dobson 2019.
141 On Keats, see also Kipling's "'Wireless'", discussed in the previous chapter. Percy Shelley plays a similar role for Rickie in *The Longest Journey*.

He has been writing a book "for the last six months", as the red-headed woman informs Joe, but the manuscript is "all covered with illegible hopeless scribblings" (156). He has left everything he owns to her, but his manuscript will never be turned into a published book. Lucian Taylor has tortured himself in vain, while dreaming, drugging, and writing himself into insanity.

As a *künstlerroman*, *The Hill of Dreams* is so different from Gissing's *New Grub Street*, with which it shares its Bloomsbury setting, that it is difficult to fathom that it was written a mere five years later. Underneath its highly polished linguistic surface, it develops the gothic realism of Stevenson, Wilde, and Kipling into a weird, supernatural, gaslit fantasy while advancing to psychological and symbolic complexities that prefigure the writings of Forster and Lawrence. It combines the atmosphere of 1890s decadence with a psychological study of a writer's mind delving ever deeper into the occult. Moreover, it combines virtuoso performances of a highly sensuous style and some programmatic poetological passages with a cautionary tale of the "fury of literature" (58) that replaces ideas of progression, self-formation, and growth with ideas of degeneration, decadence, and decline. Lucian's early purchase of De Quincey's *Confessions* foreshadows his own addiction to opium, and the cultivation of his lurid imagination to the point of self-torture and an ascetic abnegation of the body leads to loss of reality and loss of self in a grotesque maelstrom of occult fantasies. The novel remains somewhat ambivalent about these fantasies, which it describes in a highly sensuous, often erotic and, for a Victorian audience, morally dubious manner. Yet Machen's close association of writing with physical pain and transgressive, antisocial fantasies marks an end point of an entire literary tradition, in many ways far more radical in its view of art as opposed to society's values than *New Grub Street*. In its "coupling [of] the act of fictional composition with the progressive decomposition of reality" (Camara 2014, 12), it is a morbid, mordant parody of the tradition of the literary *bildungsroman*, which it directly invokes in alluding to Thackeray's *Pendennis* as well as in its hero's spatial movement from the provinces to London.

In his 1923 introduction to the novel, Machen describes *The Hill of Dreams* as "a picaresque of the mind" (522) and "a *Robinson Crusoe* of the soul" (523) that takes place in London instead of on a desert island. He does not mention the fact that his 'Robinson' character does not survive his isolation; also, the term 'picaresque', while encapsulating the hero's anti-social stance, would imply his survival in the face of numerous adventures and difficulties. There is, however, no rescue for Lucian Taylor, who dies ignominiously in a London garret. In its persistent positioning of the isolated artist against society, *The Hill of Dreams* is an extreme example of the anti-*künstlerroman* in the nineteenth century – more extreme, even, than Melville's *Pierre*. Wanting to become a writer and pursuing art over life is Lucian's death sentence. Only at the very end is it made clear that *The Hill of Dreams* is not only an anti-*bildungsroman* but also a descant on the aesthetic movement. It is not a pure celebration of literary decadence but an investigation into its values, its limitations and deceptions. As Lucian follows in the footsteps of Pater and Wilde, he gives up all contact with reality for completely imaginary sensuous experiences, losing himself in feverish fantasies. His death might thus also be read as a symbolic "exploration" of the potentially lethal consequences of 'art for art's sake',[142] and as a signal that Machen was already striving beyond the aesthetics of *fin de siècle* decadence. In doing so, he created one of the best horror stories on the topic of literary authorship.[143]

E. M. Forster's *The Longest Journey* (1907)

Like Machen's *The Hill of Dreams*, with which it shares the date of publication in book form and a number of neo-Pagan themes, E. M. Forster's second novel, *The Longest Journey* (1907), explores how literary talent "stays in and goes bad" (Connolly 2008, 116). In the 1930s, Cyril Connolly singled out Forster as one of the "true innovators" in the field of literature, stating that "[n]ovels like *The Longest Journey* [...] established a point of view, a technique, and an attitude to the reader that were to be followed for the next thirty years by the psychological novelists" (2008, 27). While this novel now no longer commands the same attention among Forster's writings, and Forster himself is widely regarded as rather a transitional author than an innovator (Schneider 2017, 175), *The Longest Journey*'s blend of realism and symbolism is an important step in the development of the 'author novel' in the early twentieth century.[144] The novel follows its protagonist, Frederick Elliot, commonly known as 'Rickie', from his student days at Cambridge to his early death in a train accident. The orphaned Rickie, soon to come into his own money, is intent on choosing writing as his profession, albeit not the kind of writing that makes money (he mentions Marie Corelli in this context). His ambition is to pro-

---

142 "[L]iterature is always an exploration", as Machen writes in his 1923 introduction to *The Hill of Dreams* (Machen 2019, 525). It is certainly suggestive, although speculative, to consider a link between this implicit critique of aestheticism in Machen's novel and Wilde's trial and imprisonment, which occurred while Machen was conceiving and writing *The Hill of Dreams*.
143 For more on authorship horror, → ch. 15.
144 For the view that *The Longest Journey* attempts a "circumvention of the modern", see May 1996, 235. May also evaluates this novel as "one of the most purely transitional documents of its time" (236), a "conflicted and partial passage to modernism" (251), and a "self-interfering" text (251) that wavers undecidably between "the emancipatory myth of Edwardian psychic and natural unity" and an "ironist intuition of fragmentation" (236).

duce "art", which he contrasts with "drudgery". In this model, the idea of a literary apprenticeship is foreign to him, since "the artist is not a bricklayer at all, but a horseman, whose business it is to catch Pegasus at once, not to practice for him by mounting tamer colts" (Forster 2006, 15). Physically weak, Rickie likes to read and write stories, and is endowed with a rich and susceptible imagination; but he is also prone to periods of emotional instability and insecurity. Lame in one leg, he lacks the energy that would make him "acute and heroic" enough to be able to overcome the limitations of his world, not to "experience" merely but to "be an experience" (61). He writes stories based on the "idea of getting into touch with Nature" (71), involving mythological creatures like "Fauns" and a "Dryad" (71), and scenarios of metamorphic transformation. He is encouraged to submit his stories to magazines, and later to try a collection in book form under the title *Pan Pipes*, but nothing comes of this during his lifetime.

Rickie's pursuit of mystical experiences of a more profound reality behind the veil of everyday suburban life strikingly resembles Lucian's in *The Hill of Dreams*, also in its musicality: "He stood at the springs of creation and heard the primeval monotony" (Forster 2006, 40). But in Forster the veil is not torn to reveal unspeakable horrors beneath. Rickie's experiences are, for the most part, less overwhelming than Lucian's. They are culturally mediated by a blend of Greek, Christian, and Wagnerian mythologies, and despite his pursuit of reality they remain filtered by the philosophical idealism and metaphysics that he imbibed as a student at Cambridge. Lucian, unlike Rickie, has no need to "actually believe[]" in the reality of the Faun that attacks him in the forest (Forster 2006, 71). For Rickie, such belief in the reality of "Fauns" (71) is not only culturally mediated, and thus already a form of self-conscious pretence, but it is also soon suppressed by the conventions of modern bourgeois life and of changing literary tastes. Rickie turns away from his early enthusiasm for nineties-style decadence, as is illustrated by the brief summary of his short story "The Bay of the Fifteen Islets", a gothic story that could have been written by Machen (60). He has, as he tells his future wife Agnes Pembroke, "changed those follies for others" (71) – most notably, for an interest in "people who are well-made and beautiful" (69). Such 'healthy' masculine heroism as Rickie admires is represented first by Agnes's lover Gerald Dawes and later by Rickie's half-brother Stephen Wonham.

The editor of the *Holborn* magazine offers him the perennial advice to "[s]ee life [...] and then send us another story" (144), which leaves Rickie confused: "'But what does he *mean*?' Rickie was saying. 'What does he *mean* by life?" (152, emphasis original). In his view, he has already gone past the stage of finding experience useful:

> He loved, he was loved, he had seen death and other things; but the heart of all things was hidden. There was a password and he could not learn it, nor could the kind editor of the *Holborn* teach him. He sighed, and then sighed more piteously. For had he not known the password once – known it and forgotten it already? (144)

Experience has nothing to offer him, as the novel continues, other than disappointment. Instead of unlocking "the heart of all things", experience moves Rickie further away from genuine knowledge. Reality and truth remain as mysterious, as unknowable as the cow in the famous metaphysical discussion that opens the novel ("The cow is there" [3]). The only time that an experience of supernatural "horror" is allowed to pierce the bourgeois carapace of normality is when Rickie and Agnes see the menacing "two figures [...] of enormous size" watching them from the Cadover Rings (132); this passage also foreshadows Rickie's fatal accident when the sound of an approaching train makes Agnes pull him away from the scene (ibid.).

Instead of rising to be an artist, Rickie is bogged down in conventions and conformity. His marriage to Agnes quickly cools his love for her. She "had always mistrusted the little stories", the narrator tells us: "How could Rickie, or anyone, make a living by pretending that Greek gods were alive, or that young ladies could vanish into trees?" (151). For Rickie, having attained "[t]he crown of life" (167) as a husband, his dream of a "spiritual union" (167) remains unfulfilled. Their child, a daughter, dies soon after birth. Working as a schoolmaster, he feels more and more "that the cow was not really there", that he lives under a "cloud of unreality" (176), oppressed by his bourgeois existence without ever "an influx of interest" or "of passion" (190). Switching abruptly to the present tense, the narrator comments: "Henceforward he deteriorates. [...] He has lost the work that he loved, his friends, and his child. He remained conscientious and decent, but the spiritual part of him proceeded towards ruin" (193). The change to present, perfect, and back to past tense possibly serves to emphasise that this is the narrator's viewpoint, not Rickie's own, introducing a greater distance to the character than before and already preparing for Rickie's exit from the novel.

Out of this spiritual ruin, Rickie is lifted briefly when he acknowledges his half-brother Stephen and decides to support and follow him. Stephen is revealed to be a child of Rickie's mother, the result of "one brief embrace" but also, more symbolically, "the child of poetry and rebellion", invested with "a cloudless spirit" (242). Stephen, uneducated and prone to drink, with no respect for conventional morality or bourgeois (i.e., suburban middle-class) values, appears to Rickie like a genuine revival of "the candour of the Greek" (267), a representative of a Dionysian, ecstatic life force: "Stephen was a hero. He was a law to himself, and rightly. He was great enough to despise our small moralities. He was attaining love" (279). Yet Rickie's hero-worship is again disappointed when Stephen breaks his promise not to drink again. Rickie can barely save his intoxicated half-brother from being run over by a train near the Rings, but in doing so he is himself severely injured and dies soon after.

In the eyes of his aunt, the eccentric Mrs Failing, Rickie is "one who has failed in all he undertook" (282). Yet, in the final chapter, we learn that Rickie's brother-in-law Herbert and his half-brother Stephen come to an agreement about publishing Rickie's book, *Pan Pipes*. Stephen is now in possession of the Cadover estate, and he has a wife and a daughter who shares Rickie's and Stephen's mother's name, but he is otherwise unchanged. Rickie's fall and Stephen's rise provide a new pattern that moves *The Longest Journey* away from a conventional novel of formation. At the end, Rickie's literary creations turn out to be far less important than his singular act of self-sacrifice in saving Stephen's life. The turn from Rickie to Stephen is one from literature to life, from weakness to strength, from unheroic failure to heroic victory, from cloudy idealism to "cloudless" realism (242) – or in other words from the metaphysical "night in which [...] all cows are black" (Hegel 2018, 10) to the cow in all its stark, brute, undeniable, unmetaphysical, and ultimately unfathomable reality.

If Forster has found a way of moving from art to life, this affirmative closure to *The Longest Journey* comes at the cost of Rickie's death and his displacement by Stephen. Whereas Rickie struggles to find his place in life and art, Stephen, it seems, arrives fully formed and is in no need of further education or study, in no need even of reflection or of getting 'in touch with Nature' – he *is* Nature. Stephen stands outside of conventional society, and yet, by means of his fatherhood, he is the conduit through which society, even humanity, will be continued into the future: "He was alive and had created life. By whose authority? Though he could not phrase it, he believed that he guided the future of our race, and that, century after century, his thoughts and his passions would triumph in England" (Forster 2006, 289). As passages like this show, *The Longest Journey* in its symbolic structure and some of its ideas anticipates the novels of D. H. Lawrence. Rickie's literature is sterile, a symbol of infirmity like his lameness, whereas Stephen is complete and fertile – he can walk the earth without the need of writing as a prosthesis, although one might argue that his character's function in the novel depends on Rickie's disability as a "narrative prosthesis" (Mitchell/Snyder 2001), a flaw that he can be seen to fix. Stephen, as Forster presents him, does not require any form of mediation to access reality, nor any external authority to change it. The novel's shift of focus from the tragic story of the weak Rickie Elliot to the story of Rickie's heroic, virile counterpart is at the same time a shift in genre, from a literary (anti-)*bildungsroman* to a novel of generations and of spiritual, sexual, and moral renewal.

Its visibly disabled author character has to die so that something new, someone new and 'better' can be born.[145]

Henry Green's *Blindness* (1926)

Forster's and others' hopes for this new 'golden generation' were of course shattered in the First World War, which mercilessly culled Britain's youth in the mud of Flanders Fields. After the War, the surviving younger generation developed a new sense of cultural and literary 'decadence' and disillusionment, now mainly associated with concepts and groups such as the 'Bright Young People', the 'Jazz Age', the 'Bloomsberries', and the 'Lost Generation' (Melchiori 1956, Green 1976, Taylor 2008). Many of their novels and stories that include authors as characters are pervaded by a profound scepticism and a satirical bitterness towards literature as a profession, which is often depicted in a cynical light – early and most famously in Aldous Huxley's *Crome Yellow* (1921), *Those Barren Leaves* (1925), and *Point Counter Point* (1928), in Evelyn Waugh's *Vile Bodies* (1930) and Anthony Powell's *What's Become of Waring* (1939), among others, some of which are to be discussed in the next chapter. The youth of these authors was certainly a selling point in itself; Marius Hentea explains that in the 1920s "publishers targeted youth, advertisements sold it and a whole series of efforts encouraged the writing of young authors" (2014, 13–14). To 'make it new', in Pound's famous phrase, at this time often meant to start young. Evelyn Waugh, in 1920, diagnosed the media as dominated by the young, indeed "[t]he very young" (qtd. in Hentea 2014, 14).

Henry Green, at twenty-one, was certainly very young when his first novel *Blindness* was published in 1926. This *künstlerroman* contains the most sustained response of the young, postwar generation to the tradition of the literary *bildungsroman*. Green was a modernist experimenter but also an inheritor of 1890s aestheticism (Melchiori 1956, 191, 199). *Blindness*, however, reads like a direct response to Forster's *The Longest Journey*. Like Forster's novel, it has a tripartite structure, in this case based on developmental stages: "Caterpillar", "Chrysalis", "Butterfly", but like Forster's naming of the parts "Cambridge", "Sawston", and "Wiltshire", these do not actually reveal much about the protagonist's development. The first chapter presents the diary of seventeen-year-old John Haye, a pupil at 'Noat' (standing in for Eton) who is interested in the arts, is full of youthful egotism and enthusiasm,

---

[145] On *The Longest Journey* as *bildungsroman*, see also Jeffers 1988 and Wojtas 2010; on fantasy as Forster's subversion of the schematic surface of its plot, see Miracky 2002–2003. On the novel's connections to contemporary genetic theory, see Newman 2016.

and dreams of a literary career: "What fun it would be if I could write! I see myself as the English Anatole France, a vista of glory ... superb!" (Green 2008, 351) The entries read like a credible diary of a clever, somewhat immature, artistic Etonian, and they may well have been based on actual diaries Green may have kept as a schoolboy (though these did not survive; see Hentea 2012). Towards the end of the diary chapter, John reads Dostoevsky and is bowled over by the sheer power of *Crime and Punishment:* "What a force books are! This is like dynamite" (Green 2008, 364). This entry concludes his journal; on the next page, a letter from one of his fellow pupils to another friend reports that John has had a terrible accident and has lost his eyesight. The "dynamite" comparison that ends the journal foreshadows the violence of the shattered train window that blinds John. Though not directly linked to the Great War, it associates him with the many war veterans who had suffered life-changing injuries.

That accident cruelly curtails John's development. He cannot go to Oxford now. John's parents having both died, he is nursed by his stepmother, who has no literary inclinations or taste and does not understand either Dostoevsky or "the young generation" (372). He cannot read, and he cannot imagine writing anything by means of dictation to his stepmother, who he feels would not understand him. He expects a life of dullness, a permanent present without change. His existence becomes one of unlived potentialities, expressed in rhetorical questions: "Would he marry now? And would a young lady want to marry a blind young man?" (450) John flirts with a girl from the neighbourhood but insists on calling her 'June' instead of using her real name, Joan. With her, he briefly regains his ambition to "be a great writer", not to let his blindness prevent him from pursuing literature, invoking the example of Milton. "I will be a great writer one day, and people will be brought to see the famous blind man who lends people in his books the eyes that he lost, and ..." (463). Joan, however, who is the focaliser in this passage, does not see how this will be possible: "it would be so difficult when one could not see the page" (464). She tells him that her father "writes books too, only they never get written" (ibid). John is quickly disappointed by her responses: "Why had he told her about his writing? Now everything was spoilt. And of course she did not understand. She was lamentably stupid" (ibid.). Her humble class status makes her unacceptable as a companion; his later attempts at companionship are equally unsuccessful. John shows signs of a more than physical blindness, a blindness of the heart and the mind that leaves him emotionally and intellectually stunted. In other words, he prematurely mistakes his blindness for the symbol of a more profound spiritual or aesthetic insight, whereas in fact he is merely rehearsing a tired cliché of Romantic art (cf. Tripp 2014, 468). His aestheticism leads him, fatally, to misrecognise his environment, to fictionalise the persons around him, and to fail in building genuine, lasting reciprocal relationships with others, particularly with women.[146]

When his stepmother takes him to London, he is overwhelmed by the city's noise and bustle, an experience that culminates in a seizure that makes him lose consciousness. The novel ends with a letter from John to his schoolfriend B. G. in which John announces that he will "settle down to writing now" and that he is "happy" (Green 2008, 505) – a letter that is in some contrast to John's mood in the previous chapters, casting some doubt on the letter's authorship, its honesty, or at least its reliability as a prediction of John's future.

Readings of the novel that accept the optimism expressed on its final page at face value risk falling prey to what Lionel Trilling called the "myth of the sick artist" (Trilling 1955, qtd. in Aebischer 2003, 511). By this time, the reader should have come to distrust those parts of the novel that are told in letters or in first-person diaries, given the "far more powerful and immediate expressions of physical suffering" contained in its passages of "third-person narration focalized through John" (Aebischer 2003, 514–515). Other critics have likewise argued that the novel's "larger frame", its tripartite structure, "is at odds with [its] episodic development" (Brothers 1983, 411). The chapter titles within the parts are far more clearly ironic, most notably the chapter "Picture Postcardism" (Green 2008, 404), which cautions the reader against the sentimentality of John's imaginary visualisations. Instead of becoming a successful writer, in any sense of that word, and fulfilling the promise of the developmental narrative implied in the linear progression from caterpillar to chrysalis and butterfly, John remains immature and "self-absorbed" (Aebischer 2003, 523).

Against these "'ironic' interpretations", Benjamin Kohlmann (2009) reads *Blindness* in the context of French Symbolism, as mediated to Green via Maurice Bowra at Oxford; yet while he adds an important historical layer to the novel's genesis and a further layer of complication to the novel's ambivalence about literary representation, Kohlmann does not provide sufficient evidence to convince me that Green intended, or that early readers were likely to understand, his novel to endorse rather than critique the "tropes of the sick artist, of artistic maturation, of inspired poetic vision" (2009, 1197). An ironic interpretation is invited and supported by the contrast between the novel's macro-structure, which is defined by a developmental framework (and possibly by symbolist ideas), and its episodic and fragmentary narration. While not entirely resulting in a neat contradiction between form and content, the novel remains at the very least ambivalent about the

---

[146] This is a trait that John Haye shares with Lucian Taylor and Stephen Dedalus, among other young male artists *manqués* of the modernist period.

artistic nature of its hero. There is nothing in it, least of all in the diary section, that would prove that John actually has what it takes to be a great artist.

A more plausible interpretation is offered by Marius Hentea, who reminds readers that "there is no reason to think that John will be an artist" (2014, 17). He invokes the context of "professional authorship" and publishing as more pertinent for an interpretation of the novel, a context in which it is more likely that John could become not an artist, but "a young author whose life story [...] would appeal to publishers" (17). Art came early to this postwar generation of writers; so did professionalisation. Writing novels, in particular, came to be "increasingly about profit rather than art" (19). Producing novels quickly and publishing them in quick succession became yet another of Connolly's "enemies of promise". Hentea quotes Richard Le Gallienne, writing in 1927: "The old proverbial way was to starve genius in his garret. The new way is to kill him with kindness, to drown him in honey. [...] Premature laurel [...] is too apt to provoke that premature self-satisfaction which inevitably ends in premature decay".[147] In this interwar generation, the economic need to supply the public with ever new novels, most of them forgettable, stifled aesthetic innovation. Success in the literary market was predicated on putting an end to experimentation. Hentea refers to the 1920s boom in guides to authorship and novel-writing, a reprise or continuation of late nineteenth-century developments (as we have seen in the discussion of *New Grub Street*). He also indicates a further development of the *künstlerroman* that he calls "the *Bestsellerautorroman*" (19), best represented by the curious metafictional title *Best Seller: The Story of a Young Man Who Came to New York to Write a Novel about a Young Man Who Came to New York to Write a Novel* (by N. O. Youmans, 1930).[148] By this time, as Frank Kermode reminds us, the trope of the isolated artist, whether employed in a serious or comic fashion, had "become fully, not to say histrionically, self-conscious" (Kermode 1961, 22, qtd. in Kohlmann 2009, 1197).

Blindness combines its budding author's disability with a larger enquiry into visual and non-visual modes of perception and representation, possibly even with an implicit critique of literary mimesis (Tripp 2014, 467), of the "Picture Postcardism" (Green 2008, 404) provided by conventional literary fiction. In any case, the protagonist's blindness serves as a deliberate limitation for the novel's form (Aebischer 2003, 523), enabling Green to find a way beyond both aestheticism

---

[147] Richard Le Gallienne, "On the Present Inflation of Literary Values", *New Statesman*, Jan. 8, 1927, 387; qtd. in Hentea 2014, 18.
[148] By 'N. O. Youmans', 1930 [→ ch. 10]. Unfortunately, the other novel mentioned by Hentea in this context is not about authorship at all; its title is not *Well-to-Do Author* but *Well-to-Do Arthur* (by W. Pett Ridge, 1920), and its adolescent hero works first in a munitions factory and then in an architect's office; see the review in the *TLS*, Feb. 19, 1920, 123.

and conventional literary realism – beyond even the symbolism that governed the life trajectories of Forster's characters in *The Longest Journey*. While using the key trope of the isolated artist, Green's *künstlerroman* casts doubt on established myths that posit the artist against society. It pursues a different trajectory from the decadent models of James, Machen, and Forster. Instead of confirming these predecessors, *Blindness* opens out into a form that transcends aestheticist self-absorption and offers a materialist critique of the artist's isolation from his social environment. It also does so in its narrative form through introducing a number of different text types (diaries, letters) and – as in Forster – employing variable focalisation, thus opening up the novel to other subjectivities and decentring the artist character by providing alternative perspectives that highlight that character's limitations. These modernist narrative techniques – "forms of narrative immediacy, the repudiation of omniscience, the stylised modes of point of view" – can be read as formal equivalents of "the loss in the artist's representativeness" (Weimann 1988, 442). Like the conclusion of Joyce's *Portrait of the Artist*, and the open ending of Stephen's story in *Ulysses*, the promise of consummation for the blind artist of Green's *Blindness* is still open to disappointment. His isolation from the rest of society is a powerful symbol of the gulf that has opened up, in the early twentieth century, between the public and private dimensions of the author figure. This gulf, as we will see in the next chapter, not only produces aesthetically challenging literary forms – it is also a source of comedy and satire. The author who is no longer a representative public figure or no longer comfortable with "the traditional burden of authorial representativeness" (Weimann 1988, 442) can be imaginatively represented as a figure of suffering, as in *Blindness* and *The Longest Journey* – or, more mercilessly, can become a figure of ridicule.

10 "Do you seriously believe in literature?" Comic Turns from Aldous Huxley to Kingsley Amis

Nineteenth-century novels and stories rarely explore the comic potential in fictions of authorship. *Pendennis,* despite its genial tone, is more satirical and sentimental than comic. *The Hand of Ethelberta,* subtitled *A Comedy in Chapters,* is a rare exception, although Hardy's comedy is rather too subdued to merit the label of a 'comic novel'. Early twentieth-century authorship novels mainly follow the realist mainstream, with occasional forays beyond its boundaries into the gothic or grotesque, even into horror, or into symbolic schemata of myth, as we have seen in the previous chapter. This changes after the First World War, when a new comic tone emerges: many English novels that deal with authorship during the interwar years are often humorous to the extent of being cynical about literature and publishing. The young urban professionals of postwar London have grown sceptical about narratives of growth, development, and social integration; they have also grown disillusioned about the value and meaning of literature in an increasingly commercialised and competitive market and a wider cultural field that is marked by popular journalism with its gossip columns and celebrities (cf. Taylor 2008; DeCoste 2013). The age of the 'man of letters as hero' was over, but the age of the man of letters as a comic anti-hero was just beginning.

Aldous Huxley captures this shift in one of his short stories in the 1922 collection *Mortal Coils,* "Nuns at Luncheon", in which a (woman) journalist asks a (male) short story writer: "do you seriously believe in literature?" (Huxley 1955, 129). They touch on the strangeness of their "business" (130) as they are having lunch together. She tells him an anecdote from a German hospital, presenting it to him as material for a sensational story about an affair between a nun and an escaped convict. This, the journalist tells the writer, is "ready-made literature" (133), but neither of them seems to think it has any value beyond the commercial use of a 'good story'. "You can write that up easily and convincingly enough. But it's the sort of thing that bores me so frightfully to do", explains the journalist: "That's why I can never bring myself to write fiction. What is the point of it all?" (131).

This cynical side of the "business" of literature (ibid., 130) can also be exploited, as Huxley does here, for meta-reflexive short stories and novels that are often farcical. Huxley's first published work of fiction, the short story "The Farcical History of Richard Greenow" (1920), even carries the self-descriptive adjective in its title. This is a *doppelgänger* story about a male intellectual whose body is temporarily possessed by a popular woman novelist (cf. Sheets 1993), a story in the comic-gothic mode of Max Beerbohm [→ ch. 9]. Some interwar novels take up a self-reflexive attitude to the world of publishing, in particular to the production and marketing of 'bestsellers'. This approach is perfectly summed up in the subtitle of the American novel *Best Seller* by 'N. O. Youmans' (1930): *The Story of a Young Man Who Came to New York to Write a Novel about a Young Man Who Came to New York to Write a Novel* (discussed below). The template for many such humorous or satirical novels about the publishing industry is still recognisably the literary *bildungsroman*, particularly as inflected by Thackeray's *Pendennis*, though this has been copied so often by now that authors need not be familiar with the original to create further imitations. There is an abundance of novels and stories about young men (occasionally women) coming to New York or London to write a novel in the late nineteenth and the twentieth century, and they are still going strong today. Rarely, however, were they as funny as in the 1920s and 1930s.

The novels by Powell and Amis show younger authors moving away from the centres of publishing to seek out elusive older writers and to question established models of authorship that have reached a point of culmination. Here, the comedy is one of distance, not between success and failure but between generations: between an older generation of writers, whose style has become ridiculous, and a younger generation in search of new forms and new authorial identities. If their template is Henry James rather than Thackeray or Dickens, they turn Jamesian irony into farce, and James himself can become, in Amis's *I Like It Here*, the idol of a spent generation of modernists.

"Humble Heroisms": Aldous Huxley's *Crome Yellow* (1921), Evelyn Waugh's *Vile Bodies* (1930) and *Scoop* (1938)

The standard recipe for a young author's self-reflexive novel is satirically summed up in Aldous Huxley's *Crome Yellow* (1921). The disaffected young poet Denis Stone has been invited to stay at Crome, the country house of the Wimbush family. Among the party of guests are the Byronic painter Gombauld, the bestselling author Barbecue-Smith, and the lizard-like intellectual Scogan (often said to be based on Bertrand Russell). Denis is self-conscious of his youth and uneasy about his writing and his general direction in life. Throughout the novel, his desire to see himself and to be seen by others as "a man of action" (Huxley 2004, 2) is frustrated by circumstances and his own indolence. His affections for Henry Wimbush's doll-like niece Anne are not returned at first, and by the time she is fed up with Gombauld and sends the appropriate signals in his direction, Denis has already taken the wrong kind of action, which precipitates his return to London. Half a year earlier, Denis has had a volume of poems published. The taste of his talents given in the novel show him to be more of a Georgian imitator than a modernist innovator (cf. 4, 121). This is particularly evident in his poem on the occasion of a country fair at Crome, a pastiche of pretentious clichés (150–151). Poetry, at least the kind of poetry Denis is producing, no longer seems worthwhile or culturally relevant; it joins the ranks of the numerous society pastimes and activities that are satirised in *Crome Yellow*. The novel's comedy derives from puncturing the artistic, intellectual, and utopian pretensions of an *haut-bourgeois* social set, which likes to decorate itself with artists and authors.

Confronted with the handsome and successful painter Gombauld, Denis feels himself to be "still only potential" (122) – an unfulfilled promise. When asked what he is writing, he answers evasively "just verse and prose" (13). Denis is embarrassed to be made to talk about his novel, having written only two chapters so far. He says it is "about the usual things, you know" (13), which makes Scogan groan and embark on a description of "the usual things", which amounts to the perfect capsule description of an author novel:

> I'll describe the plot for you. Little Percy, the hero, was never good at games, but he was always clever. He passes through the usual public school and the usual university and comes to London, where he lives among the artists. He is bowed down with melancholy thought; he carries the whole weight of the universe upon his shoulders. He writes a novel of dazzling brilliance; he dabbles delicately in Amour and disappears, at the end of the book, into the luminous Future. (13)

Denis is even more embarrassed at this point, because Scogan "had described the plan of his novel with an accuracy that was appalling" (13). By now, the blueprint of *Pendennis* can no longer claim any originality. Scogan deplores how young writers "continue to write about things that are so entirely uninteresting as the mentality of adolescents and artists" (13–14), and he goes on to say that "[a] serious book about artists regarded as artists is unreadable; and a book about artists regarded as lovers, husbands, dipsomaniacs, heroes, and the like is really not worth writing again" (14). By implication, a comic novel about a young writer as a would-be lover and would-be hero of his own life – like *Crome Yellow* – could be just the thing to write in the postwar era of the early 1920s.

Books, in this world, may no longer be a way of establishing connections but of escaping from people, as the misanthrope Henry Wimbush explains to Denis (158–159). For Denis, by contrast, they are obstacles to real-life experience. He feels weighed down by his education: "Books [...]. One reads so many, and one sees so few people and so little of the world" (18). This intensifies Denis's sense of isolation, of his inability ever to know others intimately, that accompanies him throughout the novel – a sense of existential loneliness even in the midst of company, which is one of the key affects in a romantic view of modern life. Whereas the strict rationalist Scogan speculates about utopian methods of social engineering for the mass society of the future, in ways that prefigure Huxley's *Brave New World*, in particular about "dissociating love from propagation" (23), Denis proves to be a hopeless romantic. His view of literature as proceeding from "inspiration" (26) is ridiculed, first, by the imitative plot of his autobiographical novel, and secondly in his confrontation with Barbecue-Smith, the celebrity author of bestselling self-help books, including *Humble Heroisms*, a title that takes up the theme of the non-heroic hero, or the hero failing to act heroically, that sums up Denis's existence as a writer and lover. For Barbecue-Smith, as for Denis, the source of writing is inspiration, but he takes a perfectly unromantic view of it, having learned to "produce a literary composition unconsciously" (28) by means of self-induced hypnosis, which allows him to write 3,800 words in one and a half hours (26). The perennial point that the kind of pointless advice books Barbecue-Smith writes can be produced by bypassing the conscious mind, through "automatic writing" (28), also underlines the difference between commercial mass authorship and the romantic self-image of the young writer. Whereas the bestselling books are mindless productions without genuine ideas, the young poet-novelist has ideas but is unable to get them down in writing, or to publish them successfully. He may show promise or "potential" (122), but whether he will ever achieve the hoped-for integration of his ambitions and abilities is doubtful. So far, this author, who believes in the authenticity and sincerity of his own work – in his own "authenticity of expression" (Moore 2012, 269), has not created anything that amounts to more than weak imitations of existing models.

Denis, like so many *bildungsroman* heroes before him, is all potential, but unlike his many literary forebears he is not likely ever to realise this potential, at least as far as we can tell from the parodic samples of his poetry. As a comic novel of ideas, *Crome Yellow* is not about the writer's formation or development; its central mode is not a sense of movement, of opening out to the world, but of stasis, stagnation, and spatial and temporal confinement. That sense or mood prevails in Huxley's novels of the 1920s, in which some poets earn their living by editing the *Rabbit Fanciers' Gazette*, while some popular novelists exploit their own amorous affairs for literary material (as in *Those Barren Leaves*, 1925).

This is the stuff of comic fiction also for Evelyn Waugh's *Vile Bodies* (1930), in which the aspiring young novelist Adam Fenwick-Symes takes on a job as a gossip columnist among the 'Bright Young Things' of the Jazz age (Taylor 2008), finding that a novelist's imagination helps fill the column of 'Mr Chatterbox' with sensational stories about his celebrity friends and even about invented people, blurring the lines between fiction and reporting because "people did not really mind *whom* they read about provided that a kind of vicarious inquisitiveness into the lives of others was satisfied" (Waugh 2003a, 112, emphasis original). At one point he has his friends write his column for him, which gets him the sack. The novel ends with war being declared and Adam finding himself in France on "the biggest battlefield in the history of the world" (220), in an eerie anticipation of the Second World War. Like Denis Stone in *Crome Yellow*, Adam Fenwick-Symes is something of a cipher, a type instead of a personality: "There was nothing particularly remarkable about his appearance. He looked exactly as young men like him do look" (13). Not only is his inward development as a person entirely irrelevant for the novel, the narrator even refuses to describe his external features. The destruction of the manuscript of Adam's book, apparently an autobiography, by British customs officers on his return from France at the beginning of the novel makes a shambles of any attempt at establishing himself as a serious writer from the very outset and precipitates his turn towards journalism. There is no indication that Adam is ever going to make an effort to return to writing books.

Most notably, however, the novel's instant success turned its real author, Evelyn Waugh, into the kind of literary celebrity that *Vile Bodies* appears to satirise, but which had been the goal Waugh had set for himself. The novel itself shifts in its narrative organisation and tone between "the intrusive, knowing voice of the Society pages [...] and the detached, impersonal orchestrator of modernist aesthetics" (DeCoste 2013, 6), embodying in its form a split between two distinct types of modern authorship which are nonetheless joined at the seams. In this world, the press has become the dominant cultural force, whereas no one seems to read novels anymore (cf. DeCoste 2013, 10). The literary energies of fiction-making are invested in gossip columns, whereas the voice of the modernist novelist, embodied by Waugh's self-effacing third-person narrator, is devoid of affect, aiming for a flat, matter-of-fact style or, in the chapters consisting solely of dialogue on the telephone, doing without any narratorial voice or focalisation at all.

While this flattening is at its most radical in the more experimental *Vile Bodies*, the diagnosis about the lost cultural relevance of novels is also borne out by Waugh's later, more conventional novel *Scoop* (1938), subtitled 'a novel about journalists'. This novel owes more to P. G. Wodehouse than to T. S. Eliot or Henry Green. Here, a minor young journalist named William Boot is mistaken for his distant cousin, fashionable novelist John Courteney Boot. This Boot's "novels sold 15,000 copies in their first year and were read by the people whose opinion [he] respected" (Waugh 2003b, 201), as he is introduced in what amounts to a neat distinction between sales figures and actual readers. He moves in London's high society and takes care to keep "his name sweet in intellectual circles with unprofitable but modish works on history and travel" (ibid.). Yet, when his name comes up in the search for a foreign correspondent at the *Daily Beast* newspaper to cover a war in East Africa, his young cousin William is hired by mistake. By chance and despite his total inexperience, William manages to land a scoop in Africa and becomes a news sensation. Back home, he prefers to return to his eccentric family in the country to continue writing his nature column. The knighthood intended for him is conferred upon his cousin, the novelist, in a reversal of the earlier mistake, while his uncle sits in for him at the banquet held in his honour by the *Daily Beast*. In the age of mass-produced novels and newspapers, commercial novelists, travel-writers, and journalists exist in a continuum, and their roles are easily doubled, reversed, or exchanged. As both Huxley and Waugh knew, this continuum could be exploited for the sake of authorial self-promotion, but only at the cost of no longer 'believing in literature' in an emphatic sense.

"Hidden Souls": Authorial Celebrity in W. A. Darlington's *Wishes Limited* (1922) and William Caine's *The Author of "Trixie"* (1924)

In 1920, William Aubrey Cecil Darlington (1890–1979) had a major commercial success with his novel *Alf's Button*, a story about a British soldier who finds a magic button he can use to summon a genie to fulfil his wishes. *Alf's Button* sold more than 180,000 copies in a mere two years. In *Wishes Limited* (1922), W. A. Darlington – long-term drama critic for the *Daily Telegraph* – used a similar fantasy formula for a fast-paced farce about literary celebrity involving a unionised flapper fairy godmother and a man turned into a black beetle. *Wishes Limited* is partly a send-up of the publishing world and the frenzy of celebrity in the era of the Bright Young Things, partly a comic fantasy with panto qualities – including the striking transformation of a man into a beetle, familiar to modern readers from Kafka's *Metamorphosis*. Kafka's story was written in 1915 but not translated into English before the 1930s, making it unlikely that Darlington knew it when writing this novel. A likelier influence is the horror novel *The Beetle* by Richard Marsh (1897), which was made into a British film in 1919. Darlington must have realised the comic potential of this theme of transformation.

Like Huxley's Denis, Darlington's John Benstead wants to be a "Man of Action" (Darlington 1922, 10), even in capital letters, but fails rather miserably. He has left Cambridge and has £150 a year of his own money, not enough to marry his girlfriend Beth, who is used to a more comfortable lifestyle: "I'm not the love-in-a-cottage, bread-and-cheese-and-kisses type", she tells him (15). He is determined to make a living as a writer but so far has not earned more than £50 by it (14). The only solution, as Beth sees it, is for him to "write a successful novel" (19). She grants him a month to finish a book that will make him rich and famous. John sits down immediately: "That was undoubtedly how all the best books were written – at top speed with a red-hot brain" (25), he thinks, taking inspiration from Shakespeare and trusting in received ideas of genius and inspiration; but he finds himself unable to compose as much as the first sentence of his novel. He revises his earlier view of creative writing: "As if books could be written at white heat like that! No really great book had ever been complete without painful, unremitting toil" (31). Hard work, not spontaneous inspiration is what gets novels written, but this insight does not help him either when he tries to reconcile his imagined characters to the "machine-made plot" he has planned for them (34).

John is at his wits' end and in some despair when suddenly Florinelle, his fairy godmother, appears and offers him supernatural help. Very young and dressed like a "flapper" (38), Florinelle grants his wish to make him into a celebrated novelist. This very modern fairy is dressed in "high-heeled shoes, silk stockings, a skimpy yellow frock cut low at the neck", she has "long fair plaits, a floppy black hat and a brilliant sunshade" (38). Modern times have also reached Fairyland in other ways: "The old Kingdom of Faery is done for", she tells him: "We have become a Republic run on strict Trade Union lines" (46), which means that her "staff of djinns" (47) would go on strike if asked to work too much. As it is, she can only grant one wish per month, "so long as it conforms to the Union scale" (49), and that wish must not be longer than twelve words. John promptly wishes "to be the author of a successful novel, so that I can get married" (49–50), and his wish is granted.

After a few weeks, just before Beth's deadline, his novel is already published – without his hand having been involved in it in any way. He sees the advertisement in the *Daily Gazette* for *Hidden Souls*, "the most wonderful first novel ever written", a "marvellously subtle psychological study by a new author of genius" (87), and at first believes that "there must be another John Benstead" (ibid.). But the book, as far as the public is concerned, is indeed his. He reads it and finds that it has no connection at all to the story he had planned to write. Instead, he finds out to his "horror" that

> this was one of those modern books. Daphne, the heroine, was the worst kind of bad hat. By page 4 she was convicted of drink and suspected of drugs. Her relations with Paul (whom John stigmatised instantly as a blot and a blight) were not such as any respectable author would encourage in a heroine; and there seemed on page 6, to be a broad hint that both Lucien and Monro enjoyed her favours equally with Paul. (94)

Hidden Souls becomes a sensational bestseller, fulfilling John's wish to become a successful author in one fell swoop and without any labour involved. But the book he is now famous for has nothing at all to do with him and is not 'his' in the modern sense of authorship and ownership established, among others, by John Locke: i.e., he has not "mixe[d] his labor with" the materials found in nature

(Rose 1993, 114). In this case, book and author are quite distinct: djinns have taken words from the English language and generated a text based on popular expectations; they have merely added John's name to it, so he is the declarative but not the executive author of 'his' work.

There is an ethical complication to this because John does not object to being made into an author without his personal involvement in writing a text published in his name, but he does object to the moral atmosphere presented in the book. John Benstead's morals are conventional and conservative. As his name suggests, he has so far been very steady and set in his ways. The word "modern", for him, is evidently not a term of praise. Yet, 'his' novel is a sensational page-turner, "one of those modern books" (Darlington 1922, 94). He is shocked to find himself compared in reviews to "our leading realist", one Spencer Delaney (105), and to be called "[r]ather a perverse genius" (106). The book is "banned by the libraries" (156), i.e., the circulating libraries, which makes it even more of a bestseller because people have to buy it to read it.

Having been magically engineered to be a success on the book market, this 'modern' book bears no connection to John's actual personality or his creative ideas (limited as they are). His wish had been "to be the author of a successful novel" (49), not to write that novel. With this magic trick, *Wishes Limited* stages the split between author and work that is characteristic of modern celebrity authorship: the author's fame takes on a life of its own, independent from the author's actual writing. He gets piles of fan letters and becomes a newsworthy personality in the papers: "The blessed rag's full of you. You're the latest sensation. You're News, my lad. England's going to be made to sit up and take notice which side you brush your hair and when you were last vaccinated. It's on their posters to-day! 'Famous Footballer Turns Naughty Novelist.'" (144)[149]

The act of creating the work is severed from the act of writing or from any conscious endeavour on the author's part: like the memory of past lives in Kipling's "The Finest Story in the World", like the ghostly return of John Keats in Kipling's "'Wireless'", or the idea of automatic writing under hypnosis in Huxley's *Crome Yellow*, *Wishes Limited* cuts off the biographical person of the author from the work ascribed to that author. Because that work has been created by magic, by Florinelle's "staff of djinns" (47), Darlington presents 'modern' authorship as a pure

---

[149] A related case of authorship by magic is mentioned, if only very marginally, in Sylvia Townsend Warner's *Lolly Willowes* (1926), in which "one of these brilliant young authors" (Warner 2020, 157) sells his soul to the Devil not "in order to become a great writer" (158) but, taking "a short-cut" (ibid.), "on the condition that he should be without doubt the most important person at a party" (157).

fulfilment of a Foucauldian 'author function': John Benfield is an author with a novel to his name but without a work of his own making.

John's main concern with this, however, is not about his *not* having written what is supposed to be 'his' novel, but about the social repercussions of being associated with *this* novel as his. He is particularly worried about his reputation among his family and in his hometown of Wetherbridge, "a backwater to which the main stream of modern life seldom penetrated" (106). For "people such as Mrs Purcell and John's Aunt Susan, the growth of modern realistic fiction was held to be a scandalous thing which ought to be put down by law" (106). His younger friends cannot understand how he could "write that particular brand of tripe" (115): "[W]hy the hell didn't you leave it to some blighter with long hair and – and dirty nails?" his friend Peter asks him (115), implicitly if perhaps unconsciously opposing such low-brow authorship to Joyce's (Stephen's) model of the detached and invisible author whose fingernails are clean and manicured.

To make matters even worse, his publishers expect him to deliver a second novel in the same vein as soon as possible, but since he is disgusted with his literary début, he explains that he wrote it while being ill, and – channelling Jonathan Swift via Matthew Arnold – resolves to make his next novel "a masterpiece of sweetness and light that should wipe from people's minds the very memory of 'Hidden Souls'" (158).[150] First, though, he employs a secretary to take care of his abundant mail. A list shows letters of praise and abuse in equal measure, including eight "Hurt letters from relations", nineteen "Disgusted letters from friends", and nine "Love letters" (164).

Parallel to the plot of restoring his reputation runs the affair of John's neighbour, Mr Spalding. When she first made her way into John's apartment, Florinelle had accidentally come across Mr Spalding and turned him into a black beetle because he frightened her. Since her union regulations only allow her to grant one wish per month, John must wait thirty days before asking her to return Mr Spalding to human form. Meanwhile, he has to look after the black beetle and take care not to lose it (or him). His keeping a pet black beetle adds to his celebrity status, somewhat like the pet lobster did for Nerval. Since he is now in the public eye, he cooks up a plan to keep Mr Spalding's re-transformation a secret. Not the best part of this plan is to do this on a train, not considering that Mr Spalding was wearing his pyjamas and a colourful dressing gown when Florinelle transformed him, and that naturally he would still be wearing this outfit when he is returned to normal. His appearance on the platform of Waterloo Station causes quite a stir. He is

---

150 The phrase 'sweetness and light' originates in Swift's *Battle of the Books* (1704) and was famously used by Matthew Arnold in *Culture and Anarchy* (1869).

arrested, and John is called up as a witness in court. A farcical court room scene ensues, in which John manages to wriggle himself out of his predicament with a series of rhetorical tricks, avoiding any reference to the supernatural. Fortunately, Florinelle's djinns have gone on strike and have "wiped out" (310) any memory of what they have done. There is no trace of *Hidden Souls* anymore, and no recollection of Mr Spalding's absence. John's wealth is gone, too, but he is ready to start again, and as it turns out his publishers have just accepted the manuscript of his second – that is, first – novel.

Wishes Limited gives a comic turn to the classic literary *bildungsroman* formula that was all about achieving a compromise between author and society. John's (re)integration into respectable society at the end is achieved only when all memory of his once being a scandalous novelist has been erased. The *bildungsroman* here only succeeds by dispensing with the *künstlerroman* idea, which pits the artist against society. John gives up on being a socially controversial artist, and instead is happy to become a purveyor of socially harmless fiction with a "clean, open-air atmosphere" (311). He clearly prefers honest work and a peaceful, quiet life to the controversial, exposed existence of a celebrity author. Already at the beginning, he had doubts whether authorship was his "true vocation in life or just a pleasant hobby" (78), and these doubts are resolved as they are in *Pendennis*, in the model of gentleman authorship that is not a "vocation" at all, not indicative of serious artistic ambition, but merely a stepping stone to something much better – a gentlemanly life of leisure.

The mechanical *dea ex machina*, Florinelle the fairy godmother, in her flapper costume, is an embodiment of the modern age that splits off the author's person and work from the author's public image, constructed for the consumption of a news-hungry, newspaper-reading "Society of the Burning Eyes", as John calls it (232). That society, as quick to celebrate as to condemn and as quick to forget as to remember, is contrasted with the 'organic' community of Wetherbridge with its local, personal, and much more traditional rhythms of daily life, which here serves a very similar function as the family home of Boot Magna does in Evelyn Waugh's *Scoop* (1938), or the more famous Blandings Castle in the works of P. G. Wodehouse: to stand for the antithesis of anything remotely 'modern'.

Next to its comic use of the supernatural, in splitting off the author from the work and transforming a lawyer into a cockroach, *Wishes Limited* also contains references to modern technologies of communication, whose uncanny sense of non-human agency is cautiously defused by comedy: the telephone, for example, is at one point said to have its own personality and to "repl[y] in a surprised tone. [...] John rang off before the telephone had even time to ask what it was all about" (142). Modern technology disconnects people from their bodies, disembodies the human voice by mediating it through communications technology, and thus deprives them of agency and control of their own identity, as it does in Waugh's *Vile Bodies* and other modernist texts (cf. Berensmeyer 2022, 165–166). Possibly the fictional book title *Hidden Souls* also hints at this Freudian predicament of the loss of integrity between soul and body, most drastically staged by the transformation of Mr Spalding, which explores the boundary between humans and animals rather than between humans and technology.

In the guise of light humour and supernatural fantasy farce, *Wishes Limited* explores the limits of the human in modernity, as mediated by super- and nonhuman technologies of alienation. Its conventional, anti-modernist plot and style of narration creates an interesting tension against the modern themes that are negotiated within it and the modernist imagery that is employed (from telephonic voices to the metamorphosed beetle). It explores these limits less in the mode of discussing ideas (as in Huxley) than in presenting absurd scenes of social comedy in a manner that would later be perfected by Waugh. While its views on authorship and the production of books are conservative, harking back as far as Thackeray (at least by implication), its mode of presentation embraces the modern even as it condemns its extremes.

Herbert Jenkins Ltd., Darlington's publishers, specialised in light humour. Their list included P. G. Wodehouse as their star author. They were apparently interested in novels that presented literary authorship and modern literary phenomena of author-making in a humorous light. Two years after *Wishes Limited*, they published William Caine's *The Author of "Trixie"* (1924), another now forgotten comic novel whose only claim to modernist fame is its being included in a list of Sebastian Knight's favourite books in Vladimir Nabokov's *The Real Life of Sebastian Knight* (1941). Here, an archdeacon's dignity and reputation as a clergyman is endangered by his having written a bestselling novel, *Trixie*. He cannot allow his name to appear on the book's cover, so he finds a strawman in the pretentious young poet Bisham Dunkle, a "Shakespeare" to his "Bacon" (Caine 1924, 21). Dunkle's price is the archdeacon's daughter's hand in marriage and a generous sum of money. To everyone's horror, the book is not only a "Winner", in publishers' terms, but a "Best Seller" (64), indeed "an instantaneous success" (74). Dunkle and wife quickly tear through the money and find themselves in debt. Financial considerations demand a second novel by Bisham Dunkle, though he would much prefer building a reputation as a poet rather than novelist. He tries and fails to produce a successor to *Trixie*, so he turns to his father-in-law to persuade him to produce another novel. The archdeacon, however, has decided to admit to his authorship of *Trixie* and to enjoy literary fame. Many further complications ensue, in which the clergyman's daughter Chloe turns out to be a much more effective blackmailer than her ineffectual poet-husband. The pitfalls of modern author-making, especially the excesses of celebrity worship, are satirised even more effectively in Caine's

The Author of "Trixie" than they are in *Wishes Limited*, and in this case a previously unsuccessful author is showered with the effects of celebrity without any supernatural intervention:

> Dunkle was hunted off his legs. Invitations poured in upon him – to lunch, dine, and sup with perfect strangers; to address the Literary Societies of Polytechnic Institutions; to be the guest of the Fulle Jugges, of the Adullamites, of the Tupper Club and other festive societies; to give away the prizes at academies for the sons of gentlemen; to kick off in charity football matches; to lay foundation-stones; to open bazaars and swimming-baths; to pay their rent for unsuccessful writers, painters, sculptors, musicians, tailors; to take shares in cinematograph palaces; to borrow anything from £ 1 to £ 100,000 on his sole note of hand; to be photographed gratis; to become the husband of unknown women; to stand for Parliament; to lecture in America; to appear on the programmes of music-halls; to buy out-of-date Encyclopædias Britannicas; to subscribe to mumps hospitals, testimonials to retiring pugilists, monuments to philanthropists, missions to ploughmen, cats' homes, brass bands, Societies for the Discouragement of Fiction Reading; [...] (160–161)

This list continues for another page, its sheer length signalling the excess of unwholesome attention paid to a celebrity author. Interestingly, the list also includes invitations to "write testimonials" and thus to use the advertising potential of celebrity for a diverse range of goods including "fountain pens, ever-sharp pencils, loose-leaf notebooks, safety razors, strops, shaving-soaps, corn-cures, boot-polishes, corrugated-iron summer-houses, photographic cameras, player-pianos, ice-cream freezers, bicycles, cork jackets, tinned soups, baseball bats, shampoo powders, sardines, vacuum cleaners, Virginian cigarettes, hair dyes" (161–162). The commercial aspect of modern popular fiction publishing, and its cross-pollination with other commercial products, could not be summed up in any better way.

At the end, archdeacon Roach is offered the bishopric of Pontefract and henceforward gives up any further literary ambitions, ceding the authorship of *Trixie* to his son-in-law. Both Darlington's and Caine's comic novels present the making of modern authorial reputations as a manufacturing of celebrity and explore its social repercussions.

Author Hunting: N. O. Youman's *Best Seller* (1930), Anthony Powell's *What's Become of Waring* (1938), and Kingsley Amis's *I Like It Here* (1958)

Jasper Watts, motivated by his love of books, goes to New York to find a job in publishing, and he joins the sales force of B. H. Johnson and Sons. He learns quickly "that selling books is a tough racket" (Youmans 1930, 64) and that publishing is a "form of gambling" (239). As Jasper notes after his first sales conference and the subsequent drinks party:

> Years of close association with books had left these men cynical and a little calloused. Their perceptions had been blunted; to them books were so much more merchandise; they no longer saw in the printed page a concrete record of some one's creative urge. Once, perhaps, they had felt toward the literature just as he did now – it was all very sad when one came to think about it after ten drinks. (68)

Best Seller (1930) was written under a pseudonym by a business insider, Allen Clarke Marple, who had worked at Harper's in the 1920s. The novel was advertised as "a galuptious harlequinade cast in the publishing world of New York [...] written by a man in the heart of the business" (Youmans 1930, front inside jacket flap). It contains many realistic depictions of the inner workings of mass-market publishing and bookselling in the 1920s, including a lot of liquid lunches, all-night parties, and speakeasies. From the sales force, Jasper Watts moves up into the advertising department, while writing a largely autobiographical novel on the side, embellished with fiction: "[W]here his life had been dull it was a simple matter to insert things he had always wanted to do" (108). He takes care to spice up the story of his alter ego, Henry, knowing "the value of sex interest" (110) in making a book sell. But he is uncertain of the ending:

> After various vicissitudes Henry came to New York, of course, and settled down to write a novel. Jasper wasn't quite sure just what happened to it. In most stories the young man's novel became a success and made his fortune, just when he had given up hope; but Jasper thought it might make a more artistic ending if Henry's book turned out to be a flop. Not a critical flop, naturally, but a book which just somehow never got started.
> But he wasn't absolutely sure; he didn't want to tack on an unhappy ending just to please the critics. (110)

Knowing the written and unwritten laws of the trade, here is an author who is ready to tailor his novel to those laws. He does not carry the first name 'Jasper' in vain, but in homage to the anti-hero of Gissing's *New Grub Street*. Jasper wants the novel within the projected novel to be a critical success by making it into a commercial failure, a "flop"; but on the other hand, he does not want *his* novel to be a commercial failure "just to please the critics" by writing "an unhappy ending". This passage acutely points up the double bind of modern literary authorship, torn between the conflicting imperatives of commercial and critical values. He even considers writing two different versions of the novel, one for magazine serialisation (which demands a happy ending) and one for book publication. "Every one else writes about the young fellow whose novel succeeds just when he has given up hope – but I'm going to be different", he tells one of his women friends. "After all, most first novels flop – two thousand five-hundred is about as far as they go", he explains to her (228).

Jasper shows *Young Sacrifice* to an experienced editor, who dismisses it as too run-of-the-mill: "[T]here are twenty books a year in which the hero is a young fellow who appreciates the finer things and is hurt by the brutality of life" (230). Nevertheless, the novel does get published and is even selected for a book club, the Book Lovers' League (loosely based on the Book of the Month Club, founded in 1926). He has his picture taken, with an open collar and no tie, and a smart publicity agent gets him into the major newspapers with fantastic made-up stories about his life:

> He had already been a prize-fighter, a stoker on a ship, and an All-American football player; he knew that he had left college because he had rebelled against authority; he had discovered with varying emotions that he worked only after one A.M.; that he ran three miles every morning before breakfast, that he thought Americans were doing the only really fine writing; and that he invariably ate a can of sardines before going to bed. (288–289)

Jasper has landed a bestseller and plans his next novel along the same lines as his début. In a market as oversaturated as this, where books are being sold but rarely read, this is apparently not a problem. Books are merchandise, "like potatoes or beer" in Henry James's memorable phrase ("The Next Time", James 1999, 2: 243) [→ ch. 8], and authors are easily replaced by new ones. In his new position at the publishing house, Jasper in the last chapter welcomes a young man with similar ambitions as his own and finds a job for him in the sales department. The novel thus ends as it began, implying an endless cycle of production, not only of books but of positions in the publishing industry, from authors to salespersons. *Best Seller*, which apparently sold "exceptionally well",[151] combines its jaded view of the publishing business with salacious "sex interest" (Youmans 1930, 110) and its fictional author's fairy-tale success story. The topos of a Midwestern journalist coming to New York to seek his fortune in literature was already very common by then in American literature, the writer as a kind of "Horatio Alger character" having already been parodied by William Dean Howells in *The World of Chance* in 1893 (Dennis 1980, 282).

In its jaded view of New York's publishing scene, *Best Seller* resembles Q. D. Leavis's contemporary jeremiad against the decline of literary and cultural standards in *Fiction and the Reading Public* (Leavis 1979 [1932]), but 'Youmans' exploits this diagnosis for a racy narrative that would only have confirmed Leavis's worst nightmares.

---

[151] According to a notice in *Variety*, Nov. 12, 1930, 72. The book has otherwise sunk without trace.

In Anthony Powell's fifth novel, *What's Become of Waring* (1939), a fledgling author named Hudson is hired by a publisher to write a life of the recently deceased bestselling travel writer T. T. Waring. He finds out that the reclusive Waring is actually Alec Pimley, the black sheep of an upper-middle-class family, who has been living in the south of France and going by the name of 'Robinson'. What is worse, Hudson also finds out that 'Waring' never travelled to the exotic countries he describes in his books but that he has been plagiarising and embellishing earlier anonymous or foreign-language travel narratives. Waring's readers should have been warned by his name, which derives from Robert Browning's poem "Waring" (1842) about an author who has suddenly absconded:

> What's become of Waring
> Since he gave us all the slip,
> Chose land-travel or seafaring,
> Boots and chest, or staff and scrip,
> Rather than pace up and down
> Any longer London-town?
>   (Browning 2018, 97, l. 1–6)

These first lines of the poem also serve as the epigraph to Powell's novel, which combines a Wavian comedy of upper-middle-class manners with more realistic vignettes of the publishing world and London's literary bohemia in the 1930s. This world is peopled by Dickensian caricatures like the brothers Hugh and Bernard Judkins, who run a publishing firm together but are constantly at each other's throat, or the struggling writers Handsworth and Minhinnick, the latter known – or rather unknown – for his epic poem *Aristogeiton*.

The unnamed narrator, a former advertising copy writer, now works as a reader for the Bloomsbury-based publishing company of Judkins and Judkins, while trying to write a book titled *Stendhal: and Some Thoughts on Violence*. The success of the Waring books makes it impossible for them to publish Hudson's revelations; they publish a posthumous Waring book instead, which does not sell as well as the earlier ones and receives worse reviews (Powell 2015, 234). Since the notional author has been presumed dead, and the real author has died in a boating accident, the Waring craze – based as it was on the mystery of the author's personality – quickly peters out. Waring, the narrator notes, had been "a master of the science of building up a literary personality" (27), and it was this personality, not the writing as such, that sold the books: a heroic author image of "Youth Triumphant" (27). The writing itself is described as "the almost perfect exemplar of a form of woolly writing that appeals irresistibly to uncritical palates" (27), a kind of middlebrow writing, in other words, that is not a guarantee but also no hindrance to success. Like *Wishes Limited*, or in somewhat different form *Scoop*, which was published in the same year, *What's Become of Waring* inherits from Henry James's "The Private Life" and earlier tales the split of an authorial self as a contrast between a celebrated author's public image and his real, private self, and gives this split a comic turn.

After Hudson's discovery, the narrator professes himself "not unduly surprise[d]" by Waring's plagiarism (132). His relaxed attitude is attributable to his professional experience in the publishing industry, about which he has no illusions. Material needs and money are the prime motivators for most characters in the novel except Hudson, whose commitment to his job sprang from genuine admiration for Waring's books. The real Waring, however, only wrote them out of "the need to earn a living" (175). Authenticity has to take a back seat when it comes to this superior goal.

This is satirically emphasised by the novel's forays into spiritualism; one of the publisher brothers, Hugh Judkins, is drawn to the occult, even though he professes to be a sceptic, and the novel is framed by two séances that the narrator attends. At the first one, the spirit to be conjured up is that of George Eliot, of all people, ridiculously addressed as "Mimi" (17) and cajoled by the communal singing of "Little Brown Jug" (19). At the second, there is a genuine revelation about Waring's true identity (which had been kept a secret), but this can only occur because the Indian medium has been told by his lover, a sister of Alec Pimley. Any spiritual dimension to life has descended to the depths (both social and intellectual) of spiritualism, a materialist parody of the spiritual. As the narrator muses while falling asleep at the end of the novel, only material interests in "money" and "power" remain (235–236). Unlike in Waugh, there is no redeeming perspective such as Catholicism or another organised religion in view here; everything is subsumed in a general air of melancholy. Literature and publishing clearly cannot serve as a substitute for religion. This is made clear when Hugh Judkins suddenly decides to run his business on strict moral principles, for example firing a divorcée. This decision results in many authors quitting the firm. At the end, thoroughly disillusioned, the narrator's friend Hudson decides to give up writing: "I think I'm finished with literature for the time being, if not for life" (192), and the narrator quits his job in publishing to return to advertising (234), "where the people were worse but made more money" (141).[152]

What's Become of Waring burlesques the publishing business in the tradition of nineteenth-century visions of London's literary bohemia, whose repertoire the

---

[152] The novel was rejected by Duckworth, Powell's former publisher, and did not sell at all well when it was published by Cassell. It has not aged well in some respects, most notably in its frequent instances of casual racism.

novel revisits in a similar spirit of disillusionment; but this spirit is now no longer tragic, as it still was in Gissing and Orwell [→ ch. 11], but is mined for its comic potential. Powell skewers the idealisation of youth after the First World War in the heroic and sensational, but completely fictional, public image of 'T. T. Waring', possibly an allusion to T. E. Lawrence, who had died in 1935 at the age of 46. It is also, without knowing it, a descant on the bohemian social world of London publishing that would be destroyed by the Second World War.

I Like It Here, Kingsley Amis's third published novel (1958), picks up where Powell left off: here, too, a younger writer is sent on a mission abroad to confirm the identity of a reclusive older writer, "the one indisputably major talent to have arisen since the death of Conrad" (Amis 1968, 16). Garnet Bowen, a journalist who is "supposed to be" a dramatist and trying to write a play (8), takes up the challenge of going to Portugal, accompanied by his wife and three young children, to locate the legendary author Wulfstan Strether. Strether, named after the American abroad of Henry James's *The Ambassadors* and very much a Jamesian kind of writer, is supposed to have retired from writing since his last novel, *This Rough Magic*, published in 1946, ended with a Prospero-like farewell to literature (16); but now a fresh typescript has been sent to the publisher, and there is apparently no other way to verify its authenticity but to send Bowen as an envoy to Portugal. The main theme of the novel is the Englishman (in this case, actually Welshman) abroad, the target of Amis's satire being Bowen's chauvinism and provincialism or the alleged funniness of foreigners, or both in varying degrees. But the novel also explores the perennial theme of the younger writer's self-discovery and self-fashioning in opposition to an earlier generation of authors, in Bowen's case what he calls the last specimens of "the great-writer period", which he thinks has ended in "about 1930 […] [o]r perhaps 1939" (180). Several jokes are made at the expense of older writers like Graham Greene and Somerset Maugham, and of course Henry James. Strether's Jamesian allegiance is confirmed by his having *Portrait of a Lady* on his bookshelf; Bowen concurs "that a knowledge of Jamesiana, plus the possession of Jamesian texts, certainly befitted an indisputably major talent" (78) but that this fact alone does not prove Strether's authenticity. Strether's style, a sample of which is given in the novel (101–102), is a fine parody of James and thoroughly despised by Bowen:

> He wanted to put the man who had written that in the stocks and stand in front of him with a peck, or better a bushel, of ripe tomatoes and throw one at him for each time he failed to justify any phrase […] on grounds of clarity, common sense, emotional decency and general morality. (102)

He turns out, however, to grow increasingly fond of the older man and to enjoy his company. After many complications, he is finally convinced that this man is who he claims to be when, visiting Henry Fielding's tomb in Lisbon's British cemetery, Strether proclaims the superiority of tragedy over comedy and his own superiority as "the colossus of the twentieth [century]" (168) over Fielding as the colossus of the eighteenth. A Strether impersonator, Bowen concludes, would not have had the temerity to play up his arrogance to such an extent:

> Well then, [...] he wouldn't have dared to put himself on show as the kind of prancing, posturing phoney who'd say he was better than Fielding. Nothing to be gained by it. And far too much danger of affronting my conception of how great writers behave. He'd have been perfectly safe in sticking to humility, reverence and what-have-you. But he didn't. So that meant he couldn't have been putting on an act. (180)

Returning to London, Bowen destroys the play that he had begun to write and decides to make a fresh start as a writer, paying more attention to his own interests than to fulfilling other people's expectations.

This gesture towards freedom from previous constraints can be read as a liberation on behalf of a younger generation of writers, whose aesthetic programme – like Amis's – inclines more towards comedy, and thus harks back to the literary model of Fielding, than the earnest invocations of tragedy and seriousness voiced by Strether as a representative of a generation of authors in the wake of James, Conrad, and Lawrence, certainly including Maugham and Greene. The novel's title *I Like It Here*, besides the rather smug self-satisfaction of the Englishman abroad, also suggests a coming to terms with one's own potentials and limitations as a writer, an act of self-justification and self-location: Amis, like Bowen, signals his allegiance to the modern era, an era defined in the arts by, among other things, a taste for jazz as opposed to classical music (cf. 78) and comedy rather than tragedy. Lack of appreciation for the "light-heavyweight" in the arts, Bowen states, constitutes "a grave impoverishment of cultural life" (78).

Implicitly, too, the contemporary achievement of the English form of the minor novel is set against the failure of any grander gestures in literature that appear out of touch with the present. If Strether's "whole *persona*" is "arranged on the lines of what a reader would expect a writer to be like" (144), and thus entirely an effect of audience *cathexis* and authorial *hexis*, Bowen is engaged in a search for an alternative 'persona', a convincing and timely autopoetic self-performance and heteropoetic self-image as a writer for a new era. In its focus on a transfer of literary authority from one generation to another, Amis's *I Like It Here* is engaged in establishing its own grounds of appreciation and authorial reputation by parodying and satirising older, no longer convincing models of literature (the novel in particular) while searching for new forms of literary expression and seeking to assert a different authorial persona. Whereas earlier novels in the interwar years (*Crome Yellow, Wishes Limited*) focus on the distance between success and failure, and on the separation between authors and 'their' books in the modern marketing of bestsellers, Powell and Amis explore the distance between literary generations and different concepts of authorship. The 'belief in literature', questioned and put to the test in these narratives, is thus paradoxically or indirectly affirmed, especially by Amis, whose protagonist returns home from his trip abroad with renewed convictions about what he wants to do and is able to do – indirectly asserting Amis's poetics as a master of the minor novel and a contender for greatness as a "light-heavyweight" of literature.

11 "Writing's a mug's game": Novels of Resentment and Regeneration in the 1930s and 1940s

Ever since *New Grub Street* explored the precarity of London's literary life, the realistic depiction of authors struggling in an economically challenging *milieu* has remained an attractive proposition for novelists. There is a long list of works in Gissing's wake, mainly by younger male authors who similarly tried to rise above their own miseries by writing semi-autobiographical novels about impoverished authors, journalists, and editors. Bernard Bergonzi called *New Grub Street* a "novel of resentment" (Bergonzi 1976, 20), and his label fits these later writings even better. They are novels of resentment not only in their unregenerate pessimism about the literary world, but also about society and gender relations, and relationships with women more particularly. Tinged with misogyny, they often strike a maudlin note of self-pity and sentimentality. Their heroes are young men on the make, approaching or just past the age of thirty, unmarried and unmoored, trying mostly unsuccessfully to gain a foothold in the literary establishment while eking out a bohemian existence in or around Bloomsbury or Soho. In the 1930s, their revolt against the literary establishment takes some of them further afield, to Paris or Corfu.

This chapter is bookended by two rather typical responses to Gissing in the mid-twentieth century, one famous, the other obscure: I first trace Gissing's heritage to Orwell's late realist anti-*bildungsroman Keep the Aspidistra Flying* (1936), and I close with a reading of Roland Camberton's novel about a struggling Jewish writer in 1940s Soho, *Scamp* (1950). In their portrayal of doomed lower-middle-class literary aspirations, these novels combine a diagnosis of cultural sterility with a plot of erotic disappointment and final release. In between these readings, I place the more radical modernist energies, and the promise of a literary and cultural revitalisation, of a trio of Irish, American, and English 'bad boys' of the Thirties: Samuel Beckett, Henry Miller, and Lawrence Durrell. In their refusal to engage in 'fine writing' or to obey the niceties of polite literature, these – often aggressively masculine – writers have a sister-in-arms in Stevie Smith, whose *Novel on Yellow Paper* (1936) is similarly experimental in form and daring in its content, if not as sexually explicit as Miller's or Durrell's (whose works could not be published in Britain at the time).

Yet what exactly was the orthodoxy that these writers rebelled against? In the 1920s and 1930s, the literary field in England was severely stratified into three major zones or 'brows', carefully guarded by powerful institutions like publishers, critics, bookshops, and libraries as well as the 'new medium' of radio (cf. Brown/ Grover 2012, Macdonald/Singer 2015). While 'highbrow' modernists cultivated "a distinctive economy" (Allington 2019, 351) in small magazines, small metropolitan bookshops (Chambers 2020), and small publishing firms like the Hogarth Press (founded in 1917), they tended to denounce the wider commercial world of literary publishing as 'middlebrow'.[153]

At the lowest end of the scale, we find what would now be called 'genre fiction', at that time still tainted with a class-inflected moral opprobrium and the fear of declining cultural standards, especially because of an alleged, negatively perceived Americanisation of popular culture (cf. Leavis 1979 [1932]). This stratification of the literary field, which began in the late Victorian period, remained stable in Britain until at least the 1950s. These conditions ensured an indirect social selectivity within the literary field, while contributing to the enforcement of a legal regime of censorship against 'immoral' books like *Lady Chatterley's Lover*, which only ended after the Lady Chatterley trial of 1960. By this time, Pegasus's harness of conventional realist fiction had become rusty as well as confining.

For a middle-class readership, circulating libraries continued to be key distributors of books up to the mid-twentieth century. On the lower end of the library market, "twopenny libraries", also known as "mushroom libraries", proliferated during the interwar period. These served a lower-middle-class and working-class clientele and were often run "by small shopkeepers such as newsagents and tobacconists" (Allington 2019, 347). Their type is memorably described in George Orwell's essay "Bookshop Memories" and his novel *Keep the Aspidistra Flying*. In these texts from 1936, as elsewhere in his work, Orwell is keenly aware of the segregation of the literary marketplace, characterised by the so-called "battle of the brows" (Brown/Grover 2012). Whereas the formidable Q. D. Leavis sensed a "standardization of taste" (1979, 33) being propagated by such popular institutions as the commercial lending libraries, the book-tables at Woolworth, and the Book of the Month Club, recent critics have identified these institutions as offering spaces for alterna-

---

[153] Unfortunately, this tendency has been replicated in literary studies, where the comparatively new field of 'middlebrow studies' appears to have developed in opposition to modernist studies rather than as an integral part of it, asserting rather than discouraging the association of experimental, urban, and predominantly masculine aesthetics with 'modernism', to the detriment of the diversity of modern literary and cultural spaces, which allowed room for (among other concepts) what Alison Light has termed "conservative modernity", i.e., an acknowledgement of the middlebrow's progressive potential besides its presumably regressive politics (Light 1991, 61). Another useful concept in this context is "threshold modernism", which emphasizes "liminal sites and contested ideas" within a wider cultural spectrum (see Evans 2018, 1). For the field of middlebrow studies, see especially Humble 2001, Macdonald 2011, Macdonald/Singer 2015, Ehland/Wächter 2016.

tive forms of cultural expression below the 'highbrow' waterline. The "feminine middlebrow" (Humble 2001) but also its masculine counterpart (Macdonald 2011) have been at the forefront of this academic trend (cf. also Ehland and Wächter 2016) – books that constituted 'respectable' publications which, as Leavis acerbically comments, left their readers "with the agreeable sensation of having improved themselves without incurring fatigue" (1979, 44). The staid, conservative cultural climate that this 'middlebrow' zone stood for caused the most unease and anxiety among writers who aspired for recognition rather than commercial success, and it consequently inflects the vicissitudes of author-making from the 1930s to the 1950s.

George Orwell's *Keep the Aspidistra Flying* (1936)

In this strictly stratified field, George Orwell, neither a Bloomsbury modernist nor a literary lightweight, clearly worried about where to fit in. As he makes unmistakably clear in the autobiographical essay "Bookshop Memories" (1936) about his experience working at Booklovers' Corner in Hampstead, he did not approve of popular authors like Ethel M. Dell or Warwick Deeping. Yet he needed his own novels to be commercially viable, close enough to what he called "the ordinary, good-bad, Galsworthy-and-water stuff which is the norm of the English novel" (2002, 52). His realist novels of the 1930s are aesthetic 'compromise formations' between art and the market, which register and reflect their own uncomfortable position between these different poles. This is most explicitly the case in *Keep the Aspidistra Flying* (1936), which traces the attempts of the twenty-nine-year-old, "out at elbow", "middle-middle-class" writer Gordon Comstock to enter the literary world (Orwell 2014, 1, 9). Its first chapter overlaps with the essay "Bookshop Memories" by introducing Gordon Comstock as an assistant in Mr McKechnie's bookshop and "twopenny no-deposit" lending library (2), expanding Orwell's dire diagnosis of the book world and the class- and gender-based segmentation of the reading public:

> Eight hundred strong, the novels lined the room on three sides ceiling-high, row upon row of gaudy oblong backs, as though the walls had been built of many-coloured bricks laid upright. They were arranged alphabetically. Arlen, Burroughs, Deeping, Dell, Frankau, Galsworthy, Gibbs, Priestley, Sapper, Walpole. Gordon eyed them with inert hatred. At this moment he hated all books, and novels most of all. Horrible to think of all that soggy, half-baked trash massed together in one place. (2–3)

Here, the material quantity of novels is inversely proportionate to their quality, their sheer mass a symptom of cultural decline. Orwell uses Gordon as a mouthpiece to ventilate his own unease with the "savage Darwinian struggle" (7) that is the history of literature, as it is spatially realised "[i]n all bookshops" (6–7):

"the works of living men gravitate to eye-level and the works of dead men go up or down – down to Gehenna or up to the throne, but always away from any position where they will be noticed" (7). The quotation from Kipling's poem "The Winners" adds a layer of irony to the notion of a race for posterity in which each book or writer is a lonely contestant.[154] The lower shelves are compared to a grave in which the "extinct monsters of the Victorian age" are "quietly rotting", while the top shelves harbour "the pudgy biographies of dukes" (7). In the middle is the "trash" (3, 12), the expanded midsection of middle- and lowbrow books that actually attract customers to the shop.

Similar disgust at mass reading and its "taste for the second-rate" had been uttered half a decade earlier by Q. D. Leavis in her study of *Fiction and the Reading Public* (1979, 34). Orwell himself later, in "The Lion and the Unicorn" (1941), deplored what he saw as the "cultureless life" of the modern masses (2002, 314). It may be more surprising to find such a jeremiad about the "depressing" (62) state of popular culture and the "deteriorating" (57) quality of novels articulated in a novel. The passage quoted above implies that *Aspidistra* may in time be included in this wall of "soggy, half-baked trash" (2014, 3), but also a hope that it might rise above it. As in many of Orwell's texts, there is a very real sense of ambivalence about the value of literature in the modern world, as is also articulated in the contemporaneous essay "In Defence of the Novel" (1936), where his main target is book reviewing but where one finds the same fundamental diagnosis of the low "prestige" of the novel form combined with the belief "that the novel is worth salvaging" (Orwell 2002, 57). In *Keep the Aspidistra Flying*, the ambivalence is made explicit in Gordon Comstock's thoughts, which are often difficult to disentangle from the narrator's comments in free indirect discourse, and which sometimes move into stream of consciousness narration (cf. Fowler 1995, 146–148):

> Dull-eyed, he gazed at the wall of books. He hated the whole lot of them, old and new, highbrow and lowbrow, snooty and chirpy. The mere sight of them brought home to him his own sterility. For here was he, supposedly a 'writer', and he couldn't even 'write'! It wasn't merely a question of getting published; it was that he produced nothing, or next to nothing. And all that tripe cluttering the shelves – well, at any rate it existed; it was an achievement of sorts. (Orwell 2014, 7)

Gordon's resentment arises from "his own sterility", his lack of an oeuvre and lack of motivation, which he attributes in an extended rant to his "lack of money" (8). As in the novel's epigraph, in which Orwell changes the King James version of

---

154 Kipling's "The Winners" (1888) contains the lines "Down to Gehenna or up to the Throne / He travels the fastest who travels alone" (Kipling 2000, 16).

1 Corinthians 13 by replacing the word 'charity' with the word 'money', Gordon's thoughts frequently turn to money as the driving force of the modern world, the class system, and culture. Without some real capital, there can be no "refinement" (8), no cultural or symbolic capital. At the climax of this rant, the narration switches to the present tense and then to the first person: "Money writes books, money sells them. Give me not righteousness, O Lord, give me money, only money" (8).

Gordon has published a book of poems titled *Mice*, which has been widely ignored and is now being remaindered. He is a young writer from a "genteel as well as shabby" family (43) who has shown "exceptional promise", as he quotes from the *TLS* review of his poems (11), but he has fallen prey to the "enemies of promise" listed by Cyril Connolly (2008 [1938]). As he contemplates the impending doom that will befall the dying civilisation he lives in (Orwell 2014, 21), the energy of his resentment seems to be all that keeps him from committing suicide. That, and his attachment to his girlfriend, Rosemary Waterlow, who so far has refused to sleep with him, something he also attributes to his poverty: even "human relationships must be purchased with money" (14). In his anger and frustration, Gordon Comstock is a precursor of the 'angry young men' of the Fifties (cf. Williams 2010, 66), a talented middle-class 'superfluous man' searching for his position in life and railing against the Establishment as well as against women and the lower classes. He lives in "lower-middle-class decency" (Orwell 2014, 23) in a boarding house in Willowbed Road, N. W. (based on Willoughby Road in Hampstead). For two years, he has been working on a long poem titled *London Pleasures* (33–34) that he cannot bring himself to finish. His only friend in literary circles is Ravelston, editor of *Antichrist* magazine, "a middle- to highbrow monthly, Socialist in a vehement but ill-defined way" (88). In Bourdieuan terms, Gordon lacks the personal and cultural capital that would enable his acceptance by the literary establishment, "a coterie of moneyed highbrows" (84) that he despises and yet envies: "The sods! The bloody sods! [...] Why not say outright 'We don't want your bloody poems. We only take poems from chaps we were at Cambridge with [...]'?" (84).

Gordon's continuing decline is represented not only by his move to a "filthy kip" in the slums of old Lambeth (231) but also by his next job as an assistant at Mr Cheeseman's bookshop, which is several steps down from Mr McKechnie's establishment, being one of the cheaper "mushroom libraries" that are "deliberately aimed at the uneducated" (225; cf. Allington 2019, 347, Hilliard 2014). Gordon now considers himself "part of the slum" (228), with no longer any illusions, any hope or ambition towards a better life:

> Much of the time, when no customers came, he spent reading the yellow-jacketed trash that the library contained. Books of that type you could read at the rate of one an hour. And they

were the kind of books that suited him nowadays. It is real 'escape literature', that stuff in the twopenny libraries. Nothing has ever been devised that puts less strain on the intelligence; even a film, by comparison, demands a certain effort. (228)

Yet again, social distinctions and hierarchies are mediated via literature and literary criticism, showing Gordon's abject condition in his acceptance of "escape literature", the lowest type of commercial fiction available as a form of mindless entertainment. He sees himself has having gone "under ground" (224) in what is possibly an allusion to Dostoevsky's *Notes from Underground* (cf. Fowler 1995, 141), but he soon finds that this extreme outsider position is difficult to maintain for a longer stretch of time. Moreover, it is his "wretchedness", he thinks, that leads Rosemary "to yield to him, even if it was only once" (Orwell 2014, 247). The moment itself is passed over in a terse single sentence: "So it was done at last, without much pleasure, on Mother Meakin's dingy bed" (247). In the final paragraph of chapter 10, this sentence also marks a rare shift in focalisation from Gordon to Rosemary, recording her feelings rather than his ("dismayed, disappointed and very cold"), before the next chapter returns to Gordon's point of view. A few months later, when Rosemary tells him she is pregnant, he decides to escape the slum and "turn respectable" again (254) by going back to his former job in advertising.

Aspidistra ends with a few variations on key tropes of a coming-of-age novel: "He was thirty and there was grey in his hair, yet he had a queer feeling that he had only just grown up" (266–267). Having failed in his "rebellion" "against the money-code", he "surrenders" and feels "at peace" (267). He recognises decency and respectability in the "lower-middle-class people" he had previously despised, "behind their lace curtains, with their children and their scraps of furniture and their aspidistras" (268), but whose ranks he is now about to join. Having a real child of his own to look forward to, he destroys the manuscript of *London Pleasures* in what is expressed in drastic terms as the abortion of "a two years' fœtus which would never be born" (268).

The novel's central conflict, expressed in the symbolic aspidistra of the title (which in turn derives from Gordon's reading of Robert Tressell's *Ragged Trousered Philanthropists*, 47), is between the (artistic and personal) freedom of literary bohemia and the norms and expectations of life in 'respectable' society, which demands sacrifices to "the money-god" (51). Gordon's marriage to Rosemary and his return to the despised job in advertising that he had given up in order to become a poet is the ultimate expression of this sacrifice at the end, which is presented as a happy ending but which many critics have seen as an unsatisfying and half-hearted conclusion to the novel. Rita Felski, for example, refers to Gordon's "conversion" as "largely unmotivated and singularly unconvincing" (Felski 2000, 36); Michael Levenson calls it "melodramatic" and reports that it "has embarrassed many readers" (Levenson 2007, 69). Marriage to a woman whose maiden name is Waterlow may signal the poet's ebb-tide or his Waterloo moment, his final defeat by the forces of conformity.

Yet, it is at the same time his rescue from the slough of despond. The compromise of being *"in* the money-world, but not *of* it" (Orwell 2014, 56), an allusion to John 17.14 and a well-known tenet of Christian faith, expresses Gordon's aloofness from the cash-nexus in religious terms, but in this context it sounds more like an attempt at self-defence against the reproach of having to sacrifice one's ideals and ambitions at the altar of economic necessity and social conformity. *Aspidistra*, which at times "reads rather like a pastiche of *New Grub Street* transplanted to the London of the early nineteen-thirties" (Bergonzi 1976, 21), thus harks back to the key compromise formula of the literary *bildungsroman* but presents it as a form of personal failure rather than personal success (as it would have been for a character like Pendennis). This is because Gordon's *bildungsroman* has been contaminated, as it were, by the ideals of the *künstlerroman*, in which artist and society are at odds with each other. In order to achieve his formation as a full member of society (as expressed in his marriage), he must admit his failure as an artist, and the affective mode of this admission is resentment – a permanent emotional distance from, but powerless dissatisfaction with, the world at large and his own position in it (though not 'of it').

Orwell's later *Nineteen Eighty-Four* (1949) continues and develops some ideas from *Aspidistra*, particularly its bitterness about the cheapened and standardised products of an entertainment industry. In the totalitarian state of Oceania, among other things, "rubbishy newspapers containing almost nothing except sport, crime and astrology" brainwash the population (Orwell 2013, 50). "[S]ensational five-cent novelettes" (ibid.) are no longer written by individual authors but by committees aided by "novel-writing machines" (149), like the ones that Gissing imagined Edison inventing in *New Grub Street*. Winston Smith's decision to start writing a diary with "an archaic instrument" like a pen (9) is already an act of resistance because he returns to the older, and now forbidden, model of individual authorship with its ethical attributes of sincerity and authenticity, in revolt against the prevailing state-sponsored practices of doublethink and enforced ignorance. Here, writing can once again be imagined as a meaningful and valuable activity in an environment that seeks to suppress any sense of individuality – a possibility that the realistic, New-Objectivity-ish mode of *Aspidistra* and its prevailing money-world strikingly did not allow. For Orwell himself, the change from realism to science fiction provided him with a solution to the problem of his own authorial identity as a novelist. *Nineteen Eighty-Four* proved that he could continue to write novels in an accessible, formally unchallenging 'middlebrow' style while including experimental, avantgarde elements on the level of content – thereby making his escape from the "half-baked trash" (2014, 3) of commercial fiction and "up to the throne" (7) of immortality.

Orwell's hero, the disaffected lower-middle-class man, not only fulfils a bridging function between the late Victorian, Edwardian and post-Edwardian realist novels of Gissing and Bennett (whose first novel, *A Man from the North*, 1898, is also about a young man who gives up his literary aspirations, and whose *Riceyman Steps* from 1923, shares the setting in and around a second-hand bookshop) and the postwar 'angry young men' novels by Amis, Braine, and Sillitoe. He can also be profitably compared to the writer-protagonists in other novels of the 1930s that break out of the realist mould and, in breaking with both literary and social conventions, seek different ways of escaping from a position of resentment and immobility.

"Everything that was literature has fallen from me": Samuel Beckett, Henry Miller, and Lawrence Durrell

In 1932, Samuel Beckett wrote his first novel, *Dream of Fair to Middling Women*, for which he failed to find a publisher in Britain (it was first published posthumously only in 1993). Its protagonist is the apathetic student Belacqua Shuah, who resembles many a coming-of-age hero in his antisocial and individualist stance but who, in contrast to the *bildungsroman* foil that lies behind the novel, refuses to mature in any recognisable sense. Beckett 'revived' Belacqua in the stories collected in *More Pricks than Kicks* (1934), some of which were extracted from the *Dream* manuscript. Near the end of the story "Yellow", in which Belacqua dies on an operating table, he is characterised as "an indolent bourgeois poltroon, very talented up to a point, but not fitted for private life in the best and brightest sense" (Beckett 1993, 174). In *Dream*, he also refuses the trappings of realist fiction that are an essential part of the *bildungsroman* genre, including a 'synthetic' view of character and environment that he identifies and dismisses in the novels of Balzac and Austen as a form of polite juggling:

> Much of what has been written concerning the reluctance of our refractory constituents to bind together and give us a synthesis is true equally of Belacqua. [...] The procédé that seems all falsity, that of Balzac, for example, and the divine Jane and many others, consists in dealing with the vicissitudes, or absence of vicissitudes, of character in this backwash, as though that were the whole story. Whereas, in reality, this is so little the story [...]. To the item thus artificially immobilised in a backwash of composure precise value can be assigned. So all the novelist has to do is to bind his material in a spell, item after item, and juggle politely with irrefragable values [...]. (Beckett 1996, 118–119)

Like Gordon Comstock, Belacqua writes poetry, but he can also imagine himself a novelist, though one completely outside of this realist tradition:

> I shall write a book, he mused [...] – a book where the phrase is self-consciously smart and slick but of a smartness and slickness other than that of its neighbours on the page. The blown rose of a phrase shall catapult the reader into the tulips of the phrase that follows. The experience of my reader shall be between the phrases, in the silence, communicated by the intervals, not the terms, of the statement [...]. I shall state silences more competently than ever a better man spangled the butterflies of vertigo. (138)

This emphasis on the unsaid, on "silences", is then linked to the music of Beethoven, as it is in the story "Ding-Dong", also from *More Pricks than Kicks,* where Belacqua refers to his indolent life as "a Beethoven pause" (Beckett 1993, 40). It can also be associated with Beckett's 1937 letter to Axel Kaun, in which the silences in Beethoven's seventh symphony are singled out for comparison to the aesthetic effect that Beckett wants to achieve in his writing (Beckett 1984, 53). *Dream,* however, is decidedly not there yet.

In *Dream,* Belacqua continues: "If ever I do drop a book, which God forbid, trade being what it is, it will be a ramshackle, tumbledown, a bone-shaker, held together with bits of twine" (1996, 139). If *Dream*'s "mannered prose" (Cohn 1984, 10) offers only a weak foreshadowing of the rigorous pleasures of Beckett's postwar trilogy *Molloy, Malone Dies,* and *The Unnamable,* it resembles other late modernist attempts at overcoming the conventional strictures of narrative realism – conventions not merely of language but also of subject matter, of aesthetics as well as of morality.

Henry Miller's *Tropic of Cancer* (1934) can be singled out as most representative of this trend. What Beckett called a *"reductio ad obscenum"* (1984, 41) aimed at a literary exploration of the nature and meaning of human life underneath the veneer of civilisation and social conventions, a project whose progenitors include Thomas Hardy and D. H. Lawrence. Miller's sexual-revolutionary stance was a particularly powerful provocation in a decade characterised by "deep political divisions" (Kohlmann/Taunton 2019, 2) and a heavily politicised cultural atmosphere. The novel – which is largely autobiographical, and an early example of what would now be called autofiction – was published by the Obelisk Press in Paris, which specialised in 'dirty books'. It was banned in most Anglophone countries, in some cases as late as the 1970s.

Miller's writer-narrator seeks to liberate himself from any social constraints and obligations, a liberation made possible by his move to Paris (and the occasional cheque from his wife, who remains in the US). These constraints include what counts as literary writing: "Everything that was literature has fallen from me. There are no more books to be written, thank God. [...] This is not a book, in the ordinary sense of the word. No, this is a prolonged insult, a gob of spit in the face of Art, a kick in the pants to God, Man, Destiny, Time, Love, Beauty … what you will" (Miller 2015, 1). He has abandoned any elevated notion of literature and related author concepts like the genius: "We have no need for genius – genius is dead" (22), he insists. Instead, he considers himself to be "a writing machine" (22), the task of which is to put into words "all that which is omitted in books" (9). The idea of writing as a means of capturing personal experience, unfiltered, and its associated promise of literary and (counter-) cultural regeneration through excess, would prove to be of lasting influence on later generations of (mostly male) writers, from Jack Kerouac to Hunter Thompson. Miller in *Tropic of Cancer* is as likely to write about hunger and food as about sex and women.

Yet, it is clear that the sexual act, for Miller as well as for Durrell (see below), is the epitome of human (male) existence and heightened experience, its pleasure a metonymy for their idea of life as a fulfilment of the desire, ultimately, for freedom. In this, they radicalise the experience of the male writer from Gissing to Orwell, which consisted predominantly in sexual frustration due to his inability, for lack of money, to get married; and they celebrate the writer's liberation from such restraints in the more relaxed moral climate of 1930s Paris and the Mediterranean, even to the extent that, for the Durrell of *The Black Book*, "[t]he verb 'to fuck' has become synonymous with the verb 'to be'" (1977, 219). The price for this freedom, however, is often paid by the women and non-heterosexual characters in these texts.

Orwell, famously, felt "*understood*" by Miller: "'He knows all about me,' you feel, 'he wrote this specially for me'", he asserts in the essay "Inside the Whale" (1940), proclaiming that *Tropic of Cancer* was better than "ordinary fiction" because it dealt with "the recognisable experiences of human beings" (2002, 214, emphasis original). This impression is echoed by many readers and reviewers of today's autofiction, as is Orwell's question why "these monstrous trivialities are so engrossing" (216). He ends the essay by praising Miller as "the only imaginative prose-writer of the slightest value who has appeared among the English-speaking races for some years past" (249). Part of this understanding, though it remains unsaid, may well reside in Miller's innovative solution to the relationship of author and society, his transformation of the 'novel of resentment' into a novel of regeneration.

Among English writers, the one most clearly inspired by Miller is Lawrence Durrell, whose first novel *The Black Book* (1938), written when its author was twenty-four, was also first published by Jack Kahane's Obelisk Press. Durrell's "mannered prose" (Cohn 1984, 10) resembles the young Beckett's but is even more florid, influenced by Lawrence and Miller, among others. In fact, this style ought to be recognised as less a personal property of an author but an expression of a *zeitgeist*, a historical constellation in which this mannered language (including elliptical sentences, mixed metaphors, jumbled tenses, aphoristic pronouncements, rhetorical questions, etc.) fulfils a particular function as a signal of resistance to the mimetic conventions of the realist novel. Their use of a more poetic language and (frequently) their lack of a conventional plot can be seen as attempts to escape from these conventions and to make readerly homopoetic assimilation more difficult. For the 'author novel', such nonlinearity offers exciting new possibilities.

Like *Tropic of Cancer*, *The Black Book* is narrated in the first person, but it adds a second first-person narrator as an additional complication: the forty-year-old writer Herbert Gregory, whose diary the first narrator presents and edits in extracts that alternate with his own retrospective narration. Both men reflect on their writing in ways that complement each other and amount to a critique of conventional forms: "Dear me. This is becoming fine writing in the manner of the Sitwells" (Durrell 1977, 38), complains Gregory, and adds: "If you are afflicted by my tediousness, take heart. This might have been a novel instead of anything so pleasantly anonymous as a diary" (39). He refers to earlier attempts at writing as "literary garbage" and "[t]his lame practice for a literary career" (71). The first narrator, in drawing the reader's attention to another character, named Tarquin, does so self-consciously with the words: "Let us take a novelist-in-the-cupboard peep at Tarquin" (27), and he frequently returns to a metareflective mode on the genre of his writing: "The truth is that I am writing my first book. It is difficult, because everything must be included: a kind of spiritual itinerary which will establish the novel once and for all as a mode which is already past its *senium*" (66), i.e,. its old age. The novel is always present, in the background, as a horizon of expectations, a standard to be achieved or avoided. "I tell myself continually", the narrator continues, "that this must be something without beginning, something which will never end, but conclude only when it has reached its own genesis again" (66). The refusal of a conventional linear plot structure is thus connected to a notion of spiritual renewal and rebirth beyond the ordinary life cycle of birth and death.

In a preface of 1959, Durrell introduced the book as "a two-fisted attack on literature by an angry young man of the thirties", retrospectively aligning himself with the young generation of English novelists at the end of the fifties (Durrell 1977, 9). He also speaks of his "despair and frustration", and of trying to "break the mummy wrappings – the cultural swaddling clothes which I symbolized here as 'the English Death'" (9). For an English writer at the time, such a break with conventions, or the "escape from the chaste seminary of literature" (66) came at a high price – not being published in Britain, for one – and was perhaps only possible from a spatial distance: Lawrence's Taos, Durrell's Corfu, Connolly's Sanary-sur-Mer. Durrell's autobiographical narrator, also named Lawrence Durrell, and sometimes referring to himself as "Lawrence Lucifer" (147, 170), speaks of having escaped "the English death" (102, 241, 243) and of intending to *"revive"* England to "become, in a sense, *the first Englishman*" (136, emphases original). His England stands for a life of conformity, boredom, and stagnation. He looks back on events in London from his refuge in Greece, from where he assembles the other characters, "those others, no less spectres, who are [his] mimes" (21). He keeps Gregory's black notebook "in the cupboard downstairs" (31). About Gregory's writing, he says it has "the quiet venom of a player who has forgotten the rules" (31). There are some indications that Gregory is merely another 'mime' or fiction of the first narrator himself, representing that narrator's "tender id" (55) or the "saurian" (58) subconscious mind as opposed to his "interrogative ego", a part of his self that "take[s] a sort of hieroglyphic dictation from space" (55). While Gregory's book is handwritten in "green ink" (71), the first narrator uses a typewriter (56), thus emphasising the difference between these two kinds of writing, the informal, private character of the personal diary and the more public nature of fiction that generates a "world" for a community of readers: "this world which I am trying to hammer out *for you* on a blunt typewriter, over the Ionian" (56, emphasis added).

If this is the case, then *The Black Book* experiments with two opposed author concepts, which it places side by side, or in a more complicated manner one inside the other: the author who "take[s] [...] dictation", bypassing the conscious mind, and the author as editor, "whose function is simply to [...] annotate it, punctuate, edit" the black book (55) – one wielding a pen, the other hammering on a typewriter. This method of interlacing different narratives and different layers of mediation foreshadows the technique Durrell would perfect in his more famous postwar novels, above all in *The Alexandria Quartet* (1957–1960). There, he splits up and relativises authorial roles further among several writer characters: Arnauti, Pursewarden, and Darley, whose perspectives and reflections complement and contradict each other, with Darley, writing in the first person, coming closest to a persona of Durrell. This relativisation leads to an insight into the "limitations" of literary fiction when it comes to representing reality: "I began to see [...] that the real 'fiction' lay neither in Arnauti's pages nor Pursewarden's – nor even my own. It was life itself that was a fiction – we were all saying it in our different ways, each understanding it according to his nature and gift" (Durrell 1968, 792). This insight, in the fourth volume of the quartet, *Clea* (1960), relates to the exploration of the limits of fiction in postmodernist metafiction (Waugh 1984) [→ ch. 13].

Like Miller, Durrell wants to revolutionise and revive writing by abandoning literary conventions and aiming for an existential sense of authenticity beyond "the ancient tinned salad of the subsidised novel" (Durrell 1968, 751). Instead of the inert, dead matter of literary history – "the great domes of pulp, endless spools of marrow and garbage and cloth, woven into daily papers, sanitary towels, toilet wafers, blotting paper" (Durrell 1977, 149) – he suggests an existential revivification:

"Books should be built of one's tissue or not at all" (121). Like the bookshops in Orwell's *Aspidistra*, Durrell spatialises literary history in the arrangement and recycling of its material substrate: books and paper. The new life that 'Lawrence Lucifer' envisages, and the creation of a "new gnosis" (160), are not only contrasted to the weight of dead ancestors (cf. 157) but, implicitly and sometimes explicitly, gendered as male and pitched as the innovative utterance of a single male individual, in direct opposition to "the nervous orgasm of a million women novelists" (152) – likewise echoing Orwell's misgivings about the feminine middlebrow. The regenerative power of his writing is to be signalled by the emblem of the phoenix he intends to draw on his manuscript (193), a phoenix rising from the ashes of dead literature.

Stevie Smith's *Novel on Yellow Paper* (1936)

There is no precisely corresponding female equivalent to the bad boy authors of the 1930s. Possible contenders might include Anaïs Nin, but her early novel *House of Incest* (1936) was self-published in France and not widely read; or Leonora Carrington, whose surrealist prose from the 1940s (*Down Below*) was largely ignored in Britain. Gertrude Stein's *Autobiography of Alice B. Toklas* (1933) has recently been interpreted as a form of "self-*rewriting*" (Nugent-Folan 2022), an experimental and oblique approach to the genre of autobiography and the literary *bildungsroman*.[155] But perhaps the most neglected and unusual contender for a modernist 'author novel' by a woman writer of the Thirties is Stevie Smith's *Novel on Yellow Paper* (1936).[156] Smith creates an impressive character in the fictional woman writer Pompey Casmilus. She intervenes in the contemporary debate about the industrialisation and mechanisation of literature, and she does so as a woman writer who is carving out a niche for herself in the embattled literary field between 'highbrow' and 'middlebrow' authorship in Britain. The name 'Stevie Smith', a pseudonym of Florence Margaret ('Peggy') Smith (1902–1971), is at least as

---

[155] Nugent-Folan compares Beckett's (later) "self-*un*writing" (2022, 173) in the text *Company* (1980) to Stein's *Autobiography of Alice B. Toklas* (1933). Stein's experiments with self-writing might usefully be read against a more conventional female literary *bildungsroman* such as Storm Jameson's *Company Parade* (1934). I refrain from doing so here for reasons of space.

[156] For a reading of *Novel on Yellow Paper* in the context of experimental modernism, see Wheeler 1994, 141–161; for a critical perspective on strategies of "authorial self-construction" and "tactics of concealment" in the *Novel* and its early reception, see May 2010, 7, 115–117, who also points out that at least one early reader assumed the *Novel*'s real author to be Virginia Woolf (117). Comprehensive accounts of Smith's work include Civello 1997, Severin 1997, Huk 2005, and Walsh 2004.

ambiguous as 'George Eliot' and has confused many readers about her gender (see May 2010, 115–177), a first step of many in an unconventional direction.

Earlier in this book, we have seen how female authors responded to the masculine genre of the literary *bildungsroman* and how they explored the fundamental tension between their roles of 'woman' and 'artist'. *Novel on Yellow Paper* (1936) takes its readers into a pitched battle against literary conventions and a long tradition of gender inequality in literary authorship. Many women associated with the literary world during the later modernist period held jobs in the publishing business, mostly though as office workers, typists, or secretaries. As Lawrence Rainey points out (2009), in the early twentieth century the word "typewriter" could denote both the machine and its (usually female) operator. At the time, Smith worked as private secretary to Sir Neville Pearson with Newnes Publishing Company, a large firm that produced newspapers and magazines like *The Strand* (1891–1950) and the *Lady's Companion* (1892–1940). This situation forms the background to her first novel, whose narrator, young Pompey Casmilus, works as a secretary for a publisher called Sir Phoebus Ullwater. Her novel is written – typed – on yellow paper because, as Pompey tells the reader, she sometimes types in the office and does not want to confuse parts of her novel with the letters she has to type and post for Sir Phoebus, which are typed on blue paper (Smith 2015 [1936], 6).[157]

Like the other novels discussed in this chapter, *Novel on Yellow Paper* is a subversive variation on the *künstlerroman* genre, exactly contemporaneous with Orwell's *Aspidistra* and following on the heels of E. F. Benson's *Secret Lives* (1932), which depicts a woman writer who makes the transition from working as a secretary in an office to writing novels. Both *Secret Lives* and *Novel on Yellow Paper* set creative writing in juxtaposition to the material and technological environment of offices and their mechanical routines. In Benson's satirical take on female authorship, however, the writer can only create when she is subjected to a noisy environment, because that is what she is used to from her previous office work. In her case, writing is all about quantity rather than quality (cf. Stewart 2011, 23), reminding us of the stereotype of the "lady novelist" so viciously caricatured by Thackeray

---

[157] Whereas "Phoebus" clearly designates Apollo, God of knowledge, oracles, and the arts (and is thus an apt if certainly ironic name for a newspaper owner), the potentially "pompous" implications of "Pompey" are less unambiguously tied to Roman origins; in the 1930s, Pompey would also have been known as the nickname for Portsmouth and the name of a famous American racehorse, among other possible associations. "Casmilus" was the name of one of the Cabeiri, ancient Greek deities associated with fertility (see "Cabeiri" 2016). He was often identified with Hermes/Mercury, god of messengers and thieves. On Smith's choice of "a composite of names borrowed from two male figures" as a subversion of gender hierarchies, see Schneider 1997, 63–64.

and still very prevalent as a synonym for bad (women's) writing in the 1930s [→ ch. 6]. This is attested (to give only one example) by W. H. Auden complaining about a changed book title making his poetry appear "like work of a vegetarian lady novelist".[158] For Smith's protagonist, like Benson's, the office is an institutional space conducive to creative writing: typing on yellow paper is an enabling condition of literary expression. As for Miller's Henry in *Tropic of Cancer*, it is the symbiosis of writer and machine that allows Pompey to structure her digressive, exploratory narrative into the form of a novel.

In the modernist period, mechanisation entered the sphere of literary creativity, and many writers deplored technological and cultural changes in the literary world that, in their view, betokened a separation of authorship from inspiration or genius through its association with mechanical labour. Many of the "high priests" of modernism, such as T. S. Eliot and Wallace Stevens, knew office work at first hand and feared that the "industrialization of writing" (Latham 2019, 180) would degrade their status to that of office workers. Kipling, in one of his late stories, "Dayspring Mishandled" (1928), satirically envisages a "Fictional Supply Syndicate to meet the demand" for "standardised reading-matter" (2015, 391). In Orwell's *Nineteen Eighty-Four* (1949), such novels are mass-produced by machines, as already envisaged in *New Grub Street*. It is this change of writing "from a cultured pursuit to an industrialized and [...] increasingly mechanized activity" (Latham 2019, 173) that lies at the heart of Smith's novel. Its major insight is that, as Sean Latham argues, "authorship is no longer a self-evident category; it has become so commercialized, mechanized, and distributed that the book itself can no longer be clearly distinguished, from the memos, advertisements, articles, and correspondence that constitute the new surround of writing" (174).

Novel on Yellow Paper foregrounds the hybridity and insecurity of Pompey's/ Smith's writing in trying to find a genuine voice of her own in this context. In the process, it juxtaposes a Romantic ideal of authorship as self-expression with a modernist despair at the impossibility of realising such an ideal in the industrialised world of writing. The appeal to the reader to "read on and work it out for yourself" (Smith 2015, 1) not only opens the text up to various interpretations but also signals the writer's failure to reconcile her writing with the formal and material constraints of books in a modern book market; she tells readers, only a few lines earlier, that the word "book" means "magazine" in the newspaper business.[159] References to typing abound, for instance when Pompey self-critically re-

---

158 W. H. Auden, letter to Bennett Cerf, Nov. 1936 (Faber 2019, 119).
159 Earlier readings of *Novel on Yellow Paper* – rare as they are – have focused on the ways in which Smith handles literary form to call attention to the instability of language and meaning

veals that she can only type with one finger of each hand (15) or when she assures readers that a particular word is "no slip-up of the typewriter" (18). She frequently refers to the world of newspaper publishing and its trend for market consolidation, as when she invokes the publishing mogul Lord Beaverbrook, the "baron of Fleet Street", who "knew [his] public to a T" (21) – unlike the novel writer, who frequently imagines a reader inimical to or not interested in what she has to say, calling for this reader to put the book away (24).[160]

Yet, she also worries about her book's layout (25) and about the inability of writing to represent the spoken voice: "Oh talking voice that is so sweet, how hold you alive in captivity, how point you with commas, semi-colons, dashes, pauses and paragraphs?" (25) Here the voice is "alive" as an immediate expression of the self; it is threatened with death when it is imprisoned in what Max Weber famously called the "iron cage" of modern routines of representation, "bound to the technical and economic conditions of machine production" (Weber 1958, 181). The contrast between a Romantic cult of authorship and the modernist condition of impersonality is, in Smith's novel, literally materialised in the punctuation of a text.[161]

There are other difficulties that Pompey experiences with writing a novel and meeting an audience's taste, especially a middlebrow audience "which won't stand for highbrow nonsense" (Smith 2015, 47) and is more interested in interior decoration than in high-minded ideas. Pompey, however, gets "bored" by the expectation of having to write conventional novelistic descriptions of interior spaces: "I am not an interior decorator", she writes, and "I find it difficult to look at furniture and remember to tell other people" (47). Likewise, she is not enthusiastic about stories involving family histories, "those cradle-to-the-grave novels that never let you out under three volumes" (56). She is highly critical of Victorian novels of romance and adventure (rather arbitrarily naming Mrs Humphrey Ward and James Payn), for reasons that are ideological as well as formal (Severin 1997, 25). Instead of such old-fashioned narrative conventions, she offers her readers a feast of non-linearity

---

(Nemesvari 1991) or on her transgressive disruption of conventional narrative forms (Wheeler 1994, 142–153).

160 Max Aitken, 1st Baron Beaverbrook (1879–1964) was a major player in the British newspaper business in the early twentieth century, comparable to Rupert Murdoch's role at the beginning of the twenty-first century. He is memorably portrayed as Lord Monomark in Evelyn Waugh's *Vile Bodies* (1930).

161 William May notes that the manuscript Smith submitted to Cape was "unpunctuated" and that she "added the requisite number of full stops and speech marks" only at her publisher's behest (2010, 101). On Pompey's voice in the novel, see also Nemesvari 1991, 27, 32–33, 36.

– moving between recollections of travel in Germany and reflections on food, culture, sex, and class in Britain (for instance, Smith 2015, 111).

In a passage that anticipates Richard Hoggart's *The Uses of Literacy* (1957) by two decades, Smith/Pompey even provides a sociological analysis of popular fiction, i.e., the twopenny weeklies that are mostly read by young women (Smith 2015, 115–116). She divides these into "Fiction for the Married Woman" (115) and "stories for unmarried girls", the latter "full of pretty ideas that are all the time leading to washing-up" (117). These she despises for their ugliness and triviality, their "negation of human intelligence" (118). Later, she tells readers about a young man, a reader of Swinburne, Kipling, and the Bible, who develops a taste for writing and then turns it into a profession, working as "a Lady Novelist. The only surviving lady Novelist" (143) "writing those chic little middles for girlies' papers, the tuppenny weekly girlies' papers that are always having emotional crises, and wondering about their young man" (144). This writer has internalised the idea of writing as a job like any other: "'Oh yes you know I *write*, you know, just straightforward and honest. It's a job like any other job, isn't it? Only harder, harder than a navvy's job. It's just a job JOB JOB" (143, emphasis original).

For Pompey, by contrast, literary authorship is not a "job" but a private exertion and a compulsion to create outside of pre-existing formulas or generic conventions. As she explains towards the end, returning to the question of her book's form and format:

> People have said to me: If you must write, remember to write the sort of book the plain man in the street will read. It may not be a best seller – but it should maintain a good circulation.
>   About this I pondered for a long time and became distraught. Because I can write only as I can write only, and Does the road wind uphill all the way? Yes, to the very end. But brace up, chaps, there's a 60,000 word limit. (179)

The form of Pompey's writing, in the sense of the writing process, and the format of the published book are in conflict, just like the vivid "talking voice" (25) conflicts with the fixed format of the typed and printed text. The first-person novel as individual expression is here staged as permanently resisting the generic fixity of any established literary form, as it is in Miller and Durrell, among others.

In the years after the war, only Doris Lessing will re-focus the 'woman writer novel' on a concern with structural constraints of the novel form, while remaining within the realist tradition and the politically committed type of the socialist *bildungsroman*.[162] This seems a far cry from Smith's open embrace of a form that ap-

---

[162] See Kohlmann 2015. For the view that *The Golden Notebook* "parodies conventional realism", see Waugh 1984, 71.

pears to be formless and is certainly unpredictable. In its metafictional spirit, it is closer to Muriel Spark's debut novel *The Comforters* (1957), whose protagonist is a female writer at work on a study of *Form in the Modern Novel*, who discovers that she is herself a character in a novel (Waugh 1984, 121) [→ ch. 13]. Yet *Novel on Yellow Paper* shares with *The Golden Notebook* the confrontation of the modern predicament of female authorship. Its brutally honest diagnosis of the modern publishing world, i. e., the segregation of readerly tastes according to 'brows' and the constraints imposed on writers working in established generic moulds, make for a strong engagement with the material conditions of literary production in 1930s Britain. Moreover, its radical self-reflection and formal innovation make it a prime example of experimental modernist fiction that engages with the literary and cultural expectations of its time. Far from merely being another experimental novel that plays with linguistic indeterminacy, *Novel on Yellow Paper* critiques the material, cultural and social as well as formal and genre boundaries of literary writing in the interwar years. With its irreverent author-protagonist, Stevie Smith positioned her individual talent at the end of a long tradition of women's writing, transcending restrictive narrative conventions and intervening in contemporary debates on the impact on literature of new technologies and new audiences for fiction.

"What an abominable occupation": Roland Camberton's *Scamp* (1950)

Roland Camberton was the pen name of Henry Cohen (1921–1965), who won the 1951 Somerset Maugham award for his first novel, *Scamp* (1950).[163] *Scamp* tells the story of Ivan Ginsberg, a single man aged thirty who has been trying to break into the literary scene by writing numerous short stories, without much success. He shares a mice- and rat-infested flat with his friend Bellenger, a notorious womaniser. Ginsberg, who has been educated at Cambridge as a scholarship boy from London's East End, earns some money teaching Russian literature and giving private language lessons, and he also works as a "ghost" for the prolific journalist Bert Flogcrobber (Camberton 2010, 232), finishing and polishing articles at very low rates. His idea is to establish a magazine "for the younger generation", to be called *Scamp*. All he needs, he reasons, is money, contributors, and a printer. Despite his best efforts, he does not get very far with any of these, and due to a series of mis-

---

[163] Maugham had set up the award in 1947 with money earned from selling the film rights to *The Razor's Edge* to MGM for $250,000 (Nash 2016, 32).

haps and bad decisions, the magazine fails before even a single issue is printed. He is thoroughly disillusioned and disgusted with what London has become since the War, and the novel is filled with atmospheric descriptions of the seedy charms of Soho and a city pockmarked by bombings and postwar austerity: "Everywhere decay; truly a wasteland; without love, [...] his familiar environment was nothing but a desert, an ugly, unhealthy desert half destroyed by war and neglect" (186–187).

There is still a paper shortage, which exacerbates the situation of numerous bohemian writers like him, the "Soho bums" (37) who frequent the "shoddy Bohemia" (44) of the cafés, cheap restaurants, pubs, and all-night milk bars of Soho and Bloomsbury. Some of these write "pornography for private circulation" (48), others are novelists or poets, and some are thinly veiled pen-portraits of recognisable Soho fixtures, like the colourful 'Angus Sternforth Simms' (Julian Maclaren-Ross). Maclaren-Ross's own novel *Of Love and Hunger* (1947) could be profitably discussed in this context, as could other novels and plays of the now legendary Soho-Fitzrovia context, such as Patrick Hamilton's *Hangover Square* (1941) and Rodney Ackland's *Absolute Hell* (1952). While not particularly original in its plot or its depiction of this area and period of London, Camberton's *Scamp* offers a Jewish angle on this scene, to be set next to the writings of Simon Blumenfeld, Alexander Baron, and Bernard Kops, which focus more firmly on life in London's East End (cf. Sinclair 2010).

From the beginning of the novel, Ginsberg feels disgusted by writing:

> A story a day, that was his minimum task; two thousand words, preferably with a plot, development, a climax, and a twist. After six months of this routine, he was beginning to feel an intense hatred of the short story, in fact, of all writing. What an abominable occupation it was! What a struggle! For what meagre prizes! Only the middlemen, he felt, were to be envied: the publishers, editors, anthologists and functionaries who stood between the raw material of the writer and the public purse. (22)

The plan to become an editor is thus motivated by a hatred of writing. To be an editor would be a step up in the world, closer to the revenue streams of "the public purse". "Writing", he later tells his new friend Kathleen, is "a mug's game" (280), not worth playing. And yet this is part of his idea of who he is: "I'm nothing and nobody if I'm not a writer, and the sad fact is that I'm not" (24) – because he is "mainly an unpublished writer" (85).

His erotic disappointments need to be added to his literary ones. Ginsberg's first love, Margaret, has disappeared from his life; she may have committed suicide while pregnant with his child (91), or she may simply have left him behind. Ginsberg has been conducting an intermittent affair with Lolita, a young woman from Gibraltar, but she finally breaks it off. One of the more interesting aspects of this novel is its multicultural cast of characters and its sense of London as a city of immigrants: "After the French, the Jews, the Italians, the Greeks, the Cypriots, the Maltese, had come the Indians [...]" (250). This development causes concern and resentment on the part of disaffected white men like Flogcrobber, the journalist, who harbours antisemitic prejudices, mixed with nostalgic ideas about England, which Ginsberg shares (171, 270), and who joins the (fictional) right-wing "Association of the Freemen and Yeomen of England" (304). When Ginsberg comes to collect the money that Flogcrobber owes him, the journalist shoots at him with a revolver but misses his aim and then writes him a cheque. At the end of the novel, Ginsberg is ready to start a "new life" (302), with Kathleen, a young woman from Ireland who had sent him a story for *Scamp* and then joins him in London. He destroys many of his short stories (partly, it seems, to impress her), and his new plan is to write a novel, "*the* novel" (288, emphasis original). Their rather sudden marriage is *Scamp*'s somewhat unlikely romantic conclusion to Ginsberg's string of failures – and there is a sense of the contingent or accidental to all of this, since he might as well have been shot and killed by Flogcrobber in the final chapter as a victim of antisemitism. If the ending in marriage resembles that of *Aspidistra*, it is even less convincing here than it is in Orwell.

Jake, the hero of Camberton's second (and last) novel, *Rain on the Pavements* (1951), has published a novel – very tellingly titled *Failure*. He does not dare tell his family or friends about it. Moreover, *Rain on the Pavements* is set in pre-war Hackney, and its author-protagonist is yet another "refracted self-portrait" of Camberton (Sinclair 2010, 8). The narrator finds this obscure author's book, a "thin, ill-printed, yellow-wrapped volume" (qtd. in Sinclair 2010, 9), which is now merely a trace of a vanished past and a vanished life. Camberton himself never published anything else in his lifetime and settled down to obscurity.

In these versions of the novel of resentment from the interwar years to the late 1940s, writers are yet again depicted as champing at the bit of social, moral, and literary norms. Orwell's and Camberton's unconvincing happy endings are failed compromise formations, born out of the attempt to reconcile their heroes' (and their own) literary and erotic aspirations to the economic and cultural recession of the Great Depression and the Second World War. The name of Orwell's protagonist, Gordon Comstock, is telling not only in its associations of class ('common stock') but also of the notorious US Postal Inspector and anti-vice activist Anthony Comstock, whose name had become proverbial for censorship and bigotry. Orwell responded with admiration to Henry Miller's radical flight from the bounds of literary and social convention, though he did not follow Miller's lead in breaking the mould of the well-made novel. While Miller, the young Durrell, and the young Beckett sought to reinvigorate writing and 'make themselves new' by means of unfettered, incandescent, anti-conventional prose, we find an equally unconventional but more playful vitality in Stevie Smith's *Novel on Yellow Paper*.

The formal difference between Orwell and Camberton on the one hand, Miller and Durrell on the other, is also one between different kinds of narration: whereas *Scamp* and *Aspidistra* have a heterodiegetic narrator, who maintains an inevitable distance to the characters, *Tropic of Cancer*, *Novel on Yellow Paper*, and *The Black Book* have homo- or even autodiegetic narrators, creating an impression of directness and immediacy. They stage the processes of their own autography, their "self-writing" (Abbott 1996, ix) or "self-*un*writing" (Nugent-Folan 2022, 173) on the printed page. In doing so, they gesture towards a new schism in the literary field: the tripartite division between the 'realists', the 'fabulists', and the 'nonfictionists' (later, the autofictionists) that will emerge in the postwar literary world (Lodge 1986, 18–19, and see part IV of this book). While the realist novel continues to stagnate in its settled ways of representation and respectability, these authors write themselves out of resentment and frustration into a reprise of Romantic expressivism.

12 Working Women: Figurations of Female Authorship in Postwar Britain

The Feminine Point of View

Postwar Britain has been succinctly described as the "nadir of British feminism" (Pugh 2000, 284) because of its rollback of progressive social attitudes that had evolved before and during World War Two. One can get a fine glimpse of this in a report by the author and biographer Olwen Campbell on a conference titled *On the Feminine Point of View*, based on a series of meetings "of a group of women of varied interests and occupations" from 1947 onwards (Campbell 1952, 5). Campbell deplores women's lack of economic power (28), their lack of scope in careers (31), and "the almost complete absence of [women's] authoritative influence in the conduct of affairs" (13). She points out that women's advice in serious matters is still unwelcome, citing the rejection of one of Dorothy Sayers's short pieces by the BBC "on the ground that 'our public do not want to be admonished by a woman'" (25).[164] She also addresses the question of women's role in the arts, particularly whether there is "a feminine point of view distinguishable in literature" or whether "women writers even to-day, when they write so much" are "influenced by a masculine pattern and masculine preferences" (43). Women, in other words, no longer lack access to the literary marketplace, but they accommodate their writings to established expectations of femininity instead of "express[ing] their opinion" (43).

Mid-twentieth-century British women writers negotiated conflicting demands on gender as well as economic and aesthetic constraints on literary authorship. At this time, writing by women was still frequently and all too easily disqualified as 'middlebrow'. The categorical boundaries between 'modernist' and 'middlebrow' writing, and the complex interplay of factors such as class, taste, and gender associated with them, constituted a difficult terrain, especially for women writers, which they had to navigate in writing, publishing, and managing their public image.

The aim of this chapter is to reconstruct a rhetoric of female authorship in the late modernist period, before the social and cultural transformations of the 1960s led to radical changes in the practical, economic, and aesthetic aspects of female literary authorship. These changes would finally dispel the pernicious image of the 'lady novelist', which, through its association with sentimentalism and com-

---

[164] The quotation can be traced to Sayers 1946, 7.

mercialism, had prevented many female authors from being taken seriously in comparison with their male colleagues. In this, I follow Liz Sage's judgement that much postwar British women's writing was a self-reflexive engagement with, and opposition to, "the very concept of 'women's fiction' or 'women's writing'", categories which had become uncomfortable and confining for many (2016, 110). Yet only few women writers took up the challenge of writing an *autocritique* of their own position in the literary field – as Stevie Smith certainly did in the 1930s with her *Novel on Yellow Paper* [→ ch. 11].

The male prejudice against writing women was still strong in the early to mid-twentieth century. In *The Little Nugget* (1913), P. G. Wodehouse, for example, introduces the female crime writer Nesta Ford. She reappears in his *Piccadilly Jim* of 1917, where she is described as "familiar to all lovers of sensational fiction", as someone who writes "voluminously" and who has "a strong literary virus in [her] system" (Wodehouse 2012, 5). Her ambition to be a "Well-Known Society Leader and Authoress" (18) is a cause of much pain to her husband, as is her running a literary salon. The pathological metaphor of the "virus", the emphasis on quantity, and the focus on her husband's suffering make this a classic example of humour at the expense of a (fictional) woman writer. Another woman writer, later in the same novel, is briefly introduced as "Lora Delane Porter, the feminist writer" (146) – the epithet is probably not intended as a term of endearment in this context. Moreover, women and writing are further associated in this novel, as they are in E. F. Benson's *Secret Lives* (1932), with the typewriter and an office setting: Mr Pett, Nesta's husband, does not object against the activity of writing as such. He hears "the tapping of a typewriter" (10); the sound is not that of his wife at work, it turns out, but his niece Ann Chester "copying out a story" for her (11). To this he responds with "benevolent approval. He loved to hear the sound of a typewriter: it made home so like the office" (10). When a man's home is invaded by a literary salon, in other words, he still has an office in which to feel at home. The same possibility of escape is not afforded to women in the novel; in fact, the home library is clearly marked as a male haunt, as having "that peculiar quality which belongs as a rule to the dens of men" (10). The invasion of a masculine space by a woman writer is also the theme of Huxley's story "The Farcical History of Richard Greenow" (1920), in which the body of a male author is taken over by the personality of an aggressive woman writer, tellingly named 'Pearl Bellairs'. The list of similar examples that represent women writers as objects of satire and ridicule could be extended *ad lib*.

Novels and stories in which women writers are taken more seriously or are represented in a more positive light are few. In the first half of the twentieth century, there are a few obvious candidates among female artist novels, but there are few women writers as characters in these, or their writing is not essential for the narrative. Virginia Woolf and Dorothy Richardson present vivid accounts of female creativity and artistic activity, but in *To the Lighthouse* (1927) the artist is a painter, Lily Briscoe, and in *Pilgrimage* (1915–1938) the focus is on Miriam Henderson's inner life and perception of the world rather than her development as a writer. The events of *Pilgrimage* end in 1915, when Richardson published the first instalment of the sequence; she did not pursue her protagonist's role as a writer beyond this point. This is in keeping with the tradition of the female *bildungsroman*, as inaugurated by *Jane Eyre* and *The Young Authoress* [→ ch. 6]. Woolf's famous manifesto *A Room of One's Own* (1929) raised awareness for the predicament of women writers, but it had no immediate impact on the under-representation of female authorship in 'highbrow' literary fiction, even by women – Stevie Smith's *Novel on Yellow Paper* being a rare exception.

Expanding the view beyond High Modernism towards 'middlebrow' writing and genre fiction, one comes across a richer crop of female author fictions in the 1930s. Storm Jameson's trilogy of (semi-autobiographical) novels beginning with *Company Parade* (1934) addresses the self-formation of a woman writer, but it does so in a conventional realist manner that is unlikely to have impressed her more experimentally inclined peers. There is also the example of Agatha Christie's Ariadne Oliver, a writer of detective novels who resembles her author in many details (as Christie invented the Belgian detective Hercule Poirot, her fictional alter ego invents a Finnish detective called Sven Hjerson). She makes her first appearance in the story "Parker Pyne Investigates" (1932) and subsequently features in a number of Poirot novels between 1936 and 1972. Roughly contemporaneously, Angela Thirkell's Barsetshire novels (1933–1961) feature the popular novelist Laura Morland as an idealised self-portrait.

In the 1950s, we see the rise of the 'angry young men', kitchen-sink drama, neo-realist cinema, and the Movement Poets. The 'angries' celebrated aggressive masculinity as a form of social renewal and anti-establishment revolt (most fully embodied in the character of Jimmy Porter in John Osborne's 1956 play *Look Back in Anger*), pushing women authors even further to the detested margins of a middlebrow culture perceived as feminine, inert, and stagnant. 'Woman writer' or, worse, 'lady novelist' could be an uncomfortable category for women who wanted to be taken seriously as writers. Yet, among the 'career novels' that aimed to advertise various professions for young women (Spencer 2000), quite a few dealt with the book world, from *Shirley: Young Bookseller* (1956) by Valerie Baxter to *Juliet in Publishing* by Elizabeth Churchill (1956).[165] One of these is

---

[165] For a list of such novels published between 1952 and 1961, see https://www.peakirkbooks.com/page/career-stories. Last access 21 Feb. 2023.

Jane: Young Author (Baxter 1958), first published in 1954. Its fledgling woman novelist learns the ropes at a literary agency before working for a publisher and then as a (male) author's secretary; the novel mainly presents practical advice for budding writers in the form of fiction. While the conversations Jane Fanshawe has with her last employer, the author Stephen Traill, are rather one-sided in the manner now commonly described as 'mansplaining', the book maintains an optimistic view of Jane's opportunities in the literary world, even though her romantic first novel *What the Heart Desires* is turned down by an agency. Instead, the novel implies that Jane's "next book" is going to be about her learning process and is going to be called *Jane: Young Author* (Baxter 1958, 191). This self-reflexive flourish opens up the possibility of success that the novel had previously denied to its protagonist. The realism of *Jane: Young Author*, however, is also evinced by the fact that Jane is only able to support her literary ambitions because of a substantial inheritance.[166]

There are comparatively few women writers as characters in British postwar fiction before Doris Lessing's *The Golden Notebook* (1962). Lessing's writer-protagonist Anna Wulf, whose several notebooks in different colours combine personal journals and recollections with political reflections and a novel in progress, may well be the first fully imagined fictional woman novelist in the twentieth-century English novel. Lessing reinvigorates the idea of a woman writer as a literary heroine. In *The Golden Notebook,* she applies techniques of fragmentation and nonlinearity to a subject that embodies nothing less than the antithesis to masculine – as well as impersonal and self-effacing – modernist authorship (Spencer 1973, Worthington 2004). She achieves a compromise between experimental and realist (even middlebrow) techniques and thus contributes to the subversion of the gendered hierarchy of value that dominated English literature at the time.

The originality of this formal breakthrough can be better assessed in comparison to Lessing's predecessors and contemporaries, whose rhetoric of authorship mostly remains confined to the comic or the melodramatic mode, or a combination of the two. Sometimes women writers as characters are drawn in realistic fashion, sometimes in a way that borders on the grotesque. As Sharon Spencer reminds us, "women whose desire for self-expression is so strong and so consistent that they define themselves as artists" were long considered deficient in their femininity, at best a ridiculous oddity, at worst a menace to society (1973, 247). If one expands the scope beyond the refined sphere of literary art, even female writer characters in romances by women suffer from the cultural and social constraints placed upon

---

[166] *Jane: Young Author* was written by the prolific Laurence Meynell (1899–1989) under the pseudonym of Valerie Baxter (see Morse 2004). I am grateful to Leonie Kappus for drawing my attention to this book.

them – and here these constraints become even more visible (see Stewart 2011). In fiction by Elizabeth Taylor, Mary Renault, Kathleen Farrell, and others, one can recognise glimpses of alternative forms of feminine authority and community that push beyond the confines of established views of modernism. If *The Golden Notebook* can be read as a document of women's hard-won liberation (also as authors) in the early 1960s, her immediate postwar predecessors and peers offer a similar, though not yet sufficiently explored, record of their struggle against conventions and categorisations like that of the sentimental 'lady novelist'. Looking back on her early career, Muriel Spark wrote in c. 1991: "[A]bove all I didn't want to become a 'lady novelist' with all the slop and sentimentalism that went with that classification" (Spark 2014, 29).

In one of the most sustained investigations of narrative voice in fiction by women, Susan Lanser explored the connections between discursive authority and social power, and the textual practices of gendered self-authorisation employed by women writers. Her study *Fictions of Authority* examines such practices across three major types of narrative voice: authorial, personal, and communal. Most pertinently, Lanser asserts that the crisis of realism in the modernist novel was a crisis of "overt authoriality" and a failure of "masculine realism", which Woolf attempted to sidestep by pursuing an aesthetics of anonymity, distancing, and impersonality, in marked contrast to Richardson's more personal voice, shaped in response to the same crisis (Lanser 1992, 109, 106). Yet Lanser's book ends without considering the inheritors of this presumptive legacy of modernist crisis in the years leading up to and including *The Golden Notebook*.

The question of a feminine point of view is taken up one year after Campbell's report in Vera Brittain's *History of Women from Victoria to Elizabeth II* (1953). A veteran of the profession, Brittain finds it in women writers who follow a tradition established by Olive Schreiner in the nineteenth century:

> During the 20th century this [feminine] view has struggled increasingly for expression, but has not yet found it on a large enough scale or with sufficient public appreciation of its saving value.
> In the writing of books (as distinct from their work as journalists) women have not only achieved equality with men but have sometimes surpassed them, both from the standpoint of their earnings and in status, recognition, and power. (Brittain 1953, 216)

Brittain goes on to assert that "[w]ith some feminine authors brought up in an older tradition it was fashionable to admire only the work of men and take pride in themselves as exceptions to the general rule of female futility" (219) but that this is now about to change as women writers will increasingly acknowledge the influence of their female predecessors and contemporaries. For Vera Brittain, the real problem facing women writers is structural and practical: how to reconcile literary work with marriage and child-rearing (she proposes, among other things, financial support for "home helps" for writers who have "proved [their] value," 221). Such proposals, though they seem quaint today, reflect the progressive zeitgeist of the late 1940s and 1950s, in the wake of sociological studies on *Women and Work* and *Women and a New Society*, leading up to Myrdal and Klein's pathbreaking book *Women's Two Roles*.[167] In their day-to-day lives and the social and economic practicalities of writing as a profession, the reality for women still looked grim. A few years earlier, in 1947, the same Vera Brittain had been more sceptical: in her book *On Becoming a Writer*, she emphasized that being "a man or woman of letters" was "by no means the same thing," and asserted that "[t]he scales of opportunity still tend to be weighted against women":

> [T]he beginner will find, if she is a woman, that authorship especially in its more creative branches, offers her the advantages of relative sex-equality. This equality, as I have said, is not yet absolute; it is still rare to find women holding high positions on newspapers or magazines read by both sexes, and the appointment of a woman as editor of a London or even a provincial daily would be an unusual event. (Brittain 1947, 29–30)

The extent to which the mid-century literary marketplace was segregated according to gender is still under-researched. But the consensus is that the "stagnant" literary world of the later 1940s and 1950s was not particularly welcoming to women, despite Iris Murdoch being "marked down as an honorary Angry Young Man" (Taylor 2016, 224, 270). In her memoir *Stet*, the editor Diana Athill recalls first being assigned to oversee the cookery list because of her gender (2000, 62) and also notes the gender pay gap: "All publishing was run by many badly-paid women and a few much better-paid men: an imbalance that women were, of course, aware of, but which they seemed to take for granted" (56). Her diagnosis of gender stereotypes and attitudes towards working women is worth quoting more fully:

> Among people of my grandparents' generation and, to a slightly lesser extent, my parents' it was taken for granted that men were to be preferred to women in responsible jobs because they were in better control of their emotional lives. A woman might be as intelligent as a man, but her intelligence could not be relied on because if, for instance, she was crossed in love she would go to pieces. Menstrual moodiness was not actually mentioned, but the idea of it lurked: women, poor things, were so designed that they couldn't be expected to overcome their bodies' vagaries. To my generation [Athill was born in 1917] this was not true, but it was still present as something which needed to be disproved. (81)

---

[167] See Williams 1945, Luetkens 1946, Myrdal/Klein 1956.

There are indications that the attention given to women writers in literary journals like the *TLS* was considerably less than that accorded to their male competitors (Berensmeyer/Trurnit 2022). There was a declining market for short stories with fewer literary magazines to publish them (Taylor 2016, 247, 256). Focusing on literary prizes rather than sales as a basis of recognition, the situation for women is even worse: out of sixteen different literary prizes in Britain between 1945 and 1960, only a quarter were awarded to women.[168] Based on anecdotal evidence, one also finds male writers and editors often patronising their female colleagues and assuming that women write for a female audience only. Lawrence Durrell, in a letter to 'Edward Lane', alias Kay Dick, editor of *The Windmill*, on learning that he is dealing with a woman rather than a man, expresses the hope that she is "not one of the vinegar-bearing lady-novelists".[169] When Elizabeth Jane Howard interviewed Evelyn Waugh for the BBC in 1964, Waugh reportedly asked between takes: "When is Miss Howard going to take her clothes off?" (Stannard 1992, 477) Examples like these could be extended *ad lib*. In a rejection letter from the editor of *Lilliput: The Pocket Magazine for Everyone*, Storm Jameson's agent is informed in 1951 that

> [t]his magazine is read by the two sexes, as far as we know, in a proportion of six men to four women. In consequence, I am afraid that the Storm Jameson story you sent me is too womanly for us. By this I mean that, while a woman reader might find some sympathy with the heroine and understand her emotional storm, to me she seemed a rather trying and hysterical girl and I was not very anxious to follow her story.[170]

Whether or not the editor is deliberately making fun of the author's name here, he rejects the "emotional storm" as "too womanly" in a gesture that fits the general trend of gendering fiction at mid-century as either serious and manly or romantic and womanly. It is this ideological gendering of fiction but also its economic repercussions that postwar British women writers explore when they create fictional authors in novels and stories. While they do not share an ideological agenda and do not present positive role models, they do question and subtly undermine stereotypical attitudes towards the 'woman writer' as idea and reality in mid-twentieth century Britain.

---

168 This information is based on a total of 191 prize-giving events between 1945 and 1960; 142 were awarded to men, 49 to women (25.6%).
169 Lawrence Durrell, undated letter to 'Edward Lane', Harry Ransom Center, Kay Dick archive, box 6, folder 4.
170 Jack Hargreaves, letter to A. D. Peters, 6 July 1951, Harry Ransom Center, Storm Jameson archive, box 10, folder 1.

Exorcism of the 'Lady Novelist': Elizabeth Taylor's *A View of the Harbour* (1947) and *Angel* (1957)

A View of the Harbour, Elizabeth Taylor's third novel, is set in a small seaside town shortly after the Second World War. Narrated in an authorial voice, typically (for Taylor) modelled on the ironic style and free indirect discourse of Jane Austen's mature fiction, the novel presents a cross-section of postwar provincial society: a young widow, a recent divorcee, the local pub owner, a doctor and his family, the family's housekeeper, and so on. Bertram Hemingway, a retired army officer, has come there to capture the titular 'view of the harbour' in a painting. The doctor's wife, Beth, is a novelist whose greatest difficulty is reconciling fiction and actuality, the world she creates in her imaginative writing with the real world of her everyday married life. While reviewers praise her "perception" and "her broad humanity" (Taylor 2018 [1947], 19), Beth finds it difficult to engage with a more particular humanity in the form of her children, Prudence and Stevie. When she is working on a novel, Beth is "happy" to have "the words pouring out of her own darkness" (31), organising an invented world. The fiction she writes seems to owe a considerable debt to the tradition of Victorian and Edwardian realism, whose clichés the narrator mercilessly unpicks:

> [S]he had taken her characters for a nice country walk and brought them back successfully, drawn them together at meal-times and let them talk (but not eat) and now, her eyes burning hotly, was hoping to have an only child dead before luncheon. 'Oh, God save her!' cried the mother, wringing her hands, and Beth would have wrung her own if they had been less busy. Instead, she wept, but was relentless in intention. (31–32)

At this moment, her creative process is interrupted by her daughter Stevie, who has come home from school early. The conflict between the imaginary and the real child is clearly laid out: "with the dying child still on her mind, Beth could not bring herself to welcome this living one" (32). She feels "haunted" by "[t]he imaginary people" who populate her fiction (57), and she feels "guilt about her writing" (57). "'*Men* look upon writing as *work*,'" she tells herself (57, italics original) – implying that women do not, or that men do not look upon women writers as 'working' in the same way as they do. Beth's unhappiness with her predicament is palpable. On the train to London to visit her publisher (also a woman, as is revealed in a conversation with Beth's friend Tory), she reflects again on her "guilt" and "shame" (178) and clearly diagnoses the gender imbalance of her upbringing:

> 'A man,' she thought suddenly, 'would consider this a business outing. But, then, a man would not have to cook the meals for the day overnight, nor consign his child to a friend, nor leave half-done the ironing, nor forget the grocery order as I now discover I have forgotten it. The

artfulness of men,' she thought. 'They implant in us, foster in us, instincts which it is to their advantage for us to have, and which, in the end, we feel shame at not possessing.' (178)

Her husband, in turn, considers her writing "a disease, a madness" that he, the doctor, would like to have "cured" long ago (122). The novel portrays their marriage as functioning without much affection, reminiscent perhaps of the marriage between Laura and her stolid husband Fred in David Lean's film *Brief Encounter* (1945), with the exception that it is not Beth who is having an affair but her husband, Robert, who is in an extramarital relationship with Beth's best friend, Tory, their divorcée neighbour next door. At the end of the novel, Tory decides to get married again, to the interloper Bertram Hemingway, and to move to London to escape her unlucky attachment to Robert. In contrast to her daughter Prudence, Beth remains unaware of the affair to the end. Her perception is clearly less good than her critics assume. As catastrophe is narrowly averted, Beth completes her next novel with a fleeting sense of "bliss, a second only, before all the doubts and anxieties begin again and other people step in. [...] [H]er heart turned over painfully as she laid down her pen" (314).

A View of the Harbour is a novel with no central protagonist. Its focus is on multiple connections between people in a small town. The novel's acute observation of these relationships amounts to a portrait of contemporary provincial society – in contrast to the insulated and unrealistic fictional world created by the intrafictional novelist Beth Cazabon. That Taylor, in her third novel, should be doubting the value of her own chosen profession is clear in her choice of first name for this fictional author. Beth (= Elizabeth) is a distorted mirror of herself. Beth's family name, moreover, may allude to *Middlemarch*, the most famous English novel of provincial life, in which Dorothea Brooke's unworldly husband is called Casaubon. Taylor uses the character of Beth mainly to establish an ironic distance between her own literary writing and a less ambitious (feminine middlebrow) form of the novel, and thus to establish and secure narrative authority for herself. The novel within the novel, like a play within a play, serves to emphasize a distinction between different kinds of literature, and to establish a hierarchy of values between them.

Ten years later, her novel *Angel* (1957) similarly centres on a woman writer to criticise a particular kind of female authorship in favour of another. This time, the distance is also established by means of literary periodisation. *Angel* is an early example of neo-Victorian or rather, in this case, neo-Edwardian fiction. It not only "de-romanticise[s] the process of writing" (Mantel 2008, 6) but speaks out against a particular kind of woman writer: the successful 'lady novelist' and author of romantic bestsellers in the vein of Marie Corelli or Amanda Ros, whose biographies, published in the early 1950s, Taylor used as a model (Stewart

2011, 25).[171] Ten years after her portrayal of a contemporary woman novelist in *A View of the Harbour*, who when she travels to see her publisher is described as looking "not [...] at all like [...] what reviewers sometimes call 'lady novelists'" (Taylor 2018, 175), Taylor returned to reflect on just the type and on the recent history of a particular kind of women's writing. With the character of Angelica Deverell, born in 1885, she presents a vivid caricature of a popular woman writer, but also a psychological portrait of an author whose powers of imagination, while at first enabling her to escape from the ordinary world and to rise in society, ultimately imprison her – and her husband, the painter Esmé – in a golden cage of her own making. The triumph of the imagination over reality, embodied in her success as a novelist, also severs her connection to the real world. Angelica refuses to see that this world is changing. At the end, during the Second World War, she is a lonely old lady in a crumbling country house, completely out of touch with what might be going on outside its walls.

The novel traces, in carefully observed scenes, how Angelica's visual imagination and her passionate nature overpower any physical or social discomfort. She desires "to dominate the world" (Taylor 2008, 18) and to have "power over many different kinds of men" (27), and she acts out this longing in elaborate daydreams. When she puts pen to paper and lets her imagination take over, the novels resulting from this naive wish-fulfilment become bestsellers, beginning with *The Lady Irania*, and their success gives the author real – economic as well as social – power. Her own family watch Angel's "superior airs" (38) with suspicion, regarding writing as a "strange indulgence, peculiar, suspect" (39) and fearing for Angel's sanity. The novel regularly stages her writing as an auto-erotic act, equating her self-empowerment with sexual pleasure.

Angel's first novel becomes "an escape-thread spun out of herself" (41), but it is a form of escape that puts increasing emotional pressure. She begins to resent the successes of other writers, particularly women: "she was afraid that while she rested she might be forgotten. The publication of some other woman's novel would send her scurrying back to her study: men writers did not affect her so strongly," as the narrator laconically remarks, who also clearly labels her as suffering from "self-delusions" (75). Later, these extend as far as her unhappy relationship with her husband:

> Like many romantic, narcissistic women she shied away from the final act of love-making. She would have lived in a world of courtship and hand-kissing if she could. Sex seemed to have nothing to do with her. It was a sudden reversal, not a continuation, of the delights

---

[171] Another model may have been Clare Leighton's 1947 biography of her mother, the novelist Marie Connor Leighton: *Tempestuous Petticoat: The Story of an Invincible Edwardian*.

of being wooed. [...] That desperate communication with herself in which she writes, holds good in love as well, he thought. (155; cf. 205)

Esmé becomes a prisoner in her golden cage: "He had not come to love his captivity; he had only lost the courage to escape" (180). As the house and garden crumble to their ruin, Angelica seems unaware of the "prodigious collapse" around her (212); the war is "a personal annoyance [...] but nothing more" (215). Towards the end, in her damp house under the cobwebbed chandelier, she appears like a ruined relic, a second Miss Havisham. As Taylor lays on her hallmark gothic imagery (cf. Berensmeyer 2015, 478–479), Angelica is presented as the ghostly and feared but also pitied Other of contemporary women writers: a woman out of touch with the modern world, egotistic, self-deluded, lost in a romantic fantasy of her own making. The novel emphasises the contrast between the literature of the past and the present by making strategic use of gothic imagery and literary allusions to Victorian fiction. Although it follows the traces of a female *bildungsroman* and begins almost with a celebration of the literary imagination, it ends on a melodramatic note, showing the failure of this imagination to square up to reality and fully engage with the world. Imagination and reality drift further and further apart, leaving Angelica Deverell an empty husk. Her tragedy is that she remains true to herself but loses touch with modernity and the changing taste of her audience. Taylor's ironic aesthetic, the form in which she "embraces the styles, themes, and narratives" of 'women's fiction' only to interrogate its "stereotypes" (Sage 2016, 113) allows her to explore Angelica's predicament, the discrepancy between her romanticism and her reality, from a reflexive distance. Such a dated conception of female authorship, she appears to argue, is hardly possible or desirable anymore. *Angel* is not only a profound reflection on the psychology of literary creativity but a descant on a literary world that has been lost – and, for Taylor herself, possibly an exorcism of a particular type of novelist she feared and abhorred: the ever-productive but inwardly hollow 'lady novelist'.

Meeting *The Cost of Living* (1956): Diana Gardner and Kathleen Farrell

Diana Gardner (1913–1997) worked in publishing as a reader and editor; her only novel, *The Indian Woman*, appeared in 1954. She wrote the short story "The Woman Novelist" in 1950 but did not publish it during her lifetime; it was added to a posthumous edition of her 1946 story collection *Halfway Down the Cliff* (Gardner 2006, 53–67). The new publication turned it into the title story of that collection – a strategic choice that emphasises the oddity and rarity of a story that self-consciously reflects on the condition of being a woman novelist. The story is about Madeleine Filmer, a woman who supports her extended family by writing but who feels let down by her husband Wykham, who receives a state grant after leaving the Army to study law. Their genteel family has come down in the world, and she worries about their financial and social stability. Madeleine watches with suspicion as her husband, whose name perhaps alludes to the ne'er-do-well George Wickham from Austen's *Pride and Prejudice*, neglects his domestic duties, such as tending to their garden, in favour of socialising with the local gentry. Like a practical illustration of *A Room of One's Own*, the story describes "[t]hose two and a half hours in the afternoon, when the children were at school, and the two old ladies, the mothers-in-law, were withdrawn, resting in their bedrooms." These hours "were hers – hers for herself. […] She could carry on – the family was secure – if she were certain of those two and a half precious hours" (54–55). But the other family members and household duties keep encroaching on the time she has to herself, and she worries about not getting enough time to write not only because writing provides her "solace" (58) but also because it is her "job" (54) that pays the rent for a house that is too big and too expensive: "She wondered how long they would be able to afford to live here" (57). While her husband retreats to "his study" (60), her place for writing is more exposed: the dining room or the conservatory (58). After lunch, she begins to write "under pressure", "almost perspiring" (62). In the debate about literary writing as a form of art or a form of work, she takes up a middle ground; she is "under pressure" from external constraints, but she appears to be using a pen – a token of literary creativity – rather than a typewriter, the symbol of mechanisation.

While Madeleine is writing in the conservatory, we learn (in a rather abrupt switch in focalisation) that her husband awkwardly propositions their domestic help, Beryl, in the garden – something that the reader then learns is also very much on Madeleine's mind, as her writing is interrupted by anxiety and fear of being left alone without Beryl if her husband "were to make a pass at" her (66). The story ends with Madeleine continuing her writing with regained confidence, as a "beam of sunlight […] [strikes] across the white page" (67).

Gardner's story shows a powerful, creative woman writer encumbered by social and economic circumstances beyond her control. Towards the end, it remains open whether her work will indeed enable her to overcome these constraints or whether it merely makes it easier for her to ignore her husband's shortcomings. Next to her husband's first name and its allusion to Austen's good-for-nothing Wickham, the family name, Filmer, may be a reference to early modern political theory: Sir Robert Filmer's *Patriarcha*, a classic of seventeenth-century patriarchalist political thought. This was published in a modern edition in 1949 that Gardner might have noticed (Filmer 1949). At the heart of this story, then, is not Madeleine's pride in her own work as a novelist but her submission to her husband's expectations and aspirations, including even his extramarital interest in younger women. The distinguishing formal feature of this story, however, is its adherence to a strictly personal point of view without authorial commentary. The conflict that is hinted at remains unresolved in the story's open ending, with the symbol of the white page hit by sunlight indicating a note of optimism that fails to convince, given the obstacles in Madeleine's path.

Money, or rather lack thereof, is also the topic of Kathleen Farrell's long-forgotten novel *The Cost of Living*, published by Macmillan in 1956. The author of five novels, Farrell (1912–1999) is better known as a fixture of literary London's social life at mid-century and as a catalyst for other writers' works (De-la-Noy 1999). In this novel, we meet the typist Marianne, who types other people's novels rather than writing her own, while closely observing the artistic career, or lack thereof, of her painter friend Alexandra. For both, as the novel makes clear from the outset, earning a living as an artist is "near to impossible" (Farrell 1956, 1). Their limited means are summed up in the wine that Marianne buys for a party: "six bottles of a harsh red wine optimistically labelled Bordeaux" (3). A contemporary review notes the novel's "neat and funny" take on "[d]omestic trivia and abortive adventures with young men called Peter discussed over cocoa" (Johnson 1956). This is true, but it ignores the more serious aspect to the novel's depiction of female artists who are famished for success in life. In this aspect, *The Cost of Living* resembles *Jane: Young Author*, whose writer-protagonist also shares a flat with a visual artist, but Farrell's novel is much more concerned with the economic aspects of such a bohemian life, and her protagonists are certainly poorer.

Narrated in the first person, *The Cost of Living* is particularly good at depicting Marianne's troubles with the manuscripts she has got to type: first, a book on ceramics that is easy to do because she "did not have to understand the wretched thing – I had merely to type it"; then, a "very long, very intimate" novel whose manuscript turns out to be nearly illegible (37). Here, the words "I began on a novel" (ibid.) refer not to the act of creative writing but to typing somebody else's work. Like Gardner's woman novelist, Marianne's efforts of 'getting down to' this novel (51) keep being disturbed by people barging in on her. Her principal affect is fatigue: she is "tired of the novel which had to be typed; tired of sandwiches and weak tea and cheap wine. Tired of living alone [...]; tired of the misery of losing interest in [her]self" (53). The wearisome novel that she has got to type is described more closely in the following passage:

> By that time I had nearly finished the novel. It seemed to get longer and longer towards the end; and sadder, too, and much sillier. There was only one woman in it, and she spent most of

her life retching and clinging to park railings; and when she wasn't doing that she was leaning her forehead against the wall in some dark alley-way. Leaning her forehead against the wall was to stop her being completely overcome by nausea. I can't remember that it ever did. I wondered how such young men managed to make women feel so sick, so often. And I thought, poor young men, how they suffer. (102)

This passage is striking for its sarcastic observation of the limited experience of literary "young men" when it comes to depicting female characters, whereas women in Marianne's view, as she goes on to explain, are much more resilient when it comes to the challenges of life. Her conclusion is that "the young men who wrote novels were better when they wrote about themselves" (103) – affirming the gendered separation of fiction into books by and for men and books by and for women, but also the narrative situation of the novel in which Marianne is herself the narrator, thus justifying her personal voice and discursive authority. But she is not, apparently, moved at this point to write novels of her own; later, in conversation with Marius, an editor, she says she lacks the necessary "enthusiasm" for writing and establishing a literary reputation (115).

The novel concludes with an assertion of friendship between the two failing artists, Alexandra and Marianne, planning another party, this time with "a passably good imitation hock at five bob a time", "[v]ery dry and in the right-shaped bottles" (233). Here, then, we have a novel by a woman about a woman writer who decides against authorship. A beam of sunlight on a white page, a party to look forward to – the authorial authority of both Madeleine in "The Woman Novelist" and Marianne in *The Cost of Living* is weak, though in their very weakness, their assertion of low status, may reside the potential for new forms of subaltern feminine authority and community beyond modernist individualism and impersonality.

Multiple Narrative Identities: Mary Renault's *The Friendly Young Ladies* (1944)

When she wrote *The Friendly Young Ladies,* Mary Renault was still emerging as an author of novels conventionally labelled as 'romance' but containing disruptive elements that subverted generic conventions. As Jesi Egan explains, Renault's early novels, published between 1939 and 1953, "are unusual in that they deliberately highlight the genre's native ambiguities", principally through exploring her characters' "fluid rather than fixed" sexual orientations (Egan 2016, 463, 469). Set in 1937, *The Friendly Young Ladies* centres on two women, Leo Lane and Helen

Vaughan, who share a houseboat in London.[172] Their bohemian cohabitation (as explicit a homosexual relationship as is possible in a mid-twentieth century English novel) is interrupted by the arrival of seventeen-year-old Elsie, Leo's younger sister, who wants to escape from the stifling atmosphere of her Cornwall home. Elsie has had literary ambitions since childhood. Now she learns that her sister is in fact a published author – if only of Western novels with titles like *Silver Guns* or *Quick on the Draw*, published under the male pseudonym Tex O'Hara – the name perhaps concealing the author's femininity in alluding to the protagonist of *Gone with the Wind* (though that might be too early for the time in which the novel is set, only one year after Mitchell's book was published). Leo prefers to think of herself as "a competent hack" rather than a "famous author" (Renault 2014 [1944], 98, 99); she has no literary ambitions beyond 'enjoying herself' (cf. 99) and making some money: "I do what I like doing, and do it as well as I can, and make a living at it; and you can't ask much more of life than that, can you?" she says (99). We learn later that this kind of writing comes easily to her and is even "[r]ather boring", "just clerical work: I could almost do it straight on the typewriter" (179).

Scenes and discussions of writing pervade the novel. Penning a letter to her friend Peter, Elsie is proud to call her sister a novelist, but she regrets the fact that Leo does not write more intellectual books "with a title like, say, *The Problem of Sex*, or *Whither Womanhood?*" rather than another page-turner called *Rustlers' Roundup* (109). She soon meets another acquaintance of Leo's, Joe, who "really writes," i. e., literary fiction and not genre fiction, and she soon finds herself reading this 'J. O. Flint's novel *Remission*, which includes "a clear and meticulous description of a dead baby [...], terrifyingly quiet and cool" (133). The reading comes as a shock to her, and she begins to resent "the whole armour of masculine impersonality" that Leo presents to the world (134). In a moment perhaps best described as queer, she begins to question the former certainties, norms, and unspoken rules that she has grown up with, including human sexuality: Elsie feels "an unsettling suspicion that one was living on a brittle surface, and that underneath it things might be other than what they seemed" (134). She even admits to Peter that "Leo's interested in all sorts of queer things" (232). Nevertheless, she does not fully acknowledge the implications of this queerness for the environment she now finds herself in, as the novel makes clear in a scene of reading when Elsie is disappointed by Shakespeare's sonnets and fails to realise that many of

---

172 The name 'Helen Vaughan' perhaps accidentally echoes Arthur Machen's *The Great God Pan* (1894); there are no further parallels between Renault's novel and Machen's story. Thanks to Gero Guttzeit for pointing this out to me.

them are addressed to a man rather than a woman (209–211). Turning away from Shakespeare, she returns to romantic clichés, "thinking of cypresses, of fountains, of moonlight and viols and nightingales" (211).

Despite her sister being "an authoress" (112), Elsie feels left out of the "literary talk" between Leo and Joe. Alone on a punt, both Leo and Joe work on their texts; then, after discussing Milton and Shakespeare, Leo asks Joe to read what he has written, and he complies with her request. In her response, she tries to sound masculine ("boyish and hard," 183), suppressing any emotion; this leads to Joe making an erotic advance, but her gaze repels him ("She was looking at him as if she had surprised him with a knife levelled at her heart," 184) and he withdraws. Leo is described as containing both 'woman' and 'boy' (cf. 194), and her writing of Western novels, a decidedly masculine genre, can be seen as a form of acting out the masculine part of her sexual identity and her bisexual orientation. In a later conversation with Peter, Leo asserts her 'oddness' but also insists on her privacy, on "keeping [her] oddities for the few people who are likely to be interested" (203). It is the down-to-earth character of her friend Helen, a nurse, who defends this privacy and their living arrangements against intruders like Peter, the novel's embodiment of social conformity and heteronormative masculinity (cf. 249; on p. 250 he refers to Helen as "normally sexed"). However, at the end, Leo decides to follow Joe to America; she leaves Helen, arguably in part because the convention of romance forces this ending on Renault's novel but perhaps also, as Stewart has argued, "to be with another writer" (2011, 31).

Leo, author of genre fiction, is perhaps the most original fictional woman writer in the novels and stories considered in this chapter. But her position is interesting in particular because it is depicted in Renault's novel as problematic and sexually as well as artistically queer. Leo writes Western fiction, one might argue, to explore the masculine aspect of her sexual identity, but she quickly – too quickly – concedes that she does not deserve to be taken seriously as an author, that she is merely a "competent hack" (Renault 2014, 98). These judgements may well reflect Renault's own doubts about the merits of middlebrow romance authorship and her uneasy explorations of this form.[173] Literary authorship of the serious kind is coded as masculine in the novel, and it is embodied in the dispassionate coolness and impersonality of Joe's authorial persona J. O. Flint. Joe's modernist persona is contrasted with the literary attitudes of the women in the novel: Elsie, who harbours naive romantic notions about poetry and the literary life, and Leo, who ac-

---

[173] They are certainly echoed in a reader's report for Knopf rejecting Renault's novel *North Face* in 1948: "Mary Renault seems to me to be a capable writer of merchandise love fiction dressed up and dignified a bit with 'artistic' touches to pass as literature" ('EG', 9 Dec. 1948, Harry Ransom Center, Knopf archive, box 656, folder 6). See also Egan 2016 and Zilboorg 2001.

tively tries to suppress her emotions when she talks to Joe to appear more 'masculine' in literary conversations.

In an oblique way, the novel's own narrative voice situates authority in a gender-neutral 'safety zone' of authorial distance – the novel's title, *The Friendly Young Ladies*, can be read as embodying such detachment. The bohemian community that Renault allows her readers to envisage in this novel is undermined from the start by internal fissures as well as external influences from the heteronormative society that surrounds it – leaving the very act of authorship hobbled by the gendered constraints that regulate the literary field.

"A fine woman bashing away at a typewriter": Muriel Spark's *The Girls of Slender Means* (1963)

Muriel Spark's novel *The Girls of Slender Means* (1963) looks back to the end of the Second World War. Its central observer-character, Jane Wright, is one of several young women who live in the May of Teck Club, a London boarding house "for the Pecuniary Convenience and Social Protection of Ladies of Slender Means below the age of Thirty Years" (Spark 2013, 9). She is associated with the literary life and the publishing business through her work as the only assistant to a small publisher, Huy Throvis-Mew Ltd., which is actually run by someone called George Johnson, with the hint that this is not his real name but that he is in "the habit of changing his name after a number of years" (38) to escape his creditors. During wartime and the early months of postwar austerity, Jane performs what the narrator refers to as "brain-work" (37), which includes writing letters to famous authors for another person associated with the literary world, the "pale foreigner" Rudi Bittesch (37), in order to get these authors to reply with an autograph letter or at least a letter with an autograph signature that Bittesch can then sell for ready cash— a money-making ploy that, as the novel implies, is used so frequently that few authors still fall for it. She later fakes a letter from Charles Morgan on behalf of her friend, the anarchist writer and later Catholic convert Nicholas Farringdon, to raise his market value in the publisher's eyes. (Spark may be implying that Morgan's literary reputation is already in decline at this time.).

The narrator reveals that Jane, who is of slender means but not slim of figure – even "fat" (123) –, later becomes a gossip columnist, but that in 1945, part of her "brain-work" has to do with the fact that she is an aspiring poet: "secretly, she wrote poetry of a strictly non-rational order, in which occurred, in about the proportion of cherries in a cherry-cake, certain words that she described as 'of a smouldering nature', such as loins and lovers, the root, the rose, the seawrack and the shroud" (37) – a brilliant caricature of the sub-Georgian poetry celebrated and published by the Poetry Society, with which Spark herself was involved in the late 1940s.

The only other female character associated with writing, and the only one to be associated with poetry in this novel, is the rector's daughter Joanna Childe, who teaches the other girls elocution lessons using mostly poems by Donne, Wordsworth, Tennyson, Hopkins, and the Georgian favourite "Moonlit Apples" by John Drinkwater. Many of the poems cited in the novel combine religious and erotic registers, often ironically matching the sometimes more, sometimes less repressed sexuality of the "girls of slender means", but many of them involve death, as the lines on Chatterton from Wordsworth's "Resolution and Independence" that recur in the novel (43, 61). Many can also be read as foreshadowing, in their "smouldering" tone, their romanticisation of death and catastrophe ("the seawrack and the shroud"), the very real catastrophe at the novel's ending, when Joanna dies in the collapse of the house after a forgotten German bomb explodes in the garden. Smouldering words portend smouldering ruins. Ironically, one of Joanna's favourite poems was Hopkins's "The Wreck of the *Deutschland.*" Farringdon's only recording of her reciting this poem is erased after her death so that the tape can be re-used. Nothing remains of her engagement with poetry, and we also never get to read any of Jane's, beyond Spark's mischievous description quoted above. As the novel implies, her life in the May of Teck Club and her experience in working for a publisher turns her away from her earlier, romantic and idealistic view of poetry and towards the emotional detachment of the gossip columnist, from a secret passion for poetry towards divulging other people's secrets.

This resembles Spark's own swerve from poetry to prose fiction in the 1950s, and her disillusionment with the coterie circle of the Poetry Society. Spark's involvement in this society in 1947 and 1948, and her role in its 'war of the poets', which made newspaper headlines at the time, has been subject to some debate. As Martin Stannard reports in his biography, a twenty-nine-year old Spark, a woman with new ideas, obvious talent and, like Jane, an "aspiring brain", provoked the male establishment in ways that not only concerned poetry (Stannard 2009, 72; see also 78–98).[174] While she was attracted to some of the poets, as well as their poetry, and entered into relationships first with Howard Sergeant and then with Derek Stanford, she also suffered what would now be called sexual harassment. As Stannard diplomatically puts it, "[v]arious poetic gentlemen in, or beyond, middle life were invigorated by her presence" (2009, 81), a situation that Spark exploited but that soon also caused much discomfort until she was sacked

---

174 On Spark's involvement with the Poetry Society, see also Sheridan 2009.

as secretary of the society and editor of the *Poetry Review* in November 1948. In *The Girls of Slender Means*, all this and more may be implied in the following sarcastic description of the poetry scene of 1945 and its gender politics: "Some days later he [Nicholas] took Jane to a party to meet the people she longed to meet, young male poets in corduroy trousers and young female poets with waist-length hair, or at least females who typed the poetry and slept with the poets, it was nearly the same thing" (2013, 61).

The activities of typing and sex are linked as a female support system for the benefit of male poets: "young female poets" becomes a euphemism for this support system that combines sexual favours with a free typing service. The modern Muse may call herself a 'female poet', but the narrator's comment that "it was nearly the same thing" as a secretary implies a significant gender gap between the male and female poets of 1945. This Muse not only kisses the poet but has to prepare his scribblings for publication. As in Farrell's *The Cost of Living*, aspiring women writers are reduced to typists. Emphasising the erotic aspects of women typing, the diabolical Dougal Douglas exclaims in Spark's *The Ballad of Peckham Rye* (1960): "There is no more beautiful sight [...] than to see a fine woman bashing away at a typewriter" (Spark 1999, 129).[175] Less diabolical, but no less revealing of gender bias is this comment by Digby, one of the anthropologists in Barbara Pym's *Less than Angels* (1955): "A woman who can cook *and* type – what more could a man want, really?" (Pym 2010, 70).

Beyond the merely autobiographical, the move away from poetry and towards the novel echoes the trajectories of many modernist authors, some of whom (in German letters, Thomas Mann would be the most famous example) deliberately made this transition to step away from personal involvement towards impersonality and ironic detachment in order to achieve a post-realist authorial authority. The typewriter is a mechanical embodiment of such distancing, symbolising writing as a form of exteriority rather than the presumably natural, though not less technical, use of a pen and its allegedly closer connection to hand and heart. (We also saw this contrast enacted in Durrell's *Black Book*, and the notion of the writer as a machine in *Tropic of Cancer*, in ch. 11.)

Writing is rarely envisaged as a profession in novels and stories by mid-century women writers. In most cases, fictional women writers are young women just embarking on a career: on the cusp of taking life into their own hands, like the adolescent diarist Cassandra Mortmain in Dodie Smith's *I Capture the Castle* (1949; a writer's daughter whose journal is in part about struggling free from

---

[175] Dougal's mischievous schemes lead to the brutal murder of Merle Coverdale, the head of the typing pool at the nylon textile manufacturer Meadows, Meade & Grindley.

her father's austere modernist classic *Jacob Wrestling*),[176] or young women working as secretaries or freelance typists, as in *Novel on Yellow Paper* or *The Cost of Living*. If they are published authors, they often doubt the value of their work, like Mary Renault's Leo, unless they are pathological egocentrics, like Elizabeth Taylor's Angelica Deverell or, less extremely, her Beth Cazabon. This is also the case of Catherine Oliphant in Barbara Pym's *Less than Angels* (1955), one of that author's outwardly submissive but quietly subversive 'excellent women', who at the age of thirty-one "earned her living writing stories and articles for women's magazines" (Pym 2010, 1) but who feels limited by the constraints of her medium: "There was a page in her typewriter, half typed, and she sat down, hoping to finish the story she was writing. But the inspiration seemed to have gone and the falsely happy ending she had planned seemed unbearably trite and removed from life" (21).[177]

Many end up in other professions, like Muriel Spark's Jane, who becomes a gossip columnist. Realistic depictions of mature women writers are few and far between; Diana Gardner's "The Woman Novelist" is a rare exception that focuses on the woman writer as a breadwinner trying to make ends meet, almost despairing under the burden of having to support her less than supportive family. It is a telling fact that this story remained unpublished until recently. For women authors, the writing life did not seem a topic worth writing about. While there may be various reasons for this (lack of commercial interest in the topic being one of them), it may at least in part be attributed to the precarious discursive authority of women writers in postwar Britain, where a "feminine point of view" was not wanted and the "public [did] not want to be admonished by a woman" (Campbell 1952, 25).

In late modernist British fiction, the woman writer as a literary character appears to be condemned to a spectral existence, even in works by women writers, but nevertheless – or for this very reason – she remains a haunting figure of sheer possibility and promise. The novels and stories discussed here allow us to re-evaluate the terrain out of which works like *The Golden Notebook* or A. S. Byatt's (later) Frederica quartet emerged. Studying female authorship as a theme in narrative fiction offers ample scope for reflecting on the complex interplay of social, cultural, political, economic, and human factors that make up literature and the literary

---

[176] Moreover, at the end Cassandra closes her journal for good, leaving writing behind rather than considering it as a career. As the title indicates, the novel has a first-person narrator, though its narratee is private rather than public (the novel is in the form of a personal diary); see Lanser 1992 for this important distinction.

[177] Thanks to Leonie Kappus for pointing me to Pym's *Less than Angels*. Beyond these few remarks, the fact of Catherine being a writer is of little importance to the novel.

life. Given the gender segregation of the literary field in late modernism, in which 'womanly' writing was associated with the middlebrow and the commercial form of romance whereas 'manly' writing was considered serious and literary, the predicament of female authorship is rarely explored in fiction. But when it is, fictional women authors point up the constraints and limits of a 'feminine' aesthetic of literary creativity. They allow us to reconstruct a rhetoric of female authorship out of the narrative strategies used by women us to negotiate the difficulties of literary creation and production. These difficulties were real and not merely imaginary, and while their male colleagues certainly experienced difficulties too, they tended to be of a different kind. Women writers in postwar Britain developed a complex and critical attitude towards established clichés that they could not quite overcome before the cultural rejuvenation, the rise of second-wave feminism, and the boom in women authors (such as Angela Carter, Iris Murdoch, Margaret Drabble, A. S. Byatt) from the 1960s onwards.

From the late nineteenth century to the late modernist era, author fictions become increasingly self-conscious about their authors' placement or "position-taking" (Bourdieu 1996, 231) in the literary field. This is due on the one hand to the large quantity of novels in mass-market publishing after the collapse of the 'triple-decker' format in the 1890s, which makes it more difficult for authors to achieve distinction and recognition. On the other hand, economies of authorship begin to diversify more strictly into the 'art novel' and commercial fiction. As a consequence, authorial positions in the field become more insecure and fraught with tensions and doubts about one's 'correct' placement as either a serious artist or a popular entertainer. We saw this tension about authorial 'rank' being played out in the stories of James, Kipling, and Beerbohm, frequently as a question of the very possibility of authentic, original, personal expression in an era of mechanisation and the competition of new communications media from newspapers to radio waves [→ ch. 8]. The generic framework of the literary *bildungsroman* came to be fragmented and modified in stories about literary failure rather than success, in narratives of stunted growth and thwarted expectations that suggest "the erosion of representativeness" of the figure of the artist around 1900 (Weimann 1988, 439), a loss that corresponds to a change in narrative techniques towards impressionism, stylisation, and degrees of impersonality. Author characters in novels by Arthur Machen, E. M. Forster, and Henry Green are to be pitied rather than admired [→ ch. 9].

The other side of this development is the ridicule to which they are subjected by writers like Aldous Huxley and Evelyn Waugh [→ ch. 10]. For these writers, literature has finally turned from a contested 'profession' (Dickens, Thackeray) via a dubious 'trade' (Gissing) into a cynical 'business' (Huxley) in which markets determine authors instead of vice versa. Obviously, satires of this business of literature are still being written because their authors have not quite given up on the idea of, or belief in, literature as having a symbolic value that transcends its material, commercial value. It is this idea that comes to be institutionalised in modernist 'highbrow' literature – a radicalisation of the art novel – that is deliberately placed in opposition to 'lowbrow' and 'middlebrow' forms of writing, exacerbating earlier anxieties about commercial fiction and its value by adding an intermediate category that is easily mistaken as more valuable than it actually is, and allowing the arbiters of taste more leeway in assigning their fellow writers to this contemptuous category. The 'novel of resentment' takes part in this culture war of embattled stratifications, uneasily trying to reconcile elements of realist and modernist aesthetics – most notably in Orwell's novels of the 1930s. Others escape this battlefield by pitching their tents outside England and outside the limitations of the conventional novel, aiming towards forms of autofictional writing that is liberated from economic and cultural constraints and hoping for a regeneration of literature through sheer Dionysian (masculine) energy.

This hierarchy of values entrenches a gendered opposition between 'masculine' and 'feminine' kinds of writing. If the 'bad boys' of the 1930s and the 'angry young men' of the 1950s identified the Establishment they railed against, and its middlebrow forms of literary expression, as 'feminine', female authors struggled to represent their own authorship against misogynist stereotypes of 'vinegar-bearing lady-novelists' (Durrell) or common clichés about 'women's fiction'. (Some) women writers of the 1950s and early 1960s develop a rhetoric of female authorship that points towards escape routes from such stereotypes, sometimes from within the very fiction that is stigmatised as 'middlebrow', imagining new forms of community, representativeness, and (in Lessing) political agency.

In the next part, we will explore the development of scenarios of literary authorship against the background of further diversification of the market and new hierarchies of the literary field from the 1950s to the present.

Part IV **From Postmodernist Metafiction to Contemporary Autofiction**

Ian McEwan is an unlimited company [...]
Copyright page

13 The Validity of Authorship: Postwar British Metafiction from Muriel Spark to William Golding

Ten years before Roland Barthes proclaimed the death of the author, Muriel Spark imagined a posthumous form of female authorship. The narrator of her story "The Portobello Road" (1958) is an aspiring woman writer whose literary aspirations can only be fulfilled after she has died. As a young woman, Needle – as she is called, having found one in a haystack in her youth – goes "to London to see life, for it was my ambition to write about life, which first I had to see" (Spark 2018, 500). But her literary career does not advance much beyond "writing speeches for absorbed industrialists" in "a job with a publicity man" (501), echoing an episode in Spark's own life. It is only after being murdered (and hidden, as it happens, in a haystack) and returning to the world as a ghost that Needle can realise her ambitions and write: "Of course, I did not live to write about life as I wanted to do. Possibly that is why I am inspired to do so now in these peculiar circumstances" (501). It is only the "peculiar circumstances" of her physical death that set the author free – from life – and enable her to gain the supposedly necessary distance to "write about life" (501). Killed by a man, Needle is the ghost of a woman writer speaking from the other side of death, whose posthumous narration is her only claim to literary authorship and narrative control over a life otherwise dominated by happenchance.

In the 1960s and 1970s, literature sought new ways out of the perceived impasse of a modernist "literature of exhaustion" towards a postmodernist "literature of replenishment" (Barth 1982). This was accompanied by a turn towards metafiction, i.e., in its two classic definitions, "fiction about fiction – that is, fiction that includes within itself a commentary on its own narrative and/or linguistic identity" (Hutcheon 1980, 1), or "fictional writing which self-consciously and systematically draws attention to its status as an artefact in order to pose questions about the relationship between fiction and reality" (Waugh 1984, 2). Needle's story is a case in point, as Spark's narrative combines elements of realism with generic features of the fairy tale and the ghost story to reflect on the relationship between life and literature, feminine and masculine social roles, authorship and power. Patricia Waugh has described the main thrust of postmodernist metafiction as "a celebration of the power of the creative imagination together with an uncertainty about the validity of its representations" (Waugh 1984, 2), and Spark's story similarly oscillates between affirming the power of authorship and doubting its value in and for life. After the exhaustion or implosion of avantgarde modernist experiments, from impressionism and impersonality to multiple points of view and stylistic plurality, authors of postmodernist metafiction now returned to the old questions of art and life.

Postmodernist metafiction radicalised the impression, already firmly established in modernism, "that any attempt to represent reality could only produce selective perspectives, fictions, that is, in an epistemological, not merely in the conventional literary, sense" (Pfeiffer 1978, 61). Metafiction is literary fiction that lays bare the constructedness and selectivity of everyday reality. It reveals "the ontological status of all literary fiction: its quasi-referentiality, its indeterminacy, its existence as words and world" (Waugh 1984, 101). It replaces a dominant focus on knowledge of things within a given world to a focus on the ontological status of the world or worlds that writing can access or create (McHale 1987, 10).

Patricia Waugh argues that metafictional frame-breaking in the Victorian realist novel was used to reinforce rather than weaken the conventions of fictional representation; her example is George Eliot's *Adam Bede*. Chapter 17 of this novel, "In Which the Story Pauses a Little", famously consists of an essay in which the author addresses her goals and intentions to tell the truth about her characters. Yet, there are other examples of metafictional and author-fictional frame-breaking in nineteenth-century literature, and earlier too, perhaps less well known or more subtle; examples in which the validity of representation and the authority of the author are contested rather than confirmed in the light of sceptical attitudes towards the "selective perspectives" of literary worldmaking (Pfeiffer 1978, 61). On the other hand, one might question the hypothesis that such frame-breaking in postmodernism *always* serves the purpose of weakening the validity of representations. It is not the use of metalepsis as such that defines its meaning and function, but the manner in which it is employed (cf. Levin 2016).

In postmodernism, some authors explicitly returned to Victorian conventions in order to point out their inherent fragility, most notably John Fowles in *The French Lieutenant's Woman* (1969) with his liberation-theological revision of the 'omniscient author'.[178] In some cases, however, as in Muriel Spark, the ironic, self-conscious use of generic tropes and plot patterns, "lay[ing] bare the process of imposing form upon contingent matter through the discursive organization of 'plot'" (Waugh 1984, 17), may actually have the opposite effect – namely, to strengthen the superior position of the actual author vis à vis her fictional characters and the fictional world more generally. Waugh refers to this as a "quasi-omniscient

---

[178] See the famous passage in this novel in which Fowles pointedly addresses the convention he has been working in and argues that "[t]he novelist is still a god, since he creates [...]; what has changed is that we are no longer the gods of the Victorian image, omniscient and decreeing; but in the new theological image, with freedom our first principle, not authority" (Fowles 1996, 99).

author" who is not a "benevolent" presence but a sinister, inscrutable, "disturbing authority" (74). Similarly, in Nabokov, there is a sense that characters are at the mercy of an autocratic author: "my characters cringe when I come near with my whip" (Nabokov qtd. in Tammi 1985, 100). Obviously, all fictional characters are inventions; George Eliot's are no different from Nabokov's in this respect. But the attitudes with which they are treated by their authors are conveyed to audiences as radically different.

A median position is taken in Julio Cortázar's *Hopscotch* (*Rayuela*, 1963, English translation 1966), one of the signature novels of late modernist experimentalism and the Latin American 'boom' (cf. McHale 1987, 193). Here, a bohemian group of characters in the novel's first part, set in postwar Paris, forms a club that idolises the work of an elusive author named Morelli, whose ambitious ideas and notes towards a yet-to-be-written novel form part of the 'expendable chapters' gathered in the third section of *Hopscotch*. One of these chapters, for example, contains "one of the many endings to [Morelli's] unfinished book" (Cortázar 2014, 380); others reflect on the relationship between author and reader, author and work, and on what a modern novel should or should not contain – he discards, for example, "hedonistic and prechewed novels, with *psychologies*" (486) and instead wants to achieve "experiential immediacy" for the reader (405). Morelli reflects on the different attitudes of authors, from "the romantic novelist", who "wants to be understood for his own sake or for that of his heroes", to "the classical novelist", who "wants to teach", to a new novelist, or 'antinovelist' (cf. 404), whose goal is to "mak[e] an accomplice of the reader" (405). This novelist would be neither benevolent nor disturbing in his or her authority, but "a coparticipant and cosufferer" (405) of experiences shared with the reader in an "opening" of conventional literary order towards "incongruity" and a liberated "imagination in the service of no one" (404). Even this creed in search of new (hetero- and homopoetic) models of literary authorship bears an ironic colouring, since the absent-minded Morelli has been hit by a car and is in hospital while his literary admirers discuss these enigmatic pronouncements. Moreover, the conceptual structure of the novel *Rayuela* as a whole mirrors some of Morelli's ideas but not all of them and not in an entirely systematic way; there are parallels between Morelli and Cortázar, the novel's actual author, but the two are not identical.[179]

Postmodernist fiction, then, does not constitute a radical break with older (modernist and pre-modernist) forms but a more self-aware use of these forms. Possibly, this signals the arrival of "a new type of author [...] who knows about

---

[179] Cortázar later developed one of Morelli's ideas into another novel, *62: A Model Kit* (1968); see McHale 1987, 253 n. 27

the inauthenticity of his [sic] production but who nonetheless continues producing" (Boris Groys, qtd. in Ingold 1992, 349). This amounts to a "'double coding' of authorship" (Berensmeyer 2000, 66). The very act of questioning or subverting the validity, even the very possibility, of authorship can serve as an act of stabilisation and legitimation, even in some cases a "return to authoritative omniscience and superiority" (ibid.). Viewed in this light, postmodernist metafiction in Britain responds to a crisis of fiction, a crisis that mainly concerns the attractiveness of imaginative literature compared to other modern media, and its potential for doing justice to the complexities of the modern world. These texts negotiate the position of the author as a figure of authority inside and outside the fiction, trying out different options between forms of mystification and disavowal. If they introduce author figures within their fictions, it is less with a realist or realistic sense of literature as a social field or a market, but rather with a view to literature as a source of moral or cultural authority. Thereby, they already implicitly affirm the symbolic value of literature while ignoring, to a large extent, the material, social, and political institutions that make its very existence possible by supporting the writing and publishing of these texts. Consequently, there is a revival of the Romantic position of authorial expression as an individual, original, authentic act – despite all protests to the contrary. Another price to be paid for the renewed legitimation of fiction in postmodernism, it seems, is the invisibilisation of its institutional foundations.

Beyond the Uncertainty Principle: Muriel Spark's *The Comforters* (1957)

In Muriel Spark's first novel, *The Comforters* (1957), the literary critic Caroline Rose writes her first novel and develops hallucinations: she hears a typewriter tapping in her head. She is even able to hear what this author of her own narrative is writing: a text that predicts the story of her life as it progresses. By means of metalepsis, the author-character is dissociated from the narrative in which she plays a part. *The Comforters* breaks with the postwar realist consensus in British narrative fiction, taking inspiration from the French *nouveau roman* in its disruption of mimetic illusion and point of view. Michael Gardiner describes this as "a destruction of myths of depth and of cinematic ideologies of perception" (2010, 29). As an experiment with the selectivity of limited perspectives, *The Comforters* questions and subverts the norms of social realism in the novel, if not "the fundamental intellectual principles of British consensus" (ibid., 28) based on empiricism and logical positivism.

Spark's experiments with perspective and metafiction in *The Comforters* culminate in those scenes in which Caroline Rose becomes aware of an authorial presence telling her story. Thus, as Gardiner explains, "the writing *of* scenes is linked to the writing done *in* scenes, complicating perspective by turning perspective itself into narrative" (2010, 29). Evelyn Waugh's description of these scenes in his review of the novel is particularly perceptive:

> The area of Caroline's mind which is composing the novel becomes separated from the area which is participating in it, so that, hallucinated, she believes she is observant of, observed by, and in some degree under the control of, an unknown second person. In fact she is in the relation to herself of a fictitious character to a story-teller. (Waugh 1957, qtd. in Stannard 2009, 179)

The disembodied storyteller's voice, however, is accompanied by the mundane sound of a typewriter; it is "a voice that is quite certainly not numinous" (Lyons 2010, 87) but de-romanticised and quite secular. It is not the artist as a Tolkienesque "sub-creator" of a fictional world (Tolkien 1983, 155) but rather as a craftsman or -woman whose fictional creations can gain the ability to stand their own ground, as Caroline does when she tells her boyfriend, Laurence Manders:

> I won't be involved in this fictional plot if I can help it. In fact, I'd like to spoil it. If I had my way I'd hold up the action of the novel. It's a duty. [...] I intend to stand aside and see if the novel has any real form apart from this artificial plot. I happen to be a Christian. (Spark 2009, 93)

Like Caroline in the novel, Spark had recently – in 1954 – converted to Catholicism, and the topic of the relationship between the free will of human beings and the will of God is clearly mapped onto Caroline's hallucinatory experience with 'her' author in the novel.

In terms of style and form, *The Comforters* is an indirect critique of what Evelyn Waugh derisively termed "the Amis-Wain-Braine" school of social realism (qtd. in Patey 1998, 321). This is discernible in Spark's choice of protagonists, her focus on an aspiring woman artist, and above all in her experiments with narrative voice and the novel form, all of which are in stark contrast to the prevailing realism of the mid-1950s. In the choice of a female protagonist who is an intellectual interested in "Form in the Modern Novel" (Spark 2009, 47), and in its genre-bending mixture of "detective story, crime, social satire, adventure, violence, psychological novel, young love, domestic tale, gothic novel",[180] it is a highly original and unusual

---

[180] Manuscripts of *The Comforters*, McFarlin Library, University of Tulsa, Oklahoma, Muriel Spark Collection, box 13.6, 26.

contribution to the literature of the late fifties. From an early stage in the novel's conception, Spark emphasises the metafictional aspects of confronting a character with her place in a fictional plot, of "[t]rying to make a plot out of a life | Giving our lives a *plot* | *Plotting* our lives".[181] Moreover, she repeatedly refers in her working notes to Heisenberg's principle of uncertainty: the principle "that it is forever impossible in the nature of things to determine the position and velocity of an electron at the same time for by the very act of observing its position is changed" (ibid., 38) The interference between the observer (in this case, the author) and the observed (in this case, the character) becomes audible in the novel as the sound of the mechanical typewriter: "Caroline hears typewriter tapping. 'They are changing us merely by observing us. They can never know what we are really like [...] or what we were doing before they started observing.['] Heisenberg's Principle of Uncertainty" (ibid., 39).[182]

Spark confronts the author as character with a superior if "deromanticized authorial presence" articulated by the technological device of the typewriter (Berensmeyer 2016, 180).[183] This distancing technique, however, not only breaks with realist conventions but also implies that the (female) author as creative individual is disempowered. At the same time, it strengthens the discursive and narrative authority of the actual author, Muriel Spark. In writing her own first novel, she addresses the "anxiety of authorship" (Gilbert/Gubar 2000, 49) head-on; the auditory hallucinations mirror an episode in her own life, thus associating herself with Caroline, while at the same time splitting herself off from this character and her first-novel-within-a-first-novel.

Compared to the more recent trend of autofiction, which blurs the roles of author, narrator, and character, Spark offers a case study of authorial doubling that is closer to the labyrinthine halls of mirrors in the work of Nabokov, Barthelme, or Fowles. As if to demonstrate her power over her characters, Spark has the tellingly named and grossly physical character of Mrs Hogg disappear when she is not publicly visible to other characters; she only becomes visible as the story requires (cf. Waugh 1984, 55–56). She goes beyond the diagnosis of late modernist female authorial fatigue towards an aesthetic programme of playful postmodernism that begins to reassert the act (and art) of writing and the practices of literary authorship.

---

[181] Muriel Spark Collection, box 13.7, notebook 1, 15, emphasis changed from underlining to italics.
[182] The Heisenberg reference is not included in the published version of the novel. On metafiction and the uncertainty principle see also Waugh 1984, 3.
[183] See also Gardiner 2010 and Lyons 2010, Bailey 2021. The metafictional device of a character hearing the sound of a typewriter also features in a 1940 science fiction story by L. Ron Hubbard, *Typewriter in the Sky*, first published in *Unknown* magazine. There was a UK book edition in 1952, so it is at least theoretically possible that Spark was aware of this title.

While French poststructuralists begin to declare the 'death of the author', metafictional writing devises ways and means towards a resurrection.

"Telling the literal truth": Julian Mitchell's *The Undiscovered Country* (1968)

In Spark's *The Comforters*, the storyworld is embedded in a superordinate reality and thereby unmasked as fiction. It is written into being by an invisible, omnipotent, and omniscient author beyond it, the 'Typing Ghost' whose voice Caroline hears and against whom she tries to rebel. There is, in British postwar metafiction, a tendency to distrust fictionality and to attempt to find ways of legitimising it vis à vis other forms of public discourse that are regarded as more serious or worthwhile. There is also a concurrent tendency to express scepticism about the value of literary fiction compared to more recent and in some respects more effective audiovisual media, especially film and television.

Both tendencies come together in the work of B. S. Johnson, for example, who gave perhaps the clearest expression of the second tendency and had radical views about the first. Asking "why should anyone who simply wanted to be told a story spend all his spare time for a week or weeks reading a book when he could experience the same thing in a version in some ways superior at his local cinema in only one evening?", Johnson saw the only way forward for literature was to forgo description and focus solely on "the inside of [the novelist's] skull", placing an emphasis on style and form over events and subject matter (Johnson 1977, 151–152). As to the first tendency, however, he took the radical Platonic view that fiction is nothing but lies, interrupting his novel *Albert Angelo* (1964) with the authorial interjection "fuck all this lying" (Johnson 1964, 167). In his subsequent writing, however, Johnson did not turn to documentary nonfiction but to more radical experiments with literary form, as in *The Unfortunates* (1969), an unbound text that can be read in random order (Lodge 1986, 12–14) – possibly inspired by the non-linear sequence of chapters in *Hopscotch*.

Competing modes of literary fiction attempted to come to terms with the perceived crisis of the novel in postwar Britain. David Lodge, in 1971, saw English novelists "at the crossroads" (1986, 18), having to decide between three conflicting options: one, the conventional "realistic novel" with its "compromise between fictional and empirical modes" (18); two, the "nonfiction novel" (19); and three, "fabulist" metafiction (19). Between these radical positions, there are awkward compromises to be made, leading some novelists explicitly to address the problems associated with these choices and their uncertainties about literary form in the novels they write. What Lodge calls "the problematic novel" (24) existed to some extent already in the nineteenth century, but he is right to point out their increasing self-consciousness in late modernism and postmodernism.

One now largely forgotten novel that Lodge discusses in this context is Julian Mitchell's *The Undiscovered Country* (1968). Mitchell's novel is split down the middle between a conventional realistic and largely autobiographical first-person narrative in part one, titled "A Friend in Need", and a fragmentary, satirical, 'fabulist' first-person narrative in part two, titled "The New Satyricon". The first part tells the story of 'Julian Mitchell', who becomes an author of four novels, and his best friend Charles Humphries. They first meet at a prep school during World War Two and again ten years later at a cricket match. At that time, Charles is more or less openly homosexual whereas Julian has 'moved on' to girls. They meet again as students at Cambridge, trying and not quite succeeding to find the romance of Oxbridge they have read about in Waugh's *Brideshead Revisited*. Julian embarks on a Commonwealth fellowship to California, meeting Charles in Los Angeles. On his return to England, he finds Charles increasingly erratic and suicidal. Finally, Charles commits suicide and leaves the manuscript of his novel "The New Satyricon" to Julian, who then edits it.

Conversations between Julian and Charles, interspersed throughout part one of the novel, return again and again to the sorry state of literature and to their living in what Charles calls a "post-literary age" (Mitchell 2010, 63). Julian turns away from writing poetry that imitates the high modernists to writing respectable but not very interesting novels. Charles, the more radical of the two, thinks like B. S. Johnson that "television's the new medium. We should all be thinking in visual terms, not verbal ones" (64). Charles then works in Hollywood for a spell before returning to England. But he does not give up writing; he turns into what Robert Scholes called a 'fabulator', a writer who discards realism for a postmodernist blend of allegory and satire (Lodge 1986, 6, with reference to Scholes 1967).

The outcome of this effort, "The New Satyricon", parodies the style of contemporary literature, as Julian explains in his editorial preface. Using an "inflated" style is a technique of "distancing", which "enables Charles to mock the whole business of writing. Literature is only fantasy, he wants us to realize, and both reader and writer are observers like everyone else. Through the style, he satirizes himself as a satirist" (Mitchell 2010, 199). In modelling his work on the *Satyricon* of Petronius, Charles also engages with the zeitgeist of the 1960s, especially sexual liberation and "*sex for sex's sake*" (210, emphasis original), although it must be said that his satire is rather coy compared to contemporary American examples of this kind, such as *Naked Lunch* (which receives a name-check in Mitchell), *Candy*, or *Myra Breckinridge*. The autodiegetic narrator of this second novel-within-the novel calls himself 'Henry'; he pursues an enigmatic beloved through an enormous hotel in which a society of 'Encolpians' (named after Encolpius, the principal character of the *Satyricon*) are celebrating their mysterious sexual rites, and he is forced into their company, subjected to torture, and undergoes possibly several changes of gender (348) before being killed.

The result of stitching together these two opposing forms into one novel is an awkward yet interesting hybrid between a minor realistic novel and a work of metafictional fabulation, made perhaps even more interesting by the fact, noted by Lodge, that "the author's full name is Charles Julian Humphrey Mitchell" (1986, 31) so when 'Julian' refers to 'Charles' as "my oldest friend, my alter ego, my doppelganger, my secret sharer" (Mitchell 2010, 149) he exposes the actual author's dual, conflicted aesthetic position – echoing a familiar technique of authorial doubling [→ ch. 8]. This position may be one of discontent with his previous four novels, which are all name-checked with their actual titles in *The Undiscovered Country*, and of uncertainty about how to proceed with his writing. Charles, then, is the embodiment of 'Julian''s and the real Julian Mitchell's inner critic, whose own alternative aesthetic is expressed as a radical break with conventional realism. The relationship between, and even the ontological status of, Julian and Charles is uncertain, as when Julian first mentions Charles's death, he remarks: "*I am a minor novelist, telling the literal truth. I am a character in one of my own books. Yet I feel I am really a character in one of his. He never wrote it, and I don't know what to do or say.* [...] *I am no Orpheus. It is my own ghost I must bring back to life*" (92, italics original).

These italicised passages, which occasionally interrupt the realistic autodiegetic narration of part one, constitute a metalepsis between author and character ("*I am a character in one of my own books*") that is impossible to disentangle, other than indeed taking it as "*the literal truth*": Julian Mitchell has made himself a character in one of his own books. But whose voice are we supposed to be hearing in this passage: that of the actual author or that of the character 'Julian'? The metaleptic confusion of diegetic levels makes this undecidable. Moreover, the "conflict" of the novel between two opposing aesthetics remains unresolved at the end (Lodge 1986, 32). Lodge's critique of *The Undiscovered Country* still stands: "On the literary level, the realistic compromise between fact and fiction is abandoned in favour of two diametrically opposed alternatives – the nonfiction novel of Part I and the fabulation of Part II – but all the counter-double-bluffing cannot conceal the fact that neither is entirely satisfactory" (ibid.). *The Undiscovered Country* was to be Julian Mitchell's last novel. This novelist, standing at the crossroads, found yet another path and turned to writing successful plays and screenplays – thus confirming B. S. Johnson's and others' scepticism towards the validity and viability of the literary medium in the age of audiovisual media.

Fiction as a Tool of Knowledge: Iris Murdoch's *The Black Prince* (1973)

The authority of fiction and its potential for knowledge are also in question in Iris Murdoch's *The Black Prince* (1973), her fifteenth novel. The narrative centres on fifty-eight-year-old Bradley Pearson, who considers himself a serious novelist in contrast to his more successful and prolific friend and protégé Arnold Baffin. Baffin writes popular novels without thinking too much about art, pretentiously titled novels like *The Woeful Forest* or *The Gauntlets of Power*. Bradley, envious of Arnold and secretly admiring him, embarks on an affair with Arnold's wife Rachel but then falls in love with their daughter Julian. He neglects his troubled sister Priscilla and, instead of helping her, elopes with Julian. They separate and he returns to London. Priscilla commits suicide. Bradley buys a set of Arnold's complete works, a "huge compact mountain of smugly printed words" (Murdoch 2019, 416), only to destroy them. When Arnold is found dead, Bradley is arrested and sentenced for murder. In prison, he writes *The Black Prince: A Celebration of Love* – the novel we have been reading.

This novel is framed by multiple paratexts: an editor's preface by 'P. A. Loxias', a foreword by Bradley Pearson, a postscript by same, by his former wife Christian, his friend and psychoanalyst Francis Marloe, Arnold's widow Rachel, Julian, and Loxias. The novel within the novel, hedged in by these multiple and never quite converging perspectives, has a conventional plot that is enriched by essayistic reflections and further asides that address questions of love, art, and morality. Bradley's novel within Iris Murdoch's *The Black Prince* (1973) is an extended attempt at making sense of chaotic events by means of art. As Hilda Spear explains:

> Only through his narrated autobiography does Bradley's life take on meaning and reality both for himself and his readers; only by examining each event is he able finally to distinguish reality from appearance; only, even within the narrative, by reinterpreting art itself, is he able to make sense of the contingency of the events which come upon him and finally, only by the act of writing his memoirs is he able to realise himself as novelist and artist. (Spear 1995, 79)

This becomes clear, above all, in an early extended metafictional aside, when Bradley addresses the narratee directly and comments on his own tendency to accompany his story with a running "commentary" (Murdoch 2019, 85), explaining that his book is "about art" but simultaneously "a work of art" (85). He reflects on the novel as a darkly comic form (86), on irony as a "necessary tool" (86), and on writing as a form of self-defence but also, possibly, self-knowledge (87). The emotions generated by erotic love in the novel give rise to blindness *and* genuine insights about the self, moments of egotism as well as impulses of altruism

(Nussbaum 2004). In this case, then, metafiction is not used to cast doubt on the validity of representation but as a tool of knowledge – moral as well as epistemic.

These reflections on the nature of love and the purpose of art form the philosophical core of this darkly romantic novel, whose principal object of romance is ultimately the novel form itself, with its double duty of "tam[ing] the world by generalizing" (Murdoch 2019, 87) and of discovering truths about the self that unsettle these generalisations. It is only the experience of love in all its suddenness and superior reality that gives weight to Bradley's otherwise rather hollow assertions of being an artist. As he writes in his postscript:

> At some point in a black vision I apprehended the future. I saw this book, which I have written, I saw my dearest friend P.L., I saw myself a new man, altered out of recognition. I saw beyond and beyond. The book had to come into being because of Julian, and because of the book Julian had to be. [...] She somehow was and is the book, the story of herself. (445)

Julian, however, breaks free from Bradley's attempt to possess her, asserting her individuality in her own postscript. Bradley's self-knowledge only goes so far. Moreover, like a character in a Spark novel, Bradley feels caught up in a plot that is not of his own making: "I felt that everything that was happening to me was not just predestined but somehow actively at the moment of its occurrence *thought* by a divine power which held me in its talons" (445, emphasis original).

This "divine power" may of course be the actual author, Iris Murdoch, thinking about what will happen to her character in Sparkian fashion, but in this novel such power over the characters is ceded to another divine figure: P. A. Loxias. 'Loxias' is one of the names of the Greek god Apollo, who, as the editor of Bradley's memoir, personifies the doubleness of art as a force of order as well as chaos in human lives (Spear 1995, 76–77), one 'Black Prince' among many possible contenders for the person named in the novel's title. (Another notable one is the allusion to *Hamlet* and other plays by Shakespeare that run through the novel.)

In foregrounding the writtenness of Bradley's novel-within-the-novel with its sudden emotional turning points and crises, Murdoch emphasises that the artist's work is not "governed by preestablished rules" but that "the artist and the writer [...] are working without rules in order to formulate the rules of what *will have been done*" (Lyotard 1997, 81). In this, she inscribes Bradley into the tradition of the *bildungsroman*; as Nussbaum notes, "just as, in Charles Dickens's *David Copperfield*, we need to understand that the quality of mind that narrates the entire story [...] is who David has become" (2004, 704), we need to realise Bradley's personality as one that, as lover and artist, is in the process of formation and transformation – and that achieves clarity only in retrospect. Murdoch's Bradley, like Spark's Caroline, are author figures whose subjectivity or whose 'true' nature is not pre-established; on the contrary, they need to work it out for themselves, in a human-all-too-human fashion, imperfectly and painfully, in the process of writing, which then becomes the text that audiences are given to read.

Yet Bradley's sincerity in his first-person narration is at least somewhat undermined by his unreliability, and brusquely denied by the postscripts, which project different, competing, and conflicting views on Bradley's character. Commentary and meta-commentary amount to the impression that this novel is at the same time searching for truth and generating suspicion on the very possibility of telling the truth (cf. Moraru 2020). Nevertheless, there is a sense that Murdoch's gadgetry in *The Black Prince* in the final analysis merely gestures towards postmodernist relativism while in fact acknowledging, and intending readers to acknowledge, the validity of Bradley's own (though imperfect) soul-searching (cf. Dooley 2004). Since the postscripts in their contradictory perspectives cancel each other out, they leave the bulk of the book, Bradley's narrative, relatively untouched.

There is, however, one further aspect of *The Black Prince* that casts doubt on the centrality of Bradley Pearson's narrative. This is the fact, observed by Valentine Cunningham, that it is Arnold Baffin – and not Bradley Pearson – who appears like a "Murdoch lookalike novelist" in this novel: an author criticised for "his over-production, his never blotting a line, his producing yet again 'the mixture as before', yet one more Murdochian affair about a stockbroker who wants to become a monk", and so on (Cunningham 2002, 158). Bradley's destruction of Arnold's pile of books, then, would appear to be a kind of self-ironic *auto-da-fé* on Murdoch's part, a signal of her awareness of her shortcomings as a serious novelist, and of the gap between her ideals and their execution. In this aspect, then, *The Black Prince* contains a self-referential, allegorical, and parodic author fiction: the kind of authorial "shadow self" (Kenner 1976, 178–179) Murdoch may have feared to have become at this point of her literary career. The formal inventiveness of this novel, then, also amounts to a strategy of authorial self-reinvention for its actual author.

Yet, this self-parodic authorial allegory merely casts an oblique sidelight on the novel's actual author. For most readers, it is to be expected that Bradley Pearson's narrative, however diminished in its authority by the external postscripts and the internal signals of narratorial unreliability, remains the most profound – and the only reliable – source for understanding Bradley as a character. He remains the only meaningful object of readerly sympathy in *The Black Prince*. Even though this narrative is hedged by an array of contrasting points of view, it remains the centre of attention and thus preserves a fairly conventional narrative unity to this novel. Despite its metafictional bells and whistles, then, *The Black Prince* implicitly – and in parts explicitly – asserts the authority and the (moral and cultural) value of a personal, person-centred authorial narrative. Even though the self that is presented in Bradley's narrative is processual and never entirely transparent, its moral unity is not in question. Instead of the 'death of the author' – and in perfect alignment with Iris Murdoch's moral philosophy, as well as her search for "a new vocabulary of experience and a truer picture of freedom" in literature (1961, 20) – the novel remains based on the notion of the integrity of the individual self.

"Orpheus on the National Health": Russell Hoban's *Kleinzeit* (1974)

Another way of approaching and asserting the validity of fiction is by relating it to the authority of myth. Even if this happens in a playful way that acknowledges the unavailability of timeless truths, recourse to myth is one way of working towards a "reenchantment of the world" (Berman 1981) – whether in forms of magic realism (spawned by the Latin American boom of the 1960s and 1970s), in allegorical fables such as John Barth's *Giles, Goat-Boy* (1966), or in works of science fiction and fantasy. Russell Hoban's approach to myth in *Kleinzeit* (1974), however, is less stabilising than decentring and anarchic. This neglected gem of British postmodernism was written by an American expatriate best known for his post-apocalyptic science fiction novel *Riddley Walker* (1980). In response to the crisis of literary fiction, as discussed above, *Kleinzeit* lends a mythic authority and a supernatural agency to the power of 'Word', of language as a personified mythic presence. Hoban thus replaces the expressivist paradigm of modern authorship – which we have seen to be alive and well in *The Black Prince* – with a radical sense of boundless, boundaryless textuality. Like Roland Barthes and Julia Kristeva, he imagines a textuality without authors. Instead of the "self-creation of the author through his work" (Cortázar 2014, 405), the writer-protagonist of *Kleinzeit* experiences authorship as a process of decreation.

After losing his job as a writer of advertising copy in London, Kleinzeit feels a strange kind of pain. He is admitted to hospital, where doctors recommend an operation to remove his hypotenuse, his asymptotes, and his stretto. Kleinzeit escapes from and returns to the hospital repeatedly and spends time busking on a glockenspiel in the corridors of the Underground. He also embarks on an erotic relationship with one of the hospital nurses, who is referred to as 'Sister' throughout. As the musical and mathematical names of his inner organs already indicate, the story is set in a strangely altered world, a world in which spaces, objects and abstract concepts have voices and a kind of agency of their own. 'Hospital' repeatedly talks to Kleinzeit, as does his mirror, as does God; Death manifests as a hairy ape; Action is shown smoking a cigarette, and so on. The world of this novel is animated by the myth of Orpheus, of whom Kleinzeit is a modern version. Kleinzeit is tasked with finding "the hidden soul of harmony" (in a quote from Milton's "L'Allegro", 1631; Hoban 2021, 161) and to "remember" (172), that is re-integrate and return to their old order, the dispersed and disintegrated parts of himself and of the modern world.

Kleinzeit pens the commercial that gets him fired on a sheet of yellow paper that he picked up in a corridor of the Underground. He subsequently finds more paper there, deposited by a man he calls Redbeard. The paper – described as "Ryman. 64 mill hard-sized thick din A4. Duplicator paper" (88) –has a voice and an agency of its own, attaching itself to its owner and suggesting nonsense phrases like "harrow full of crocks" (14) or "borrow fool's pox" (36) or "Morrow's cruel mock" (41). Kleinzeit feels attracted by the yellow paper, even in a sexual way, and gets hold of a supply. He imagines himself as a heroic writer, possibly induced by his reading of Thucydides, and he imagines the writing process as a violent sexual act:

> [Kleinzeit] smiled as he thought of the yellow paper waiting for him, how he would throw himself upon it like a tiger. Rape. The yellow paper would love it. Redbeard simply hadn't been man enough. [...] Kleinzeit went into the living room, rubbing his hands and chuckling, lit the candle, stripped the flimsy Ryman bag from the yellow paper. The yellow paper lay before him naked. Yes yes oh yes, it murmured. Never like this before, no one like you before. Yes yes oh yes. Now now now. (101)

The paper is anthropomorphised ("naked") and is given a voice ("it murmured"). By alluding to the last words of Joyce's *Ulysses*, Molly Bloom's orgasmic "and yes I said yes I will Yes" (Joyce 1987, 644), the passage also clearly feminises the paper and emphasises its (or Kleinzeit's, or both) modernist literary aspirations, in a way that recalls, for example, Lawrence Durrell's metaphors for writing as a sexual act [→ ch. 11].

When he starts writing, however, the tables are turned: the paper, not the writer, is revealed to be "a tiger": "He opened the door of the yellow paper's cage, and it sprang upon him. Over and over they rolled together, bloody and roaring. [...] He wrote the first line while the yellow paper clawed his guts, the pain was blinding. It'll kill me, said Kleinzeit" (Hoban 2021, 103). But he masters the writing, finishes a paragraph that "danced and sang" (104), and leaves the paper tamely "purring" (104). Like Orpheus placating the wild animals, Kleinzeit's writing has pacified the yellow paper's predatory nature. The paper now tells him it is "pregnant": "I'm carrying your novel inside me" (110), further emphasizing its co-creative femininity, and the metaphorical masculinity of the act of writing. The novel's preliminary title is simply "Hero" (103). The writer-as-hero, this suggests, is born in the writing process, having been conceived by the union of pen and paper.

Yet, this potentially heroic aspect of authorship is soon undermined. Kleinzeit, as his name already indicates (it means 'small time' in German), is a rather unheroic writer-hero. He crosses out the word "Hero" as his novel's title, calling it "[r]idiculous" (167). Some of his fellow patients in the hospital are also (failed) writers, who remind him that "the world is full of people who write a few chapters" (115), no matter on what kind of surface. One of the patients, Drogue, writes short lyric poems on Rizla cigarette paper. He aims for "[u]niversal subjects", which is why he has chosen Rizla as a "universal paper" to write on: "yellow paper and foolscap may be universal in their way but they're not universal the way Rizla is" (131). However, this striving for the universal only results in bland, cliché-ridden rhymes and slogans similar to commercial advertising (130–131). It may be impossible to achieve meaningful universality in a meaningless world. When Kleinzeit asks what it all means, Hospital tells him: "How can there be meaning? [...] Meaning is a limit. There are no limits" (146). In the animistic world of myth to which the world of *Kleinzeit* has returned, the lack of limits also touches the human subject, the I: "[e]ven Orpheus wasn't *I*" (145, emphasis original).

The yellow paper yearns for the return of her "lover" Kleinzeit (160) when she is visited by Word, who injects his "seed" into her. This episode demonstrates that authorship is always tied to intertextuality: "Nobody does it all himself, said Word. Nobody does it unless I have shot my seed as well" (160). The "mind" of Word is "full of every kind of nonsense", like the phrases mentioned earlier, which Word explains as mnemonics that serve to recall the "hidden soul of harmony" (161). Word stresses the agency of language in the semiosphere and in the act of writing. Creativity arises from this agency of language in interaction with the medium of writing – in this case, the yellow paper – and the individual agency of the writer, whose role is far less important than the other two: "I don't know what his name is, said Word, and I don't care. Whoever it is that writes on you, let him get on with it. It's in you now" (162). The next time Kleinzeit tries to write on the yellow paper, his words will not stay on it; the paper informs him that he has to "find what's there and let it be" (169), that is, not follow an expressivist model of authorship but tap into the divine power of 'Word' as a superior authority. *Kleinzeit* thus imagines a postheroic scenario of writing without the writer as hero, an author fiction without authors in the conventional sense; one in which, finally, the poststructuralist ideal of authorship after the 'death of the author' has been realised as a vision of the boundless intertextuality of language.

Back in hospital, Kleinzeit is left with the task of re-membering himself. When a new fellow patient recites Milton to him, he feels a moment of restored harmony, though his physical suffering returns quickly. Harmony, the hospital tells him, is only ever momentary, a passing experience, while the "[p]lace of dismemberment" is "[e]verwhere, all the time" (182). He is soon discharged, suffering the same pain as before. Sister moves in with him. He writes some more, apparently without a hitch. As a present from Death, he receives the gift of being able to draw a perfect black circle on the yellow paper. This image "sums up both the cyclical pattern of Orpheus and Kleinzeit's personal achievement: the effortless, Zen-like expression of interior harmony which makes it possible for him to be a whole person and a poet" (Branscomb 1986, 33).

In this postmodernist version of the Orpheus myth, the world has become a place of dismembered experiences, painfully longing to re-establish a lost harmony, something that can only ever be achieved for a few precious moments, at best held on to as a memory. This may be symbolised in the *ensō*, the Zen circle Kleinzeit draws at the end. Writing, at first presented as an act of male heroism, is revealed to work best when giving up any sense of the ego and 'letting be' what one finds is there – setting oneself adrift, giving oneself over to the power of Word (of intertextuality) and the medium of the paper. *Kleinzeit* decentres the agency of the author in favour of a model of creativity in which the creative impulses come from outside the writer's person – returning to a model of (divine) external inspiration. Thus the novel combines, with some satirical zest, a postmodernist diagnosis of a dismembered, meaningless world dominated by commercial interests and the military-industrial complex (as instanced by names like "Napalm Industries" or "Sodom Chemicals", 19), with a nostalgic yearning for the "hidden harmony", a return to the unity of mathematics and music, and the poetic universalism of myth.[184] This the modern-day "Orpheus on the National Health" (185) will be unable to restore, but he will be able to keep his Eurydice and live with her in what is perhaps an unexpected happy ending (which also, at least obliquely, echoes the ending of Orwell's *Keep the Aspidistra Flying*).

Kleinzeit radically decentres or deconstructs authorial authority in a strong denial of individual authorship. Instead, it invests the medium of writing – paper –with a pure, irrefragable, archaic power. This is the power to bring back old, half-forgotten myths and to reenchant the technologised modern world with wild forms of poetic thinking. *Kleinzeit* presents perhaps the farthest-reaching narrative deconstruction of authorship, this side of complete textual disintegration, in postmodernist literary fiction published in Britain. Experience has been fragmented; acts of authorship have been relocated away from a human subject to a weird

---

[184] Hoban reprised this Orphic theme in *The Medusa Frequency* (1987), where the protagonist is the unsuccessful novelist Herman Orff, at work on his third novel, while his day job is writing speech balloons for comics. The novel leads him to the underworld of literary creation, which is ruled by a giant squid.

array of material objects and spiritual forces charged with an animistic energy; and beyond this lies a yearning for a dissolution of the rational, industrialised modern world and for a future that is also the past of myth, a timeless universal harmony.[185]

The 'Isness' of Reality: William Golding's *The Paper Men* (1984)

Paper is also a crucial medium in William Golding's late novel *The Paper Men* (1984), and here too it is a medium of creativity as well as a source of danger to the person writing on it. It fixes that person into a biographical artefact that can be exploited and abused. In this, Golding takes up the topic of the relationship between authors and their biographers at which Henry James had excelled [→ ch. 8].

As an author novel, *The Paper Men* is remarkable also because it is one of very few novels that deal with the aging writer. It is narrated in the first person by Wilfred Barclay, an English author who is in his early fifties at the beginning of the book and in his sixties at its end. Modelled in some respects on its actual author (see Carey 2010, 423), who turned 73 the year the book was published, Barclay had one early sensational success with his first novel *Coldharbour*. Since then, he has enjoyed a respectable but otherwise unremarkable literary career. 'Wilf' is persecuted by his nemesis, the boorish and relentless American professor of English Literature, Rick L. Tucker from the University of Astrakhan, Nebraska. Tucker is dead set on writing Barclay's biography. Barclay first meets him one morning in front of his house in the act of rifling through the author's rubbish in search of valuable material for the book. From that moment on, the author's life takes a turn to the burlesque and the picaresque. Freshly divorced and on the move, he travels the world to escape his pursuer. He is "happy not to want fame" (Golding 2013, 88). There are things in his past that he does not want to see printed in a book: "There were authors enough to go round after all, authors by the thousand; and all with foreheads of such brass or lives of such impenetrable rectitude they could afford the deadliest of all poisons about themselves, the simple truth. Whereas I –" (41).

Barclay fears being turned into a laughingstock by "a really modern biography [...]. Cheap printing in Singapore, ten million pulp copies from a backstreet factory in Macao" (67). His dislike of the idea takes on epic, paranoid proportions: He imag-

---

185 In other words, it progresses from Weberian disenchantment to Bermanian reenchantment, or from the *Dialectic of Enlightenment* to Kittler's *Musik und Mathematik*.

ines Tucker as a "Boswell" with "access to [...] not just paper, not just tapes, videos, discs, crystals with their hideous, merciless memories, but others, snifters, squinters, reconstitutors, mechanisms doubtless that listened in a room and heard echoes of every word, saw shadows of every image that were trapped on walls" (68).

Tucker, meanwhile, like a revenant of the narrator of "The Aspern Papers", tries to get access to Wilf's archive through the author's ex-wife Liz and their daughter Emmy. Barclay and Tucker meet at a hotel in Switzerland, where Tucker is accompanied by his beautiful young wife and former student, Mary Lou. Tucker tries to persuade Barclay to sign an agreement to make him his official biographer. Barclay, however, still does not understand why this professor is so interested in him. As he tells Mary Lou, "You see, writers are ten a penny. A hundred a penny. There are probably more writers than there are professors, seeing that some of each are also the other" (78). The professor even attempts – at least that is how Barclay interprets it – to use Mary Lou to seduce him into signing the agreement. Tucker's research, it turns out, is funded by an American billionaire and book collector named Halliday, who soon lures Mary Lou away from him. After seven years, the funding runs out, and Tucker is left with nothing.

Barclay's narrative becomes increasingly erratic as he tends to drink too much, and the fog of alcohol and advancing age makes his story increasingly unreliable. At one point, in Rome, he has a mild stroke that further impairs his judgement and his writing. There is even the possibility that he killed someone in a road accident in South America (68). After several flights and rental car journeys through Greece, Italy, and Yugoslavia, among other places, he meets Tucker again in the same Swiss hotel and turns the tables on him, forcing Tucker to demean himself and lap up wine from a saucer like a dog. "No wine in the saucer, no authorized biography. No letters from MacNeice, Charley Snow, Pamela, oh a whole chest full of goodies! Variant readings. [...] Tucker, when you get your claws into it [...] [t]he pearly gates will open" (192).[186] Yet, despite having humiliated his would-be biographer and whetted his appetite even more, Barclay still withholds the agreement.

The professor is increasingly desperate, having staked his whole career, his entire life on the Barclay biography. Instead, the author decides to write the biography himself (cf. 234). We are given to understand that the text we are reading *is* that biography and that Tucker has become its principal narratee, the book's "re-

---

[186] The references are to the poet Louis MacNeice and novelists C. P. Snow and Pamela Hansford Johnson (Lady Snow), names that help anchor the fictional 'Wilfred Barclay' in the real literary life of twentieth-century Britain.

cipient" (210), sometimes addressed in the second person. Consider this sentence from chapter XI: "On that ferry (I was watching an Italian cruise ship I think the Italians said she was the *Cristoforo Colombo* so for my biography I mean our biography you can find the exact place and date) I tried with my mind to think the word 'end'" (162). The (now auto-)biography, written by Barclay, turns into a kind of double biography, "our biography" (162), "a duet" (196).

Finally, Barclay is invited back to England by his ex-wife and learns that she suffers from terminal cancer. Her new partner, Capstone Bowers, has left her. In London, Barclay meets with a couple of old friends in the Random Club when Tucker appears, more dishevelled than ever, and the scene ends in a public brawl that gets Barclay expelled from the club. After Liz's death, he decides to stage a "rite of passage" in the garden and to burn all his papers. Among the trees, he sees Rick Turner watching him through some instrument before realising that the instrument is a gun and that Rick has shot him. The novel ends in mid-sentence and mid-word with the question "How the devil did Rick L. Tucker manage to get hold of a gu [sic]" (246).

Most likely, the gun belonged to Capstone Bowers, the man who had moved in with Liz after Barclay had moved out, not a paper man but somebody who went in for big-game hunting. When Barclay moved back in, he noticed the mark on the wall where that gun had been hanging. The analogy with a tiger or a lion turns the author into a trophy for the academic. The novel thus inserts itself into the tradition of Henry James's stories of persecuted literary celebrities, like "The Death of the Lion" or "The Real Right Thing" [→ ch. 8], and of course "The Aspern Papers", with the difference that Golding and his Wilfred Barclay are painfully aware of the academic cottage industries that have sprung up around individual authors in the twentieth century.

Unlike David Lodge's *Small World* or *Changing Places*, and unlike Malcolm Bradbury's *The History Man*, *The Paper Men* only marginally touches upon the academic world in the satirical mode of the campus novel, and it offers no reflections on or parodies of modern literary theory. Also, as John Carey notes, the novel is "in essence [...] not humorous" (2010, 424), though it does have moments of the blackest of black humour, quite in contrast to most campus fiction, and its high points are much darker than one might expect at first. What it does reflect is the return of biography as a respectable scholarly and literary pursuit, which it seeks to disparage and discredit. Part of the real-life background to *The Paper Men* is Golding's growing impatience with James R. Baker, professor of English in San Diego and author of *William Golding: A Critical Study* (1965). Golding found Baker's persistent claims on himself increasingly less bearable over the years (Carey 2010, 408).

In his climactic argument with Tucker, Barclay refers to both of himself and the scholar as "paper men" (196) – as both less solid or weaker than other people and preoccupied or obsessed with paper and writing, even as "paper men" in the sense of fictional characters who only exist, as it were, 'on paper', in the pages of a novel. All the characters, including the narrator, are fairly 'flat' characters, to the point of being caricatures. Barclay's questionable solidity may already be hinted at in his name, as in having 'feet of clay'. Papery insubstantiality is also a key attribute of the God-or devil-like figure of the American billionaire Halliday: his entry in *Who's Who* is empty: "just blank, white paper" (205).

References to paper thus pervade the novel, as is only to be expected. Paper in *The Paper Men* is, on the one hand, a valueless substance, rubbish, dead matter. It can, however, bear treacherous traces of the past, like the papers Barclay heedlessly throws away and that Tucker retrieves from the bin, thereby unearthing the memory of Barclay's former lover Lucinda that will lead his wife to divorce him. On the other hand, the novel shows us papers in the form of valuable documents in the author's archive that are the biographer's bread and butter. The archive is "the paperweight of a whole life" (Golding 2013, 245). Then there is the paper on which Barclay types the agreement that he then refuses to sign, using it to tease and torment his would-be biographer. Finally, there is the paper on which he writes his own last book, the text we are reading, "a book for keeping a journal" (209) that he buys in Rome.

The novel itself is a kind of paper trail of Barclay's scattershot journey and life, a double biography of himself and his scholarly nemesis. Barclay is intent on separating his life, his value as a person, from its objectification in the media of writing and printing on paper, such as the imagined "ten million pulp copies" of his biography. "To know myself accepted, endured not even as in honest whoredom, for money, but for *paper!*" he exclaims after he sees through (or projects) Mary Lou's and Tucker's intentions (93).

The Paper Men shows its credentials as postmodernist metafiction not only in its denigration of paper, and thus by extension of the insubstantiality of literary fiction, but also in its reflections on reality. When Barclay "brood[s] on the isness", that is on the experiential quality of the real (210), and when he attributes the pain he feels in his hands and feet to a miracle, as a development of (invisible) stigmata, he is asserting, or trying to assert, his existence in what he calls "quote reality unquote" (210), an existence legitimised by a higher power. This religious or supernatural dimension in the novel has invited much critical comment (e. g., Simon 1991, Delbaere 1991, Wöhrer 1995). Having studied the novel's genesis, Carey dismisses these elements as extraneous to its original conception (2010, 426). Yet, the 'Great Dream' that is ascribed to Barclay in the novel (and that echoes through many works of Golding's late phase) very much resembles the life-changing dream of building bridges between generations on the Spanish Steps that helped Golding out of his severe crisis, an intense and very long writer's block, in the early 1970s (Kendall 2018). This may be interpreted as a mystical experience, but through the biographical connection its presence in the novel is directly linked to the enigma of literary creativity and the theme of writing and authorship. It also resonates with an echo, however distant, of Muriel Spark's engagement with a superior level of reality in *The Comforters*.

"However minor" *The Paper Men* may seem compared to Golding's masterpieces, Tim Kendall explains, it "is also central, because it is Golding's most direct attempt to explain his own creative processes and their relationship to dreaming" (2018, 478). In transferring his healing dream and his subsequent acceptance of mortality to his fictional author character, Golding invests Barclay with the superior status of a literary alter ego. Autobiographical details add depth to the 'papery' caricature of an aging writer. The dream episode, moreover, attributes to Barclay an encounter with a higher reality, or at least the idea of having been touched by a divine "isness": a vision of Halliday on the Spanish Steps (Golding 2013, 205–207). The final version of the novel leaves much of this unsaid; "[t]here is no celebration of creativity in the face of impending death" (Kendall 2018, 484) in the published text.

In contrast to Golding, whose writing flourished as a consequence of his dream, Barclay is not so lucky. He continues to disappoint himself in his writing. This is the point at which their identities finally diverge. The function of these metaphysical or religious passages in the novel, then, should perhaps not be interpreted as statements of a belief in the beyond, but as fulfilling a literary and a metaliterary function: they serve to show Barclay's limitations as a man (a fictional person) and as a 'paper man', i.e., a literary character in a novel. Here, then, is a paper man, a fictional character, desperately trying to gain control over his life and trying to establish, ultimately unsuccessfully, that his reality is actual and substantial, that he is more than a figment, more than a character in a novel.

Postwar British metafiction negotiates a crisis of literary fiction concerningist authority, validity, and representativeness. It does so by questioning its author characters and submitting them to trials of knowledge and experience. These works document profound uncertainty about the value of fiction while also celebrating literary writing as a superior instrument of psychological insight, moral knowledge, and critique of reality. Paradoxically, the weakening of authorial authority *within* the fiction can lead to an empowering of the actual author's superior position. Far from confirming the 'death of the author', these novels affirm authorship as a powerful cultural institution – from Spark's godlike position vis à vis her creation to Golding's salvage of the creative core of his selfhood. Others invite their readers to evaluate the moral failings of their author characters, as in Murdoch's *The Black Prince*, or imagine a reenchantment of the fragmented modern world through recourse to the unifying power of myth, like Hoban's *Kleinzeit*.

More recent narrative texts that proceed in a similar vein, inheriting this tradition, continue its dialectic between subversion and affirmation of authorial authority and the legitimacy of fiction. For example, works by Nicola Barker (*I am Sovereign*, 2019), Joshua Cohen (*Book of Numbers*, 2015) or Steven Hall (*Maxwell's Demon*, 2021) attest to a continuation, in the twenty-first century, of a postmodernist sensibility of textual experimentalism and the playful undermining of conventional narrative patterns. However, the critical dominance of postmodernist metafiction was relatively short-lived, as its dispersal of authorial singularity in the boundless sea of intertextuality or in what Jonathan Lethem memorably called "the ecstasy of influence" (2007) was almost immediately countered by the rise of "witness literature" (Engdahl 2002, Craps 2012) and a 'new sincerity' (cf. Voelz 2016). In this formation, authors take on the role of guarantors of authentic and representative experience. Yet, in fact, non-experimental modes of literary storytelling never disappeared – nor did they merely eke out an existence in the domains of science fiction, fantasy, and other popular genres. Especially in the US and Canada, realist narrative techniques were vigorously reintroduced in the 1970s, in work by Alice Munro and Raymond Carver, among others. Their approaches to the representation of authors and authorship will be the main concern of the next chapter.

14 "The unreckoned consequences of art": Authorial Realism in Munro, Carver, Roth, and Moore

Among several literary developments that one might highlight from the 1970s onwards, a return to realist traditions of narrative is one of the most conspicuous and sustained trends. Many authorship narratives in the mode of autofiction, for example [→ ch. 17], adhere to forms of post-ironic realism or a 'new sincerity' (cf. Voelz 2016) that is believed to require a concealment of narrative art. Even forms of authorial omniscience – the bugbear of literary modernism – have been revived in "'post-postmodern' modes of [...] narration" that perform "narrative authority" by invoking "a historically specific figure of authorship" (Dawson 2013, 247).

This revival of literary realism does not mean that radical experiments with authorship metafiction are no longer being written. Mark Z. Danielewski's *House of Leaves* (2000), Jeanette Winterson's *The PowerBook* (2000), Doug Dorst's and J. J. Abrams's *S.* (2013), or Jonathan Safran Foer's *Tree of Codes* (2010) are only a few examples of works that address the digital media environment of contemporary writing or that use multimodal techniques of presentation and technologies of book production in self-referential ways. In reduced form, elements of metafiction are also likely to be present in autofiction despite its generally less overtly playful or less poignantly sceptical tone.

Another perennial genre that survives to this day and that depends on elements of formal realism is authorship satire, which is usually concerned with authorial rivalries, competition and frustration, and the uncertainties of the literary marketplace. Such novels, not discussed in this book, include Martin Amis's *The Information* (1995) and Edward St Aubyn's *Lost for Words* (2014) as well as Ian McEwan's story *My Purple Scented Novel* (2016).[187]

The stories discussed in this chapter, written and published in the US and Canada in the 1970s and 1980s, comprise forms of 'authorial realism' in that they deal frankly and critically with the often exploitative relationship between art and life, and with the costs involved in using the lives of others (as well as the writer's own

---

[187] My reason for not including them is firstly one of space, and secondly of theoretical interest. Most of these texts do little else than repeat rather tired scenarios and tropes of authorial rivalry or engage in thinly veiled *roman à clef* depictions of authorial competitiveness in the market for publicity, sales figures, awards, and attention. In the case of Amis's *The Information*, the novel's publishing history is even more outrageous than any plot element in that novel itself (cf. Howard 1996).

life) as material for literature. While the stories by Alice Munro and Raymond Carver can be associated with American minimalism, with what Mark McGurl has called "lower-middle-class modernism" (2009, 273), the texts by Philip Roth and Lorrie Moore exhibit more 'maximalist' tendencies of "verbal pride" rather than minimalist self-retracting "shame", in McGurl's terminology (ibid., 301). Nonetheless, despite these superficial differences in style and form, they are remarkably similar in their realist emphasis of *milieu*, in their embrace of modernist techniques of narrative reduction and condensation (along the lines of the 'iceberg principle'), and their – explicit and implicit – view of authorship as a socially marginal, deviant, and potentially harmful professional (de-)formation.

A Bad Smell in the House of Fiction: Alice Munro's "Material" (1973)

The narrator of Alice Munro's short story "Material" (1973) describes herself as a "middle-aged wom[a]n" (1997, 99). Married to an engineer named Gabriel, she works part-time teaching history at a private girls' school in Vancouver. A new collection of short stories by her ex-husband, the writer Hugo Johnson, revives her memory of their time together. They used to live in a rented apartment in town, with their landlady's daughter, 'Dotty', occupying a flat in the basement. They condescend to Dotty but are also fascinated by her colourful impoverished existence, which they tend to romanticise: "This is life, I thought, fresh from books, classes, essays, discussions. Unlike her mother, Dotty was flat-faced, soft, doughy, fashioned for defeat, the kind of colorless puzzled woman you see carrying a shopping bag, waiting for the bus" (106). They even suspect her of prostituting herself. Hugo, who needs silence for his writing, is disturbed by the noise from the pump that keeps Dotty's flat from flooding. One night he shuts it off, with the result that the basement is indeed damaged by the water coming in. The couple quarrel over who is responsible for this. Soon after, Dotty moves into her recently deceased mother's house, and the narrator and Hugo move away too. But the quarrel has driven a wedge between them that ultimately destroys their marriage. The narrator reproaches herself with not having taken any initiative herself and switched the pump back on:

> I could have told somebody, if I thought it was that important, pushed Hugo out into the unpleasant world and let him taste trouble. But I didn't, I was not able fully to protect or expose him, only to flog him with blame, desperate sometimes, feeling I would claw his head open to pour my vision into it, my notion of what had to be understood. (114)

Now, Hugo has moved on to wife number three. The narrator clearly resents the smugness of the (largely male) literary world of which he has become a part: "He looks", she notes when contemplating a photo of him, "at the same time, woebegone and cheerful. [...] Outrageous writers may bounce from one blessing to another nowadays, bewildered, as permissively reared children are said to be, by excess of approval" (103). She describes him as a member of a group of "vain quarrelsome men" who are "cosseted by the academic life, the literary life, by women" who ascribe "power" to them" (99). It becomes clear that she includes herself, at least her younger self, in this category of a female admirer, carer, and enabler who has pampered Hugo's ego and nurtured his vanity, and who is now reproaching herself for this. The adjective "quarrelsome" on the story's first page foreshadows the central quarrel of the story that precipitates the parting of their ways. She also dismisses Hugo as childish or child-like when she compares him to "permissively reared children", with the implication that she had taken a motherly role towards him and been too 'permissive' in shielding him from "the unpleasant world" (114).

One of the stories in Hugo's new collection includes a character who has obviously been modelled on some signature mannerisms and accoutrements of Dotty. The narrator describes the story as "very good", "honest": "There is Dotty, lifted out of life and held in light, suspended in the marvellous clear jelly that Hugo has spent all his life learning how to make" (115). But her praise for the story is laced with irony; she refers to "tricks" (115), a word that she and Hugo used earlier in referring to their suspicions of Dotty's prostitution. And when she drily notes that Dotty "has passed into Art" with a capital A, something that "doesn't happen to everybody" (115), there is unspoken resentment in these "[i]ronical objections" of which she confesses herself to be "half-ashamed" (116). She decides to write a letter of "[a]cknowledgement" to Hugo, but in writing it she reaches a sudden moral clarity about her situation in relation to the men in her life, men who have "authority" and hold power to decide "what to do about everything they run across in this world, what attitude to take, how to ignore or use things" (116) – a situation of "unhappiness" about being subjected to the social and familial expectations of a male-dominated world. What she writes is three terse sentences: "*This is not enough, Hugo. You think it is, but it isn't. You are mistaken, Hugo*" (116, italics original). The implication is that she will not post this letter and keep her "unhappiness" (116) to herself.

As a work of author fiction, this story is remarkably Jamesian in its shift of focus from the author to an observer character, a woman who has lived with the author in his formative years and who is one of the nurturing women who have enabled this man to fulfil his dreams of becoming an established, successful author. The story's title, "Material", not only refers to Hugo's use of the Dotty episode as material for a later story, to the relationship between life and art; arguably, it can also be associated with the material support without which art cannot be made. Thus, material is not only subjected to art as the stuff out of which art is made; one can also realise, as the narrator does, that the true material foundations of the writer's life consist of those practical, economic, and social support structures that benefit men and disadvantage women. These structures are 'material' in the sense of 'essential' for enabling (male) creativity. There may even be an allusion to women's motherly, nurturing social role in the etymological derivation of the word 'material' (Latin *materia*, 'matter') from the Latin *mater* (mother). The narrator's maternal role has been the material that has made possible Hugo's production of "Art" and his own self-production as a writer.

The story depicts the end result of this self-production in the narrator's response to the biographical profile that accompanies Hugo's new book, which uses reality as material for a fictional, streamlined author biography in which only those aspects are preserved or highlighted that create a particular masculine author image: Hugo is presented as having worked odd jobs "*as a lumberjack, beer-slinger, counterman, telephone lineman, and sawmill foreman*" (104, emphasis original), items the narrator mercilessly unpicks as "not only fake but out-of-date" (105). Why, for instance did he not mention also being an "*examination marker*" or "*recorder player*" (105)? Hugo here assumes "the hyper-masculine identity of the working-class laborer" (McIntyre 2015, 166), an identity that he also takes in the narrator's and his *Lady Chatterley* roleplay in which he casts himself as the sexually potent gardener Mellors from Lawrence's novel (Munro 1997, 110). Even the author's image is a part of the fiction-making process, using life as material, selectively tailored to the expectations and demands of fellow authors and audiences in the literary field. The rather unlovely dishonesty with which such authors exploit other people as material for their "Art" (115) extends to the way they grow accustomed to lying to and about themselves.

If the author bio gives the lie to his self-presentation, and the narrator reproaches herself with her supporting role in this process of character (de-)formation, Dotty in her basement flat becomes symbolic for the debased role of those women who end up as collateral damage in the process of male empowerment. In order for Hugo's creative juices to flow, the water pump had to be turned off, resulting in irreparable damage to the house. The narrator now recognises herself to have been an accomplice in these events. The nasty smell (by implication, of the narrator's guilty conscience) is never going to go away.

The spatial arrangements of the house take on symbolic significance also when we relate them to Munro's own comparison between the process of writing a short story and exploring the physical space of a house: "Everybody knows what a house does, how it encloses space and makes connections between one enclosed space and another and presents what is outside in a new way. This is the nearest I can come to explain what a story does for me, and what I want my stories to do for other people" (Munro 1993, 825). In "Material", the act of writing is directly linked to the "basement", the foundations of the house in which the writer lives; but this writer, Hugo, has been careless of these foundations, making the house inhabitable and leaving a bad smell in the 'house of fiction'.[188]

Munro's house of fiction has internal structural weaknesses and is liable to flooding, but its inhabitants are incapable of taking adequate measures to prevent disaster. "Material" uses the metaphor of the house to express the narrator's, and Munro's, scepticism about the material, ethical, and aesthetic arrangements of a literary world that pampers men and depends on caring women, while relegating 'useless' women of a lower class, like Dotty, to the basement and ignoring their suffering. In the process of the story, the narrator also realises that her current domestic arrangements depend on her continuing complicity with her current husband's preferences and silences.

The precious "jelly" (115) that Hugo has poured over his selective memories of their shared past in turning it into literature "is not enough" (116) precisely because he continues to ignore these foundational, basic, material realities – the more important story of his own authorpoiesis and its entanglement with the narrator's female role. The story "Material", as told by the narrator, is thus turned into a much better counter-narrative to the "very good" but unnamed story by Hugo that is only briefly described in it.[189] It thus moves beyond a statement of the narrator's moral failure towards an indirect "affirmation of the power of literature and even a key to Munro's ability to make peace with the morality and efficacy of her work [...] embracing the power of literary creation and the ethical risk it

---

188 Henry James's phrase in his preface to *The Portrait of a Lady* in the New York Edition (1908). The interesting contrast between James's and Munro's metaphor is that, for James, the purpose of the house of fiction is to have as many windows as possible looking out on reality, whereas Munro emphasises "enclosed spaces" (1993, 825) within the house and arguably, in line with the story discussed here, focuses more on the actual building and its interior structures, and thus its limits of capturing reality.
189 See McIntyre 2015 for a summary of existing criticism on this story, which is divided over the question whether the narrator of "Material" is herself a writer or not, and whether her "short jabbing sentences" (Munro 1997, 116) constitute "a rival aesthetic" (McIntyre 2015, 162). The story does not specify this, and I would argue that Munro would have specified it if it mattered; what matters, I think, is that the narrator derives at self-knowledge and a powerful critique of Hugo's art. Whether she is a writer or not, she reveals herself to be a competent critic of (a certain kind of) literature and its lack of 'honesty'. – At least two other Munro stories, "Family Furnishings" (2001) and "Fiction" (2009), not considered here, deal with related metaliterary concerns; see Bernstein 2019.

carries" (McIntyre 2015, 161). The voice of the narrator, while ostensibly not a writer herself, tends to be anaclitically propped onto Munro's writerly voice, indirectly expressing Munro's doubts and beliefs about the power of fiction and the literary world of her time. The story is not meant to be read as written by the character of the narrator; but, as a written artefact, its rhetoric of minimalist simplicity and ostensive artlessness, in combination with the story's subject matter, constitutes a counter-aesthetic to Hugo's transformation of life into art that relates the 'material' to the act of fiction-making in a very different way.

Raymond Carver's "Put Yourself in My Shoes" (1972) and "Intimacy" (1986)

In "Put Yourself in My Shoes", first published in 1972 and then included in Carver's first collection *Will You Please Be Quiet, Please?* (1976), a young writer named Myers and his wife Paula pay a spontaneous Christmas visit to the Morgans, a middle-aged couple from whom they once rented a house without ever meeting them, an experience that did not go well because the Morgans complained about the Myerses' keeping a cat in the house in breach of their agreement. Like Munro's "Material", this story is about the relationship between the – ironically named – "ivory tower" and "the real world" (Carver 2009, 101). Myers has quit his job and is now a writer, but he lives in poverty in an apartment that he no longer shares with Paula. He is "between stories" and feeling "despicable" (102), desperate to find new material for his writing.

    The material is willingly provided by the Morgans, who regale their guests with stories from their life that illustrate, above all else, the Morgans' narrow-minded self-righteousness. The first story is about an academic who has "an affair with one of his students" and is physically attacked and injured by his son (107). The Morgans encourage Myers to imagine writing this story from the perspective of the errant husband, the betrayed wife, the guilty son, or "that eighteen-year-old coed who fell in love with a married man" (108), with Edgar Morgan claiming that "[i]t would take a Tolstoy to tell it and tell it *right*" (108). The Morgans' improvised creative writing workshop moves on from Tolstoyesque unhappy families to a tale of their trip to Munich, the narrative "raw material" (110) in this case consisting of a lost wallet and the sudden death of its finder, an Australian lady who returned the wallet to Mrs Morgan but had taken the cash out of it. Instead of pitying the Morgans' "disappointment" at this betrayal, however, all Myers can do is laugh, upon which Edgar Morgan accuses Myers of not really being a writer, because he lacks understanding and empathy.

Things take a turn towards *Who's Afraid of Virginia Woolf* when Edgar Morgan starts ventilating his anger about the Myerses not having abided by the terms of their agreement when they rented the house, which he describes as a kind of invasion: "That's the *real* story that is waiting to be written" (114). The Myerses leave, with Paula summing up the Morgans as "crazy" and "scary" (115). Myers, however, knows that he has struck gold: no longer "between stories" (102), he is now "at the very end of a story" (115). This, the final sentence, metafictionally closes the story and reveals what we have been reading to be a record of, indeed to *be* the transformation of "raw material" (110) into a story.

The young writer's laughter is the knowing laugh, the last laugh that will shut up the Morgans' endless tirades and replace them with a few well-crafted and perfectly arranged sentences, turning the "raw material" (110) of their anger, their lurid accusations, and their blistering sense of "disappointment" into art. The Morgans are deftly characterised not only in their habit of telling stories about others to raise themselves up as moral authorities, but also in the callousness and carelessness with which they react to Myers being brought to a fall in their driveway when he is attacked by their dog (who is not allowed inside the house), and their passive-aggressiveness throughout the Myerses' visit. Despite (or even because of) his destitute, precarious, subaltern economic position, the author Myers can assert his autonomy over against the Philistine social world of the Morgans. The author's technique, assumed by the Morgans to be at the centre of fiction writing – putting oneself in the shoes of others, imagining their mental world, and developing empathy for them – is turned against them when, instead of being empathic, Myers reveals their ethical limitations. In doing so, he asserts his own (emotional) intelligence to be superior, and this act of assertion is part of his self-making as an author. He has reached "the very end of a story" not only in the temporal sense of an ending, but also in the sense of its ethical and authorpoietic purpose, in the sense of writing a story that creates and legitimises its (that is, his very own) authorial point of view. The events of the story have ended, and now its writing can begin (cf. May 2006). We can assume that, when he will have written down the story, Myers will be satisfied with it, before once again feeling "despicable" about being "between stories" and continuing the cycle of literary creation.

There is a much less assured sense of the moral legitimacy of using autobiographical material for fiction in Carver's late story "Intimacy" (1986). The story also recounts a surprise visit, but this time the story is narrated in the first person and in the present tense by a middle-aged writer who pays an unannounced visit to his ex-wife. It becomes clear very soon that she still feels hurt by his betrayal, which led to their separation and divorce some years earlier. The story gives ample scope to her accusations, with the narrator barely responding to what his ex-wife has to say. It is, in many ways, her story, or at least her side of the story; the intimacy of the title also comes from her description of their former closeness: "We were so *intimate* once upon a time I can't believe it now" (Carver 2009, 562), with the words "once upon a time", associated as they are with the opening of a fairy tale, possibly emphasising this lack of credibility. Her distrust culminates in the suspicion that the purpose of his visit to her may be "hunting for *material*" (563). She complains about his having "held [her] up for display and ridicule in [his] so-called work" (565). "But what do I know? they'll say in a hundred years. They'll say, Who was she anyway?" (565), imagining readers and critics interpreting the narrator's "so-called work" long after their deaths.

After a while, the narrator gets down on his knees and touches the hem of her dress in a gesture of humility that he says he cannot quite explain: "What am I doing on the floor? I wish I could say" (566). Guessing his need for being forgiven for his trespasses on their shared life in his writing, she says she forgives him. As he gets up to leave, she approaches him very closely – reminding him of their former intimacy – and says: "You just tell it like you have to, I guess, and forget the rest. Like always. You been doing that for so long now anyway it shouldn't be hard for you" (567). Her husband will be home soon for his dinner, so the narrator leaves. He notices that the front door had been open all the time during their conversation. The last thing she tells him before he says goodbye is: "Maybe it'll make a good story [...]. But I don't want to know about it if it does" (568). The narrator walks away, noticing how the leaves have untidily piled up on the sidewalk.

The story's autumnal setting and the falling leaves at the end certainly contribute to an overall sense of melancholy and loss, of paths not taken or not cleared up properly, so that the memory of past hurt (inflicted, we gather, rather than incurred by the writer-narrator) impinges on the present and slows down the narrator's progress: "I can't take a step without putting my shoe into leaves" (568). Since he was the one who left her, the word "leaves" may also provide a verbal allusion to this act of desertion – an effect that is created on the level of the textual composition, thus revealing an implicit authorial perspective that the narrator himself is not aware of and that lies above or beyond his shortcomings and short-sightedness. Obviously, the story presents the narrator's perspective despite giving so much verbal space to the ex-wife and her feelings as expressed towards him, with his own responses very minimal and poorly understood ("I wish I could say"). Much remains unsaid here, in Carver's trademark elliptical style, which is contrasted with her more natural and emotional speech. When she encourages him to "just tell it like you have to" (567), one might expect her to say "just tell it like it is". What first appears like an intimate encouragement and a statement of forgiveness actually turns into, or can be read as, an expression of slow-burning anger, possibly resignation (knowing that this is what he 'has to' do in order to be the writer he is). The story may be entirely fictional, but it still makes for uncomfortable reading as a story about the relationship between art and life even if we do not consider it as being in any sense 'about' the real Carver and his ex-wife, Maryann Burk Carver. (The couple separated in 1978.)

Here, then, is a fictional author using his own life, and the life of his ex-wife, as material for a story about a writer and his ex-wife. Even though the narrator claims to his ex-wife that "[r]egret [...] doesn't interest [him] much" (563), the emotional resonance of the story gives the lie to that claim. The result is no longer laughter and the affirmation of artistic autonomy, as in "Put Yourself in My Shoes", but a sense of resignation and regret about putting someone into such a preposterous situation. What is more, the story leaves an uncomfortable aftertaste in that it is not only ethically but aesthetically problematic, and that it knows this but ploughs ahead regardless, like its narrator wading through the leaves at the end. It seeks to acknowledge and understand the ex-wife's legitimate accusations, but it turns them into yet another story nevertheless. Certainly, it shows the fictional author-narrator humiliating himself in front of her and begging for her forgiveness; and certainly, also, the narrator establishes both "ambiguity" and "distance" towards himself and his own feelings (Amir 2010, 50). But, in transforming this into literature, the story also pleads for the reader to forgive this trespass to its actual author because he has turned this material into "a good story" (Carver 2009, 568) – a Carver story. Coming to "Intimacy" after reading Munro's "Material", one cannot but feel that there is something not quite right here: an element of the "jelly" that Munro describes as the writer's technique of encapsulating life into art (1997, 115), and something of a bad smell, produced by the elements of exploitation (even though it is also self-exploitation) and sensationalism, that damages the story's artistic integrity.[190]

"The rest was so much fiction": Philip Roth's *The Ghost Writer* (1979)

In 1956, twenty-three-year-old Nathan Zuckerman of Newark, New Jersey, a young writer, pays a visit to his idol, the "famous rural recluse" (Roth 2007, 3) E. I. Lonoff. The first volume of Philip Roth's Zuckerman novels, *The Ghost Writer* reflects on Zuckerman's admiration for the older Jewish author, whom he reverently refers to as a "master" (4, 31) and "a visionary" (11) in the field of American letters. Zuckerman has got himself into trouble with Newark's Jewish community for publishing

---

[190] See Scofield 1999 for a more sanguine reading of this story, also in relation to "Put Yourself in My Shoes" and others.

a controversial short story that, in their view, confirms antisemitic stereotypes and "would [...] warm the heart of a Julius Streicher or a Joseph Goebbels" (67). Zuckerman is a "spiritual son" in search of "patriarchal validation" (7). He seeks approval as an artist and the kind of moral support that Lonoff can offer as an established author and potential father figure. Also in the house are Lonoff's wife Hope and Amy Bellette, a young Jewish refugee from Europe who works at Harvard University Library sorting Lonoff's archive for a future deposit there. Zuckerman notices that Amy bears a striking resemblance to Anne Frank. While spending the night at Lonoff's remote house in the Berkshires, he concocts an elaborate fiction about Amy, the "girl-woman" (11), actually being Anne Frank. Were he to marry her, his reputation among his family and the entire Jewish community would become unassailable.

Henry James's "The Middle Years" [→ ch. 9] functions as an important hypotext to this novella about "the madness of art" (Roth 2007, 50). This central quotation from James's story decorates Lonoff's study. Nathan reads the story twice during the night, wondering about its meaning. He also provides a detailed summary (72–75). There are obvious parallels between Lonoff and James's Dencombe. Like Dencombe, Lonoff is a recluse and an inveterate reviser of his work. By way of a paralepsis, we learn that Lonoff, like Dencombe, is going to die from a severe illness five years after the events of *The Ghost Writer* (10). However, unlike Dencombe, he is married, and Zuckerman (or Roth) prefers to ignore the homoerotic element that characterises the relationship between Dencombe and his young admirer, Doctor Hugh.

Lonoff describes his daily routine as "turn[ing] sentences around" (12), an occupation that is fundamentally incompatible with everyday life and that puts an enormous strain on his wife, the "self-effacing" Hope (20). Hope is not only ironically named; there are hints at her own authorship (which she may have given up for the sake of her husband) in the six framed "short nature poems signed 'H. L.', copied in delicate calligraphy and decorated with watercolor designs" (30). These have taken on an ornamental function in the kitchen "above the breakfast table" (30). If Hope's domestically framed poems represent nature, something that Lonoff no longer cares for, as he explains – when he takes a walk, he no longer even "see[s] the trees" (102) – it is art, and the Jamesian "madness of art", that has taken over his life. In Roth's novella, life is being sacrificed for art, but – as we also saw in Munro and Carver – this is no longer a beautiful sacrifice. There is something "terrible" in the author's "triumph" (48). Lonoff suffers from his self-imposed isolation for the sake of art, but his wife suffers even more. Like her poems, her own nature, her own creative potential has been confined in the domestic space of the kitchen. Whereas at first her submissive comportment is perceived by Zuckerman in a gender-stereotypical and exoticising manner ("aging geisha", 21), she breaks out of this frame the next morning when she threatens to leave her husband for good. Even though this escape is implied to be merely temporary, it does gesture towards Hope's potential for agency beyond the confinement of her marriage. The pursuit of art as practiced by Lonoff is a madness that exerts intolerable pressures on everyone involved.

For Zuckerman, who observes all this and finally begins to transform it into a story, taking notes for what presumably will become *The Ghost Writer*, there is intense discomfort in his own situation as a renegade in the eyes of his community. *The Ghost Writer*, already in its first sentence, repeatedly invokes the tradition of the *bildungsroman* (cf. ibid., 3, 51). Joyce's *Portrait of the Artist as a Young Man* is another powerful subtext here, as is *The Diary of Anne Frank*. If Anne/Amy is the spiritual sister of Kafka or "his lost little daughter" (109), Zuckerman sees himself in analogy to Joyce's Stephen, seeking "a flaming Dedalian formula to ignite *my* soul's smithy" (32). Their association is made unmistakably clear in the title of the novella's second part, "Nathan Dedalus" (49). There is the threat of exile, of banishment from his community. As Zuckerman reflects, "literary history was in part the history of novelists infuriating fellow countrymen, family, and friends". His (Joycean) model of what it means to be a writer includes such conflict: if Lonoff has to isolate himself from any and all humanity in order to write, for Zuckerman there is a keen sense of a more specific isolation from his family and the Jewish community: "writers weren't writers", he thinks, "if they didn't have the strength to face the insolubility of that conflict and go on" (71).

Willingness to sustain this conflict for the sake of art (and the writer's autonomy) is combined with a wish-fulfilling dream of achieving an unassailable position in Zuckerman's fantasy of Amy being Anne Frank and himself her future husband. Zuckerman encourages himself to "invent as presumptuously as real life" (78) and engages in a long flight of fancy, a fiction within the fiction, that develops Amy's/Anne's story in the novella's third part, "Femme fatale". This fantasy is certainly even more provocative than anything in Zuckerman's fictional and Roth's real stories published so far. The author Anne Frank, here imagined as a Holocaust survivor, furnishes yet another model of authorship for Zuckerman, being "of all the Jewish writers [...] the most famous" (98), a writer who has experienced what Kafka merely imagined. Yet this is self-consciously unmasked as Zuckerman's flight of fancy: "The rest was so much fiction" (110), as he asserts after spending a sleepless night in Lonoff's study.

Roth presents a rich tapestry of intertextual allusions and models of authorship in *The Ghost Writer:* from James, Kafka, Joyce, and Isaac Babel to Saul Bellow and Bernard Malamud (thinly disguised as Lonoff and Abravanel), from the posthumous fame of Anne Frank to the notoriety and scandal caused by Roth's own earlier work. Zuckerman presents authorship as a mode of filiation, of an ideal paternity that creates new bonds between writers and that replaces their natural families and relationships in ordinary life. He is in search of a father figure; he dreams about founding a literary dynasty with Amy Bellette; and he thinks of Anne Frank as Kafka's lost daughter. Zuckerman embodies the conflict between the rebellious younger writer and his community, whereas Lonoff projects a fatalistic image of the future for Zuckerman, the future of a writer who has rejected life for the sake of a "religion of art" (112). These different possible futures and desired pasts, however, are shown to be illusory fictions of a fantastic paternity and, ultimately, revealed as male fantasies of authority and power. The women in this novel, both Amy (whose name associates love) and Hope (whose name is simply telling), present a female alternative that resists being implicated in a patriarchal nexus of filiation whose principal virtue is faith – the belief in a strong, Harold-Bloomesque concept of authorship as struggle in which women are enlisted merely as helpmeets or as part of the supporting cast (Bloom 1973).

The last chapter, "Married to Tolstoy", turns the tables on Lonoff, who has apparently terminated his relationship with Amy but who is surprised, possibly not for the first time, by Hope's attempt to leave him. Hope has packed a suitcase; failing to start his car, she starts walking through the snow – a scene that triggers Lonoff's comment about being "married to Tolstoy" (Roth 2007, 116). Though Zuckerman sees her journey as "doomed" (ibid.), implying that she will return, this sudden agency on the part of Hope contradicts his earlier view of her as the submissive wife whose sole purpose in life is to support her husband. Implicitly, it also contradicts his fantasy of winning Amy's/Anne's hand in marriage and securing her absolute moral authority for the cause of his writing. If Amy/Anne is the 'ghost writer' of the novella's title, a ghost brought back to life briefly in the mode of fiction and then laid to rest again, the ending resists Zuckerman's desire to be united with that ghost, as it resists his dream of patriarchal acknowledgement as Lonoff's "spiritual son" (7). This ghostly succession, tempting though it may be, will have to be overcome to fulfil Zuckerman's Joycean *bildungsroman* of authorial independence. If he has the strength to continue as an author and risk the rupture with his family and friends, he will have to establish his own authority and prove his stamina in dealing with "the unreckoned consequences of art" (Roth 2007, 611).[191]

---

[191] This theme, which runs through many of Roth's novels, is continued in *Zuckerman Unbound*, which deals with what Roth, in an explanatory note to a limited edition of that novel, called "the consequences of a literary vocation" (2007, 619), in particular the fallout from Zuckerman's controversial novel *Carnovsky* (which resembles Roth's *Portnoy's Complaint*) and his subsequent celebrity.

Zuckerman's key conflict in this novel is about the responsibility of an author to his community and his art. Were he to give in to the moralising expectations of his father and the eminent Judge Wapter, who pressure him to rethink the representation of Jews in his work, he would not only sacrifice his ideal of artistic autonomy but also risk the cultural trivialisation of the Holocaust. Yet there is another conflict underlying this: that between a Joycean and a Jamesian view of the artist, or between rebellious self-realisation and tragic self-denial, the poles represented in the novel by youthful Zuckerman and aging Lonoff. If Zuckerman is "Nathan Dedalus" (Roth 2007, 49), the hero of his own Joycean *bildungsroman* in search of approval for his autonomy as an author, Lonoff is "the master" (4), a monument of American letters and a model (on the surface at least) of resigned asceticism, someone who has sacrificed his life to his art. If the Joycean model stands for ambitious youth, the Jamesian paradigm represents the sacrifice, respectability, and resignation of the seasoned author, in or beyond 'the middle years'.

Yet, realising what goes on in Lonoff's bedroom forces Zuckerman to revise his idealised picture of "the master". Different authorial stances are being probed here, including the surprising analogy between Hope Lonoff and Tolstoy; however, the even more fundamental conflict in this novel seems to be that between reality and fiction itself. Confronted with "the originality and excitement of what actually goes on" (78), Zuckerman attempts to outdo real life in the mode of fiction by concocting an imaginary past and future for Amy and himself out of the little he knows about her, spliced with the biographical facts about Anne Frank. This literary creation, and the entire novel, can thus be regarded "as Zuckerman's bid for authority" (Hadar 2016/2017, 33). The entire novel is narrated in retrospect by an older Zuckerman who artfully inhabits or recreates his younger self, and who stands in as a fictional correlate for his actual author, Roth, in a "play of authorial disclosure and erasure" (Mills 2018, 395). *The Ghost Writer* complicates the conventions of literary realism by pointing out the extent to which they depend on fantasy and imagination. Real life keeps coming up with scenarios that are more 'presumptuous' (cf. Roth 2007, 78) than anything a writer might invent.

The Ghost Writer presents an alternative reading of Henry James that differs from Lionel Trilling's influential interpretation, which defined how James was viewed by an entire generation of authors and critics in the 1950s and 1960s. It contains an implicit critique of the "tragic maturity" that, according to Trilling, was the ethical goal to be achieved by reading James (qtd. in Mills 2018, 389). Instead of celebrating "the redemption of suffering in the light of suffering's capacity to clarify the self" (ibid., 389), Roth's novel shows artistic and moral conflict as inescapable and irresolvable. His protagonists, here and elsewhere, may achieve clarity about themselves, but this only rarely ends or relieves or redeems their suffering, which is often unjust and meaningless. As the trilogy progresses via *Zuckerman*

Unbound (1981) to *The Anatomy Lesson* (1983), Zuckerman's literary *bildungsroman* makes him increasingly aware of the limits and boundaries to which he is subject. Instead of being liberated from "his family, his memories, his people, and his past by the work" (Roth 2007, 631), Zuckerman is even more bound by them than he can imagine in *The Ghost Writer* – to the extent that, at the age of forty, in *his* 'middle years', he decides to give up writing and to study medicine instead.

The later novels, especially *Zuckerman Unbound*, engage more directly with the modern media culture of celebrity, which is not exactly absent in *The Ghost Writer* but remains a comparatively marginal concern there. Yet already in *The Ghost Writer* Zuckerman struggles to preserve his artistic integrity in the light of the three major conflicts of authority and allegiance I highlighted in my reading: the conflict between the artist and his family/community, between different authorial self-images and aesthetic programmes, and between fiction and reality. These conflicts are not presented in the raw, as it were, but in a form that strongly invokes the tradition of the literary *bildungsroman* and *künstlerroman*, including the avoidance of autobiography by means of creating an 'alter ego' or "shadow self" (Kenner 1976, 178–179): Nathan Zuckerman is to Roth what Stephen Dedalus is to Joyce – an authorial 'ghost', a distancing persona that can alleviate the suffering while keeping it in view and making it accessible to the reader, a filter through which the "raw material" (Carver 2009, 110) of reality can be processed into the "marvellous clear jelly" (Munro 1997, 115) of fiction.

Postmodernist pastiche it may be, but Roth uses different authorial intertexts and literary techniques not for the sake of muddying the waters but to achieve an authorial position above and beyond mere ironic playfulness. The struggle of his characters is presented in carefully honed prose, in a style so polished that "every *a*, *an*, and *the* [is] perfectly in place" (Pinsker 2014, 343). Such a style gestures towards the aesthetic sublation of conflict and thus affirms belief in the power of art – a power that, on the level of form, balances out the apparent irony with which that power is contested in the narrative.

"Tell them you're a walking blade": Lorrie Moore's "How to Become a Writer" (1982)

Lorrie Moore's "How to Become a Writer" (first published in 1982, then included in her collection *Self-Help*, 1985) is the rare example of a story about a writer narrated in the second person. It is one of several you-narratives in this collection, which also includes the "faux-advice" narratives "How to Be an Other Woman" and "How to Talk to Your Mother (Notes)".[192] The title alludes to creative writing programmes and 'how-to' guides, and it is in this spirit that the narrative interpellates a budding writer in mostly short sentences that, for the most part, either describe this person ("You are great with kids"), exhort her to do one thing or another ("Decide to experiment with fiction"), or speculate about a certain state of affairs ("Perhaps your creative writing isn't all that bad") (Moore 2020, 222–223). The story does this in a largely facetious and clearly parodic manner, making fun of the often nonsensical and useless advice given to writers. Yet, it also outlines quite clearly how its protagonist, Francie, develops into a writer largely in spite of the advice given to her by various authority figures from parents to teachers and peers. Sentences like "Early, critical disillusionment is necessary" (222) masquerade as advice while doing double duty as depictions of Francie's slow and arduous progress towards her vocation.

The story imposes some order onto Francie's chaotic and contingent experiences, metafictionally staging the process of shaping art out of life and of giving it a literary form. Francie's own writing is said to suffer from a lack of plotting, a lack of direction. These missing qualities are teasingly supplied by the story's form of the writing guide and its implicit evocation of a *bildungsroman* trajectory, condensed into a few pages of a short story that follows Francie from high school to college and beyond that to her becoming a freelance writer. Major events in her life barely even receive a mention, such as the loss of her virginity, her parents' divorce, and her brother's severe injury in the Vietnam war (226). Yet, they do furnish an important backdrop to her writing. One of the repeated motifs in her stories is people dying outrageous accidental deaths or blowing themselves up; but she cannot directly write about her brother's trauma: "Your typewriter hums. You can find no words" (226).

During her education, Francie is confronted with several competing theories about the origins of literary creativity (e. g., "You will read somewhere that all writing has to do with one's genitals", 227), none of which ever provide a satisfactory explanation for her sense of having to write, of not wanting or not being able to do anything else. She feels the need to justify this odd choice of profession, to defend her decision against studying child psychology or law, in conversations with other people, who cannot understand that her choice was not a choice but a calling:

> Sooner or later you have a finished manuscript more or less. People look at it in a vaguely troubled sort of way and say, "I'll bet becoming a writer was always a fantasy of yours, wasn't it?" Your lips dry to salt. Say that of all the fantasies possible in the world, you

---

[192] For the term "faux-advice book" in relation to these stories, its significance with regard to gender, and Moore's use of humour, see Vogel 2011, 75.

can't imagine being a writer even making the top twenty. Tell them you were going to be a child psychology major. "I bet," they always sigh, "you'd be great with kids." Scowl fiercely. Tell them you're a walking blade. (228)

Despite the continuing self-doubts that accompany the writing life, Francie sticks with it. Her lack of direction is finally contrasted, in the story's last sentence, with the gesture of her date, whose "face" is described as "blank as a sheet of paper" and who "smooth[s]" "his arm hairs [....] always, in the same direction" (229). His gesture of orderly arrangement may be a substitute for ordering the writerly chaos that resists accommodation to the usual, plot-driven directedness of human social lives. If his face is compared to a writing surface, on which nothing is and perhaps never will be written, that accentuates the writer's habit of thinking in metaphors and similes, as part of her professional formation or deformation. Similar to Carver's "Put Yourself in My Shoes" in this respect, the story asserts the position of writers as social oddities, placed in the margins of ordinary, suburban middle-class society, a position from which they lack certain kinds of recognition (the respect awarded to child psychologists and other more directly useful professions) but may achieve others. "How to Become a Writer" may be making fun of advice given to writers, but in doing so it also reasserts the writer's pride in her "pain and suffering" (222), and ultimately in her achievement of self-formation against the odds.

These narratives, though they certainly contain elements of metafiction, integrate these elements into a largely realist paradigm. They are committed to modes of social and moral realism, close and precise observation of human behaviour, and attention to detail, while also paying close attention to matters of literary form. While their techniques sometimes pay homage to postmodernist effects of frame-breaking or pastiche, they also return to a position beyond the corrosive ironies of postmodernism that reinvests these techniques with a renewed seriousness of subject matter as well as form – thus anticipating a later trend that is widely associated with the work of David Foster Wallace and the 'post-postmodernist' abdication of irony since the 1990s (Wallace 1993). Far from celebrating pure surface and the 'death of the author', the texts discussed in this chapter are invested in character as an expression of moral personhood, and in authorship as an ideal of artistic excellence and communicative authority that may be seldom achieved but is nonetheless worth striving for.

The minimalism of Carver and Munro establishes an intense focus on their characters' moral shortcomings within a precisely outlined social environment. Roth's and Moore's return to the template of the *bildungsroman*, though laced with irony, speaks to that form's perennial attractiveness as a means of interpreting the experiences and anxieties of young writers. These texts can be funny, witty, or sarcastic, but at bottom they treat their characters with respect and take their ambitions and weaknesses seriously. They also revive certain patterns of nineteenth-century author novels in engaging with the economic and cultural aspects of writing and author-making that link them not only to James but also, at least indirectly, to Gissing.

But the realist paradigm does not mean a wholesale return to traditional narrative forms and conventions. All the texts discussed in this chapter experiment with narrative form and point of view. In these examples, literary realism – including a realistic assessment of the possibilities and problems, and the moral responsibilities, of literary authorship – is more a question of genre than of form.

The preoccupation with genre is also paramount in the authorship horror novels of Stephen King (discussed in the next chapter), as well as in the fields of suspense fiction and autofiction. The hierarchical distinction between the 'art novel' or 'literary fiction' and popular genres has significant consequences for the autopoetic self-fashioning and allopoetic *hexis* of authors as well as for the kind of discursive and cultural authority to which they can lay claim. In recent years, the *rapprochement* of literary fiction and genre fiction, while not entirely overcoming this opposition, complicates and at times subverts the established hierarchy of the literary field. This ongoing process of change also involves new ways of producing, distributing, and marketing both fiction and the authors who write it in the age of platform capitalism (cf. Laquintano 2016, McGurl 2016), together with new regimes of visibility powered by social media. The pleasures and horrors that this brave new world holds in store for authors as well as audiences are as yet difficult to predict with any degree of confidence. In the next two chapters, I turn to exemplary author representations in horror and suspense fiction from the later twentieth and early twenty-first century before moving on to autofiction and related recent literary trends.

15 Authorship Horror: Stephen King's *Misery* (1987)

Whereas Raymond Carver and Alice Munro revive a version of literary realism, Stephen King stands for the revival of realism's gothic undertow in the field of genre fiction. In this chapter and the next, I examine the representation of authors and authorship in modern horror and suspense fiction, beginning with a close reading of Stephen King's 1987 novel *Misery*. If Melville's *Pierre* is the epitome of 'authorship horror' in the nineteenth century [→ ch. 5], and Kipling's and Machen's stories are key developments of this style around the turn of the twentieth [→ ch. 8, 9], King explores it in new and exciting ways in a late twentieth-century and contemporary American setting.

Surprisingly many works in the King canon feature authors as characters. These include, most notably, the novel *The Shining* (1977) with its central character, would-be author Jack Torrance, grandiosely daydreaming about being known as "Jack Torrance, bestselling author. Jack Torrance, acclaimed playwright and winner of the New York Critics Circle Award. John Torrance, man of letters, esteemed thinker, winner of the Pulitzer Prize at seventy for his trenchant book of memoirs, *My Life in the Twentieth Century*" (King 2011a, 420). They also include the short story "Word Processor of the Gods" (1983), in which a man discovers the word processor's magical power of 'revising' reality itself – another Kingian study of more than autonomous authorship that extends to the self-creation of a (male) subject – the other side of the decreation that happens to Jack Torrance in *The Shining* and that Paul Sheldon in *Misery* is threatened by.[193]

The Dark Half (1989), "Secret Window, Secret Garden" (1990), *Bag of Bones* (1998), *Lisey's Story* (2006), *Duma Key* (2008), and *Joyland* (2013) are also centrally concerned with authors and authorship (cf. Feleki 2014). Further author characters in King's early fiction are featured in *It* (1986), *The Tommyknockers* (1987), and "Umney's Last Case" (1993; see Thoss 2013). More recently, King has negotiated his own authorship metafictionally in the *Dark Tower* series (Allan 2021, 284–289). There is thus a continuous and coherent strand in King's oeuvre that is concerned with the powers of storytelling and writing, and the discursive authority of

---

[193] See Kirschenbaum 2016, 77–85 for a discussion of "Word Processor of the Gods". A variation on this formula, involving the Amazon Kindle, is the basis of King's *UR* (2009), a short story "created and released solely through and for the e-reader Kindle" (Feleki 2014, 7).

the author.[194] Yet *Misery* (1987) has rightly been called Stephen King's "most thorough and complex exploration [...] of the powers of the artist, of the pressures of the audience, and of the workings of creativity" (Lant 1997, 92).[195]

Paul Sheldon, an author of bestselling historical romance novels, is kidnapped by his "number-one fan" (King 2011b, 22). Annie Wilkes, a mentally deranged woman, forces him to write a continuation to a series of successful books that he had decided to terminate by allowing the heroine of that series, Misery Chastain, to die. Annie relishes the escapist appeal and identificatory pleasures of the Misery novels. After rescuing Sheldon from the wreck of his crashed car and nursing him back to consciousness, Annie burns the only manuscript of his latest work, *Fast Cars*, in front of him. She refuses to respect his wishes to write a more literary and, thematically, more masculine novel set in the present. Rendered immobile and dependent on the opiates she feeds him, Sheldon – named, apparently, after the bestselling US novelist Sidney Sheldon (1917–2007) – has no choice but to bring his fictional heroine back to life in a new novel, *Misery's Return*, written exclusively for his kidnapper.

Sheldon experiences authorship under duress, in a variant of the tales of Scheherazade (survival by means of serial narration), referenced at several points in the text. Yet, interestingly, as the novel progresses, he begins to take pleasure in the escape that literary creativity offers, when he can "see through the paper" (136) into the world of his imagination. At the end, he regains an ambivalent freedom from the tortures inflicted on him. He does so by vanquishing his kidnapper first in fiction, where he transforms her into an analogue of Henry Rider Haggard's African goddess She-who-must-be-obeyed (from *She*, 1887). He overcomes her in real life by only pretending to burn the manuscript in front of her and later, after his liberation and Annie's death, publishing it very successfully. His freedom is ambivalent, however, because he is still haunted by his fear of Annie's return (as a goddess, she would be immortal) but also because he has fulfilled her desire to have Misery resurrected and thus continued his career as a romance writer. However, at the very end of the novel, he sets out to write a work that he hopes will count as a serious literary effort.

The novel offers a haunting reflection on the ambivalences and ambiguities of authorial creativity. These are ambivalences of genre, wavering between personal literary ambition (the desire to be recognised as a more 'serious' writer) and the

---

194 On storytelling in King's later fiction, see Perry 2019. For a systematic overview of King's author characters, see Anderson 2020. The most sustained analysis so far of how King has turned authorship into a "horror trope" is d'Hont 2021.
195 The geography of *Misery* is linked to *The Shining* when Annie tells Sheldon about the reporter she killed, Andrew Pomeroy, who planned to investigate the Overlook hotel (King 2011b, 232–233).

production of commercial fiction, of "bestselling bodice-rippers" (King 2010, 165), which is here depicted as a form of captivity, but which is nevertheless allowed to contain its own potential for a form of liberation within and by means of writerly imaginative pleasure. The text's ambiguities relate to the opposition of sanity and insanity, as literary production is depicted as a form of temporary escape from reality and also as its own kind of madness or addiction, in analogy to the opiates Sheldon is fed by Annie. His kidnapper, the female monster who demands total imaginative absorption in the story of the fictional heroine Misery, embodies the threat of psychological abnormality, described in the novel in now somewhat dated terms as a manic-depressive disorder.

Annie can be read as embodying an author's fear of completely losing touch with reality and succumbing to psychosis, whereas Sheldon's literary activity has so far only been a temporary access of some kind of 'madness', a mental journey into a different space, the imaginary world 'behind' the paper – a space that King, in a particularly felicitous phrase in his memoir *On Writing*, refers to in spatialised terms as "unreal estate" (King 2010, 212). Annie can also be read, in a more narrowly biographical perspective, as a manifestation of either King's alcoholism or his discomfort with celebrity, or both. In *On Writing*, King reflects on his addiction to alcohol and cocaine and on his fiction from the 1970s and 1980s being a cry "for help [...] through my monsters" (2010, 96). "As sick with drugs and alcohol as I was much of the time, I had such fun with that [novel]", he tells us (2010, 169). This is not to interpret the character of Annie as a mere allegory of alcohol and drug abuse or the depredations of fandom, but to point out her association with the kinds of dependencies and pressures that may keep a writer caught in a cycle that both fuels and inhibits literary creativity.[196]

Despite King's claims of Annie Wilkes being "almost as much to be pitied as to be feared" (King 2010, 168), the novel has very little pity or sympathy for her. When Sheldon finally overcomes her, this is explicitly figured as rape (King 2011b, 347) and as an act of revenge for his having been "raped back into life by the woman's stinking breath" after his accident (7, cf. ibid., 5). She is all too simply a monster. The horrors of *Misery* are not supernatural, and they are ultimately less physical (though Annie severs Sheldon's left foot and thumb, etc.) than they are semantic, both metaphoric and metonymic: madness, obesity, poverty, dependency, and historical romance fiction are gendered feminine in the novel as well as being exoticised, spatialised, and racialised by association with the Victorian colonial adventure novels of H. Rider Haggard, which inspire Sheldon's new novel. Sheldon

---

[196] For some examples of King's personal experiences with obsessive fans of his work in the 1980s, see Lant 1997, 90–91.

applies Haggard's depiction of a cruel African goddess to help him make sense of, reframe, and finally overcome his sick captor and tormentor.[197]

Such strategies of othering are the obverse of Sheldon's slow recovery of the autonomy that had been taken from him, and they are closely interwoven with the novel's focus on authorship, which is represented as wavering between alienation and self-determination. As Sheldon regains his physical and creative powers, he has to fight for his liberty by means of writing and an act of authorship that is personal as well as literary.[198]

Annie's othering in the novel (and in the novel within the novel) is the price of Sheldon's (self-)authoring. As the novel progresses, Annie's character turns into something of a showcase for a stereotypic and multiple, even obsessive process of othering the social opposites of masculinity, sanity, wealth, success, slimness, independence, restraint, good taste, etc. By implication, this hierarchy of values replicates and reinforces the division in the literary field between popular, commercial, and literary fiction, and the accompanying "distaste towards mass culture" (Birke 2014, 526) that the writer Sheldon feels for his own bestselling novels. Sheldon is described as having a split authorial identity, writing "novels of two kinds, good ones and best-sellers" (King 2011b, 7).

This fundamental division between 'good' and 'bad', familiar from gothic and fantasy fiction but also from religious laws and the Puritan strand in American culture (Bercovitch 1976), is neatly mapped onto other aspects of the novel to create a hierarchy of binary oppositions that order its world. For example, not far from his place of captivity is a "Presbyterian church" whose bells help Paul Sheldon keep track of time (King 2011b, 136).[199] His name, 'Paul', is also deeply embedded in Christianity and associated with one of the most 'literary' and prolific writers included in the New Testament. The evil that Annie embodies poses a diabolical threat to this symbolic order, like the Lacanian real that is beyond representation. Paul's ultimate victory over her, despite occurring in reality, is more imaginary

---

[197] As King himself tells the story of the first longhand draft of the novel, he began writing at Brown's Hotel in London on what he was told "had been Rudyard Kipling's desk" (King 2010, 166) – possibly this explains some of the more Kiplingesque features of *Misery*, where the female of the species is also deadlier than the male.

[198] See Arnzen 1998 for a deconstructive reading of the novel within the novel as "a battle for mastery over the text and over meanings" and as "a battle of the sexes" (240); cf. Berkenkamp 1992 for an earlier reading, informed by reader-response theory, that tends to neglect the violence involved in Sheldon's and Wilkes's "collaborative writing exercise" (210). However, their collaboration is rather like that between a writer and his editor than by two authors; an editor, moreover, who "lacks any formal understanding beyond her enthusiasm for Paul's books" (d'Hont 2021, 180).

[199] How Paul can tell by the sound of its bells that it is a Presbyterian church remains the narrator's secret.

than real to him, and leaves a haunting remainder of terror. As an other, she is wholly Other – a force beyond the powers of human reason and understanding. In the novel's moral economy, she represents an evil that threatens the very idea of order – that is, as Zygmunt Bauman has summarised the modern struggle for order, the idea of "determination against ambiguity, of semantic precision against ambivalence, of transparency against obscurity, clarity against fuzziness", against "the randomness of chaos" (Bauman 1991, 6–7). Annie thus comes to represent *absolute* evil.

Her greatest threat lies in Sheldon's colluding with and succumbing to her vampiric desires, the threat of "autocannibalism" that she poses (King 2011b, 363). In the context of literary authorship, Annie can be interpreted as the physical embodiment of a kind of authorial self-hatred. As she turns from "Constant Reader" to "Merciless Editor" (117), taking a more active part in the creative process, she reveals her savvy as more than just a fan or a passive consumer but a real connoisseur of the delights and pitfalls of romance fiction. For example, she forces Sheldon to rethink his first solution to the quandary of bringing Misery back from the grave, which fails to convince her. She wields power over him not only physically but mentally and emotionally. Already in the novel's earliest pages, as she recounts how she found him and nursed him, she makes him feel "like a character in a story or a play, a character whose history is [...] created like fiction" (12).

Annie Wilkes is the author of Sheldon's narrative, an author-goddess who wields absolute power over the boundaries of his physical body and of his authorial and personal identity, and whom he needs to destroy to free himself and regain control over these boundaries. As she literally cuts off pieces of his body, she reduces and remakes his physical boundaries, just as her editorship over his writing determines the literary boundary work that the novel *Misery* performs between serious and popular, 'good' and 'bad' fiction. Her othering throughout the novel is the enabling condition of possibility for Sheldon's renewed self-authoring as a person, a man, and a writer. The novel's plot with its central confrontation between these two characters thus enacts the struggle between different kinds of literary authorship that King himself felt so keenly during the 1980s, when he was reaching for the top in terms of commercial success but was not taken seriously by reviewers and critics, who categorised him as an author of genre fiction, despite his attempts to escape this category by also writing realistic stories like the novellas collected in *Different Seasons* (1982).[200]

---

[200] King was one of six authors who dominated the fiction bestseller lists in the US from the mid-1980s to the mid-1990s; the other five being Tom Clancy, Michael Crichton, John Grisham, Dean Koontz, and Danielle Steele (Epstein 2002, 33). By 1988, eleven Stephen King novels had reached the top of the *New York Times* bestseller list (Allan 2021, 291 n. 2).

Despite the ambivalent mixture of pleasure and pain that characterises their collaborative creative process, the "collusion" between Paul and Annie in producing *Misery's Return* (Birke 2014, 527) cannot ultimately overcome the "deep-rooted [...] negative imagery associated with the 'popular'" (Birke 2014, 528) that dominates King's novel.[201] This is because the split between 'good' literary fiction and 'bad' popular fiction, like the split between good and bad reading, is part of the unshakeable foundational hierarchy of values in the novel. Paul's struggle for recognition as a serious writer, like King's, remains unfulfilled because the manuscript of his novel *Fast Cars* is destroyed, and the novel he publishes after his ordeal is *Misery's Return*, the continuation of his historical romance series. If the resolution of the plot is a form of wish-fulfilment, it fails to resolve the ambivalence surrounding Sheldon's status in the literary world. Annie's de facto co-authorship of *Misery's Return* is only acknowledged in the "world-wide headlines generated by the bizarre circumstances under which the novel had been written" (King 2011b, 362), the media buzz that will make the book even more of a bestseller, adding the sensational thrill of a real-life story behind the fiction. At the end of the novel, Sheldon sits down at his word processor and begins another novel, a 'serious' one, in solitary authorship, re-entering the literary imaginary "in gratitude and in terror" (369).

Some critics have been aware of how protagonist and antagonist, Sheldon and Annie, both share aspects of "monstrousness" (Schopp 1994, 29), though clearly the only one allowed to escape from the cycle of torment at the end, the only one to overcome the monstrous within himself, is Paul Sheldon. He is aware of the "terror" of writing itself (King 2011b, 369) and its "autoerotic side" (267), but the point for him, and for King's novel, is that it is necessary to maintain control over the boundaries of sanity and sexuality that are threatened by artistic creativity, and thereby uphold civilisation itself. The novel thus revisits the antibourgeois problematic of the *künstlerroman*, the artist as a threat to society, as someone who negates, or threatens to negate, its core values, and it recasts that form's classic compromise in the mould of horror fiction – more precisely, by externalising that threat in the character of the mad goddess, the omnivorous Muse who demands total absorption in the pleasure of fiction and who, as a murderess, embodies absolute irresponsibility and the annihilation of social norms.

The above-noted hierarchy of values that is central to this novel's moral and narrative economy is also visible in its geography, which replicates a conventional

---

201 Cf. Berkenkamp 1992, 210. See also Dowling 2011 for an interesting discussion of *Misery* as a response to King's neglect at the hands of literary critics, compared to Melville's in *Pierre*; cf. Arnzen 1998, Meyer 2004, Allan 2021.

American division between metropolitan and cultured New York City (Sheldon's home) and the 'wasteland' of rural Colorado, where Annie keeps Sheldon captive, in addition to the imaginary England and Africa to which Sheldon (and Annie) escape in writing and reading fiction. Annie's last name, Wilkes, associates her with John Wilkes Booth, Confederate sympathiser and assassin of Abraham Lincoln, further entrenching the Northeast vs. Midwest topography of the novel. This is not to equate the Midwest with the American South, since Colorado was not a state during the Civil War, yet the name Wilkes does provide a strong enough link to the Confederate South as yet another manifestation of a threatening difference from Sheldon's perspective.

The depths that are probed in Sheldon's (and, by extension, King's) rather bathetic metaliterary experiment within the novel turn out to be a racialised and feminised monstrosity, a mad African goddess as the ultimate vision of horror. While the gendered and sexualised aspects of this reflection of authorship have been discussed in detail in earlier criticism,[202] the colonialised and racialised imagery in *Misery* has escaped systematic attention. It has also, perhaps wisely, been left out of Rob Reiner's 1990 film adaptation. Yet it is arguably the culmination point of the ambivalence the novel explores between literary creation as a liberating mental journey to a place of otherness and the enslavement of the author at the hands of a monstrous African goddess, the idol of the Bourka tribe. The epigraph to the novel already hints at this: "goddess / Africa" (King 2011b, n. p.). While Annie is not Black, her stand-in within *Misery's Return* is a tribal goddess that needs to be defeated by a British 'crew of light', like Ayesha in Rider Haggard's *She*.

The functions of the exoticised 'Africa' in *Misery* merit further scrutiny. Already at the beginning, the connection between Annie and Africa is established in Sheldon's mind: "The image of Annie Wilkes as an African idol out of *She* or *King Solomon's Mines* was both ludicrous and queerly apt", we are told, and this is then connected to the "large but unwelcoming", "big but not generous" shape of her body (King 2011b, 8) and its idol-like "solidity", like a Deleuzian body without organs, indeed "as if she might not have any blood vessels or internal organs" (8). She is thus dehumanised, othered from the very start. She is also animalised, having "the nostrils of an animal scenting fire" (79), and referred to as a "bitch" (ibid.). Like "a tribe in one of those Rider Haggard stories", Sheldon feels the need to "placate[]" the "goddess when she [is] angry, by making sacrifice to her effigy" (79). The Africa invoked in the novel is the "dark continent" (262) of Victorian col-

---

[202] "The horror in the novel resides in King's own view of the creative process and, primarily, in the sexual roles he imposes upon that process" (Lant 1997, 93); cf. Schroeder 1996, Keesey 2002.

onial adventure fiction, a throwback to a pagan, tribal, and matriarchal or matrifocal past, with Annie represented as the "dark goddess", "looming black over the jungle green" (262). Geoffrey, the fictional hero of *Misery's Return*, must save Misery from the Bourka tribe and its bee goddess, and the novel within the novel emphasises the religious and theological groundwork of its host narrative by contrasting African polytheism with Christian monotheism:

> But his ideas about God – – like his ideas about so many things, had changed. They had changed in Africa. In Africa he had discovered that there was not just one God but many, and some were more than cruel – – they were insane, and that changed all. Cruelty, after all, was understandable. With insanity, however, there was no arguing. [...] He had always known and accepted the fact that the gods were hard; he had no desire, however, to live in a world where the gods were insane. (340)[203]

There may be no arguing with insanity, the absolute Other in King's novel. Yet one may nevertheless find its figural association with femininity, "dark" Africa (262), and non-Christian religions deeply troubling. Another, less obvious, association is established between Annie and Native Americans when we learn that the car Annie drives is a Jeep "Cherokee" (128), adding a further tribal, native, and in the novel's moral economy 'savage' attribute to her character and its function in the novel's moral universe. Sheldon's wrecked car, by contrast, is a Chevrolet Camaro, a name that connotes camaraderie or male homosocial bonds.

Another aspect that highlights the symbolic order of *Misery* is the representation of physical books in the novel. Paul Sheldon's already printed books, the typescript of *Fast Cars* that is burned by Annie, the combination of typescript and manuscript that is to be the new novel – all of these are mentioned or featured in the text. As to the novel within the novel, hardly any author fiction in literary history has ever been so insistent on how *painful* the physical act of writing can be. Sheldon is forced to work on an old broken typewriter that keeps losing letters. These must be filled in by hand and are reproduced in the printed text in a different, manuscript-facsimile typeface. Only towards the end, Sheldon abandons this quasi-Oulipian instrument and continues writing in longhand despite the pain in his hands. The decreasing functionality of the mechanical instrument and the return to the pen instead of the typewriter reassert Paul's natural gift as a creative writer, someone who is trying to escape from the repetitive mechanisms of commercial writing. His creativity is also gendered masculine, as is emphasised by his constant, and not entirely unjustified, castration anxiety, while the typewriter

---

[203] I have refrained from attempting to reproduce the typographical peculiarities in the text, which replicates the mixture of type- and handwritten letters of the manuscript.

is feminised as "as solid as the woman, and also damaged" (68).²⁰⁴ The typescript is to be, according to Annie's plan, the only edition of *Misery's Return*, written exclusively for her (she intends to bind it in the skin of her pig, also named Misery). In an early draft of *Misery* as a horror story rather than a novel, this book was to have been bound in Paul Sheldon's skin (King 2010, 168). This is the manuscript that he pretends to burn in front of Annie, replacing most of the text by empty pages, and which is subsequently published to become another bestseller. At the end, Sheldon's career is envisaged as continuing as that of a 'serious' writer, and he sets out to write his new novel on a word processor that costs 15,000 dollars (King 2011b, 363).²⁰⁵

In contrast to these paraphernalia of professional identity, which emphasise the "business" aspect of writing that Annie deplores (81), there is the big book she keeps in her living room, her self-made scrapbook of newspaper clippings. When Sheldon finds it, it is his (and the reader's) access to a public record of her mental and criminal history. This confrontation between serial writing and serial killing (cf. Jaber 2021, 167) helps to underline how the making of books, in *Misery*, reflects the production of temporality itself through repeated acts of violence. As Sheldon tells Annie, "[w]riting a book is a little like firing an ICBM" – an intercontinental ballistic missile – "only it travels over time instead of space" (King 2011b, 306). However, Annie's self-authorship in her scrapbook is fundamentally different from Sheldon's in his writing. She has collected newspaper clippings and reassembled them to create a narrative timeline of her life as a nurse and a murderer. Her creativity consists and exhausts itself in taking and rearranging what others have written (about her or, unwittingly, for her). While not entirely passive, her 'authoring' the scrapbook is another result of editing rather than writing – an 'uncreative' form of creativity. Similarly, in *The Shining*, Jack Torrance finds out about the history of the Overlook hotel (the palatial 'monster' of that novel) from a scrapbook containing newspaper clippings that he finds in the basement. It becomes a source for his plan to write a book about the hotel, after abandoning his play *The Little School*, and leads him to grandiose dreams of authorial fame (King 2011a, 420). Like in *The Shining*, the monster's history is made available to its victim via a scrapbook. While the projected book in *The Shining* remains unwritten, it is the essential means of the hero's liberation in *Misery*.²⁰⁶

---

204 On the modernist tradition of feminising typewriters → ch. 11, 12. For another dual manuscript/typewriter composition, see the section on Durrell's *The Black Book* in ch. 11.
205 The price tag corresponds to that of Stephen King's own Wang System 5 word processor which he purchased in the early 1980s (Kirschenbaum 2016, 74–77) and which is preserved in a photograph by Jill Krementz (see the cover of *On Writing*, King 2010).
206 On the scrapbook in *Misery* as a site of struggle, see Palko 2007.

Next to the difference between scrapbook and printed book, and between typescript and manuscript, the difference between oral and written narrative is significant (cf. Perry 2019, 21). The power Annie wields is the immediate one of the spoken word (and, of course, the deed) whereas Sheldon's power resides in the delayed effect of writing, which like the missile strikes long after it has been fired. The novel replicates this in its first pages, when Sheldon cannot yet make out the words that Annie is saying to him, and they are written in phonetic approximation to their sound, somewhat resembling the opening of Joyce's *Portrait of the Artist as a Young Man* – a further hint at the *künstlerroman*, the horror version of which *Misery* undoubtedly is, and also evidence of King's literary ambition for this novel. When Sheldon finally overcomes Annie, he stuffs her mouth with burning paper in a drastic gesture of silencing her oral narrative power. The manuscript "becomes Paul's literal and figurative weapon against Annie" in what has been called "a grotesque parody of Annie's insatiable appetite to consume Paul's fiction" (Allan 2021, 281). In fighting his captor to the death, Sheldon uses both the text and the typewriter as weapons, going one better over Howard Ingham in Highsmith's *Tremor of Forgery* [→ ch. 16] when it comes to killing the Other with a typewriter. Ingestion and defecation are also metaphors for reading and writing. Some critics have noted the anal nature of writing that King repeatedly alludes to in his work, its representation as "corporeal ex-pression" by means of defecation (Willbern 2013, 107). The production of text is a physical activity, and as such it becomes amenable to the tropes of body horror.

From a literary-sociological vantage point, the horror explored in *Misery* is that of a writer unable to escape from the 'prostitution' that is writing commercial fiction and being dependent on his ability to continue providing an audience with the drug they desire. "You might as well call yourself a whore", Annie tells Sheldon at one point (2011b, 81). This condition of authorial doubleness, the split between pulp fiction and literary fiction, is also enacted, if more crudely, in *The Dark Half* (1989). Here, an author's pseudonymous doppelgänger refuses to stay dead and buried; he rises from his symbolic grave in physical form to go on a killing spree. Here, the author's 'dark' double is an evil twin, a monster, explicitly related in the novel to gothic tales like *The Strange Case of Dr Jekyll and Mr Hyde* and *Frankenstein* (cf. d'Hont 2021, 183), emphasising once more King's view of the dual and alienated nature of modern authorship, in yet another exploration of the 'great divide' between literature as art and literature as mass culture (cf. Huyssen 1986, Arnzen 1998, Meyer 2004, Landais 2012), a divide that has been exacerbated by the "financialization" of fiction, including genre fiction, since the 1980s, as conglomerate publishing companies have been privileging monetary over artistic or literary value (Allan 2021, 273).

Riding the wave of this cultural and economic transformation of authorship, King was highly aware, early on, of becoming a "brand-name author" and the limits this imposed on his "artistic freedom", confining him to the production of horror fiction (Allan 2021, 275). The other authorial doppelgängers in his fiction are usually ghosts. *Misery* is the only authorship novel in the King canon that has no need for the supernatural (d'Hont 2021, 183).[207] The miseries of *Misery* are exclusively of this world.

In *Misery*, Stephen King engaged in a realistic (though disturbingly brutal) way with the question of an artist's freedom and "professional identity" (Allan 2021, 281). At the centre of the novel is the fictional and actual author's relationship with publishers, critics, and fans, and the associated question who owns a literary product or brand. The source of horror, for King's fictional authors, lies not in the process of creation itself but in the fear of a "loss of control over their creative output" (d'Hont 2021, 184). *Misery* provides King's most sustained and complex, if not entirely sympathetic, reflection of the ambiguity and ambivalence of modern authorship between commerce and art, between alienation and self-authoring, allo- and autopoetics.

---

[207] On authorial doppelgängers in King, see also Landais 2013, who, however, limits her discussion to *The Dark Half* and "Secret Window, Secret Garden".

16 The Tremor of Genre: Making and Unmaking Writers in Suspense Fiction

How does popular literature represent authors and authorship? In contemporary culture, the distinction between 'genre fiction' and 'literary fiction' has become more fluid than it used to be, but it has not entirely disappeared. The distinction is not necessarily made on the basis of textual cues or signals but is frequently defined by context, such as a novel's publishing and marketing, the author's reputation or previous publications, and visual cues on the cover. In some cases, the difference may be based on not much more than the question whether a novel is published by Dell or Faber.

The focus of this chapter is on novels that inhabit different places along the "literary/genre fiction continuum" (cf. Kardos 2019, 220) and that, yet again, place stories of authorship centre stage. Along this continuum, there is not only a marked interest in "the genres of genre fiction" on the part of literary fiction, which deploys genre tropes as a resource for different purposes of critique and distinction (Rosen 2018). Writers of genre fiction, in their turn, also occasionally demonstrate a fascination with the conventions and institutions of literary fiction, especially with authors and authorship. Since around the year 2000, the topic of literary authorship has become more noticeably prominent in the thriller and crime genre and other popular genres, including romance, while at the same time there has been a *rapprochement* between literary fiction and genre fiction.

Already in the 1980s, Stephen King turned to the topic of literature and to metafictional devices within suspense and horror fiction, possibly with a view towards adding a 'literary' quality and thus a higher symbolic value to his commercially extremely successful thrillers [→ ch. 15]. King, as well as other thriller writers like Robert Harris and John Le Carré, have been aiming (with varying success) to escape the category of genre fiction and to be recognised as 'serious' writers.

On the other hand, 'literary' authors coming from the other end of the spectrum have increasingly been attempting to spice up their fiction with thriller-like features or genre tropes. These are not too clearly marked categories. The fusion of literary and genre fiction is a wider trend that has been noted by critics as a "genre turn in contemporary literary fiction" (Dorson 2017), part of the wider tendency to make literary fiction more popular for a (potentially) larger audience, possibly even signalling "a wholesale reorganization of the literary field" (ibid., n. 1). For example, Colson Whitehead wrote a 'literary' Zombie novel, *Zone One* (2011); Kazuo Ishiguro, winner of the Nobel Prize in Literature, has been adding elements of both fantasy (*The Buried Giant*, 2015) and science fiction/young adult fiction to his novels (*Klara and the Sun*, 2021); while Booker Prize winner Marlon James has turned to fantasy with his *Dark Star* trilogy from 2019 onwards.

Reading genre fiction alongside literary novels about authorship means to negotiate the shifting boundaries between these "subsets of the larger literary field and marketplace" (Rosen 2018, n. p.). Although they come at this topic from different sides of the field and with different sets of rules and expectations, they all address similar crises and instabilities in the making of authors. Each in their own way responds to the question of the risks, responsibilities, and discursive authority of authorship and, more generally, fiction in the contemporary world.

Authors as Detectives and Criminals: Patricia Highsmith's *The Tremor of Forgery* (1969)

In crime fiction since the Golden Age, author characters have often been cast as writer-detectives, and there is frequently a degree of self-awareness in which this can be used to reflect on the plot that is being written and the plot that is being uncovered by the detective. As Linda Hutcheon pointed out, "[t]here is almost inevitably within the novel also a conversation about how such events as are then under discussion occur in detective stories but never in real life (that is, in that novel)" (Hutcheon 1980, 31). Examples of writer-detectives include Harriet Vane in Dorothy Sayers's *Strong Poison* (1930) and other novels as a partner to Lord Peter Wimsey; Ariadne Oliver, featured in several stories and novels by Agatha Christie; Ellery Queen, who is both a character and a pen name created by Frederic Dannay and Manfred Bennington Lee in 1928; P. D. James's Adam Dalgliesh, who is a poet as well as a police inspector. There is also Jessica Fletcher, mystery writer and heroine of the long-running American TV series *Murder, She Wrote* (1984–1996). Within the storyline of that series, the fictional 'J. B. Fletcher' is said to have written at least 39 novels; in real life, this fictional writer has 'co-authored' a total of 55 spin-off novels since 1989 in an ongoing series with three different (real) authors.[208] Similarly, the fictional mystery novelist Richard Castle, hero of the TV series *Castle* (2009–2016), has some real books under his belt.

More rarely, writers in crime fiction are victims of crime, and even more rarely are they its perpetrators. The film *Knives Out* (2019) manages to combine both

---

[208] A list of the titles of Fletcher's real and fictional novels can be found on Wikipedia. – Transmedia franchises that include real books by fictional authors are not limited to the genre of detective fiction; for example, the US TV dramedy series *Jane the Virgin* (2014–2019) spawned a romance novel, *Snow Falling* (2017), purportedly written by the series' heroine, romance writer Jane Gloriana Villanueva. I would like to thank Rim Khaled for drawing my attention to this.

positions, as, in its own way, does Gilbert Adair's *The Death of the Author* (1992), a novella in which a literary critic – modelled on the notorious Paul de Man – devises a theory that denies that texts have meaning; he is ready to kill to prevent the revelation of dark secrets from his past, and is himself murdered at the end. Among these rare examples is Patricia Highsmith's *The Tremor of Forgery* (1969). This is the second Highsmith novel, after *A Suspension of Mercy* (1965), to feature a novelist as a central character. Published in the US as *The Story-Teller*, *A Suspension of Mercy* is a complex psychological thriller in which an expatriate novelist's fantasies about killing his wife lead to several deaths. *The Tremor of Forgery*, while outwardly less experimental in its form, may be the more interesting in terms of its plot and its author character.

In this novel, the American writer Howard Ingham has travelled to Tunisia to work on a screenplay when he learns that the film's director has just committed suicide. Ingham decides to stay in Tunisia and to work on a crime novel, prospectively titled *The Tremor of Forgery*, featuring an amoral embezzler named Dennison. This fictional character shows some significant parallels to Highsmith's most famous criminal, Tom Ripley from *The Talented Mr. Ripley* (1955) and its sequels. As he imagines "the ultimate crumbling of Dennison" in his novel (Highsmith 2015, 147), Ingham's own personality and moral orientation begin to come apart in the unfamiliar environment of Tunisia. His moral relativism (cf. 197) is emphasised by contrast to his neighbour and fellow American, the patriotic Francis Adams, who produces pro-American propaganda broadcasts and whose moral standards present a clear (if unsympathetic) moral and political counterpoint to Ingham's wavering. Ingham's moral relativism slides into nihilism as he contemplates that "whatever was right and wrong [...] was what people around you said it was" (155). One night, as an Arab tries to enter his bungalow, Ingham throws his typewriter against the intruder's head. The novel never specifies whether he has actually killed the Arab. The body disappears, and the crime (if such it was) is hushed up by the locals who service the bungalows.

Ingham now finds himself "in a curiously delicate condition" (216). Yet he is more concerned about getting his typewriter repaired than about what has happened to Abdullah, the intruder. Highsmith's biographer notes that the Olympia Deluxe typewriter featured in the novel is identical to Highsmith's own, and that her "pleasure in the act [of murder] is all too palpable" (Schenkar 2009, 386). In finishing his novel, Ingham embraces Dennison's moral nihilism – far from "crumbling", as he had originally envisaged, his hero is allowed to emerge from prison unchanged, and to "start the same financial manoeuvrings all over again" (246). Ingham never faces his crime of alleged manslaughter, and as he leaves Tunisia to return to New York, his lack of guilt is given an objective correlative in the typewriter's – the murder weapon's – lightness as he walks towards his plane: "Even the typewriter in his hand weighed nothing at all now" (258).

In this pseudo-existentialist variation on Camus's *The Stranger* (1942), set against the backdrop of the Six-Day War of 1967, Highsmith most poignantly examined the darker side of her own creativity and the ambivalent relationship between crime fiction and ethics (cf. Stolarek 2018, 151–155). She shows an author turning into an amoral murderer in real life as well as in his fiction; inviting strong parallels to herself and her fictional character, Ripley, the novel self-reflexively addresses its actual author's personal moral universe and projects a nihilistic stance that forces readers to check their own sympathies for Ingham and to question their own value system in being confronted with that most amoral character of all: a criminal author of crime fiction.

The Tremor of Forgery may well be the most radical author-crime fiction ever written. Most of the other authorship thrillers (at least those that I have read) turn out to be comparatively harmless. Their central plot motif is usually not murder but an accidental death that leads one hopeful author to appropriate the manuscript of a better writer just deceased. This 'stolen novel' plot has been around for a long time. An early example of an author stealing his friend's work is F. Anstey's novel *The Giant's Robe* (1884). The title plays on a quotation from *Macbeth*: "Now does he feel his title / Hang loose about him, like a giant's robe / Upon a dwarfish thief" (5.2.20–22), which also serves as the novel's epigraph. As summed up by John Sutherland, the novel's "hero is Mark Ashburn, a schoolteacher and failed novelist, who assumes ownership of the manuscript of a more gifted friend, supposed dead at sea. When the friend returns, Mark is disgraced but lives to redeem himself as a drudging lawyer" (Sutherland 2009, 22). In a preface, Anstey (i.e., Thomas Anstey Guthrie, 1856–1934) traces his idea for this novel "to a short tale, published some time ago in one of the Christmas numbers", about a "German student who, having found in the library of his university an old scientific manuscript, by a writer long since dead and forgotten, produced it as his own" (Anstey 1884, n. p.). Without obvious irony, the author identifies the stolen manuscript idea as itself lifted from something he has read and asserts his "honest and independent work" in reshaping this plot idea into a new novel (ibid.). Nevertheless, he was accused of having plagiarised his idea from W. W. Follett Synge's *Tom Singleton, Dragoon and Dramatist* (1879) (Sutherland 2009, 22).

Ever since, the stolen novel or the stolen plot have become staples of the novelistic imagination. In the modern era, as literature becomes a form of property in which authors have rights, both moral and monetary, plagiarism becomes a threat to an authorial economy based on originality. While the concept of literary plagiarism, and the very word itself, were known in antiquity, the stakes involved for both the perpetrators and the victims of plagiarism, forgery, and other forms of literary fraud are much higher in modernity, as authors depend on the ownership of their literary products for their economic and moral livelihood (cf. Lynch 2019, Rose 1993).

Famous authors are regularly accused of plagiarism, often based on spurious evidence or accidental verbal similarities (as in the case of *The Legend of Rah and the Muggles,* a self-published book that anticipated a name used in the *Harry Potter* books). Some of the more outrageous cases are themselves worthy of literary treatment, as when a woman accused Joyce Carol Oates and Stephen King of having entered her home to photograph her private papers – an incident that Oates used for her novel *Jack of Spades: A Tale of Suspense* (2015). Writers tend to worry they may be 'plagiarising' someone without knowing it, because of some idea or phrase they have unconsciously memorised. The anxiety surrounding literary theft has been explored by writers in many forms, sometimes as comedy or satire, sometimes (as in Oates's *Jack of Spades*) as suspense fiction.

Similar questions of literary ownership, authenticity, and autonomy harbour numerous possibilities for mystery, secrecy, and suspense that can be exploited along genre-typical lines. One of the better-known contemporary authorship thrillers, Robert Harris's *The Ghost* (2007) is a thinly veiled *roman à clef* about former British Prime Minister Tony Blair. It dramatises the plight of a professional ghostwriter who has been hired to pen the former PM's autobiography. The unnamed 'ghost' comes under increasing pressure in a conflict of loyalties as the former PM is indicted for war crimes by the International Criminal Court. The novel is presented as a memorandum written by the ghost. It was adapted into a film titled *The Ghost Writer* in 2010. Its political animus has quickly been overtaken by more recent events and scandals in British and global politics. It is perhaps worth noting that Harris wrote it between instalments of his Roman trilogy based on the life of Cicero (*Imperium,* 2006; *Lustrum,* 2009; *Dictator,* 2015), whose story is told through his secretary, Tiro; thus there is a thematic link between the modern ghost-writer and the Roman secretary in that both are writing the life of a politician.

The Stolen Plot: John Colapinto's *About the Author* (2001) and Jean Hanff Korelitz's *The Plot* (2021)

Other authorship thrillers have been dealing more directly with matters of writing and publishing. Many of them also employ, like Harris's *The Ghost,* the metafictional device of staging the text as a record, memorandum, or memoir written by the author-narrator him- or herself. This is the case, for example, in John Colapinto's *About the Author* (2001), which, for better or worse, embodies the subgenre of the authorship thriller to perfection and can serve as a template for the analysis.

The story begins with Cal Cunningham, a hopeful young writer in New York City, who shares an apartment with a law student, Stewart Church. Cal is confident and arrogant about his future success, but he suffers from writer's block. He finds out that Stewart is actually a writer himself but has given up on the idea of a literary career under pressure from his parents. When Cal reads one of Stewart's short stories, he is certain of being in the presence of a master and painfully aware of his own lack of talent. He is even more surprised when he learns that Stewart has completed a novel based on Cal's bohemian exploits in New York, titled *Almost Like Suicide*. When Stewart has a lethal traffic accident, Cal approaches an agent and publishes Stewart's novel as his own – it is, after all, based on *his* life, and thus he rationalises the theft by arguing that Stewart somehow stole it from him in the first place. The novel is – as invariably happens in these plots – a major hit, Hollywood buys the film rights (as it would for Colapinto's novel, although no film has yet been made), and Cal is suddenly rich. Out of curiosity, he tracks down Stewart's former girlfriend Janet in a small town in Vermont – and falls in love with her. He compares seeing her for the first time with a Joycean epiphany – yet another Stephen who falls in love with his own words and thinks himself an artist, though in this case the erotic charge of seeing the girl is rather bathetically expressed:

> I felt like Stephen Dedalus at the turning point of *Portrait of the Artist as a Young Man*, when he sees the bird-girl wading on the strand, her skirt dovetailed around her waist, her legs bare to his gaping eyes. 'Heavenly God!' Stephen's soul exclaims – and I knew just what his soul meant. Less abstractly, I felt my bound-down penis stir quickly to life in my hot underwear, stiffening and prodding insistently at the front of my fly. I readjusted my stance. (Colapinto 2001, 82)

Cal, as narrator, is drawn to literary allusions and sometimes rather elaborate literary language that does not always do his bidding. The novel seems alternately overwritten and underwritten. There are several such stylistic 'readjustments' of the narrator's "stance" in the text, which alternates stylistically between the plain language of action that drives the plot and a more 'literary' language that 'stirs to life' and 'prods insistently' at the conventions of the genre but, like the narrator's penis, is not allowed to get up and out. It is hard to say whether these involuntarily comic passages are merely bad writing or a deliberate strategy of characterisation on Colapinto's part, demonstrating that Cal is indeed a mediocre writer. One would hope the latter but fears the former.

As Highsmith's Ripley turns himself into the murdered Dickie Greenleaf, Cal begins to take over Stewart's personality as well as his novel. He moves into Janet's house, and they get married. He has dark forebodings about Stewart's ghost rising from the dead to accuse him, particularly when he first sees a portrait of his former roommate painted by Janet: "As if pushing through a mesh of bloodied gauze bandages, Stewart's face suddenly reared up from its dark background, a face looming from shadow into lamplight, glaring out at me accusingly" (Colapinto 2001, 82). Joyce is invoked again when Cal imagines Stewart standing between himself and his wife like "the deceased boy" in "Joyce's short story 'The Dead'" (91). But Stewart is and remains dead. Meanwhile, the novel sells "[l]ike iced bottles of Coca-Cola in mid-July" and receives rave reviews to boot (98). On his book tour, Cal feels like "an impersonator of an impersonator" (99). He tries to settle into his new identity as "a writer [living] in a rural hamlet" but, as before, realises that he "lack[s] the patience for literary work" (104).

The inevitable twist comes when Cal is blackmailed by a former one-night stand of his, Lesley (Les) Honecker, who had stolen Stewart's laptop and some manuscripts from their apartment before his death and thus has proof of his fraudulent deed. He tries to pay her off with $ 25,000, but she keeps coming back for more and finally even moves to the small town where he lives. To increase the pressure on Cal, Les befriends Janet and gives her Stewart's diary to read; this makes Janet rediscover her love for Stewart and to move to her parents' place temporarily. Cal has a meeting with his agent in which he pitches his idea for a new novel based on recent events but dressed as fiction. In this central metafictional conversation about a "plot involv[ing] a blocked writer who steals his deceased roommate's manuscript and makes a million bucks" (169), Cal tries to make his agent come up with an appropriate ending. The agent argues that the author-thief must not kill his blackmailer because that would make the novel impossible to sell to Hollywood, to its "[e]nd-user" (170): "You gotta picture Tom Cruise, or whoever, reading this thing and saying, 'They want me to play some blocked writer who steals his friend's book and then *kills* someone?' Tom'll throw the thing in the crapper" (170). Asked to suggest a solution "[w]ithout a thought of commercial considerations", the agent does propose murder.

More complications ensue, however, which make this radical act unnecessary. Cal believes that Les has been killed by a drug gang. He fails to locate the laptop in her deserted home but thinks that he is safe nonetheless. He feels the need to admit to his crimes by writing a lengthy confession, which he intends to destroy on completion. This turns out to be the book we have been reading so far, and it is "the most honest, and thus the finest, thing I will ever write" (209). From this point forward, the novel reaches the narrative present and goes into the mode that Samuel Richardson called "writing to the moment" (Richardson 1964, 289), adding a sense of urgency to its final pages and eventful dénouement. The metafictional emphasis on the book's writtenness, however, does not exactly help to speed up the pace of the narrative, and the element of suspense is drained away from the ending. Cal is accused of murder, but he can now clear his name because he has been able to take possession of the laptop, and his new manuscript exonerates him further. The criminal proceedings add to his celebrity, making him into a "literary-world O. J. [Simpson]" (Colapinto 2001, 245). *Almost Like Suicide* is published under Stewart's name. Cal's new book is published as a memoir. As his agent informs him, this is because "fiction's dead – check the sales of your beloved Roth and Updike and Bellow" (251). Titled *About the Author*, a pun "on the idea that I was 'just *about* the author' of the famous novel published under my name" (253), the new book is (obviously) another runaway bestseller, enabling Cal to settle his debts and to reconcile with Janet.

The happy ending leaves a rather stale aftertaste to this novel, which is rather too clever for its own good – an attempt at writing in a popular form while also striving to fill that form with more 'literary' qualities, an attempt that fails not only on the level of style but also on the level of plot and story, because the narrator's ethical and psychological quandaries never attain a sufficient level of credibility. *About the Author* entirely lacks the moral seriousness of Highsmith's Ripley novels, and the ease with which the narrator is allowed to escape into a happy ending feels unearned. Its metafictional elements are not entirely without interest or fun, especially in the way they self-consciously reflect on the "end-user" of contemporary fiction – i.e., the film and TV industry (Colapinto 2001, 47, 170) – and weave required set-pieces into the thriller plot accordingly. When Cal's agent describes *Almost Like Suicide* as "a fin de siècle *Bright Lights, Big City*, with a Gen X twist and some post-po-mo juju thrown in for good measure" (47), we may feel that we have read this novel. But these are ultimately half-hearted appeals to reconcile the genre-specific requirements of the thriller with a more literary sensibility, resulting in a kind of genre/literary hybrid, a 'meta-thriller' that turns out to be a rather unconvincing compromise. Moreover, the insistent male-gaze voyeurism, culminating in a lesbian sex scene between Les (!) and Janet, strikes a false note that is wholly unlike Proust but would fit neatly into an erotic thriller movie from the 1990s along the lines of *Basic Instinct*.

Twenty years later, *The Plot* by Jean Hanff Korelitz (2021) follows this template with some interesting variations.[209] Jacob Finch Bonner, a "once promising author" (3) who has had two books published without particular success and whose career is in steady decline, teaches creative writing in a bottom-of-the-barrel low-residency MFA programme in northern Vermont. There Jake meets a gruff, unpleasant student who is at first unwilling to share the plot of his projected novel because

---

[209] These variations seem to be inexhaustible indeed: not considered here, for reasons of space, are further variations on the 'stolen novel' plot such as John Boyne's *A Ladder to the Sky* (2018) and Andrew Lipstein's *Last Resort* (2022).

he claims it to be so original that the book will be a huge success. In a private session, the student reveals the story to Jacob despite his earlier misgivings. Years later, Jacob learns that the student has died and that his novel, if it was ever completed, has not been published. He writes a novel based on the student's story, titled *Crib*, and the former student's prophecy comes true – the novel is a critical and commercial success, conquering the bestseller lists and catapulting its author into the limelight. Yet Jacob is anxious about the possibility of being found out, and soon an anonymous accuser sends messages via Jacob's contact form on his website and goes public with his accusations on Facebook and Twitter soon after. Jacob tries to find out who the accuser is, and he discovers the real-life, true-crime origin of the mother-daughter-story that he had thought of as literary fiction.

Korelitz, like Colapinto, embeds the complications of literary ownership in a suspense novel. She shows the conflict between the empty promise, institutionalised in the ethos of creative writing programmes, that "anybody can be a writer" (Korelitz 2021, 3), and the contrasting tenet "Only you can tell your singular story with your unique voice" (132; cf. 320). Both are conventional principles of, and clichés about, creative writing, institutionalised in MFA programmes (McGurl 2009), but the novel demonstrates that they form a contradiction between the general and the singular. This contradiction frames the novel, and it will be Jacob's undoing. He has appropriated a story that was not his to tell (and, as it turns out, not his former student's either). The story belongs to (is part of) someone else's life and the secret of that life. As it turns out, the story's original and unique owner takes revenge on any "anybody" who sees fit to divulge it, mistaking fact for fiction.

In contrast to Colapinto's novel, the blackmailer is the one who feels she 'owns' the story that someone else has published, adding a much more powerful motivation than mere greed to this character. Korelitz's fictional author is less criminally guilty in having stolen merely a story and not an entire manuscript – the writing in this case is indeed his, whereas Colapinto's Cal merely felt he had a right to it because it was based on *his* life. What Korelitz's Jake has done is not technically plagiarism – as his publisher's legal team remind him and us, there would be no new novels "if you could copyright a plot" (Korelitz 2021, 149). Yet, in this case, the novel has no happy ending in store for its protagonist. These variations raise the stakes of *The Plot* and make it a much more satisfying read. Moreover, in Korelitz's case, the "theft of story" (Korelitz 2021, 232), is briefly aligned in the novel with "the anxieties we have around appropriation" (231) in the age of identity politics. This aspect shows the cultural distance that separates these two American novels published twenty years apart. While Jake asserts the novelist's freedom to tell and retell stories that others have invented, his partner Anna voices her scepticism that "what you writers think of as some kind of spiritual exchange looks like plagiarism to the rest of us" (232). In their disagreement and in the fate that awaits Jake as punishment for his unwitting trespass on another person's "unique" story, the novel registers the unease about fiction and the autonomy of literature that has become a major undercurrent of literary conversations in this century.

Romance Authorship: Colleen Hoover's *Verity* (2018) and the Dangers of Fiction

Another (and commercially the most viable segment) of contemporary suspense fiction is the romance thriller, which merges a mystery plot with elements of romance fiction. In the highly competitive market of 'new adult fiction', Colleen Hoover is a "TikTok sensation with over 200,000 five-star reviews" (Hoover 2018, back cover). Her 2018 novel *Verity* combines the psychological thriller with a romance plot and a generous amount of pornography and solecisms in equal measure. Lowen Ashleigh, thirty-one years old, is a struggling author in New York City with, so far, little luck in her private and professional life when she is hired by the husband of the bestselling romance writer Verity Crawford, with a view to adding new volumes to a contracted book series that his wife had started but is now unable to complete. The books are special because they are written from the villain's point of view (Hoover 2018, 134). Verity has been incapacitated in a car accident, but her publishers have been keeping the extent of her life-changing injuries a secret. Lowen, who has just been evicted from her apartment, moves to the Crawfords' rural home to work in Verity's study, while Verity is comatose in an upstairs bedroom.

This being a work of romance fiction, Lowen of course falls in love with Verity's husband Jeremy; she also connects with their five-year-old son, Crew. Two older daughters have died in two separate accidents. Lowen's work in the study is interrupted when she stumbles upon a manuscript that contains Verity's autobiography. This text reveals Verity's hateful personality: she hated her children out of jealousy for Jeremy's love and attention, and she deliberately tipped the canoe to make one of her daughters drown. Reading this autobiography makes Lowen fall even more deeply in love with Jeremy. She suspects that Verity only simulates her catatonic condition and that in fact she secretly communicates with her son Crew. This is indeed the case, and when Lowen and Jeremy discover this, they kill Verity. It is only after Verity's death that Lowen finds a letter that reveals the autobiography to be the very opposite of what it pretended to be. Instead of telling the truth, it was a writing exercise in "antagonistic journaling" (Hoover 2018, 298) to help Verity find the right mindset and tone for the villain in her book series. To protect her love for Jeremy and the unborn child she now carries, Lowen decides to destroy the letter and conceal the truth.

While Hoover's writing resembles that of E. L. James, the plotting invites associations to Daphne Du Maurier's *Rebecca* (1938) and one of Du Maurier's own inspirations for that book, Charlotte Brontë's *Jane Eyre*. In both these novels, as in *Verity*, we have a female first-person narrator who falls in love with her employer; in both cases, the employer's first wife plays a significant role in blocking the narrator's romantic fulfilment. Imagine Jane Eyre finding the memoirs of the first Mrs Rochester, finding a *Wide Sargasso Sea*-like counter-narrative to her own story in that novel, and you have grasped the basic plot mechanism in *Verity*. Here, by contrast to *Rebecca* and *Jane Eyre*, the (fictional) revelations about Mrs Crawford accelerate the female protagonist's attachment to her erotic object, the Rochester/Maxim de Winter-like Jeremy. If the reader pities Verity's sad fate as her authorship of a fictionalised alternative account of her life dooms her to a cruel death, all the sensation of this final revelation is drained of its potential ethical impact and aesthetic payoff as we are invited to connive with Lowen's destruction of Verity's final letter, the letter that reveals the truth about her life. As Lowen suggests at the very end, perhaps the letter provides only another version of 'Verity' (*nomen est omen*, obviously). "No matter which way I look at it", she muses, "it's clear that Verity was a master at manipulating the truth. The only question that remains is: Which truth was she manipulating?" (314).

Lowen turns out to be a bad reader of fiction when she cannot accept that Verity's ability to simulate villainy – the one characteristic that made her books so appealing – is not based on biography but on artistry:

> I still don't technically know her, but I know the Verity who wrote the autobiography. It's apparent that the way she wrote the rest of her novels wasn't a unique approach for her. After all, they say *write what you know*. I'm beginning to think Verity writes from a villainous point of view because she's a villain. Being evil is all she knows. (134)

In drawing on one of the tritest clichés of creative writing workshops, Lowen reduces art to life and equates the implied and the actual author; however, in accordance with Lejeune's "autobiographical pact" (Lejeune 1975), she may be forgiven for mistaking the intentions of Verity's manuscript. At the end, however, even when she is confronted with the truth, she only acknowledges this as another possibility, perhaps another self-invention by Verity, whose true personality remains elusive. She thus confirms the old saying 'once a liar, always a liar' – if you can fake your autobiography once, you can do it twice.

The foul aftertaste of all this, however, springs mainly from the fact that Lowen profits from casting doubt on the truth of Verity's final epistolary revelation. In doubting this truth, she exonerates herself from the role she played in Verity's death, from which she stands to gain not only emotionally and sexually but also economically. But perhaps this, too, is narrated from a villain's point of view? *Verity* searches for a shock effect that reveals the powers and dangers of fiction-making, as one author discovers to her horror that her own voice is powerless against the text that she has written, an alternative autobiography so credible in its tone (we must believe) that her husband is immediately convinced that he has been married to a psychopath all along. Verity's creativity as an author has condemned her to death. She did not 'write what she knew' but freely invented a different personality for herself, an act for which she is cruelly punished. The co-author brought in to complete the series has at the end of the novel not only taken over Verity's book series but her husband and her son as well; she has taken over her entire life, and she is more than willing to let Verity – and truth itself – die for her own happiness. The moral indifference of all this is almost as shocking as the bad grammar in both Lowen's and Verity's narratives.

Verity is a cynical farewell to an older Romantic and romance tradition that invested characters with at least a minimum of emotional credibility and dignity. Its true romance is in the sales figures it imagines for Verity's novels and for itself, which have surely been surpassed beyond belief at the time you are reading this.[210]

Powerful Fictions of the Real: Chris Power's *A Lonely Man* (2021) and Hari Kunzru's *Red Pill* (2020)

The idea of a stolen story, combined with the ghost-writer plot element, and the relationship between truth and fiction also feature in Chris Power's *A Lonely Man*, published by Faber in 2021. *A Lonely Man* combines elements of the spy novel with literary fiction in homage to John Le Carré and Roberto Bolaño. In this case, the thieving writer is Robert Prowe, an Englishman living in Berlin with his Swedish wife and their two young daughters. (The fictional author's last name is an anagram of the actual author's.) By chance, he meets Patrick Unsworth, who trusts him with his story of having worked as a ghost-writer for a Russian oligarch. The oligarch has since been found dead in London. Patrick is on the run, feeling threatened and persecuted by Putin's henchmen. Robert, who has been stuck in his work on a new novel, senses that this is highly welcome literary

---

[210] In early December 2022, three of Colleen Hoover's novels were among the top five on the *New York Times* bestseller list; *Verity* had already spent fifty weeks on the list by then.

material, and secretly records his conversations with Patrick. The narrative segues from passages focalised through Robert to retrospective passages focalised through Patrick, which are revealed to have been written and embellished by Robert. Initially, Robert does not believe in the veracity of Patrick's narrative, which helps him relieve his conscience in using his story as the basis for a novel. When Patrick finds out that Robert has been stealing from him, he is indignant; but not for long, since it turns out that they are in fact both being monitored by shady Russians. Robert receives a phone call that indirectly threatens his family. Patrick's apartment is raided, and he flees to Blanes – the Spanish hideaway of Roberto Bolaño, over whose book *Antwerp* the two men had bonded when they first met. Only Robert knows where he is. Robert takes his family to their second home in Sweden, where he feels safer; but he is trapped by two Russians who force him to reveal Patrick's location.

This novel employs its thriller plot to reflect on the changing relationship between fact and fiction, which has lost its usefulness and authority as cultural discourse – repeating and deepening the diagnosis of Cal's agent in *About the Author*. The distinction between truth and fiction comes under pressure on several levels: Russian oligarchs and their ghost-writers create new realities by making things up; Putin's henchmen get to decide what is real and what is not; Robert uses aesthetic license in fictionalising what he learns from Patrick, and in doing so gets caught up in a very real net of political persecution. A story purportedly told by Vanyashin, Patrick's Russian employer, turns out to have been copied from the (real) oligarch Boris Berezovsky (cf. Power 2021, 240, 244). Robert registers a widespread dissatisfaction with fictional narrative, telling his Berlin friends at one point that the story would "probably be a better magazine article than a novel" (226) and that, unlike a doctor's explanations to a patient, which involve a similar arrangement and selection of facts into a story, "the kinds of stories I tell don't help anyone" (226). Instead of stopping, however, he begins to see his novel as a "tribute" to "Patrick's experience" (249); thus ennobling his theft, he ignores the real risks involved in his actions, risks which have less to do with Patrick than with Patrick's pursuers.

The novel's homage to Roberto Bolaño can also be seen in the fictional author's first name (Robert, almost Roberto) and in the fact that his last name is an anagram of the real author's last name, 'Prowe' instead of 'Power'. Bolaño's work similarly features fictional versions of himself, sometimes under the name 'Belano' etc. Several themes, including the exploration of male ambition and versions of toxic masculinity, mesh with key interests in the Chilean writer's oeuvre, while the Berlin setting and the Russian agents are clearly marking Le Carré territory (who is also namechecked in the novel at one point). Although the novel is ultimately too conventional to reach the quality of Bolaño, it does contain some interesting reflections on literary writing as a form of theft, persecution, and loss of reality. Power's novel explores how fact-based or research-based realist fiction can paradoxically result both in an intensification (through embellishment) and a de-realisation of reality. In searching for the truth by means of organising facts, it ignores that reality itself (understood as the result of acts of realisation) is based on acts of fiction-making, that the world is always being shaped by fictions that determine what is perceived as real or not. In this, *A Lonely Man* follows (perhaps somewhat too) faithfully in the generic footsteps of spy fiction, as analysed for instance by Luc Boltanski in *Mysteries and Conspiracies* (2014).

When the narrator refers to seeing "life [...] as [...] a series of stacked realities" rather than "as a vast sprawl" (Power 2021, 283), he sums up what Robert thinks he has learned from his experience. In these "stacked realities", the manipulation of facts by means of *literary* fiction is the least problematic and the least powerful. It is the *real* fictions that determine what will become true, as Robert painfully learns when he is forced into betraying Patrick's hiding place.

A Lonely Man shares this sense of persecution with Hari Kunzru's *Red Pill* (2020). Similar to Power's, Kunzru's novel combines literary fiction with elements of the spy genre. As one perceptive reviewer noted, Kunzru has "grafted a taut psychological thriller onto an old-fashioned systems novel of the sort Don DeLillo or Thomas Pynchon used to write" (Offill 2020, 33). Kunzru's protagonist embarks on a residency fellowship at a sleek new institute in a suburb of Berlin, named the Deuter Center after its founder. The unnamed narrator plans to work on a book about the construction of the lyric self, but he soon gets sucked into a dystopian philosophical maelstrom of personal anxiety, intellectual and emotional dependencies and persecutions. He is disconcerted when he finds out that all his writing and other activities are being closely monitored and surveilled by the Center. He meets a woman who tells him her story of being a victim of the East German *Stasi*, and he links her experiences to his own sense of being undermined by those who observe and control him. He also becomes addicted to watching a violent cop show on TV.

Against the background of the 2016 US elections, the writer is drawn further into dark thoughts about the future, and he gradually loses control as he slides into a delusional disorder. Instead of writing his book on the construction of self in poetry, he experiences the disintegration of his own personality. He meets Anton, the racist creator of the cop show, who offers him a view of the world completely different from his liberal beliefs, a view that is described in analogy to the 'red pill' offered to Neo in *The Matrix*, an initiation into the world's true nature. As the narrator becomes both attracted and disgusted by Anton's right-wing views, he also grows increasingly unreliable. He pursues Anton first to Paris and then to a remote Scottish island. He fills notebooks with ruminations on "pointlessness, the utter ruin of all my projects, the supercession of all that I was or could ever be" (Kunzru 2020, 227). Instead of a final confrontation with Anton, however, he returns home to his partner and their children and undergoes psychotherapy. Having abandoned the search for an ultimate higher truth and having recognised the red-pill "realism" of Anton as "just the cynical operation of power" (283), he comes to cherish a fragile and unstable vision of human "solidarity" (283).

This interest in making and unmaking authors in suspense fiction, and in literary fiction like Power's and Kunzru's that works with thriller tropes, betrays an ongoing concern with the fragility of authorship and its cultural status in the present. Authors are both revered and suspect as providers of powerful narratives – hence their appeal as ghost-writers in the political thriller, authors whose conscience is challenged by moral pressures between their artistic autonomy and their need to earn money. When it does not serve a useful purpose, fiction is frowned upon (in these works of fiction) as an economically and artistically unstable type of discourse, at best frivolous, at worst downright damaging or even lethal as in *Verity.*

In a world destabilised by filter bubbles, fake news, and other (more) powerful fictions, literary fiction has a hard time staking and maintaining a claim to discursive authority. Commercially, it is also apparently less and less viable compared to nonfiction books and other forms like the memoir, as Cal's agent in Colapinto's *About the Author* already explains in 2001 with a look at dwindling sales of authors like Updike and Roth (Colapinto 2001, 251). This might be one reason for the increasing attractiveness, for writers and publishers, of autofiction – to be discussed in the next chapter – which claims (or pretends) to be based on the facts of the author's life, on experience rather than invention. In the mode of the nonfiction novel, Norman Mailer wrote about himself in the third person in *The Armies of the Night* (1968). Philip Roth's *The Facts* (1988) claims to be "a novelist's autobiography" (subtitle) and is the first of his so-called 'Roth books'. Similarly, J. M. Coetzee's *Boyhood* (1997), *Youth* (2002), and *Summertime* (2009) blur the distinctions between fiction and autobiography into "*autre*biography" (Lenta 2003, 157). Yet, whereas the genre of authorial autobiography is obviously much older, there is a sense, since the turn of the millennium, that autofiction and forms of documentary realism are on the rise because the literary mode of fiction is undergoing an economic and aesthetic crisis. The next chapter will situate these forms in their cultural and economic contexts and examine how they attempt to re-establish the discursive authority of individual authorship.

17 Economies of Authorship in Contemporary (Auto-)Fiction: Between Expressivism and Institutionalism

The early 2000s saw a proliferation of autobiographies, memoirs, autoethnographies, and autofiction (cf. Hayes 2021). Postmodernist irony had become exhausted, and words like 'reality' and 'sincerity' could be invoked with impunity "as terms of revitalization" in the literary field (Leypoldt 2017, 55). It was possible again now to take literally that venerable mantra of creative writing workshops, 'write what you know', as a precept for producing allegedly immediate, intimate records of personal experience instead of telling fictional stories. Thus, in autofiction, the novel form merges with the confessional mode and the authenticity claims of memoir. The genre boundaries between these modes have always been fluid. The term 'autofiction' was coined by Serge Doubrovsky in 1977, but the practice of autobiographical fiction is of course much older. Like the autobiography, autofiction pulls the reader more directly into a dialogue with the actual author and focuses on the author's personal life. Yet, for the most part, autofiction is closer to the novel in its style and presentation (see Burgelin/Grell/Roche 2010, Dix 2018, Wagner-Egelhaaf 2012). Indeed, one might say that autofiction also conforms to another old mantra: 'show, don't tell'.

Through its insistence on the illusion of immediacy and authenticity, autofiction not only generates a *rapprochement* of fiction and nonfiction. It collapses the boundaries between these two categories. It tends to invite the warmth of moral judgement rather than the coolness of aesthetic distance. Such a tendency towards de-aestheticisation could already be observed in some forms of nineteenth-century realist and naturalist writing. In these cases, new forms of distinction or boundary work become necessary. Sometimes, these forms are directly, programmatically, even aggressively addressed in a book's title, as in Gerhard Henschel's *Künstlerroman* (2015) or Julie Myerson's *Nonfiction: A Novel* (2022).

Among other recent literary trends, autofiction is symptomatic of a growing suspicion or distrust of fiction in the literary field itself. Authenticity and sincerity have come to be appreciated as 'post-postmodern' authorial values, just as autobiographical or autoethnographical narration has been hailed as a source of empowerment for underprivileged and marginalised communities. Moreover, democratic societies that have suffered crises of accountability and political divisiveness through the cancerous growth of 'fake news' or 'alternative facts' may have good reasons to cherish narratives that privilege notions of personal honesty, responsibility, and truthfulness. Forms of testimony, based on authenticity of experience and expression (cf. Moore 2002), are welcomed as modes of witnessing that give a voice and a face to previously unacknowledged and unrepresented social groups. While this is all to the good, an unwelcome side effect is an increasing distrust of fictionality altogether. Witness literature is predicated on the homology of author and story, just as autofiction privileges the 'auto' over the 'fiction', staking its claim for the authenticity of the unfeigned. If authors can adequately and rightfully only tell – or show – their own life's story, the literary license to invent freely – "the right to say everything and [...] the right of everything to be said" (Bourdieu 1996, 91) – is under threat. In such a climate, fiction needs new defences, new defenders, who remind their readers of the value of non-assertive imaginative discourse (cf. Smith 2019). A literature predicated on identity and topicality is at risk of losing its distinctiveness as a mode of writing based on possibility and imagination, and to become so attached to past traumatic experiences that it neglects to help design a future that would be worth living for.

The conflict between individual expression and institutional formation is expressed in contemporary discourses of authenticity and responsibility, but it is simultaneously embedded in socio-economic conditions of literary creation and production in a "dissociated" literary marketplace (Hartling 2009, 10) and a "creative economy" (Brouillette 2014) in which audiences are increasingly compartmentalised and fragmented. In the contemporary setting, some 'name economy' authors have become entrepreneurs. A few even delegate the actual writing – their "executive authorship" (Love 2002, 39) – to small armies of assistants. Ian McEwan – who can still, as far as I know, be trusted to do his own writing – has incorporated himself as an unlimited company in England and Wales. Others have followed the siren call of digital platforms such as Wattpad or Amazon that promise visibility to new writers (Laquintano 2016). These platforms have scaled up the analogue-era cottage industries of vanity presses and service providers seeking hopeful authors who would be willing to spend money to get published. The dissociation of literary publishing also affects literary form: on the one hand, there has been a return to the long novel, "vast narratives generated by a single brain" (Lethem 2017, 61) – Knausgård, Ferrante, Bolaño, Yanagihara – distributed by traditional publishing houses; on the other hand, the 'Kindle single', short, often serial narrative fiction distributed by no-name authors via Amazon (McGurl 2016).

In this diversified world of publishing, divided between five dominant global players (Thompson 2012), a host of independent and small publishers, and a growing sphere of nontraditional digital platforms, only a tiny minority of authors achieve visibility on a historically unprecedented global scale. Vast numbers of aspirational writers hope to "see [their] story get published"²¹¹ by posting content for free on digital platforms that specialise in fan fiction, such as Archive of Our Own, or by seeking commercial distribution in the e-book market via Amazon Publishing (McGurl 2016). This situation, though predicated on new technologies, is not new in principle; it resembles the eighteenth-century divide between geniuses and Grub Street hacks. The key difference is one of scale and technology. Instead of the rapacious 'brain-sucking' bookseller who exploits starving authors (cf. Oswald 1787, Berensmeyer/Guttzeit/Jameson 2015), digital corporations now monetise the 'free' creativity of hopeful writers to generate advertising revenue. In addition to writing, authors find themselves coerced to establish a lively social media presence to maintain their audiences' attention: "Tweet or Perish" is a more recent slogan for creative writers (Lethem 2017, 61). In the social and economic logic of the contemporary literary marketplace, only very few "star authors" (Moran 2000) transcend this diversification. Hypervisibility for a select few comes at the price of invisibility for the vast majority.

Autofiction has become such an important genre, I would argue, for at least two reasons: its promise of authenticity in a climate of distrust towards fiction, and its affordance of attracting attention towards authors in their struggle for cultural visibility. Thus we see a return to the author as the pivot of literary worldmaking, in at least two varieties: as a revival of Wordsworth's 'egotistical sublime' (in Eggers, for example, and Knausgård) or as a return to the 'negative capability' of Keats (in the writings of Rachel Cusk).²¹² In these autobiographies that read like novels, or vice versa, the writer becomes an exemplary form of self-fashioning, a format of subject formation, representing the "ideal of the creative self" for a contemporary society that celebrates and demands creativity as a key competence of coping with the modern world (Reckwitz 2012, 89). But if that is the case, how can authors preserve some of their former professional and social distinction? If they are now 'normal people' (as in the title of Sally Rooney's bestselling novel of 2018), ordinary creative labourers, they will have to seek to obtain distinction and visibility by other means.

Whereas 'author autofiction' has in the meantime become a staple of this kind of literary self-reflection, it cannot be the sole focus here. The Nobel Prize for Annie Ernaux in 2022 was clear evidence of the build-up of critical praise and commercial success, indicating that autofiction has become a prestigious form in the literary field. But the concern with the boundaries between fiction and reality, and with the validity, purpose, and sustainability of authorship as a career in a di-

---

211 Wattpad landing site, https://www.wattpad.com, accessed 26 Nov. 2022.
212 See Keats 1988, 539, 547.

versified society and an economically difficult market, driven by new technologies and new forms of unpredictability, can also be detected in two other fascinating 'comebacks': on the one hand, in the revival of the *bildungsroman* in the novels of Sheila Heti and Lily King, among others; on the other hand, in the return of the novel of resentment and regeneration that expresses a critique of the socio-economic conditions of the literary field. As representatives of this latter trend, I will turn to works by Percival Everett and Rachel Cusk.

The Authenticity of Suffering: Dave Eggers's *A Heartbreaking Work of Staggering Genius* (2000)

Published at the turn of the millennium, *A Heartbreaking Work of Staggering Genius* broke new ground in merging the techniques of postmodernist fiction with the tropes of the "misery memoir", a genre based on personal (and allegedly authentic) reminiscences of suffering and trauma that became commercially attractive in the 1990s (Hayes 2021), especially after the worldwide success of Jung Chang's *Wild Swans* (1992) and Frank McCourt's *Angela's Ashes* (1996). Eggers's book combines a Whitmanesque expansiveness and stylistic multiplicity with an earnest focus on the author's harrowing experiences of personal loss. Like Knausgård's *My Struggle*, it stages the author primarily as a suffering individual. The suffering, however, is not only and not even for the most part related to being a writer or an artist, but to being a brother, a friend, a person embedded in a network or what Eggers refers to as a "lattice" of social connections (Eggers 2007, 211, 237, 339, 436). There is clearly much more at stake in autofiction than the mere activity of writing, for which the bare statement 'I am writing' would after all suffice (cf. Kittler 1990, 15).

In a preface, the author explains that some events and characters have been fictionalised. In a section titled "Acknowledgements", readers uncomfortable with "the idea of this being real" are encouraged to read the work as fiction (Eggers 2007, n. p.). Eggers even invites readers to write to him for a digital copy so that they can change characters' names by "using the search-and-replace function" (n. p.) on their computer. Knowingly, the text both extols and defuses its nonfictional nature early on as a form of "self-flagellation" and "self-aggrandizement", even as an attempt at "self-canonization disguised as self-destruction" (n. p.). Like Anthony Trollope in his autobiography, Eggers includes a break-down of his earnings from the book in this section. In the tradition of the literary *bildungsroman*, he includes the processes of his own author-making in the form of the work. He asserts these processes while also appearing to undermine them by postmodernist pyrotechnics that place them in a context of humour and light-hearted irony.

For example, there are passages within dialogues where the author/narrator-as-character comments on his literary performance and technical difficulties of realistic representation, as happens in this conversation between Dave Eggers and his brother Toph:

> This is just a caricature, this, the skeleton of experience – I mean, you know this is just one slivery, wafer-thin slice. To adequately relate even five minutes of internal thought-making would take forever – It's maddening, actually, when you sit down, as I will once I put you to bed, to try to render something like this, a time or place, and ending up with only this kind of feebleness – one, two dimensions of twenty. (115)

Yet the overall tone of the text is anti-postmodernist (or post-postmodernist) and serious despite these "gimmicks, bells, whistles" (115). The ultimate impression it gives is one of successful reintegration after and in spite of the disintegration of experience and of literary form. After the early death of both parents, the Eggers siblings support each other and seek to make a life for themselves on their own terms. By means of the narrator's conversational and semi-spontaneous voice, anger at the world's injustice and the thousand natural shocks of the flesh are transformed into a text that strives towards a sense of wholeness, a totality of personal and social experience that integrates the individual into a reconstructed family and a wider social network of friends and colleagues within the cultural scene of San Francisco in the 1990s.

Formally, the text combines conventional first-person narrative in the present tense with formal "gimmicks" (115) like the film script and the interview, plus an extended unpaginated section of paratexts at the beginning. These "gimmicks" introduce a humorous tone, already on the modified copyright page that, for those readers with eyes still sharp enough to read the fine print, introduces uncertainty in the categories of fictionality and factuality. Yet these devices from the arsenal of postmodernist fiction arguably fulfil a merely decorative function, without destabilising the work's narrative core or its aesthetic coherence – they are the icing on the cake, establishing a jokey tone that lightens the narrative without taking away from its overall earnestness. The self-reflexive commentary supports rather than disrupts the work's emotional impact (cf. Polvinen 2013). Viewed from a rhetorical standpoint, it works together with the paratexts to establish real "interpersonal communication", "a heart-to-heart between writer and reader" (Jensen 2014, 149), or an alignment of auto- and heteropoetic strategies of author representation.

In form and content, *Heartbreaking Work* is, like a conventional *bildungsroman*, based on the integration of the individual within society rather than insisting, as does the *künstlerroman*, on their separation from it. But this integrative ideal is now emotionally charged, even to the point of overt sentimentality, to appeal to the authorial audience's empathic sensibility (*cataclisis* and *cathexis*). The novel culminates in a vision of social connections as a "lattice" (Eggers 2007, 436), a mutually supporting network in which its autobiographical subject is held and comforted even as he rages against society's "stupid rickety scaffolding" (437) and clamours for "attention" (ibid.). "The lattice", Eggers as narrator explains in an interview situation in the novel, "is the connective tissue. The lattice is everyone else, the lattice is my people, collective youth, people like me [...]. The lattice is everyone I have ever known [...]. I see us as a one, as a vast matrix, an army, a whole, each one of us responsible to one another, because no one else is" (211).[213] He also declares, in a hyperbolic expansion of this image, that he wishes to become "the center of the lattice", a beating heart "pumping blood to everyone" (237). It is a key symbol of connectivity that recurs at crucial points in the narrative, as when the narrator's colleague Shalini is hospitalised after a freak accident and Eggers realises that "what Shalini needs is the connection, the pumping of blood, the use of the lattice" (339).

This focus on the self as embedded in networks of family and friends also shows in the depiction of the narrator's early literary efforts as part of a group of like-minded youngsters founding and editing *Might* magazine, a San Francisco-based journal that ran from 1994 to 1997: "All together, our floor, our building, it has something, is bursting, is not just a place where people are working but a place where people are creating and working to change the *very way we live*" (Eggers 2007, 170).[214] This sentence sums up the new ethos of the creative economy and the idealism of those involved, as do the following sentences with their characteristic hyperbole: "[T]his will be [...] the very first meaningful magazine in the history of civilization, [and] it will be created *by and for us twentysomethings*" (172).

> We want everyone to follow their dreams, their hearts (aren't they bursting, like ours?); we want them doing things that we will find interesting. Hey Sally, why work at that silly claims adjusting job – didn't you used to sing? Sing, Sally, *sing!* We feel sure that we speak for others, that we speak for millions. If only we can get the word out, spread the word, with this, this magazine ... (173)

Somewhat more realistically, the expectations are to use *Might* as a "springboard" for those involved "to get themselves in *Time* and *Newsweek*" (174), to obtain a foothold in the publishing world. Significantly, in these passages, the narrator does not present himself as a solitary artist but as part of a creative team trying to make

---

[213] In the book's list of symbols (Eggers 2007, n. p.), "Lattice" is glossed as "Transcendental-equivalent", possibly referring to the transcendence of individuality in a wider social formation, as indicated in the passage just quoted (211).
[214] Emphases in quotations from Eggers 2007 are original.

ends meet and to produce something that is both artistically and somehow also economically valuable (cf. 169–172, 367, 417). He and his fellow editors want to preserve a bohemian lifestyle in a capitalist world:

> After all, the last thing we want from this, or at least the last thing I want from all this, is some kind of *job*. We have to avoid that kind of cruelly ironic fate – that we, the loudmouths who so cloyingly espouse the unshackling of one's ideas about work and life themselves become slaves to something, to a schedule, obligated to advertisers, investors, keeping regular hours – (240, emphasis original)

The magazine is also a way of getting in touch with other artists, authors, and celebrities, establishing a community of sorts, or at least the impression of a community. Other writers are solicited for the magazine and celebrated for their eccentricity, as in the cameo appearance of William T. Vollmann (283), and the magazine also invents fake authors like twenty-six-year-old 'Kevin Hilllman', alleged author of a book titled *Slacker? Not Me*, which resembles the design of Eggers's book in being composed of "the transcribed recordings of a week's worth of conversations between Hillman and his friends, captured by accident on a tape recorder" (285). Authorship by accident seems like a consummation of Generation X's ideals and beliefs. Soon, however, the group's experiences among the tech start-ups of the 1990s and their cultural scene turns into a disappointment when the "grind" sets in (287) and life in the offices of *Might* magazine turns into a bad "routine" (ibid.). After a couple of years, the venture unravels, and Eggers moves to New York.

As the book develops from its "slightly less self-conscious" first half to an "increasingly self-devouring" second half (Eggers 2007, 200), Eggers as author and narrator continues to temper his self-aggrandising impulses with the more down-to-earth comments of his siblings and friends, culminating in his final conversation with the suicidal John, who accuses him of committing a form of abuse by incorporating them in his book: "I'm just another one of the people whose tragedies you felt fit into the overall message", he tells him (423), decrying the "whole enterprise" of writing the book as "disgusting" (424), as an exploitation of "real people" for the sake of "entertainment" (ibid.) – similar, by implication, to MTV's *The Real World*, a reality television show for which Eggers unsuccessfully auditioned earlier in the text. The preface explains that 'John' is an "amalgam", a fictional character, but his accusations of Eggers's 'cannibalism' (cf. 424) are none the less powerful for this. Eggers is more protective of some elements of his own privacy than is Knausgård, by comparison; he does not, for instance, reveal his complete phone number (362). But even though the conversation with John, or whatever may have been its real-life equivalent, provides an occasion for self-criticism and the kind of "self-devouring" element mentioned earlier (200), it obviously did not stop Eggers from going ahead. Arguably, it adds to the 'reality effect' of his text, giving credibility to its authenticity by voicing objections against it – even though readers know that these authenticating words have been placed into the mouth of a fictional or fictionalised character by the author.[215]

This is very much a young person's book, written when Eggers was merely twenty-one, a memoir that reads like a coming-of-age novel with occasional touches of postmodernist irony. By comparison, Knausgård's *My Struggle* (2009–2011) is almost entirely free of such self-conscious distancing. Knausgård writes from the vantage point of advancing middle age; his text is more nostalgic in tone and, apart from its sheer length and often essayistic character, not challenging from a technical point of view, though extremely immersive and "highly bingeable" (Leypoldt 2017, 63). *My Struggle*'s assertion of individuality is, however, extremely provocative in its Scandinavian context because it rebels against the social conformity encompassed in *'Janteloven'*, the Law of Jante, as laid down by Aksel Sandemose in 1933, which mandates that no one is entitled to think they are special or in any way better than others. In Norway, the series was a *succès de scandale* for this reason; possibly, its commercial and critical success outside Norway, particularly the US and Britain, can be attributed to more relaxed cultural attitudes to self-centredness in these countries but also to the text's performative marking of a direction of the literary field that was recognised as innovative and invigorating (Leypoldt 2017).

For Eggers, the American autobiographical tradition from Franklin to Twain and Didion provides a more welcoming cultural environment. *Heartbreaking Work* tempers its assertion of individuality through a range of techniques and tricks that resemble the repeated emphasis on the Eggers brothers' virtuosity in throwing and catching a Frisbee (cf. Eggers 2007, 430–436). Among these are the many instances of self-consciousness, self-referentiality, and frame-breaking in the text, as well as the many direct appeals to the narratee, who is invited to identify with the protagonist as early as the novel's epigraph (ibid., n. p. [v]).

Many autofictional narratives share this conversational and confessional rhetoric, establishing the impression of a direct communication between author and reader. As in Eggers, techniques of metalepsis and self-reflexiveness are frequently used to establish an emotional sense of authenticity, a bond of shared knowingness between author and reader, rather than to draw the text's authenticity into question. Beyond the technical flourishes, it is the experience of suffering that provides the foundational matter of concern, an experience that is worthy of being shared

---

[215] On *Heartbreaking Work* and strategies of authentication, see Nünning 2005b, Korthals Altes 2008, Funk 2011 and 2015. On authenticity and authentication in the arts more generally, see also Moore 2002 and 2012.

with others. For example, in *I Love Dick* by Chris Kraus (1997), the autobiographical narrator suffers from an erotic obsession for the British academic Dick Hebdige, and the resulting book is an innovative and striking combination of personal reminiscence and theoretical ruminations, now sometimes referred to as 'autotheory' (Fournier 2021); but its central concern is the narrator's disruptive *amour fou*. Joan Didion's *The Year of Magical Thinking* (2005) is a memoir of the grief suffered by Didion after her husband passed away.

Similarly, in Sigrid Nunez's memoir *The Friend* (2018), the writer-narrator's prime subject matter is the suffering of grief combined with reflections on writing, reading, and dog-keeping. In Nunez, as in Eggers or Didion, the literary expression of personal suffering does not serve as a sign of uniqueness or distinction but as a signal of universality and relatability. Likewise, the banal details of everyday routines in Knausgård s *My Struggle* assert the author's similarity to 'normal people' and their equally banal daily lives, though arguably with a more gender-specific bias. The confessional manner as well as the inordinate length of *My Struggle* contribute to an impression of getting to know this character/author very intimately, possibly even more intimately than members of one's own family. In autofiction, authors thus turn themselves into *relatable* individuals, as if they were the reader's personal acquaintances or even friends. 'I am like you', they say; 'you are like me'. The epigraph to Eggers's *Heartbreaking Work* really puts it best: "First of all: / I am tired. / I am true of heart! / And also: / You are tired. / You are true of heart!" (Eggers 2007, n. p. [v]) They intensify the trend towards authentication that we observed in the return to (minimalist) realism of the 1970s and 1980s, but now directly addressing and implicating the actual reader in textual processes of communication.

Paratexts and other co-texts, such as an author's website or social media presence, frequently add to this personal relatability. The boundaries between authors and their texts are made more permeable as the work becomes less a static object of art than a rhetorical performance intended to establish communication between authors and readers. Instead of the modernist creed of impersonality or invisibility, authors now strive for, or are pushed towards, personality (in the sense of relatability, with an emphasis on normality) and hypervisibility. Instead of the distance between the bourgeois and the artist, they invite identification as a different, seemingly more intimate, low-threshold form of admiration. They also, in some cases, emphasise their belonging to a particular social, cultural, or ethnic identity. Fiction can take a back seat to such assertions of authenticity and credibility; but arguably it is the fictionality of the narrative – its formal artifice of being 'written like a novel' – that enhances the performative impression of authenticity and that encourages readers to experience it as such. In this literary and cultural process, the figure of the author becomes the central focal point of the text and its connection to the world.

Bildungsroman Revisited: Sheila Heti's *How Should a Person Be?* (2012) and Lily King's *Writers & Lovers* (2020)

In an era characterised by anxieties over 'fake news' and crises of confidence in established mainstream media, the boundary work performed by autofiction between fictionality and factuality calls for a clear distinction between the two while also demonstrating the cultural fluidity of these categories.[216] Their distinction is not merely a matter of correctly labelling a text as either 'memoir' or 'novel' – as in the notorious case of James Frey's *A Million Little Pieces* (2003), which was first sold as nonfiction but later as a novel when substantial parts of it had been found to be fabricated. Eggers's work, though consistently marketed as nonfiction (e. g., on the back cover of the 2007 edition), has many features that make it read like a novel. For Eggers, this may have been a strategy to expand the formal features of the memoir. Other autofictionists, such as Knausgård and Kraus, use such flourishes only sparingly and prefer to give their texts an essayistic (rather than novelistic) quality.

What many writers of autofiction share, however, to varying degrees, is a dissatisfaction with 'pure' or 'mere' literary fiction. Sheila Heti expressed this discontent in 2007: "it seems so tiresome to make up a fake person and put them through the paces of a fake story. I just – I can't do it" (qtd. in Leypoldt 2017, 65). Certainly, disavowals of fiction are nothing new and have indeed accompanied fiction-making from its very beginnings (witness Plato's partial ban of poets from the ideal community in the *Republic*); but in the present context they become part of a push towards an aesthetic renewal that is frequently associated with a 'new sincerity' (Voelz 2016). Yet, when witnessing becomes the principal purpose of writing, the freedom of literary invention is curtailed, and fiction may therefore be cast in a morally dubious light: as a merely playful, frivolous undertaking, a "fake story" that lacks a clear goal. Witnessing requires strategies of authentication and authorisation that anchor the text in the real world (cf. Moore 2002). This can be accomplished by referring to the authority of the text's actual author, based on their experience and their role as a witness of universal or more individual experiences, or their ownership of a social, ethnic, or cultural identity. As a cultural ideal, the author as witness thus embodies forms of author-making that

---

[216] For a wider context to such debates, see Ryan/Fludernik 2019.

connect the writing process and its products even more closely to the person of the actual author. While some authors fully embrace this ideal, others are more wary of its implications and consequences, questioning the boundaries of the autofictional genre and its processes of communicative authentication with a renewed sense of intellectual critique.

An earlier – fictionalised – instance of this dissatisfaction can be found in A. L. Kennedy's 1999 novel *Everything You Need*. The novel is set in a small writers' colony on an island off the Welsh coast, where Nathan Staples, a successful middle-aged author in a creative and personal crisis, berates himself for his lack of perseverance and, in doing so, hints at a more general distrust of making art out of life:

> You never do exorcise anything. You don't even manage that other thing: the making of the silk purse from the pig's shit, from the wreckage of yourself. It doesn't work. In the end, you only put things down to say they happened, to say **you** happened, and to hope you have a chance of making it all less real. Even if you never manage, even if you always still remember, anyway. (Kennedy 2000, 521, italics and emphasis original)

Here, writing is a potential means of working through personal problems, an attempt to salvage "the wreckage of [the] self", a way of translating into fiction and thereby distancing, transforming, and overcoming the narrow confines and shortcomings of the writer's life, of generalising (and redeeming) the bad infinity of the merely individual. For Kennedy's writer protagonist, this transformation is doomed to fail – "It doesn't work", at least not for him – and this failure is also signalled in his scatological variation of the proverb 'making a silk purse out of a sow's ear' (i.e., turning something worthless into something valuable). What his writing achieves is nothing more than a documentation of events ("put things down to say they happened"), a verbal assertion of the existence of the self ("to say *you* happened"), and an attempt to keep what is unbearable at bay by derealising these events ("making it all less real") in the mode of fiction.

Fiction feeds on the real; but this writer, even though he deplores his ultimate failure to achieve it, nonetheless regards fiction as a mode of release from the pains and pressures of his life. It is through his writing that he manages to establish a connection to his daughter Mary, another budding writer, who comes to the island without knowing that he is her father. Connection – love – is finally established as the human "need" that the title of the novel, in its possible allusion to one of the Beatles' most famous songs, proclaims as superior to all other needs. Yet these reflections near the end of the text, as quoted above, also register a dissatisfaction with fiction that had been a companion to the modern novel and its cultural perception for a long time but that, at the end of the 1990s, was growing more insistent and pervasive.

Sheila Heti's *How Should a Person Be?* (2012) is the direct result of Heti's unease with making up "fake stories" about fictional characters (Leypoldt 2017, 65). First published in a slightly different version in 2010, when Heti was thirty-four, this autofictional novel is possibly one of the closest approximations of what could be called a contemporary *künstlerroman*. The novel, which is mainly set in Toronto, centres on events from the personal and professional lives of the actor and playwright Sheila Heti and her friend, the painter Margaux Williamson. Some passages resemble transcribed conversations among friends in the form of a play script, including stage directions. In some chapters, emails or letters are presented in the form of numbered sentences. Chapters are short and scene-like, and the dramatic form is also evoked by their being gathered into five acts, a prologue, and an intermission. The events of the novel are framed by a competition to paint the ugliest painting, which is planned in the first chapter and decided in the last one.

Sheila is divorced after a brief marriage and now lives in her own apartment. In this 'room of her own' (cf. Heti 2014, 41), she works on a play that has been commissioned by "a feminist theater company", but she finds the work far from easy, and the pressure to be an artist, combined with the uncertainty of what a (woman) artist should be like, weighs heavily on her:

> I had spent the past few years putting off what I knew I had to do – leave the world for my room and emerge with the moon, something upon which the reflected light of my experience and knowledge could be seen: a true work of art, a real play. (Heti 2014, 40)

In subsequent ruminations on her writing, she notes the gap she feels between her original intentions for the play and her present situation: "Finishing it now felt like an impossibility. Any direction I might take with it seemed as likely as any other. I didn't know what mark on earth I should make" (46). She feels a "psychological block" (67), feels that the play "does not serve [her] life" (71). In a later, more upbeat mood, she exaggerates the potential impact her play will have on the world, replacing the personal purpose of art for the artist with the social purpose of a literature of commitment:

> If with this play the oil crisis is merely averted and our standard of living maintains itself at its current level, I will weep into my oatmeal. If this play does anything short of announcing the arrival of the next cock – I mean, messiah – I will shit into my oatmeal. (87)

This passage, which gives a good example of Heti's salty language and humour, illustrates the author's wavering between hubris and self-abasement. Neither affect feels entirely convincing (to the narrator), and the only thing that can bring her to complete her work is neither its personal value nor an abstract social value that resides somewhere in the future, but the present context of personal friendship. In the end, it is her friend Margaux who pushes her to finish her work, and to do it in a way that will yield an "answer [to the] question – about how a person should be" (262). Yet the implication is that it will not be in the form of a play but will be the book we have been reading (ibid.). The friendship with Margaux is the book's focus. Kn a central episode, they travel to the Miami art fair together. After the fair, however, Sheila goes to New York City, which she thinks is a better environment for her development as a genuine artist, but she soon returns to Toronto. Moreover, she parts ways with a man named Israel, with whom she was having an increasingly toxic sexual relationship. This act of separation from an overly assertive man strengthens the bond of her female friendship with Margaux, who had felt betrayed by Sheila's departure for New York, and it marks Sheila's newly found freedom and independence: "it felt like the first choice I had ever made not in the hopes of being admired" (273).

The question of artistic expression and its social purpose pervades the novel, as does the central question of how to live a good life and of what kind of person to be as an artist – in short, the search for an appropriate model of an artist for the twenty-first century. In contrast to men, there are (she argues) no available role models for women artists: "we haven't too many examples yet of what a genius looks like. It could be me" (4). This radical uncertainty can be sensed throughout the text. Questions about the connection between ethics and aesthetics, art and life abound: does the production of art make the artist, or does the artist's personality shape the work? "[I]f I want my life to be a work of art, then if I make bad work, it tarnishes my life", Sheila reasons (73).

She worries about self-care and self-cultivation, about how to "build your soul" (2), a word that she keeps misspelling as "sould" (5, 186), indicating the dangers of self-exploitation and self-commercialisation (processes which, obviously, are at the very core of any autofictional project such as this one). Revealing the soul is compared to public exposure of one's nakedness, which Sheila describes as one of the social function of artists: "Some of us have to be naked, so the rest can be exempted by fate" (61). Her Jungian analyst explains to her that work is more important than fantasising "about being *the person who worked*" (85), and that a life without suffering is "a life empty of all those things that make a human life meaningful" (84).

At this moment, it becomes particularly obvious that Heti is responding to the literary model of the *bildungsroman* and its assumptions about the individual's life as a process of growth and a quest for meaning. While the novel does not stage this process in its plot, it clearly invokes this model as a reference point for thinking about human life and the life of the artist. It also evokes a different model: instead of the idea of the genius as a guiding concept, the key value is solidarity among a group of (artist) friends in a somewhat bohemian cultural environment. The distinction between art and artists is blurred (cf. 103) as the artists' performance of themselves becomes a crucial part of the work. In this, the text registers the modern expansion of creativity beyond the arts into other social fields (cf. Reckwitz 2012). Its response to this is to reject the objectification of the artist and to embrace in its stead the idea of "the art impulse" as "a gesture" and "as a reproduction" (Heti 2014, 184): "We are gestures, but we less resemble an original painting than one unit of a hundred thousand copies of a book being sold" (185). As the token of a human type, the artist's individuality is dissolved in almost Benjaminian fashion into a reproducible form of subjecthood. The principal gain that comes out of this is a newly found freedom from wanting to be admired (cf. 273), yet the remaining challenge is to use this freedom responsibly: "We have found that, in our freedom, we have wanted to be like coke to the coke addict, food to the starving person, and the middle of the night to thieves" (184). But this path leads to "cheating", being untruthful to oneself and others (185).

While the novel offers no final conclusions or solutions to this problem of aesthetic and/as ethical freedom in a Western society, Sheila's return to Toronto and her embrace of friendship at least indirectly point to an assertion of group solidarity in favour of playing at being a solitary artist. Whereas, earlier in the text, Sheila had felt the desire to be special and had toyed with the idea of being a genius (cf. 4, 94), she now begins "to light up [her] soul" when she abandons this idea and decides to write again instead (277), in the knowledge that friendship is a higher good than any (ultimately self-deluding) idea of being chosen.

Heti's text has been read as an example of confessional writing (Bloom 2019), of the 'new sincerity' (Voelz 2016) and the 'new audacity' (Cooke 2020). Yet, while none of these descriptions are wrong, it is perhaps best understood as engaging with the form of the *künstlerroman* and the literary *bildungsroman:* an autobiographical novel about a contemporary woman writer who struggles with the contradictions that beset the idea of art and the self-concept of how to be an artist in late capitalist liberal democracies.

This conflict between "economic and creative values" (Kovach 2020, 185), explored further by Heti in *Motherhood* (2018), also forms the core of Lily King's fifth novel, *Writers & Lovers* (2020). Here, the emphasis of the question 'how to live as an artist' is less philosophical than economic. Though this is not a work of autofiction, it invites comparison with *How Should a Person Be?* because of its similar focus on a struggling woman writer in her early thirties and its first-person narration. Casey Peabody's story is set in Boston; a brief mention of the death of Princess Diana (King 2021, 80) places it clearly in the mid- to late 1990s. In contrast to *How Should a Person Be?*, *Writers & Lovers* is less concerned with the depiction of a singular individual but of a representative experience: of what it is like to be a woman writer working on her first novel while waiting tables in a restaurant to make ends (barely) meet. As the title already indicates, this is not about one writer in particular but about writers more generally and their search for emotional and financial stability as well as for an environment conducive to literary creativity.

Casey has been estranged from her father after her parents' divorce, and her mother has recently died, so there is no support to be expected from her immediate family. On the contrary, in one poignant scene, her father even demands that she hand over a sapphire ring that belonged to her mother. This ring has talismanic power for Casey and is an important element in her writing routine, of which she is very protective (cf. King 2021, 1, 81). She spends eight weeks in a writers' colony, where she meets Luke and is ready to fall in love, only to discover that he is still married. Her writer friend Muriel introduces her to an eligible young man named Silas, to whom Casey feels powerfully attracted but who disappears on a long trip shortly after their first date. She begins a relationship with the older writer Oscar Kolton, a widowed father of two boys. Oscar is an established and respected author, and his children are delightful, and yet Casey begins to feel that he is not quite right for her. Despite his success, he is deeply insecure, very competitive, and in need of constant admiration. When Casey accompanies him to a public reading, she witnesses his outrage when he realises that a female colleague, Vera Wilde, is drawing a bigger audience. This confirms her earlier impression that Oscar is one of those "men who wrote tender, poetic sentences that tried to hide the narcissism and misogyny of their stories" (51).

Casey's first novel, *Love and the Revolution*, is about Cuba, based in part on her mother's experiences among the revolutionary Left. Writing for her is not a means to an end but an essential part of her identity, something that gives meaning to her life: "I don't write because I think I have something to say. I write because if I don't, everything feels even worse" (3):

> What I have had for the past six years, what has been constant and steady in my life is the novel I've been writing. This has been my home, the place I could always retreat to. The place I could sometimes even feel powerful [...]. The place where I am most myself. (310)

While she struggles with various medical and financial difficulties, she completes the novel after six years of writing and finds an agent who is interested, even enthusiastic about it. But she loses her restaurant job, has a crisis of confidence, and applies for a position as an English teacher. She withstands the temptation of moving in with Oscar, even though she is about to lose her tiny apartment and is desperate to find a 'room of her own': "It's impossible not to think that I could write better with just a little more space and light. I wish my own room of my own wasn't so claustrophobic" (166). Waiting to hear from her agent, she realises that time is the only resource that she has left: "I have nothing but time now" (273) – echoing a very similar observation made by Balzac in *Lost Illusions* about the precarious lives of authors. Yet King's novel has a conventional happy ending in store for its protagonist: Casey's manuscript becomes the object of a bidding war between several publishers, allowing her finally to rid herself of her $73,000 debt and begin to plan her next novel. She even gets the teaching job, her cancer scare turns out to be a false alarm, and she finally hooks up with Silas, her 'Mr Right'.

This happy ending may appear escapist, the outcome of a desire to reward the heroine in the manner of a fairy tale, but readers may well sense that this reward is also extended to them in exchange for their sympathy with Casey's suffering. It shows this novel's much more conventional literary form, a female *bildungsroman* combined with elements of romance. However, in this novel, the writing life and ist economic and personal constraints are depicted more realistically and in greater detail than in Heti's text. There is a greater awareness of financial precariousness and personal sacrifice involved in the choice of being a writer, including romantic and reproductive choices in a woman writer's life cycle. There is also a greater emphasis on the economic aspect of authorship in the detailed depiction of Casey's interactions with her agent and of the agent's negotiation tactics in selling the manuscript to a publisher. The financial windfall she experiences at the end may not be quite realistic for a first novel, though no concrete figure is given, but the novel shows a healthy awareness that the life of a woman writer (Casey/King avoids the word 'artist' in this context) depends on economic and institutional aspects beyond her control. In this, *Writers & Lovers* continues the realist focus of Roth's, Carver's, and Munro's works from the 1970s and 1980s [→ ch. 14] but marries it to a heavily romanticised ending – similar, in this respect, to Chimamanda Ngozi Adichie's *Americanah* (2013).

As Dan Sinykin argues, "autofiction expresses the conditions of its production and negotiates those conditions to pry from them symbolic and financial capital" (2017, 475). This holds true for other contemporary authorship narratives as well, including more conventional novels like *Writers & Lovers*, which also "express[ ] the contemporary pressures of authorship" (ibid.) and discuss the economic and symbolic values of literary writing. In these texts, the characters of authors turn into "symbolic markers" to which audiences are encouraged to develop an affective attachment (cf. Reckwitz 2012, 245). As media of empathy and identification, these character-narrators, who exist by and in writing, represent a still powerful myth of the self as an expressive individual. As in the older *bildungsroman*, they tend to achieve some sort of resolution against all odds in the end.[217]

These authorship narratives revitalise the Romantic idea of the expressive and creative self while engaging with the expansion of the "creative ethos" (Florida 2003, 21) into a new social norm for society at large (cf. Reckwitz 2012). They do not ignore the economic contexts of contemporary authorship in the "conglomerate era" (Sinykin 2017, 474), but, by focusing on individual authors, they still take the author as a model for a particular type of modern subject formation (Kyora 2014): a producer of commodities that have cultural and personal as well as material and financial value. As authorpoietic fictions, these narratives celebrate "the creative imagination" (Taylor 1992, 198) even as they doubt its chances for survival in the modern world. They perform an uneasy – not always aesthetically convincing or entirely satisfying – alliance between the authorship model of expressivism and that of institutionalism. They beg the question to what extent authors 'make themselves' or are produced by institutions – the theatre company that commissions Sheila's play, the writers' colony that welcomes Casey, or the agency that takes her on. If a novel is not the place to arrive at sociological or economic conclusions, it is a significant site for the negotiation and accumulation of the symbolic capital of literature as a cultural good. This is why these texts foreground the expressivist model of authorship, accentuating individualism against all the odds of modernity and with a fairy-tale touch. Literary and social form in these texts cannot be made to cohere anymore in the novel's narrative progression. The gap between them needs to be filled or, absent that possibility, camouflaged by an escape into other generic forms: confessional discourse in autofiction, romance in Adichie's and Lily King's novels, disappearance into the stories of others in Cusk's *Outline* trilogy (see below), or an asymmetric double plot about the imbalances of power and privilege in Halliday's *Asymmetry*.

Authorship and the (In)Authenticity of 'Race': Percival Everett's *Erasure* (2001)

If the revitalised literary *bildungsroman* and *künstlerroman* can no longer convincingly fill the gap between individual expression and social formation, a logical consequence of this is a return to the novel of resentment – a form that unsparingly

---

[217] This is less obvious in Lisa Halliday's novel *Asymmetry* (2018), which I cannot discuss here for reasons of space but which would make for an interesting comparison.

emphasises the painful consequences of this disjunction without seeking to conceal them within pat compromises. One such novel is Percival Everett's *Erasure* (2001).

Thelonious 'Monk' Ellison is a recognised author of experimental fiction. Having published four novels and a volume of short stories, he is now, in the mid-1990s, a professor of English at UCLA. He is also Black, though this fact has not had much influence on his writing: in his journal, which forms the basis of Percival Everett's 2001 novel *Erasure*, Ellison notes early on that he "hardly ever think[s] about" and indeed does not "believe in race" (Everett 2021, 4). Coming from a wealthy family, he has been "refusing complicity in the marginalization of 'black' writers" (238). He is equally unwilling "to have [his] art be defined as an exercise in racial self-oppression" (ibid.). Instead, he has written a retelling of Euripides's *The Persians* and "parodies of French poststructuralists" (4). However, his fellow postmodernists in the *Nouveau Roman* Society hate him for having written and published one moderately successful realistic novel, *Second Failure*, about a young Black man who turns into a terrorist killing racists. This is a novel that Ellison himself now despises (69–70).

He is even more contemptuous of authors like Juanita Mae Jenkins, writers who enjoyed a privileged education and use it to create fiction about impoverished Black communities written in a grotesque caricature of Black English. While Ellison's agent is unable to sell his recent 'unreadable' work and tells him "you're not black enough" (49, cf. 48), Ellison learns that Jenkins's bestselling novel *We's Lives In Da Ghetto* earns her accolades as well as money (cf. 46). Out of sheer contempt and to prove a point, Ellison sits down to write *My Pafology*, a pastiche of "remembered passages of *Native Son* and *The Color Purple* and *Amos and Andy*" (70), an even more grotesque and violent caricature of underprivileged Black lives than Jenkins's – and he names its protagonist 'Van Go Jenkins'. Ellison makes his agent offer this "demeaning and soul-destroying drivel" (156) to publishers under the authorial pseudonym 'Stagg R. Leigh' (named after the traditional American murder ballad 'Stagger Lee'). Random House offers $ 600,000 for the rights, praising its authenticity ("true to life", 155).

Ellison reflects on his situation:

> I tried to distance myself from the position where the newly sold piece-of-shit novel had placed me vis-à-vis my art. It was not exactly the case that I had sold out, but I was not, apparently, going to turn away the check. [...] In my writing my instinct was to defy form, but I very much sought in defying it to affirm it, an irony that was difficult enough to articulate, much less defend. (159)

Having to care for his mother, who is suffering from dementia, after the violent death of his sister (a doctor, shot and killed by an anti-abortion activist), Ellison can certainly use the money. As to his artistic and aesthetic ideals, he will tell himself that he has been writing 'against the grain', a mode with which he is familiar from his woodworking hobby (cf. 4–5, 159) and his work on poststructuralist semiotics (cf. 18–22).

But with the novel's further financial and critical success comes increasing disgust. Ellison senses that he has sacrificed his artistic integrity. Even his decision to rename his novel *Fuck* shortly before publication can do nothing to halt its progress as it is selected for several book clubs, reaches the top of the bestseller list, receives a rave review in the *New York Times*, and is optioned as a film for the proud sum of three million dollars. Ellison agrees to masquerade as 'Stagg R. Leigh' to meet the Hollywood producer, convincing him that he is "da real thing" (248), a taciturn ex-convict. In creating this anti-novel, Ellison has created a monstrous version of himself as a stereotypical Black writer, wearing blackface to enhance a cliché of Blackness. He even agrees to impersonate Stagg Leigh on national television, if only as a silhouette behind a screen.

From this moment on, Ellison's journal traces his disintegration and the 'erasure' of his personal and artistic identity as references to Ralph Ellison's *Invisible Man* (1952) and its surreal confidence man, Rinehart, pile up (cf. Butler 2018, Gibson 2010). "Behold the invisible!" (Everett 2021, 238, 245), Ellison exclaims as he descends into the underworld of New York City, shortly before *Fuck* wins the National Book Association's annual award – against Ellison's own minority vote as a member of the panel of judges. 'His' novel, which he compares to a chair rather than a work of art as being no more than "a functional device" (234), meets with universal approval, and it creates its own author almost by default, threatening to erase Ellison's own identity in the process. As his mother descends further into dementia, Ellison's own sanity and sense of identity appear to be similarly compromised. Inevitably, he is in for defeat:

> [T]here was no such person [as Stagg R. Leigh] and yet there was and he was me. I had not only made him, but I had made him well enough that he created a work of so-called art. I felt like god considering Hitler or any number of terrorists or Congressmen. [...] I had to defeat myself to save myself. I had to toss a spear through the mouth of my own creation, silence him forever, kill him, press him down a dark hole and have the world admit that he never existed. (287)

Erasure contains one of the most cogent reflections on the question of race and representation in recent US fiction. It "satirizes", according to Rachel Farebrother, "America's eagerness to consume racialized images of the ghetto, especially within an increasingly commodified literary marketplace" (2015, 117). Whereas its Black protagonist, conspicuously named Thelonious Ellison after two of the most celebrated Black American artists of the twentieth century, fails to achieve recognition as a (moderately exciting) experimental postmodernist, his bitter parody of racialised stereotypes in literature is immediately and without friction accepted as 'authentic' by publishers, film producers, and other cultural institutions. He is, in effect, passing as "black(er)" (Moynihan 2010, 25), profiting from a desire for a commodified and racialised visibility in the media. Instead of presenting an invisible man, *Erasure* critiques a regime of mediated and mediatised appearances.

The demand for authenticity, for "da real thing" (Everett 2021, 248), is simply too strong to brook any dissent in the matter. The novel brings forth its own fictional author, Stagg R. Leigh, a Frankensteinian 'Being'[218] whom Ellison at first enjoys impersonating but whose persona soon becomes unbearable to him. As Robert Butler notes in this context, "such 'success' traps the winner by tying him to a socially constructed role that violates the deepest promptings of his core self" (2018, 146). Although Ellison created both the novel and its author by putting the name 'Stagg R. Leigh' on the title page, they are both, in an emphatic sense, products of those institutions that dominate the market of cultural representations of race. It is these institutions, from publishing houses to reviewers and television talk show hosts, that hold the allopoetic, paraclitical power to erase Ellison and put Leigh in his place.

Forgery, Author Fiction, and the Canon: Arthur Phillips's *The Tragedy of Arthur* (2011)

Arthur Phillips's novel *The Tragedy of Arthur* (2011) looks at the economic and symbolic authority of contemporary authorship from yet another angle. In a variation on the autofictional paradigm, Phillips explores the potential entanglements of a contemporary writer with the towering canonical presence of Shakespeare. The question here is how contemporary authors can develop and maintain their own literary authority vis à vis 'the Bard', particularly when faced with those institutional pressures that define the economic and cultural weight of tradition in relation to emerging individual talents.

The Tragedy of Arthur imagines what would happen if someone discovered a new play by Shakespeare. In the novel, "the first certain addition to Shakespeare's canon since the seventeenth century" (Phillips 2011, vii) is a play about the legendary British king titled *The Tragedy of Arthur*. The play in Phillips's book is a quarto print from a private collection. What makes this find so remarkable is the fact that the quarto dates from 1597, which would make it the very first play that identifies

---

[218] As noted in ch. 1, 'Being' is the term that was used by Percy Shelley to describe what is more commonly called Frankenstein's 'creature'; cf. Groom 2019, xi.

Shakespeare as its author on the title page. The preface to this publication speculates that the play's topic may have been too "politically dangerous" (ibid.) for it to be included in the First Folio of 1623. Random House is only too eager to pick it up and turn it into a publishing sensation.

The closest model for this is Nabokov's *Pale Fire* (1962), in which the story is told through an editor's comments on a narrative poem by a fictional poet. Like *Pale Fire*, *The Tragedy of Arthur* also contains a complete text within the novel, in this case a play in blank verse, but this time not by a fictional writer but – ostensibly – by Shakespeare (Phillips acknowledges Nabokov's influence in Reilly 2013, 6). The play – a clever and credible pastiche – takes up about of a quarter of the book. But it does not merely imitate a Shakespeare play, it imitates the *edition* of a Shakespeare play in its physical form: it comes with stage directions added in square brackets and explanatory notes to the text, like an Arden, Oxford, or Cambridge edition, and a lengthy introduction, in this case an excessive 256 pages in 48 chapters, signed by 'Arthur Phillips'. Some notes to the text are by this Arthur Phillips, others by one (fictional) Professor Roland Verre. While Arthur uses his notes to state his case that the play is a forgery, Professor Verre argues in favour of the play's authenticity.[219]

In the introduction, Arthur Phillips introduces himself as a novelist whose father was a convicted forger, who had been incarcerated for a long time and who, towards the end of his life, revealed what he claims to be the genuine discovery of a previously unknown Shakespeare play. Arthur's father wishes for Arthur and his twin sister Dana to publish this text as authentic Shakespeare. It gradually becomes clear that Arthur, who had always seen his father as a failed artist and as a failure in general, is now almost ready to believe him. Arthur's father has a credible story: he claims that he discovered this Shakespeare quarto in an English country house in the late 1950s and that he kept it in a bank safe in order to give his children a better future. Moreover, it is quite possible that Shakespeare might have written a play based on the Arthurian chapters in Holinshed's *Chronicles*, a source that he also used for numerous other plays, most notably the histories. This single surviving copy, then, like the famous first quarto of *Hamlet* that was only discovered in 1823, had been bound together with other play texts and then forgotten on the shelves of a private library. The book contains a facsimile of the title page of this quarto, dated 1597, "as it hath beene diuers times plaide by the right / Honourable the Lord Chamberlaine His Seruants", and also the information that

---

[219] Although Roland Verre is no Oxfordian, his name has an uncanny resemblance to Edward de Vere; it might also be a pun on Latin *vere* ('truly') or a number of other Latin words beginning with 'ver' such as *vereor* ('to worry', 'to fear', 'to worship') or *verres* ('boar').

the photo copyright of this facsimile belongs to "2011 Arthur Phillips" (Phillips 2011, xi).[220]

Arthur's publishing company, Random House, agrees to release the new Shakespeare play if the quarto passes all the available scientific tests. Paper, ink, individual letter forms are examined for their authenticity. Numerous genuine Shakespeare experts, including the renowned linguist David Crystal and Columbia University professor James Shapiro, confirm the likelihood that the text is indeed a Shakespeare play from the late 1590s. But then the tables are turned when Arthur discovers among the papers of his deceased father a note card that hints at an earlier draft of the play (Phillips 2011, 202). This is incontrovertible evidence that the play *is* a forgery by Arthur's father after all. But now Random House is no longer willing to stop the publication. The novel also contains another facsimile: a letter by the Senior Vice President of Random House responding to Arthur's wish to destroy the forged play, or rather what this letter calls "the original edition of the play" (253). The letter threatens Arthur with litigation if he does not comply with his contract, which stipulates that he must write an introduction – i.e., the text that we have been reading. Arthur has been forced to confirm his father's forgery against his better knowledge and against his will.

Obviously, the novel's title refers not only to the (edition of) the play included in the book but also to the tragedy, at least in the colloquial sense of the term, of 'Arthur Phillips', whose illusions about his father – and about ethical standards in publishing– have been shattered. The father's ultimate success in producing the perfect forgery is the son's final disappointment. Arthur as author is no king in this narrative, as the elision of the word 'king' from the book's title already suggests; instead, he is bound by the terms of his contract.

The novel's metafictional juxtaposition of elements of reality and fiction, truth and falsehood, authenticity and deception also draws on the long history of literary forgery and its modernist and postmodernist legacies (see, e.g., Dutton 1983, Stewart 1994, Lynch 2019). Its take on the problems of authorship and authenticity is informed by the history of Shakespeare scholarship, including the notorious forgeries of John Payne Collier (1789–1883) in the mid-nineteenth century, who inserted forged manuscript corrections into genuine copies of early printed texts (see

---

220 *The Tragedy of Arthur* is part of a more general trend in contemporary literary fiction to make use of book history and the format of the material book in order to create new kinds of reading experience by manipulating the physical space of the page and the codex format, such as J. J. Abrams's and Doug Dorst's *S.* (2013), Jonathan Safran Foer's *Tree of Codes* (2010), or Mark Z. Danielewski's *Only Revolutions* (2006). These multimodal works also explore the possibilities of the material book to probe (possibly unique) epistemological affordances of imaginative literature and the format of the book as an artefact and a medium (cf. Gibbons 2012; Hallet 2014).

Freeman/Freeman 2004). Phillips's experimental approach to writing a play that Shakespeare might have written raises pertinent questions about literary originality, authority, and property. It also sheds light on the economics of commercial publishing, turning book history into a sounding board for fiction: what *would* happen if a new play by Shakespeare were to be discovered today, even if its provenance proved to be dubious, or more than dubious? In the novel, the publishing giant insists on Shakespeare's authorship of the play. Whereas, in the case of Everett's *Erasure*, discussed in the previous section of this chapter, the institutional demand for the authenticity of the fictional author destroys the real author, similar institutional powers force the editor figure in *The Tragedy of Arthur* to present a forged work as authentic.

Applying the scale model of authorial positions to this novel [→ table 3 in ch. 1], one can even see several author functions competing in this text. Firstly, there is the strong heteronomy of Arthur Phillips junior, who is forced by his publisher to assemble the text. We also find the author as a weakly heteronomous producer of a text conforming to rules and conventions: Arthur senior, the forger, clings closely to the precursor Shakespeare as a model author to write a 'new' play by Shakespeare. Shakespeare is declared to be the creator of the work *The Tragedy of Arthur*, which is made materially present in the text (weak autonomy and declarative authorship). Finally, the position of strong autonomy, of authorship as sovereign ownership of the work, resides in this case with Random House. It is the publisher who decides, based on expert advice, that the play is genuine – it is Shakespeare and not "Fakespeare" (Phillips 2011, 168). Authenticity, then, is shown to be the product of an institution, based on authenticating procedures as well as economic and legal deliberations and, of course, on the vast prestige of Shakespeare's name: "anyone walking into a publishing house bearing a newly discovered Shakespeare play would be whisked to the top floor" (227) simply because of the enormous financial and symbolic capital involved in such a discovery. Such value, Arthur muses, results from Shakespeare's having become, through sheer force of time, "the standard of all truth and beauty" (227), his hypercanonical reputation (cf. Damrosch 2006) "inflated" (Phillips 2011, 226) "out of all sane proportion" (225).

Ironically, it is the lawyers, not the scholars or publishers, least of all the editor, who have the last word on the question of authenticity. On yet another level of irony, the actual author Arthur Phillips finds a way to frame his imitation of a full-fledged Shakespearean tragedy as a text worthy of consideration by contemporary readers, thus asserting his own authority and confirming the fictional Arthur Phillips's democratic view of Shakespeare as "one of many writers" (225).

In combination, these two levels of irony connect the – by now somewhat tired – mode of Nabokovian postmodernist experiment to the material book as a physical object and to the economic realities of contemporary authorship and publishing. Like a Shakespeare portrait, this novel is a fiction that "work[s] with the idea of the real, arranging a series of motifs [...] into a synthetic image" (Pointon 2006, 217). It uses the cultural capital of Shakespeare – similar to Ellison's use of the cultural capital of racialised stereotypes in Everett's *Erasure* – to draw our attention to the institutions and processes of constructing, mediating, and claiming literary authorship and textual authority in the twenty-first century. *The Tragedy of Arthur* explores formal qualities and functional features of the material book and its history (layout, typography, and the affordances of the codex) for non-traditional narrative and stylistic purposes. It confronts the authority of Shakespeare with the budding prospects of an emerging modern author, reflecting on questions of originality, imitation, and attribution. It pits the (cultural and economic) value of authenticity against deceit through forgery and the literary fake, and it creates an elaborate literary game for its audience, leaving readers less deceived at the end.

In their critique of the socio-economic conditions of the literary field, Everett and Phillips revisit the modernist novel of resentment and regeneration, adding a self-reflexive postmodernist awareness of literary form and the material book as artefact. A similar affective response to the world of literary publishing is combined with a critique of autofictional oversharing in Rachel Cusk's engagement with contemporary author-making.

The Lives of Others: Rachel Cusk's *Outline* Trilogy (2014 – 2018)

The narrator and protagonist of Rachel Cusk's *Outline* trilogy (*Outline*, 2014; *Transit*, 2016; *Kudos*, 2018) is a writer who remains nameless until a few pages before the end of the first volume, when her first name, Faye, is briefly mentioned. In *Transit*, likewise, her name only comes up once. Faye lives through the aftermath of a divorce, about which we learn very little except that it has financial as well as personal repercussions. In *Outline*, she travels to Athens to teach a creative writing course in a summer school, and the novel consists mostly of conversations she has with strangers she meets during her trip, with her students and fellow writers. She reports these conversations in a flat, unemotional tone, hardly ever allowing her own feelings to be recorded in her narrative. The effect of this narrative strategy of indirectness is that her own character only becomes visible as an outline (hence the title of the first book), the mere trace of a personality that can only be inferred from her reports of the stories other people tell her.[221] Quite in con-

---

[221] As Claire Messud notes (2017, 28), this technique resembles W. G. Sebald's in *The Emigrants* (1996).

trast to the self-centred narratives of autofiction, which tend to embrace a strategy of oversharing, Faye's – and Cusk's – approach is marked by self-effacement and erasure. The inner life of the narrator-protagonist remains a blank – as if her own experiences, her own feelings are too traumatic to be faced head-on. Faye is almost completely passive and lets herself drift through whatever Athens has in store for her. She reasons that she believes in "the virtues of passivity, and of living a life as unmarked by self-will as possible" (Cusk 2016a, 170).

On the plane, she encounters a man who is consistently identified as 'the neighbour', a wealthy Greek who has spent much of his time in London. She allows him to take her out on his boat, but when she realises that he feels attracted to her she refuses his advances in what amounts to the most decisive action she ever manages to perform: "he had to understand, I said, that I was not interested in a relationship with any man, not now and probably not ever again" (Cusk 2016a, 178). Apart from this exchange, Faye is always present but strangely absent from the novel, a mere recorder of the stories of others. The narration segues seamlessly between her words and those of her interlocutors, making it difficult sometimes to distinguish who is actually speaking (e. g., 44). This effect is intensified by the near-consistent absence of quotation marks for passages of direct speech. The fuzzy boundaries between her consciousness and the memories of others are also addressed by one of her writing students, who says she is so full of other people's memories "that she was frightened [...] of the boundaries separating these numerous types of mental freight, the distinctions between them, crumbling away until she was no longer certain what had happened to her and what to other people she knew" (154).

A similar condition is mentioned by a character in *Transit*, who finds it difficult to distinguish between what she has experienced and what she has merely read in fiction (Cusk 2016b, 244). While these boundaries never actually collapse for Faye, her obsession with other people's stories may indicate a troubling avoidance of facing up to her own past, or the professional deformation of the fiction writer, or both. Still, many if not all of the stories shed an indirect light on Faye's personal situation and mental condition.

Cusk's technique of indirectness and inference allows her to relate many of the episodes to Faye's sense of loss, as for example in this passage, when her Irish colleague Ryan tells her about his difficulties with writing, comparing them to a marriage:

> He doesn't quite know how it happened; all he knows is that he doesn't recognise himself in those stories any more, though he remembers the bursting feeling of writing them, something in himself massing and pushing irresistibly to be born. He hasn't had that feeling since; he almost thinks that to remain a writer he'd have to become one all over again, when he

might just as easily become an astronaut, or a farmer. It's as if he can't quite remember what drove him into words in the first place, all those years before, yet words are what he still deals in. I suppose it's a bit like a marriage, he said. You build a whole structure on a period of intensity that's never repeated. (Cusk 2016a, 45)

This passage performs several functions at once: it mirrors Faye's disappointment in marriage and the breakdown of that "structure", and it also echoes her self-doubt about her own writing, although this is only implied. She never actually responds to what Ryan tells her, and the chapter ends before we learn her answer to Ryan's question about her own work. We can only infer that Faye, like Ryan, has doubts about writing and being a writer, and that she knows what he is talking about when he refers to writing as a "concept of transmuted pain" (2016a, 43).

Outline is about writers in mid-career, who find it hard to reconnect to "what drove [them] into words in the first place" (Cusk 2016a, 45). Faye is more interested in tourism and boat trips with strangers, it seems, but she is also judging the stories others tell her, as if evaluating them from a literary perspective and collecting them for her own future work: for example, "this was a story", she tells 'the neighbour' in response to his representation of his first marriage, "in which I sensed the truth was being sacrificed to the narrator's desire to win" (30). *Outline* is very much aware of the fact that the stories we tell ourselves and others are motivated by different kinds of desire, first and foremost that of self-justification. In such stories, the truth is often unavailable: "there was no single truth any more [...]. There was no longer a shared vision, a shared reality even. Each of them saw things now solely from his own perspective: there was only point of view" (83).

This Jamesian insight, which may well come from Faye's literary training, is particularly acute in the way her own point of view is consistently elided. The novel acquires a retro-modernist sense of authorial detachment as the reader needs to piece Faye's backstory together from the fragments and mirror-like reflections in the stories told by other characters. Here the *künstlerroman* turns into a kaleidoscope of apparently random glimpses in a reprise of modernist impersonality. Yet, combined with this is a negation of any sense of specialness for the writer. As in many examples of contemporary author fiction, writing, and the life of the writer, are presented as mundane and banal. As one of her interlocutors, Paniotis, puts it: "Writers need to hide in bourgeois life like ticks need to hide in an animal's fur: the deeper they're buried the better" (97). The same thought recurs in *Kudos* as a statement of belief in literary realism (Cusk 2019, 183). Paniotis also professes his dissatisfaction with the idea that life should be like a novel, like a *bildungsroman:* "this sense of life as a progression is something I want no more of" (Cusk 2016a, 99). This is certainly echoed in the plot of *Outline*, which offers no progression or development for Faye. Her own story resembles the suggestion of one of her students, Georgeou, who tells the class "that a story might merely be a series of events we believe ourselves to be involved in, but on which we have absolutely no influence at all" (137). The very same question about the relationship between a life and its narrative shape recurs in all three novels, framed most insistently in *Kudos* as a debate about personal freedom (cf. Cusk 2019, 71, 174, 179, 190).

With regard to the legitimacy of fiction, *Outline* positions itself on a middle ground. The key to this is in Faye's first session with her students, which ends with one angry student leaving the class and calling Faye "a lousy teacher" (Cusk 2016a, 158). In a central passage, scepticism about the value of fictionalising actual experiences is countered with an assertion of "possibility" and "probability" as "useful thing[s]" (139), and the distinction between witnessing an event from an external point of view as opposed to experiencing the event from within, subjectively (cf. 137–139). Only from within can we know "what the story really [is]" (138). And this inside view of other people's consciousness, one might add, is only available in imaginative literature. The radical experiment that underlies Cusk's *Outline*, then, is to deny herself this resource, to understand "the role of the artist" as "merely [...] that of recording sequences" (206), and to provide readers with access to her narrator's point of view on the world only indirectly, through her matter-of-fact recording of observations and the stories other people tell her.

This concern with "passivity" and the "erosion of individuality" is continued in *Transit*, the second volume of the trilogy (Cusk 2016b, 197, 4). Again, we see Faye mainly in the others she interacts with. Here, however, she also takes action herself and buys a run-down former council flat in London that she decides to have refurbished. Supervising the builders and arguing with her downstairs neighbours, a nasty elderly couple, now fills much of her time. She also goes on a date with a chance acquaintance, attends a panel at a literary festival outside London and allows herself to be kissed by the panel chair, goes to the hairdresser to have her hair dyed, and teaches creative writing both as a private tutor and in a classroom setting. Again, there is no conventional plot. Instead, the novel is filled with the stories of Faye's friends and acquaintances. While *Outline* focuses on her passivity, *Transit* is concerned with change and the idea of freedom: with the boundaries between the wills and desires of one person and those of others. For the writer, such change can also, as one of Faye's fellow authors at the festival explains, come about by means of writing: "he was actively and by small degrees becoming distanced from the person he had been, while becoming by the same small degrees someone new" (104). Indirectly, we can infer from the text that Faye realises she cannot simply wait for important changes to happen to her, she needs to do something to bring them about:

> For a long time, I said, I believed that it was only through absolute passivity that you could learn to see what was really there. But my decision to create a disturbance by renovating my house had awoken a different reality, as though I had disturbed a beast sleeping in its lair. I had started to become, in effect, angry. I had started to desire power, because what I now realised was that other people had had it all along, that what I called fate was merely the reverberation of their will, a tale scripted not by some universal storyteller but by people who would elude justice for as long as their actions were met with resignation rather than outrage. (Cusk 2016b, 198)

This act of rebellion resembles that of Caroline Rose in Spark's *The Comforters*, the character who tries to subvert the plot that is given to her by an omnipotent and omniscient narrator [→ ch. 13]. Faye similarly rejects the idea that her life story is "scripted [...] by some universal storyteller" (ibid.); instead, she takes the first steps towards overcoming her passivity and regaining control over her own life.

There is no explicit indication in the first two novels that this renunciation of passivity involves the shaping of a new writing project, apart from the fact that *Outline* and *Transit* are narrated by Faye as their fictional author and might be taken as a product of this resolution. Yet, by the time of *Kudos*, Faye has not only married again but published a new work of fiction. One quotation from *Outline* is brought up by an interviewer in *Kudos* as something "he had recently read [...] somewhere" (Cusk 2019, 183), so we can safely assume that Faye is to be taken as the supposed author of these novels in the fictional world of the trilogy. *Kudos* opens up this world to discussions of the economic and cultural value of literature and the making and marketing of books. Faye travels to a literary festival abroad, possibly in Germany, and to a writers' conference in Southern Europe, possibly Portugal. Again, the novel consists mostly of conversations in which she reveals very little while her interlocutors open up about their life stories. Thoughts about the contingency of human lives (e. g., 64) alternate with concerns for the future of literature in an age of shrinking margins and cultural shifts towards other kinds of pursuits and pastimes.

The "thirty-five-year-old salesman" (36), for example, who now runs a prestigious publishing house explains to Faye that their most profitable publications are now Sudoku, while authors of "unprofitable literary novels" have been let go for more mediocre ones: "those writers who performed well in the market while maintaining a connection to the values of literature; in other words, who wrote books that people could actually enjoy without feeling in the least demeaned by being seen reading them" (37). Without naming it as such, this editor describes the contemporary equivalent of the middlebrow: a cultural product that reproduces the "connotations" of great literature but without "making [...] demands and inflicting [...] pain" on its readers (40). Consumption, even "combustion" of culture is the key (38), as opposed to the slower-burning, longer-lasting values embodied in the literary canon, a new attitude that is perfectly in tune, according to this editor, with the age's "pursuit of freedom from strictures or hardships of any kind" (39).

While Faye, who believes in "the small rock of authentic literature" (105), objects to the injustice of this economic formation, she knows she can do little to change it. She notes in passing that the push towards more aggressive literary marketing has created "a literature of its own" (105) that favours authors who are good at public appearances but whose works are not quite up to the mark. She is also aware of the sheer fragility of literary publishing, which she fears might vanish in an instant when the public decide to spend their money on other things (105).

Ryan, the brooding Irish writer from *Outline*, returns in *Kudos* like a walk-on illustration of these changes, having transformed himself into a bestselling author who co-writes with a younger woman under a shared pseudonym. Ryan has given up on his literary ideals and focuses now on making public appearances, for the sake of which he has lost weight and self-monitors his nutrition and physical activity. The gain of freedom in one aspect of one's life necessitates a new set of constraints in others – a lesson that is repeated by many characters in *Kudos*.

As its title indicates, the main theme of this novel is recognition or acclaim (cf. Cusk 2019, 98, 189), and the different ways in which these kinds of social acknowledgement are expressed and, frequently, withheld – in particular with regard to gender differences between male and female authors. For instance, one of Faye's female interlocutors observes that "honesty" is praised in men who write about themselves but "scorned" in women (147). The value of literature is one topic that runs through *Kudos*; the other is the relative value of male and female work, and the invisibility of women in cultural fields, culminating in the drastic final image of Faye bathing in the sea while a man on the shore is exposing himself to her and urinating into the water.

Faye is again only named once in this novel, this time in a phone call with her son in England (Cusk 2019, 227). There is no indication that Faye is a mere stand-in for the actual author, Rachel Cusk, though there are some biographical parallels between them. The *Outline* trilogy is not a work of autofiction but a more indirect, fictionalised exploration of Cusk's life as a writer and, especially in *Kudos*, her convictions and beliefs about literature and its conditions of possibility. In Cusk's oeuvre, these novels constitute a departure from her earlier autobiographical memoirs or autofictions, *A Life's Work* (2001), *The Last Supper* (2009), and *Aftermath* (2012). While these books, like many autofictional projects, had originated in a sense of frustration with fiction, the *Outline* trilogy constitutes a return to it, and possibly signals a renewed confidence in "the screen of fiction" (Cusk 2016b, 107) as not merely protective but revelatory – a means of "tell[ing] the truth" (Cusk 2019, 182). As such, it asks urgent questions about the relationship between the writer and her text, the degree of truthfulness that is appropriate or permitted, and the degrees of subjectivity and objectivity that are available in a project like this. Cusk's use of free indirect discourse to blend conversation with reflection (cf. Valihora 2019, 25) is the perfect instrument to explore a variable distance between subjectivity and objectivity, self and others, identification and non-identification (cf. Vermeulen 2021, 89).

In the *Outline* trilogy, Cusk opposes the trend towards authorial visibility and transparency by hiding behind the persona of Faye, and thus again fictionalising the "zero point of discourse" (Iser 2013, 122), but also by leaving this persona largely blank, a mere cipher, a recipient for the stories of others (many of whom are also writers). She finds a point of reconciliation between the modernist strategy of impersonality and a contemporary sensibility that favours relatedness and intersubjectively shared narrative spaces – showing, however, that there is a cost to the creation of such spaces in fiction, and a larger material context that is beyond the individual writer's control. The auto- and heteropoetic strategies of autofiction thus merge with a critique of self-centredness and professional blindness in the literary field itself. Here the expressivism of the subject, his or her freedom to verbalise experiences, is always caught up in social constraints. Both impersonality and relatability in fiction carry a price-tag. Cusk thus arrives at a "dissociated" perspective on literary authorship (cf. Hartling 2009, 10): an interrogation of narrative structures that purport to privilege individuality but instead tend to subject individual perspectives to a universalising normative format (cf. Jensen 2018, 69), combined with a critique of the institutional structures that provide an 'outline' for the formation of authors and set limits to their access to audiences and to forms of recognition and admiration.

The strategy of denying readers access to the author-narrator-protagonist's inner life, and thus cutting her off from readerly empathy, is a striking device that pushes these novels beyond conventional fiction and autofiction into what one might call, in French, *autrefiction:* fiction that delineates the negative space around its central character, providing an outline of her narrative through the stories of others. By foregrounding Faye not as the author of her own life-story in a kind of *bildungsroman*, but as a mostly passive witness to the powerlessness of others, Cusk offers a cogent metareflection on literary representation as well as a pertinent interrogation of the contemporary conditions of possibility for literary fiction.

Conclusion

For a long time, the "return of the author" (Burke 1992, Jannidis et al. 1999) has been a much-noted phenomenon in literary studies. In literature itself, obviously, authors never left and so never needed to come back or to protest, like the still living plague victim about to be carted off in *Monty Python and the Holy Grail* (1975), "I'm not dead!" Roland Barthes, who had proclaimed "The Death of the Author" in the late 1960s, soon contradicted himself in publishing – incidentally, in the same year the Monty Python film came out – an autobiography whose title, *Roland Barthes par Roland Barthes*, almost comically insists on the identity of author and subject.

For many reasons, the relations between actual authors and (fictional) narrators, characters, and events have remained largely underexplored in literary studies. Because of the lasting influence of the New Criticism and its exclusive focus on 'the text', to do so was deemed either unnecessary or even wrong. From structuralism, narrative studies inherited a predominantly text-focused orientation, while reader-response theory, obviously more interested in the right-hand side of the communication model – the reader –, was keen to move away from conventional notions of authorial intention. This changed, gradually, in feminist and postcolonial criticism. Edward Said's *The World, the Text, and the Critic* (1983) leaves the author out of its title but returns at length to authors as 'worldly' anchors of textuality, and to style as "the recognizable, repeatable, preservable sign of an author" (Said 1983, 33). The embodied presence of authors in the world matters to any theory or critical method that understands texts as manifestations of historical, social, or political identities and constellations.

Novels and stories that contain authors as characters reflect such identities and constellations in their content and frequently in their form. From the early nineteenth century onwards, author characters have been a regular feature of narrative fiction. There are literary and material (social) reasons for their prevalence. Their numbers tend to increase when social and economic pressures challenge the self-understanding of authors, the viability of their career, and the purpose of their profession. There is demand for such stories not only when they promise a new variation of a familiar plot, but particularly, it seems, in times of transition between changing concepts, models, and practices – in short, paradigms – of literary authorship.

Though many of these 'author fictions' may justifiably be accused of "literary navel gazing" (Hill 2022), others have more to offer. They address the fragile material conditions of literary creation in the actual and symbolic economies of cultural production. Authors write (or re-write, or even un-write) themselves as well as their books, and author fiction makes this process of "autography" (Abbott 1996, Nugent-Folan 2022) explicit. In writing about the instability of authorship, through a process of aesthetic reflection, such works attain a degree of stability, a compromise of literary and social form, if only for the duration of the novel or story. Most author narratives are written by authors in mid-career.[222] It is tempting to see this as a symbolic act of representation and, in some cases, self-projection or self-justification, at least partly motivated by the psychologically and sociologically complex transitional period of middle age.

Yet authors inscribe not only their personalities or idiosyncrasies into their works; they engage with those concepts and models of authorship that are valid or dominant in their culture. They register the structuring force of available forms and genres in relation to wider social contexts: historical formations of race, class, and gender, legal and economic possibilities and constraints, and other institutional and technological infrastructures of literary creation and production. Author narratives represent the making of authors (*authorpoiesis*) while performing rhetorical, formal, and generic structures and strategies pertaining to authorship (*auto-/heteropoetics*) in front of an audience. These structures and strategies evolve historically, not in literary theory but in literature itself – in narrative texts that negotiate their conditions of origin, i.e., authorship, publishing, and related institutional contexts of literary life. Author narratives represent and, in representing, perform actual, possible, or probable (as well as improbable) manifestations of literary authorship. Such discursive negotiations in narrative fiction are productive as well as reflexive: they can bring about actual change and serve as models for others to follow or avoid.

Understanding authorpoiesis as a looped dynamic process that involves social and textual action helps to show how authors are both active agents in and "product[s]" (Pérez/Torras 2016, 42) of the literary field. Authors make literature, but literature also makes authors. As origins of literary works, they are identifiable but also to a large extent inaccessible, "an invisible point from which the books c[o]me", as the narrator of Italo Calvino's *If on a Winter's Night a Traveller* explains (Calvino 1998, 102). They are also, of course, not the sole point of origin – a "zero point of discourse" (Iser 2013, 122) that can only be imagined as a self-bootstrapping *fons et origo*, a groundless ground. Such abstractions deny the complex negotiations and "field translations" that Clayton Childress (2017) has described as governing the processes of literary creation and production, from author's manuscript to printed book or online publication. Editors, publishers, and other agents

---

[222] In the corpus assembled for this book (see appendix 1), the average age of authors who write 'author fiction' is about 47.

in the "communications circuit" (Darnton 1982; Adams/Barker 2006) are crucial contributors to the final, neat impression made by the text that audiences get to see, even if the author's name is the only immediately visible trace of that process on the title page.

Authorship scenarios in fiction negotiate the conditions of literary creation and self-creation, exploring the ambiguities and ambivalences of author-making across several fields from creation to reception. They are also performative: bringing about what can only be established ex post facto but what authors and audiences need to assume to have been there all along – the mystery of creativity, a radical improbability that is nevertheless a crucial part of the self-understanding of actual authors (cf. Amlinger 2021, 562–563, 672). They are not, however, tied firmly to their individual author's own personal circumstances. Authors do not always write about themselves when they write about authors and authorship. They certainly enjoy the privilege of fiction that allows them to write about anything and to invent freely. Yet even a novel about a completely fictional or historical author, far removed from the actual author's situation, is written from that actual author's position in the field and therefore constitutes an engagement, even if only an indirect one, with that position and its possibilities.

In this book, I have argued that any narrative at least implicitly contains an author fiction in the philosophical sense of a concept or model of authorship. Those works of fiction (in the literary sense) that place such an author fiction centre stage can then be considered as 'author fictions' in both senses: they harbour at least one model or concept of authorship, however vaguely defined, while at the same time unfolding this author fiction within a fictional story and its discourse. I have also referred to such works as 'author novels' or 'author stories'. This is not to be misunderstood as an attempt to establish a previously unknown genre. Whether such works constitute a genre would require further clarification and specification. Instead, I consider author fiction as a thematic mode that can be present in many different genres and subgenres, from the *bildungsroman* to the ghost story to the romance thriller. The very boundaries of genre, always to be negotiated within author-text-audience relations, are part of the game that literary author fictions play with audiences' expectations and cultural norms.

In their negotiations with the perennial paradoxes of personal expression and institutional constraints, author fictions perform boundary work between the real world and the world of fiction. They draw connections and distinctions between forms of authorial subjecthood, social institutions, and literary forms and genres. Balzac's *Lost Illusions* is an early novel of literary disillusionment, but for many years the literary *bildungsroman* along Goethean lines and (later) the *künstlerroman* proved to be the more influential forms of mediation between the literary and the social. Other forms gained ground as older patterns lost their cultural validity, producing further variations and counter-traditions such as the gothic and its modern equivalent, horror fiction. When the generic resources of the realist *bildungsroman* had been exhausted, towards the end of the nineteenth century, author fictions turned away from narratives of progress and individual development, towards texts that staged the breakdown of the "Victorian compromise" (Chesterton 1946, 21) between individual and society and between the upper and middle classes. Economic uncertainties widened the gap between promise and realisation, giving rise to the "novel of resentment" (Bergonzi 1976, 20) – most notably, Gissing's *New Grub Street* – and the novel of disappointment or literary failure – Forster's *The Longest Journey* and Green's *Blindness*, for example. Some authors, at their lowest ebb, engaged in fantasies of personal wish-fulfilment, like Frederick Rolfe, whose author-protagonist embarks on a new life as Pope Hadrian the Seventh.

Author fictions reflect changing aesthetic and social models of literary authorship. In addition to authors' individual "position-takings" (Bourdieu 1996, 231), a central factor in these performances are the roles of authors in relation to other people, other professions, cultural fields, or social groups – roles that are permanently contested and newly established. The Romantic genius kept the furthest possible distance from others, who could not hope to imitate his (or, more rarely, her) uniqueness; Victorian novelists were at pains to prove their belonging to a class of high-status professionals, as distinct from the "trading author" (Mill 1859, 1: 31), let alone the working class. The mid-Victorian literary *bildungsroman* was all about achieving a working compromise between different – social and anti-social – impulses. The 1880s and 1890s, a crucial period in literary history because of the increasing compartmentalisation of literature into a mass medium on the one hand and a form of art on the other, saw the rise of the literary artist as opposed to the 'mere' craftsman (e. g., Henry James as opposed to Anthony Trollope), with authors on both sides of this divide viewing themselves as performing an important public service and fulfilling a relevant social role.

The history of author fiction dovetails with the more general history of the modern novel, as modernist artists increasingly cultivated their distance and distinctness from bourgeois capitalist society. Authors who were devoted to their art as a "sacred office" (James 1984, 46) and proud of what Graham Greene memorably called "the exclusiveness of unsuccess" (2019, 122) despised the writers of popular bestsellers who embraced commercial taste and enjoyed the acclaim of the masses. In the *künstlerroman* genre, the idea of compromise broke down. To be an artist now meant to be the kind of person prepared to suffer or starve rather than give up their ideals. Modernist artistic coteries created a bohemian counterworld to the bourgeois mainstream, a subculture that was in effect an alternative social structure to support the idea of the creative artist against the collectivising pressures of an industrialised mass society. For those writers who were uncomfortable with either option, dissatisfied with the "iron cage" (Weber 1958, 181) of mass society and dubious about the ivory towers of "minority culture" (Leavis 1930), the result was often resentment, expressed in the form of the 'angry (young) author novel' by the likes of Orwell or Camberton. Resentment could also give way to satire, which made fun of these ideals and embraced the commercial appeal of the market and mass authorship, as in Waugh's *Vile Bodies*.

The conditions of mass authorship exert enormous pressure on authorial identity and upon the ideals of originality and art. This is expressed in many stories around 1900 that stage drastic scenarios of doubled or split author personalities and ghostly revenants. Modernist author fictions that present the "loss of social integration and bourgeois respectability" of the artist figure question the very "representativeness" of authors and authorship, i.e., their discursive and cultural authority (Weimann 1988, 439). Comic novels by Aldous Huxley and Evelyn Waugh (and, later, Kingsley Amis) ridicule the pretensions of authors and the vagaries of public taste. Women writers longing to escape from the narrow confines of the 'feminine middlebrow' claim equal recognition in the literary field. They revitalise some of the older forms of author fictions, most notably the *bildungsroman*, that most tenacious narrative template of modernity, as in Doris Lessing's *The Golden Notebook*.

After the Second World War, postmodernist metafiction engages with an even more severe crisis in the validity of authorial authority and the value of literature in relation to other media and other types of social discourse. Postmodernity entails an expansion of the discourse of creativity beyond the arts into wider social and industrial contexts, as well as the invention of creative industries and creative economies. It is a typical marker of such processes of deindustrialisation that Andy Warhol's art collective should be called 'The Factory' and that, a few years later, captains of industry should strive to make factories look more like art collectives. The division between the everyday bourgeois world and a bohemian *demimonde* of the arts becomes more difficult to maintain. As an artistic strategy, the assertion of authorial individuality in opposition to wider social and economic processes is now less obvious, even less so as questions of authorship and conflicts between different sorts of literary value (aesthetic/economic/political) have entered the field of genre fiction in the form of authorship thrillers or horror novels.

Without putting too much interpretative weight on this, we can observe in postmodernism a turning inwards, towards an ontological questioning of literary form in metafiction that only indirectly engages with the social and economic status of authors and authorship in real life. However, the pendulum swings back in the 1970s and 1980s in the minimalist short story but also in the novel, which returns to varieties of realism and to questions of social norms, ethics, and morality.

Frequently, these texts interrogate an author's right to use the lives of others as material for fiction, and thus question the boundaries between literature and (social) reality, (re-)establishing the author's role as both inside and outside society, as a privileged moral observer and critic, whose self-irony and understatement only serve to strengthen that position. These new forms of social realism reimagine the relationship between the artist and the 'bourgeois' (or, rather, the suburban middle class). Questions of ethnic belonging and the author's responsibility to his or her community are also addressed in this context, as in Roth's *The Ghost Writer*. These concerns are shared, among others, in the nonfiction novel, in documentary realism, and in witness literature. The new role of the author that emerges in these processes is no longer the ecstatic or resentful artist in opposition to society but the author as representative witness – a member of society or of a particular group who assumes the role of a spokesperson for that group, without claiming any kind of epistemic, economic, or social superiority.

The logical consequence of these new kinds of authorial self-consciousness is to forgo fictionality altogether and aim for a documentary autobiographical realism that asserts the truth of what it represents and that fuses the name and person of the author with that of the narrator, as in the New Journalism or in works of autofiction. Far from simply returning to the pattern of the *bildungsroman*, recent author fictions complicate the relationship between the authorial subject and its literary reflection, between the actual author and the author as narrator of him- or herself. While these two positions can never merge completely, their overlap initiates a further round of the cat-and-mouse game between reality and representation, giving authors once again the opportunity, in the words of A. L. Kennedy, "*to say [they] happened*" (2000, 521, emphasis original). Such intensification in the mode of fiction can be achieved not only in autofiction but also in the denial of a strong "self-will" (Cusk 2016a, 170), as in Cusk's *Outline* trilogy, where we only catch glimpses of the central author character and narrator in the stories she records of others, a technique I have tentatively termed *autrefiction* – a position that involves an othering or at least a distancing from the empirical author persona. These texts lead back to the perennial questions and paradoxes of authorial freedom and institutional constraints, of expressivism vs. institutionalism, as narrative fiction continues to negotiate the legitimacy of fiction-making and the writer's dependence on social structures and economic conditions of creativity.

This history of author fictions is further complicated by shifting cultural values and changing attitudes to fictionality itself – in short, from Romantic irony to Victorian sincerity to modernist/postmodernist irony and towards a 'new sincerity' in the twenty-first century (Voelz 2016). Metafiction, autobiographical writing, and autofiction blur the boundaries between fiction and reality, whereas other genres police those boundaries keenly. Social, political, economic, legal, moral, and other concerns persistently link works of literature to their authors and thus to the world outside the fiction. For this reason, the boundaries between fiction and reality are never absolute, irrespective of how hard writers, institutions, and audiences – including scholars and critics – engage in boundary work that tries to assert, shift, cross, or deny the ontological gap. For author narratives, the thin line that separates fiction from reality, and the narrative representation of that line in novels and stories about authors and authorship, is too tempting (for authors, and apparently for audiences too) to be left unexplored.

Furthermore, connections between actual and fictional authors are rarely simple or monocausal, nor are the relations between historical forces and literary forms. These are not, according to Edward Said, "reducible to an explanatory or originating theory, much less to a collection of cultural generalities" (1983, 27) but need to be described as expressions of "worldliness": "texts have ways of existing that even in their most rarefied form are always enmeshed in circumstance, time, place, and society" (35). The fictional author can be almost anything, a chronicler or a satirist, a hack, a failure, a historian, a biographer or autobiographer, a detached 'master' or a literary novice, and so on and so forth. This sheer multiplicity of staged positions might appear to be no more than a "perennial exchange of something else for something else again" (Hegel 2008, 106), i.e., a "bad infinity" in Hegel's terms (105), yet these fictional or fictionalised author roles refer to possibilities and realities of authorship in the actual world. The critic's task, then, is to find those patterns that connect individual texts to larger historical developments, relating these fictions more systematically to the scope, availability, and value of authorial roles in the literary field and in society at large. This multiplicity of authorial positions corresponds to a wide variety of literary forms in which stories about fictional authors have been told, from the pseudo-editorial preface and the frame tale to realist narrative, ghost stories, postmodernist metafiction, and autofiction. Here, too, it is imperative to establish plausible connections between text and world rather than presenting a mere parade of formal options in front of a weakly lit historical backdrop.

The conceptual challenge for the study of author fictions lies in the exploration of the interfaces between society and literature, the "contexture" (cf. Berensmeyer 2020, 8, 18–21) or "matrix" (McGurl 2009, 466) where cultural scripts and conventions are translated into literary forms, and where negotiations of narrative voice combine with struggles for literary and discursive – ultimately social – authority. Without assuming a deterministic relationship of causality between social and literary dynamics, we can perhaps also identify this as the plane of correlation between historical events and literary forms – a correlation that is more than merely an accidental temporal association but less than a definitive causal connection.

In the mode of fiction, historical social processes are propped onto literary forms, emplotted and enacted in narrative, and performatively reflected by authors as well as audiences. Under the pressures of historical and political forces, literary fiction becomes a dynamic interface for the negotiation of form-making across social and even across ontological boundaries, from the improbable to the impossible. This boundary crossing invites associations to "unnatural narratology" (cf. Alber/Heinze 2011, Richardson 2015, Alber 2016), but even more pertinently to Aristotle's concept of "probable impossibilities" in imaginative literature (*Poetics* 1460a, Aristotle 2013, 53). Jim Phelan has explained these as "*crossover phenomena in narrative progressions,* instances in which the logic of author-audience relationships trumps the logic of event sequence or of telling situations" (Phelan 2017, 4, emphasis original; cf. ibid., 32–59). Such "crossover phenomena", or discrepancies between narrative logic and real-world logic, could be regarded as similar instances of cataclitic and homopoetic boundary work, as audiences tolerate "breaks in the probability code" (49) when this adds to their enjoyment of the story. The anaclitic 'piggybacking' of authors on narrators and characters, to which audiences respond in turn with cathectic emotional attachments, may well be one of these "probable impossibilities" that, far from an error in the system, constitute one of the foundations of literary activity.

Appendix 1: An Incomplete List of Authorship Narratives, 1800–2022

This list of novels and stories that feature authors as (major) characters is ordered chronologically by date of first publication. While its focus is on books in English, it also includes some works in other languages.[223] Titles published in the same year are listed alphabetically by author.

1800–1850

Félicité de Genlis: *La femme auteur* (1802)
'Dionysius': *Adventures of a Pen* (1806)
Byron: *Childe Harold's Pilgrimage* (1812–1818)
Jean Paul: *Leben Fibels* (1812)
E. T. A. Hoffmann: *Mademoiselle de Scudéri* (*Das Fräulein von Scuderi*, 1819)
Charles-Augustin Sainte-Beuve: *Vie, poésies et pensées de Joseph Delorme* (1829)
Benjamin Disraeli: *Contarini Fleming* (1832)
Giacomo Leopardi: "Dialogo di Torquato Tasso e del suo genio familiare" (1835)
Thomas Carlyle: *Sartor Resartus* (1836)
Honoré de Balzac: *Lost Illusions* (*Illusions perdues* 1837–43)
Edward Bulwer-Lytton: *Ernest Maltravers* (1837)
Honoré de Balzac: *Béatrix* (1839)
Catherine Gore: *Cecil* (1841)
William M. Thackeray: "The Fashionable Authoress" (1841)
Thomas Miller: *Godfrey Malvern* (1842–43)
James Grant: *Joseph Jenkins* (1843)
Charles Baudelaire: *La Fanfarlo* (1847)
Rose Ellen Hendricks: *The Young Authoress* (1847)
G. H. Lewes: *Ranthorpe* (1847)
William M. Thackeray: *The History of Pendennis* (1848–50)
Edward Bulwer Lytton: *The Caxtons* (1849)
Charles Dickens: *David Copperfield* (1849–50)
Charles Kingsley: *Alton Locke* (1850)
William Wordsworth: *The Prelude* (pub. 1850)
Christina Rossetti: *Maude* (wr. 1850, pub. 1897)

1851–1900

George Borrow: *Lavengro* (1851)
Wilkie Collins: *Basil* (1852)

---

[223] Many Victorian novels listed here were found with the help of Bassett 2020. Thanks to Sonia Düwel and Sonja Trurnit for their assistance in compiling this list.

Herman Melville: *Pierre; or, The Ambiguities* (1852)
Edward Bulwer Lytton: *'My Novel' or Varieties in English Life by Pisistratus Caxton* (1853)
Fanny Fern: *Ruth Hall* (1854)
Julia Addison: *Evelyn Lascelles* (1855)
Caroline Clive: *Paul Ferroll* (1855)
Joseph Middleton: *Love versus Law* (1855)
Elizabeth Barrett Browning: *Aurora Leigh* (1856)
Selina Bunbury: *Our Own Story* (1856)
Edward Bulwer Lytton: *What Will He Do With It?* (1858)
Meir Aron Goldschmidt: *Homeless: or, A Poet's Inner Life* (1861; *Hjemløs*, 1853–57)
Mary Elizabeth Braddon: *The Doctor's Wife* (1864)
Fyodor Dostoevsky: *Notes from Underground* (1864)
Annie Thomas: *On Guard* (1865)
Edmund Yates: *Broken to Harness* (1865)
Charlotte Yonge: *The Clever Woman of the Family* (1865)
Anthony Trollope: "The Adventures of Fred Pickering" (1866)
Florence Marryatt: *The Confessions of Gerald Estcourt* (1867)
Edmund Yates: *Black Sheep* (1867)
Louisa May Alcott: *Little Women* (1868)
Catherine Helen Spence: *The Author's Daughter* (1868)
Edward Collins: *The Ivory Gate* (1869)
Ellen Wood: *Roland Yorke* (1869)
Mrs. Alexander Fraser: *Not While She Lives* (1870)
Tom Hood: *Money's Worth* (1870)
Anthony Trollope: *An Editor's Tales* (1870)
Eliza Tabor: *Diary of a Novelist* (1871)
George Eliot: *Middlemarch* (1871–72)
Charles Reade: *A Terrible Temptation* (1871)
Thomas Hardy: *A Pair of Blue Eyes* (1872–1873)
George Barnett Smith: *Alden of Aldenholme* (1873)
Fyodor Dostoevsky: "Bobok" (1873)
Anthony Trollope: *The Way We Live Now* (1874–75)
Mary Hay: *The Squire's Legacy* (1875)
Florence Marryatt: *Fighting the Air* (1875)
Thomas Hardy: *The Hand of Ethelberta* (1876)
James Payn: *Fallen Fortunes* (1876)
Walter Besant and James Rice: *The Golden Butterfly* (1876)
Dora Russell: *Beneath the Wave* (1878)
Elizabeth Owens Blackburne: *Molly Carew* (1879)
Agnes Jane Jack: *Brother and Sister* (1879)
W. Follett Synge: *Tom Singleton* (1879)
Pericles Tzikos: *Paolo Gianini* (1879)
Rhoda Broughton: *Second Thoughts* (1880)
Emily Foster: *An Author's Story, and Other Tales* (1881)
William Hale White: *The Autobiography of Mark Rutherford* (1881)
F. Anstey: *The Giant's Robe* (1883)

Walter Besant: *All in a Garden Fair* (1883)
Charlotte Riddell: *A Struggle for Fame* (1883)
Grant Allen: *Philistia* (1884)
George Gissing: *The Unclassed* (1884)
Henry James: "The Author of 'Beltraffio'" (1884)
David Christie Murray: *The Way of the World* (1884)
Annie Swan: *Ursula Vivian, the Sister Mother* (1884)
Eliza Lynn Linton: *The Autobiography of Christopher Kirkland* (1885)
William Edward Norris: *Adrian Vidal* (1885)
Mary Elizabeth Braddon: *One Thing Needful* (1886)
Wilkie Collins: *The Evil Genius* (1886)
Annie Edwards: *A Playwright's Daughter* (1886)
Octave Mirbeau: *Le Calvaire* (1886)
James Payn: *The Heir of the Ages* (1886)
Frederika Macdonald: *The Flower and the Spirit* (1887)
Sarah Grand: *Ideala* (1888)
H. Rider Haggard: *Mr. Meeson's Will* (1888)
Henry James: "The Aspern Papers" (1888)
Amy Levy: *The Romance of a Shop* (1888)
George Moore: *Confessions of a Young Man* (1888)
Susan Morley: *Dolly Loraine* (1888)
John Walter Sherer: *Helen the Novelist* (1888)
Henrietta Eliza Vaughn Stannard: *Confessions of a Publisher: The Autobiography of Abel Drinkwater* (1888)
Walter Besant: *The Bells of St. Paul's* (1889)
Marie Corelli: *Ardath: The Story of a Dead Self* (1889)
Edna Lyall: *Derrick Vaughan, Novelist* (1889)
Adeline Sergeant: *Esther Denison* (1889)
Eliza Margaret von Booth: *Sheba* (1889)
Oscar Wilde: "The Portrait of Mr. W. H." (1889)
André Gide: *Les cahiers d'André Walter* (1890)
Knut Hamsun: *Sult* (*Hunger*, 1890)
George Gissing: *New Grub Street* (1891)
Rudyard Kipling: "The Finest Story in the World" (1891)
Richard Le Gallienne: *The Book-Bills of Narcissus* (1891)
Henry James: "Greville Fane" (1892)
Henry James: "The Private Life" (1892)
Frederick Leal: *Wynter's Masterpiece* (1892)
Italo Svevo: *A Life* (*Una vita*, 1892)
Israel Zangwill: *Children of the Ghetto* (1892)
Anne Elliott: *The Winning of May* (1893)
Ernest William Hornung: "Author! Author!" (1893)
Ernest William Hornung: "A Literary Coincidence" (1893)
William Dean Howells: *The World of Chance* (1893)
Henry James: "Sir Dominick Ferrand" (1893)
Henry James: "The Middle Years "(1893)
William Edward Norris: *A Deplorable Affair* (1893)

Richard Penderel: *Wilfred Waide, Barrister and Novelist* (1893)
Francis William Lauderdale Adams: *A Child of the Age* (1894)
Rhoda Broughton: *A Beginner* (1894)
Sarah Jeanette Duncan: *A Daughter of To-day* (1894)
Ella Hepworth Dixon: *The Story of a Modern Woman* (1894)
George Gissing: *In the Year of Jubilee* (1894)
Ernest William Hornung: "The Star of the 'Grasmere'" (1894)
Henry James: "The Coxon Fund" (1894)
Henry James: "The Death of the Lion" (1894)
Dorothy Leighton: *Disillusion* (1894)
Thomas Banks Maclachlan: *William Blacklock, Journalist* (1894)
David Christie Murray: *A Rising Star* (1894)
Dora Russell: *A Great Temptation* (1894)
Emily Morse Symonds: *A Modern Amazon* (1894)
Eliza Margaret von Booth: *A Husband of no Importance* (1894)
Grant Allen: *The Woman Who Did* (1895)
Marie Corelli: *The Sorrows of Satan* (1895)
Henry James: "The Next Time" (1895)
Richard Penderel: *A Fleet Street Journalist* (1895)
May Sinclair: "A Study from Life" (1895)
Marie Corelli: *The Murder of Delicia* (1896)
Henry James: "The Figure in the Carpet" (1896)
Norma Octavia Lorimer: *A Sweet Disorder* (1896)
Arthur Machen: *The Hill of Dreams* (wr. 1895–97, pub. 1907)
Louise Mack: *The World is Round* (1896)
Anthony Blake's Experiment (1896)
Leonard Merrick: *Cynthia: A Daughter of the Philistines* (1896)
Mabel Wotton: *Day-Books* (1896)
L. Gladstone: *Neil Macleod: A Tale of Literary Life in London* (1897–1898)
Sarah Grand: *The Beth Book: A Study from the Life of Elizabeth Caldwell Maclure, Woman of Genius* (1897)
Olive P. Rayner [= Grant Allen]: *The Type-Writer Girl* (1897)
Arnold Bennett: *A Man from the North* (1898)
Ellen Thorneycroft Fowler: *Concerning Isabel Carnaby* (1898)
Ernest William Hornung: *Some Persons Unknown* (1898) [collects three earlier tales from 1893–94]
Henry James: "John Delavoy" (1898)
William Le Queux: *Scribes and Pharisees: A Story of Literary London* (1898)
Richard Marsh: "Tom Ossington's Ghost" (1898)
Richard Marsh: "That Five Hundred Pound Prize" (1898)
George Paston [= Emily Morse Symonds]: *A Writer of Books* (1898)
Guy Boothby: *Love Made Manifest* (1899)
Mary Cholmondeley: *Red Pottage* (1899)
Henry James: "The Real Right Thing" (1899)
William Edward Norris: *Giles Ingilby* (1899)
Mary Braddon: *The Infidel* (1900)
Henry Harland: *The Cardinal's Snuff-Box* (1900)
Edith Wharton: "Copy" (1900)

1901–1950

Rudyard Kipling: "Wireless" (1902)
Richard Marsh: "For Debt" (1902)
Samuel Butler: *The Way of All Flesh* (1903)
Henry James: "The Birthplace" (1903)
Thomas Mann: *Tonio Kröger* (1903)
Richard Marsh: *A Duel* (1904)
E. M. Forster: *The Longest Journey* (1907)
Richard Le Gallienne: "The Death of the Poet" (1907)
Jack London: *Martin Eden* (1909)
H. G. Wells: *Tono-Bungay* (1909)
Rainer Maria Rilke: *The Notebooks of Malte Laurids Brigge* (*Aufzeichnungen des Malte Laurids Brigge*, 1910)
May Sinclair: *The Creators* (1910)
Mrs. Wilfrid Ward: *The Job Secretary* (1911)
Algernon Blackwood: "The Whisperers" (1912)
Thomas Mann: *Death in Venice* (*Der Tod in Venedig*, 1912)
Marcel Proust: *Swann's Way* (*Du côté de chez Swann*, 1913)
P. G. Wodehouse: *The Little Nugget* (1913)
Dorothy Richardson: *Pointed Roofs* (1915)
P. G. Wodehouse: *Something Fresh* (1915)
Max Beerbohm: "Enoch Soames" (1916)
James Joyce: *Portrait of the Artist as a Young Man* (1916)
Dorothy Richardson: *Backwater* (1916)
Dorothy Richardson: *Honeycomb* (1917)
P. G. Wodehouse: *Piccadilly Jim* (1917)
Max Beerbohm: "Hilary Maltby and Stephen Braxton" (1919)
Marcel Proust: *In the Shadow of Young Girls in Flower* (*À l'ombre des jeunes filles en fleurs*, 1919)
Dorothy Richardson: *The Tunnel* (1919)
May Sinclair: *Mary Olivier* (1919)
Aldous Huxley: "The Farcical History of Richard Greenow" (1920)
Dorothy Richardson: *Interim* (1920)
Aldous Huxley: *Crome Yellow* (1921)
Marcel Proust: *The Guermantes Way* (*Le côté des Guermantes*, 1920–21)
Dorothy Richardson: *Deadlock* (1921)
W. A. Darlington; *Wishes Limited* (1922)
F. Scott Fitzgerald: *The Beautiful and Damned* (1922)
Aldous Huxley: "Nuns at Luncheon" (1922)
Marcel Proust: *Sodom and Gomorrah* (*Sodome et Gomorrhe*, 1921–22)
Ernest Raymond: *Rossenal* (1922)
Stefan Zweig: *Letter from an Unknown Woman* (1922)
L. M. Montgomery: *Emily of New Moon* (1923)
Marcel Proust: *The Prisoner* (*La Prisonnière*, 1923)
Dorothy Richardson: *Revolving Lights* (1923)
P. G. Wodehouse: *Leave it to Psmith* (1923)
William Caine: *The Author of "Trixie"* (1924)

Ivy Compton-Burnett: *Pastors and Masters* (1925)
André Gide: *The Counterfeiters* (*Les faux-monnayeurs*, 1925)
Helen Hooven Santmyer: *Herbs and Apples* (1925)
Aldous Huxley: *Those Barren Leaves* (1925)
L. M. Montgomery: *Emily Climbs* (1925)
Marcel Proust: *The Fugitive* (*Albertine disparue*, 1925)
Dorothy Richardson: *The Trap* (1925)
Henry Green: *Blindness* (1926)
Max Beerbohm: "Felix Argallo and Walter Ledgett" (1927)
L. M. Montgomery: *Emily's Quest* (1927)
Marcel Proust: *Time Regained* (*Le temps retrouvé*, 1927)
Radclyffe Hall: *The Well of Loneliness* (1928)
Aldous Huxley: *Point Counter Point* (1928)
Rudyard Kipling: "Dayspring Mishandled" (1928)
Dorothy Richardson: *Oberland* (1928)
Virginia Woolf: *Orlando* (1928)
Thomas Wolfe: *Look Homeward, Angel* (1929)
W. S. Maugham: *Cakes and Ale* (1930)
Dorothy Sayers: *Strong Poison* (1930)
Evelyn Waugh: *Vile Bodies* (1930)
N. O. Youmans (Allen Clark Marple): *Best Seller: The Story of a Young Man who Came to New York to Write a Novel about a Young Man who Came to New York to Write a Novel* (1930)
Dorothy Richardson: *Dawn's Left Hand* (1931)
Robert Musil: *The Man Without Qualities* (*Der Mann ohne Eigenschaften*, 1930–43)
Samuel Beckett: *Dream of Fair to Middling Women* (1932, first publ. 1993)
E. F. Benson: *Secret Lives* (1932)
Agatha Christie: *Parker Pyne Investigates* (1932)
Dorothy Sayers: *Have His Carcase* (1932)
Angela Thirkell: *High Rising* (1933)
Gertrude Stein: *The Autobiography of Alice B. Toklas* (1933)
Virginia Woolf: *Flush* (1933)
Storm Jameson: *Company Parade* (1934)
Henry Miller: *Tropic of Cancer* (1934)
Christina Stead: *Seven Poor Men of Sidney* (1934)
Angela Thirkell: *Wild Strawberries* (1934)
Angela Thirkell: *The Demon in the House* (1934)
Storm Jameson: *Love in Winter* (1935)
Dorothy Richardson: *Clear Horizon* (1935)
George Orwell: *Keep the Aspidistra Flying* (1936)
John Cowper Powys: *Maiden Castle* (1936)
Dorothy Sayers: *Gaudy Night* (1936)
Storm Jameson: *None Turn Back* (1936)
Stevie Smith: *Novel on Yellow Paper* (1936)
Angela Thirkell: *August Folly* (1936)
Arthur Calder-Marshall: *Pie in the Sky* (1937)
Ellery Queen: *The Doors Between* (1937)

Dorothy Sayers: *Busman's Honeymoon* (1937)
Gertrude Stein: *Everybody's Autobiography* (1937)
Angela Thirkell: *Summer Half* (1937)
J. R. R. Tolkien: *The Hobbit* (1937)
Lettice Cooper: *National Provincial* (1938)
Lawrence Durrell: *The Black Book* (1938)
Ernest Hemingway: "The Snows of Kilimanjaro" (1938)
Vladimir Nabokov: *The Gift* (1938, English trans. 1961)
Dorothy Richardson: *Dimple Hill* (1938)
Angela Thirkell: *Pomfret Towers* (1938)
Evelyn Waugh: *Scoop* (1938)
John Fante: *Ask the Dust* (1939)
Christopher Isherwood: *Goodbye to Berlin* (1939)
James Joyce: *Finnegans Wake* (1939)
Henry Miller: *Tropic of Capricorn* (1939)
Flann O'Brien: *At Swim-Two-Birds* (1939)
Anthony Powell: *What's Become of Waring* (1939)
Dorothy Sayers: *In the Teeth of the Evidence* (1939)
Angela Thirkell: *The Brandons* (1939)
Thomas Wolfe: *The Web and the Rock* (1939)
Carter Dickson (John Dickson Carr): *And So to Murder* (1940)
L. Ron Hubbard: *Typewriter in the Sky* (1940)
Angela Thirkell: *Before Lunch* (1940)
Angela Thirkell: *Cheerfulness Breaks in* (1940)
Thomas Wolfe: *You Can't Go Home Again* (1940)
Vladimir Nabokov: *The Real Life of Sebastian Knight* (1941)
Angela Thirkell: *Northbridge Rectory* (1941)
Angela Thirkell: *Marling Hall* (1942)
Maud Hart Lovelace: *Betsy and Tacy Go Downtown* (1943)
Angela Thirkell: *Growing Up* (1943)
Roger Lemelin: *Au pied de la Pente Douce* (1944)
W. S. Maugham: *The Razor's Edge* (1944)
Mary Renault: *The Friendly Young Ladies* (1944)
Angela Thirkell: *The Headmistress* (1944)
Jorge Luis Borges: "The Aleph" ("El aleph", 1945)
Hermann Broch: *The Death of Virgil* (*Der Tod des Vergil*, 1945)
Robert Charbonneau: *Fontile* (1945)
Christopher Isherwood: *Prater Violet* (1945)
Storm Jameson: *The Journal of Mary Hervey Russell* (1945)
Elizabeth Smart: *By Grand Central Station I Sat Down and Wept* (1945)
Angela Thirkell: *Miss Bunting* (1945)
Ernest Hemingway: *The Garden of Eden* (1946–1961, publ. posth. 1986)
J. B. Priestley: *Bright Day* (1946)
Angela Thirkell: *Peace Breaks out* (1946)
Storm Jameson: *Before the Crossing* (1947)
Storm Jameson: *The Black Laurel* (1947)

Julian Maclaren-Ross: *Of Love and Hunger* (1947)
Alberto Moravia: *Conjugal Love* (*L'amore conjugale*, 1947)
J. B. Priestley: *Jenny Villiers* (1947)
Elizabeth Taylor: *A View of the Harbour* (1947)
Angela Thirkell: *Private Enterprise* (1947)
Angela Thirkell: *Love Among the Ruins* (1948)
Hans Henny Jahnn: *The Ship* (*Das Holzschiff*, 1949)
George Orwell: *Nineteen Eighty-Four* (1949)
Dodie Smith: *I Capture the Castle* (1949)
Angela Thirkell: *The Old Bank House* (1949)
Mika Waltari: *A Nail Merchant at Nightfall* (*Neljä päivänlaskua*, 1949)
Georges Bernanos: *Night is Darkest* (*Un mauvais rêve*, 1950)
Robert Élie: *La fin des songes* (1950)
Diana Gardner: "The Woman Novelist" (1950)
Hans Henny Jahnn: *Die Niederschrift des Gustav Anias Horn* (1950)
Angela Thirkell: *County Chronicle* (1950)
Roland Camberton: *Scamp* (1950)
Stanley G. Weinbaum: *The Dark Other* (1950)

1951 – 2000

Samuel Beckett: *Molloy* and *Malone Dies* (1951)
Roland Camberton: *Rain on the Pavements* (1951)
Graham Greene: *The End of the Affair* (1951)
Anthony Powell: *A Question of Upbringing* (1951)
Muriel Spark: "The Seraph and the Zambezi" (1951)
Angela Thirkell: *The Duke's Daughter* (1951)
Anthony Powell: *A Buyer's Market* (1952)
Muriel Spark: "The House of the Famous Poet" (1952)
Angela Thirkell: *Happy Returns* (1952)
Angus Wilson: *Hemlock and After* (1952)
Angela Thirkell: *Jutland Cottage* (1953)
Valerie Baxter [i.e. Laurence Meynell]: *Jane: Young Author* (1954)
Ernest Buckler: *The Mountain and the Valley* (1954)
Iris Murdoch: *Under the Net* (1954)
Angela Thirkell: *What Did It Mean?* (1954)
J. R. R. Tolkien: *The Lord of the Rings* (1954)
J. R. R. Tolkien: *The Two Towers* (1954)
Anthony Powell: *The Acceptance World* (1955)
Barbara Pym: *Less than Angels* (1955)
Louis-Ferdinand Céline: *Conversations with Professor Y* (*Entretiens avec le professeur Y*, 1954)
Gabrielle Roy: *Street of Riches* (*Rue Deschambault*, 1955)
Angela Thirkell: *Enter Sir Robert* (1955)
J. R. R. Tolkien: *The Return of the King* (1955)
Kathleen Farrell: *The Cost of Living* (1956)

Appendix 1: An Incomplete List of Authorship Narratives, 1800–2022 — 393

Jean Simard: *Mon fils pourtant heureux* (1956)
Angela Thirkell: *Never Too Late* (1956)
Lawrence Durrell: *Justine* (1957)
Georgette Heyer: *Sylvester, or the Wicked Uncle* (1957)
Jack Kerouac: *On the Road* (1957)
Anthony Powell: *At Lady Molly's* (1957)
Mordecai Richler: *A Choice of Enemies* (1957)
Muriel Spark: *The Comforters* (1957)
Elizabeth Taylor: *Angel* (1957)
Angela Thirkell: *A Double Affair* (1957)
Evelyn Waugh: *The Ordeal of Gilbert Pinfold* (1957)
Kingsley Amis: *I Like it Here* (1958)
Lawrence Durrell: *Balthazar* (1958)
Lawrence Durrell: *Mountolive* (1958)
James Jones: *Some Came Running* (1958)
Muriel Spark: "The Portobello Road" (1958)
Angela Thirkell: *Close Quarters* (1958)
Alberto Arbasino: *L'Anonimo lombardo* (1959)
Julio Cortázar: "Blow-Up" ("Las babas del diablo", 1959)
Pamela Hansford Johnson: *The Unspeakable Skipton* (1959)
Grace Metalious: *Return to Peyton Place* (1959)
Angela Thirkell: *Love at All Ages* (1959)
John Barth: *The Sot-Weed Factor* (1960)
Jorge Luis Borges: *Borges and I* (*Borges y Yo*, 1960)
Lawrence Durrell: *Clea* (1960)
Anthony Powell: *Casanova's Chinese Restaurant* (1960)
Murō Saisei: *Fish of the Fire* (*Hi no Sakana*, 1960)
Muriel Spark: "The Father's Daughters" (1961)
Angela Thirkell: *Three Score and Ten* (1961)
Colin Wilson: *Adrift in Soho* (1961)
James Baldwin: *Another Country* (1962)
Émile-Charles Hamel: *Prix David* (1962)
Christopher Isherwood: *Down There on a Visit* (1962)
Doris Lessing: *The Golden Notebook* (1962)
Brian Moore: *An Answer from Limbo* (1962)
Vladimir Nabokov: *Pale Fire* (1962)
Anthony Powell: *The Kindly Ones* (1962)
Herman Wouk: *Youngblood Hawke* (1962)
Anthony Burgess: *Inside Mr Enderby* (1963)
Julio Cortázar: *Hopscotch* (*Rayuela*, 1963)
Sylvia Plath: *The Bell Jar* (1963)
Muriel Spark: *The Girls of Slender Means* (1963)
Elliott Baker: *A Fine Madness* (1964)
Saul Bellow: *Herzog* (1964)
A. S. Byatt: *The Shadow of the Sun* (1964)
Anthony Powell: *The Valley of Bones* (1964)

Patricia Highsmith: *A Suspension of Mercy* (1965)
Kurt Vonnegut: *God Bless You, Mr. Rosewater* (1965)
Nigel Balchin: *In the Absence of Mrs. Petersen* (1966)
Joseph McElroy: *A Smuggler's Bible* (1966)
Anthony Powell: *The Soldier's Act* (1966)
Macedonio Fernández: *The Museum of Eterna's Novel* (*Museo de la novela de la eterna*, 1967)
John Barth: "Anonymiad" (*Lost in the Funhouse*, 1968)
Anthony Burgess: *Enderby Outside* (1968)
Norman Mailer: *The Armies of the Night* (1968)
Julian Mitchell: *The Undiscovered Country* (1968)
Anthony Powell: *The Military Philosophers* (1968)
Mary Stewart: *The Wind Off the Small Isles* (1968)
Margaret Drabble: *The Waterfall* (1969)
Patricia Highsmith: *The Tremor of Forgery* (1969)
Kurt Vonnegut: *Slaughterhouse Five* (1969)
Brian Moore: *Fergus* (1970)
John Updike: *Bech: A Book* (1970)
Bernard Malamud: *The Tenants* (1971)
Anthony Powell: *Books Do Furnish a Room* (1971)
Paul Theroux: *Jungle Lovers* (1971)
David Ireland: *The Flesheaters* (1972)
Steven Millhauser: *Edwin Mullhouse* (1972)
Erica Jong: *Fear of Flying* (1973)
Iris Murdoch: *The Black Prince* (1973)
Anthony Powell: *Temporary Kings* (1973)
Peter Van Greenaway: *The Medusa Touch* (1973)
Kurt Vonnegut: *Breakfast of Champions* (1973)
Anthony Burgess: *The Clockwork Testament, or Enderby's End* (1974)
Raymond Carver: "Put Yourself in My Shoes" (*Will You Please Be Quiet Please?*, 1974)
Lawrence Durrell: *Monsieur* (1974)
Iain Crichton Smith: *Goodbye Mr Dixon* (1974)
Russell Hoban: *Kleinzeit* (1974)
John Irving: *The 158-Pound Marriage* (1974)
Margaret Laurence: *The Diviners* (1974)
Alice Munro: "Material" (*Something I've been Meaning to Tell You*, 1974)
J. I. M. Stewart: *The Gaudy* (1974)
Malcolm Bradbury: *The History Man* (1975)
Richard Brautigan: *Sombrero Fallout* (1975)
Anthony Powell: *Hearing Secret Harmonies* (1975)
J. I. M. Stewart: *Young Pattullo* (1975)
Ajar (Romain Gary): *Hocus Bogus* (*Pseudo*, 1976)
Margaret Atwood: *Lady Oracle* (1976)
Nicolas Born: *Die erdabgewandte Seite der Geschichte* (1976)
J. I. M. Stewart: *A Memorial Service* (1976)
Anthony Burgess: *ABBA ABBA* (1977)
Serge Doubrovsky: *Fils* (1977)

Stephen King: *The Shining* (1977)
Mario Vargas Llosa: *Aunt Julia and the Scriptwriter* (*La tía Julia y el escribidor*, 1977)
J. I. M. Stewart: *The Madonna of the Astrolabe* (1977)
Nigel Williams: *My Life Closed Twice* (1977)
A. S. Byatt: *The Virgin in the Garden* (1978)
Lawrence Durrell: *Livia* (1978)
John Irving: *The World According to Garp* (1978)
David Malouf: *An Imaginary Life* (1978)
Iris Murdoch: *The Sea, the Sea* (1978)
Isaac Bashevis Singer: *Shosha* (1978)
J. I. M. Stewart: *Full Term* (1978)
John Barth: *Letters* (1979)
Italo Calvino: *If ona Winter's Night a Traveler* (*Se una notte d'inverno un viaggiatore*, 1979)
Bernard Malamud: *Dubin's Lives* (1979)
Deborah Moggach: *Close to Home* (1979)
Jean-Benoît Puech: *La bibliothèque d'un amateur* (1979)
Philip Roth: *The Ghost Writer* (1979)
William Styron: *Sophie's Choice* (1979)
Kurt Vonnegut: *Jailbird* (1979)
John Gardner: *Freddy's Book* (1980)
Mordecai Richler: *Joshua Then and Now* (1980)
Jane Rule: *Contract with the World* (1980)
Michel Déon: *Where Are You Dying Tonight?* (*Un déjeuner de soleil*, 1981)
José Donoso: *The Garden Next Door* (*El jardín de al lado*, 1981)
Timothy Findley: *Famous Last Words* (1981)
Maggie Gee: *Dying, in Other Words* (1981)
Jennifer Johnston: *The Christmas Tree* (1981)
Philip Roth: *Zuckerman Unbound* (1981)
Muriel Spark: *Loitering with Intent* (1981)
Alexander Theroux: *Darconville's Cat* (1981)
Reinaldo Arenas: *Farewell to the Sea* (*Otra vez el mar*, 1982)
John Banville: *The Newton Letter* (1982)
Lawrence Durrell: *Constance* (1982)
John Fowles: *Mantissa* (1982)
John Updike: *Bech is Back* (1982)
Peter Ackroyd: *The Last Testament of Oscar Wilde* (1983)
Anita Brookner: *Look at Me* (1983)
Maureen Duffy: *Londoners: An Elegy* (1983)
Lawrence Durrell: *Sebastian* (1983)
William Golding: *The Paper Men* (1983)
Stephen King: "Word Processor of the Gods" (1983)
Philip Roth: *The Anatomy Lesson* (1983)
Muriel Spark: "The Executor" (1983)
Fay Weldon: *The Life and Loves of a She-Devil* (1983)
Julian Barnes: *Flaubert's Parrot* (1984)
Roberto Bolaño: *The Spirit of Science Fiction* (*El espíritu de la ciencia-ficción*, c. 1984, publ. 2018)

Anita Brookner: *Hotel du Lac* (1984)
Anthony Burgess: *Enderby's Dark Lady, or No End to Enderby* (1984)
Anita Desai: *In Custody* (1984)
Joan Didion: *Democracy* (1984)
Penelope Lively: *According to Mark* (1984)
Alison Lurie: *Foreign Affairs* (1984)
Wilbur Smith: *The Leopard Hunts in Darkness* (1984)
Paul Auster: *City of Glass* (1985)
A. S. Byatt: *Still Life* (1985)
Lawrence Durrell: *Quinx* (1985)
Lorrie Moore: "How to Become a Writer" (*Self-Help*, 1985)
Philip Roth: *The Prague Orgy* (1985)
Magda Szabó: *The Door* (*Az ajtó*, 1985)
Anne Tyler: *The Accidental Tourist* (1985)
Paul Auster: *Ghosts* (1986)
Paul Auster: *The Locked Room* (1986)
Raymond Carver: "Intimacy" (1986)
J. M. Coetzee: *Foe* (1986)
Richard Ford: *The Sportswriter* (1986)
Philip Roth: *The Counterlife* (1986)
Vikram Seth: *The Golden Gate* (1986)
Peter Ackroyd: *Chatterton* (1987)
John Barth: *The Tidewater Tales* (1987)
Bret Easton Ellis: *The Rules of Attraction* (1987)
Russell Hoban: *The Medusa Frequency* (1987)
Stephen King: *Misery* (1987)
Ian McEwan: *The Child in Time* (1987)
Stephen Marlowe: *The Memoirs of Christopher Columbus* (1987)
Michèle Roberts: *The Book of Mrs Noah* (1987)
Carol Shields: *Swann: A Mystery* (1987)
Mario Vargas Llosa: *The Storyteller* (*El hablador*, 1987)
Bernard-Henri Lévy: *Les derniers jours de Charles Baudelaire* (1988)
Amin Maalouf: *Samarkand* (*Samarcande*, 1988)
Philip Roth: *The Facts* (1998)
Mary Wesley: *Second Fiddle* (1988)
Martin Amis: *London Fields* (1989)
Michael Frayn: *The Trick of It* (1989)
Stephen King: *The Dark Half* (1989)
Muriel Spark: "Open to the Public" (1989)
Paul Theroux: *My Secret History* (1989)
A. S. Byatt: *Possession* (1990)
Stephen King: "Secret Window, Secret Garden" (1990)[224]
Jay Parini: *The Last Station* (1990)
Philip Roth: *Deception* (1990)

---

[224] Later works by Stephen King have not been included in this list.

Appendix 1: An Incomplete List of Authorship Narratives, 1800 – 2022 — **397**

Don DeLillo: *Mao II* (1991)
Alan Judd: *The Devil's Own Work* (1991)
F. Springer: *Teheran, een zwanezang* (1991)
Antonio Tabucchi: *Requiem: A Hallucination* (*Requiem: uma alucinaçao*, 1991)
Gilbert Adair: *The Death of the Author* (1992)
Leon Forrest: *Divine Days* (1992)
Robert Grudin: *Book: A Novel* (1992)
Amélie Nothomb: *Hygiène de l'assassin* (1992)
Antonio Tabucchi: *Dreams of Dreams* (*Sogni di sogni*, 1992)
Ben Elton: *This Other Eden* (1993)
Philip Roth: *Operation Shylock* (1993)
Vikram Seth: *A Suitable Boy* (1993)
Austin Wright: *Tony & Susan* (1993)
Antonio Tabucchi: *The Last Three Days of Fernando Pessoa* (*Gli ultimi tre giorni di Fernando Pessoa*, 1994)
Antonio Tabucchi: *Pereira Maintains* (*Sostiene Pereira*, 1994)
Fernando Vallejo: *Our Lady of the Assassins* (*La virgen de los sicarios*, 1994)
Martin Amis: *The Information* (1995)
Michael Chabon: *Wonder Boys* (1995)
Lydia Davis: *The End of the Story* (1995)
Penelope Fitzgerald: *The Blue Flower* (1995)
Richard Ford: *Independence Day* (1995)
David Lodge: *Therapy* (1995)
Vanna Bonta: *Flight* (1995)
Richard Powers: *Galatea 2.2* (1995)
Gerhard Roth: *Der See* (1995)
Roberto Bolaño: *Nazi Literature in the Americas* (*La literatura nazi en América*, 1996)
A. S. Byatt: *Babel Tower* (1996)
Andrei Kurkov: *Death and the Penguin* (1996, English trans. 2001)
Mark Laidlaw: *The 37th Mandala* (1996)
Muriel Spark: "Harper and Wilton" (rev. version, 1996)
J. M. Coetzee: *Boyhood* (1997)
Geoff Dyer: *Out of Sheer Rage* (1997)
Chris Kraus: *I Love Dick* (1997)
Philip Roth: *American Pastoral* (1997)
Kurt Vonnegut: *Timequake* (1997)
Douglas Cooper: *Delirium* (1998)
Michael Cunningham: *The Hours* (1998)
Peter Farrelly: *The Comedy Writer* (1998)
John Irving: *A Widow for One Year* (1998)
Jill Paton Walsh: *Thrones, Dominations* (1998)
Gerhard Roth: *Der Plan* (1998)
Philip Roth: *I Married a Communist* (1998)
John Updike: *Bech at Bay* (1998)
Barbara Vine: *The Chimney Sweeper's Boy* (1998)
Gilbert Adair: *A Closed Book* (1999)

Roberto Bolaño: *Amulet* (*Amuleto*, 1999)
Elizabeth Jane Howard: *Falling* (1999)
A. L. Kennedy: *Everything You Need* (1999)
David Lodge: *Home Truths* (1999)
Wei Hui: *Shanghai Baby* (1999)
Kate Atkinson: *Emotionally Weird* (2000)
Margaret Atwood: *The Blind Assassin* (2000)
Terence Blacker: *Kill Your Darlings* (2000)
Roberto Bolaño: *Nocturno de Chile* (*By Night in Chile*, 2000)
Helen De Witt: *The Last Samurai* (2000)
Dave Eggers: *A Heartbreaking Work of Staggering Genius* (2000)
Joanne Harris: *Blackberry Wine* (2000)
Joseph Heller: *Portrait of an Artist, as an Old Man* (2000)
Gerhard Roth: *Der Berg* (2000)
Philip Roth: *The Human Stain* (2000)
Enrique Vila-Matas: *Bartleby & Company* (*Bartleby y compañía*, 2000)

2001 – 2022

A. S. Byatt: *The Biographer's Tale* (2001)
John Colapinto: *About the Author* (2001)
Percival Everett: *Erasure* (2001)
Jonathan Franzen: *The Corrections* (2001)
F. Sionil José: *Ben Singkol* (2001)
Yasmina Khadra: *L'écrivain* (2001)
Ian McEwan: *Atonement* (2001)
Amy Tan: *The Bonesetter's Daughter* (2001)
Kim Wilkins: *Angel of Ruin* (2001)
Carlos Ruiz Zafón: *The Shadow of the Wind* (*La sombra del viento*) (2001)
Paul Auster: *The Book of Illusions* (2002)
William Boyd: *Any Human Heart* (2002)
A. S. Byatt: *A Whistling Woman* (2002)
J. M. Coetzee: *Youth* (2002)
Jonathan Safran Foer: *Everything is Illuminated* (2002)
Yasmina Khadra: *L'imposture des mots* (2002)
Orhan Pamuk: *Snow* (*Kar*, 2002)
Jill Paton Walsh: *A Presumption of Death* (2002)
Gerhard Roth: *Der Strom* (2002)
Carol Shields: *Unless* (2002)
Paul Auster: *Oracle Night* (2003)
Frédéric Beigbeder: *Windows on the World* (2003)
J. M. Coetzee: *Elizabeth Costello* (2003)
Glen Duncan: *I, Lucifer* (2003)
Daniel Kehlmann: *Ich und Kaminski* (*Me and Kaminski*, 2003)
Paul Murray: *An Evening of Long Goodbyes* (2003)

Peter Straub: *Lost Boy, Lost Girl* (2003)
Jonathan Tropper: *The Book of Joe* (2003)
Monique Truong: *The Book of Salt* (2003)
Meg Wolitzer: *The Wife* (2003)
Roberto Bolaño: *2666* (2004)
Dean Koontz: *The Taking* (2004)
David Leavitt: *The Body of Jonah Boyd* (2004)
David Lodge: *Author, Author* (2004)
Gerhard Roth: *Das Labyrinth* (2004)
Muriel Spark: *The Finishing School* (2004)
Peter Straub: *In the Night Room* (2004)
Colm Toibín: *The Master* (2004)
Julian Barnes: *Arthur and George* (2005)
Bret Easton Ellis: *Lunar Park* (2005)
Wei Hui: *Marrying Buddha* (2005)
Nicole Krauss: *The History of Love* (2005)
China Miéville: "Reports of Certain Events in London" (*Looking for Jake and Other Stories*, 2005)
Kebir Ammi: *Apulée, mon éditrice et moi* (2006)
Emma Donogue, "Speaking in Tongues" (2006)
Richard Ford: The Lay of the Land (2006)
Wolf Haas: *Das Wetter vor 15 Jahren* (2006)
Donald Tyson: *Alhazred* (2006)
Will Self: *The Book of Dave* (2006)
Walter Siti: *Troppi paradisi* (2006)
J. M. Coetzee: *Diary of a Bad Year* (2007)
M. Allen Cunningham: *Lost Son* (2007)
Samuel R. Delaney: *Dark Reflections* (2007)
Assia Djebar: *Nulle part dans la maison de mon père* (2007)
Thomas Glavinic: *Das bin doch ich* (2007)
Robert Harris: *The Ghost* (2007)
Elfriede Jelinek: *Neid* (2007)
Claire Keegan: "The Long and Painful Death" (*Walk the Blue Fields*, 2007)
David Markson: *The Last Novel* (2007)
Walter Moers: *The City of Dreaming Books* (*Die Stadt der träumenden Bücher*, 2007)
Gerhard Roth: *Das Alphabet der Zeit* (2007)
Philip Roth: *Exit Ghost* (2007)
Andrew Foster Altschul: *Lady Lazarus* (2008)
Paul Auster: *Travels in the Scriptorium* (2008)
Mark Budman: *My Life at First Try* (2008)
Candace Bushnell: *One Fifth Avenue* (2008)
Peter Handke: *The Moravian Night* (*Die morawische Nacht*, 2008)
Andrew Miller: *One Morning Like a Bird* (2008)
Miguel Syjuco: *Ilustrado* (2008)
Gary Victor: *Banal oubli* (2008)
Carlos Ruiz Zafón: *The Angel's Game* (*El juego del ángel*, 2008)
Chimamanda Ngozi Adichie: "Jumping Monkey Hill" (2009)

Nicholson Baker: *The Anthologist* (2009)
A. S. Byatt: *The Children's Book* (2009)
J. M. Coetzee: *Summertime* (2009)
Dominick Dunne: *Too Much Money* (2009)
Dean Koontz: *Relentless* (2009)
Steve Heli: *How I Became a Famous Novelist* (2009)
Daniel Kehlmann: *Ruhm* (*Fame*, 2009)
Clare Kilroy, *All Names Have Been Changed* (2009)
Barbara Kingsolver: *The Lacuna* (2009)
Karl Ove Knausgård: *A Death in the Family: My Struggle Book 1* (*Min kamp, Første bok*, 2009)
Karl Ove Knausgård: *A Man in Love: My Struggle Book 2* (*Min kamp, Andre bok*, 2009)
Karl Ove Knausgård: *Boyhood Island: My Struggle Book 3* (*Min kamp, Tredje bok*, 2009)
Haruki Murakami: *1Q84* (2009–10)
Kenzaburō Ōe: *Death by Water* (2009, English trans 2015)
Dan Simmons: *Drood* (2009)
Gerhard Roth: *Die Stadt. Entdeckungen im Inneren von Wien* (2009)
Michel Houellebecq: *La carte et le territoire* (2010)
Karl Ove Knausgård: *Dancing in the Dark: My Struggle Book 4* (*Min kamp, Fjerde bok*, 2010)
Karl Ove Knausgård: *Some Rain Must Fall: My Struggle Book 5* (*Min kamp, Femte bok*, 2010)
Nicole Krauss: *Great House* (2010)
Yann Martel: *Beatrice and Virgil* (2010)
Jay Parini: *The Passages of H. M.* (2010)
Jill Paton Walsh: *The Attenbury Emeralds* (2010)
Alessandro Baricco: *Mr Gwyn* (2011)
Elena Ferrante: *My Brilliant Friend* (*L'amica genial*, 2011)
Siri Hustvedt: *The Summer Without Men* (2011)
Karl Ove Knausgård: *The End: My Struggle Book 6* (*Min kamp, Sjette bok*, 2011)
Ben Lerner: *Leaving the Atocha Station* (2011)
David Lodge: *A Man of Parts* (2011)
Arthur Phillips: *The Tragedy of Arthur* (2011)
Deborah Levy: *Swimming Home* (2011)
Helen Oyeyemi: *Mr Fox* (2011)
Gerhard Roth: *Orkus. Reise zu den Toten* (2011)
Carlos Ruiz Zafón: *The Prisoner of Heaven* (*El prisoner del Cielo*) (2011)
Joël Dicker: *The Truth about the Harry Quebert Affair* (*La vérité sur l'affaire Harry Quebert*, 2012)
Elena Ferrante: *The Story of a New Name* (*Storia del nuovo cognomen*, 2012)
Wolf Haas: *Verteidigung der Missionarsstellung* (2012)
Felicitas Hoppe: *Hoppe* (2012)
Howard Jacobson: *Zoo Time* (2012)
Keith Ridgway: "The Spectacular" (2012)
Chimamanda Ngozi Adichie: *Americanah* (2013)
Percival Everett: *Percival Everett by Virgil Russell* (2013)
Elena Ferrante: *Those Who Leave and Those Who Stay* (*Storia di chi fugge e di chi resta*, 2013)
Richard Ford: *Let Me Be Frank With You* (2014)
Sheila Heti: *How Should a Person Be?* (2013)
Tao Lin: *Taipei* (2013)

Ruth Ozeki: *A Tale for the Time Being* (2013)
Jill Paton Walsh: *The Late Scholar* (2013)
Rachel Cusk: *Outline* (2014)
Ben Lerner: *10:04* (2014)
Ann-Marie MacDonald: *Adult Onset* (2014)
Paul Ewen: *Francis Plug: How to be a Public Author* (2014)
Elena Ferrante: *The Story of the Lost Child* (*Storia della bambina perduta*, 2014)
Julie Schumacher: *Dear Committee Members* (2014)
Edward St. Aubyn: *Lost for Words* (2014)
C. D. Rose: *The Biographical Dictionary of Literary Failure* (2014)
Marlene Streeruwitz: *Nachkommen* (2014)
Candace Bushnell: *Killing Monica* (2015)
Joshua Cohen: *Book of Numbers* (2015)
Gerhard Henschel: *Künstlerroman* (2015)
John Irving: *Avenue of Mysteries* (2015)
Klaus Modick: *Bestseller* (2015)
Joyce Carol Oates: *Jack of Spades* (2015)
Jonathan Galassi: *Muse* (2015)
Liz Fenton and Lisa Steinke: *The Year We Turned Forty* (2016)
Ian McEwan: "My Purple Scented Novel" (2016)
Nuala O'Connor: *Miss Emily* (2015)
Adam O'Fallon Price: *The Grand Tour* (2016)
Ann Patchett: *Commonwealth* (2016)
Suzanne Rindell: *Three-Martini Lunch* (2016)
Graham Swift: *Mothering Sunday* (2016)
Carlos Ruiz Zafón: *The Labyrinth of Spirits* (*El laberinto de los espíritus*) (2016)
Paul Auster: *4 3 2 1* (2017)
Rachel Cusk: *Transit* (2017)
Andrew Sean Greer: *Less* (2017)
Nicole Krauss: *Forest Dark* (2017)
Sally Rooney: *Conversations with Friend* (2017)
C. D. Rose: *Who's Who When Everyone is Someone Else* (2017)
Jeet Thayil: *The Book of Chocolate Saints* (2017)
John Boyne: *A Ladder to the Sky* (2018)
Rachel Cusk: *Kudos* (2018)
Karen Duve: *Fräulein Nettes kurzer Sommer* (2018)
Mark Edwards: *The Retreat* (2018)
Lisa Halliday: *Asymmetry* (2018)
Colleen Hoover: *Verity* (2018)
Sigrid Nunez: *The Friend* (2018)
Melatu Uche Okorie: *This Hostel Life* (2018)
Sally Rooney: *Normal People* (2018)
Mona Awad: *Bunny* (2019)
Laura Beatty: *Lost Property* (2019)
Mary Costello: *The River Capture* (2019)
Gertraud Klemm: *Hippocampus* (2019)

Salman Rushdie: *Quichotte* (2019)
Ayad Akhtar: *Homeland Elegies* (2020)
William Boyd: *Trio* (2020)
Susanna Clarke: Piranesi (2020)
Garth Greenwell: *Cleanness* (2020)
Emily Henry: *Beach Read* (2020)
Lily King: *Writers & Lovers* (2020)
Stephen King: "Rat" (2020)
Hari Kunzru: *Red Pill* (2020)
Hervé Le Tellier: *The Anomaly* (*L'Anomalie*, 2020)
Emily Segal: *Mercury Retrograde* (2020)
Chelsea G. Summers: *A Certain Hunger* (2020)
Claire-Louise Bennett: *Checkout 19* (2021)
Rachel Cusk: *Second Place* (2021)
Jean Hanff Korelitz: *The Plot* (2021)
David Laskin: *What Sammy Knew* (2021)
Patricia Lockwood: *No One is Talking About This* (2021)
Alison Moore: *The Retreat* (2021)
Chris Power: *A Lonely Man* (2021)
Sally Rooney: *Beautiful World, Where Are You?* (2021)
Mohamed Mbougar Sarr: *La plus secrète mémoire des hommes* (2021)
Colm Toibín: *The Magician* (2021)
Ruth Ozeki, *The Book of Form and Emptiness* (2021)
Sam Riviere: *Dead Souls* (2021)
Gary Shteyngart: *Our Country Friends* (2021)
Carlos Ruiz Zafón: *The City of Mist* (*La ciudad de vapor*) (2021)
Caitlin Barasch: *A Novel Obsession* (2022)
Kenny Boyle: *The Tick and the Tock of the Crocodile Clock* (2022)
Jordan Castro: *The Novelist* (2022)
Amit Chaudhuri: *Sojourn* (2022)
Lee Cole: *Groundskeeping* (2022)
Sean Thor Conroe: *Fuccboi* (2022)
John Darnielle: *Devil House* (2022)
Nina de Gramont: *The Christie Affair* (2022)
Hernan Diaz: *Trust* (2022)
David Guterson: *The Final Case* (2022)
Lauren Kate: *By Any Other Name* (2022)
Andrew Lipstein: *Last Resort* (2022)
Ian McEwan: *Lessons* (2022)
Julie Myerson: *Nonfiction* (2022)
Gunnhild Øyehaug: *Present Tense Machine* (2022)
Elissa Soave: *Ginger and Me* (2022)

Appendix 2: Quantitative Survey, 1800–2022

Based on the list provided in appendix 1, these diagrams show the quantitative development of works of author fiction from the early nineteenth century to the present.

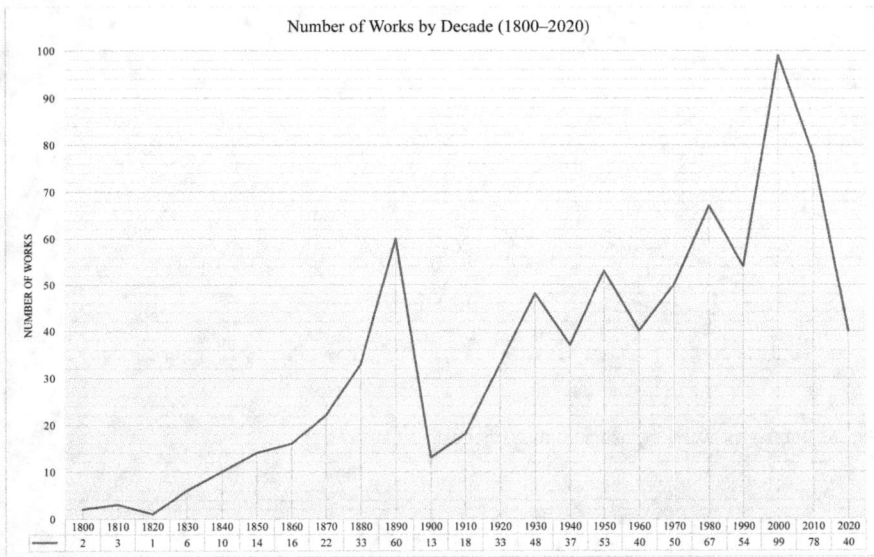

Fig. 5: Number of works by decade (1800–2020)

https://doi.org/10.1515/9783111056166-021

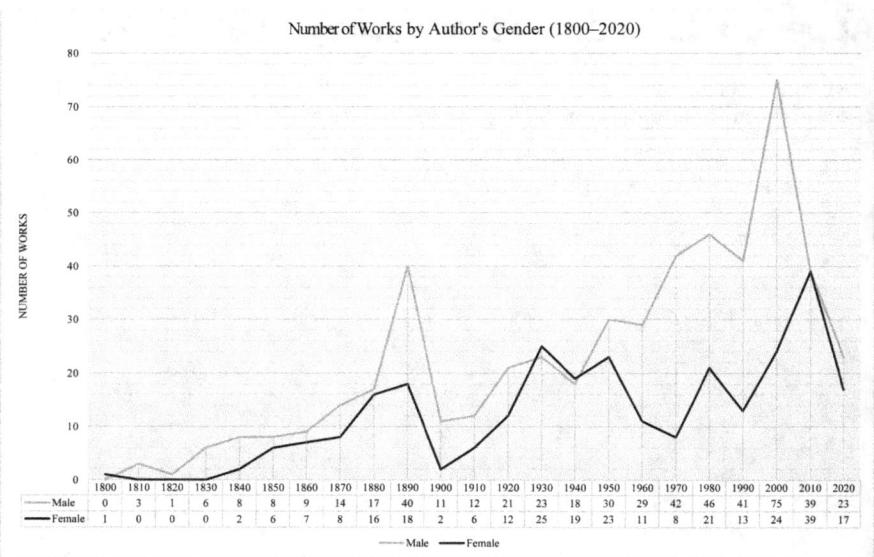

Fig. 6: Number of works by actual author's gender

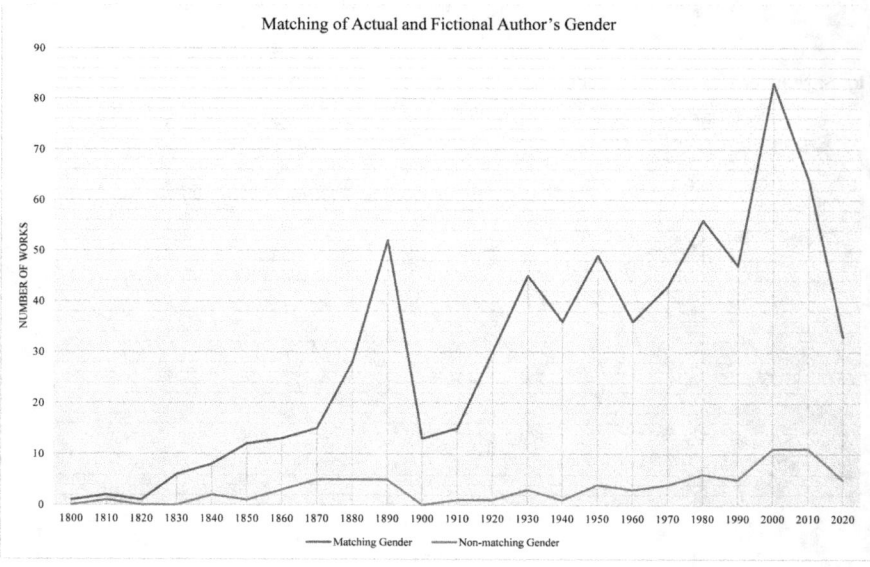

Fig. 7: Matching of actual and fictional author's gender

List of Illustrations and Tables

Fig. 1: The authorpoietic loop —— 6
Fig. 2: Acts, concepts, and models of literary authorship —— 30
Fig. 3: Constants in literary communication —— 65
Fig. 4: The interactional loop between author, work, and audience —— 76
Fig. 5: Number of works by decade (1800–2020) —— 403
Fig. 6: Number of works by actual author's gender —— 404
Fig. 7: Matching of actual and fictional author's gender —— 404

Table 1: Authorship paradigms and emergent genres or modes of 'author fiction' —— 10
Table 2: Taxonomy of author concepts —— 28
Table 3: Scale of authorship concepts —— 29

Glossary

allopoetic: vector that connects a (completed) work to its author; non-textual (social) aspect of author formation via the work's reception by audiences, confirming or disconfirming an author's (self-)image; effect or force that results in *hexis* (attribution) or *paraclisis* (transformation/deformation)

anaclisis: attachment of an abstract author fiction to textual phenomena or narrative resources, e.g., an 'authorial narrator' who comes to stand in for (a version of) the actual author; as *autopoetic anaclisis*, the (intentional) attachment or grafting of actual authors to their texts; as *heteropoetic anaclisis*, textual anticipation (or rhetorical priming) of audience response to the work and its author

author fiction: 1) literary works that engage with ideas and practices, meanings and values of literary authorship
2) abstract concept and performative expression of literary authorship, realised within the rhetorical conventions, social forms, and media infrastructures of the literary field, expressed and reflected in works of author fiction (1); an idea of how a particular literary work's performance of authorship relates to or is informed by the set of historically available concepts of authorship

authorpoiesis: author-making; self-creation of authors through their work, i.e., the reflexive and performative construction of a relational space that encompasses and includes (both fictional and real) authors, through the interaction of authors, works, and audiences, as visualised in the authorpoietic loop (fig. 5) – a dynamic process that combines social and textual dimensions

autopoetic: vector that connects an author to his or her work; textual (including paratextual) signals, writerly strategies, and other resources that authors use to perform, confirm, or invalidate models of authorship in the process of authorial self-formation; the more strictly authorial dimension in the process of *authorpoiesis*

cataclisis: placement, anticipation, or priming of an audience in relation to work and author by means of *heteropoetic* textual signals

cathexis: an audience's response or attachment to a work; cognitive, affective, and ethical engagement of audiences with fictional entities; *homopoetic* assimilation of the work and projection of an author image by an audience based on *auto-* and *heteropoetic* signals, expectations, and conventions

heteropoetic: vector that connects a work to its audience; textual signals, writerly strategies, and other resources that authors use to anticipate or position an audience in relation to the work and its author

hexis: the attribution of an aptitude, quality, ability, or prestige etc., which authors acquire by means of audience responses; the *allopoetic* formation of an author by the work and its reception (beyond the author's control)

homopoetic: vector that connects an audience to a work; non-textual (social) aspect of audience engagement with a work and its author, usually taking the form of assimilation, appropriation, attachment, or projection (*cathexis*); the effect of such assimilation or projection upon the work's reception

paraclisis: the *allopoetic* transformation or deformation that occurs when the work changes its author in (for the author) unwelcome ways

Acknowledgements

This book would not have been written, at least not so soon, without the stimulus and time provided by an *Opus magnum* grant from the Volkswagen Foundation in 2021 and 2022. I am particularly indebted to Joanna Rostek, who took over my teaching duties for three semesters as part of this generous grant, and whose own research on literature and economics yielded much additional food for thought. I am also grateful to my team at LMU Munich for discussing parts of this book as it was being written: Gero Guttzeit, Georgina Nugent, and Daniel Schneider. I would also like to thank Dorothee Birke, Gert Buelens, and Ludwig Pfeiffer for their valuable comments on some chapters, and Renate Schruff for her perceptive and careful reading of large parts of the penultimate draft. Sonja Trurnit and Sonia Düwel helped to gather and process data for the appendices, kept track of references, and prepared the index for this book. David Trotter pointed me to E. M. Forster's *The Longest Journey* at just the right moment. For stimulating conversations and exchanges over the years, I would like to thank Thomas Austenfeld, Yuri Cowan, Marysa Demoor, Tobias Döring, Christoph Ehland, Johannes Frimmel, Andrew Hadfield, Christine Haug, Andreas Höfele, Leonie Kappus, Andreas Mahler, Maria Mäkelä, Leo Mellor, Kai Merten, Helge Nowak, Ansgar Nünning, Claudia Olk, Jim Phelan, Christoph Reinfandt, Enno Ruge, Philipp Schweighauser, Martin Spies, Carlos Spoerhase, Frederik Van Dam, Uwe Wirth, and Anne Zwierlein.

Among the institutions whose resources and staff have helped me in preparing this book, I would like to thank the universities of Munich, Giessen, and Ghent; the Bodleian Library, Oxford; the British Library; the McFarlin Library at the University of Tulsa, Oklahoma, and the Harry Ransom Center at the University of Texas at Austin, whose holdings enriched my knowledge of mid-twentieth century women's writing. I would also like to thank all former members of the Ghent research group RAP (Research on Authorship as Performance), especially Isabelle Clairhout, Sören Hammerschmidt, Alise Jameson, and Jasper Schelstraete. I am grateful to the Alte Nationalgalerie (Staatliche Museen zu Berlin – Preußischer Kulturbesitz) for granting me permission to use Lesser Ury's *Frau am Schreibtisch* as a cover image. At De Gruyter, I am indebted to Ulrike Krauss, Katja Lehming, and Ulla Schmidt for shepherding the book through the production process.

Earlier versions of chapters 3, 9, and 12 have previously been published as "Books and Authors as Disposable Commodities in Balzac's *Lost Illusions*", *Im Zentrum: Das Buch*, ed. Johannes Frimmel et al. (Wiesbaden: Harrassowitz, 2022), 15–26; "'Whom the Gods Wish to Destroy': The Ambivalence of Promise in Modernist Authorship Narratives", *Poetica* 53 (2022), 106–124; and "Authors of Slender Means? Female Authorship in Mid-Twentieth-Century British Fiction",

Zeitschrift für Anglistik und Amerikanistik 70.4 (2022), 385–402. Parts of chapters 5 and 8 have been developed from an earlier article, "'An insane desire to see the author': Herman Melville, Henry James, and the Ambiguities of Gendered Authorship", *Gender and Creation: Surveying Gendered Myths of Creativity, Authority, and Authorship*, ed. Anne-Julia Zwierlein (Heidelberg: Winter, 2010), 159–174. Parts of chapter 6 and the section on Stevie Smith in chapter 11 were first laid out in "Female Authorship in Modern Fiction: Stevie Smith's *Novel on Yellow Paper* (1936) and the History of Fictional Women Writers", *Authorship* 9.1 (2020), https://www.authorship.ugent.be/article/id/63889/. An extended discussion of Arthur Phillips's *The Tragedy of Arthur* [→ ch. 17] can be found in my article "The Forger's Shakespeare Library: Authorship, Book History, and *The Tragedy of Arthur*", *AAA – Arbeiten aus Anglistik und Amerikanistik* 43.2 (2018), 125–140.

References

Abbott, H. Porter. 1996. *Beckett Writing Beckett. The Author in the Autograph*. Ithaca, NY and London: Cornell University Press.

Abel, Elizabeth, Marianne Hirsch, and Elizabeth Langland, eds. 1983. *The Voyage In. Fictions of Female Development*. Hanover, NE and London: University Press of New England.

Abraham, Adam. 2016. "Before *New Grub Street:* Thomas Miller and the Contingencies of Authorship". *Victorian Fiction Beyond the Canon*. Ed. Daragh Downes and Trish Ferguson. London: Palgrave Macmillan. 31–44.

Abrams, M. H. 1991. *Doing Things with Texts. Essays in Criticism and Critical Theory*. Ed. Michael Fischer. 1989. New York: Norton.

Adams, Thomas R., and Nicolas Barker. 2006. "A New Model for the Study of the Book". *The Book History Reader*. Ed. David Finkelstein and Alistair McCleery. 2nd ed. London and New York: Routledge. 47–65.

Adorno, Theodor W. 2019. "The Position of the Narrator in the Contemporary Novel". *Notes to Literature*. Ed. Rolf Tiedemann. Trans. Shierry Weber Nicholsen. New York: Columbia University Press. 53–58.

Aebischer, Pascale. 2003. "Creative Disability/Disabled Creativity in Henry Green's *Blindness* (1926)". *Studies in the Novel* 35.4: 510–525.

Agamben, Giorgio. 1999. "Bartleby, or On Contingency". *Potentialities: Collected Essays in Philosophy*. Trans. Daniel Heller-Roazen. Stanford: Stanford University Press. 243–271.

Aguirre, Robert D. 2002. "Cold Print: Professing Authorship in Anthony Trollope's *An Autobiography*". *Biography* 25.4: 569–592.

Alber, Jan. 2016. *Unnatural Narrative. Impossible Worlds in Fiction and Drama*. Lincoln, NE: University of Nebraska Press.

Alber, Jan, and Rüdiger Heinze, eds. 2011. *Unnatural Narratives – Unnatural Narratology*. Berlin and Boston: De Gruyter.

Allan, Angela S. 2021. "Stephen King, Incorporated: Genre Fiction and the Problem of Authorship". *American Literary History* 33.2: 271–297.

Allington, Daniel. 2019. "The Twentieth and Twenty-First Centuries". *The Book in Britain. A Historical Introduction*. Ed. Zachary Lesser. Hoboken, NJ and Chichester: Wiley Blackwell. 339–460.

Altick, Richard. 1998. *The English Common Reader. A Social History of the Mass Reading Public, 1800–1900*. 1957. 2nd ed. Columbus: Ohio State University Press.

Álvarez Amorós, José Antonio. 2008. "On Mark Ambient's Henpeckery in 'The Author of *Beltraffio*,' or How to Keep Up Narratorial Preconceptions". *JNT: Journal of Narrative Theory* 38.3: 317–341.

Amir, Ayala. 2010. *Raymond Carver's Visual Poetics*. Lanham, MD and Plymouth, UK: Lexington Books.

Amis, Kingsley. 1968. *I Like It Here*. 1958. Harmondsworth: Penguin.

Amlinger, Carolin. 2021. *Schreiben. Eine Soziologie literarischer Arbeit*. Frankfurt am Main: Suhrkamp.

Anderson, James Arthur. 2020. "Four Quadrants of Success. The Metalinguistics of Authorship in the Fiction of Stephen King". *Horror Literature from Gothic to Post-Modern. Critical Essays*. Ed. Michele Brittany and Nicholas Diak. Jefferson, NC: McFarland. 101–112.

Andrews, Malcolm. 2006. *Charles Dickens and His Performing Selves. Dickens and the Public Readings*. Oxford: Oxford University Press.

Anesko, Michael. 1986. *"Friction with the Market"*. *Henry James and the Profession of Authorship*. New York and Oxford: Oxford University Press.

Anstey, F. 1884. *The Giant's Robe*. London: Smith, Elder. Google Books. https://www.google.de/books/edition/The_Giant_s_Robe/vLsLAQAAIAAJ?hl=en&gbpv=1. Last access 21 Feb. 2023.
Aristotle. 2013. *Poetics*. Trans. Anthony Kenny. Oxford: Oxford University Press.
Arnold, Matthew. 1993. "The Function of Criticism at the Present Time". 1864. *Culture and Anarchy and Other Writings*. Ed. Stefan Collini. Cambridge: Cambridge University Press. 26–51.
Arnzen, Michael. 1998. "The *Misery* of Influence". *Paradoxa. Studies in World Literary Genres* 4.10: 237–252.
Aryan, Arya. 2020. *The Post-War Novel and the Death of the Author*. Cham: Palgrave Macmillan.
Athill, Diana. 2000. *Stet. A Memoir*. London: Granta; New York: Grove.
Auerbach, Erich. 1994. *Mimesis. Dargestellte Wirklichkeit in der abendländischen Literatur*. 1946. Tübingen and Basel: Francke.
Auerbach, Erich. 2003. *Mimesis. The Representation of Reality in Western Thought*. Trans. Willard R. Trask. 1953. Princeton: Princeton University Press.
Badura, Christian, and Melanie Möller. 2019. "Authorship in Classical Rome". *The Cambridge Handbook of Literary Authorship*. Ed. Ingo Berensmeyer, Gert Buelens, and Marysa Demoor. Cambridge: Cambridge University Press. 64–80.
Bailey, James. 2021. *Muriel Spark's Early Fiction: Literary Subversion and Experiments with Form*. Edinburgh: Edinburgh University Press.
Bakhtin, M. M. 1981. *The Dialogic Imagination. Four Essays*. Ed. Michael Holquist. Trans. Caryl Emerson and Michael Holquist. Austin, TX: University of Texas Press.
Balzac, Honoré de. 1970. *A Harlot High and Low*. [*Splendeurs et misères des courtisanes*]. 1839–1847. Trans. Rayner Heppenstall. London: Penguin.
Balzac, Honoré de. 1973. *Splendeurs et misères des courtisanes*. 1839–1847. Ed. Pierre Barbéris. Paris: Gallimard.
Balzac, Honoré de. 2004. *Lost Illusions*. 1837–1843. Trans. Herbert J. Hunt. 1971. London: Penguin.
Balzac, Honoré de. 2013. *Illusions perdues*. 1837–1843. Ed. Jacques Noiray. Paris: Gallimard.
Barrett Browning, Elizabeth. 2018. *Elizabeth Barrett Browning*. Ed. Josie Billington and Philip Davis. 21st-Century Oxford Authors. Oxford: Oxford University Press.
Barth, John. 1982. *The Literature of Exhaustion and The Literature of Replenishment*. Northridge, CA: Lord John Press.
Barthes, Roland. 1977. "The Death of the Author". 1967. *Image-Music-Text*. Trans. Stephen Heath. London: Fontana. 142–148.
Barthes, Roland. 1982. *A Barthes Reader*. Ed. Susan Sontag. New York: Hill & Wang.
Bassett, Troy J. 2010. "Living on the Margin: George Bentley and the Economics of the Three-Volume Novel, 1865–70". *Book History* 13: 58–79.
Bassett, Troy J. 2020. *At the Circulating Library. A Database of Victorian Fiction, 1837–1901*. http://www.victorianresearch.org. Last access 26 Nov. 2022.
Bauman, Zygmunt. 1991. *Modernity and Ambivalence*. Cambridge and Malden, MA: Polity Press.
Baxter, Valerie. 1958. *Jane: Young Author*. 1954. London: The Bodley Head.
Beckett, Samuel. 1984. *Disjecta. Miscellaneous Writings and a Dramatic Fragment*. Ed. Ruby Cohn. New York: Grove.
Beckett, Samuel. 1993. *More Pricks than Kicks*. 1934. London: Calder.
Beckett, Samuel. 1996. *Dream of Fair to Middling Women*. 1993. London: Calder.
Beebe, Maurice. 1964. *Ivory Towers and Sacred Founts: The Artist as Hero in Fiction from Goethe to Joyce*. New York: New York University Press.
Beerbohm, Max. 1922. *Seven Men*. 1919. London: Heinemann.

Behrendt, Stephen C. 2011. "The Romantics and Media". *Romantic Explorations. Selected Papers from the Koblenz Conference of the German Society for English Romanticism*. Ed. Michael Meyer. Trier: WVT. 7–21.
Belleau, André. 1980. *Le Romancier Fictif. Essai sur la représentation de l'écrivain dans le roman québécois*. Sillery: Les Presses de l'Université du Québec.
Beller, Anne-Marie. 2016. "Popularity and Proliferation: Shifting Modes of Authorship in Mary Elizabeth Braddon's *The Doctor's Wife* (1864) and *Vixen* (1879)". *Women's Writing* 23.2: 245–261.
Bénichou, Paul. 1996. *Le sacre de l'écrivain, 1750–1830. Essai sur l'avènement d'un pouvoir spirituel laïque dans la France moderne*. Paris: Gallimard.
Benjamin, Walter. 2006. "The Storyteller: Reflections on the Works of Nikolai Leskov". 1936. Trans. Harry Zohn. *The Novel: An Anthology of Criticism and Theory 1900–2000*. Ed. Dorothy J. Hale. Malden, MA: Blackwell. 361–378.
Bennett, Andrew. 2005. *The Author*. New York and London: Routledge.
Bennett, Andrew. 2006. "Expressivity: The Romantic Theory of Authorship". *Literary Theory and Criticism: An Oxford Guide*. Ed. Patricia Waugh. Oxford and New York: Oxford University Press. 48–58.
Benson, E. F. 1988. *Secret Lives*. 1932. London: Hogarth Press.
Benveniste, Émile. 1966. *Problèmes de linguistique génerale*. Paris: Gallimard.
Bercovitch, Sacvan. 1976. *The Puritan Origins of the American Self*. New Haven, CT and London: Yale University Press.
Berensmeyer, Ingo. 2000. *John Banville: Fictions of Order. Authority, Authorship, Authenticity*. Heidelberg: Winter.
Berensmeyer, Ingo. 2014. "Grub Street Revisited: Late Eighteenth-Century Authorship Satire and the Media Culture of Print". *Anglistentag 2013 Konstanz Proceedings*. Ed. Silvia Mergenthal and Reingard M. Nischik. Trier: WVT. 127–136.
Berensmeyer, Ingo. 2015. "'What are you like to come home to?' Domesticity in Postwar British Women's Poetry and Fiction, 1945–1960". *Anglia* 133.3: 466–488.
Berensmeyer, Ingo. 2016. "'The *musique concrète* of civilization': Responding to Technological and Cultural Change in Postwar British Literature". *REAL: Yearbook of Research in English and American Literature* 32: 169–186.
Berensmeyer, Ingo. 2020a. *Literary Culture in Early Modern England, 1630–1700. Angles of Contingency*. Berlin and Boston: De Gruyter.
Berensmeyer, Ingo. 2020b. "Methods in Hermeneutic and Neo-Hermeneutic Approaches: A Reading of Shakespeare's Sonnet 73". *Methods of Textual Analysis in Literary Studies: Approaches, Basics, Model Interpretations*. Ed. Vera Nünning and Ansgar Nünning. Trier: Wissenschaftlicher Verlag Trier. 59–83.
Berensmeyer, Ingo. 2022. *A Short Media History of English Literature*. Berlin and Boston: De Gruyter.
Berensmeyer, Ingo, Gert Buelens, and Marysa Demoor. 2012. "Authorship as Cultural Performance: New Perspectives in Authorship Studies". *ZAA: Zeitschrift für Anglistik und Amerikanistik* 60.1: 5–29.
Berensmeyer, Ingo, Gert Buelens, and Marysa Demoor, eds. 2019. *The Cambridge Handbook of Literary Authorship*. Cambridge: Cambridge University Press.
Berensmeyer, Ingo, Gero Guttzeit, and Alise Jameson. 2015. "'The Brain-Sucker: Or, the Distress of Authorship': A Critical Edition". *Authorship* 4.1. https://doi.org/10.21825/aj.v4i1.1111. Last access 15 Feb. 2023.

Berensmeyer, Ingo, and Martin Spies. 2011. "Between Romance and Realism: 'Twice-Told' Urban Gothic in Herman Melville's 'Bartleby, the Scrivener' and Related Mid-19th-Century Narratives of Modern City Life". *A History of the American Short Story: Genres – Developments – Model Interpretations.* Ed. Michael Basseler and Ansgar Nünning. Trier: WVT. 109–122.

Berensmeyer, Ingo, and Sonja Trurnit. 2022. "Post-War British Women Writers: A Quantitative Approach". *Journal of Cultural Analytics* 7.1: 81–107. https://doi.org/10.22148/001c.33994. Last access 26 Nov. 2022.

Bergonzi, Bernard. 1976. "Introduction". *New Grub Street.* By George Gissing. Ed. Bernard Bergonzi. 1968. Harmondsworth: Penguin. 9–26.

Berkenkamp, Lauri. 1992. "Reading, Writing and Interpreting: Stephen King's *Misery*". *The Dark Descent. Essays Defining Stephen King's Horrorscape.* Ed. Tony Magistrale. New York, Westport, CT, and London: Greenwood Press. 203–211.

Berman, Morris. 1981. *The Reenchantment of the World.* Ithaca, NY and London: Cornell University Press.

Bernstein, Stephen. 2019. "'The Great Unhappiness of Another': Writers and Readers in Three Stories by Alice Munro". *Short Fiction in Theory & Practice* 9.1: 17–26.

Bex, Sean. 2016. "Marketing Professionalism: The Transatlantic Authorship of Edith Wharton". *Neophilologus* 100: 503–519.

Birch, Edmund. 2018. "Literary Machines: George Gissing's Lost Illusions". *The Labour of Literature in Britain and France, 1830–1910. Authorial Work Ethics.* Ed. Marcus Waithe and Claire White. Basingstoke: Palgrave Macmillan. 187–201.

Birke, Dorothee. 2014. "Challenging the Divide? Stephen King and the Problem of 'Popular Culture'". *Journal of Popular Culture* 47.3: 520–536.

Birke, Dorothee. 2015. "Author, Authority, and 'Authorial Narration': The Eighteenth-Century English Novel as a Test Case". *Author and Narrator. Transdisciplinary Contributions to a Narratological Debate.* Ed. Dorothee Birke and Tilmann Köppe. Berlin, Munich, and Boston: De Gruyter. 99–111.

Birke, Dorothee. 2016. *Writing the Reader. Configurations of a Cultural Practice in the English Novel.* Berlin and Boston: De Gruyter.

Birke, Dorothee. Forthcoming. "Elizabeth Justice, *Amelia, Or, The Distress'd Wife* (1751)". *The Cambridge Guide to the Eighteenth-Century Novel, 1660–1820.* Ed. April London. Cambridge: Cambridge University Press.

Birke, Dorothee, and Stella Butter. 2020. "Methods of Psychoanalytic Criticism". *Methods of Textual Analysis in Literary Studies. Approaches, Basics, Model Interpretations.* Ed. Vera Nünning and Ansgar Nünning. Trier: Wissenschaftlicher Verlag Trier. 85–105.

Birke, Dorothee, and Tilmann Köppe. 2015a. "Author and Narrator: Problems in the Constitution and Interpretation of Fictional Narrative". *Author and Narrator. Transdisciplinary Contributions to a Narratological Debate.* Ed. Dorothee Birke and Tilmann Köppe. Berlin, Munich, and Boston: De Gruyter. 1–12.

Birke, Dorothee, and Tilmann Köppe, eds. 2015b. *Author and Narrator. Transdisciplinary Contributions to a Narratological Debate.* Berlin, Munich, and Boston: De Gruyter.

Blake, William. 1988. *The Complete Poetry and Prose of William Blake.* Ed. David V. Erdman. Rev. ed. New York: Anchor Books.

Bloom, Harold. 1973. *The Anxiety of Influence: A Theory of Poetry.* Oxford: Oxford University Press.

Bloom, Myra. 2019. "Messy Confessions: Sheila Heti's *How Should a Person Be?*" *Avant Canada: Poets, Prophets, Revolutionaries*. Ed. Gregory Betts and Christian Bök. Waterloo, ON: Wilfrid Laurier University Press. 173–196.
Bode, Christoph. 2011. *The Novel. An Introduction*. Trans. James Vigus. Malden, MA and Oxford: Wiley-Blackwell.
Boldrini, Lucia. 2012. *Autobiographies of Others. Historical Subjects and Literary Fiction*. New York and London: Routledge.
Bollnow, Otto F. 1979. "What Does it Mean to Understand a Writer Better than He Understood Himself". *Philosophy Today* 23.1. 16–28.
Boltanski, Luc. 2014. *Mysteries and Conspiracies. Detective Stories, Spy Novels, and the Making of Modern Societies*. Trans. Catherine Porter. Cambridge and Malden, MA: Polity Press.
Bonaparte, Marie. 1971. *The Life and Works of Edgar Allan Poe. A Psycho-Analytic Interpretation*. 1949. London: Hogarth Press.
Booth, Wayne C. 1983. *The Rhetoric of Fiction*. 1961. 2nd ed. Chicago and London: University of Chicago Press.
Bosse, Heinrich. 2014. *Autorschaft ist Werkherrschaft. Über die Entstehung des Urheberrechts aus dem Geist der Goethezeit*. Paderborn: Fink.
Boumelha, Penny. 1993. "'A Complicated Position for a Woman': *The Hand of Ethelberta*". *The Sense of Sex: Feminist Perspectives on Hardy*. Ed. Margaret R. Higonnet. Urbana: University of Illinois Press. 242–259.
Bourdieu, Pierre. 1993. *The Field of Cultural Production. Essays on Art and Literature*. Ed. Randal Johnson. New York: Columbia University Press.
Bourdieu, Pierre. 1996. *The Rules of Art. Genesis and Structure of the Literary Field*. Trans. Susan Emanuel. Cambridge: Polity Press.
Boyd, Brian. 2017. "Does Austen Need Narrators? Does Anyone?" *New Literary History* 48.2: 285–308.
Boyiopoulos, Kostas. 2013. "'The Serried Maze': Terrain, Consciousness and Textuality in Machen's *The Hill of Dreams*". *Victoriographies* 3.1: 46–63.
Boyiopoulos, Kostas. 2017. "'Use my body like the pages of a book': Decadence and the Eroticized Text". *Decadence and the Senses*. Ed. Jane Desmarais and Alice Condé. Cambridge: Legenda Books. 101–120.
Braddon, Mary Elizabeth. 2008. *The Doctor's Wife*. 1864. Ed. Lyn Pykett. Oxford and New York: Oxford University Press.
Branscomb, Jack. 1986. "The Quest for Wholeness in the Fiction of Russell Hoban". *Critique: Studies in Contemporary Fiction* 28.1: 29–38.
Brantlinger, Patrick. 1998. *The Reading Lesson. The Threat of Mass Literacy in Nineteenth-Century British Fiction*. Bloomington, IN: Indiana University Press.
Braudy, Leo. 1997. *The Frenzy of Renown. Fame and Its History*. 1986. New York: Vintage.
Braun, Rebecca. 2020a. "Introduction: Twenty-First Century Approaches to World Authorship". *World Authorship*. Ed. Tobias Boes, Rebecca Braun, and Emily Spiers. Oxford: Oxford University Press. 1–16.
Braun, Rebecca. 2020b. "Celebrity: On the Different Publics of World Authorship". *World Authorship*. Ed. Tobias Boes, Rebecca Braun, and Emily Spiers. Oxford: Oxford University Press. 31–44.
Braun, Rebecca, and Emily Spiers, eds. 2016. *Literary Celebrity*. Special issue of *Celebrity Studies* 7.4: 449–594.
Bridy, Annemarie. 2016. "The Evolution of Authorship: Work Made by Code". *Columbia Journal of Law & the Arts* 39.3: 395–401.

Brittain, Vera. 1947. *On Becoming a Writer.* London: Hutchinson.
Brittain, Vera. 1953. *Lady into Woman: A History of Women from Victoria to Elizabeth II.* London: Dakers.
Brontë, Charlotte. 1985. *Jane Eyre.* 1847. Ed. Q. D. Leavis. Harmondsworth: Penguin.
Brooks, Peter. 1976. *The Melodramatic Imagination. Balzac, Henry James, Melodrama, and the Mode of Excess.* New Haven, CT and London: Yale University Press.
Brothers, Barbara. 1983. "*Blindness*: The Eye of Henry Green". *Twentieth-Century Literature* 29.4: 403–421.
Brouillette, Sarah. 2014. *Literature and the Creative Economy.* Stanford: Stanford University Press.
Brown, Erica, and Mary Grover, eds. 2012. *Middlebrow Literary Cultures. The Battle of the Brows, 1920–1960.* Basingstoke: Palgrave Macmillan.
Browning, Robert. 2018. *Robert Browning.* Ed. Richard Cronin and Dorothy McMillan. 21st-Century Oxford Authors. Oxford: Oxford University Press.
Brunn, Alain. 2001. *L'auteur.* Paris: Flammarion.
Buckley, Jerome Hamilton. 1974. *Season of Youth. The Bildungsroman from Dickens to Golding.* Cambridge, MA: Harvard University Press.
Bucknell, Clare. 2021. "The Myth of Oscar Wilde's Martyrdom". *The New Yorker.* Oct. 4. https://www.newyorker.com/magazine/2021/10/11/the-myth-of-oscar-wildes-martyrdom. Last access 11 Feb. 2022.
Bugliani, Paolo. 2022. "Diminishing Figures: Spectral Simulacra of Authors in Henry James and Max Beerbohm's Decadent Short Stories". *Between: Journal of the Italian Association for the Theory and Comparative History of Literature* 12.24: 103–123.
Bulwer Lytton, Edward. 1893. *Ernest Maltravers; or, The Eleusinia.* 1837. Boston: Little, Brown, and Company. Google Books. https://hdl.handle.net/2027/uva.x030832709. Last access 26 Nov. 2022.
Burgelin, Claude, Isabelle Grell, and Roger-Yves Roche, eds. 2010. *Autofiction(s).* Lyon: Presses Universitaires de Lyon.
Burke, Seán. 1992. *The Death and Return of the Author. Criticism and Subjectivity in Barthes, Foucault and Derrida.* Edinburgh: Edinburgh University Press.
Butler, Robert J. 2018. "Percival Everett's Signifying on Ralph Ellison's *Invisible Man* in *Erasure*". *Canadian Review of Comparative Literature / Revue Canadienne de Littérature Comparée* 45.1: 141–152.
Byron, [George Gordon] Lord. 2008. *The Major Works.* Ed. Jerome J. McGann. Oxford: Oxford University Press.
"Cabeiri". 2016. *Encyclopaedia Britannica.* https://www.britannica.com/topic/Cabeiri#ref195535. Last access 21 Feb. 2023.
Caine, William. 1924. *The Author of "Trixie".* London: Herbert Jenkins.
Caleb, Amanda Mordavsky. 2010. "'A City of Nightmares': Suburban Anxiety in Arthur Machen's London Gothic". *London Gothic.* Ed. Lawrence Phillips and Anne Witchard. New York: Continuum. 41–49.
Calvino, Italo. 1998. *If on a Winter's Night a Traveller.* 1980. Trans. William Weaver. 1983. London: Vintage.
Camara, Anthony. 2014. "Abominable Transformations: Becoming-Fungus in Arthur Machen's *The Hill of Dreams*". *Gothic Studies* 16.1: 9–23.
Camberton, Roland. 2010. *Scamp.* 1950. London: New London Editions.
Campbell, Olwen W. 1952. *The Report of a Conference on the Feminine Point of View.* London: Williams & Norgate.

Campe, Rüdiger. 1991. "Die Schreibszene, Schreiben". *Paradoxien, Dissonanzen, Zusammenbrüche. Situationen offener Epistemologie*. Ed. Hans Ulrich Gumbrecht and K. Ludwig Pfeiffer. Frankfurt am Main: Suhrkamp. 759–772.

Carey, John. 2010. *William Golding. The Man Who Wrote* Lord of the Flies. *A Life*. 2009. London: Faber and Faber.

Carlyle, Thomas. 1986. *Selected Writings*. Ed. Alan Shelston. Harmondsworth: Penguin.

Carretta, Vincent. 2005. *Equiano, the African: Biography of a Self-Made Man*. Atlanta, GA: University of Georgia Press.

Carver, Raymond. 2009. *Collected Stories*. New York: Library of America.

Chamarat, Gabrielle, and Alain Goulet, eds. 1996. *L'auteur. Actes du Colloque de Cerisy-la-Salle 4–8 octobre 1995*. Caen: Presses Unversitaires de Caen.

Chambers, Matthew. 2020. *London and the Modernist Bookshop*. Cambridge: Cambridge University Press.

Chartier, Roger. 1994. *The Order of Books. Readers, Authors, and Libraries in Europe between the Fourteenth and Eighteenth Centuries*. Trans. Lydia G. Cochrane. 1992. Stanford, CA: Stanford University Press.

Chatman, Seymour. 1978. *Story and Discourse. Narrative Structure in Fiction and Film*. Ithaca, NY and London: Cornell University Press.

Cheadle, Brian. 2017. "*David Copperfield* and *Pendennis:* Answering Back". *Dickens Quarterly* 34.1: 14–26.

Chesterton, G. K. 1946. *The Victorian Age in Literature*. 1913. London, New York, and Toronto: Oxford University Press.

Childress, Clayton. 2017. *Under the Cover. The Creation, Production, and Reception of a Novel*. Princeton, NJ and Oxford: Princeton University Press.

Chung, June Hee. 2019. *Henry James and the Media Arts of Modernity. Commercial Cosmopolitanism*. New York: Routledge.

Civello, Catherine A. 1997. *Patterns of Ambivalence: The Fiction and Poetry of Stevie Smith*. Columbia: Camden House.

Clark, Matthew, and James Phelan. 2020. *Debating Rhetorical Narratology. On the Synthetic, Mimetic, and Thematic Aspects of Narrative*. Columbus: Ohio State University Press.

Clausen, Christopher. 1993. "Arthur Henry Hallam and the Victorian Compromise". *The Sewanee Review* 101.3: 375–393.

Cohn, Ruby. 1984. "Foreword". *Disjecta. Miscellaneous Writings and a Dramatic Fragment*. By Samuel Beckett. Ed. Ruby Cohn. New York: Grove.

Colapinto, John. 2001. *About the Author*. London: Fourth Estate.

Colclough, Stephen. 2019. "From the Nineteenth Century to the Modern Age". *The Book in Britain. A Historical Introduction*. Ed. Zachary Lesser. Hoboken, NJ and Chichester: Wiley Blackwell. 227–338.

Cole, Sarah Rose. 2007. "National Histories, International Genre: Thackeray, Balzac, and the Franco-British *Bildungsroman*". *Romanticism and Victorianism on the Net* 48. https://doi-org.emedien.ub.uni-muenchen.de/10.7202/017436ar . Last access 26 Nov. 2022.

Conary, Jennifer. 2014. "Never Great, Only Popular: Mary Elizabeth Braddon's *The Doctor's Wife* and the Literary Marketplace". *Studies in the Novel* 46.4: 423–443.

Connolly, Cyril. 2008. *Enemies of Promise*. 1938. Chicago: University of Chicago Press.

Connor, Sharon. 2018. "The Age of the Female Novelist: Single Women as Authors of Fiction". *British Women's Writing from Brontë to Bloomsbury.* Vol. 1. *1840s and 1850s.* Ed. Adrienne E. Gavin and Carolyn W. de la L. Oulton. Cham: Palgrave Macmillan. 139–151.

Cooke, Jennifer. 2020. "Ugly Audacities in Auto/biography: Genius, Betrayal, and Writer's Block". *Contemporary Feminist Life-Writing: The New Audacity.* Cambridge: Cambridge University Press. 64–92.

Cortázar, Julio. 2014. *Hopscotch. Blow-Up and Other Stories. We Love Glenda so Much and Other Tales.* Trans. Gregory Rabassa and Paul Blackburn. Everyman's Library. New York, London, and Toronto: Knopf.

Craps, Stef. 2012. *Postcolonial Witnessing: Trauma Out of Bounds.* Houndmills: Palgrave Macmillan.

Cross, Nigel. 1988. *The Common Writer. Life in Nineteenth-Century Grub Street.* 1985. Cambridge: Cambridge University Press.

Culver, Stuart. 1984. "Representing the Author: Henry James, Intellectual Property and the Work of Writing". *Henry James: Fiction as History.* Ed. Ian F. A. Bell. London: Vision Press; Totowa, NJ: Barnes & Noble Books. 114–136.

Cunningham, Valentine. 2002. "Shaping Modern English Fiction: The Forms of the Content and the Contents of the Form". *On Modern British Fiction.* Ed. Zachary Leader. Oxford: Oxford University Press. 149–180.

Currie, Gregory. 2010. *Narratives and Narrators: A Philosophy of Stories.* Oxford: Oxford University Press.

Cusk, Rachel. 2016a. *Outline.* 2014. London: Vintage.

Cusk, Rachel. 2016b. *Transit.* London: Jonathan Cape.

Cusk, Rachel. 2019. *Kudos.* 2018. London: Faber and Faber.

Damrosch, David. 2006. "World Literature in a Postcanonical, Hypercanonical Age". *Comparative Literature in an Age of Globalization.* Ed. Haun Saussy. Baltimore, MD: Johns Hopkins University Press. 43–53.

Darlington, W. A. 1922. *Wishes Limited.* London: Herbert Jenkins.

Darnton, Robert. 1982. "What Is the History of Books?" *Daedalus* 111.3: 65–83.

DaRosa, Marc. 1997. "Henry James, Anonymity, and the Press: Journalistic Modernity and the Decline of the Author". *Modern Fiction Studies* 43.4: 826–859.

Davies, Sarah. 1993. "*The Hand of Ethelberta:* De-Mythologising 'Woman'". *Critical Survey* 5.2: 123–130.

Davison, Carol Margaret. 2008. "Calvinist Gothic: The Case of Charles Brockden Brown's *Wieland, or the Transformation* and James Hogg's *The Private Memoirs and Confessions of a Justified Sinner*". *Le Gothic: Influences and Appropriations in Europe and America.* Ed. Avril Horner and Sue Zlosnik. Basingstoke: Palgrave Macmillan. 166–184.

Dawson, Paul. 2012. "Real Authors and Real Readers: Omniscient Narration and a Discursive Approach to the Narrative Communication Model". *JNT* 42.1: 91–116.

Dawson, Paul. 2013. *The Return of the Omniscient Narrator. Authorship and Authority in Twenty-First Century Fiction.* Columbus: Ohio State University Press.

Dawson, Paul. 2015. "Ten Theses against Fictionality". *Narrative* 23.1: 74–100.

Deane, Bradley. 2003. *The Making of the Victorian Novelist. Anxieties of Authorship in the Mass Market.* New York and London: Routledge.

DeCoste, Damon Marcel. 2013. "'(AND YOU GET FAR TOO MUCH PUBLICITY ALREADY WHOEVER YOU ARE)': Gossip, Celebrity, and Modernist Authorship in Evelyn Waugh's *Vile Bodies*". *Papers on Language and Literature* 49.1: 3–36.

De-la-Noy, Michael. 1999. "Obituary: Kathleen Farrell". *The Independent,* 27 Nov.
Delbaere, Jeanne. 1991. "The Artist as Clown of God: *The Paper Men*". *William Golding: The Sound of Silence.* Ed. Jeanne Delbaere. Liège: English Department, University of Liège. 116–175.
Deleuze, Gilles. 1998. "Bartleby; or, The Formula". *Essays Critical and Clinical.* Trans. Daniel W. Smith and Michael A. Greco. 1993. London: Verso. 68–90.
Deleuze, Gilles, and Félix Guattari. 1986. *Kafka. Toward a Minor Literature.* 1975. Trans. Dana Polan. Minneapolis, MN and London: University of Minnesota Press.
Dennis, Scott A. 1980. "*The World of Chance:* Howells' Hawthornian Self-Parody". *American Literature* 52.2: 279–293.
Derrida, Jacques. 1992. *Acts of Literature.* Ed. Derek Attridge. New York and London: Routledge.
Detering, Heinrich, ed. 2002. *Autorschaft. Positionen und Revisionen.* Stuttgart and Weimar: Metzler.
d'Hont, Coco. 2021. "The (Un)Death of the Author: Authorship as Horror Trope in Stephen King's Fiction". *Horror Studies* 12.2: 175–188.
Diaz, José-Luis. 2007. *L'écrivain imaginaire. Scénographies auctoriales à l'époque romantique.* Paris: Honoré Champion.
Diaz, José-Luis. 2011. *L'homme et l'oeuvre.* Paris: Presses Universitaires de France.
Dickens, Charles. 1985. *The Personal History of David Copperfield.* 1849–1850. Ed. Trevor Blount. Harmondsworth: Penguin.
Dilthey, Wilhelm. 1996. *Selected Works.* Vol. 4. *Hermeneutics and the Study of History.* Ed. Rudolf A. Makkreel and Frithjof Rodi. Princeton, NJ: Princeton University Press.
'Dionysius'. 1806. "Adventures of a Pen". *The European Magazine and London Review* 50: 23–26, 187–191, 277–282.
Disraeli, Benjamin. 1878. *Contarini Fleming. A Psychological Romance.* 1832. London: Longmans, Green, and Co.
Disraeli, Benjamin. 1985. *Sybil, or The Two Nations.* 1845. Ed. Thom Braun. Harmondsworth: Penguin.
Dix, Hywel, ed. 2018. *Autofiction in English.* Cham: Palgrave Macmillan.
Dobson, Roger. 2019. "Lucian in the Labyrinth". *Faunus: The Decorative Imagination of Arthur Machen.* Ed. James Machin et al. London: Strange Attractor Press. 129–142.
Dolin, Tim. 1997a. "Introduction". *The Hand of Ethelberta.* By Thomas Hardy. Ed. Tim Dolin. London: Penguin. xix–xli.
Dolin, Tim. 1997b. "A History of the Text". *The Hand of Ethelberta.* By Thomas Hardy. Ed. Tim Dolin. London: Penguin. 407–416.
Dooley, Gillian. 2004. "Iris Murdoch's Use of First-Person Narrative in *The Black Prince*". *English Studies* 85.2: 134–146.
Dorson, James. 2017. "Cormac McCarthy and the Genre Turn in Contemporary Literary Fiction". *European Journal of American Studies* 12.3. https://doi.org/10.4000/ejas.12291. Last access 15 Feb. 2023.
Dowling, David. 2011. "Dreams Deferred: Ambition and the Mass Market in Melville and King". *Journal of Popular Culture* 44.5: 970–991.
Downie, J. A. 2006. "Who Says She's a Bourgeois Writer? Reconsidering the Social and Political Contexts of Jane Austen's Novels". *Eighteenth-Century Studies* 40.1: 69–84.
Drucker, Johanna. 2014. "Distributed and Conditional Documents: Conceptualizing Bibliographical Alterities". *MatLit* 2.1: 11–29.
Dryden, Edgar A. 1977. *Nathaniel Hawthorne. The Poetics of Enchantment.* Ithaca, NY and London: Cornell University Press.

DuPlessis, Rachel Blau. 1985. *Writing Beyond the Ending. Narrative Strategies of Twentieth-Century Women Writers*. Bloomington: Indiana University Press.
Durrell, Lawrence. 1968. *The Alexandria Quartet. Justine Balthazar Mountolive Clea*. 1962. London: Faber and Faber.
Durrell, Lawrence. 1977. *The Black Book*. 1938. London: Faber and Faber.
Dutton, Denis, ed. 1983. *The Forger's Art. Forgery and the Philosophy of Art*. Berkeley and Los Angeles: University of California Press.
Dzieza, Josh. 2022. "The Great Fiction of AI. The Strange World of High-Speed Semi-Automated Genre Fiction". https://www.theverge.com/c/23194235/ai-fiction-writing-amazon-kindle-sudo write-jasper. Last access 29 Jan. 2023.
Easley, Alexis. 1996. "Authorship, Gender and Identity: George Eliot in the 1850s". *Women's Writing* 3.2: 145–160.
Easley, Alexis. 2004. *First-Person Anonymous. Women Writers and Victorian Print Media, 1830–1870*. Aldershot: Ashgate.
Easley, Alexis. 2018. "Gender, Authorship, and the Periodical Press". *The History of British Women's Writing*. Vol. 6. *1830–1880*. Ed. Lucy Hartley. London: Palgrave Macmillan. 39–55.
Easthope, Antony. 1983. *Poetry as Discourse*. London: Methuen.
Edel, Leon. 1962. *Henry James*. 5 vols. Philadelphia, PA and New York: Lippincott.
Edwards, Owen Dudley. 2017. "Doyle, Sir Arthur Ignatius Conan (1859–1930), Writer". *Oxford Dictionary of National Biography*. Oxford: Oxford University Press. Last access 6 Nov. 2022.
Egan, Jesi. 2016. "Cultural Futurity and the Politics of Recovery: Mary Renault's Ambivalent Romances". *Modern Fiction Studies* 62.3: 462–480.
Eggers, Dave. 2007. *A Heartbreaking Work of Staggering Genius*. 2000. London: Picador.
Ehland, Christoph, and Cornelia Wächter, eds. 2016. *Middlebrow and Gender, 1890–1945*. Leiden and Boston: Brill Rodopi.
Eibl, Karl. 2013. "Wer hat das gesagt? Zur Anthropologie der Autorposition". *Scientia Poetica* 17: 207–229.
Elfenbein, Andrew. 2020. "What Is an Author (in Literary Scholarship)?" *The Wordsworth Circle* 51.3: 281–299.
Eliot, George. 1990. "Silly Novels by Lady Novelists". 1856. *Selected Essays, Poems and Other Writings*. Ed. A. S. Byatt and Nicholas Warren. Harmondsworth: Penguin. 140–163.
Eliot, T. S. 1928. "Tradition and the Individual Talent". *The Sacred Wood. Essays on Poetry and Criticism*. 1920. London: Methuen. 47–59.
Emre, Merve. 2019. "The Cage of Authorship". *The Ferrante Letters. An Experiment in Collective Criticism*. By Sarah Chihaya, Merve Emre, Katherine Hill, and Jill Richards. New York: Columbia University Press. 297–224.
Emre, Merve. 2022. "The Illusion of the First Person". *The New York Review of Books* 69.17 (3 Nov.): 43–46.
Engdahl, Horace. 2002. *Witness Literature. Proceedings of the Nobel Centennial Symposium, Stockholm, 4–5 December 2001*. Singapore: World Scientific.
Epstein, Jason. 2002. *Book Business: Publishing Past, Present, and Future*. New York: Norton.
Evans, Elizabeth F. 2018. *Threshold Modernism: New Public Women and the Literary Spaces of Imperial London*. Cambridge: Cambridge University Press.
Everett, Percival. 2021. *Erasure*. 2001. London: Faber & Faber.
Ezell, Margaret J. M. 1999. *Social Authorship and the Advent of Print*. Baltimore, MD: Johns Hopkins University Press.

Faber, Toby. 2019. *Faber & Faber: The Untold Story*. London: Faber & Faber.
Falardeau, Jean-Charles. 2016. "Les milieux sociaux dans le roman canadien-français contemporain". 1964. *Sociologie et sociétes* 48.2: 305–324.
Fanger, Donald. 1967. *Dostoevsky and Romantic Realism*. Chicago: University of Chicago Press.
Farebrother, Rachel. 2015. "'Out of Place': Reading Space in Percival Everett's *Erasure*". *MELUS: The Journal of the Society for the Study of the Multi-Ethnic Literature of the United States* 40.2: 117–136.
Farrell, Kathleen. 1956. *The Cost of Living*. London: Macmillan.
Feleki, Despoina. 2014. "Popular Authorship Reconfigured: Stephen King's Authorial Personae from Print to Digital Environments". *Authorship* 3.1. http://dx.doi.org/10.21825/aj.v3i1.1071. Last access 26 Nov. 2022.
Felski, Rita. 2000. "Nothing to Declare: Shame, Identity, and the Lower Middle Class". *PMLA: Publications of the Modern Language Association of America* 115.1: 33–45.
Felski, Rita. 2020. *Hooked. Art and Attachment*. Chicago and London: University of Chicago Press.
Ferguson, Sam. 2018. *Diaries Real and Fictional in Twentieth-Century French Writing*. Oxford: Oxford University Press.
Fielding, Heather. 2015. "Kipling's Wireless Impressionism: Telecommunication and Narration in Early Modernism". *MFS: Modern Fiction Studies* 61.1: 24–46.
Filmer, Robert. 1949. *Patriarcha and Other Political Works by Sir Robert Filmer*. Ed. Peter Laslett. Oxford: Blackwell.
Finkelstein, David. 2002. *The House of Blackwood. Author-Publisher Relations in the Victorian Era*. University Park, PA: Pennsylvania State University Press.
Fish, Stanley. 1982. *Is There a Text in This Class? The Authority of Interpretive Communities*. Cambridge, MA: Harvard University Press.
Fisher, Judith L. 2002. *Thackeray's Skeptical Narrative and the 'Perilous Trade' of Authorship*. Aldershot and Burlington, VT: Ashgate.
Flaubert, Gustave. 1980. *Correspondance*. Vol. 2. *Juillet 1851 – Décembre 1858*. Ed. Jean Bruneau. Paris: Gallimard.
Fletcher, Angus. 2021. "Why Computers Will Never Write Good Novels". *Nautilus* 95 (10 Feb.). https://nautil.us/why-computers-will-never-write-good-novels-238122/ Last access 15 Feb. 2023.
Flint, Kate. 2004. "Symonds, Emily Morse [*pseud*. George Paston] (1860–1936)". *Oxford Dictionary of National Biography*. Oxford: Oxford University Press. Last access 15 Oct. 2021.
Florida, Richard. 2003. *The Rise of the Creative Class: And How It's Transforming Work, Leisure, Community, and Everyday Life*. New York: Basic Books.
Flothow, Dorothea, and Markus Oppolzer. 2017. "Introduction". *The Essays: Forms and Transformations*. Ed. Dorothea Flothow, Markus Oppolzer, and Sabine Coelsch-Foisner. Heidelberg: Winter. ix–xxi.
Fludernik, Monika. 2003. "The Diachronization of Narratology: Dedicated to Franz K. Stanzel on His 80th Birthday". *Narrative* 11.3: 331–348.
Flynn, Michael J. 2010. "*Pendennis, Copperfield,* and the Debate on the 'Dignity of Literature'". *Dickens Studies Annual* 41.1: 151–189.
Forster, E. M. 2006. *The Longest Journey*. 1907. Ed. Elizabeth Heine. London: Penguin.
Foster, Benjamin R. 2019. "Authorship in Cuneiform Literature". *The Cambridge Handbook of Literary Authorship*. Ed. Ingo Berensmeyer, Gert Buelens, and Marysa Demoor. Cambridge: Cambridge University Press. 13–26.

Foucault, Michel. 1977. "What Is an Author?" 1969. *Language, Counter-Memory, Practice*. Ed. Donald F. Bouchard. Ithaca, NY: Cornell University Press. 113–138.
Fournier, Lauren. 2021. *Autotheory as Feminist Practice in Art, Writing, and Criticism*. Cambridge, MA: MIT Press.
Fowler, Roger. 1995. *The Language of George Orwell*. Houndmills and London: Macmillan.
Fowles, John. 1996. *The French Lieutenant's Woman*. 1969. London: Vintage.
Fraiman, Susan. 1993. *Unbecoming Women. British Women Writers and the Novel of Development*. New York: Columbia University Press.
Franck, Georg. 2018. "The Economy of Attention". *Journal of Sociology* 55.1: 8–19.
Franssen, Gaston, and Rick Honings, eds. 2016. *Celebrity Authorship and Afterlives in English and American Literature*. London: Palgrave Macmillan.
Franssen, Paul, and Ton Hoenselaars, eds. 1999. *The Author as Character. Representing Historical Writers in Western Literature*. Madison and Teaneck, NJ: Fairleigh Dickinson University Press; London: Associated University Presses.
Freeman, Arthur, and Janet Ing Freeman. 2004. *John Payne Collier: Scholarship and Forgery in the Nineteenth Century*. 2 vols. New Haven, CT: Yale University Press.
Freud, Sigmund. 1953. "Three Essays on the Theory of Sexuality". 1905. *The Standard Edition of the Complete Psychological Works of Sigmund Freud*. Vol. 7. *A Case of Hysteria, Three Essays on Sexuality and Other Works (1901–1905)*. Ed. James Strachey. Vol. 7. London: Hogarth Press. 123–245.
Freud, Sigmund. 1959. "Creative Writers and Day-Dreaming". *The Standard Edition of the Complete Psychological Works of Sigmund Freud*. Vol. 9. *Jensen's 'Gradiva' and Other Works (1906–1908)*. Ed. James Strachey. London: Hogarth Press. 143–153.
Freud, Sigmund. 1985. *The Complete Letters of Sigmund Freud to Wilhelm Fliess, 1887–1904*. Trans. Jeffrey Moussaieff Masson. Cambridge, MA and London: Belknap Press of Harvard University Press.
Friedman, Lawrence. 2007. *Guarding Life's Dark Secrets. Legal and Social Controls over Reputation, Propriety, and Privacy*. Stanford: Stanford University Press.
Frow, John. 2021. "Authorship". *Literature. Oxford Research Encyclopedias*. https://doi.org/10.1093/acrefore/9780190201098.013.1018. Last access 27 Feb. 2021.
Fuchs, Tobias. 2021. *Die Kunst des Büchermachens. Autorschaft und Materialität der Literatur zwischen 1765 und 1815*. Bielefeld: transcript.
Funk, Wolfgang. 2011. "The Quest for Authenticity: Dave Eggers's *A Heartbreaking Work of Staggering Genius* between Fiction and Reality". *The Metareferential Turn in Contemporary Arts and Media: Forms, Functions, Attempts at Explanation*. Ed. Werner Wolf. Amsterdam: Brill Rodopi. 125–144.
Funk, Wolfgang. 2015. *The Literature of Reconstruction: Authentic Fiction in the New Millennium*. London: Bloomsbury.
Garcia-Fernandez, Erin. 2017. "The Way 'We' Died in Trollope's *An Editor's Tales*". *Victorian Periodicals Review* 50.3: 467–487.
Gardiner, Michael. 2010. "Body and State in Spark's Early Fiction". *The Edinburgh Companion to Muriel Spark*. Ed. Michael Gardiner and Willy Maly. Edinburgh: Edinburgh University Press. 27–39.
Gardner, Diana. 2006. "The Woman Novelist". *The Woman Novelist and Other Stories*. London: Persephone Books. 53–67.
Gaskell, Elizabeth. 2005. *North and South*. 1854. Ed. Alan Shelston. New York: Norton.
Genette, Gérard. 1983. *Narrative Discourse. An Essay in Method*. Trans. Jane E. Lewin. Ithaca, NY: Cornell University Press.

Genette, Gérard. 1997. *Paratexts. Thresholds of Interpretation*. Trans. Jane E. Lewin. Cambridge: Cambridge University Press.
Gervais, Daniel J. 2020. "The Machine as Author". *Iowa Law Review* 105: 2053–2106.
Gibbons, Alison. 2012. *Multimodality, Cognition and Experimental Literature*. New York: Routledge.
Gibson, Scott Thomas. 2010. "Invisibility and the Commodification of Blackness in Ralph Ellison's *Invisible Man* and Percival Everett's *Erasure*". *Canadian Review of Comparative Literature / Revue Canadienne de Littérature Comparée* 37.4: 354–370.
Gilbert, Sandra, and Susan Gubar. 1988–1994. *No Man's Land. The Place of the Woman Writer in the Twentieth Century*. 3 vols. New Haven, CT: Yale University Press.
Gilbert, Sandra, and Susan Gubar. 2000. *The Madwoman in the Attic: The Woman Writer and the Nineteenth-Century Literary Imagination*. 1979. New Haven, CT and London: Yale University Press.
Gissing, George. 1978. *George Gissing on Fiction*. Ed. Jacob and Cynthia Korg. London: Enitharmon Press.
Gissing, George. 2016. *New Grub Street*. 1891. Ed. Katherine Mullin. 2nd ed. Oxford: Oxford University Press.
Gittings, Robert. 1975. *Young Thomas Hardy*. London: Heinemann.
Glass, Loren. 2004. *Authors Inc. Literary Celebrity in the Modern United States, 1880–1980*. New York and London: New York University Press.
Golding, William. 2013. *The Paper Men*. 1984. London: Faber and Faber.
Grabes, Herbert. 2008. "Cultural Memory and the Literary Canon". *Cultural Memory Studies. An International and Interdisciplinary Handbook*. Ed. Astrid Erll and Ansgar Nünning. Berlin: De Gruyter. 311–320.
Graham, Sarah, ed. 2019. *A History of the Bildungsroman*. Cambridge: Cambridge University Press.
Grausam, Daniel, 2011. *On Endings: American Postmodern Fiction and the Cold War*. Charlottesville, VA and London: University of Virginia Press.
Green, Henry. 2008. *Nothing. Doting. Blindness*. Ed. D. J. Taylor. London: Vintage.
Green, Martin. 1976. *Children of the Sun. A Narrative of 'Decadence' in England after 1918*. New York: Basic Books.
Greene, Graham. 2019. *The End of the Affair*. 1951. London: Vintage.
Griem, Julika. 2021. "From Product Placement to Boundary Work: Further Steps towards an Integrated Sociology of Literary Communication". *ZAA* 69.1: 57–76.
Grimes, Hilary. 2011. *The Late Victorian Gothic. Mental Science, the Uncanny, and Scenes of Writing*. Farnham and Burlington: Ashgate.
Grimm, Gunter E., and Christian Schärf, eds. 2008. *Schriftsteller-Inszenierungen*. Bielefeld: Aisthesis.
Groom, Nick. 2019. "Introduction". *Frankenstein or The Modern Prometheus. The 1818 Text*. By Mary Shelley. Ed. Nick Groom. 2018. Oxford: Oxford University Press. ix–l.
Gross, John. 1973. *The Rise and Fall of the Man of Letters. Aspects of English Literary Life since 1800*. 1969. Harmondsworth: Penguin.
Grüttemeier, Ralf, ed. 2016. *Literary Trials. Exceptio Artis and Theories of Literature in Court*. London: Bloomsbury.
Guillory, John. 2022. *Professing Criticism. Essays on the Organization of Literary Study*. Chicago and London: University of Chicago Press.
Guttzeit, Gero. 2017. *The Figures of Edgar Allan Poe. Authorship, Antebellum Literature, and Transatlantic Rhetoric*. Berlin and Boston: De Gruyter.
Guttzeit, Gero. 2018. "Authoring Monsters: Mary Shelley, Edgar Allan Poe and Early Nineteenth-Century Figures of Gothic Authorship". *Forum for Modern Language Studies* 54.3: 279–292.

Guttzeit, Gero. 2021. "The Invisible Author, Then and Now". Unpublished conference paper.
Guy, Josephine M. 1996. *The Victorian Social-Problem Novel. The Market, the Individual and Communal Life*. Houndmills and London: Macmillan.
Habermas, Jürgen. 1997. "Modernity: An Unfinished Project". 1980. *Habermas and the Unfinished Project of Modernity*. Ed. Maurizio Passerin d'Entrèves and Seyla Benhabib. Cambridge, MA: MIT Press. 1–38.
Hack, Daniel. 1999. "Literary Paupers and Professional Authors: The Guild of Literature and Art". *Studies in English Literature 1500–1900* 39.4: 691–713.
Hadar, David. 2016/2017. "A Course in Ghost Writing: Philip Roth, Authorship, and Death". *Connotations* 26: 14–38.
Hallet, Wolfgang. 2014. "The Rise of the Multimodal Novel: Generic Change and its Narratological Implications". *Storyworlds across Media: Toward a Media-Conscious Narratology*. Ed. Marie-Laure Ryan and Jan-Noel Thon. Lincoln: Nebraska University Press. 151–172.
Hanley, Ryan. 2018. "The Equiano Effect: Representativeness and Early Black British Migrant Testimony". *Migrant Britain: Histories and Historiographies. Essays in Honour of Colin Holmes*. Ed. Jennifer Craig-Norton, Christhard Hoffmann, and Tony Kushner. London and New York: Routledge. 262–271.
Hanson, Clare. 2000. *Hysterical Fictions: The 'Woman's Novel' in the Twentieth Century*. Basingstoke: Macmillan.
Hardy, Florence Emily. 2011. *The Early Life of Thomas Hardy, 1840–1891*. 1928. Cambridge: Cambridge University Press.
Hardy, Thomas. 1997. *The Hand of Ethelberta*. 1876. Ed. Tim Dolin. London: Penguin.
Hardy, Thomas. 2005. *A Pair of Blue Eyes*. 1872–1873. Ed. Pamela Dalziel. London: Penguin.
Harputlu Shah, Zeynep. 2019. "Passive Resistance in George Gissing's *New Grub Street* and Knut Hamsun's *Sult*". *Nordic Journal of English Studies* 18.1: 95–120.
Hartley, Daniel. 2016. *The Politics of Style: Towards a Marxist Poetics*. Leiden: Brill.
Hartling, Florian. 2009. *Der digitale Autor. Autorschaft im Zeitalter des Internets*. Bielefeld: transcript.
Hartman, Geoffrey. 1975. "Nature and the Humanization of the Self in Wordsworth". 1970. *English Romantic Poets. Modern Essays in Criticism*. Ed. M. H. Abrams. London, Oxford, and New York: Oxford University Press. 123–132.
Harvey, Giles. 2022. "The History Boy". Review of *Lessons* by Ian McEwan. *The New York Review of Books* 69.17 (3 Nov.): 16–18.
Hassan, Ihab. 2003. "Beyond Postmodernism: Toward an Aesthetic of Trust". *Modern Greek Studies* 11: 303–316.
Hatton, Nikolina. 2020. *The Agency of Objects in English Prose, 1789–1832. Conspicuous Things*. Basingstoke: Palgrave Macmillan.
Hawthorne, Nathaniel. 1982. *Tales and Sketches*. Ed. Roy Harvey Pearce. New York: Library of America.
Hawthorne, Nathaniel. 1987. *The Centenary Edition of the Works of Nathaniel Hawthorne*. Vol. 17. *The Letters, 1853–1856*. Ed. Thomas Woodson et al. Columbus, OH: Ohio State University Press.
Hayes, Patrick. 2021. *The Oxford History of Life Writing*. Vol. 7. *Postwar to Contemporary, 1945–2020*. Oxford: Oxford University Press.
Hayman, David. 1982. *Ulysses. The Mechanics of Meaning*. 1970. Rev. ed. Madison, WI: University of Wisconsin Press.
Haynes, Christine. 2005. "Reassessing 'Genius' in Studies of Authorship". *Book History* 8: 287–320.

Haynes, Christine. 2010. *Lost Illusions. The Politics of Publishing in Nineteenth-Century France.* Cambridge, MA and London: Harvard University Press.
Hayot, Eric. 2012. *On Literary Worlds.* Oxford: Oxford University Press.
Hegel, Georg Wilhelm Friedrich. 2008. *Lectures on Logic.* Trans. Clark Butler. Bloomington: Indiana University Press.
Hegel, Georg Wilhelm Friedrich. 2018. *The Phenomenology of Spirit.* Trans. Michael Inwood. Oxford: Oxford University Press.
Helle, Sophus. 2019. "What Is an Author? Old Answers to a New Question". *Modern Language Quarterly* 80.2: 113–139.
Henderson, Desirée. 2017. "Windows on Writing: Susanna Rowson and the Scene of Female Authorship". *Studies in the Novel* 49.2: 149–169.
Hendriks, Rose Ellen. 1847. *The Young Authoress.* London: Darling.
Henkle, Roger B. 1980. *Comedy and Culture. England 1820–1900.* Princeton: Princeton University Press.
Hentea, Marius. 2012. "The Fiction of Blindness and Real Life: The Diary Portion of Henry Green's *Blindness* (1926)". *Notes and Queries* 59.3: 421–424.
Hentea, Marius. 2014. *Henry Green at the Limits of Modernism.* Brighton, Chicago, and Toronto: Sussex Academic Press.
Herman, David. 2008. "Narrative Theory and the Intentional Stance". *Partial Answers* 6.2: 233–260.
Hesford, Walter. 1982/1983. "'Do you know the author?' The Question of Authorship in *Wieland*". *Early American Literature* 17.3: 239–248.
Heti, Sheila. 2014. *How Should a Person Be?* 2012. London: Vintage.
Hibbitt, Richard. 2006. *Dilettantism and its Values. From Weimar Classicism to the fin de siècle.* Abingdon and New York: Routledge.
Highsmith, Patricia. 2015. *The Tremor of Forgery.* 1969. London: Virago.
Hill, Matt Rowland. 2022. "Last Resort by Andrew Lipstein review – a hipster literary romp". *The Guardian* 10 Mar. https://www.theguardian.com/books/2022/mar/10/last-resort-by-andrew-lipstein-review-hipster-literary-romp-millennial-brooklyn. Last access 29 June 2022.
Hilliard, Christopher. 2014. "The Twopenny Library: The Book Trade, Working-Class Readers, and 'Middlebrow' Novels in Britain, 1930–1942". *Twentieth-Century British History* 25.2: 199–220.
Hilliard, Christopher. 2021. "Authors and Artemus Jones: Libel Reform in England, 1910–52". *Literature & History* 30.1: 62–76.
Hirsch, Pam. 2003. "What's in a Name: Competing Claims to the Authority of George Eliot". *George Eliot Review* 35: 7–17. https://georgeeliotreview.org/items/show/601. Last access 26 Nov. 2022.
Hoban, Russell. 2021. *Kleinzeit.* 1974. London: Penguin.
Hobbs, Katherine. 2019. "Sensational Autobiography: Female Authorship, Marriage, and Melodramatic Self-Representation in 1850s England". *ELH: English Literary History* 86.3: 699–728.
Hoberman, Ruth. 2002. "Women in the British Museum Reading Room during the Late-Nineteenth and Early-Twentieth Centuries: From Quasi- to Counterpublic". *Feminist Studies* 28.3: 489–512.
Hochman, Barbara. 1996. "Disappearing Authors and Resentful Readers in Late-Nineteenth Century American Fiction: The Case of Henry James". *ELH: English Literary History* 63.1: 177–201.
Hollowell, John. 1977. *Fact and Fiction. The New Journalism and the Nonfiction Novel.* Chapel Hill, NC: University of North Carolina Press.
Hoover, Colleen. 2018. *Verity.* London: Sphere.

Howard, Gerald. 1996. "Slouching towards Grubnet: The Author in the Age of Publicity". *Review of Contemporary Fiction* 16.1: 44–53.
Howe, Suzanne. 1930. *Wilhelm Meister and His English Kinsmen: Apprentices to Life.* New York: Columbia University Press.
Howells, William Dean. 1893. "The Man of Letters as a Man of Business". *Scribner's* 14: 429–446.
Hughes, Kathryn. 2001. *George Eliot. The Last Victorian.* New York: Cooper Square Press.
Hughes, Linda L. 2005. "Constructing Fictions of Authorship in George Eliot's *Middlemarch*, 1871–1872". *Victorian Periodicals Review* 38.2: 158–179.
Hühn, Peter. 1995. *Geschichte der englischen Lyrik.* 2 vols. Tübingen and Basel: Francke.
Huk, Romana. 2005. *Stevie Smith: Between the Lines.* Basingstoke: Palgrave Macmillan.
Humble, Nicola. 2001. *The Feminine Middlebrow Novel, 1920s to 1950s. Class, Domesticity, and Bohemianism.* Oxford: Oxford University Press.
Hutcheon, Linda. 1980. *Narcissistic Narrative: The Metafictional Paradox.* Waterloo, Ontario: Wilfrid Laurier University Press.
Hutcheon, Linda. 2013. *A Theory of Adaptation.* 2006. 2nd ed. London and New York: Routledge.
Huxley, Aldous. 1955. *Mortal Coils. Five Stories.* 1922. Harmondsworth: Penguin.
Huxley, Aldous. 2004. *Crome Yellow.* 1921. London: Vintage.
Huyssen, Andreas. 1986. *After the Great Divide. Modernism, Mass Culture, Postmodernism.* Indianapolis: Indiana University Press.
Ingold, Felix Philipp. 1992. *Der Autor am Werk. Versuche über literarische Kreativität.* Munich: Hanser.
Irwin, William, ed. 2002. *The Death and Resurrection of the Author?* Westport, CT: Greenwood Press.
Iser, Wolfgang. 1974. *The Implied Reader. Patterns of Communication in Prose Fiction from Bunyan to Beckett.* Baltimore, MD and London: Johns Hopkins University Press.
Iser, Wolfgang. 1978. *The Act of Reading. A Theory of Aesthetic Response.* Baltimore, MD and London: Johns Hopkins University Press.
Iser, Wolfgang. 2006. *How to Do Theory.* Malden, MA and Oxford: Blackwell.
Iser, Wolfgang. 2013. *Emergenz. Nachgelassene und verstreut publizierte Essays.* Ed. Alexander Schmitz. Konstanz: Konstanz University Press.
Izzo, David Garrett, and Daniel T. O'Hara, eds. 2006. *Henry James against the Aesthetic Movement. Essays on the Middle and Late Fiction.* Jefferson, NC: McFarland.
Jaber, Maysaa Husam. 2021. "Trauma, Horror and the Female Serial Killer in Stephen King's *Carrie* and *Misery*". *Critique: Studies in Contemporary Fiction* 62.2: 166–179.
Jakobson, Roman, and Peter Bogatyrëv. 1982. "Folklore as a Special Form of Creativity". 1929. *The Prague School. Selected Writings, 1929–1946.* Ed. Peter Steiner. Austin, TX: University of Texas Press. 32–46.
James, Henry. 1984. *Literary Criticism. Essays on Literature. American Writers. English Writers.* New York: Library of America.
James, Henry. 1987. *The Complete Notebooks of Henry James.* Ed. Leon Edel and Lyall H. Powers. New York and Oxford: Oxford University Press.
James, Henry. 1996a. *Complete Stories 1892–1898.* New York: Library of America.
James, Henry. 1996b. *Complete Stories 1898–1910.* New York: Library of America.
James, Henry. 1999. *Collected Stories.* Ed. John Bayley. 2 vols. New York: Knopf.
James, Simon. 2003. *Unsettled Accounts: Money and Narrative in the Novels of George Gissing.* London: Anthem Press.
Jameson, Fredric. 2006. *The Political Unconscious. Narrative as a Socially Symbolic Act.* 1981. London and New York: Routledge.

Jannidis, Fotis, Gerhard Lauer, Matias Martinez, and Simone Winko, eds. 1999. *Rückkehr des Autors. Zur Erneuerung eines umstrittenen Begriffs*. Tübingen: Niemeyer.
Jeandillou, Jean-François. 2001. *Supercheries littéraires. La vie et l'œuvre des auteurs supposés*. 1989. Geneva: Droz.
Jeffers, Thomas L. 1988. "Forster's *The Longest Journey* and the Idea of Apprenticeship". *Texas Studies in Literature and Language* 30.2: 179–197.
Jeffers, Thomas L. 2005. *Apprenticeships. The* Bildungsroman *from Goethe to Santayana*. New York and Houndmills: Palgrave Macmillan.
Jensen, Meg. 2018. "How Art Constitutes the Human: Aesthetics, Empathy and the Interesting in Autofiction". *Autofiction in English*. Ed. Hywel Dix. Cham: Palgrave Macmillan. 65–83.
Jensen, Mikkel. 2014. "A Note on a Title: *A Heartbreaking Work of Staggering Genius*". *The Explicator* 72.2: 146–150.
Joch, Markus, and Norbert-Christian Wolf, eds. 2005. *Text und Feld. Bourdieu in der literaturwissenschaftlichen Praxis*. Tübingen: Niemeyer.
John-Wenndorf, Carolin. 2014. *Der öffentliche Autor. Über die Selbstinszenierung von Schriftstellern*. Bielefeld: transcript.
Johnson, B. S. 1964. *Albert Angelo*. New York: New Directions.
Johnson, B. S. 1977. "Introduction to *Aren't You Rather Young to be Writing Your Memoirs?*" 1973. *The Novel Today: Contemporary Writers on Modern Fiction*. Ed. Malcolm Bradbury. Manchester: Manchester University Press. 151–168.
Johnson, Marigold. 1956. "Plain and Fancy". *Times Literary Supplement* 2834 (22 June): 373.
Johnson, Samuel. 2020. *Samuel Johnson*. Ed. David Womersley. 2018. Oxford: Oxford University Press.
Joyce, James. 1987. *Ulysses*. Ed. Hans Walter Gabler, with Wolfhard Steppe and Claus Melchior. Harmondsworth: Penguin.
Joyce, James. 2000. *A Portrait of the Artist as a Young Man*. 1916. Ed. Jeri Johnson. Oxford: Oxford University Press.
Juhl, P. D. 1980. "Life, Literature, and the Implied Author". *Deutsche Vierteljahrsschrift für Literaturwissenschaft und Geistesgeschichte* 54.2: 177–203.
Jullien, Dominique. 2020. "Vernacular, Unacknowledged Multilingualism, and Esoteric Code: Failed Revelations in J. L. Borges's 'Averroës' Search' and R. Kipling's 'The Finest Story in the World'". *Textual Practice* 34.5: 841–860.
Jung, Daun. 2017. "Critical Names Matter: 'Currer Bell,' 'George Eliot,' and 'Mrs. Gaskell'". *Victorian Literature and Culture* 45: 763–781.
Jürgensen, Christoph, and Gerhard Kaiser, eds. 2011. *Schriftstellerische Inszenierungspraktiken. Typologie und Geschichte*. Heidelberg: Winter.
Kaenel, André. 1992. *"Words are Things": Herman Melville and the Invention of Authorship in Nineteenth-Century America*. Berne and Berlin: Peter Lang.
Kania, Andrew. 2005. "Against the Ubiquity of Fictional Narrators". *Journal of Aesthetics and Art Criticism* 63.1: 47–54.
Kardos, Michael. 2019. "The Literary/Genre Fiction Continuum". *Critical Creative Writing: Essential Readings on the Writer's Craft*. Ed. Janelle Adsit. London: Bloomsbury Academic. 220–222.
Keats, John. 1988. *The Complete Poems*. Ed. John Barnard. 3rd ed. London: Penguin.
Keen, Paul, ed. 2014. *The Age of Authors. An Anthology of Eighteenth-Century Print Culture*. Peterborough, Ontario: Broadview Press.
Keene, Donald. 2023. "Japanese Literature". 1998. *Encyclopaedia Britannica*. https://www.britannica.com/art/Japanese-literature/Modern-literature - ref319950. Last access 5 Feb. 2023.

Keesey, Douglas. 2002. "'Your Legs Must Be Singing Grand Opera': Masculinity, Masochism, and Stephen King's *Misery*". *American Imago: Psychoanalysis and the Human Sciences* 59.1: 53–71.
Kelleter, Frank. 2004. "Ethnic Self-Dramatization and Technologies of Travel in *The Interesting Narrative of the Life of Olaudah Equiano, or Gustavus Vassa, the African, Written by Himself* (1789)". *Early American Literature* 39: 67–84.
Kendall, Tim. 2018. "William Golding's Great Dream". *Essays in Criticism* 68.4: 466–487.
Kennedy, A. L. 2000. *Everything You Need*. 1999. London: Vintage.
Kenner, Hugh. 1976. "The Cubist *Portrait*". *Approaches to Joyce's 'Portrait': Ten Essays*. Ed. Thomas Staley and Bernard Benstock. Pittsburgh: University of Pittsburgh Press. 171–184.
Kermode, Frank. 1961. *Romantic Image*. 1957. London: Routledge.
Kermode, Frank. 2000. *The Sense of an Ending. Studies in the Theory of Fiction. With a New Epilogue*. 1966. Oxford: Oxford University Press.
Kern, Stephen. 2019. "Wireless World". *Communication in History. Stone Age Symbols to Social Media*. Ed. Paul Heyer and Peter Urquhart. 7th ed. London and New York: Routledge. 145–148.
Kerr, Lucille. 1992. *Reclaiming the Author. Figures and Fictions from Spanish America*. Durham, NC and London: Duke University Press.
Kindt, Tom, and Hans-Harald Müller, eds. 2006. *The Implied Author: Concept and Controversy*. Trans. Alastair Matthews. Berlin and Boston: De Gruyter.
King, Lily. 2021. *Writers & Lovers*. 2020. London: Picador.
King, Stephen. 2010. *On Writing. A Memoir of the Craft*. 2000. New York: Scribner.
King, Stephen. 2011a. *The Shining*. 1977. London: Hodder and Stoughton.
King, Stephen. 2011b. *Misery*. 1987. London: Hodder and Stoughton.
Kiparski, Frederik. 2018. "Contemporary French-Language Theories of Literary Authorship". *Dealing with Authorship. Authors between Texts, Editors and Public Discourses*. Ed. Sarah Burnautzki, Frederik Kiparski, Raphaël Thierry, and Maria Zannini. Newcastle: Cambridge Scholars. 2–20.
Kipling, Rudyard. 1965. *Rudyard Kipling to Rider Haggard. The Record of a Friendship*. Ed. Morton Cohen. London: Hutchinson.
Kipling, Rudyard. 1987. *A Choice of Kipling's Prose*. London and Boston: Faber and Faber.
Kipling, Rudyard. 1994. *Collected Stories*. New York: Knopf.
Kipling, Rudyard. 2000. *Selected Poems*. Ed. Peter Keating. London: Penguin.
Kipling, Rudyard. 2015. *Stories and Poems*. Ed. Daniel Karlin. Oxford: Oxford University Press.
Kirkland, Richard. 1996. *Literature and Culture in Northern Ireland Since 1965. Moments of Danger*. London and New York: Longman.
Kirschenbaum, Matthew. 2016. *Track Changes: A Literary History of Word Processing*. Cambridge, MA and London: Belknap Press of Harvard University Press.
Kittler, Friedrich. 1990. *Discourse Networks, 1800/1900*. 1985. Trans. Michael Metteer and Chris Cullens. Stanford: Stanford University Press.
Klancher, Jon P. 1987. *The Making of English Reading Audiences, 1790–1832*. Madison, WI: University of Wisconsin Press.
Knights, Ben. 1978. *The Idea of the Clerisy in the Nineteenth Century*. Cambridge: Cambridge University Press.
Knox, Marisa Palacios. 2014. "'The Valley of the Shadow of Books': George Gissing, New Women, and Morbid Literary Detachment". *Nineteenth-Century Literature* 69.1: 92–122.
Kohlmann, Benjamin. 2009. "'The Heritage of Symbolism': Henry Green, Maurice Bowra, and English Modernism in the 1920s". *Modern Language Notes* 124.5: 1188–1210.

Kohlmann, Benjamin. 2015. "Toward a History and Theory of the Socialist Bildungsroman". *Novel: A Forum on Fiction* 48.2: 167–189.
Kohlmann, Benjamin, and Matthew Taunton. 2019. "Introduction: The Long 1930s". *A History of 1930s British Literature*. Ed. Benjamin Kohlmann and Matthew Taunton. Cambridge: Cambridge University Press. 1–14.
Köppe, Tilmann, and Jan Stühring. 2011. "Against Pan-Narrator Theories". *Journal of Literary Semantics* 40.1: 59–80.
Korelitz, Jean Hanff. 2021. *The Plot*. New York: Celadon Books.
Korthals Altes, Liesbeth. 2008. "Sincerity, Reliability and Other Ironies: Notes on Dave Eggers' *A Heartbreaking Work of Staggering Genius*". *Narrative Unreliability in the Twentieth-Century First-Person Novel*. Ed. Elke d'Hoker and Gunther Martens. Berlin: De Gruyter. 107–128.
Korzybski, Alfred. 1958. *Science and Sanity. An Introduction to Non-Aristotelian Systems and General Semantics*. 1933. 4th ed. Lakeville, CT: International Non-Aristotelian Library.
Kovach, Elizabeth. 2020. "Collapsing the Economic and Creative Values of Contemporary Literature in Sheila Heti's *Motherhood* and Ben Lerner's *10:04*". *REAL: Yearbook of Research in English and American Literature* 36: 185–200.
Kraver, Jeraldine R. 2001. "All about 'Author-ity': When the Disciple Becomes the Master in 'The Author of *Beltraffio*'". *"The Finer Thread, the Tighter Weave". Essays on the Short Fiction of Henry James*. Ed. Joseph Dewey and Brooke Horvath. West Lafayette, IN: Purdue University Press. 30–42.
Kreknin, Innokentij. 2014. *Poetiken des Selbst. Identität, Autorschaft und Autofiktion am Beispiel von Rainald Goetz, Joachim Lottmann und Alban Nikolai Herbst*. Berlin/Boston: De Gruyter.
Kripke, Saul. 2013. *Reference and Existence. The John Locke Lectures*. Oxford: Oxford University Press.
Kristeva, Julia. 1980. *Desire in Language. A Semiotic Approach to Literature and Art*. Ed. Leon S. Roudiez. Trans. Thomas Gora, Alice Jardine, and Leon S. Roudiez. New York: Columbia University Press.
Künzel, Christine, and Jörg Schönert, eds. 2007. *Autorinszenierungen: Autorschaft und literarisches Werk im Kontext der Medien*. Würzburg: Königshausen & Neumann.
Kunzru, Hari. 2020. *Red Pill*. London and New York: Scribner.
Kyora, Sabine, ed. 2014. *Subjektform Autor. Autorschaftsinszenierungen als Praktiken der Subjektivierung*. Bielefeld: transcript.
Lackey, Joanna. 2012. "'I use the woman's figure naturally': Figuring Women's Work in Elizabeth Barrett Browning's *Aurora Leigh*". *Nineteenth-Century Gender Studies* 8.3. http://www.ncgsjournal.com/issue83/lackey.html. Last access 15 Feb. 2023.
Lackey, Michael. 2022. *Biofiction: An Introduction*. London and New York: Routledge.
Lamarque, Peter. 2009. *The Philosophy of Literature*. Malden, MA and Oxford: Blackwell.
Lamarque, Peter, and Stein Haugom Olsen. 1994. *Truth, Fiction, and Literature: A Philosophical Perspective*. Oxford: Oxford University Press.
Landais, Clotilde. 2012. "Le représentation littéraire de l'écrivain comme reflet de l'imposture de l'institution littéraire chez Stephen King". *Imaginaires de la vie littéraire. Fiction, figuration, configuration*. Ed. Björn-Olav Dozo, Anthony Glinoer, and Michel Lacroix. Rennes: Presses Universitaires de Rennes. 339–353.
Landais, Clotilde. 2013. *Stephen King as a Postmodern Author*. New York: Peter Lang.
Lanser, Susan Sniader. 1992. *Fictions of Authority. Women Writers and Narrative Voice*. Ithaca, NY and London: Cornell University Press.

Lant, Kathleen Margaret. 1997. "The Rape of Constant Reader: Stephen King's Construction of the Female Reader and Violation of the Female Body in *Misery*". *Journal of Popular Culture* 30.4: 89–114.
Laporte, Charles. 2013. "*Aurora Leigh, A Life-Drama*, and Victorian Poetic Autobiography". *SEL: Studies in English Literature 1500–1900* 53.4: 829–851.
Laquintano, Timothy. 2016. *Mass Authorship and the Rise of Self-Publishing*. Iowa City: University of Iowa Press.
Larkin, Philip. 2002. *Trouble at Willow Gables and Other Fictions*. Ed. James Booth. London: Faber and Faber.
Latham, Sean. 2009. *The Art of Scandal: Modernism, Libel Law, and the Roman à Clef*. Oxford: Oxford University Press.
Latham, Sean. 2019. "Industrialized Print: Modernism and Authorship". *The Cambridge Handbook of Literary Authorship*. Ed. Ingo Berensmeyer, Gert Buelens, and Marysa Demoor. Cambridge: Cambridge University Press. 165–182.
Latour, Bruno. 2005. *Reassembling the Social. An Introduction to Actor-Network-Theory*. Oxford: Oxford University Press.
Law, Graham. 2012. "The Professionalization of Authorship". *The Oxford History of the Novel in English*. Vol. 3. *The Nineteenth-Century Novel 1820–1880*. Ed. John Kucich and Jenny Bourne Taylor. Oxford: Oxford University Press. 37–55.
Layne, Bethany, ed. 2020. *Biofiction and Writers' Afterlives*. Newcastle: Cambridge Scholars.
Lazzaro-Weis, Carol. 1990. "The Female 'Bildungsroman': Calling it into Question". *NWSA Journal* 2.1: 16–34.
Leavis, F. R. 1930. *Mass Civilisation and Minority Culture*. Cambridge: The Minority Press.
Leavis, Q. D. 1979. *Fiction and the Reading Public*. 1932. Harmondsworth: Penguin.
Legleitner, Rickie-Ann. 2021. *Women Writing the American Artist in Novels of Development from 1850–1932. The Artist Embodied*. Lanham, MD: Lexington Books.
Lejeune, Philippe. 1975. *Le pacte autobiographique*. Paris: Seuil.
Lenta, Margaret. 2003. "*Autre*biography: J. M. Coetzee's *Boyhood* and *Youth*". *English in Africa* 30.1: 157–169.
Lesser, Margaret. 2012. "Ellen Marriage and the Translation of Balzac". *Translation and Literature* 21.3: 343–363.
Lessing, Doris. 2007. *The Golden Notebook*. 1962. London: Harper Perennial.
Lethem, Jonathan. 2007. "The Ecstasy of Influence. A Plagiarism". *Harper's Magazine* 314.1881: 59–71.
Lethem, Jonathan. 2017. *More Alive and Less Lonely. On Books and Writers*. Ed. Christopher Boucher. New York and London: Melville House.
Levenson, Michael. 2007. "The Fictional Realist: Novels of the 1930s". *The Cambridge Companion to George Orwell*. Ed. John Rodden. Cambridge: Cambridge University Press. 59–75.
Levin, Yael. 2016. "Metalepsis and the Author Figure in Modernist and Postmodernist Fiction". *Twentieth-Century Literature* 62.3: 289–308.
Levine, Caroline. 2015. *Forms. Whole, Rhythm, Hierarchy, Network*. Princeton and Oxford: Princeton University Press.
Levinson, Marjorie. 2007. "What Is New Formalism?" *PMLA: Publications of the Modern Language Association of America* 122.2: 558–569.
Lewes, Darby, ed. 2006. *Auto-poetica. Representations of the Creative Process in Nineteenth-Century British and American Fiction*. Lanham, MD: Lexington Books.
Lewes, G. H. 1847. *Ranthorpe*. Leipzig: Tauchnitz.

Leypoldt, Günter. 2016. "The Artist as Hero: Nineteenth-Century Concepts of Authorship in a Transatlantic Perspective". *Traveling Traditions: Nineteenth-Century Cultural Concepts and Transatlantic Intellectual Networks.* Ed. Erik Redling. Berlin and Boston: De Gruyter. 95–110.
Leypoldt, Günter. 2017. "Knausgaard in America: Literary Prestige and Charismatic Trust". *Critical Quarterly* 59.3: 55–69.
Leypoldt, Günter. 2021. "Spatial Reading: Evaluative Frameworks and the Making of Literary Authority". *American Journal of Cultural Sociology* 9.2: 150–176.
Light, Alison. 1991. *Forever England: Femininity, Literature and Conservatism between the Wars.* London and New York: Routledge.
Lilti, Antoine. 2014. *Figures publiques. L'invention de la célébrité (1750–1850).* Paris: Fayard.
Linley, Margaret. 1999. "Dying to Be a Poetess: The Conundrum of Christina Rossetti". *The Culture of Christina Rossetti: Female Poetics and Victorian Contexts.* Ed. Mary Arseneau, Anthony H. Harrison, and Lorraine Janzen Kooistra. Athens, OH: Ohio University Press. 285–314.
Lodge, David. 1986. *The Novelist at the Crossroads and Other Essays on Fiction and Criticism.* 1971. London and New York: ARK Paperbacks.
Lodge, David. 2002. *Language of Fiction. Essays in Criticism and Verbal Analysis of the English Novel.* 1966. London and New York: Routledge.
Longolius, Sonja. 2016. *Performing Authorship. Strategies of 'Becoming an Author' in the Works of Paul Auster, Candice Breitz, Sophie Calle, and Jonathan Safran Foer.* Bielefeld: transcript.
Love, Harold. 2002. *Attributing Authorship: An Introduction.* Cambridge: Cambridge University Press.
Lovejoy, Arthur O. 2019. "On the Discrimination of Romanticisms". 1924. *Essays in the History of Ideas.* 1948. Baltimore: Johns Hopkins University Press. 228–253.
Lubbock, Percy. 1926. *The Craft of Fiction.* 1921. London: Jonathan Cape.
Lucas, John. 1974. *Arnold Bennett. A Study of His Fiction.* London: Methuen.
Luetkens, Charlotte. 1946. *Women and a New Society.* London: Nicholson & Watson.
Luhmann, Niklas. 2000. *Art as a Social System.* Trans. Eva M. Knodt. Stanford, CA: Stanford University Press.
Lukács, Georg. 1971. *Die Theorie des Romans. Ein geschichtsphilosophischer Versuch über die Formen der großen Epik.* 1920. Darmstadt and Neuwied: Luchterhand.
Lukács, Georg. 1972. "Balzac: 'Verlorene Illusionen'". 1952. *Schriften zur Literatursoziologie.* Ed. Peter Ludz. 5th ed. Neuwied, Darmstadt, and Berlin: Luchterhand. 349–357.
Lukács, Georg. 2000. "From *The Theory of the Novel*: A Historico-Philosophical Essay on the Forms of Great Epic Literature". *Theory of the Novel. A Historical Approach.* Ed. Michael McKeon. Baltimore, MD and London: Johns Hopkins University Press. 185–218.
Lyas, Colin. 1983. "The Relevance of the Author's Sincerity". *Philosophy and Fiction: Essays in Literary Aesthetics.* Ed. Peter Lamarque. Aberdeen: Aberdeen University Press. 17–37.
Lycett, Andrew. 1999. *Rudyard Kipling.* London: Weidenfeld and Nicolson.
Lynch, Jack. 2019. "Plagiarism and Forgery". *The Cambridge Handbook of Literary Authorship.* Ed. Ingo Berensmeyer, Gert Buelens, and Marysa Demoor. Cambridge: Cambridge University Press. 354–370.
Lyons, Paddy. 2010. "Muriel Spark's Break with Romanticism". *The Edinburgh Companion to Muriel Spark.* Ed. Michael Gardiner and Willy Maly. Edinburgh: Edinburgh University Press. 85–97.
Lyotard, Jean-François. 1997. *The Postmodern Condition. A Report on Knowledge.* Trans. Geoff Bennington and Brian Massumi. Manchester: Manchester University Press.
Macdonald, Kate, ed. 2011. *The Masculine Middlebrow, 1880–1950: What Mr. Miniver Read.* Basingstoke: Palgrave Macmillan.

Macdonald, Kate, and Christoph Singer, eds. 2015. *Transitions in Middlebrow Writing, 1880–1930*. Basingstoke: Palgrave Macmillan.
Machen, Arthur. 2019. *Collected Fiction*. Vol. 2. *1896–1910*. Ed. S. T. Joshi. New York: Hippocampus Press.
Maier, S. E. 2007. "Portraits of the Girl-Child. Female Bildungsroman in Victorian Fiction". *Literature Compass* 4.1: 317–335.
Maingueneau, Dominique. 2004. *Le discours littéraire. Paratopie et scène d'énonciation*. Paris: Armand Colin.
Maingueneau, Dominique. 2016. *Trouver sa place dans le champ littéraire. Paratopie et création*. Louvain-la-Neuve: Academia.
Maitra, Julian. 2020. "Shakespeare's Verified Facebook Page: How Authorship Patterns Survive and Thrive in the Digital Sphere". *Kodex. Jahrbuch der Internationalen Buchwissenschaftlichen Gesellschaft*. Vol. 10. *Im digitalen Jenseits der Literatur. Towards the Digital Beyond of Literature*. Ed. Vincent Kaufmann. Wiesbaden: Harrassowitz. 111–128.
Maner, Martin. 1991. "Beerbohm's *Seven Men* and the Power of the Press". *English Literature in Transition, 1880–1920* 34.2: 132–151.
Mann, Thomas. 1990. "Joseph und seine Brüder. Ein Vortrag". 1942. *Gesammelte Werke in dreizehn Bänden*. Vol. 11. *Reden und Aufsätze 3*. Frankfurt am Main: S. Fischer. 654–669.
Mantel, Hilary. 2008. "Introduction". *Angel*. By Elizabeth Taylor. London: Virago. 1–6.
Mantrant, Sophie. 2013. "'All London Was One Grey Temple of an Awful Rite': Londres dans *The Hill of Dreams* d'Arthur Machen (1907)". *Cahiers Victoriens et Edouardiens* 77. https://doi.org/10.4000/cve.344. Last access 26 Nov. 2022.
Marcus, Sharon. 1995. "The Profession of the Author: Abstraction, Advertising, and *Jane Eyre*". *PMLA: Publications of the Modern Language Association of America* 110.2: 206–219.
Margree, Victoria. 2016. "Metanarratives of Authorship in Fin-de-Siècle Popular Fiction: 'Is That All You Do, Write Stories?'" *English Literature in Transition 1880–1920* 59.3: 362–389.
Martin, Andy. 2015. *Reacher Said Nothing. Lee Child and the Making of* Make Me. London: Bantam.
Martin, Andy. 2019. *With Child. Lee Child and the Readers of Jack Reacher*. Cambridge: Polity.
Martin, Jean-Pierre, ed. 2010. *Bourdieu et la littérature*. Nantes: Cécile Defaut.
Martus, Steffen. 2007. *Werkpolitik. Zur Literaturgeschichte kritischer Kommunikation vom 17. bis ins 20. Jahrhundert mit Studien zu Klopstock, Tieck, Goethe und George*. Berlin and New York: De Gruyter.
Mattacks, Kate. 2009. "Mary Elizabeth Braddon's Secret: An Antifeminist amongst the New Women". *Antifeminism and the Victorian Novel. Rereading Nineteenth-Century Women Writers*. Ed. Tamara S. Wagner. Amherst, NY: Cambria. 217–230.
Maturana, Humberto, and Francisco Varela. 1980. *Autopoiesis and Cognition. The Realization of the Living*. Dordrecht: Reidel.
Maturana, Humberto, and Francisco Varela. 1988. *The Tree of Knowledge*. Boston: Shambhala.
May, Brian. 1996. "Modernism and Other Modes in Forster's *The Longest Journey*". *Twentieth Century Literature* 42.2: 234–257.
May, Charles E. 2006. "Putting Yourself in the Shoes of Raymond Carver". *Journal of the Short Story in English* 46: 31–42.
May, William. 2010. *Stevie Smith and Authorship*. Oxford: Oxford University Press.
McAlpine, Erica. 2020. *The Poet's Mistake*. Princeton: Princeton University Press.
McBride, Margaret. 2001. *Ulysses and the Metamorphosis of Stephen Dedalus*. Lewisburg: Bucknell University Press; London: Associated University Presses.

McCarthy, Tom. 2016. "Foreword: On Being the Subject of a Conference or, What Do I Know?" *Tom McCarthy. Critical Essays*. Ed. Dennis Duncan. Canterbury: Gylphi. 1–2.

McDonell, Jennifer. 2015. "Henry James, Literary Fame, and the Problem of Robert Browning". *Critical Survey* 27.3: 43–62.

McGann, Jerome J., ed. 2008. *Lord Byron. The Major Works*. Oxford: Oxford University Press.

McGill, Meredith. 2003. *American Literature and the Culture of Reprinting, 1834–1853*. Philadelphia: University of Pennsylvania Press.

McGurl, Mark. 2009. *The Program Era. Postwar Fiction and the Rise of Creative Writing*. Cambridge, MA and London: Harvard University Press.

McGurl, Mark. 2016. "Everything and Less: Fiction in the Age of Amazon". *Modern Language Quarterly* 77.3: 447–471.

McHale, Brian. 1987. *Postmodernist Fiction*. New York and London: Routledge.

McIntyre, Timothy. 2015. "'This Is Not Enough': Gesturing Beyond the Aesthetics of Failure in Alice Munro's 'Material'". *American Review of Canadian Studies* 45.2: 161–173.

McPherson, Sue. 2017. "Gissing's *New Grub Street* and the Wider Concerns of Impoverishment". *English Literature in Transition, 1880–1920* 60.4: 490–505.

Meizoz, Jérôme. 2007. *Postures littéraires. Mises en scène modernes de l'auteur*. Geneva: Slatkine.

Meizoz, Jérôme. 2011. *La fabrique des singularités: Postures littéraires II*. Geneva: Slatkine.

Meizoz, Jérôme. 2016. *La littérature 'en personne'. Scène médiatique et formes d'incarnation*. Geneva: Slatkine.

Melchiori, Giorgio. 1956. *The Tightrope Walkers. Studies of Mannerism in Modern English Literature*. London: Routledge & Kegan Paul.

Melville, Herman. 1993. *Correspondence*. Ed. Lynn Horth. Evanston and Chicago, IL: Northwestern University Press and The Newberry Library.

Melville, Herman. 1996. *Pierre; or, The Ambiguities*. 1852. Ed. William C. Spengemann. Harmondsworth: Penguin.

Melville, Herman. 2002. *Melville's Short Novels*. Ed. Dan McCall. New York and London: Norton.

Melville, Herman. 2014. "Hawthorne and His Mosses". *Shakespeare in America. An Anthology from the Revolution to Now*. Ed. James Shapiro. New York: Library of America. 123–141.

Menke, Richard. 2013. "The Medium Is the Media: Fictions of the Telephone in the 1890s". *Victorian Studies* 55.2: 212–221.

Menke, Richard. 2018. "*New Grub Street*'s Ecologies of Paper". *Victorian Studies* 61.1: 60–82.

Menke, Richard. 2019. *Literature, Print Culture, and Media Technologies, 1880–1900. Many Inventions*. Cambridge: Cambridge University Press.

Meres, Francis. 1598. *Palladis Tamia. Wits Treasury [...]*. London: P. Short, for Cuthbert Burbie. Folger Shakespeare Library, STC 17834 copy 1. https://shakespearedocumented.folger.edu/resource/document/palladis-tamia-one-earliest-printed-assessments-shakespeares-works-and-first. Last access 31 Jan. 2022.

Messud, Claire. 2017. "Fierce, She Got Outside the Moment". Review of *Transit* by Rachel Cusk. *The New York Review of Books* 64.5 (23 Mar.): 28–30.

Meyer, Michael J. 2004. "Stephen King's Writers: The Critical Politics of Literary Quality in *Misery* and *The Dark Half*". *Literature and the Writer*. Ed. Michael J. Meyer. Leiden: Brill. 97–117.

Micevska, Teona. 2021. *Modernist Women Dandies. Poetry, Photography, Authorship*. Berlin: Peter Lang.

Mill, John Stuart. 1859. *Dissertations and Discussions Political, Philosophical, and Historical*. 2 vols. London: John W. Parker and Son.

Miller, D. A. 2003. *Jane Austen, or the Secret of Style*. Princeton and Oxford: Princeton University Press.

Miller, Henry. 2015. *Tropic of Cancer.* 1934. London: Penguin.
Miller, J. Hillis. 1970. *Thomas Hardy: Distance and Desire.* Cambridge, MA: Belknap Press of Harvard University Press.
Miller, J. Hillis. 1975. "Optic and Semiotic in *Middlemarch*". *The Worlds of Victorian Fiction.* Ed. Jerome H. Buckley. Harvard English Studies 6. Cambridge and London: Harvard University Press. 125–145.
Miller, J. Hillis. 1977. "The Critic as Host". *Critical Inquiry* 3.3: 439–447.
Miller, Thomas. 1844. *Godfrey Malvern; or, The Life of an Author.* 1842. 2nd ed. London: Thomas Miller.
Mills, Adelais. 2018. "Authorial Enchantments in the Fictions of Henry James, Philip Roth, and Joshua Cohen". *CounterText* 4.3: 382–405.
Milne, Leah A. 2021. *Novel Subjects. Authorship as Radical Self-Care in Multiethnic American Narratives.* Iowa City: University of Iowa Press.
Milton, John. 1957. *Complete Poems and Major Prose.* Ed. Merritt Y. Hughes. New York: Odyssey Press.
Miracky, James J. 2002–2003. "Pursuing (a) Fantasy: E. M. Forster's Queering of Realism in *The Longest Journey*". *Journal of Modern Literature* 26.2: 129–144.
Mitchell, David T., and Sharon L. Snyder, 2001. *Narrative Prosthesis. Disability and the Dependencies of Discourse.* Ann Arbor, MI: University of Michigan Press.
Mitchell, Julian. 2010. *The Undiscovered Country.* 1968. London: Capuchin Classics.
Montaigne, Michel de. 1915. *The Essays of Michael Lord of Montaigne.* 1910. Trans. John Florio. 1632. 3 vols. London and Toronto: Dent; New York: Dutton.
Moore, Allan F. 2002. "Authenticity as Authentication". *Popular Music* 21.2: 209–223.
Moore, Allan F. 2012. *Song Means: Analysing and Interpreting Recorded Popular Song.* Farnham: Ashgate.
Moore, Lorrie. 2020. *Collected Stories.* New York: Knopf.
Moran, Joe. 2000. *Star Authors. Literary Celebrity in America.* London and Sterling, VA: Pluto Press.
Moraru, Christian. 2020. "Murdoch *after* Postmodernism: Metafiction, Truth, and the Aesthetic of Presence in *The Black Prince*". *Études britanniques contemporaines* 59: 78–84.
Moretti, Franco. 1988. *Signs Taken for Wonders. Essays in the Sociology of Literary Forms.* 1983. Trans. Susan Fischer, David Forgacs and David Miller. London and New York: Verso.
Moretti, Franco. 2000. *The Way of the World. The* Bildungsroman *in European Culture.* 1987. Trans. Albert Sbragia. London and New York: Verso.
Moretti, Franco. 2013. *The Bourgeois. Between History and Literature.* London and New York: Verso.
Morley, John. 1877. *On Compromise.* 1874. 2nd ed. London: Chapman and Hall.
Morse, Elizabeth J. 2004. "Meynell, Laurence Walter (1899–1989)". *Oxford Dictionary of National Biography.* Oxford: Oxford University Press. Last access 18 Aug. 2022.
Morton, Timothy. 2007. *Ecology without Nature: Rethinking Environmental Aesthetics.* Cambridge, MA: Harvard University Press.
Moynihan, Sinéad. 2010. *Passing into the Present. Contemporary American Fiction of Racial and Gender Passing.* Manchester: Manchester University Press.
Mullan, John. 2007. *Anonymity. A Secret History of English Literature.* Princeton, NJ and Oxford: Princeton University Press.
Mullen, Richard, and James Munson. 1996. *The Penguin Companion to Trollope.* Harmondsworth: Penguin.
Munro, Alice. 1993. "What Is Real?" *The Art of Short Fiction. An International Anthology.* Ed. Gary Geddes. Toronto: HarperCollins. 824–827.

Munro, Alice. 1997. "Material". 1973. *A Wilderness Station. Selected Stories, 1968 – 1994.* New York: Vintage International. 99 – 116.
Murdoch, Iris. 1961. "Against Dryness. A Polemical Sketch". *Encounter* 16: 16 – 20.
Murdoch, Iris. 2019. *The Black Prince.* 1973. London: Vintage.
Myrdal, Alva, and Viola Klein. 1956. *Women's Two Roles: Home and Work.* London: Routledge.
Nabokov, Vladimir. 1996. *Novels and Memoirs 1941 – 1951. The Real Life of Sebastian Knight. Bend Sinister. Speak, Memory.* Ed. Brian Boyd. New York: Library of America.
Nash, Andrew. 2016. "The Material History of the Novel I: 1940 – 1973". *The Oxford History of the Novel in English.* Vol. 7. *British and Irish Fiction Since 1940.* Ed. Peter Boxall and Bryan Cheyette. Oxford: Oxford University Press. 21 – 36.
Nemesvari, Richard. 1991. "'Work it Out for Yourself': Language and Fictional Form in Stevie Smith's *Novel on Yellow Paper*". *The Dalhousie Review* 71.1: 26 – 37.
Newman, Daniel Aureliano. 2016. "Kin Selection, Mendel's 'Salutary Principle' and the Fate of Characters in Forster's *The Longest Journey*". *Fact and Fiction: Literary and Scientific Cultures in Germany and Britain.* Ed. Christine Lehleiter. Toronto, Buffalo, and London: University of Toronto Press. 247 – 271.
Nietzsche, Friedrich. 2007. *Ecce Homo. How To Become What You Are.* Trans. Duncan Large. Oxford: Oxford University Press.
Noiray, Jacques, ed. 2013. *Illusions perdues.* By Honoré de Balzac. Paris: Gallimard.
Nugent-Folan, Georgina. 2022. "Self Re-writing and Self Un-writing. Reconsidering Gertrude Stein's Marginalisation in Discussions of Samuel Beckett's Autographic Writing". *Samuel Beckett Today / Aujourd'hui* 34: 163 – 176.
Nünning, Ansgar. 1993. "Renaissance eines anthropomorphisierten Passepartouts oder Nachruf auf ein literaturkritisches Phantom? Überlegungen und Alternativen zum Konzept des *'implied author'*". *Deutsche Vierteljahrsschrift für Literaturwissenschaft und Geistesgeschichte* 47.1: 1 – 25.
Nünning, Ansgar. 1997. "Deconstructing and Reconceptualizing the Implied Author". *Anglistik* 8.2: 95 – 116.
Nünning, Ansgar. 2005a. "Reconceptualizing Unreliable Narration". *A Companion to Narrative Theory.* Ed. James Phelan and Peter J. Rabinowitz. Malden, MA: Blackwell. 89 – 107.
Nünning, Ansgar. 2005b. "Fictional Metabiographies and Metaautobiographies: Towards a Definition, Typology and Analysis of Self-Reflexive Hybrid Metagenres". *Self-Reflexivity in Literature.* Ed. Werner Huber, Martin Middeke, and Hubert Zapf. Würzburg: Königshausen & Neumann. 195 – 209.
Nussbaum, Martha. 2004. "'Faint with Secret Knowledge': Love and Vision in Murdoch's *The Black Prince*". *Poetics Today* 25.4: 689 – 710.
Oates, Joyce Carol. 1996. "The Madness of Art: Henry James's 'The Middle Years'". *New Literary History* 27.2: 259 – 262.
Offill, Jenny. 2020. "Seeing Too Clearly". Review of *Red Pill* by Hari Kunzru. *The New York Review of Books* 67.18 (19 Nov.): 33 – 35.
O'Malley, Gregory E. 2014. *Final Passages. The Intercolonial Slave Trade of British America, 1619 – 1807.* Chapel Hill, NC: University of North Carolina Press.
Onslow, Barbara. 2000. *Women of the Press in Nineteenth-Century Britain.* Houndmills: Macmillan.
Orwell, George. 2002. *Essays.* Ed. John Carey and Peter Davison. New York: Everyman's Library.
Orwell, George. 2013. *Nineteen Eighty-Four. The Annotated Edition.* 1949. London: Penguin.
Orwell, George. 2014. *Keep the Aspidistra Flying.* 1936. London: Penguin.

Oswald, John. 1787. "The Brain-Sucker, or the Distress of Authorship". *The British Mercury* 1–2: 14–27, 43–48.
Palko, Amy. 2007. "Poaching the Print: Theorising the Scrapbook in Stephen King's *Misery*". *The International Journal of the Book* 4.3: 57–60.
Parker, Hershel. 1996. *Herman Melville: A Biography*. Vol. 1. *1819–1851*. Baltimore, MD: Johns Hopkins University Press.
Pasco, Allan H. 2016. *Balzac, Literary Sociologist*. Basingstoke: Palgrave Macmillan.
Paston, George (Emily Morse Symonds). 1999. *A Writer of Books*. 1898. Chicago, IL: Academy Chicago Publishers.
Patey, Douglas Lane. 1998. *The Life of Evelyn Waugh. A Critical Biography*. Oxford and Malden, MA: Blackwell.
Patron, Sylvie. 2009. *Le narrateur: Introduction à la théorie narrative*. Paris: Armand Colin.
Patron, Sylvie. 2019. *The Death of the Narrator and Other Essays*. Trier: WVT.
Patron, Sylvie, ed. 2021. *Optional-Narrator Theory: Principles, Perspectives, Proposals*. Lincoln, NE: University of Nebraska Press.
Pérez Fontdevila, Aina, and Meri Torras Francés. 2016. "Hacia una *biografía* del concepto de autor". *Los papeles del autor/a. Marcos teóricos sobre la autoría literaria*. Ed. Aina Pérez Fontdevila and Meri Torras Francés. Madrid: Arco Libros. 11–51.
Perry, Michael. 2019. "Storytelling and a Story Told. Stephen King's Narrators in *From a Buick 8, The Colorado Kid,* and *Blaze*". *The Modern Stephen King Canon. Beyond Horror*. Ed. Philip L. Simpson and Patrick McAleer. Lanham, MD: Lexington Books. 21–32.
Peterson, Linda H. 1999. *Traditions of Victorian Women's Autobiography: The Poetics and Politics of Life Writing*. Charlottesville: University of Virginia Press.
Peterson, Linda H. 2009. *Becoming a Woman of Letters: Myths of Authorship and Facts of the Victorian Market*. Princeton: Princeton University Press.
Pfeiffer, Helmut. 2021. *Das zerbrechliche Band der Gesellschaft. Diagnosen der Moderne zwischen Honoré de Balzac und Henry James*. Paderborn: Brill Fink.
Pfeiffer, K. Ludwig. 1978. "The Novel and Society. Reflections on the Interaction of Literary and Cultural Paradigms". *PTL: A Journal for Descriptive Poetics and the Theory of Literature* 3: 45–69.
Pfeiffer, K. Ludwig. 1981. *Bilder der Realität und die Realität der Bilder. Verbrauchte Formen in den Romanen George Merediths*. Munich: Fink.
Phelan, James. 1996. *Narrative as Rhetoric. Technique, Audiences, Ethics, Ideology*. Columbus, OH: Ohio State University Press.
Phelan, James. 2005. *Living to Tell about It. A Rhetoric and Ethics of Character Narration*. Ithaca, NY: Cornell University Press.
Phelan, James. 2011. "The Implied Author, Deficient Narration, and Nonfiction Narrative: Or, What's Off-Kilter in *The Year of Magical Thinking* and *The Diving Bell and the Butterfly?*" *Style* 45.1: 119–137.
Phelan, James. 2017. *Somebody Telling Somebody Else. A Rhetorical Poetics of Narrative*. Columbus: Ohio State University Press.
Phelan, James. 2018. "Authors, Resources, Audiences: Toward a Rhetorical Poetics of Narrative". *Style* 52.1–2: 1–34.
Phillips, Arthur. 2011. *The Tragedy of Arthur*. New York: Random House.
Pinsker, Sanford. 2014. "Anne Frank and the 'What If' School of Fiction". *Sewanee Review* 122.2: 340–344.
Plato. 1993. *Republic*. Trans. Robin Waterfield. Oxford: Oxford University Press.

Plato. 2002. *Phaedrus*. Trans. Robin Waterfield. Oxford: Oxford University Press.
Poe, Edgar Allan. 1984. *Essays and Reviews*. Ed. G. R. Thompson. New York: Library of America.
Pointon, Marcia. 2006. "National Identity and the Afterlife of Shakespeare's Portraits". *Searching for Shakespeare*. By Tarnya Cooper, with essays by Marcia Pointon, James Shapiro, and Stanley Wells. New Haven, CT: Yale University Press. 217–225.
Polvinen, Merja. 2013. "Affect and Artifice in Cognitive Literary Theory". *Journal of Literary Semantics* 42.2: 165–180.
Poovey, Mary. 1988. *Uneven Developments: The Ideological Wok of Gender in Mid-Victorian England*. Chicago: University of Chicago Press.
Powell, Anthony. 2015. *What's Become of Waring*. 1939. London: Arrow.
Power, Chris. 2021. *A Lonely Man*. London: Faber and Faber.
Prendergast, Christopher. 1978. *Balzac. Fiction and Melodrama*. London: Edward Arnold.
Puech, Jean-Benoît. 1982. "L'auteur supposé. Essai de typologie des écrivains imaginaires en littérature". Unpublished doctoral thesis. Paris: EHESS.
Pugh, Martin. 2000. *Women and the Women's Movement in Britain, 1914–1999*. 2nd ed. Basingstoke: Macmillan.
Pulkki, Eveliina. 2018. "Failing Authorship in Knut Hamsun's *Sult* (1890)". *Forum for Modern Language Studies* 54.3: 293–306.
Puskar, Jason. 2019. "Institutions: Writing and Reading". *The Cambridge Handbook of Literary Authorship*. Ed. Ingo Berensmeyer, Gert Buelens, and Marysa Demoor. Cambridge: Cambridge University Press. 429–443.
Pym, Barbara. 2010. *Less than Angels*. 1955. London: Virago.
Quinn, Vincent. 2007. "Jane Austen, Queer Theory and the Return of the Author". *Women: A Cultural Review* 18.1: 57–83.
Rabinowitz, Peter J. 1976. "Truth in Fiction: A Reexamination of Audiences". *Critical Inquiry* 4: 121–141.
Radford, Andrew. 2011. "A Novel of 'Balanced Sensations'? Decoding *The Hand of Ethelberta* (1876)". *The Thomas Hardy Yearbook* 39: 3–16.
Rainey, Laurence. 2009. "Pretty Typewriters, Melodramatic Modernity: Edna, Belle, Estelle". *Modernism/modernity* 16.1: 105–122.
Reader, W. J. 1966. *Professional Men: The Rise of the Professional Classes in the Nineteenth Century*. London: Weidenfeld and Nicolson.
Reckwitz, Andreas. 2012. *Die Erfindung der Kreativität. Zum Prozess gesellschaftlicher Ästhetisierung*. Frankfurt a. M.: Suhrkamp.
Reilly, Charlie. 2013. "An Interview with Arthur Phillips". *Contemporary Literature* 54.1: 1–22.
Reinfandt, Christoph. 2003. *Romantische Kommunikation. Zur Kontinuität der Romantik in der Kultur der Moderne*. Heidelberg: Winter.
Renault, Mary. 2014. *The Friendly Young Ladies*. 1944. London: Virago.
Richardson, Brian. 2015. *Unnatural Narrative. Theory, History, and Practice*. Columbus, OH: Ohio State University Press.
Richardson, Samuel. 1964. *Selected Letters of Samuel Richardson*. Ed. John Carroll. Oxford: Clarendon Press.
Rimmon-Kenan, Shlomith. 2002. *Narrative Fiction: Contemporary Poetics*. 1983. London and New York: Routledge.
Roberts, Patrick. 1994. "Ethelberta: Portrait of the Artist as a Young Woman: Love and Ambition". *The Thomas Hardy Journal* 10.1: 87–94.

Rose, Mark. 1993. *Authors and Owners: The Invention of Copyright*. Cambridge, MA: Harvard University Press.

Rosen, Jeremy. 2018. "Literary Fiction and the Genres of Genre Fiction". *Post45* 7 Aug. https://post45.org/2018/08/literary-fiction-and-the-genres-of-genre-fiction/. Last access 26 Nov. 2022.

Ross, Trevor. 2019. "Censorship". *The Cambridge Handbook of Literary Authorship*. Ed. Ingo Berensmeyer, Gert Buelens, and Marysa Demoor. Cambridge: Cambridge University Press. 400–414.

Rossetti, Christina. 1897. *Maude: Prose and Verse*. Chicago: Herbert S. Stone.

Rossetti, W. M. 1897. "Prefatory Note". *Maude: Prose and Verse*. By Christina Rossetti. Chicago: Herbert S. Stone. 1–6.

Roth, Philip. 2007. *Zuckerman Bound: A Trilogy and Epilogue 1979–1985. The Ghost Writer. Zuckerman Unbound. The Anatomy Lesson. The Prague Orgy*. New York: Library of America.

Roth, Philip. 2017. *Why Write? Collected Nonfiction 1960–2014*. New York: Library of America.

Rowe, Karen E. 1983. "'Fairy-born and human-bred': Jane Eyre's Education in Romance". *The Voyage In. Fictions of Female Development*. Ed. Elizabeth Abel, Marianne Hirsch, and Elizabeth Langland. Hanover, NE and London: University Press of New England.

Ruth, Jennifer. 2006. *Novel Professions. Interested Disinterest and the Making of the Professional in the Victorian Novel*. Columbus, OH: Ohio State University Press.

Ryan, Marie-Laure, and Monika Fludernik, eds. 2019. *Narrative Factuality. A Handbook*. Berlin and Boston: De Gruyter.

Ryan, Susan M. 2016. *The Moral Economies of American Authorship. Reputation, Scandal, and the Nineteenth-Century Literary Marketplace*. Oxford: Oxford University Press.

Sage, Liz. 2016. "Women's Fiction after the War". *The Oxford History of the Novel in English*. Vol. 7. *British and Irish Fiction Since 1940*. Ed. Peter Boxall and Bryan Cheyette. Oxford: Oxford University Press. 110–127.

Said, Edward W. 1983. *The World, the Text, and the Critic*. Cambridge, MA: Harvard University Press.

Saint-Amand, Denis, and David Vrydaghs. 2011. "Retours sur la posture". *COnTEXTES* 8. https://doi.org/10.4000/contextes.4712. Last access 7 Feb. 2022.

Saint-Amour, Paul K. 2003. *The Copywrights. Intellectual Property and the Literary Imagination*. Ithaca, NY and London: Cornell University Press.

Salmon, Richard. 1997. *Henry James and the Culture of Publicity*. Cambridge: Cambridge University Press.

Salmon, Richard. 2012. "The English Bildungsroman". *The Oxford History of the Novel in English*. Vol. 3. *The Nineteenth-Century Novel 1820–1880*. Ed. John Kucich and Jenny Bourne Taylor. Oxford: Oxford University Press. 90–105.

Salmon, Richard. 2013. *The Formation of the Victorian Literary Profession*. Cambridge: Cambridge University Press.

Salmon, Richard. 2019. "The Bildungsroman and Nineteenth-Century British Fiction". *A History of the Bildungsroman*. Ed. Sarah Graham. Cambridge: Cambridge University Press. 57–83.

Sapiro, Gisèle. 2011. *La responsabilité de l'écrivain. Littérature, droit et morale en France (XIXe – XXIe siècle)*. Paris: Seuil.

Sapiro, Gisèle. 2020. *Peut-on dissocier l'œuvre de l'auteur?* Paris: Seuil.

Sapiro, Gisèle, and Cécile Rabot, eds. 2017. *Profession? Écrivain*. Paris: CNRS Éditions.

Saunders, David, and Ian Hunter. 1991. "Lessons from the 'Literary'. How to Historicise Authorship". *Critical Inquiry* 17.3: 479–509.

Saunders, John W. 1964. *The Profession of English Letters*. London: Routledge and Kegan Paul.

Savu, Laura E. 2009. *Postmortem Postmodernists: The Afterlife of the Author in Recent Narrative*. Madison and Teaneck, NJ: Fairleigh Dickinson University Press.

Sayers, Dorothy. 1946. *Unpopular Opinions*. London: Gollancz.

Sayers, Philip. 2021. *Authorship's Wake: Writing After the Death of the Author*. New York and London: Bloomsbury Academic.

Schaffrick, Matthias, and Markus Willand, eds. 2014. *Theorien und Praktiken der Autorschaft*. Berlin and Boston: De Gruyter.

Scheiding, Oliver. 2018. "Charles Brockden Brown, *Wieland; or, The Transformation. An American Tale* (1798)". *Handbook of the American Novel of the Nineteenth Century*. Ed. Christine Gerhardt. Berlin: De Gruyter. 157–173.

Schellenberg, Betty A. 2019. "The Eighteenth Century. Print, Professionalization, and Defining the Author". *The Cambridge Handbook of Literary Authorship*. Ed. Ingo Berensmeyer, Gert Buelens, and Marysa Demoor. Cambridge: Cambridge University Press. 133–146.

Schenkar, Joan. 2009. *The Talented Miss Highsmith. The Secret Life and Serious Art of Patricia Highsmith*. New York: Picador.

Scherr, Alexander, and Ansgar Nünning. 2020. "Methods of New Sociological Approaches to Literature". *Methods of Textual Analysis in Literary Studies: Approaches, Basics, Model Interpretations*. Ed. Vera Nünning and Ansgar Nünning. Trier: Wissenschaftlicher Verlag Trier. 229–249.

Schmid, Wolf. 2010. *Narratology: An Introduction*. Trans. Alexander Starritt. Berlin and Boston: De Gruyter.

Schmid, Wolf. 2013. "Implied Author (revised version; uploaded 26 January 2013)". *The Living Handbook of Narratology*. Ed. Peter Hühn, Jan Christoph Meister, John Pier, and Wolf Schmid. Hamburg: Hamburg University. http://www.lhn.uni-hamburg.de/article/implied-author-revised-version-uploaded-26-january-2013. Last access 10 Feb. 2022.

Schneider, Karen. 1997. *Loving Arms. British Women Writing the Second World War*. Lexington, KY: University Press of Kentucky.

Schneider, Ralf. 2017. "E. M. Forster, *A Passage to India* (1924)". *Handbook of the English Novel of the Twentieth and Twenty-First Centuries*. Ed. Christoph Reinfandt. Berlin and Boston: De Gruyter. 175–194.

Scholes, Robert. 1967. *The Fabulators*. Oxford: Oxford University Press.

Schopp, Andrew. 1994. "Writing (with) the Body: Stephen King's *Misery*". *LIT: Literature Interpretation Theory* 5.1: 29–43.

Schroeder, Natalie. 1996. "Stephen King's *Misery*: Freudian Sexual Symbolism and the Battle of the Sexes". *Journal of Popular Culture* 30.2: 137–148.

Schweik, Robert. 2002. "Hardy's 'Plunge in a New and Untried Direction': Comic Detachment in *The Hand of Ethelberta*". *English Studies* 83.3: 239–252.

Scodel, Ruth. 2019. "Authorship in Archaic and Classical Greece". *The Cambridge Handbook of Literary Authorship*. Ed. Ingo Berensmeyer, Gert Buelens, and Marysa Demoor. Cambridge: Cambridge University Press. 46–63.

Scofield, Martin. 1999. "Story and History in Raymond Carver". *Critique: Studies in Contemporary Fiction* 40.3: 266–280.

Selig, Robert L. 1970. "'The Valley of the Shadow of Books': Alienation in Gissing's *New Grub Street*". *Nineteenth-Century Fiction* 25.2: 188–198.

Sennett, Richard. 1999. *The Corrosion of Character. The Personal Consequences of Work in the New Capitalism*. New York: Norton.

Sennett, Richard. 2002. *The Fall of Public Man*. 1977. London: Penguin.
Severin, Laura. 1997. *Stevie Smith's Resistant Antics*. Madison: University of Wisconsin Press.
Severn, Stephen E. 2010. "Quasi-Professional Culture, Conservative Ideology, and the Narrative Structure of George Gissing's *New Grub Street*". *Journal of Narrative Theory* 40.2: 156–188.
Sheets, Robin A. 1993. "'The Farcical History of Richard Greenow': Aldous Huxley and Anxieties of Male Authorship". *Journal of Narrative and Life History* 3.2–3: 197–208.
Sheridan, Susan. 2009. "In the Driver's Seat: Muriel Spark's Editorship of the 'Poetry Review'". *Journal of Modern Literature* 32.2: 133–142.
Shields, David. 2010. *Reality Hunger. A Manifesto*. New York: Knopf.
Showalter, Elaine. 1972. *A Literature of Their Own. British Women Novelists from Brontë to Lessing*. Princeton, NJ: Princeton University Press.
Sidney, Sir Philip. 1973. "A Defence of Poetry". *Miscellaneous Prose of Sir Philip Sidney*. Ed. Katherine Duncan Jones and Jan van Dorsten. Oxford: Clarendon Press. 73–121.
Simenon, Georges. 2016. *Maigret's Memoirs*. 1951. Trans. Howard Curtis. London: Penguin.
Simon, Irène. 1991. "Vision or Dream? The Supernatural Design in *The Paper Men*". *William Golding: The Sound of Silence*. Ed. Jeanne Delbaere. Liège: English Department, University of Liège. 176–185.
Sinclair, Iain. 2010. "Man in a Macintosh: Roland Camberton, the Great Invisible of English Fiction". *Scamp*. By Roland Camberton. London: New London Editions. 5–18.
Sinykin, Dan. 2017. "The Conglomerate Era: Publishing, Authorship, and Literary Form, 1965–2007". *Contemporary Literature* 58.4: 462–491.
Siskin, Clifford. 1998. *The Work of Writing: Literature and Social Change in Britain, 1700–1830*. Baltimore, MD: Johns Hopkins University Press.
Skov Nielsen, Henrik. 2010. "Natural Authors, Unnatural Narration". *Postclassical Narratology. Approaches and Analyses*. Ed. Jan Alber and Monika Fludernik. Columbus: Ohio State University Press. 275–301.
Smith, Stevie. 2015. *Novel on Yellow Paper*. 1936. London: Virago.
Smith, Zadie. 2019. "Fascinated to Presume: In Defense of Fiction". *The New York Review of Books* 66.16 (24 Oct.): 4–9.
Spark, Muriel. 1999. *The Ballad of Peckham Rye*. 1960. London: Penguin.
Spark, Muriel. 2009. *The Comforters*. 1957. London: Virago.
Spark, Muriel. 2013. *The Girls of Slender Means*. 1963. London: Penguin.
Spark, Muriel. 2014. *The Informed Air: Essays by Muriel Spark*. Ed. Penelope Jardine. New York: New Directions.
Spark, Muriel. 2018. *The Complete Short Stories*. Edinburgh: Canongate.
Spear, Hilda D. 1995. *Iris Murdoch*. Houndmills: Macmillan.
Spencer, Sharon. 1973. "'Femininity' and the Woman Writer: Doris Lessing's *The Golden Notebook* and the *Diary* of Anais Nin". *Women's Studies* 1: 247–257.
Spencer, Stephanie. 2000. "Women's Dilemmas in Postwar Britain: Career Stories for Adolescent Girls in the 1950s". *History of Education* 29.4: 329–342.
Spivak, Gayatri C. 1996. "Subaltern Studies: Deconstructing Historiography?" 1985. *The Spivak Reader*. Ed. Donna Landry and Gerald MacLean. London and New York: Routledge. 203–237.
Spoerhase, Carlos. 2018. *Das Format der Literatur. Praktiken materieller Textualität zwischen 1740 und 1830*. Göttingen: Wallstein.
Stang, Richard. 1959. *The Theory of the Novel in England, 1850–1870*. New York: Columbia University Press.

Stannard, Martin. 1992. *Evelyn Waugh: No Abiding City. 1939–1966*. London: Dent.
Stannard, Martin. 2009. *Muriel Spark. The Biography*. London: Weidenfeld and Nicolson.
Stanzel, Franz K. 1984. *A Theory of Narrative*. Trans. Charlotte Goedsche. 2nd rev. ed. Cambridge: Cambridge University Press.
Stanzel, Franz K. 1987. *Typische Formen des Romans*. 1964. Göttingen: Vandenhoeck & Ruprecht.
St Clair, William. 2004. *The Reading Nation in the Romantic Period*. Cambridge: Cambridge University Press.
Sterry, Emma. 2017. *The Single Woman, Modernity, and Literary Culture. Women's Fiction from the 1920s to the 1940s*. Basingstoke: Palgrave Macmillan.
Stetz, Margaret D. 1999. "Introduction". *A Writer of Books*. By George Paston (Emily Morse Symonds). Chicago, IL: Academy Chicago Publishers. v–xiv.
Stetz, Margaret D. 2015. "Internationalizing Authorship: Beyond *New Grub Street* to the *Bookman* in 1891". *Victorian Periodicals Review* 48.1: 1–14.
Stewart, David H. 1988. "Kipling's Portraits of the Artist". *English Literature in Transition, 1880–1920* 31.3: 265–283.
Stewart, Susan. 1994. *Crimes of Writing. Problems in the Containment of Representation*. 1991. 2nd ed. Durham, NC: Duke University Press.
Stewart, Victoria. 2011. "The Woman Writer in Mid-Twentieth Century Middlebrow Fiction: Conceptualizing Creativity". *Journal of Modern Literature* 35: 21–36.
Stiénon, Valérie. 2008. "Notes et remarques à propos de Jérôme Meizoz, *Postures littéraires. Mises en scène modernes de l'auteur*". *COnTEXTES*. http://contextes.revues.org/833. Last access 7 Feb. 2022.
Stolarek, Joanna. 2018. "Fluid Identities and Social Dislocation in the Face of Crime, Guilt and Ethics in Patricia Highsmith's *The Talented Mr Ripley* and *The Tremor of Forgery*". *Brno Studies in English* 44.2: 145–156.
Stougaard-Nielsen, Jakob. 2012. "'No absolute privacy': Henry James and the Ethics of Reading Authors' Letters". *Authorship* 1.2. https://doi.org/10.21825/aj.v1i2.765. Last access 7 Feb. 2022.
Stougaard-Nielsen, Jakob. 2019. "The Author in Literary Theory and Theories of Literature". *The Cambridge Handbook of Literary Authorship*. Ed. Ingo Berensmeyer, Gert Buelens, and Marysa Demoor. Cambridge: Cambridge University Press. 270–287.
Sutherland, J. A. 1976. *Victorian Novelists and Publishers*. London: The Athlone Press.
Sutherland, John. 1995. "Introduction". *Later Short Stories*. By Anthony Trollope. Oxford and New York: Oxford University Press. vii–xxii.
Sutherland, John. 2006. *Victorian Fiction. Writers, Publishers, Readers*. 1995. 2nd ed. Houndmills: Palgrave Macmillan.
Sutherland, John. 2009. *The Longman Companion to Victorian Fiction*. 1988. 2nd ed. London and New York: Routledge.
Sutherland, John, ed. 1994. *The History of Pendennis*. By William Thackeray. Oxford: Oxford University Press.
Symons, A. J. A. 1979. *The Quest for Corvo. An Experiment in Biography*. 1934. Harmondsworth: Penguin.
Tabor, Eliza. 1871. *Diary of a Novelist*. London: Hurst and Blackett.
Taft, Joshua. 2011. "'New Grub Street' and the Survival of Realism". *English Literature in Transition, 1880–1920* 54.3: 362–381.
Tammi, Pekka. 1985. *Problems of Nabokov's Poetics. A Narratological Analysis*. Helsinki: Suomalainen Tiedeakatemia.

Taylor, Charles. 1992. *Sources of the Self. The Making of the Modern Identity.* 1989. Cambridge: Cambridge University Press.
Taylor, D. J. 2008. *Bright Young People. The Rise and Fall of a Generation 1918–1940.* London: Vintage.
Taylor, D. J. 2016. *The Prose Factory. Literary Life in England Since 1918.* London: Vintage.
Taylor, Elizabeth. 2008. *Angel.* 1957. London: Virago.
Taylor, Elizabeth. 2018. *A View of the Harbour.* 1947. London: Virago.
Thackeray, William Makepeace. 1945–1946. *The Letters and Private Papers.* Ed. Gordon N. Ray. 4 vols. Oxford: Oxford University Press.
Thackeray, William Makepeace. 1993. *A Shabby Genteel Story and Other Writings.* Ed. D. J. Taylor. London: Dent.
Thackeray, William Makepeace. 1994. *The History of Pendennis.* 1848–1850. Ed. John Sutherland. Oxford: Oxford University Press.
Theile, Verena, and Linda Tredennick, eds. 2013. *New Formalisms and Literary Theory.* London: Palgrave Macmillan.
Thompson, G. R. 1993. *The Art of Authorial Presence. Hawthorne's Provincial Tales.* Durham, NC and London: Duke University Press.
Thompson, Graham. 2019. "Realism and the Profession of Authorship". *The Oxford Handbook of American Literary Realism.* Ed. Keith Newlin. Oxford: Oxford University Press. 303–320.
Thompson, John B. 2012. *Merchants of Culture. The Publishing Business in the Twenty-First Century.* 2010. 2nd ed. New York: Plume.
Thoss, Jeff. 2013. "There's No Place Like Fiction. Narrative Space and Metalepsis in Stephen King's 'Umney's Last Case'". *Placing America: American Culture and its Spaces.* Ed. Michael Fuchs and Maria-Theresia Holly. Bielefeld: transcript. 91–101.
Tillotson, Geoffrey. 1963. *Thackeray the Novelist.* 1954. London: Methuen.
Tillotson, Kathleen. 1959. *The Tale and the Teller.* London: Rupert Hart-Davis.
Titolo, Matthew. 2003. "The Clerks' Tale: Liberalism, Accountability, and Mimesis in *David Copperfield*". *ELH: English Literary History* 70: 171–195.
Tokarczuk, Olga. 2019. "Nobel Lecture. The Tender Narrator". Trans. Jennifer Croft and Antonia Lloyd-Jones. Stockholm: Nobel Foundation. https://www.nobelprize.org/uploads/2019/12/tokarczuk-lecture-english-2.pdf. Last access 16 Feb. 2022.
Tolkien, J. R. R. 1983. "On Fairy-Stories". *The Monsters and the Critics and Other Essays.* Ed. Christopher Tolkien. London: George Allen and Unwin. 109–161.
Treglown, Jeremy. 1994. *Roald Dahl: A Biography.* New York: Farrar, Straus and Giroux.
Trilling, Lionel. 1955. "Art and Neurosis". *The Liberal Imagination: Essays on Literature and Society.* London: Secker and Warburg. 160–197.
Tripp, Ronja. 2014. "Visualisierung und Narrativierung in Erzähltexten der Moderne (H. Green: *Blindness*)". *Handbuch Literatur und visuelle Kultur.* Ed. Claudia Benthien and Brigitte Weingart. Berlin and New York: De Gruyter. 462–477.
Trollope, Anthony. 1994. *The Way We Live Now.* 1875. Ed. Sir Frank Kermode. Harmondsworth: Penguin.
Trollope, Anthony. 1995. *Later Short Stories.* Ed. John Sutherland. Oxford and New York: Oxford University Press.
Trollope, Anthony. 1996. *An Autobiography.* 1883. Ed. David Skilton. London: Penguin.
Trotter, David. 1993. *The English Novel in History 1895–1920.* London and New York: Routledge.
Trotter, David. 2020. *The Literature of Connection. Signal, Medium, Interface, 1850–1950.* Oxford: Oxford University Press.

Tuchman, Gaye, and Nina E. Fortin. 2012. *Edging Women Out. Victorian Novelists, Publishers, and Social Change*. London: Routledge.

Underwood, Ted, David Bamman, and Sabrina Lee. 2018. "The Transformation of Gender in English-Language Fiction". *Journal of Cultural Analytics* 3.2. https://doi.org/10.22148/16.019. Last access 26 Nov. 2022.

Uspensky, Boris. 1973. *A Poetics of Composition. The Structure of the Artistic Text and Typology of a Compositional Form*. Trans. Valentina Zavarin and Susan Wittig. Berkeley, Los Angeles, and London: University of California Press.

Valihora, Karen. 2019. "She Got Up and Went Away: Rachel Cusk on Making an Exit". *English Studies in Canada* 45.1–2: 19–35.

van der Weel, Adriaan. 2019. "Literary Authorship in the Digital Age". *The Cambridge Handbook of Literary Authorship*. Ed. Ingo Berensmeyer, Gert Buelens, and Marysa Demoor. Cambridge: Cambridge University Press. 218–233.

Vermeulen, Pieter. 2021. "Against Premature Articulation. Empathy, Gender, and Austerity in Rachel Cusk and Katie Kitamura". *Cultural Critique* 111: 81–103.

Vernon, John. 1984. *Money and Fiction: Literary Realism in the Nineteenth and Early Twentieth Centuries*. Ithaca, NY and London: Cornell University Press.

Viala, Alain. 1985. *Naissance de l'écrivain. Sociologie de la littérature à l'âge classique*. Paris: Minuit.

Villa, Luisa. 1988. "Verso/attraverso *The Hill of Dreams*: Walter Pater, Arthur Machen, l'oggetto estetico e la decadenza". *Textus: English Studies in Italy* 1.1: 101–146.

Vinogradov, Viktor Vladimirovich. 1930. *About Art Prose*. Moscow and Leningrad: State Publishing House.

Voelz, Johannes. 2016. "The New Sincerity as Literary Hospitality". *Security and Hospitality in Literature and Culture: Modern and Contemporary Perspectives*. Ed. Jeffrey Clapp and Emily Ridge. New York: Routledge. 209–226.

Vogel, Elizabeth. 2011. "'I Don't Know Why I Joke. I Hurt': Pain, Humor, and Second-Person Narration in Lorrie Moore's 'How to Be an Other Woman'". *Studies in American Humor* 24: 71–82.

Vonnegut, Kurt. 2011. "The Art of Fiction". Interview by David Hayman, David Michaelis, George Plimpton, and Richard Rhodes. *The Paris Review* 69 (1977): 57–103. *The Last Interview and Other Conversations*. Ed. Tom McCartan. New York: Melville House. 5–63.

Wagner-Egelhaaf, Martina, ed. 2012. *Auto(r)fiktion. Literarische Verfahren der Selbstkonstruktion*. Bielefeld: Aisthesis.

Waithe, Marcus, and Claire White, ed. 2018. *The Labour of Literature in Britain and France, 1830–1910. Authorial Work Ethics*. Basingstoke: Palgrave Macmillan.

Wallace, Anne D. 1997. "'Nor in Fading Silks Compose': Sewing, Walking, and Poetic Labor in *Aurora Leigh*". *ELH: English Literary History* 64.1: 223–256.

Wallace, David Foster. 1993. "E Unibus Pluram: Television and U. S. Fiction". *Review of Contemporary Fiction* 13.2: 151–194.

Walsh, Jessica. 2004. "Stevie Smith: Girl, Interrupted". *Papers on Language and Literature* 40.1: 57–87.

Walsh, Richard. 2007. *The Rhetoric of Fictionality*. Columbus, OH: Ohio State University Press.

Walton, Priscilla. 1992. "'There had to be some way to show the difference': Authorial Presence and Supplementarity in James's 'The Private Life'". *Victorian Review* 18.1: 13–23.

Wargen, Joanna. 2010. "All Eyes Are on the City: Arthur Machen's Ethnographic Vision of London". *Literary London* 8.1. http://literarylondon.org/the-literary-london-journal/archive-of-the-literary-london-journal/issue-8-1/all-eyes-are-on-the-city-arthur-machens-ethnographic-vision-of-london/. Last access 26 Nov. 2022.

Warhol, Robyn. 1989. *Gendered Interventions. Narrative Discourse in the Victorian Novel*. New Brunswick, NJ: Rutgers University Press.
Warner, Sylvia Townsend. 2020. *Lolly Willowes or The Loving Huntsman*. 1926. London: Penguin.
Warning, Rainer. 1999. *Die Phantasie der Realisten*. Munich: Fink.
Waugh, Evelyn. 1957. "Something Fresh: *The Comforters*". *Spectator* 6713 (22 Feb.): 256.
Waugh, Evelyn. 2003a. *Vile Bodies*. 1930. London: Penguin.
Waugh, Evelyn. 2003b. *Black Mischief, Scoop, The Loved One, The Ordeal of Gilbert Pinfold*. London: Everyman's Library.
Waugh, Patricia. 1984. *Metafiction. The Theory and Practice of Self-Conscious Fiction*. London and New York: Routledge.
Weber, Max. 1958. *The Protestant Ethic and the Spirit of Capitalism*. Trans. Talcott Parsons. New York: Scribner's.
Weimann, Robert. 1988. "Text, Author-Function, and Appropriation in Modern Narrative: Toward a Sociology of Representation". *Critical Inquiry* 14.3: 431–447.
Weinrich, Harald. 1964. *Tempus. Besprochene und erzählte Welt*. Munich: Beck.
Wells, Chauncey W. 1929. "Thackeray and the Victorian Compromise". *University of California Publications in English*. Vol. 1. *Essays in Criticism*. Ed. W. H. Durham, M. J. Flaherty, and Chauncey W. Wells. 179–199.
Wetzel, Michael, ed. 2022. *Grundthemen der Literaturwissenschaft: Autorschaft*. Berlin and Boston: De Gruyter.
Wheeler, Kathleen. 1994. *'Modernist' Women Writers and Narrative Art*. Basingstoke: Palgrave Macmillan.
Widdowson, Peter. 1989. *Hardy in History: A Study in Literary Sociology*. London and New York: Routledge.
Wilde, Oscar. 1994. *Complete Works of Oscar Wilde*. Glasgow: HarperCollins.
Wilkes, Joanne. 2017. "The Women of Anthony Trollope's *An Editor's Tales*". *Essays in Criticism* 67.2: 136–153.
Willbern, David. 2013. *The American Popular Novel After World War II. A Study of 25 Best Sellers, 1947–2000*. Jefferson, NC and London: McFarland.
Williams, David. 1991. *Confessional Fictions: A Portrait of the Artist in the Canadian Novel*. Toronto: University of Toronto Press.
Williams, Gertrude. 1945. *Women and Work*. London: Nicholson & Watson.
Williams, Raymond. 1977. *Marxism and Literature*. Oxford: Oxford University Press.
Williams, Raymond. 2001. "The Writer: Commitment and Alignment". 1980. *The Raymond Williams Reader*. Ed. John O. Higgins. Oxford: Blackwell. 208–217.
Williams, Raymond. 2010. *Tenses of Imagination. Raymond Williams on Science Fiction, Utopia and Dystopia*. Ed. Andrew Milner. Oxford: Peter Lang.
Willson, Andrew. 2017. "Vagrancy and the Fantasy of Unproductive Writing in *David Copperfield*". *Nineteenth-Century Literature* 72.2: 192–217.
Wimsatt, W. K., and Monroe C. Beardsley. 1954. "The Intentional Fallacy". *The Verbal Icon. Studies in the Meaning of Poetry*. Ed. William K. Wimsatt. Lexington: University of Kentucky Press. 3–20.
Wirth, Uwe. 2008. *Die Geburt des Autors aus dem Geist der Herausgeberfiktion. Editoriale Rahmung im Roman um 1800: Wieland, Goethe, Brentano, Jean Paul und E. T. A. Hoffmann*. Munich: Fink.
Wirth-Nesher, Hana. 1984. "The Thematics of Interpretation: James's Artist Tales". *The Henry James Review* 5.2: 117–127.

Wodehouse, P. G. 2012. *Piccadilly Jim*. 1917. N. p.: The Floating Press. Google Books. Last access 26 Nov. 2022.
Wöhrer, Franz. 1995. "'Face to Face with the Indescribable, Inexplicable, the Isness': Intimate Relationships with the Divine in *The Paper Men*". *Fingering Netsukes: Selected Papers from the First International William Golding Conference*. Ed. Frédéric Regard. Saint-Étienne: Publications de l'Université de Saint-Étienne, with Faber. 151–181.
Wojtas, Paweł. 2010. "E. M. Forster's Uneasy Bildungsroman: Exploring the Meanders of Existential Aporias in *The Longest Journey*". *New Aspects of E. M. Forster*. Ed. Krzysztof Fordoński. Warsaw: Instytut Kulturologii i Lingwistyki Antropocentryzcnej Uniwersytetu Warszawskiego; International E. M. Forster Society. 31–51.
Womble, Todd. 2018. "Roth Is Roth as Roth: Autofiction and the Implied Author". *Autofiction in English*. Ed. Hywel Dix. Cham: Palgrave Macmillan. 219–236.
Woodmansee, Martha. 1984. "The Genius and the Copyright: Economic and Legal Conditions of the Emergence of the 'Author'". *Eighteenth-Century Studies* 17.4: 425–448.
Woodmansee, Martha. 1994. *The Author, Art, and the Market: Rereading the History of Aesthetics*. New York: Columbia University Press.
Woodmansee, Martha, and Peter Jaszi, eds. 1994. *The Construction of Authorship: Textual Appropriation in Law and Literature*. Durham, NC and London: Duke University Press.
Woolf, Virginia. 1985. *Moments of Being*. Ed. Jeanne Schulkind. 1975. 2nd ed. London: Hogarth Press.
Woolf, Virginia. 2008. "Modern Fiction". 1925. *Selected Essays*. Ed. David Bradshaw. Oxford: Oxford University Press. 6–12.
Wordsworth, William. 1850. *The Prelude, or Growth of a Poet's Mind. An Autobiographical Poem*. London: Edward Moxon.
Worthington, Marjorie. 2004. "The Novel Construction of the Writer: Symbiotic Texts, Parasitic Authors in *The Golden Notebook*". *Literature and the Writer*. Ed. Michael J. Meyer. Amsterdam and New York: Rodopi. 59–78.
Youmans, N. O. 1930. *Best Seller. The Story of a Young Man Who Came to New York to Write a Novel about a Young Man Who Came to New York to Write a Novel*. Indianapolis: Bobbs-Merrill.
Zilboorg, Caroline. 2001. *The Masks of Mary Renault*. Columbia, MO: University of Missouri Press.
Zwierlein, Anne-Julia, ed. 2010. *Gender and Creation. Surveying Gendered Myths of Creativity, Authority, and Authorship*. Heidelberg: Winter.

Index

62: A Model Kit (Cortázar novel)   281

abolition   79, 102
About the Author (Colapinto novel)   335, 338, 343, 345, 398
Abrams, J. J.   301, 368
– S.   301, 368
Absolute Hell (Ackland play)   251
abstraction   26, 48, 81, 378
Ackland, Rodney   251
– *Absolute Hell*   251
act   36, 39, 45, 60, 63, 79, 116, 122, 131, 133, 156, 174, 192, 199, 202, 206, 230, 264, 282, 284, 294–295, 307–308, 321, 327, 333, 337, 342, 344, 358, 359, 374, 378
– act of authorship   26, 29–31, 46, 53, 271, 294, 322
– act of creation   36–37, 65, 220
– act of fiction-making   306, 344
– Act of Parliament   110
– act of reading   120
– act of resistance   239
– act of transgression   183
– act of writing   21, 26–27, 53, 79, 220, 264, 267, 284, 288, 292–293, 305, 326
– authorial act   26
– creative act   19, 58
– extrarepresentational act   62–63
– intentional act   57
– Married Women's Property Act   167
– performative act   80
– sexual act   242, 292
– speech act   67, 80
action   4, 23, 27, 41, 54, 61, 75, 80, 108, 125, 143, 157, 187, 214, 218, 283, 291, 336, 343, 371, 373–374, 378
Adair, Gilbert   333, 397
– *The Death of the Author*   333, 397
Adam Bede (Eliot novel)   112, 148–149, 280
Addison, Joseph   33
Addison, Julia   130, 386
– *Evelyn Lascelles*   130, 386
Adeline (Vincent novel)   8

Adichie, Chimamanda Ngozi   362–363
– *Americanah*   362
Adorno, Theodor W.   40–41
– "The Position of the Narrator in the Contemporary Novel"   40
adventure *or* adventurer   117, 121, 144, 154, 156, 202, 248, 267, 283, 321, 326
– "Adventures of a Pen"   35, 385
– "The Adventures of Fred Pickering" (Trollope tale)   154, 166, 386
– *The Adventures of Philip* (Thackeray novel)   110
advertisement *or* advertising   130, 165, 181, 186, 207, 219, 224–225, 227–228, 238, 247, 257, 291, 293, 349, 353
Aeschylus   8
aesthetic   1, 6, 9, 11, 20–22, 24, 27, 30, 33, 39, 43–47, 53, 67, 69, 71, 75, 79, 104, 112–114, 120, 160, 172, 174, 176, 1, 178–179, 191, 197, 200, 203, 208, 210–211, 217, 230, 234–235, 241, 255, 259, 265, 275–276, 284, 287, 305–306, 309, 314, 341, 343, 345, 347, 351, 356, 359–360, 363–364, 378, 380–381
aestheticism   115, 118, 173–178, 195–196, 199, 203, 207–208, 210–211
affirmation   51, 133, 143, 162, 300, 305, 309
affordance   349, 368, 370
Africa   217, 320, 322, 325–326
Aftermath (Cusk novel)   375
Against Nature (Huysmans novel)   200
Agamben, Giorgio   125
age   12, 32, 34, 49, 74, 90, 97, 112–113, 128, 134, 137, 164, 169, 180, 195, 199, 213, 218, 229, 233, 243, 271, 274, 287, 296, 317, 339, 374–375, 378
– coming of age   188, 238, 240, 354
– Golden Age   138, 168, 332
– Jazz Age   207, 216
– middle age   196, 302, 306–307, 354, 357, 378
– modern age   222
– post-literary age   286
– Victorian age   3, 113, 127, 150–151, 236

– *The Victorian Age in Literature* (Chesterton) 113
agency   4, 7, 9, 20–22, 25, 29, 46–48, 53, 71, 74, 81, 127, 222–223, 258, 276, 291–294, 311–312, 314, 363
– distributed agency   21
agent   4, 6–7, 12, 20, 22–23, 59–61, 78, 80–81, 106, 139, 148, 165, 226, 261, 336–338, 343, 345, 361–362, 364, 378
ahistoricism   20
AI   46–47
Aitken, Max, 1st Baron Beaverbrook   248
À la recherche du temps perdu (Proust novel)   68
Albert Angelo (Johnson novel)   285
alcohol *or* alcoholism   143, 158, 166, 186, 296, 321
Alexandria Quartet (Durrell novels)   244
Alf's Button (Darlington novel)   218
algorithm   46
allegory   38, 123, 125, 141, 146, 286, 290–291, 321
Allen, Grant   128, 387–388
– *The Type-Writer Girl*   128
allopoetic   7, 45, 49, 77–78, 81, 114, 115, 118, 126, 317, 366, 406
allusion   62, 108, 121, 144, 176, 229, 238, 239, 265, 266, 289, 304, 308, 336, 357
– intertextual allusion   311
alter ego   14, 225, 257, 287, 299, 314
Alton Locke (Kingsley novel)   100, 112, 385
amateur *or* amateurism   31, 100, 104, 107, 138, 145, 155
– *La bibliothèque d'un amateur* (Puech novel)   21, 395
Amazon   46, 319, 348–349
Ambient, Mark (character in James's "The Author of 'Beltraffio'")   176–177
ambiguity   54, 59, 61, 65–66, 86, 105, 122–123, 125, 173–174, 178, 182–183, 192, 246, 268, 309, 320–321, 323, 329, 379
– *Pierre or The Ambiguities*   115–126, 202, 319, 324, 386
ambition   35, 51, 88, 90, 94–95, 100–101, 107, 116, 130, 133, 136, 145–146, 150, 154, 164, 184, 186, 191, 197–199, 203, 208, 216, 222, 224, 226, 237, 239, 256, 258, 269, 279, 317, 320, 328, 343
Amelia, or the Distress'd Wife (Justice novel)   129
America *or* American   44, 61, 106, 121, 124, 129, 175–177, 185, 214, 224, 226, 229, 233, 246, 270, 286, 291, 295–296, 298, 302, 309, 313, 319, 322, 325, 332–333, 339, 354, 364–365
– Black American   365
– Latin America   3, 281, 291
– Native American   326
– South America   296
Americanah (Adichie novel)   362, 400
American Dirt (Cummins novel)   70
Americanisation   234
Amis, Kingsley   214–215, 229–231, 240, 283, 381
– *I Like It Here*   214, 229–230, 393
Amis, Martin   301, 396, 397
– *The Information*   301, 397
Amos and Andy (radio sitcom)   364
anaclisis or anaclitic   9, 75–78, 80, 101, 118, 306, 384, 406
analogue   320, 348
analogy   9, 39, 76, 186, 297, 311, 313, 321, 344
The Anatomy Lesson (Roth novel)   314, 395
Anderson, Lindsay [Alexander Christie]   128
Angel (Taylor novel)   263–265, 393
Angela's Ashes (McCourt memoir)   350
Anglo-Canadian   51
Anglo-Indian   5
angry young man *or* men   237, 240, 243, 257, 260, 276
animal   71, 181, 223, 292, 325, 372
Anlehnung, see anaclisis
Anstey, F. [Thomas Anstey Guthrie]   334, 386
– *The Giant's Robe*   334, 386
antagonist   94, 324, 340
anthropologist   273
anthropomorphism   54, 292
antiquity   334
antisemitism   74, 252
antithesis   136, 222, 258
Antwerp (Bolaño novel)   343
anxiety   137, 158, 161, 187, 192, 235, 263, 266, 276, 316, 335, 339, 344, 356

– anxiety of authorship   121, 131, 137, 150, 161, 284
– anxiety of influence   187
– castration anxiety   326
apprenticeship   155, 170
– literary apprenticeship   100, 129, 171, 196, 204
– *Wilhelm Meister's Apprenticeship* (Goethe novel)   99
appropriation   77, 339, 406
– cultural appropriation   69
Arabella (Lennox character)   129
archive   261, 270, 296, 298, 310
– Archive of Our Own   349
Argosy (magazine)   154
aristocracy, see also intellect   88, 99, 109, 113, 143–145, 190–191
Aristophanes   8
– *The Frogs*   8
Aristotle   64, 384
– *Poetics*   64
Arlen, Michael   235
army   157, 262, 266, 348, 352
– *The Armies of the Night* (Mailer novel)   345, 394
Arnold, Matthew   20, 221
– *Culture and Anarchy*   221
arrangement   66, 115, 127, 145, 245, 270, 304, 305, 316, 343
art *or* arts, see also autonomy, form, freedom, lover, madness, novel, power, religion, work   10–11, 14, 21, 35, 37, 43, 45, 47–48, 50, 53, 75, 92, 100–102, 105–106, 109, 113–114, 119, 133–135, 140, 150–151, 160–163, 172–179, 186, 189, 192, 196–197, 199–200, 202, 204, 206–207, 210, 230, 235, 242, 246, 255, 258, 266, 280, 284, 288–289, 301, 303–307, 309–313, 315, 329, 341, 354–355, 357–360, 364–365, 380–381
– art for art's sake   173, 203
– art of fiction   11
– "The Art of Fiction" (Besant essay)   101
– "The Art of Fiction" (James essay)   101, 162, 179
– art of living   113
– art of storytelling   40
– good art   198

– gospel of art   176, 195
– Guild of Literature and Art   105
– literary art *or* literature as art   48, 140, 160, 168, 174, 199, 258, 328
– Romantic art   208
– sensuous art   200
– spagyric art   200
artifice   37, 146, 355
artificial intelligence, see AI
artist, see also novel   10–13, 19, 29, 37–38, 43–44, 47–49, 85, 91, 101, 130–131, 134–136, 150, 153, 160, 168, 176–177, 179–180, 188–189, 192, 196–199, 201–202, 204–205, 209–211, 215, 222, 239, 246, 257, 267, 275, 283, 288–289, 310, 313–314, 320, 324, 329, 336, 350, 352, 353, 355, 358–360, 362, 365, 373, 380–382
– artist *manqué*   209
– failed artist   268, 367
– isolated *or* solitary artist
– literary artist   380
– modern *or* modernist artist   3, 380
– *A Portrait of the Artist as a Young Man* (Joyce novel)   43, 197, 211, 311, 328, 336, 389
– visual artist   267
– woman artist   133–135, 150, 246, 258, 267, 283, 359
artistry   11, 341
Ashleigh, Lowen (character in Hoover's *Verity*)   340–342
"The Aspern Papers" (James tale)   175, 179, 296–297, 387
Asymmetry (Halliday novel)   363, 401
attention, see also economy   3–4, 8, 12, 22–24, 29, 33, 36–37, 44, 46, 49–50, 60, 62, 72–73, 99, 116, 119, 129, 141, 146, 166, 171, 175, 177–178, 180–182, 186, 190, 203, 224, 230, 243, 247, 258, 261, 279, 290, 301, 316, 325, 340, 349, 352, 370
Athill, Diana   260
– *Stet*   260
The Atonement of Leam Dundas (Linton novel)   142
Aubrey, John   19
– *Brief Lives*   19
Auden, W. H.   247

audience 1, 4–7, 9, 12, 15, 23, 25, 30, 40, 44–47, 49, 51, 54–55, 57–59, 62–67, 70–81, 101, 104, 118–119, 130, 137, 143–144, 151, 153, 160, 162, 177, 180, 202, 230, 248, 250, 265, 281, 290, 304, 317, 320, 328, 331, 348–349, 361–362, 370, 376, 378–379, 383–384, 406
- authorial audience 6, 76, 79, 118, 130, 351
- female audience 261
- mass audience 13, 44, 49, 107
- middlebrow audience 180, 248
- narrative audience 76, 130
- target audience 37, 133
audiobook 66
Auerbach, Erich 115–116
Augustine, Saint 32
- *Confessions* 32
Augustus Caesar 31
Aurora Leigh (Barrett Browning) 3, 113, 130–131, 133–137, 151, 195, 386
Austen, Jane 39–40, 58–59, 67, 129–130, 168, 240, 262, 266
- *Pride and Prejudice* 40, 59, 130–131, 148, 266
auteur supposé 7, 9, 21
autheme 26, 34
authentication 45–46, 354–357
authenticity 9–12, 45–46, 70–71, 73, 79, 89, 91, 216, 228–229, 239, 244, 335, 347–350, 354–355, 364, 366–370
- authenticity of experience 46, 71, 73, 347
- authenticity of expression 45, 71, 216
author, *see also* death, narrator, protagonist, *passim*
- *About the Author* (Colapinto novel) 335, 338, 343, 345, 398
- abstract author 58
- actual author 1–2, 4–5, 7–9, 13–14, 32, 39–40, 42, 45, 50–51, 53–55, 57–59, 62–63, 67–68, 71, 73–82, 101, 130, 159, 280–281, 284, 287, 289–290, 295, 299, 309, 313, 329, 334, 341–342, 347, 356–357, 369, 375, 377, 379, 382, 404, 406
- "The Author" (Churchill poem) 35
- *The Author* (Crouch play) 3
- author concept 26–28, 47, 51, 101, 242, 244

- author-making 5–6, 8–9, 30, 35, 38, 81, 97, 132, 137, 150–151, 174, 223, 235, 317, 350, 356, 370, 379, 406
- "The Author of 'Beltraffio'" (James tale) 176–179, 387
- *The Author of "Trixie"* (Caine novel) 218, 223–224, 389
- bestselling author 149, 214, 319, 375
- brand-name author 329
- female author, *see also* woman author 126, 129–130, 138, 140, 150–151, 246, 256–257, 276, 284, 375
- fictional author 1, 5, 8, 13–14, 21, 27, 50–51, 78, 81–82, 173, 196, 226, 261, 263, 299, 309, 329, 332, 339, 342–343, 366, 369, 374, 383, 404
- implied author 4–5, 7, 53–55, 57–59, 64, 66, 87
- *Jane: Young Author* (Baxter novel) 128, 258, 267, 392
- male author 63, 128, 131, 137, 140, 233, 256, 258
- no-name author 348
- omniscient author 60, 178, 280–281, 285
- *The Sale of Authors* (Campbell dialogue) 35
- *Six Characters in Search of an Author* (Pirandello play) 3
- *The Truth about an Author* (Bennett) 198
- woman author, *see also* female author 130
authoress 127, 138, 256, 270
- "The Fashionable Authoress" (Thackeray) 138, 385
- *The Young Authoress* (Hendriks novel) 130, 133, 257, 385
authoriality 62, 259
authorisation, *see also* self 131, 356
authority 5, 27, 32–33, 43–44, 51, 62–63, 73, 85–86, 96, 115–119, 125, 159, 178, 188, 206, 226, 271, 280–282, 290–291, 293, 299, 303, 312–315, 343, 356, 366, 369–370, 383
- authorial authority 62, 73, 268, 273, 294, 299–300, 381
- authority of fiction 288
- authority of myth 291
- communicative authority 316
- cultural authority 282, 317, 381

- discursive authority   62–63, 259, 268, 274, 284, 317, 319, 332, 345, 381, 383
- feminine authority   259, 268
- *Fictions of Authority* (Lanser)   259
- literary authority   230, 366, 369, 383
- moral authority   86, 106, 117, 282, 312
- narrative authority   2, 11, 38, 40, 51, 62–63, 86, 116, 118, 159, 172, 178, 263, 284, 301

authorpoiesis   3–7, 9, 11, 34, 38, 80–81, 107, 114, 118, 305, 307, 363, 378, 406

authorpoietic loop   6–7, 52, 75, 406

authorship, *see also* act, horror, paradigm, writing, *passim*
- authorship studies   21
- celebrity authorship   118–119, 146, 220
- concept of authorship   2, 8, 13, 26, 29, 31, 70, 231, 312, 379, 406
- contemporary authorship   335, 362–363, 366, 369
- declarative authorship   26, 369
- executive authorship   26, 29, 348
- female authorship   14, 63, 126–127, 129, 131, 140–141, 145, 246, 250, 255–276, 279
- folklore authorship   28
- heroic authorship   119
- literary authorship   1–3, 7, 13–14, 19–52, 63, 78, 81–82, 87, 95, 119, 126, 138, 145, 176, 186, 188, 191–192, 203, 223, 225, 246, 249, 255, 270, 276, 279, 281, 284, 317, 323, 331, 370, 376–378, 380, 406
- mass *or* mass-market authorship   46, 159–160, 192, 216, 381
- modern authorship   217, 220, 291, 328–329
- *Myths of Authorship* (Peterson)   47
- precursory authorship   26
- revisionary authorship   146, 327
- self-authorship   146, 327
- social authorship   34

autobiography   10, 26, 32, 36–37, 45, 55, 72–73, 79, 81, 99, 108, 122, 130–131, 133–134, 136, 166, 182, 184, 195, 198, 217, 235, 245, 273, 286, 288, 299, 307, 314, 335, 340–342, 345, 347, 349–350, 352, 354–355, 360, 375, 377, 382–383
- *Autobiography* (Martineau)   131
- *Autobiography* (Trollope)   101, 139, 155, 158–159, 350

- *The Autobiography of Alice B. Toklas* (Stein)   245, 390
- *The Autobiography of Christopher Kirkland* (Linton novel)   128, 387

autodiegesis   32, 68, 173, 253, 286–287
autoethnography   347
autofiction   2, 9–10, 12, 31, 41, 45–46, 54, 63, 68, 71–72, 81, 241–242, 253, 276, 284, 301, 317, 345, 347–350, 354–360, 362–363, 366, 370–371, 375–376, 382–383
autograph   53, 121, 180, 271
autography   53, 253, 387
autonomy   10, 12, 22, 26–29, 34–36, 38, 40, 44, 53, 69, 71, 75, 79, 85, 125, 189, 307, 311, 313, 319, 322, 335, 340, 369
- autonomy of art   27, 75
- artistic autonomy   10, 44, 309, 313, 345
- authorial autonomy   27–28
- literary autonomy *or* autonomy of literature   27, 53, 69, 340
- personal autonomy   10
- Romantic autonomy   11, 38, 40
- strong autonomy   27–29, 369
- weak autonomy   29, 369

autopoetic   3–5, 9, 32, 39, 45, 49–51, 63, 75–79, 118, 133, 137, 174, 230, 317, 329, 406
autopoiesis   3
autotelic   69
*autre*biography   345
*autre*fiction   376, 382

Babel, Isaac   311
Bacon, Sir Francis   223
Baffin, Arnold (character in Murdoch's *The Black Prince*)   288–290
Bag of Bones (King novel)   319
Baines, Roland (character in McEwan's *Lessons*)   14
Baker, James R.   297
Bakhtin, Mikhail   59, 61, 67, 115
ballad   364
- *The Ballad of Peckham Rye* (Spark novel)   273
Balzac, Honoré de   56, 85–97, 103, 109–110, 114–117, 121, 163, 167, 172, 240, 362, 379, 385
- *Comédie Humaine*   85, 87, 92, 117
- *Cousin Pons*   167

– *A Harlot High and Low*   86
– *Lost Illusions*   85–97, 103, 109, 114, 121, 163, 362, 379, 385
– *Père Goriot*   56, 117
Banville, John   24
– *Snow*   24
Barclay, Wilfred (character in Golding's *The Paper Men*)   295–299
Barker, Nicola   300
– *I am Sovereign*   300
Baron, Alexander   251
Baron Corvo, *see* Rolfe, Frederick
Barrett, *see under* Browning
Barth, John   279, 291, 393, 394–396
– *Giles, Goat-Boy*   291
Barthelme, Donald   284
Barthes, Roland   11, 20, 46, 55–56, 279, 291, 377
– "The Death of the Author"   20, 279, 377
– *Roland Barthes par Roland Barthes*   377
Bartleby (character in Melville's "Bartleby, the Scrivener")   122, 124–125
"Bartleby, the Scrivener" (Melville tale)   124–125
Basic Instinct (film)   338
battle   6, 33, 88, 91, 131, 217, 246, 276, 322
– *The Battle of the Books* (Swift satire)   33, 221
– battle of the brows   13, 127, 160, 234
– battle of the sexes   322
Bauman, Zygmunt   323
Baxter, Valerie [Laurence Meynell]   128, 257–258
– *Jane: Young Author*   128, 258, 267, 392
– *Shirley: Young Bookseller*   257
BBC   128, 255, 261
Beardsley, Aubrey   188
"The Beast in the Jungle" (James tale)   182
The Beatles   357
Beatrice   176
beauty   151, 156, 176–177, 242, 369
Beckett, Samuel   42, 233, 240–242, 245, 252, 390, 392
– *Company*   245
– *Dream of Fair to Middling Women*   240–241, 390
– *Malone Dies*   241, 392
– *Molloy*   241, 392
– *More Pricks than Kicks*   240–241,

– *The Unnamable*   241
– "Yellow"   240
Beerbohm, Max   8, 174, 178, 184, 188–192, 214, 275, 389
– "Enoch Soames"   8, 188, 191, 389
– "Felix Argallo and Walter Ledgett"   191, 390
– "Hilary Maltby and Stephen Braxton"   188, 190–191, 389
– *Seven Men*   188–192
Beethoven, Ludwig van   241
The Beetle (Marsh novel)   191, 218
beginning   36, 102, 120, 143, 149, 164, 168, 188, 191, 196, 213, 217, 222, 243, 248, 251, 257, 264, 295, 325, 351, 356
Belacqua Shuah (Beckett character)   240–241
belief   9, 37, 53, 67, 76, 95, 156, 185, 188–189, 204, 231, 236, 276, 299, 306, 312, 314, 342, 344, 353, 372, 375
Bell, Currer   127
Bell, Laura (Thackeray character)   74
Bellow, Saul   311, 338, 393
The Belton Estate (Trollope novel)   179
Bénichou, Paul   20
Benjamin, Walter   9, 40–41, 360
– "The Storyteller"   40–41
Bennett, Arnold   128, 198, 240, 388
– *A Man from the North*   198, 240, 388
– *Riceyman Steps*   240
– *The Truth about an Author*   198
Benson, E. F.   246–247, 256, 390
– *Secret Lives*   246–247, 256, 390
Benstead, John (character in Darlington's *Wishes Limited*)   218–222
Benthamism   146, 148, 150
Benveniste, Émile   42, 61
Bergonzi, Bernard   169, 233
Berlin   342–344
Berman, Morris   295
Besant, Walter   13, 101, 162
– "The Art of Fiction"   101
Besetzung, see cathexis
bestseller, *see also* author, book, novel   12, 165, 214, 219–220, 223, 226, 231, 263–264, 322–324, 327, 338–339, 342, 365, 380
– *Best Seller* (Youmans novel)   210, 214, 224–226, 390
– *Bestsellerautorroman*   210

– bestseller list 323, 339, 342, 365
Bible, *see also* New *and* Old Testament 249
– King James Bible 26, 236
La bibliothèque d'un amateur (Puech novel) 21, 395
Biffen, Harold (character in Gissing's *New Grub Street*) 113, 165–166, 168, 198
Big Five 49
Bildung 196–197
bildungsroman, *see also* novel 2–3, 10, 13–14, 37–38, 49, 51, 85, 99–114, 122–127, 129–135, 137, 142, 151, 154, 159, 172–173, 175, 184, 192, 196, 198, 202, 206–207, 214, 216, 222, 239–240, 245–246, 257, 265, 275, 301, 311–316, 350–351, 356, 359–360, 362–363, 372, 376, 379–382
– anti-*bildungsroman* 125–126, 203, 206, 233
– author-*bildungsroman* 13, 85, 101, 114, 117, 126, 130, 137
– female *bildungsroman* 130, 132–133, 245, 257, 265, 362
– literary *bildungsroman* 3, 10, 49, 51, 85, 99–100, 102–103, 129, 135, 154, 159, 172–173, 184, 196, 198, 202, 207, 214, 222, 239, 245–246, 275, 314, 350, 360, 363, 379–380
biofiction 8
biographer 175, 255, 295–296, 298, 333, 383
Biographia Literaria (Coleridge) 100
biography 19, 71–72, 142, 182–183, 189, 254, 263, 272, 295–298, 304, 341
– *Dictionary of National Biography* 189
– double biography 297–298
Birke, Dorothee 2, 62–63, 80, 129, 149
– *Writing the Reader* 2
birth 37, 99, 205, 243
– birthday 132
– "The Birthplace" (James tale) 182, 389
– rebirth 243
Black, Benjamin (Banville pseudonym) 24
Blackadder (sitcom) 128
The Black Book (Durrell novel) 13, 242–244, 253, 273, 327, 391
The Black Prince (Murdoch novel) 288–291, 299, 394
Blackwood (publisher) 148, 153
Blackwood, John 148
Blair, Tony 335

Blake, William 29–30
– *The Four Zoas* 30
– *Jerusalem* 30
– *Milton* 30
The Blazing World (Cavendish novel) 32, 129
Bleak House (Dickens novel) 125, 169
blindness 136, 198, 208, 210, 288, 376
– *Blindness* (Green novel) 198, 207–211, 380, 390
Bloom, Harold 187, 312
Bloom, Leopold (Joyce character) 197
Bloom, Molly (Joyce character) 292
Bloomsberries 207
Bloomsbury 167, 201–202, 227, 233, 235, 251
Blumenfeld, Simon 251
Bode, Christoph 54
Bodley Head 188
body 1, 39–40, 190–191, 200–202, 213, 222–223, 256, 260, 323, 325, 328, 333
– *Vile Bodies* (Waugh novel) 43, 70, 207, 214, 216–217, 223, 248, 381, 390
Bohemia 74
bohemia *or* bohemianism 107, 109, 146, 227–229, 233, 238, 251, 267, 269, 271, 281, 336, 353, 360, 380–381
Bolaño, Roberto 342–343, 348, 395, 397–399
– *Antwerp* 343
Boldwood, Stella (character in Braddon's *One Thing Needful*) 150
Boltanski, Luc 344
– *Mysteries and Conspiracies* 344
Bonaparte, Marie 19
Bonner, Jacob Finch (character in Korelitz's *The Plot*) 338
book, *see also* form, history, market, production, review, trade, world *passim*
– advice book 128, 165, 216, 315
– audiobook 66
– *The Battle of the Books* (Swift satire) 33, 221
– bestselling book 216
– *The Black Book* (Durrell novel) 13, 242–244, 253, 273, 327, 391
– book collector 296
– book cover 68, 223
– book club 226, 365
– book of Genesis 42
– Book of the Month Club 226, 234

- *Book of Numbers* (Cohen novel)   300, 401
- book series   340–342
- book-table   234
- book title   223, 247, 347
- book tour   25, 337
- children's book   74
- dirty book   241
- e-book   349
- Google Books   112
- *Leaves from the Life-Book of Walter Lorraine* (fictional novel)   108
- manuscript book   132
- material book   21, 368–370
- National Book Association   365
- nonfiction book   345
- notebook   11, 177–178, 180, 183, 224, 244, 258, 284, 344
- *The PowerBook* (Winterson novel)   301
- printed book   64–65, 86, 120, 169, 326, 328, 378
- published book   202–203, 249
- scrapbook   327–328
- self-help book   216
- self-published book   335
- *A Writer of Books* (Paston novel)   153, 161, 170–171, 388
- writing-book   132
- *The Yellow Book* (magazine)   180, 188
Booklovers' Corner   235
bookseller   23, 25, 35, 38, 49, 87, 90–91, 134, 349
- *Shirley: Young Bookseller* (Baxter novel)   257
- bookselling   224–225
bookshop   234–235, 237, 240, 245
- "Bookshop Memories" (Orwell essay)   234–235
Boot, William (character in Waugh's *Scoop*)   217
Booth, John Wilkes   325
Booth, Wayne C.   54
Boothby, Guy   16
Borges, Jorge Luis   187
- "Pierre Menard"   187
boundary, *see also* work   5–6, 12–13, 24, 30, 48–49, 52, 62, 68–69, 72, 74–75, 79, 104, 106, 109, 111, 113, 131, 160, 173, 188, 199, 213, 223, 250, 255, 291, 314, 323–324, 332, 347, 349, 355–357, 371, 373, 379, 382–384
Bourdieu, Pierre   2, 4, 15, 20–21, 23, 47–48, 69, 77, 80–81, 159–161, 180, 237, 275, 348, 380
bourgeois   19, 41–42, 88, 94, 96, 106, 109, 135, 138, 148, 183, 191, 196, 204–205, 240, 355, 372, 380–382
- anti-bourgeois   11, 324
- haut-bourgeois   215
Bowen, Garnet (character in Amis's *I Like It Here*)   229–230
Bowra, Maurice   209
Boyhood (Coetzee 'autrebiography')   345, 397
Boyne, John   8, 338, 401
- *A Ladder to the Sky*   8, 338, 401
Bradbury, Malcolm   297, 394
- *The History Man*   297, 394
Braddon, Mary Elizabeth   140, 149–151, 165, 168, 386–388
- *The Doctor's Wife*   149–150, 368
- *Lady Audley's Secret*   145
- *The Lady's Mile*   149
- *One Thing Needful*   150, 387
"The Brain-Sucker" (Oswald satire)   35, 100
Braine, John   240, 283
Braudy, Leo   31, 37
Braun, Rebecca   21–22
Brave New World (Huxley novel)   216
Brawne, Fanny   186
Braxton, Stephen (character in Beerbohm's "Hilary Maltby and Stephen Braxton")   190
Brideshead Revisited (Waugh novel)   286
Brief Encounter (Lean film)   263
Brief Lives (Aubrey)   19
Bright Lights, Big City (McInerney novel)   338
Bright Young People *or* Things   43, 207, 216, 218
Britain *or* British, *see also* English, museum   14, 20, 44, 48–49, 94, 106, 109–110, 112, 114, 117, 119, 127, 160, 207, 217–218, 230, 233–234, 240, 243, 245, 248–250, 255, 261, 274, 282, 285, 294, 291, 296, 299, 325, 335, 354–355, 366
- Asian British   73
- postwar Britain   255–256, 258, 261, 274–275, 285, 299

- Regency Britain   128
- Victorian Britain   100, 106, 113
Brittain, Vera   259–260
- *History of Women from Victoria to Elizabeth II*   259
- *On Becoming a Writer*   260
broadcast   333
Broch, Hermann   8, 391
- *The Death of Virgil*   8, 391
Brockden Brown, Charles   38
- *Wieland*   38
Brontë, Charlotte   127, 130, 136, 341
- *Jane Eyre*   112, 130, 136, 257, 341
- *Life of Charlotte Brontë* (Gaskell)   131
The Brothers Karamazov (Dostoevsky novel)   54
Brown (character in Trollope's "Josephine de Montmorenci")   156–157
Brown's Hotel   322
Browning, Elizabeth Barrett   3, 85, 130, 133–136, 150, 195, 386
- *Aurora Leigh*   3, 113, 130–131, 133–137, 151, 195, 386
Browning, Robert   85, 183–184, 227
- "Waring"   227
Buelens, Gert   174
Bulwer-Lytton, Edward   38, 99, 101–103, 105, 130, 385–386
- *Ernest Maltravers*   99, 102–103, 385
The Buried Giant (Ishiguro novel)   331
Burney, Fanny   130
- *Evelina*   130
Burroughs, Edgar Rice   235
business   34, 90–91, 96, 109, 121, 136, 139, 151, 153, 158, 162–164, 166–167, 169–170, 204, 213, 225–226, 228, 246–248, 262, 271, 275, 286, 327
- business of literature   109, 151, 163, 170, 213, 275
- "The Man of Letters as a Man of Business" (Howells essay)   161
butler   128, 142
Butler, Robert   366
Butts, Thomas   30
Byatt, A. S.   274–275, 393, 395–398, 400
Byron, George Gordon, Lord   17, 36–38, 45, 88, 107, 214, 385
- *Childe Harold's Pilgrimage*   36, 385

Caine, William   223–224, 389
- *The Author of "Trixie"*   223–224, 389
Calvino, Italo   80, 378, 395
- *If on a Winter's Night a Traveller*   378, 395
Camberton, Roland [Henry Cohen]   233, 250–253, 381, 392
- *Rain on the Pavements*   252, 392
- *Scamp*   233, 250–253, 392
Cambridge   107, 203–204, 207, 218, 237, 250, 286, 367
Campbell, Archibald   35
- *The Sale of Authors*   35
Campbell, Olwen   255, 259, 274
- *On the Feminine Point of View*   255, 259
Camus, Albert   334
- *The Stranger*   334
Canada *or* Canadian   3, 51, 300–301
Candy (Terry Southern novel)   286
canon   20, 49, 122, 319, 329, 366, 369, 375
The Canterbury Tales (Chaucer)   32
Canzoniere (Petrarch)   32
capital   10, 37, 89–90, 117, 125, 166, 237
- cultural capital   13, 77, 141, 237, 370
- financial capital   141, 362, 369
- symbolic capital   237, 362–363, 369
capitalism   41, 85–87, 89, 92–93, 165, 174, 317, 353, 360, 380
Carbury, Lady (character in Trollope's *The Way We Live Now*)   138–139
career, *see also* novel   14, 34, 94, 105, 107–108, 121, 127, 130–134, 139, 154–156, 159, 161, 163–164, 168, 171, 175, 191, 196, 199, 208, 243, 255, 257, 259, 267, 273–274, 279, 290, 295–296, 320, 327, 336, 338, 349, 372, 377–378
Carey, John   297–298
Carlyle, Thomas   38, 99–100, 104, 110–111, 118–120, 169, 385
- *On Heroes, Hero-Worship, and the Heroic in History*   100
- *Sartor Resartus*   38, 99, 120–121, 385
Carrington, Leonora   245
- *Down Below*   245
Carter, Angela   275
Carver, Maryann Burk   309
Carver, Raymond   172, 300, 302, 306–310, 316, 319, 362, 394

- "Intimacy" 307–309, 396
- "Put Yourself in My Shoes" 306–307, 309, 316, 394
- *Will You Please Be Quiet, Please?* 306, 394

The Case of Authors (Ralph pamphlet) 34–35
Casmilus, Pompey (character in Smith's *Novel on Yellow Paper*) 245–249
castle 157
- Blandings Castle 222
- *Castle* (TV series) 332
- *The Court of Kellyon Castle* 140
- *I Capture the Castle* (Smith novel) 273, 392
Castle, Richard 332
cataclisis 76–77, 81, 118, 133, 351, 384, 406
cathexis 9, 77–78, 81, 118, 230, 351, 384, 406
Catholicism 48, 113, 189, 228, 271, 283
Catullus 31
Cavendish, Margaret 32, 129
- *The Blazing World* 32, 129
Cazabon, Beth (character in Taylor's *A View of the Harbour*) 263, 274
celebrity, *see also* authorship 11, 26, 31, 36, 43–44, 50, 87, 90, 103, 118–119, 140–142, 146–149, 160, 175, 179–182, 189, 213, 216–224, 228, 297, 312, 314, 321, 338, 353
Céline, Louis-Ferdinand 51, 74–75, 392
censor *or* censorship 25–26, 67, 69, 234, 252
Cervantes, Miguel de 68, 89
- *Don Quixote* 89
Chang, Jung 350
- *Wild Swans* 350
change 2, 7, 15, 26–27, 32, 47, 71, 87, 102, 109, 111, 116–117, 148, 191, 205, 208, 239, 247, 255, 275, 287, 317, 373, 375
Changing Places (Lodge novel) 297
chaos 289, 316, 323
character *passim*
- artist as character 197, 211
- author as character 2, 8, 12–15, 32–33, 45, 50–51, 63, 81–82, 101, 118, 128–129, 133, 161, 184, 195, 197, 207, 275, 282, 299, 319–320, 332–333, 351, 355, 362, 377, 382
- character-focaliser 130
- character formation 304
- character-narrator 362
- female character 129, 258, 268, 272
- fictional *or* fictitious character 36, 45, 58, 66, 76, 81–82, 280–281, 283, 298–299, 333–334, 353–354, 358
- 'flat' character 298
- literary character 106, 156, 274, 299
- lower-class character 104
- minor character 95, 139
- narrator as character 3, 351
- non-heterosexual character 242
- observer-character 271, 303
- poet-character 32
- poetic character 99
- *Six Characters in Search of an Author* (Pirandello play) 3
- woman as character 139, 141, 242, 256, 258
- writer as character 79, 139, 141, 165, 188, 244, 256, 258
Chardon, Lucien (character in Balzac's *Lost Illusions*) 85–97, 109, 114
Charyn, Jerome 8
- *The Secret Life of Emily Dickinson* 8
Chatterton, Thomas 272
Chaucer, Geoffrey 32, 68
- *The House of Fame* 32
- *The Canterbury Tales* 32
Chénier, André 88–89
Chesterton, G. K. 44, 110, 113
- *The Victorian Age in Literature* 113
Child, Lee 25
Childe Harold's Pilgrimage (Byron poem) 36, 385
Childress, Clayton 22, 378
Cholmondeley, Mary 128, 388
- *Red Pottage* 128, 388
Christ 123
Christian *or* Christianity 136, 176, 200, 204, 239, 283, 322, 326
Christie, Agatha 257, 332, 390
- "Parker Pyne Investigates" 257, 390
Christie, Alexander 128
Chryses (character in Homer's *Iliad*) 55
Chudleigh, Cosima (character in Paston's *A Writer of Books*) 170–171
church 123, 186, 190, 322
- Church of England 110, 155
Churchill, Charles 35
- "The Author" 35

Churchill, Elizabeth   257
– *Juliet in Publishing*   257
cinema   224, 257, 282, 285
Cinna (character in Shakespeare's *Julius Caesar*)   32
circulation   181, 249, 251
city   88, 90, 93, 185–186, 200–201, 251–252
– *Bright Lights, Big City* (McInerney novel)   338
– *The Devil in the White City* (Larson book)   70
– *A Tale of Two Cities* (Dickens novel)   57
civilisation   116, 163, 237, 241, 324, 352
Clancy, Tom   323
class   14, 31, 35, 56, 63, 72, 101, 104, 106, 109, 131, 143, 144–145, 158, 160, 162, 166–167, 171, 208, 234, 249, 252, 255, 373, 378, 380
– class barrier *or* boundary   104, 111, 142, 144–145
– class differences
– class-passing   144
– lower class   104, 106, 109, 144, 158, 165–166, 237, 305
– middle class   34, 44, 104, 106–107, 109–110, 113, 127, 142, 144, 158, 160, 162–165–166, 183, 205, 227, 233–235, 237–238, 240, 302, 316, 380, 382
– underclass   162
– upper class   44, 100, 109–110, 144–145, 380
– working class   100–101, 144, 166, 234, 304, 380
classic   49, 128–129, 132, 174, 222, 266, 274
classicism   28
Clea (Durrell novel)   244, 393
The Clever Woman of the Family (Yonge novel)   128, 386
cocaine   321
Coetzee, J. M.   345
– *Boyhood*   345, 397
– *Summertime*   345, 400
– *Youth*   345, 398
Cohen, Henry, *see under* Camberton
Cohen, Joshua   300, 401
– *Book of Numbers*   300, 401
Colapinto, John   335–339, 345, 398
– *About the Author*   335–338, 343, 345, 398
Cole, Sarah Rose   109
Coleman, Brunette [Philip Larkin]   128

Coleridge, Samuel Taylor   67, 100, 200
– *Biographia Literaria*   100
Collier, John Payne   368
Collins, Wilkie   85, 385, 387
– *The Woman in White*   118
colonialism   321, 325
The Color Purple (Walker novel)   364
column   213, 216–218
columnist   216, 271–272, 274
Comédie Humaine (Balzac)   85, 87, 92, 117
comedy   141–142, 145, 147, 190, 211, 213–215, 222–223, 227, 230, 335
– comedy of manners   141
– *Divine Comedy* (Dante)   32
– Restoration comedy   143–144
– social comedy   223
The Comforters (Spark novel)   8, 250, 282–285, 299, 374, 393
commentary   41, 60–62, 117, 189, 279, 288, 351
– authorial commentary   267
– meta-commentary   60–62, 290
commerce, *see also* art   45, 47–48, 95, 108, 160, 175, 179, 192
commodity, *see also* product   86–88, 90, 97, 105, 108, 119, 153, 169, 363
communication   68–69, 81, 178, 222, 265, 354–355, 377
– communications circuit   21, 23, 379
– communications media   275
– interpersonal communication   351
– linguistic communication   62
– literary communication   4, 55, 65–66, 68, 70, 76, 78
– narrative communication   4, 54, 64
– textual communication   54, 64, 78, 355
community   11, 28, 33, 35, 40, 70–71, 222, 259, 268, 271, 276, 311–314, 347, 353, 356, 382
– Black community   364
– Jewish community   309–311
– reading community *or* community of readers   65, 244
Company (Beckett text)   245
Company Parade (Jameson novel)   245, 257, 390
competition   24, 33–34, 70, 86, 90–94, 96, 101, 106, 109, 275, 301, 358

complexity   10, 27, 31, 48, 68, 112, 159, 202, 282
composition   55, 87, 133, 202, 327
– literary composition   35, 197, 216
– original composition   120
– textual composition   39–40, 118, 308
compromise   11, 22, 38, 40, 96–97, 99–100, 104–106, 109–115, 117, 124–125, 135–136, 145–147, 150, 164, 167–168, 172, 175, 185, 187, 222, 235, 239, 252, 258, 285, 287, 324, 338, 364–365, 378, 380
– *On Compromise* (Morley)   113
– Victorian compromise   44, 113–114, 144, 151, 192, 380
computer   47, 350
Comstock, Anthony   252
Comstock, Gordon (character in Orwell's *Keep the Aspidistra Flying*)   14, 235–239, 241, 252
confession   32, 51, 72, 111, 337, 347, 354–355, 360, 363
– *Confessions* (Augustine)   32
– *Confessions of an English Opium-Eater* (De Quincey)   199, 202
– *The Confessions of Nat Turner* (Styron novel)   70
– *Private Memoirs and Confessions of a Justified Sinner* (Hogg novel)   38
Connolly, Cyril   198, 203, 210, 237, 243
Connor, Sharon   138
Conrad, Joseph   42, 54, 229–230
– *Heart of Darkness*   118
– *Youth*   42
consciousness   37, 39, 43, 58, 116, 119, 188, 195, 201, 209, 320
– double-consciousness   6
– self-consciousness   109, 141, 144, 146–148, 168, 188, 192, 204, 210, 214, 241, 243, 266, 275, 279–280, 286, 311, 338, 353–354, 382
– stream of consciousness   236, 354, 371, 373
Constable, Archibald   162
consumption (*econ.*)   7, 97, 143, 158, 169, 222, 374
consumption (*med.*)   186
Contarini Fleming (Disraeli novel)   99, 385
contextualism   27–30

convention   2, 6, 23, 25–27, 30, 51, 56, 59, 64, 66–67, 77–79, 86, 118, 120–121, 123, 131, 134, 141, 145–146, 151, 159, 163, 168, 170, 173, 177, 204–205, 240–241, 243–244, 246, 248–250, 252, 259, 268, 280, 284, 313, 317, 331, 336, 369, 383, 406
conversion   32, 238
Copperfield, David (character in Dickens's *David Copperfield*)   103–107, 109–111, 114, 130, 289
copy   64, 108, 128, 132, 160, 187, 191–192, 195, 199, 217–218, 256, 295, 298, 360, 367–368
– advertising copy   227, 291
– digital copy   350
copyright   21, 23, 57, 187, 277, 339, 351, 368
– copyright law *or* legislation   10, 37
Corelli, Marie   170, 203, 263, 387–388
– *The Sorrows of Satan*   170, 388
Cornhill (magazine)   141–142, 146–147, 159
Cortázar, Julio   1–2, 281, 393
– *62: A Model Kit*   281
– *Hopscotch*   1, 281
Corvo, *see* Rolfe, Frederick
The Cost of Living (Farrell novel)   265–268, 273–274, 392
country, *see also* house   111, 132, 134–135, 176, 201, 215, 218, 262
– *The Undiscovered Country* (Mitchell novel)   285–287, 394
Cousin Pons (Balzac novel)   167
court   25, 69, 185, 222
– International Criminal Court   335
"The Coxon Fund" (James tale)   175, 180, 388
craft *or* craftsmanship   11, 13, 22, 27, 30, 34, 101–102, 163, 283, 380
The Craft of Fiction (Lubbock)   56
creation   7, 15, 19, 22–23, 25, 27, 30, 36–38, 43, 45, 47, 50, 53, 64–66, 72, 78, 81, 87, 89, 93, 123, 204, 245, 283, 299, 329, 365, 376–377, 379
– artistic creation   19
– literary creation   1–2, 10, 21, 36, 38, 164–165, 206, 275, 294, 305, 307, 313, 325, 348, 378–379
– novelistic creation   39
– poetic creation   29, 37

– self-creation   1, 3–4, 15, 36, 37–38, 76, 131, 133, 146, 291, 319, 379, 406
creativity   2, 19, 31, 34, 38, 63, 89, 104, 128, 135, 138, 187, 192, 293–295, 299, 304, 320, 324, 326–327, 334, 342, 349, 360, 379, 381–382
– artificial creativity   46
– authorial creativity   320
– female creativity   257, 275
– literary creativity   184, 195, 247, 265–266, 275, 299, 315, 320–321, 361
– male creativity   304, 326
creator   1–2, 7–8, 15, 28–29, 38–39, 44, 75, 77, 146, 162, 344, 369
– self-creator   151
– sub-creator   283
creature   38–39, 91, 131, 163, 204, 366
Crichton, Michael   323
crime   10, 24, 48, 74, 239, 256, 283, 331–335, 337
– *Crime and Punishment* (Dostoevsky novel)   208
– true-crime   339
crisis   15, 148, 158–159, 192, 259, 282, 285, 291, 298–299, 345, 357–358, 361, 381
critic   4, 20, 25, 28, 33–34, 44, 49, 53–54, 56, 60, 70, 73, 85, 103–104, 106, 117, 119, 124, 134, 141, 144, 147, 175, 180–182, 187, 189–190, 209, 225, 234, 238, 263, 287, 305, 308, 313, 323–324, 328–329, 331, 339, 382–383
– cultural critic   11
– drama critic   218
– literary critic   175, 282, 324, 333
– New Critics   20
– New York Critics Circle Award   319
– *The World, the Text, and the Critic* (Said book)   377
criticism   19, 33, 138, 142, 179, 182, 305, 325
– biographical criticism   19
– feminist criticism   129, 377
– genetic criticism   19
– literary criticism   3, 22, 43, 50, 62, 72, 110, 129, 238
– New Criticism   4, 61, 72, 377
– postcolonial criticism   377
– psychoanalytic criticism   19

– "The Science of Criticism" (James essay)   179
– self-criticism   353
critique   94, 113, 143, 159, 171, 198, 203, 209–210, 211, 243, 283, 287, 299, 305, 313, 331, 350, 357, 370, 376
– *autocritique*   256
Crome Yellow (Huxley novel)   207, 214–217, 220, 231, 389
Crouch, Tim   3
– *The Author*   3
Crystal, David   368
cultural studies   21, 80
culture, *see also* war   7, 28, 47, 69–70, 81, 86, 116, 236–237, 247, 249, 322, 331, 374, 378
– *Culture and Anarchy* (Arnold)   221
– global culture   116
– literary culture   34, 178, 188
– mass culture   322, 328
– media culture   314
– middlebrow culture   257
– minority culture   381
– national culture   33, 35
– popular culture   147, 234, 236
– print culture   100, 127
– subculture   380
Cummins, Jeanine   70
– *American Dirt*   70
Cunningham, Cal (character in Colapinto's *About the Author*)   336–339, 343
Cunningham, Valentine   290
Currie, Gregory   58
Cusk, Rachel   1, 15, 160, 172, 349–350, 363, 370–376, 382, 401–402
– *Aftermath*   375
– *Kudos*   160, 172, 370, 372–375, 401
– *The Last Supper*   375
– *A Life's Work*   375
– *Transit*   370–371, 373–374, 401
– *Outline*   363, 370–376, 382, 401
cynicism   50, 90, 109, 124, 150, 161, 167–168, 207, 213, 225, 275, 342, 345

Dacre, Jean (character in Tabor's *Diary of a Novelist*)   173
Dahl, Roald   74–75
Daily Telegraph   218
Daisy Miller (James novel)   65

Danielewski, Mark Z. 301, 368
- *House of Leaves* 301
- *Only Revolutions* 368
Dante Alighieri 32, 68, 176
- *Divine Comedy* 32
The Dark Half (King novel) 319, 328–329, 396
Dark Star (Marlon James novels) 332
Dark Tower (King novels) 319
Darlington, William Aubrey Cecil 218, 220, 223–224, 389
- *Alf's Button* 218
- *Wishes Limited* 218–224, 227, 231, 389
Das bin doch ich (Glavinic novel) 8
data 5, 46, 116
Datatron 47
David Copperfield (Dickens novel) 13, 49, 81, 102–107, 110–111, 118, 124, 138, 163, 173, 176, 289, 385
"Dayspring Mishandled" (Kipling story) 247, 390
de-aestheticisation 347
Deane, Bradley 11, 107
death 90, 92–93, 97, 122, 132–134, 141–142, 163, 176–178, 183, 195–196, 202–203, 205–206, 229, 243, 248, 272, 279, 287, 291, 294, 297, 299, 306, 308, 315, 320, 328, 333–334, 337, 340–342, 351, 360, 364
- *Death in Venice* (Mann novel) 196, 389
- death of the author 11, 20, 279, 285, 291, 293, 299, 316
- *The Death of the Author* (Adair novel) 333, 397
- "The Death of the Author" (Barthes essay) 20, 279, 377
- "The Death of the Lion" (James tale) 128, 180, 297, 388
- *The Death of Virgil* (Broch novel) 8, 391
- English death 243–244
decadence 196, 198, 202–204, 207
deception 73, 203, 368
decline 14, 35, 40, 85, 118, 158, 173, 197, 202, 237, 271, 338
- cultural decline 226, 235
deconstruction 61, 127, 159, 184, 198, 294, 322
decreation 291, 319
'Dedalus, Nathan' (section title in Roth's *The Ghost Writer*) 311, 313

Dedalus, Stephen (character in Joyce's *Portrait* and *Ulysses*) 74, 197, 209, 314, 336
Deeping, Warwick 235
Defoe, Daniel 68, 144
- *Robinson Crusoe* 68, 202
deformation 78, 90, 115, 118, 123, 125, 171, 316, 371, 406
degeneration 149, 158, 199, 202
de Genlis, Félicité 129, 385
- *La femme auteur* 129, 385
deindustrialisation 381
Delavoy, John (character in James's "John Delavoy") 180–181
Deleuze, Gilles 125, 325
DeLillo, Don 344, 397
Dell, Ethel M. 235
de Man, Paul 333
De Morgan, William 61
Dencombe (character in James's "The Middle Years") 181, 195–197, 201, 310
De Quincey, Thomas 199–200, 202
- *Confessions of an English Opium-Eater* 199, 202
derealisation 344
de Rochequillon, Rosalie (character in Hendriks's *The Young Authoress*) 130–131
Derrida, Jacques 69–70
de Rubempré, Lucien (character in Balzac's *Lost Illusions*) 85, 87, 93, 95
des Esseintes, Jean (character in Huysmans's *À rebours*) 200
desire 4, 19, 24, 45, 54, 72–73, 90, 99, 104, 120, 135, 137, 146, 156, 175, 181, 196, 214, 242, 258, 312, 320, 326, 328, 360, 362, 366, 372, 374
detective, *see also* fiction, novel, story 7, 48, 160, 257, 332
- writer-detective 332
development, *see also* Bildung, formation 10, 20, 37, 40–42, 72, 85, 99–100, 104, 106–107, 111–112, 114, 125, 129–131, 132, 143, 159, 162, 172, 174, 184, 188, 191, 196–198, 203, 207–210, 213, 216–217, 251–252, 257, 275–276, 298, 301, 319, 359, 372, 380, 383, 403
Deverell, Angelica (character in Taylor's *Angel*) 264–265, 274

device   5, 133, 284, 331, 335, 351, 365, 376
devil   189–190, 220, 297–298
– *The Devil in the White City* (Larson book)   70
dialectic   11, 40, 53, 300
– *Dialectic of Enlightenment* (Horkheimer and Adorno)   295
dialogue   35, 56, 61, 106, 164, 217, 347, 351
Diana, Princess of Wales   360
diary   207–211, 239, 243–244, 274, 337
– *The Diary of Anne Frank*   311
– *Diary of a Novelist* (Tabor novel)   173, 386
Diaz, José-Luis   20–21
Dickens, Charles   1, 13, 25, 38, 49–50, 55–57, 101–111, 113–115, 124–125, 130, 144, 159–160, 166, 169, 214, 227, 275, 289
– *A Tale of Two Cities*   57
– *Bleak House*   125, 169
– *David Copperfield*   13, 49, 81, 102–107, 110–111, 118, 124, 138, 163, 173, 176, 289, 385
– *Great Expectations*   114
– *Hard Times*   57, 112
– *Little Dorrit*   57
– *The Pickwick Papers*   107
Dictator (Harris novel)   335
dictionary   33
– *Dictionary of National Biography*   189
– *Oxford English Dictionary*   112
Didion, Joan   70, 354–355, 396
– *The Year of Magical Thinking*   355
Different Seasons (King collection)   323
dilettante *or* dilettantism   138, 145, 151
Dilthey, Wilhelm   20
disability   136, 156, 197, 199, 206–207, 210
discontent   132, 148, 198, 287, 356
discourse   20, 33, 39, 69, 102, 131, 149, 172, 196–197, 345, 348, 379, 381
– authorial discourse   59, 67
– confessional discourse   363
– cultural discourse   343
– *Discourse Networks* (Kittler)   21
– free indirect discourse   39, 43, 236, 262, 376
– imaginative discourse   348
– many-voiced discourse   61
– narrative discourse   86
– public discourse   285
– social discourse   381
– zero point of discourse   20, 23, 376, 378

discovery   65, 74, 228, 367, 369
– self-discovery   37, 229
disillusionment   87, 95, 100, 106, 108, 110, 134, 156, 170, 184, 207, 213, 228–229, 251, 272, 315, 379
dislocation   109, 197
Disraeli, Benjamin   99, 101–102, 112
– *Contarini Fleming*   99, 385
– *Sybil*   112
dissociation   12, 50, 173, 187–188, 216, 282, 348, 376
dissonance   178
distance *or* distancing   5, 7, 11, 13, 39–40, 67, 81, 92, 94–95, 104, 111, 115, 138, 186–188, 195, 205, 214, 217, 231, 239, 243, 253, 259, 263, 265, 273, 279, 284, 286, 299, 309, 314, 354–355, 357, 364, 373, 376, 380, 382
– aesthetic distance   347
– authorial distance   271
– cultural distance   339
– ironic distance   40, 111, 263
– spatial distance   186, 243
distinction   4, 12, 32, 37, 39, 45, 47–48, 51, 54–56, 58, 70–71, 87, 100, 119–120, 130, 158, 160, 176, 217, 238, 263, 274–275, 317, 331, 345, 347, 349, 355, 360, 371, 373, 379
– distinction between art and commerce   48, 160
– distinction between author and narrator   4, 39, 51, 53–55, 60, 67, 130
– distinction between fact *or* truth and fiction   69, 343, 356
– distinction between text and work   65
– social distinction   238, 349
distribution   34, 46, 64, 87, 161–162, 234, 247, 317, 348–349
diversity   32–33, 34, 44, 61, 72, 115, 159, 224, 234
Divine Comedy (Dante poem)   32
division   13, 47, 158–160, 253, 322, 325, 381
– division of labour   184
– political division   44, 241
divorce *or* divorcee   167, 228, 262–263, 295, 298, 307, 315, 358, 361, 370
Dixon, Ella Hepworth   162, 388
– *The Story of a Modern Woman*   162, 388
Doctor Faustus (Marlowe play)   64

The Doctor's Wife (Braddon novel)   149–150, 386
document   22, 35, 38, 54, 64–66, 118, 203, 259, 298, 357
Dolin, Tim   144
Donne, John   111, 272
Don Quixote (Cervantes novel)   68, 89, 187
doppelgänger, *see also* double   190–192, 213, 287, 328, 329
Dorst, Doug   301, 368
- *S.*   301, 368
Dostoevsky, Fyodor M.   54, 208, 238
- *The Brothers Karamazov*   54
- *Crime and Punishment*   208
- *Notes from Underground*   238, 386
double, *see also* biography, consciousness, doppelgänger, plot, reflection, standard   35–36, 122, 173–174, 184, 189–190, 192, 218, 289, 315, 328, 381
- counter-double-bluffing   287
- double bind   225
- double coding   282
- double-take   130
- doublethink   239
- doubling   38, 185–186, 284, 287
doubt   12, 22, 32, 95, 105, 108, 118, 132, 155, 159, 161, 178, 182, 195, 198, 209, 211, 222, 263, 270, 274–275, 279, 289–290, 306, 316, 341, 342, 363, 372
Doubrovsky, Serge   347, 394
Dowden, Edward   56
Down Below (Carrington)   245
Down the Road, Worlds Away   73
Doyle, Arthur Conan   7
Drabble, Margaret   275, 394
Dracula (Stoker novel)   118, 191
drama, *see also* melodrama   3, 32, 39, 145, 218, 358
- dramatisation   60, 182, 335
- dramatist   229
- kitchen-sink drama   257
- *Tom Singleton, Dragoon and Dramatist* (Follett Synge novel)   334, 387
dream   95, 97, 168, 173, 184, 190, 201–202, 205, 208, 298–299, 303, 311–312, 327, 352
- 'artist-dream'   135, 150
- daydream   200, 264, 319

- "The Dream of Duncan Parrenness" (Kipling story)   184
- *Dream of Fair to Middling Women* (Beckett novel)   240–241, 390
- *The Hill of Dreams* (Machen novel)   198–204, 388
Drinkwater, John   272
- "Moonlit Apples"   272
Dubliners (Joyce)   197
Ducks, Newburyport (Ellmann novel)   49
Duma Key (King novel)   319
Dumas, Alexandre   95
Du Maurier, Daphne   341
- *Rebecca*   341
The Dunciad (Pope poem)   33
Dunkle, Bisham (character in Caine's *The Author of "Trixie"*)   223–224
Durrell, Lawrence   13, 233, 240, 242–245, 249, 252–253, 261, 273, 276, 292, 327, 391, 393–396
- *The Alexandria Quartet*   244
- *The Black Book*   13, 242–244, 253, 273, 327, 391
- *Clea*   244, 393
Duyckinck, Evert   120
Dylan, Bob   33
- *Blood on the Tracks*   33
- "Idiot Wind"   33
dynamism   85, 96
The Dynasts (Hardy)   145

Easley, Alexis   127
economics   21–22, 161, 369
economy   12, 113, 165, 234
- authorial economy   334
- creative economy   12, 348, 352
- economy of attention   23
- economy of authorship   46, 153
- economy of literary forms   24
- economy of literature   35
- gig economy   153
- intellectual economy   182
- literary economy   162
- moral economy   323–324, 326
- name economy   49, 119, 348
- narrative economy   324
Edel, Leon   183–184

editing   19, 26, 132, 216, 327, 352
edition   57, 64, 102, 136, 142, 176, 189, 191, 265–266, 284, 312, 327, 356, 367–368
– New York Edition (James)   305
editor   22, 25–26, 46–47, 74, 81, 104, 108, 120, 128, 134, 139, 141–142, 154–159, 169, 171–172, 180–181, 204–205, 226, 233, 237, 244, 251, 260–261, 265, 268, 273, 286, 288–289, 322–323, 353, 367, 369, 374, 378, 383
– An Editor's Tales (Trollope)   139, 153–159, 172, 386
education   33, 108, 134, 148, 153, 166–167, 184, 205–206, 215, 237, 250, 315, 364
– Sentimental Education (Flaubert novel)   44, 81
Egan, Jesi   268
Eggers, Dave   12, 15, 349–356, 398
– A Heartbreaking Work of Staggering Genius   12, 350–356, 398
Eliot, George [Marian Evans]   48, 56, 100, 112, 117, 127, 136, 138, 148–149, 151, 153, 157, 160, 163, 228, 246, 280–281
– Adam Bede   112, 148–149, 280
– Middlemarch   43, 112, 117–118, 147–149, 263, 386
Eliot, T. S.   11, 25, 27, 29, 217, 247
Elliot, Frederick (character in Forster's The Longest Journey)   203–207
Ellison, Ralph   365
– Invisible Man   365
Ellison, Thelonious 'Monk' (character in Everett's Erasure)   364–366, 370
Ellmann, Lucy   49
– Ducks, Newburyport   49
Emerson, Ralph Waldo   118
The Emigrants (Sebald novel)   370
emotion   6, 9, 15, 49, 91, 94, 96, 125, 145, 148, 165, 204, 208, 226, 229, 239, 249, 260–261, 264, 270–272, 288–289, 307–309, 323, 342, 344, 351, 354, 361, 370, 384
empowerment   133, 136, 264, 284, 299, 304, 347
The End of the Affair (Greene novel)   48, 392
ending   86, 118, 123, 136, 147, 177, 190–191, 225, 252, 270, 272, 281, 294, 312, 337, 351, 362
– happy ending   109, 168, 225, 238, 252, 274, 294, 338–339, 362
– open ending   211, 267
– romance or romanticised ending   145, 362
– sense of an ending   40, 307
– surprise ending   201
– unhappy ending   225
England or English, see also church, death   9, 19, 23, 38–39, 50, 85, 97, 99, 105, 112, 128, 130, 134–135, 138, 140, 142, 146, 148–149, 158, 160–161, 176, 185, 188, 190–191, 197, 199, 199, 206, 208, 213, 218, 220, 229–230, 233, 235, 242–244, 252, 258, 263, 269, 276, 281, 285–286, 295, 297, 325, 342, 348, 361, 364, 367, 375, 385
– Black English   364
– British English   112
– English Illustrated Magazine   176
– Oxford English Dictionary   112
Enlightenment   94
– Dialectic of Enlightenment (Horkheimer/Adorno)   295
"Enoch Soames" (Beerbohm story)   8, 188–191, 389
enounced, the   39
ensō   294
enthusiasm   22, 85, 88, 168, 204, 207, 248, 268, 322, 361
enunciation   39–40, 42, 61
environment   30, 34, 133, 143, 159, 170, 208, 211, 239–240, 246, 251, 269, 301, 316, 333, 354, 359–361
epistemology   55, 66, 116, 280, 368
Equiano, Olaudah   79
– The Interesting Narrative   79
Erasure (Everett novel)   15, 44, 363–366, 369–370, 398
Ernaux, Annie   50, 349
Ernest Maltravers (Bulwer novel)   99, 102–103, 385
eroticism   142, 195
essay   33, 40, 42, 63–64, 113, 120, 128, 138, 154, 161, 168, 174, 234–236, 242, 280, 288, 302, 354, 356
Esther Waters (Moore novel)   118
ethics   110, 143, 200, 334, 359, 381
ethnicity   31, 72
Eugene Onegin (Pushkin poem)   115

Euripides   8, 364
– *The Persians*   364
Europe *or* European   36, 85, 102, 114, 182, 310, 374
Eurydice   294
Evelina (Burney novel)   130
Evelyn Lascelles (Addison novel)   130, 386
The Eve of St. Agnes (Keats poem)   186
event   19, 42, 55, 61, 64, 72–73, 76, 85–86, 117–118, 123, 161–162, 177–178, 188, 244, 257, 260–261, 285, 288, 304, 307, 310, 315, 332, 335, 337, 350, 357–358, 373, 377, 383–384
Everett, Percival   15, 44, 350, 363–366, 369–370, 398
– *Erasure*   15, 44, 363–366, 369–370, 398
Everything You Need (Kennedy novel)   357, 398
evolution   91
expectation   6, 24–25, 45, 77–78, 111, 119, 127, 135, 139, 156, 162, 220, 230, 238, 243, 248, 250, 255, 267, 275, 303–304, 313, 332, 352, 379, 406
– *Great Expectations* (Dickens novel)   114
experience, *see also* authenticity   11–12, 22, 29, 30–32, 37, 41, 44, 64, 69, 71, 73, 75, 79, 90, 106, 116, 157, 171, 173, 176, 184, 188, 197, 199–200, 203–205, 209, 215, 228, 235, 241–242, 268, 272, 281, 283, 289, 291, 293–294, 299–300, 306, 315–316, 321, 343–345, 347, 350–351, 353–354, 356, 358, 360–361, 371, 373, 376
– mystical experience   199, 204, 299
– reading experience   368
– representative experience   71, 73, 300, 360
– traumatic experience   11, 70, 348
expression, *see also* authenticity, freedom   1, 3, 15, 21, 27, 29–30, 47, 51, 63, 69, 71–72, 87, 89, 113, 144, 164, 170, 191, 209, 230, 235, 238, 242, 247–249, 259, 275–276, 282, 285, 294, 308, 316, 348, 355, 359, 363, 379, 383, 406
– self-expression   10, 29, 32, 37–38, 149, 174, 247, 258
expressivism   27–30, 43, 92, 253, 347, 363, 376, 382
eyewitness   79
Eyre, Jane (character)   136, 341

Facebook   339
The Facts (Roth autobiography)   345, 396
failure   23, 48, 88, 95, 101, 118, 122, 124, 147, 154–155, 157, 159, 161, 166–167, 171, 179, 182, 191, 196, 198, 206, 214, 225, 230–231, 239, 247, 252, 259, 265, 275, 305, 357, 367, 380, 383
– *Failure* (fictional novel)   252
– *Second Failure* (fictional novel)   364
faith   48, 131, 184, 239, 312
fallacy
– fallacy of misplaced concreteness   58
– intentional fallacy   4, 20
fame   24, 32, 35, 37, 90, 93, 95, 101, 120, 133–136, 149, 155, 166, 174–175, 180, 182, 189, 220, 223, 295, 311, 327
– hall of fame   31
– *The House of Fame* (Chaucer poem)   32
– *A Struggle for Fame* (Riddell novel)   128–129, 387
family   88, 94–95, 132, 137, 139–140, 142–143, 146–148, 155, 163–164, 182, 214, 218, 221–222, 227, 237, 248, 252, 262–263, 264, 266, 274, 306, 310–312, 314, 343, 351–352, 355, 361, 364
– *The Clever Woman of the Family* (Yonge novel)   128, 386
– "Family Furnishings" (Munro story)   305
fan *or* fandom, *see also* fiction, letter   176, 320–321, 323
Fanshawe, Jane (character in Baxter's *Jane: Young Author*)   258
fantasy   38, 104, 171, 184, 199, 201–203, 207, 218, 223, 265, 286, 291, 300, 311–313, 315, 322, 331–333, 380
farce   115, 213–214, 218, 222–223
"The Farcical History of Richard Greenow" (Huxley story)   191, 213, 256, 389
Farebrother, Rachel   365
Far from the Madding Crowd (Hardy novel)   141–142
Farrell, Kathleen   259, 265, 267–268, 273, 392
– *The Cost of Living*   265, 267–268, 273–274, 392
fascination   1, 44, 102, 133, 157, 186, 187, 199, 302, 331, 350
The Fatal Kiss (Whalley poem)   128

Faye (character in Cusk's *Outline* trilogy)   370–376
"Felix Argallo and Walter Ledgett" (Beerbohm story)   191, 390
Felski, Rita   238
The Female Quixote (Lennox novel)   129
femininity   130, 135, 137, 177, 199, 255, 258, 269, 292, 325–327
feminism   14, 44, 62, 72, 127, 129, 145, 198, 255, 256, 358, 377
– second-wave feminism   275
La femme auteur (de Genlis novel)   129, 385
Fenwick-Symes, Adam (character in Waugh's *Vile Bodies*)   216–217
Ferrante, Elena   73, 348, 400–401
feuilleton   93
– *roman feuilleton*   95
Fichte, Johann Gottlieb   100
fiction, see also art, authority, autofiction, biofiction, metafiction, nonfiction, work *passim*
– adventure fiction   326
– antirealist fiction   41
– "The Art of Fiction" (Besant essay)   101
– "The Art of Fiction" (James essay)   101, 162, 179
– author fiction   1–4, 6–10, 14–15, 30, 35, 50–51, 78, 82, 85, 101, 103, 118, 125, 172, 191–193, 257, 275, 280, 290, 293, 303, 326, 372, 377–383, 403, 406
– authorpoietic fiction   107, 363
– autobiographical fiction   45, 347
– *autrefiction*   376, 382, 376, 382
– campus fiction   297
– comic fiction   216
– commercial fiction   15, 119, 149, 168, 238, 240, 275–276, 320, 328
– *The Craft of Fiction* (Lubbock)   56
– crime fiction   24, 332, 334
– detective fiction   332
– editorial fiction   104
– experimental fiction   250, 364
– fan fiction   7, 10, 46, 349
– fantasy fiction   322
– "Fiction" (Munro story)   305
– *Fiction and the Reading Public* (Leavis)   226, 236
– *Fictions of Authority* (Lanser)   259
– formula fiction   119
– genre fiction   10, 12–14, 24, 47, 49, 119, 174, 234, 257, 269–270, 317, 319, 323, 328, 331–332, 381
– gothic fiction   121–122
– historical fiction   186, 321
– horror fiction   317, 324, 329, 331, 380
– literary fiction   12–13, 24, 45, 47, 49, 51, 55, 69, 71, 121, 149, 210, 244, 257, 269, 280, 285, 291, 294, 298–299, 317, 322, 324, 328, 331, 339, 342, 344–345, 356, 368, 376, 384
– middlebrow fiction   10, 13, 118
– modern *or* modernist fiction   41, 112, 172, 250, 274, 381
– narrative fiction   1–3, 9, 51, 53, 55, 68, 79, 126, 172, 274, 282, 348, 377–378, 382
– new adult fiction   340
– New Woman fiction   171
– "The Place of Realism in Fiction" (Gissing essay)   168
– popular fiction   131, 140, 150, 175, 199, 224, 249, 324
– postmodernist fiction   281–282, 298, 350–351, 381, 383
– prose fiction   157–158, 272
– pulp fiction   119, 328
– quasi-fiction   188
– realist fiction   138, 159, 221, 234, 240, 344
– romance fiction   321, 323, 340
– science fiction   1, 32, 239, 284, 291, 300, 331
– science of fiction   168
– sensational fiction   158, 256
– sentimental fiction   79
– serial *or* serialised fiction   114, 147, 348
– serious fiction   168
– short fiction   158–159
– spy fiction   344
– suspense fiction   317, 319, 331, 335, 340, 345
– Western fiction   270
– women's fiction   256, 265, 276
– young adult fiction   332
fictionality   4–5, 8, 42, 52, 55–60, 63, 66–69, 72–73, 76–78, 118–119, 123, 129, 131, 138, 149, 157, 191, 208, 229, 263, 280–285, 299, 332, 341, 343, 347–348, 350–351, 354–357, 373, 375–379, 382–383, 406

field   3, 14, 19–20, 22–23, 47–51, 63, 73, 78, 80–81, 154, 177, 179, 203, 234–235, 309, 317, 319, 332, 379, 381
– battlefield   217, 276
– cultural field   213, 375, 380
– field of cultural production   180
– field translation   378
– literary field   1–2, 7–8, 12, 14–15, 21–23, 25, 33, 47–50, 63, 78, 80–81, 87–88, 92–93, 96, 106, 127, 138–139, 159–161, 165, 171, 198, 203, 233–234, 245, 253, 256, 271, 275–276, 304, 317, 322, 331–332, 347, 349–350, 354, 370, 376, 378, 381, 383
– social field   78, 282, 360
– subfield   21
Fielding, Henry   230
Fifty Shades of Grey (E. L. James novel)   46
figure   1–2, 5, 34, 36, 53, 58, 87, 108, 122, 125, 127, 155, 188–189, 196, 201, 205, 211, 246, 271, 274–275, 282, 289, 298, 301, 356, 362
– artist figure   196, 381
– author figure   1, 32, 78, 114, 211, 282, 289
– authority figure   315
– editor figure   369
– father figure   310, 312
– "The Figure in the Carpet" (James tale)   175, 178–179, 388
– multistable figure   5
– narrator figure   40
– public figure   80, 103, 174, 211
– reflector figure   195
– sales figures   217, 301, 342
film   102, 218, 238, 250, 263, 285, 325, 332–333, 335–336, 338, 351, 365–366, 377
Filmer, Madeleine (character in Gardner's "The Woman Novelist")   266
Filmer, Sir Robert   266
– *Patriarcha*   266
fin de siècle   15, 160, 169, 172, 174, 188, 203, 338
"The Finest Story in the World" (Kipling story)   184, 186–187, 220, 387
Fitzcarraldo (publishing house)   50
Flaubert, Gustave   11, 40–42, 43, 81, 149
– *Madame Bovary*   149
– *Sentimental Education*   44, 81
Fleet Street   248

Florence   135
focalisation   42, 163, 172, 201, 209, 217, 238, 266, 343
– external focalisation   50
– variable focalisation   211
– zero focalisation   42, 50
focaliser   8, 118, 208
– character-focaliser   130
Foer, Jonathan Safran   71, 301, 368, 398
– *Tree of Codes*   301, 368
Follett Synge, W. W.   334, 386
– *Tom Singleton, Dragoon and Dramatist*   334, 387
Ford, Nesta (character in Wodehouse's *The Little Nugget*)   256
forgery   121, 334, 366–368, 370
– *The Tremor of Forgery* (Highsmith novel)   328, 332–334, 394
form   3–5, 9, 15, 17, 24–25, 34–36, 38–39, 44–45, 49–50, 53, 61, 78, 81, 95, 112, 114–116, 119, 123–124, 137–138, 146, 155, 159, 168, 172, 174, 192, 198, 209, 211, 214, 217, 230, 233, 235, 243, 249, 265, 266, 270, 280–281, 283, 285, 287, 302, 315–317, 333, 338, 345, 349, 351, 364, 377–379, 383–384
– artistic form   87, 174
– *bildungsroman* as form   10, 123, 137
– book form   203–204
– destruction of form   41
– dramatic form   358–359
– fiction as form   258
– form of art   168, 266, 380
– form of narration   42, 50, 115, 172
– generic form   6, 363
– human form   221
– *künstlerroman* as form   360
– letter form   368
– literary form   2–3, 7, 21, 23–25, 39, 41, 78–79, 117, 146, 150, 177–178, 211, 247, 249, 285, 315–316, 348, 351, 362, 370, 381, 384
– material form   64–66
– minor form   63
– narrative form   2, 41, 62, 178, 211, 248, 317
– novel form   11, 38–39, 41, 95, 100, 115, 123, 210, 230, 236, 247, 249–250, 263, 281, 283, 288–289, 347, 381

- physical form   328, 367
- play-script as form   358–359
- romance form   145–148, 274
- serial form   125, 199
- short story as form   178
- social form   2, 13, 22, 41, 43, 83, 137, 172, 363, 378, 406
- symbolic form   99, 113
- textual form   64
- verbal form   42
- volume form   155
format   64, 95, 123, 162, 249, 349, 368, 376
- codex format   368
- one-volume format   162
- three-decker *or* triple-decker format   162, 275
formation, *see also* Bildung, deformation, development, novel   11, 20–21, 38, 78, 85, 90, 99–101, 106, 110, 137, 171, 191, 196–197, 216, 239, 289, 300, 302, 304, 316, 406
- author formation   198, 376, 406
- compromise formation   99–100, 114, 235, 252
- cultural formation   26
- discursive formation   78
- historical formation   41, 378
- institutional formation   3, 348
- self-formation   37–38, 49, 77, 123, 202, 257, 316, 406
- social *or* socio-economic formation   2, 85, 352, 363, 375
- subject formation   64, 349, 363
formalism   22, 58
formula   71, 119, 137, 140, 159, 170, 218, 222, 239, 249, 311, 319
Forster, E. M.   172, 195, 197, 202–207, 211, 275, 380, 389
- *The Longest Journey*   198, 201, 203–207, 211, 380, 389
Forster, George   109
fortune   85, 94, 101, 155, 225–226
- *The Wheel of Fortune* (fictional novel)   139
Forward, Toby   73
Foster, Edgar   165
- *How to Write a Novel*   165
Foster, Maude (character in Rossetti's *Maude*)   132–133

Foucault, Michel   20, 53
The Four Zoas (Blake poem)   30
Fowles, John   280, 284, 395
- *The French Lieutenant's Woman*   280
fragmentation   38, 203, 209, 258, 275, 286, 294, 299, 348, 372
frame *or* framework, *see also* tale, 27–29, 116, 172, 177, 209, 209, 228, 275, 288, 310–311, 358, 369, 373
- frame-breaking   280, 316, 354
France *or* French   7, 19–21, 44, 51, 56, 61, 85–89, 96, 99, 106, 110, 129, 139, 143, 149, 157, 168, 217, 227, 245, 252, 282, 376
- *The French Lieutenant's Woman* (Fowles novel)   280
- French *nouveau roman*   282
- French poststructuralism   285, 364
- French Revolution   113
- French Symbolism   209
France, Anatole   208
Francie (character in Moore's "How to Become a Writer")   315–316
Frank, Anne   310–313
- *The Diary of Anne Frank*   311
Frankau, Gilbert   235
Frankenstein (Shelley novel)   37–39, 328
Frankenstein, Victor (character)   38–39, 366
Franklin, Benjamin   354
Frankfurt School   41, 69
freedom, *see also* art, speech   8, 29, 40–41, 43–46, 69–70, 87, 104, 146, 151, 171, 230, 238, 242, 280, 291, 320, 329, 339, 356, 359–360, 373, 375–376, 382
- freedom of art   68–69
- freedom of expression   45
- freedom of speech   69
The French Lieutenant's Woman (Fowles novel)   280
Freud, Sigmund   9, 19, 29, 75, 77, 223
Frey, James   356
- *A Million Little Pieces*   356
Friedman, Lawrence   113
The Friend (Nunez novel)   355, 401
The Friendly Young Ladies (Renault novel)   268–271, 391
The Frogs (Aristophanes play)   8
Fuller, Margaret   120

future 3, 89–90, 92, 135, 143, 170, 189, 201, 206, 209, 215–216, 289, 295, 312–313, 336, 344, 348, 359, 367, 372, 374

Galley Beggar Press 49
Galsworthy, John 235
game 92, 132, 215, 233, 251, 370, 379, 382
Gardner, Diana 265–267, 274
– *Halfway Down the Cliff* 265
– *The Indian Woman* 265
– "The Woman Novelist" 265–267, 274, 392
Gaskell, Elizabeth 131
– *Life of Charlotte Brontë* 131
– *Mary Barton* 112
– *North and South* 112
gender 14, 31, 63, 72, 101, 104, 121–122, 127–131, 135, 137, 139, 148, 150, 156, 160, 171, 177, 233, 235, 245–246, 255, 258–262, 268, 271, 273, 275–276, 287, 310, 315, 321, 325–326, 355, 375, 378, 404
– gender pay gap 260
– gender politics 273
– gender stereotypes 14, 130, 260
generation, *see also* degeneration, regeneration 2, 31, 43, 206–208, 210, 214, 229–231, 242–243, 250, 260, 298, 313
– Generation X 353
– golden generation 207
– Lost Generation 207
Genesis, *see also* Bible 42
Genette, Gérard 23, 56–57, 60
genius 9–10, 13–14, 19–20, 26–27, 29, 31, 33–37, 43, 74, 85, 88, 91–92, 105, 107, 120, 131, 154–157, 162, 176–177, 183, 210, 219–220, 242, 247, 349, 359–360, 380
– *A Heartbreaking Work of Staggering Genius* (Eggers novel) 12, 350–356, 398
genre, *see also* fiction 2–3, 10, 12–13, 24–25, 35, 49–51, 63–66, 73–74, 78, 80–81, 85, 99, 106, 114, 119, 121, 127, 130, 133, 137, 141, 145–146, 172, 175, 192, 206, 240, 243, 245–246, 250, 268, 270, 283, 300, 301, 317, 320, 331–332, 335–336, 338, 344–345, 347, 349–350, 357, 378–382
gentleman 34, 105, 109–111, 158, 176, 189, 222, 224
– gentleman authorship 34, 222

geography 3, 320, 324
Georgian 215, 272
German *or* Germany 21, 33, 39, 60, 106, 108, 116, 213, 249, 272–273, 293, 334, 344, 374
gestalt 5
ghost, *see also* story 25, 123, 182–184, 186, 188, 190, 220, 250, 265, 279, 287, 312, 314, 329, 335–336, 381
– *The Ghost* (Harris novel) 335, 399
– ghost-writer *or* -writing 29, 142, 312, 335, 342–343, 345
– *The Ghost Writer* (film) 335
– *The Ghost Writer* (Roth novel) 309–314, 382, 395
– Typing Ghost 285
giant 294, 334, 369
– *The Buried Giant* (Ishiguro novel) 331
– *The Giant's Robe* (Anstey novel) 334, 386
Gibbs, Philip 235
Gilbert, Isabel (character in Braddon's *The Doctor's Wife*) 149
Gilbert, Sandra 129, 131–132, 137
– *The Madwoman in the Attic* 131
Ginsberg, Ivan (character in Camberton's *Scamp*) 250–252
The Girls of Slender Means (Spark novel) 271–273, 393
Gissing, George 11, 13, 97, 100, 113, 153, 160–174, 187, 198, 202, 225, 229, 233, 239–240, 242, 275, 317, 380, 387–388
– *New Grub Street* 11, 13, 97, 100, 113, 125, 153, 160–173, 177, 192, 198, 202, 210, 225, 233, 239, 247, 380, 387
– "The Place of Realism in Fiction" 168
Glavinic, Thomas 8, 399
– *Das bin doch ich* 8, 399
God *or* gods 11, 29, 32, 43, 54, 88, 100, 115, 134, 185, 198, 205, 241–242, 246, 262, 280, 283, 289, 291, 298–299, 319, 326, 336, 365
– demi-god 102
– goddess 320, 322–326
– "The Great God Pan" (Machen tale) 199, 269
– money-god 238
Godfrey Malvern (Miller novel) 100–101, 385
Goebbels, Joseph 310

Goethe, Johann Wolfgang von   3, 38, 85, 99, 102, 112, 126, 171, 379
– *Torquato Tasso*   3
– *Wilhelm Meister's Apprenticeship*   85, 99
The Golden Notebook (Lessing novel)
Golding, William   279, 295–300, 395
– *The Paper Men*   295–300, 395
Goldsmiths Prize   49–50
Gone with the Wind (Mitchell novel)   269
Gosse, Edmund   48, 160, 177
gossip   181, 213, 216–217, 271–272, 274
GPT   47
Great Expectations (Dickens novel)   114
"The Great God Pan" (Machen tale)   199, 269
Greece or Greek   31, 56, 76–77, 168, 184–185, 204–205, 244, 246, 252, 289, 371
– *The Metres of the Greek Dramatists* (fictional study)   158
– "Ode on a Grecian Urn" (Keats)   187
Green, Henry [Henry Vincent Yorke]   195, 207–211, 217, 275, 380
– *Blindness*   198, 207–211, 380, 390
Greene, Graham   13, 24, 229–230, 380
– *The End of the Affair*   48, 392
– *Loser Takes All*   24
Greenleaf, Dickie (character in Highsmith's *The Talented Mr. Ripley*)   336
Greg, W. R.   138
– "False Morality of Lady Novelists"   138
Gregory, Herbert (character in Miller's *Tropic of Cancer*)   243–244
"Greville Fane" (James tale)   140, 175, 387
Grisham, John   323
Grub Street   33–34, 46, 162–163, 349
Gubar, Susan   129, 131–132, 137
– *The Madwoman in the Attic*   131
Guild of Literature and Art   105
Gulliver's Travels (Swift novel)   169
Guttzeit, Gero   80, 269
Guy, Josephine   133

Habermas, Jürgen   69
habit   7, 23, 35, 107, 158, 271, 307, 316
habitus   23, 77
hack   29, 31, 33–34, 91, 93, 100, 105, 108, 269–270, 349, 383

Hadrian the Seventh (Rolfe novel)   13, 174, 191, 380
Haggard, Henry Rider   187, 320–322, 325
– *She*   320, 325
Halfway Down the Cliff (Gardner collection)   265
Hall, Steven   300
– *Maxwell's Demon*   300
Halliday, Lisa   363, 401
– *Asymmetry*   363, 401
Hamilton, Patrick   251
– *Hangover Square*   251
Hamlet (Shakespeare play)   19, 66, 289, 367
Hamlet (character)   124
Hamsun, Knut   161, 197, 387
– *Hunger*   161
The Hand of Ethelberta (Hardy novel)   140–147, 150–151, 213, 386
handwriting   121, 200
Hangover Square (Hamilton novel)   251
happiness   91, 111, 163, 198, 342
Hard Times (Dickens novel)   57, 112
Hardy, Thomas   1, 128, 140–150, 164, 167, 213, 241, 386
– *The Dynasts*   145
– *Far from the Madding Crowd*   141–142
– *The Hand of Ethelberta*   140–147, 150–151, 213, 386
– *A Laodicean*   141
– *A Pair of Blue Eyes*   128, 141–142, 386
A Harlot High and Low (Balzac novel)   86
Harris, Robert   331, 335, 399
– *Dictator*   335
– *The Ghost*   335, 399
– *Imperium*   335
– *Lustrum*   335
Harry Potter (Rowling book series)   335
Hartman, Geoffrey   37
Hawthorne, Nathaniel   56, 68, 137, 178, 200
– *Mosses from an Old Manse*   56
"Hawthorne and his Mosses" (Melville essay)   120
Hawthorne, Sophia   124
Haye, John (character in Green's *Blindness*)   207–210
heart   91–92, 145, 147, 161, 174, 205, 208, 225, 247, 263, 270, 273, 310, 351–352, 355

- *A Heartbreaking Work of Staggering Genius* (Eggers novel) 12, 350–356, 398
- *Heart of Darkness* (Conrad novel) 118
- *Trials of the Human Heart* (Rowson novel) 129
- *What the Heart Desires* (fictional novel) 258
heaven 88, 91, 122, 336
Hebdige, Dick 355
The Heir of the Ages (Payn novel) 129, 387
He Knew He Was Right (Trollope novel) 139
Helle, Sophus 29
Hemingway, Ernest 24, 42, 391
- "The Killers" 42
- *Winner Take Nothing* 24
Hendriks, Rose Ellen 127, 130–131, 133
- *The Young Authoress* 130–131, 133
Henschel, Gerhard 347, 401
- *Künstlerroman* 347, 401
Hentea, Marius 207, 210
Hercules 91
Herman, David 58
hermeneutics 19–20
hero 19, 33, 35–36, 100–103, 106–107, 110–111, 114, 118–121, 124–125, 134, 137, 151, 198, 202, 205, 210, 213, 215–216, 226, 233, 240, 252, 281, 292–293, 313, 327, 332–334
- anti-hero 36, 213, 225
- coming-of-age hero 240
- *On Heroes, Hero-Worship, and the Heroic in History* (Carlyle) 100
- tragic hero 168
heroine 112, 130, 137, 141–143, 146–148, 162, 219, 258, 261, 320–321, 326, 332, 362
heteroglossia 61, 115
heteronomy 27–29, 34–35, 369
heteronormativity 270–271
heteropoetic 6–8, 76–79, 81, 101, 118, 133, 137, 230, 351, 376, 378, 406
Heti, Sheila 15, 350, 356–361, 400
- *How Should a Person Be?* 356–360, 400
- *Motherhood* 360
hexis 77–78, 80–81, 137, 230, 317, 406
hierarchy 23, 49, 55, 127, 147, 150, 158, 238, 246, 258, 263, 276, 317, 322, 324
Highsmith, Patricia 1, 74–75, 328, 332–334, 336, 338
- *The Story-Teller* 333

- *A Suspension of Mercy* 333, 394
- *The Talented Mr. Ripley* 333
- *The Tremor of Forgery* 328, 332–334
"Hilary Maltby and Stephen Braxton" (Beerbohm story) 188, 190–191, 389
The Hill of Dreams (Machen novel) 198–204, 388
historicism 72
- New Historicism 41
history 1–3, 5, 10, 14, 19–23, 28, 31, 34, 41–43, 47, 62, 72, 79, 82, 113, 217, 248, 264, 302, 326–327, 352, 367–368, 370, 380, 382
- book history 19, 21, 34, 368–369
- "The Farcical History of Richard Greenow" (Huxley story) 191, 213, 256, 389
- *The History Man* (Bradbury novel) 297, 394
- *The History of Pendennis* (Thackeray novel) 74, 85, 102–110, 112, 118, 138–139, 163, 199, 202, 213–215, 222, 385
- *History of Women from Victoria to Elizabeth II* (Brittain) 259
- literary history 2, 19, 22, 30–31, 51, 68, 82, 235, 244–245, 311, 323, 326, 380
- media history 21
- world history 31
Hoban, Russell 291–295, 299, 394, 396
- *Kleinzeit* 291–295, 299, 394
- *The Medusa Frequency* 294, 396
- *Riddley Walker* 291
Hobbs, Katherine 131
Hogarth Press 234
Hogg, James 38
- *Private Memoirs and Confessions of a Justified Sinner* 38
Hoggart, Richard 249
- *The Uses of Literacy* 249
Holinshed, Raphael 367
- *Chronicles* 367
Hollywood 286, 336–337, 365
Holmes, Sherlock 7
Homer 55, 74
- *Iliad* 55
- *Odyssey* 56
homoeroticism 195–196, 310
homopoetic 6, 9, 77, 118, 243, 281, 384, 406
honour 77, 99, 105, 149, 179–180, 218

Hoover, Colleen   46, 340–342, 401
– *Verity*   340–342, 345, 401
Hopkins, Gerard Manley   272
– "The Wreck of the *Deutschland*"   272
Hopscotch (Cortázar novel)   1, 281
Horace (Quintus Horatius Flaccus)   31
horror, see also fiction, novel, story   10, 38, 79, 121, 190, 199, 204–205, 213, 219, 223, 317, 320–321, 325, 327–329, 342
– authorship horror   203, 317, 319
– body horror   328
house   7, 107–108, 122, 134, 142–143, 224, 265, 272, 295, 302, 304–307, 310, 336, 374
– *Bleak House* (Dickens novel)   125, 169
– boarding house   56, 237, 271
– country house   143, 176, 214, 264, 367
– House of Commons   110
– *The House of Fame* (Chaucer poem)   32
– *House of Incest* (Nin novel)   245
– *House of Leaves* (Danielewski novel)   301
– prison-house   169, 171
– publishing house   148, 226, 348, 366, 369, 374
Howard, Elizabeth Jane   261, 398
Howells, William Dean   161, 226, 387
– "The Man of Letters as a Man of Business"   161
– *The World of Chance*   161, 226, 387
How Should a Person Be? (Heti novel)   356–360, 400
"How to Become a Writer" (Moore story)   314–316, 396
How to Write a Novel (Foster)   165
Hubbard, L. Ron   284, 391
– *Typewriter in the Sky*   284, 391
Hudson (character in Powell's *What's Become of Waring*)   227–228
Hughes, Linda K.   148–149
Hühn, Peter   39
human being   35, 177, 242, 283
humanity   62, 89, 102, 125, 134–135, 201, 206, 262, 311
Humbert, Humbert (character in Nabokov's *Lolita*)   54, 69
humour   104, 121, 159, 174, 181, 190–192, 213–214, 223, 256, 297, 315, 350–351, 358

Humphries, Charles (character in Mitchell's *The Undiscovered Country*)   286–287
hunger   70, 94, 135–136, 242
– *Hunger* (Hamsun novel)   161, 192, 387
– *Of Love and Hunger* (Maclaren-Ross novel)   251, 392
– reality hunger   45, 70
Hutcheon, Linda   332
Huxley, Aldous   191, 207, 213–216, 218, 220, 223, 256, 275, 381, 389–390
– *Brave New World*   216
– *Crome Yellow*   207, 214–217, 220, 231, 389
– "The Farcical History of Richard Greenow"   191, 213, 256, 389
– *Mortal Coils*   213
– "Nuns at Luncheon"   213, 389
– *Point Counter Point*   207, 390
– *Those Barren Leaves*   207, 216, 390
Huysmans, Joris-Karl   200
– *À rebours* (*Against Nature*)   200
hypotext   310

I am Sovereign (Barker novel)   300
I Capture the Castle (Smith novel)   273, 392
iceberg principle   302
idea, see also novel, world   1–3, 6, 8, 10, 12, 14, 24, 26–29, 35, 37, 39, 41–43, 47, 61–64, 75–76, 87, 89, 92, 100–101, 104–106, 108, 110, 112, 115, 123–125, 137, 154–155, 157, 161, 163, 169, 178, 182–183, 188, 191, 198–200, 202, 204, 206, 209, 216, 219–220, 222–223, 234, 239, 242, 247–252, 258, 260–261, 272, 276, 281, 295, 299, 323, 326, 334–338, 342, 350, 353, 359–360, 363, 370, 372–374, 380
ideal or idealism   11, 14, 28, 44, 51, 64, 81, 89–90, 103–104, 109, 136–137, 149, 164, 168, 171, 174, 176, 196, 199, 201, 204, 206, 229, 239, 247, 257, 272, 290, 293, 311, 313, 316, 349, 351–353, 356–357, 364, 375, 380–381
identity, see also politics   5, 11, 23, 32, 44–45, 67–69, 71, 73, 75, 81, 122, 127–128, 148, 150, 157, 182–183, 185, 188, 223, 228–229, 279, 299, 304, 337, 348, 361, 365, 377
– authorial identity   75, 172, 214, 239, 268, 322–323, 381

- collective identity   100
- cultural identity   356
- ethnic identity   63, 355
- group identity   12, 44, 100
- personal identity   110, 114, 323, 365
- professional *or* vocational identity   23, 85, 100, 154, 162, 185, 327, 329
- sexual identity   270
- social identity   110, 145, 150
- split identity   188

ideology   104, 137, 145, 248, 261, 282

If on a Winter's Night a Traveller (Calvino novel)   378

Iliad (Homer)   55

I Like It Here (Amis novel)   214, 229–230, 393

illness   91, 96, 109, 195–197, 310

illusion, *see also* disillusionment   41, 90, 92, 96, 175, 228, 237, 282, 347, 368

- *Lost Illusions* (Balzac novel)   85–97, 103, 109, 114, 121, 163, 362, 379, 385

I Love Dick (Kraus novel)   355, 397

image   5, 58, 75, 89, 101, 119, 122–123, 147, 156, 177, 179, 182, 216, 230, 255, 280, 294, 296, 312, 314, 352, 365, 370, 375

- author image   24, 49, 51, 58, 77–78, 107, 120, 151, 156, 182, 222, 227, 228, 304
- public image   23, 101, 121, 181, 222, 228–229, 255

imagery   89, 122, 223, 265, 324–325

imaginary   21, 51, 135, 203, 209, 262, 275, 313, 321–322, 324–325

- *An Imaginary Life* (Malouf novella)   8, 395

imagination   7, 12, 65–66, 104, 113, 117, 129, 141, 146, 151, 157, 173–174, 185, 199–202, 204, 216, 264–265, 279, 281, 313, 320, 334, 348, 363

imitation   31, 33, 66, 130, 141, 144, 180, 188, 192, 214–216, 268, 286, 367, 369–370, 380

immediacy   211, 253, 281, 347

immortality   89–92, 120, 240, 320

Imperium (Harris novel)   335

impersonality   10–12, 31, 39, 42–44, 50, 54, 59, 61, 70, 85, 159, 164, 217, 248, 258–259, 268–270, 273, 275, 280, 355, 372, 376

impression   5, 43, 45, 115, 178, 191, 199–200, 242, 253, 280, 290, 353–355, 361, 379

impressionism   174, 188, 275, 280, 351

inauthenticity   70, 282

India *or* Indian   5, 88, 228, 252

- *The Indian Woman* (Gardner novel)   265

individuality   120, 239, 289, 352, 354, 360, 373, 376, 381

individualism   27, 268, 363

industrialisation   10, 245, 247

influence   5–6, 29, 50, 102, 106, 108, 133, 158, 176, 188, 218, 242, 255, 259, 271, 364, 367, 373, 377

- anxiety of influence   187
- ecstasy of influence   300

information   31, 66–67, 74–75, 77, 80, 155, 175, 261, 367

The Information (Amis novel)   301, 397

infrastructure   14, 23, 25, 99, 378

- media infrastructure   2, 406

Ingham, Howard (character in Highsmith's *The Tremor of Forgery*)   328, 333–334

innovation   10, 49, 169, 187, 192, 210, 250

The Inquisitor (Rowson novel)   129

"Inside the Whale" (Orwell essay)   242

inspiration   3, 29, 36, 122, 184, 186–187, 216, 219, 247, 274, 282, 294, 341

- divine inspiration   36, 89, 91

institution   3, 11, 14–15, 20–23, 25–27, 30, 34–35, 40, 45, 47, 53, 69, 78, 80, 86–87, 96, 99, 105, 108, 122, 170, 233–234, 247, 276, 282, 299, 331, 339, 348, 362–363, 366, 369–370, 376, 378–379, 382–383

institutionalism   12, 21, 27–30, 32, 43, 92, 347, 363, 382

intellect   103, 105, 113–114, 162

- aristocracy of intellect   99

intellectual   213–214, 283

intention   19, 27, 47, 57–59, 62, 65–66, 78, 116, 142, 175, 180, 262, 280, 298, 341, 358, 377, 406

- anti-intentionalism   58, 61–62
- intentional act   57
- intentional agent   59, 61
- intentional fallacy   4, 20
- intentionalism   22, 58

interaction   25–26, 72, 75–77, 80–81, 179, 293, 362, 406

interpretation   19–20, 31, 41, 62, 127, 130, 209–210, 247, 313

intertextuality 10–12, 44, 66, 293–294, 300, 311, 314
"Intimacy" (Carver story) 307–309, 396
invisibility, see also visibility 22, 36, 43, 50, 80, 116, 138, 156–157, 221, 282, 285, 298, 349, 355, 365–366, 375, 378
Invisible Man (Ellison novel) 365
Ireland *or* Irish 28, 108, 155, 197, 233, 252, 371, 375
irony 11, 32, 39–42, 59, 61, 63, 70–71, 86, 90, 92, 96, 104, 110–111, 115, 118, 124, 131, 144, 148, 159, 171, 174–175, 180–181, 185, 187, 203, 209, 214, 236, 246, 262–263, 265, 272–273, 280–281, 288, 290, 301, 303, 306, 310, 314, 316, 334, 347, 350, 353–354, 364, 369, 382
Iser, Wolfgang 5, 65, 175
Ishiguro, Kazuo 331–332
– *The Buried Giant* 331
– *Klara and the Sun* 332
isolation 85, 111, 116, 198, 200–202, 211, 215, 310–311
It (King novel) 319
Italian *or* Italy 135, 190–191, 252, 296–297
ivory tower 70, 306, 381

Jack of Spades (Oates novel) 335, 401
James, E. L. 46, 341
– *Fifty Shades of Grey* 46
James, Henry 11, 13, 43, 47, 64, 83, 101–102, 128, 140, 147, 160–162, 172–184, 191–192, 195–198, 201, 211, 214, 226, 228–230, 275, 295, 297, 303, 305, 310–311, 313, 317, 372, 380, 387–389
– *The Ambassadors* 229
– "The Art of Fiction" 101, 162, 179
– "The Aspern Papers" 175, 179, 296–297, 387
– "The Author of 'Beltraffio'" 176–179, 387
– "The Beast in the Jungle" 182
– "The Birthplace" 182, 389
– "The Coxon Fund" 175, 180, 388
– *Daisy Miller* 65
– "The Death of the Lion" 128, 180, 297, 388
– "The Figure in the Carpet" 175, 178–179, 388
– "Greville Fane" 140, 175, 387
– "John Delavoy" 180–182, 388
– "The Jolly Corner" 182

– "The Middle Years" 173, 181, 195, 310, 387
– *The Middle Years* 195
– "The Next Time" 161, 175, 180, 226, 388
– "The Papers" 181–182
– *The Portrait of a Lady* 147, 229, 305
– "The Private Life" 183–184, 191, 228, 387
– "The Real Right Thing" 182, 297, 388
– *Roderick Hudson* 178
– *The Sacred Fount* 178
– *The Turn of the Screw* 118, 177
– *What Maisie Knew* 118
James, Marlon 332
– *Dark Star* trilogy 332
Jameson, Anna 136
Jameson, Fredric 41, 86
Jameson, Storm 245, 257, 261, 390–391
– *Company Parade* 245, 390
Jane Eyre (Brontë novel) 112, 130, 257, 341
Jane the Virgin (TV series) 332
Jane: Young Author (Baxter novel) 128, 258, 267, 392
Janteloven ('law of Jante') 354
Japanese 102
jazz 207, 216, 230
Jenkins, Herbert (publisher) 223
Jenkins, Juanita Mae (character in Everett's *Erasure*) 364
Jerusalem (Blake poem) 30
"John Delavoy" (James tale) 180–182, 388
Johnson, B. S. 285–287
– *Albert Angelo* 285
– *The Unfortunates* 285
Johnson, Hugo (character in Munro's "Material") 302
Johnson, Pamela Hansford 296, 393
Johnson, Samuel 19, 32, 34
– *Lives of the Poets* 19
"The Jolly Corner" (James tale) 182
Jones, William Alfred 119–120
Joseph and his Brothers (Mann novel) 61
"Josephine de Montmorenci" (Trollope tale) 139, 156, 159
journal 44, 93–94, 97, 181, 208, 258, 261, 273–274, 298, 340, 352, 364–365
journalist *or* journalism 44, 48, 57, 87–88, 90–91, 93–95, 109, 119, 154, 167, 175, 181–

182, 189, 213, 217–218, 226, 229, 233, 250, 252, 259
– New Journalism   70, 382
journey   36, 89, 296, 298, 312, 321, 325
– *The Longest Journey* (Forster novel)   198, 201, 203–207, 211, 380, 389
journeyman   154–155
Joyce, James   11, 14, 42–43, 74, 116, 118, 197, 211, 221, 292, 311–314, 328, 336–337, 389, 391
– "The Dead"   337
– *Dubliners*   197
– *A Portrait of the Artist as a Young Man*   43, 197, 211, 311, 328, 336, 389
– *Ulysses*   58, 65, 116, 197, 211, 292
Joyland (King novel)   319
Juliet in Publishing (Churchill novel)   257
Julius Caesar (Shakespeare play)   32
Justice, Elizabeth   129
– *Amelia, or the Distress'd Wife*   129

Kaenel, André   119–120
Kafka, Franz   218, 311–312
– *Metamorphosis*   218
Kahane, Jack   242
Keats, John   65, 74, 186–187, 201, 220, 349
– *The Eve of St. Agnes*   186
– "Ode on a Grecian Urn"   187
Keep the Aspidistra Flying (Orwell novel)   125, 165, 233–239, 245–246, 252–253, 294, 390
Kehlmann, Daniel   8, 398
Kendall, Tim   299
Kenneally, Thomas   70
– *Schindler's Ark*   70
Kennedy, A. L.   357, 382, 398
– *Everything You Need*   357, 398
Kenner, Hugh   14, 51, 290, 314
Kermode, Frank   40, 210
Kerouac, Jack   242, 393
Khan, Rahila [Toby Forward]   73
– *Down the Road, Worlds Away*   73
"The Killers" (Hemingway story)   42
Kindle   319, 348
King, Lily   172, 350, 360–362, 402
– *Writers & Lovers*   12, 172, 356, 360–362, 302

King, Stephen   1, 13, 24, 38, 317, 319–329, 331, 335, 395–396, 402
– *The Dark Half*   319, 328–329, 396
– *Bag of Bones*   319
– *Dark Tower* series   319
– *Different Seasons*   323
– *Duma Key*   319
– *It*   319
– *Joyland*   319
– *Lisey's Story*   319
– *Misery*   13, 319–329, 396
– *On Writing*   321, 327
– "Rat"   402
– "Secret Window, Secret Garden"   319, 329, 396
– *The Shining*   319–320, 327, 395
– *The Tommyknockers*   319
– "Umney's Last Case"   319
– *UR*   319
– "Word Processor of the Gods"   319, 395
King James Bible   26, 236
Kingsley, Charles   100, 385
– *Alton Locke*   100, 385
Kipling, Rudyard   5, 38, 54, 162, 172–174, 178, 184–188, 191–192, 201–202, 220, 236, 247, 249, 275, 319, 322, 387, 389–390
– "Dayspring Mishandled"   247, 390
– "The Dream of Duncan Parrenness"   184
– "The Finest Story in the World"   184–187, 220, 387
– *Kim*   5
– "The Winners"   236
– "'Wireless'"   186–187, 201, 220, 389
Kittler, Friedrich   21, 295, 350
– *Discourse Networks*   21
– *Musik und Mathematik*   295
Klara and the Sun (Ishiguro novel)   322
Klein, Viola   260
– *Women's Two Roles*   260
Kleinzeit (Hoban novel)   291–295, 299, 394
Knausgård, Karl Ove   12–13, 348–350, 353, 356, 400
– *My Struggle*   13, 350, 354–355, 400
Knight, Sebastian (Nabokov character)   14, 223
Knives Out (film)   332
Kohlmann, Benjamin   209
Koontz, Dean   323, 399–400

Korelitz, Jean Hanff   335, 338–340, 402
– *The Plot*   335, 338–340, 402
Kops, Bernard   251
Kraus, Chris   355, 356, 397
– *I Love Dick*   355, 397
Krementz, Jill   327
Kripke, Saul   8, 66
Kristeva, Julia   11, 61, 291
Kudos (Cusk novel)   160, 172, 370, 372–375, 401
künstlerroman, *see also* novel   11, 13, 49, 51, 85, 130, 161, 172, 192, 197, 202, 207, 210–211, 222, 239, 246, 314, 324, 328, 351, 358, 360, 363, 372, 379–380
– anti-*künstlerroman*   199, 202
– *Künstlerroman* (Henschel novel)   347, 401
Kunzru, Hari   342, 344–345, 402
– *Red Pill*   342, 344–345, 402

labour   30, 34–35, 89, 104–105, 108–109, 134, 164, 167, 184, 219
– creative labour   99, 349
– mechanical labour   247
– mental labour   105–106
– wage-labour   100, 105
A Ladder to the Sky (Boyne novel)   8, 338, 401
lady, *see also* novelist   33, 140, 156, 208, 264, 306
– *The Friendly Young Ladies* (Renault novel)   268–271, 391
– *Lady Anna* (Trollope novel)   141
– *Lady Audley's Secret* (Braddon novel)   145
– Lady Carbury (Trollope character)   138–139
– *Lady Chatterley's Lover* (Lawrence novel)   234, 304
– *The Lady Irania* (fictional novel)   264
– *Lady's Companion* (magazine)   246
– *The Lady's Mile* (Braddon novel)   149
– *The Portrait of a Lady* (James novel)   147, 229, 305
language   25, 33, 51, 59, 61–62, 64–65, 89–90, 196, 220, 227, 241, 243, 247, 250, 291, 293, 336, 358, 385
– language model   47
– literary language   62, 336
– poetic language   243

Lanser, Susan S.   62–63, 79–80, 259
– *Fictions of Authority*   259
A Laodicean (Hardy novel)   141
Larkin, Philip   74, 128
– *Trouble at Willow Gables*   128
Larson, Erik   70
– *The Devil in the White City*   70
Last Resort (Lipstein novel)   338, 402
The Last Supper (Cusk novel)   375
Latham, Sean   247
Latin   32, 304, 367
Latin America   3, 281, 291
Latinx   70
law   69, 75, 87, 154, 205, 221, 225, 266, 315, 336
– copyright law   23
– Gresham's law   180
– Law of Jante   354
– libel law   69
– obscenity law   69
– religious law   322
– universal law
Lawrence, D. H.   202, 206, 230, 241–243, 304
– *Lady Chatterley's Lover*   234, 304
Lawrence, T. E.   229
lawyer   107, 124–125, 154, 222, 334, 369
Lean, David   263
– *Brief Encounter*   263
Learned Hand, Billings   187
Leavis, Q. D.   226, 234–236
– *Fiction and the Reading Public*   226, 236
Le Carré, John   331, 342–343
Lectures on Subjects Connected with Literature and Life (Whipple)   120
Le Gallienne, Richard   210, 387, 389
The Legend of Rah and the Muggles (Stouffer novel)   335
legitimacy   92, 106, 300, 307, 373, 382
legitimation   71, 89, 99, 131, 282
Leigh, Aurora (character in Barrett Browning's *Aurora Leigh*)   133–137, 150
Leighton, Clare   264
– *Tempestuous Petticoat*   264
Leighton, Frederic   183
Lejeune, Philippe   32, 71, 341
Lennox, Charlotte   129
– *The Female Quixote*   129

Lessing, Doris   249, 258, 276, 381, 393
- *The Golden Notebook*   249–250, 258–259, 274, 381, 393
Lessons (McEwan novel)   14, 402
Less than Angels (Pym novel)   273–274, 392
letter   30, 35, 43, 74, 88, 90, 97, 105, 120, 123–124, 134, 136, 138, 148–149, 156, 160, 175, 187, 208–209, 211, 213, 221, 241, 246–247, 261, 269, 271, 296, 303, 326, 340–341, 358, 368
- autograph letter   271
- fan letter   220
- man *or* woman of letters   10, 13, 100–101, 105, 118, 129, 161, 213, 260, 319
- "The Man of Letters as a Man of Business" (Howells essay)   161
- republic of letters   33, 35
Levenson, Michael   238–239
Lewes, G. H.   99, 102, 105, 148, 385
- *Ranthorpe*   99, 385
liberalism   91, 94, 174, 344, 360
library   25, 56, 143, 169, 177, 220, 234, 237, 334
- circulating library   108, 138, 144, 162, 166, 180, 220, 234
- Harvard University Library   310
- home library   256
- lending library   234–235
- McFarlin Library   283
- mushroom library   234, 237–238
- private library   367
- public library   31
- twopenny library   234, 238
- university library
license   69, 73, 343, 348
life, *see also* story, style, *passim*
- bohemian life *or* lifestyle   267, 353
- *Brief Lives* (Aubrey)   19
- counterlives   14
- *The Counterlife* (Roth novel)   13, 396
- cultural life   230
- double life   173–174
- *An Imaginary Life* (Malouf novella)   8, 395
- inner life   37, 257, 371, 376
- *Leaves from the Life-Book of Walter Lorraine* (fictional novel)   108
- *Lectures on Subjects Connected with Literature and Life* (Whipple)   120

- life cycle   243, 362
- life force   205
- *Life of Charlotte Brontë* (Gaskell)   131
- *Life of Thomas Hardy* (Hardy)   142
- *A Life's Work* (Cusk novel)   375
- lifetime   75, 142, 169, 195, 204, 252, 265
- life-writing   79
- literary life   43, 90, 92, 100, 108, 114, 125, 139, 148, 153, 158, 161, 166, 171–172, 174–176, 233, 270–271, 274–275, 296, 303, 378
- *Lives of the Poets* (Johnson)   19
- married life   262
- *My Life in the Twentieth Century* (fictional memoir)   319
- private life   43, 148, 173–174, 181, 240, 340
- "The Private Life" (James tale)   183–184, 191, 228, 387
- professional life   340, 358
- provincial life   263
- *The Real Life of Sebastian Knight* (Nabokov novel)   160, 223, 391
- *Scenes of Clerical Life* (Eliot)   148
- *The Secret Life of Emily Dickinson* (Charyn novel)   8
- *Secret Lives* (Benson novel)   246, 256, 390
- social life   267, 316
- suburban life   204
- unlived life   182, 195
- writing life   195, 274, 316, 362
Liggins, Joseph   148
Light, Alison   234
Lilliput (magazine)   261
Limbert, Ralph (character in James's "The Next Time")   180
Lincoln, Abraham   325
linguistics   27, 62, 89, 111, 202, 250, 279
Linton, Eliza Lynn   128
- *The Atonement of Leam Dundas*   142
- *The Autobiography of Christopher Kirkland*   128
lion   180, 297
- "The Death of the Lion" (James tale)   128, 180, 297, 388
- "The Lion and the Unicorn" (Orwell essay)   236
Lipstein, Andrew   338, 402
- *Last Resort*   338, 402
Lisey's Story (King novel)   319

literacy 153, 170
– *The Uses of Literacy* (Hoggart) 249
literary studies 19, 21–22, 55, 58, 61, 234, 377
– cognitive literary studies 19
literature, *see also* art, autonomy, business, work *passim*
– American literature 106, 226
– capitalisation of literature 86
– commodification of literature 86, 104, 173
– contemporary literature 3, 46, 286
– dignity of literature 13, 92, 100, 105–106
– English literature 258, 295
– escape literature 238
– German literature 108
– good literature 169
– great literature 160, 374
– Guild of Literature and Art 105
– highbrow literature 276
– imaginative literature 282, 368, 373, 384
– *Lectures on Subjects Connected with Literature and Life* (Whipple) 120
– literature as a profession 154, 207
– literature of commitment 358
– literature of exhaustion 279
– literature of replenishment 279
– models of literature 92, 95, 230
– modern *or* modernist literature 61, 116
– popular literature 331
– production of literature 19, 47, 189
– Romantic literature 88, 94
– Russian literature 250
– value of literature 51, 91, 236, 282, 374–375, 381
– *The Victorian Age in Literature* (Chesterton) 113
– Victorian literature 191
– witness literature 11, 45, 70, 72, 300, 348, 382
Little Dorrit (Dickens novel) 57
The Little Nugget (Wodehouse novel) 256, 389
Lives of the Poets (Johnson) 19
Locke, John 219
Lodge, David 8, 13, 61, 285–287, 297, 397–400
– *Changing Places* 297
– *A Man of Parts* 8
– *Small World* 297

Lolita (Nabokov novel) 70
Lolly Willowes (Townsend Warner novel) 220
London 30, 55, 104–105, 108–109, 132, 134, 141–142, 154, 161, 166, 170, 190, 197–202, 209, 213–215, 217, 227–230, 233, 239, 244, 250–252, 260, 262–263, 267, 269, 271, 279, 288, 291, 297, 322, 342, 371, 373
– *London Pleasures* (fictional poem) 237–238
London, Jack 101, 118, 389
– *Martin Eden* 101, 118, 389
A Lonely Man (Power novel) 342–344, 402
The Longest Journey (Forster novel) 198, 201, 203–207, 211, 380, 389
Lonoff, E. I. (character in Roth's *The Ghost Writer*) 309–313
Look Back in Anger (Osborne play) 257
loop 5–7, 25, 52, 72, 75–76, 80, 378, 406
Lorna Doone (Blackmore novel) 142
Loser Takes All (Greene novella) 24
loss 38, 96, 156, 184, 196, 202, 211, 223, 275, 308, 315, 329, 343, 350, 371, 381
– self-loss 4, 202–203
Lost for Words (St. Aubyn novel) 301, 401
Lost Illusions (Balzac novel) 85–97, 103, 109, 114, 121, 163, 362, 379, 385
Lotte in Weimar (Mann novel) 8
love 88, 93, 122, 133–136, 143, 145, 150–151, 165, 167–168, 175, 179, 185, 205, 216, 218, 224, 242, 251, 260, 264–265, 283, 288–289, 292, 306, 312, 336–337, 340–341, 357, 361
– erotic love 288
– *I Love Dick* (Kraus novel) 355, 397
– *Love and the Revolution* (fictional novel) 361
– love fiction 270
– love letters 221
– love-making 264
– love triangle 32
– *Of Love and Hunger* (Maclaren-Ross novel) 251, 392
– romantic love 167
Love, Harold 26
Lovejoy, A. O. 10
lover 32, 57, 95, 141, 182, 204, 215–216, 228, 256, 271, 289, 293, 298
– art lover 177
– Booklovers' Corner 235

- Book Lovers' League   226
- *Lady Chatterley's Lover* (Lawrence novel)   234, 304
- *Writers & Lovers* (King novel)   85–97, 103, 109, 114, 121, 163, 362, 379, 385
low-brow   221
Lowell, Robert   14
Lubbock, Percy   56, 60–62
- *The Craft of Fiction*   56
Lukács, Georg   38–40, 69–70, 85, 87, 92, 112, 170
- *Theory of the Novel*   38
Lustrum (Harris novel)   335
lyric   3, 87, 142, 145, 293, 344

Macbeth (Shakespeare play)   334
Machen, Arthur   172, 195, 197–204, 211, 269, 275, 319, 388
- "The Great God Pan"   199, 269
- *The Hill of Dreams*   198–204, 388
machine   46, 94–95, 165, 168–169, 186, 219, 246–248, 273
- literary machine   169
- writing machine   193, 239, 242
Mackenzie, Julius (character in Trollope's "The Spotted Dog")   158
Maclaren-Ross, Julian   251, 392
- *Of Love and Hunger*   251, 392
Macleod, Fiona [William Sharp]   128
MacNeice, Louis   296
Madame Bovary (Flaubert novel)   149
madness   195–196, 201, 263, 310–311, 321
- madness of art   195–196, 310
- *The Madwoman in the Attic* (Gilbert/Gubar)   131
magazine   108, 120, 128, 141–142, 147, 153, 155, 157–159, 166, 181, 204, 225, 234, 237, 246–247, 250–251, 260–261, 274, 284, 343, 352–353
- *English Illustrated Magazine*   176
- *Lilliput: The Pocket Magazine for Everyone*   261
magic, *see also* realism   1, 187, 189, 218, 220, 319
- *The Magic Mountain* (Mann novel)   198
- *This Rough Magic* (fictional novel)   229
- *The Year of Magical Thinking* (Didion memoir)   355

Maigret, Jules (Simenon character)   7, 9
Maigret's Memoirs (Simenon novel)   7
Mailer, Norman   70, 345, 394
- *The Armies of the Night*   345, 394
Maingueneau, Dominique   20, 23
Malamud, Bernard   311, 385, 394
Malet, Lucas   128
Malone Dies (Beckett novel)   241, 392
Malouf, David   8, 395
- *An Imaginary Life*   8, 395
Maltby, Hilary (character in Beerbohm's "Hilary Maltby and Stephen Braxton")   190–191
Maltravers, Ernest (character in Bulwer-Lytton's *Ernest Maltravers*)   101–103
man *or* men   11, 14, 32–33, 53, 56–57, 83, 90–91, 93, 100, 102–103, 105, 107–108, 121, 127–128, 134, 138, 149, 154, 163, 171, 176–177, 181, 184, 195, 214, 217, 225, 233, 236, 240, 242, 252, 256, 259–264, 267–268, 270, 273, 279, 292, 303–305, 323, 359, 361, 364, 366, 371, 375
- angry young man   237, 240, 243, 257, 260, 276
- confidence man   120, 365
- *The History Man* (Bradbury novel)   297, 394
- *Invisible Man* (Ellison novel)   365
- *A Lonely Man* (Power novel)   342–344, 402
- *A Man from the North* (Bennett novel)   198, 240, 388
- man in the street   249
- man of action   214, 218
- man of genius   74, 176–177
- man of the crowd   122
- man of letters   10, 13, 100, 105, 118, 213, 260, 319
- "The Man of Letters as a Man of Business" (Howells essay)   161
- *A Man of Parts* (Lodge novel)   8, 400
- man without qualities   88, 92
- married man   306
- New Man   171
- paper man   297, 299
- *The Paper Men* (Golding)   295–300, 395
- *A Portrait of the Artist as a Young Man* (Joyce novel)   43, 197, 211, 311, 328, 336, 389
- representative man   118
- *Seven Men* (Beerbohm)   188–192

– single man   250
– superfluous man   237
manifesto   257
Mann, Thomas   8, 41–42, 61, 115, 118, 196–197, 273, 389
– *Death in Venice*   196, 389
– *Joseph and his Brothers*   42, 61
– *Lotte in Weimar*   8
– *The Magic Mountain*   198
– *Tonio Kröger*   42, 389
manuscript, *see also* autograph   36, 53, 104, 124, 132, 148, 155–156, 158, 164–165, 168, 173, 177, 180, 190, 199–200, 202, 217, 222, 238, 240, 245, 248, 267, 283, 286, 315, 320, 324, 326–328, 334, 337–341, 362, 368, 378
Mardi (Melville novel)   121
Marianne (character in Farrell's *The Cost of Living*)   267–268
Marius the Epicurean (Pater novel)   200
Marlow, Charles (character and narrator in works by Joseph Conrad)   54
Marlowe, Christopher   64
– *Doctor Faustus*   64
market *or* marketplace, *see also* value   9, 11, 24, 35, 41, 47, 50, 71, 85, 87, 90, 100–101, 104–106, 114, 120, 127, 149, 151, 153, 161–163, 169, 174, 180, 199, 213, 226, 234–235, 248, 261, 271, 275–276, 282, 301, 332, 340, 350, 366, 374, 381
– book market   33, 47, 220, 247
– e-book market   349
– labour-market   167
– literary market *or* marketplace   25, 34, 85, 97, 103–105, 122, 144, 147–149, 154, 158–159, 162–163, 166, 168–169, 210, 234, 255, 260, 301, 348, 349, 365
– market-gardener   142
– market participation   104, 139
– marriage market   141, 143–144, 150, 171
– mass market   107, 159–160, 174, 225, 275
marketing   45, 49, 57, 70, 87, 106, 119–121, 185, 214, 231, 317, 331, 356, 374–375
marriage   110, 129–130, 136, 140–144, 147–148, 150, 164, 167, 171, 177, 179, 191, 195, 205, 223, 238–239, 252, 260, 263, 302, 311–312, 358, 371–372

Marsh, Richard   218
– *The Beetle*   218
Martineau, Harriet   131
– *Autobiography*   131
Martin Eden (London novel)   101, 118, 389
Marx, Karl   105
Marxism   41, 72
Mary Barton (Gaskell novel)   112
"Mary Gresley (Trollope tale)   139, 155–156
masculinity   122, 127, 129, 131, 135–137, 150, 164, 171, 177, 204, 233–235, 246, 255–259, 269–271, 276, 279, 292, 304, 320, 322, 326, 343
"Material" (Munro story)   13, 302–306, 309, 394
materialism   85, 135–136, 139
materiality   39
mathematics   291, 294
– *Musik und Mathematik* (Kittler)   295
matrix   15, 22, 31, 79, 137, 352, 383
– *The Matrix* (film)   344
Maude (Rossetti story)   132–133, 385
Maugham, W. Somerset   48, 229–230, 250, 390–391
– *Of Human Bondage*   198
– *The Razor's Edge*   250
Maupassant, Guy de   168
maximalism   302
Maxwell, John   165
Maxwell's Demon (Hall novel)   300
May of Teck Club   271–272
McCourt, Frank   350
– *Angela's Ashes*   350
McEwan, Ian   14, 277, 301, 348, 396, 398, 401–402
– *Lessons*   14, 402
– *My Purple Scented Novel*   301, 401
McGurl, Mark   3, 5, 15, 22, 31, 49, 79, 137, 302, 383
– *The Program Era*   3, 22
meaning   1, 7, 10, 19–20, 23, 26–29, 61, 63, 65, 76, 81, 94, 100, 113, 116, 122–123, 144, 180, 213, 241, 247, 280, 288, 293, 310, 322, 333, 359, 361, 406
Mears, Charlie (character in Kipling's "The Finest Story in the World")   184–186, 191
mechanisation   245, 247, 266, 275

480 — Index

media, *see also* culture, history, infrastructure 21, 24–25, 45–46, 70, 121, 153, 169, 188, 207, 275, 282, 298, 324, 332, 356, 362, 366, 381
- audiovisual media   285, 287
- digital media   301
- mass media   11, 43
- media studies   34
- social media   12, 46, 49–50, 57, 317, 349, 355

mediation   26, 28, 44, 60, 68, 78, 94, 99, 172, 204, 206, 222–223, 238, 244, 370, 379
medieval   140–141, 200
medium   10, 27–29, 31, 34, 135, 146, 185, 187, 228, 234, 274, 286–287, 293–295, 368, 380
The Medusa Frequency (Hoban novel)   294, 396
Meizoz, Jérôme   20, 80
Melville, Herman   38, 115–126, 172, 202, 319, 324, 386
- "Bartleby, the Scrivener"   124–125
- "Hawthorne and His Mosses"   120
- *Mardi*   121
- *Moby-Dick*   120, 122, 124
- *Pierre or The Ambiguities*   115–126, 202, 319, 324, 386
- *Omoo*   121
- *Redburn*   121
- *Typee*   121
- *White-Jacket*   121

Melmotte, Augustus (character in Trollope's *The Way We Live Now*)   139
melodrama   86, 117, 147, 170, 238, 258, 265
memoir   45, 71, 73, 181, 198, 260, 288–289, 319, 321, 335, 338, 341, 345, 347, 354–356, 3751
- *Maigret's Memoirs*   7
- misery memoir   350
- mock-memoir   188
- *Private Memoirs and Confessions of a Justified Sinner* (Hogg novel)   38
memory   185–186, 188, 220–222, 294, 296, 298, 302, 305, 308, 314, 335, 371
- "Bookshop Memories" (Orwell essay)   234–235
Meredith, George   112, 117, 146
- *The Ordeal of Richard Feverel*   112, 117
Messud, Claire   370

metafiction   10, 70, 72, 163, 166, 197, 210, 244, 250, 279–285, 287–290, 298–301, 307, 315–316, 319, 331, 335, 337–338, 368, 381–383
metalepsis   9, 280, 282, 287, 354
Metamorphosis (Kafka novella)   218
metanarrative   161
metaphor   9, 59, 65, 77, 89, 117–118, 121, 127, 148, 171, 181, 187, 243, 256, 292, 305, 316, 321, 328
metaphysics   156, 204–206, 299
metonymy   34–35, 242, 321
Meynell, Laurence, *see* Baxter
MFA   338–339
middlebrow   10, 13, 118, 147, 160–162, 180, 227, 234–235, 239, 245, 248, 255, 257–258, 270, 275–276, 374, 381
- feminine middlebrow   235, 245, 263
Middlemarch (Eliot novel)   43, 112, 117–118, 147–149, 263, 386
"The Middle Years" (James tale)   173, 181, 195, 310, 387
The Middle Years (James autobiography)   195
Might (magazine)   352–353
milieu   233, 302
Mill, John Stuart   101, 143, 380
- *Utilitarianism*   147
Miller, D. A.   40
Miller, Henry   13, 193, 233, 240–242, 244, 247, 249, 252–253, 390–391
- *Tropic of Cancer*   13, 241–243, 247, 253, 273, 390
Miller, J. Hillis   117, 141
Miller, Thomas   100–101, 385
- *Godfrey Malvern*   100–101, 385
A Million Little Pieces (Frey)   356
Milton, John   150, 154, 197, 208, 270, 292–293
- "L'Allegro"   292
- *Lycidas*   197
Milton (Blake poem)   30
Milvain, Jasper (character in Gissing's *New Grub Street*)   162–168, 225
mimesis   76, 78–79, 191, 210, 243, 282
minimalism   26, 302, 306, 316, 355, 381
mirror   125, 188, 190, 263, 281, 284, 291, 372
Misery (King novel)   13, 319–329, 396
Misery (Reiner film)   325

misogyny   143, 177, 195, 233, 276, 361
Miss Angel (Thackeray Ritchie novel)   142
Miss Emily (O'Connor novel)   8
Mitchell, Julian   285–287
– *The Undiscovered Country*   285–287, 394
Mitchell, Margaret   269
– *Gone with the Wind*   269
mobility
– social mobility   85, 146
– upward mobility   145, 149
Moby-Dick (Melville novel)   120, 122, 124
modernism   3, 10–11, 13, 22, 27–29, 31, 41–44, 50, 69–70, 115–116, 118, 125, 127, 160–161, 169, 172, 174, 188, 191–192, 197–198, 203, 207, 209, 211, 214–215, 217, 223, 233–235, 241, 245–248, 250, 255, 258–259, 268, 270, 273–276, 279–280–281, 292, 301–302, 327, 355, 368, 370, 372, 376, 380–382
– anti-modernism   198, 223
– high modernism   172, 257, 286
– late modernism   13, 44, 241, 255, 274–275, 281, 284, 286
– retro-modernism   372
– threshold modernism   234
modernity   2, 10, 21, 28, 30–31, 40, 47, 49, 69, 88, 147, 176, 178, 223, 265, 335, 363, 381
– conservative modernity   234
Molloy (Beckett novel)   241, 392
money, *see also* god, world   88, 90, 93–95, 100–101, 103, 105, 108, 134, 139–140, 142, 154–155, 164–167, 169, 175, 187, 198–199, 203, 218, 223, 228, 236–239, 242, 250, 252, 267, 269, 271, 298, 345, 348, 364, 375
– paper-money   139
monologue   43
Monomark, Lord (Waugh character)   248
monotheism   326
monster   91, 236, 321, 327–328
monstrousness *or* monstrosity   38–39, 242, 324–325, 365
Montaigne, Michel Eyquem de   56, 79
Monty Python   377
Monty Python and the Holy Grail (film)   377
Moore, Allan F.   45–46, 71, 73, 216, 348, 356
Moore, Lorrie   301–302, 314–316
– "How to Be an Other Woman"   314

– "How to Become a Writer"   314–316, 396
– "How to Talk to Your Mother (Notes)"   315
– *Self Help*   314, 396
More Pricks than Kicks (Beckett collection)   240–241
More, Thomas   32
– *Utopia*   32
Morelli (character in Cortázar's *Hopscotch*)   1–2, 281
Moretti, Franco   41–42, 50, 86, 88, 92, 96, 99–100, 112–113, 117
Morley, John   113
– *On Compromise*   113
Morning Chronicle (newspaper)   105
Mortal Coils (Huxley collection)   213
Mosses from an Old Manse (Hawthorne)   56
Motherhood (Heti novel)   360
mot juste   188
"Mr. Bennett and Mrs. Brown" (Woolf essay)   157
"Mrs. Brumby" (Trollope tale)   139, 157, 159
MTV   353
multiplicity   41, 96, 115–116, 125, 350, 383
multitude   162
Munro, Alice   13, 172, 300–306, 309–310, 314, 316, 319, 362
– "Family Furnishings"   305
– "Fiction"   305
– "Material"   13, 302–306, 309, 394
Murder, She Wrote (TV series)   332
Murdoch, Iris   1, 260, 275, 288–291, 299, 392, 394–395
– *The Black Prince*   288–291, 299
Murdoch, Rupert   248
Muse   61, 122, 273, 324
museum   7
– British Museum   154, 169–170, 185, 189
– Lahore Museum   5
music *or* musician   143, 204, 224, 241, 291, 294
– classical music   230
– popular music   33, 45
Musik und Mathematik (Kittler book)   295
Myers (character in Carver's "Put Yourself in My Shoes")   306–307
Myerson, Julie   347, 402
– *Nonfiction: A Novel*   347, 402

My Purple Scented Novel (McEwan story)   301, 401
Myra Breckinridge (Vidal novel)   286
Myrdal, Alva   260
– *Women's Two Roles*   260
mystery   121–123, 185, 227, 332, 335, 340, 379
My Struggle (Knausgård novel)   13, 350, 354–355, 400
myth *or* mythology, *see also* authority   1, 19, 42, 47, 120, 138, 148, 203–204, 209, 211, 213, 282, 291, 293–295, 299, 363
– *Myths of Authorship* (Peterson)   47

Nabokov, Vladimir   13, 28, 54, 69, 115, 160, 223, 281, 284, 367, 369, 391, 393
– *Lolita*   70
– *Pale Fire*   367, 393
– *The Real Life of Sebastian Knight*   160, 223, 391
Naked Lunch (Burroughs novel)   286
name, *see also* economy, pseudonym   8–9, 23, 32, 34, 36, 49, 55, 57, 63, 68, 87–91, 94–95, 103, 105, 108, 110, 119, 127–128, 130, 134, 136, 138–139, 143, 149–150, 156–157, 164, 166, 176, 180, 186, 188–189, 196, 206, 208, 217, 220–221, 223, 225, 227, 229, 239, 245–246, 252, 256, 263, 266, 269, 271, 284, 286–287, 289, 291, 293–294, 296, 298, 306, 310, 312, 320, 322, 325–327, 335, 337–338, 342–343, 348, 350, 364–367, 369–370
– author's name   23, 31, 68, 119, 148, 261, 379, 382
– brand-name   329
– nickname   107, 124, 176, 246
– pen name   128, 250, 332
– proper name   8, 189
namelessness   46, 61, 176, 370
narration, *see also* form   40–42, 50, 56, 58, 60, 79, 87, 96, 115, 159, 172, 176, 185, 223, 236, 237, 253, 301, 371
– authorial narration   60, 62–63, 117, 290
– autobiographical narration   347
– autodiegetic narration   287
– autoethnographical narration   347
– deficient narration   54
– episodic narration   209
– first-person narration   50, 290, 360
– fragmentary narration   209
– impersonal narration   42
– instance of narration   32, 115
– overt narration   43
– posthumous narration   279
– realist *or* realistic narration   172, 287
– retrospective narration   243
– scenic narration   60
– second-person narration   50
– serial narration   86, 146, 320
– third-person narration   50, 111, 209
– unnatural narration   59
– unreliable narration   54, 176
narrative, *see also* audience, authority, fiction, perspective, representation, theory, voice *passim*
– anti-romantic narrative   153
– author *or* authorship narrative   51, 197, 301, 362–363, 378, 383, 385
– autobiographical narrative   99
– autofictional narrative   354
– counter-narrative   305, 341
– fictional narrative   59, 63, 67, 73, 343
– first-person narrative   286, 351
– *The Interesting Narrative* (Equiano)   79
– it-narrative   35
– metaliterary narrative   172
– narrative logic   384
– narrative-making   55, 58
– narrative progression   131, 133, 363, 384
– narrative situation   59–60, 172, 268
– narrative-telling   55, 58
– oral narrative   328
– pure narrative   55
– realist narrative   383
– serial narrative   146
– slave narrative   79
– travel narrative   227
– unnatural narrative   64
– unreliable narrative   38, 178
– written narrative   328
– you-narrative   314
narratology   5, 59, 61
– classical narratology   60
– diachronic narratology   41
– feminist narratology   62

- rhetorical narratology   67
- unnatural narratology   384
narrator, *see also* theory *passim*
- author-narrator   56–57, 178, 309, 335, 376
- authorial narrator   5, 9, 59–60, 62, 87, 96, 115, 118, 120, 123–124, 172, 406
- autobiographical narrator   243, 355
- autodiegetic narrator   32, 68, 173, 253, 286
- character-narrator   362
- editor-narrator   159
- extradiegetic narrator   59
- fictional narrator   57–58, 79, 377
- first-person narrator   56, 178, 183, 188, 243, 274, 341
- heterodiegetic narrator   59, 68, 253
- homodiegetic narrator   59, 115, 253
- impersonal narrator   59
- intradiegetic narrator   59, 159
- marginal narrator   175
- narrator-observer   178
- omniscient narrator   40, 42, 59, 115, 159, 374
- operal narrator   61
- personal *or* personalised narrator   60, 115, 118
- "The Position of the Narrator in the Contemporary Novel" (Adorno essay)   40
- suprapersonal narrator   42
- tender narrator   41
- third-person narrator   217
- writer-narrator   48, 241, 308, 355
Native Son (Wright novel)   364
Needle (character in Spark's "The Portobello Road")   279
network   1, 11, 23, 29, 34, 164, 166, 350, 352
- actor-network   22
- *Discourse Networks* (Kittler)   21
- neural network   46
- social network   25, 351
The Newcomes (Thackeray novel)   110
New Criticism   4, 61, 72, 377
New Grub Street (Gissing novel)   11, 13, 97, 100, 113, 125, 153, 160–173, 177, 192, 198, 202, 210, 225, 233, 239, 247, 380, 387
New Historicism   41
New Journalism   70, 382
Newnes, George   166
- *Tit-Bits*   166

Newnes Publishing Company   246
new normal   12
New Objectivity   239
newspaper   100, 104, 107, 180–181, 217–218, 222, 226, 239, 246–248, 260, 272, 275, 327
New Testament, *see also* Bible   322
New Woman   167, 171
New York (City)   119, 122, 124, 161, 182, 210, 214, 224–226, 325, 333, 336, 340, 353, 359, 365
- "The Literati of New York City" (Poe essay)   119
- New York Critics Circle Award   319
- New York Edition (Henry James)   305
- *New York Times*   142, 323, 342, 365
"The Next Time" (James tale)   161, 175, 180, 226, 388
Nin, Anaïs   245
- *House of Incest*   245
Nineteen Eighty-Four (Orwell novel)   239, 247, 392
Nobel lecture, *see also* prize   42
nobility   138
nom de plume, *see also* pseudonym   24
nonfiction, *see also* novel   12, 67, 70, 73, 131, 171, 188, 253, 285, 287, 345, 347, 350, 356, 382
- *Nonfiction* (Myerson novel)   347, 402
norm *or* normativity   19–20, 27, 32, 45, 47, 58, 63, 86, 99, 127, 135, 146, 162, 175, 235, 238, 269, 282, 376
- cultural norm   379
- heteronormativity   270–271
- social norm   12, 160, 252, 324, 363, 381
normalisation *or* normality   12, 86, 205, 221, 270, 349, 355
- *Normal People* (Rooney novel)   12, 349
North and South (Gaskell novel)   112
Northern Ireland   28
North Face (Renault novel)   270
Norway *or* Norwegian   12, 354
Notes from Underground (Dostoevsky novel)   238, 386
nouveau roman   282, 364
novel, *see also* bildungsroman, form, *künstlerroman*, machine, *nouveau roman*, *roman à clef*, *roman feuilleton passim*

– anti-novel   365
– art novel   99, 160, 275–276, 317
– artist novel, *see also künstlerroman*   3, 10–11, 49, 51, 85, 99, 256
– author novel *or* authorship novel   51, 63, 163, 203, 213, 215, 243, 245, 295, 317, 329, 379, 381
– autobiographical novel   51, 128–129, 216, 225, 233, 257, 360
– autofictional novel   358
– bestselling novel   223, 322, 349
– bourgeois novel   96
– campus novel   297
– career novel   257
– comic novel   213, 215–216, 223–224, 381
– coming-of-age novel   238, 354
– crime novel   74, 333
– detective novel   24, 257
– epistolary novel   118, 128
– fictional novel   332
– first-person novel   249
– gothic novel   38, 79, 283
– historical novel   90, 200, 320
– horror novel   218, 317, 381
– *How to Write a Novel* (Foster)   165
– "In Defence of the Novel" (Orwell essay)   236
– literary novel   332, 374
– long novel   348
– mass-market novel   160
– metaliterary novel   170
– middlebrow novel   160
– minor novel   230–231
– modern *or* modernist novel   40–42, 259, 281, 357, 370, 380
– *My Purple Scented Novel* (McEwan story)   301, 401
– nonfiction novel   285, 287, 345, 382
– novel of development   130, 198
– novel of formation   90, 118, 199, 206
– novel of ideas   216
– novel of regeneration   13, 242, 370
– novel of resentment   10, 13, 125, 170, 172, 233, 242, 252, 276, 350, 363, 370, 380
– *Novel on Yellow Paper* (Smith novel)   233, 245–250, 253, 256–257, 274, 390
– novel-poem   133
– novel-teller   144
– novel within the novel   263, 284, 286, 288–289, 322, 326
– "The Position of the Narrator in the Contemporary Novel" (Adorno essay)   40
– problematic novel   285
– realist *or* realistic novel   5, 44, 100, 115, 125, 235, 240, 243, 253, 280, 285, 287, 364
– romance novel   320, 332
– science fiction novel   1, 32, 291
– sensation novel   142, 144, 149
– serial novel   95
– short novel
– silver-fork novel   108
– social problem novel   112, 133
– sporting novel   199
– spy novel   342
– stolen novel   334, 338
– suspense novel   339
– systems novel   344
– *Theory of the Novel* (Lukács)   38
– three-volume novel   153, 162, 164
– verse novel   3, 24, 133, 136
– Western novel   269–270
– woman writer novel   249
– women's novel   138
– Zombie novel   331
novelette   239
novelist   1, 9, 11,14, 42, 48–49, 57, 61, 83, 96, 101–102, 104, 107, 124, 128–129, 137, 140, 143–144, 157, 160–161, 165, 175, 181, 203, 216–220, 222–223, 233, 239–241, 243, 251, 257, 262–265, 267, 269, 280–281, 285, 287–288, 290, 294, 296, 311, 320, 332–334, 339, 345, 367, 380
– antinovelist   281
– *Diary of a Novelist* (Tabor novel)   173, 386
– female novelist   129, 150, 191
– "False Morality of Lady Novelists" (Greg essay)   138
– lady novelist   14, 137–140, 246–247, 249, 255, 257, 259, 261–265, 276
– woman novelist   168, 173, 213, 245, 258, 264, 266–267
– "The Woman Novelist" (Gardner story)   265–267, 274, 392
novella   128, 196, 310–312, 323, 333

novelty   119, 143
Nugent-Folan, Georgina   197, 245, 253, 378
Nunez, Sigrid   355, 401
– *The Friend*   355, 401
"Nuns at Luncheon" (Huxley story)   213, 389
Nussbaum, Martha   289

Oates, Joyce Carol   196, 335, 401
– *Jack of Spades*   335, 401
Obelisk Press   241–242
objectivity   4, 39–41, 61, 72, 115–117, 168, 170, 188, 376
– New Objectivity   239
obscurity   46, 125, 252, 323
observation   9, 15, 39–40, 86, 157, 168, 175, 195–196, 263, 268, 283–284, 316, 344, 362, 373
– empirical observation   56
– first-order observation   39, 118
– second-order observation   39, 118, 164
observer   32, 39, 95, 115, 168, 174, 284, 286, 382
– narrator-observer   178
– observer-character   271, 303
Occam's razor   54, 59
O'Connor, Nuala   8, 401
– *Miss Emily*   8, 401
"Ode on a Grecian Urn" (Keats poem)   187
Odyssey (Homer)   56
Oedipus complex   19
oeuvre   21, 43, 89, 178, 236, 319, 343, 375
Of Human Bondage (Maugham novel)   198
Of Love and Hunger (Maclaren-Ross novel)   251, 392
Old Testament, *see also* Bible   42
Oliphant, Catherine (character in Pym's *Less than Angels*)   274
Olympia Deluxe   333
Olympia Press   70
omniscience   40, 42, 59–61, 86, 115, 159, 178, 211, 280, 282, 285, 301, 274
Omoo (Melville novel)   121
On Becoming a Writer (Brittain)   260
On Compromise (Morley)   113
One Thing Needful (Braddon novel)   150, 387
On Heroes, Hero-Worship, and the Heroic in History (Carlyle)   100

Only Revolutions (Danielewski novel)   368
On the Feminine Point of View (Campbell)   255, 259
ontology   5, 9, 53, 55–57, 62, 66, 68–69, 71–72, 74–75, 79, 130, 280, 287, 381, 383–384
On Writing (King memoir)   321, 327
OpenAI   47
optimism   38, 153, 170, 209, 258, 267
The Ordeal of Richard Feverel (Meredith novel)   112, 117
order, *see also* observation   20, 96, 106, 144, 281, 285, 289, 292, 315, 316, 323
– social order   41
– symbolic order   322, 326
originality   11, 24, 27, 29, 33, 36, 47, 103, 120, 134, 147, 150, 169, 180–181, 192, 215, 251, 258, 270, 275, 282–283, 298, 313, 334, 339, 360, 369–370, 381
Orpheus   287, 291–294
Orwell, George   1, 14, 165, 172, 189, 229, 233–240, 242, 245–247, 252–253, 276, 294, 381, 390, 392
– "Bookshop Memories"   234–235
– "In Defence of the Novel"   236
– "Inside the Whale"   242
– *Keep the Aspidistra Flying*   125, 165, 233–239, 245–246, 252–253, 294, 390
– "The Lion and the Unicorn"   236
– *Nineteen Eighty-Four*   239, 247, 392
Osborne, John   257
– *Look Back in Anger*   257
Other   265, 323, 326, 328
othering   322–323, 382
Outline (Cusk novel)   363, 370–376, 382, 401
Ovid   8, 31
ownership   23, 47, 219, 334–335, 339, 356, 369
Oxbridge   107
Oxford   107, 128, 208–209, 367
– *Oxford English Dictionary*   112

page   13, 102, 122, 138, 140, 158, 182, 189, 200, 208–209, 217, 219, 224, 241, 244, 266–268, 274, 298, 303, 315, 323, 328, 337, 367–368, 370
– copyright page   277, 351

- empty page 327
- page-turner 220, 269
- printed page 225, 253
- title page 57, 104, 148, 366–367, 379
painter 143, 214–215, 224, 257, 264, 267, 358
painting 34, 123, 176, 262, 358
A Pair of Blue Eyes (Hardy novel) 128, 141–142, 386
Pale Fire (Nabokov novel) 367, 393
Pamela (Richardson novel) 145
pamphlet 34, 124
"The Panjandrum" (Trollope tale) 157, 159
paper, *see also* money 11, 22, 33, 80, 87, 94, 97, 132, 158, 163, 181–183, 200, 244–247, 249, 264, 292–299, 316, 320–321, 328, 335, 368
- "The Aspern Papers" (James tale) 175, 179, 296–297, 387
- cigarette paper 293
- newspaper 100, 104, 107, 180, 217–218, 220, 222, 226, 239, 246–248, 260, 272, 275, 327
- *Novel on Yellow Paper* (Smith novel) 233, 245–250, 253, 256–257, 274, 390
- paperback 1
- paper industry 95
- papermaking 87, 88, 94, 97, 163
- *The Paper Men* (Golding novel) 295–300, 395
- "The Papers" (James tale) 181–182
- paper shortage 251
- paperweight 298
- *The Pickwick Papers* (Dickens novel) 107
paraclisis 77–78, 80–81, 118, 133, 366, 406
Paraday, Neil (character in James's "The Death of the Lion") 180
paradigm 2, 7, 11, 28, 30, 37, 49, 79, 82, 96, 137, 195, 313
- authorship paradigm 4, 7, 10, 15, 81–82, 164, 291, 377
- autofictional paradigm 366
- expressivist paradigm 291
- modernist paradigm 192
- paradigm change *or* shift 27, 30, 85
- realist paradigm 11, 85, 191, 316–317
- Romantic paradigm 12, 28, 150, 172
paradox 11, 30–31, 43–44, 133, 166, 231, 299, 344, 379, 382

paratext 23, 57, 63, 73, 75, 77, 288, 351, 406
paratopia 20
Paris 88, 90, 93–95, 189, 233, 241–242, 281, 344
Paris Review 1, 44
"Parker Pyne Investigates" (Christie story) 257, 390
parody 141, 143, 146, 148, 163, 168, 188, 202, 216, 228–230, 249, 286, 290, 297, 315, 328, 364–365
- self-parody 32, 122, 146, 290
passion 177, 195–196, 205–206, 264, 272
pastiche 141, 215, 239, 314, 316, 364, 367
Paston, George [Emily Symonds] 153, 161, 170–171, 388
- *A Writer of Books* 153, 161, 170–171, 388
Pater, Walter 200, 203
- *Marius the Epicurean* 200
- *The Renaissance* 200
paternity 38, 312
Paternoster Row 109
Patriarcha (Filmer) 266
patriarchy 145, 266, 310, 312
patron *or* patronage 25, 30, 34–35, 95, 121
Paul, Jean [Johann Paul Friedrich Richter] 33, 385
Payn, James 129, 248, 386–387
- *The Heir of the Ages* 129, 387
Peabody, Casey (character in King's *Writers & Lovers*) 360–363
Pearson, Bradley (character in Murdoch's *The Black Prince*) 288–291
Pearson, Sir Neville 246
Pegasus 138, 204, 234
pen, *see also* name, portrait 22, 34–35, 121, 140, 155, 169, 201, 239, 244, 263–264, 266, 273, 292, 326
- "Adventures of a Pen" 35, 385
- fountain pen 224
Pendennis, Arthur (character in Thackeray's *History of Pendennis*) 102, 105, 107–112, 114, 239
penny dreadful 25, 158–159
perception 5, 71, 176, 178, 201, 210, 225, 257, 262–263, 282, 357
Père Goriot (Balzac novel) 56, 117

performance   2, 5, 7, 8, 13, 15, 23, 26 – 27, 29, 34 – 35, 45, 49, 51, 80 – 81, 137, 143 – 145, 188, 196, 202, 374, 378, 380, 406
– authorial performance   7, 81
– literary performance   145, 351
– narrative performance   143
– reflexive performance   101
– rhetorical performance   355
– self-performance   32, 147, 230, 360
performativity   1, 3 – 4, 7, 13, 15, 22, 51, 79 – 82, 114, 133, 137, 172, 354 – 355, 379, 384, 406
performer   45, 143, 146
– self-performer   147
Pericles (Shakespeare play)   32
periodical   14, 90, 93 – 94, 100, 103, 127, 141, 144, 146, 159, 161, 167, 170, 180, 182
peritext   27
The Persians (Euripides play)   364
person *or* personage   4 – 5, 8, 23, 26 – 27, 31, 36, 42, 44 – 45, 49, 53 – 57, 59 – 60, 64, 69, 71 – 74, 79, 99, 101 – 102, 111, 116, 119, 128, 147, 156, 164, 183, 187, 217, 220, 222, 271, 289 – 290, 294 – 295, 299, 315 – 316, 323, 340, 350, 356 – 357, 359 – 360, 373, 380, 382
– creative person   10
– first person   60, 155, 157, 159, 237, 243 – 244, 267, 295, 307
– historical person   27, 89
– *How Should a Person Be?* (Heti novel)   356 – 360, 400
– non-person   42
– second person   283, 297, 314
– third person   42, 130, 345
persona   60, 69, 119, 128, 157, 183, 191, 230, 244, 270, 314, 366, 376
– author(ial) persona   4, 6 – 7, 23, 31, 150, 182, 184, 231, 270, 382
– narrative persona   148
– narrator-persona   60
– public persona   148, 151
personality, *see also* impersonality   10 – 11, 19, 24, 27, 31, 37, 43 – 44, 49, 60, 75, 119, 121, 183, 189, 191, 217, 220, 222, 227, 256, 289, 333, 336, 340 – 342, 344, 355, 359, 370, 378, 381
– split personality   172 – 173
personification   42, 61, 177, 289, 291

perspective   5, 13, 22, 37, 42, 47, 51, 70, 76, 79, 95 – 96, 100, 117 – 118, 125, 159, 163, 171, 175, 192, 211, 228, 244 – 245, 280, 282 – 283, 288, 290, 308, 321, 325, 372, 376
pessimism   41, 111, 153, 170 – 171, 174, 233
Peterson, Linda   47, 100, 127, 129
– *Myths of Authorship*   47
Petherwin, Ethelberta *or* Berta (character in Hardy's *The Hand of Ethelberta*)   142 – 148, 150, 164
Petrarch   32
– *Canzoniere*   32
Petronius, Gaius   286
– *Satyricon*   286
Phaedrus (Plato)   62
Phelan, James   4, 6, 53 – 54, 64 – 67, 76, 81, 384
– Phelan's shaver   54
phenomenon   1, 8, 44, 48, 60, 99, 118, 162, 223, 377
– crossover phenomena   384
– textual phenomena   9, 75
philistinism   176 – 178, 307
Phillips, Arthur   366 – 370, 400
– *The Tragedy of Arthur*   366 – 370, 400
philosophy   2, 57, 62, 111, 113, 117, 121, 204, 289, 291, 344, 360, 379
photograph *or* photography   120 – 121, 181, 224, 303, 327, 335, 368
Piccadilly Jim (Wodehouse novel)   256, 389
Pickering, Fred (character in Trollope's "The Adventures of Fred Pickering")   154
The Pickwick Papers (Dickens novel)   107
picture   186, 226
– *The Picture of Dorian Gray* (Wilde novel)   43, 174, 188, 191
– picture postcardism   209 – 210
– *Sheldon v. Metro-Goldwyn Pictures*   187
Pierre (character in Melville's *Pierre*)   121 – 125
"Pierre Menard" (Borges story)   187
Pierre or The Ambiguities (Melville novel) –   115 – 126, 202, 319, 324, 386
Pilgrimage (Richardson novel)   257
Pirandello, Luigi   3
– *Six Characters in Search of an Author*   3
plagiarism   148, 199, 227 – 228, 334 – 335, 339
Plato   55 – 56, 62, 356
– *Phaedrus*   62

– *Republic* 55–56, 356
Platonism 136, 285
play, *see also* roleplay, screenplay 3, 23, 32, 48, 229–230, 251, 257, 287, 289, 313, 323, 327, 358–359, 363, 366–369
– authorship play 3
– play script 358
– play within a play 263
– Shakespeare play 32, 289, 366–369
playwright 8, 179, 184, 319, 358
pleasure 61, 65, 104–105, 138, 146, 195, 238, 241–242, 317, 320–321, 324, 333
– *London Pleasures* (fictional poem) 237–238
– sexual pleasure 264
plot 50, 85–87, 92, 114–115, 117, 123, 129, 145, 163, 165, 171, 181, 190, 207, 215–216, 219, 221, 223, 233, 243, 251, 280, 283–284, 288–289, 301, 315–316, 323–324, 332–342, 359, 372–374, 377, 384
– apprenticeship plot 171
– double plot 363
– inheritance plot 167
– marriage plot 130, 148
– *The Plot* (Korelitz novel) 335, 338–340, 402
– stolen plot 334–335, 338
– subplot 170
– thriller plot 338, 343
– vocation plot 135–136
Pnin (Nabokov character) 14
Poe, Edgar Allan 19, 119–120, 178, 200
– "William Wilson" 190
poem 23, 29–30, 32, 35–38, 48, 74, 123, 128, 132–133, 136, 138, 186–187, 214–215, 227, 236–237, 272, 310
– autobiographical poem 136
– epic poem 3, 143, 145, 227
– long poem 29, 237
– lyric poem 142, 293
– narrative poem 367
– nature poem 310
– novel-poem 133
– pastoral poem 154
poet 3, 8, 10, 14, 19, 24, 26, 28, 31–32, 34, 37, 67, 88–89, 92–96, 105, 107–109, 113, 133–134, 136, 144, 149, 175, 187, 214, 223, 238–239, 251, 271–273, 294, 296, 332, 356
– distressed poet 33

– epic poet 28
– female poet 133, 273
– fictional poet 367
– *Lives of the Poets* (Johnson) 19
– male poet 273
– Movement Poets 257
– *poeta doctus* 27
– *poeta faber* 27
– *poeta vates* 26
– poet-novelist 216
– *The Poor Poet* (Spitzweg painting) 34
– Romantic poet 11, 144
– society poet 147
– woman poet 132–133, 136, 139
poetics 3, 200, 202, 231, 294, 329
– allopoetics 329
– autopoetics 3
– rhetorical poetics 68
Poetics (Aristotle) 64, 384
poetry, *see also* society, review 3, 24, 34, 39, 55, 88–90, 107, 124, 132, 134, 138, 148, 160, 184–186, 205, 215–216, 241, 247, 270–273, 344
Point Counter Point (Huxley novel) 207
point of view 40, 43, 94–96, 164, 174–175, 203, 211, 238, 255, 259, 267, 274, 282, 307, 317, 340–342, 354, 372–373
– *On the Feminine Point of View* (Campbell) 255, 259
politics 110, 114, 234
– gender politics 273
– global politics 335
– identity politics 11, 44, 70, 339
polysemy 61
The Poor Poet (Spitzweg painting) 34
Poovey, Mary 49, 103–104, 107
pope 14, 380
Pope, Alexander 33–34, 108
– *The Dunciad* 33
popularity 45, 48, 102, 159–161
pornography 251, 340
Portnoy's Complaint (Roth novel) 312
"The Portobello Road" (Spark story) 279, 393
portrait 87, 120, 122–123, 181, 188, 251, 263–264, 336, 370
– pen-portrait 251

Index — 489

- *A Portrait of the Artist as a Young Man* (Joyce novel)   43, 197, 211, 311, 328, 336, 389
- *The Portrait of a Lady* (James novel)   147, 229, 305
- self-portrait   92, 114, 144, 164, 252, 257
postcolonialism, *see also* criticism, theory   70, 72, 121
postmodernism   10–11, 24, 27–29, 31, 70, 244, 277, 279–282, 284, 286, 290–291, 294, 298, 300, 314, 316, 347, 350–351, 354, 364–365, 368–370, 381–383
- anti-postmodernism   351
- post-postmodernism   301, 316, 347, 351
poststructuralism   20, 41, 44, 61, 285, 293, 364–365
posture   20, 80
Pound, Ezra   54, 74, 207
poverty   34, 88, 91, 155, 167–168, 237, 306, 321
Powell, Anthony   207, 214, 224, 227–229, 231, 391–394
- *What's Become of Waring*   207, 224, 227–229, 391
power, *see also* empowerment   62–63, 90, 93, 96, 99, 104, 126, 131, 147, 166, 187, 196, 201, 208, 228, 245, 259, 264, 279, 284, 289, 291, 294, 298–299, 303, 305–306, 312, 314, 319–320, 322–323, 328, 342, 345, 361, 363, 366, 369, 374
- authorial power   122
- class power   35
- discursive power   26, 159
- divine power   289, 293
- economic power   255, 264
- *The Gauntlets of Power* (fictional novel)   288
- poietic power   12
- political power   15
- *The PowerBook* (Winterson novel)   301
- power of art   314
- social power   15, 70, 259, 264
- supernatural power   189
The PowerBook (Winterson novel)
Power, Chris   342–345, 402
- *A Lonely Man*   342–344, 402
praeceptor populi   27
preface   36–37, 43, 56, 102–103, 174, 243, 286, 288, 305, 334, 350, 353, 367, 383
pregnancy   122, 238, 251, 292
prejudice   137, 156, 252, 256
- *Pride and Prejudice* (Austen novel)   40, 59, 130–131, 148, 266
The Prelude (Wordsworth poem)   37, 106, 136, 385
premodernity   28, 44, 51
presentation   79, 118, 147, 176, 223, 301, 347
- self-presentation   106, 304
press   32, 35, 181, 217
- Galley Beggar Press   49
- Hogarth Press   234
- Obelisk Press   241–242
- Olympia Press   70
- periodical press   93–94, 100, 159, 182
- printing press   120, 163
- Stanhope press   94
- Virago Press   73
- yellow press   181
pride   75, 181, 200, 259, 267, 316
- LGBTQ+ pride   75
- *Pride and Prejudice* (Austen novel)
- verbal pride   302
Priestley, J. B.   235
print *or* printing   26, 33–34, 90, 94, 97, 119, 123, 134, 161, 166, 169–170, 251–252, 288, 295, 298, 366
- blueprint   215
- fine print   351
- misprint   64, 74
- print culture   32–33, 100, 127
- print publication
- reprint   119
- small print   163
printer   34, 87, 94, 123, 250
- printer-bookseller   87
- printer-publisher   34
privacy   150, 183, 270, 353
"The Private Life" (James tale)   183–184, 191, 228, 387
Private Memoirs and Confessions of a Justified Sinner (Hogg novel)   38
prize   23, 46, 50, 107, 181, 224, 251, 261
- Booker Prize   332
- Nobel Prize   50, 331, 349
- Pulitzer Prize   70, 319

product, *see also* commodity   4, 22, 47, 87, 104–105, 119, 146, 224, 239, 329, 335, 357, 366, 369, 374, 378
– by-product   4, 23
– cultural product   160, 374
– waste-product   23
production   3, 7, 9, 19, 22, 25, 33–35, 46–47, 49, 53, 72, 78, 80–81, 87, 153, 165, 169, 214, 216, 223, 226, 282, 304, 321, 327, 329, 348, 359, 362, 378
– book production   301
– cultural production   180, 377
– industrialised production   147
– literary production   1, 9, 19, 21, 30, 34, 85, 104, 107, 147, 149, 153, 155, 158, 168, 170, 189, 250, 275, 321, 378
– machine production   248
– mass production   40, 85, 149, 173
– mechanical *or* mechanised production   101, 149
– overproduction   137, 169, 172, 290
– self-production   304
– text(ual) production   34–35, 58, 62, 328
productivity   104, 119
profession   14, 21, 30, 33, 100–102, 104–108, 127, 136, 139, 142, 148, 153–156, 161, 162, 166, 168–170, 175, 179, 186, 196–197, 203, 207, 249, 257, 259–260, 263, 273–275, 315–316, 377, 380
– *The Case of Authors by Profession* (Ralph pamphlet)   34)
professionalisation *or* professionalism   10, 34–35, 101, 105, 138–139, 151, 153, 155, 157–159, 169, 171, 210
profit   24, 47, 90, 107–109, 140, 144, 162, 210, 374
The Program Era (McGurl)   3, 22
progression   123, 131, 133, 202, 209, 363, 372, 384
property   28, 124, 242, 334, 369
– Married Women's Property Act   167
prose   117, 144, 157–158, 186, 199, 215, 241–242, 245, 253, 272, 314
protagonist   14, 79, 85, 102, 105, 113, 124–125, 129, 132–133, 145, 154, 177, 179, 200, 203, 207, 210, 231, 240, 247, 250, 252, 257–258, 263, 267, 269, 283, 291, 294, 313, 315, 324, 339, 341, 344, 354, 357, 362, 364–365, 370, 371, 376, 380
– author-protagonist   113, 250, 252, 380
– writer-protagonist   133, 240, 258, 267, 291, 357
Proust, Marcel   41, 338, 389–390
– *À la recherche du temps perdu*   68
Prowe, Robert (character in Power's *A Lonely Man*)   342–344
pseudo-bibliography   190
pseudo-existentialism   334
pseudonym, *see also nom de plume*   23–24, 127–129, 140, 148, 225, 245, 258, 269, 328, 364, 375
pseudo-religion   197
pseudo-utilitarian(ism)   143, 146
psychoanalysis   19, 288
psychology   12, 25, 58, 92, 103, 125, 165, 172, 198, 202–203, 219, 264–265, 281, 283, 299, 321, 338, 358, 378
– child psychology   315–316
– gestalt psychology   5
public, *see also* discourse, figure, image, library, school   23, 35, 37, 45, 57, 73, 89, 103, 119, 129, 133, 148, 173, 178, 184, 210, 219, 248, 255, 274, 339, 375
– public sphere   21
– reading public   33, 63, 142, 160, 235
publicity   50, 121, 150, 180, 183, 226, 279, 301
publication   7, 27, 44–46, 103, 119, 142, 148, 155–158, 176, 189, 203, 225, 235, 264–265, 273, 331, 365, 367–368, 374, 378, 385
publisher   12, 19, 23, 25, 34, 46–47, 49–50, 71, 73, 81, 87, 90, 95, 103, 105, 108–109, 119–121, 124, 154–155, 160, 162, 164–165, 199, 207, 210, 221–223, 227–229, 233, 240, 246, 248, 251, 258, 262, 264, 271–272, 329, 339–340, 345, 348, 362, 364, 366, 369, 378
– bookseller-publisher   91
– independent publisher   49, 348
– printer-publisher   34
publishing   3, 15, 21–22, 24, 41, 44, 49, 57, 80, 87, 100, 103, 119, 127, 149–150, 161–162, 166, 171–172, 206, 210, 213–214, 218, 224–225, 227–229, 234, 248, 250, 255, 260, 265, 282, 301, 309, 320, 331, 335, 348, 352, 367–370, 375, 377–378

– Amazon Publishing   349
– *Juliet in Publishing* (Churchill novel)   257
– mass(-market) publishing   49, 163, 225, 275
– Newnes Publishing Company   246
– newspaper publishing   248
– publishing business *or* company *or* corporation *or* firm *or* industry   47, 108–109, 121, 168, 214, 226–228, 234, 246, 271, 328, 368
– publishing house   148, 226, 348, 366, 369, 374
– self-publishing   15, 46, 245, 335
– trade publishing   46
– web-based publishing   46
Puech, Jean-Benoît   20–21, 395
– *La bibliothèque d'un amateur*   21, 395
pun   196, 338, 367
Pushkin, Alexander   115
– *Eugene Onegin*   115
"Put Yourself in My Shoes" (Carver story)   306–307, 309, 316, 394
Pym, Barbara   273–274, 392
– *Less than Angels*   273–274, 392
Pynchon, Thomas   344

queer   72, 269–270

Rabinowitz, Peter J.   76
race   14, 45, 201, 206, 236, 242, 363–366, 378
racism   74, 228
radio   186, 234, 275
The Ragged Trousered Philanthropists (Tressell novel)   238
Rain on the Pavements (Camberton novel)   252, 392
Rainey, Lawrence   246
Ralph, James   34–35
– *The Case of Authors*   34–35
Ralph the Heir (Trollope novel)   141
Random House   364, 367–369
Ranthorpe (Lewes novel)   99, 385
rape   292, 321
The Razor's Edge (Maugham novel)   250, 391
reader *or* readership, *see also* audience, theory *passim*
– gentle reader   117, 120
– implied reader   57
– woman reader   261
– *Writing the Reader* (Birke study)   2
reading   2–4, 6, 9, 14–15, 19–20, 31, 38, 46, 58–59, 61, 64–65, 72, 75, 81–82, 86, 88, 114, 120, 134–135, 139, 149, 153–154, 162–163, 166, 168–170, 175, 179, 181, 185, 189, 196, 209, 222, 224, 233, 237–238, 269, 285, 288, 292, 296, 298, 307–308–309, 313–314, 324–325, 328, 332, 337, 340, 342, 355, 359, 368, 374
– act of reading   120
– close reading   82, 319
– *Fiction and the Reading Public* (Leavis)   226, 236
– mass reading   236
– novel reading   2
– public reading   44, 49, 57, 144, 361
– reading community *or* group   25, 65
– reading matter   97, 119, 162, 247
– reading public   33, 63, 142, 160, 235
– rhetorical reading   5
realism   10, 40–41, 85, 109, 115–117, 143, 146, 168, 172, 174, 186, 203, 206, 239, 249, 258–259, 262, 279, 286–287, 319, 345, 355, 381–382
– authorial realism   301
– documentary realism   345, 382
– formal realism   301
– gothic realism   202
– literary realism   114, 168, 174, 211, 301, 313, 317, 319, 372
– magic realism   10, 291
– moral realism   316
– narrative realism   241
– novelistic realism   85
– "The Place of Realism in Fiction" (Gissing essay)   168
– post-ironic realism   301
– Romantic realism   117
– social realism   282, 283, 316, 382
reality, *see also* television   6, 8–9, 27, 37, 47, 50, 56, 66, 68, 71–72, 74–75, 80, 88, 95–96, 104, 107, 115–117, 123, 125, 146, 153–154, 162, 173, 199–200, 202–206, 240, 244, 260–261, 264–265, 279–280, 285, 288–289, 295, 298–299, 304–305,

313–314, 319, 321–322, 343–344, 347, 349, 368, 372, 382–383
- economic reality   23, 34, 369, 374
- reality effect   184, 354
- reality hunger   45
- social reality   21, 23, 96, 382

The Real Life of Sebastian Knight (Nabokov novel)   160, 223, 391

"The Real Right Thing" (James tale)   182, 297, 388

The Real World (MTV show)   353

Reardon, Edwin (character in Gissing's *New Grub Street*)   160, 164–168, 173

Rebecca (Du Maurier novel)   341

Rebecca (character in Scott's *Ivanhoe*)   89

reception   4, 7, 19, 21, 30, 34, 58, 70, 77–78, 80–81, 85, 106, 245, 379, 406

Reckwitz, Andreas   12, 19, 44, 49, 349, 360, 362–363

recognition   7, 15, 23–24, 39, 50, 63, 77, 81, 99, 135, 171, 179, 182, 189–191, 235, 259, 261, 275, 289, 316, 324, 365, 375–376, 381

reconstruction   5, 58, 65, 80

Redburn (Melville novel)   121

Red Pill (Kunzru novel)   342, 344–345, 402

Red Pottage (Cholmondeley novel)   128, 388

reference   8, 66, 96, 110, 144, 184, 187, 222, 247, 266, 284, 296, 298, 320

reflection   14, 21, 25, 41, 53, 59, 62, 70, 80, 94, 111, 138, 174, 190, 206, 244, 249, 258, 265, 288–289, 297–298, 320, 325, 329, 343, 355, 357, 365, 372, 376, 378, 382
- double reflection   39
- meta-reflection   48, 376
- self-reflection   141, 250, 349

Reiner, Rob   325

Reinfandt, Christoph   46

religion   110, 228, 312, 326
- religion of art   197, 312

The Renaissance (Pater)   200

Renault, Mary   259, 268–271
- *The Friendly Young Ladies*   268–271, 391
- *North Face*   271

report   54, 60, 62, 216, 238, 255, 259, 270, 370

representation   1, 10, 19, 37, 41, 44–45, 48, 55–56, 63–64, 66, 78–81, 85, 107, 115, 124, 129, 149, 170, 172, 183, 191, 209–210, 248, 253, 279–280, 289, 300, 313, 317, 319, 322, 326, 328, 351, 365–366, 372, 376, 378, 382–383
- fictional representation   48, 63, 280
- narrative representation   9, 383
- literary representation   209, 376

reproduction   2, 80, 160, 181, 185, 187, 326, 360, 374

Republic (Plato)   55–56, 356

reputation   7, 23–24, 34–35, 37, 48–49, 74–75, 90, 93, 106–108, 110–111, 114, 119, 131, 142, 148, 159–160, 166, 182, 195, 221, 223–224, 230, 268, 271, 310, 331, 369

review *or* reviewer   1, 23, 25, 33, 48, 70, 93–94, 103, 106, 120, 136, 140, 179, 199, 210, 220, 227, 236–237, 242, 262, 264, 267, 283, 323, 337, 340, 344, 365–366
- book review   25, 199, 236
- *National Review*   138
- *Paris Review*   1, 44
- *Poetry Review*   273
- *Westminster Review*   100, 136

revolution   44, 109, 112, 244
- digital revolution   46
- French revolution   44, 113
- *Love and the Revolution* (fictional novel)   361
- *Only Revolutions* (Danielewski novel)   368
- sexual revolution   241

rhetoric   2, 11, 61–64, 68, 73, 78, 80, 107, 124, 222, 306, 351, 378, 406
- confessional rhetoric   354
- rhetoric of authorship   154, 255, 258, 275–276

Richardson, Dorothy   257, 259, 389–391
- *Pilgrimage*   257

Richardson, Samuel   89, 337
- *Pamela*   145

Riceyman Steps (Bennett novel)   240

Riddell, Charlotte   128, 387
- *A Struggle for Fame*   128–129, 387

Robinson Crusoe (Defoe novel)   68, 202

Roderick Hudson (James novel)   178

role   3, 6, 11, 23, 27, 30, 33–34, 48–49, 60, 64, 69, 78, 95–96, 106, 129, 131, 134, 143, 147, 149, 155, 173, 176, 184, 218, 246, 255, 257, 272, 284, 293, 300, 303–305, 342, 356, 366, 373, 380, 382

- agential role 6, 78,
- authorial role 10, 172, 244, 383
- role model 261, 359
- roleplay 304
- social role 23, 50, 135, 182, 279, 304, 380
- *Women's Two Roles* (Myrdal and Klein book) 260
Rolfe, Frederick 13, 174, 380
- *Hadrian the Seventh* 174
Roland Barthes par Roland Barthes 377
Roman, *see* Rome
roman à clef 174, 301, 335
romance, *see also* fiction, form, plot, writer 10, 145–147, 248, 258, 268, 270, 275, 286, 289, 320, 331–332, 340–342, 362–363
- historical romance 320–321, 324
- medieval romance 140–141
- middlebrow romance 270
- periodical romance 141
- sensational romance 145
roman feuilleton 95
Romanticism 9–13, 19, 21, 24, 27–29, 33, 35–36, 38, 40, 49, 85, 87–89, 92, 94, 100, 105–106, 108, 113, 117–118, 120, 125, 143–144, 146, 148–150, 172, 208, 247–248, 252–253, 265, 282, 342, 362–363, 380, 382
Rome *or* Roman 8, 31, 199, 200–201, 246, 296, 298, 335
A Room of One's Own (Woolf) 257, 266
Rooney, Sally 12, 349, 401–402
- *Normal People* 12, 349
Ros, Amanda 263
Rose, Caroline (character in Spark's *The Comforters*) 282–284, 374
Rossetti, Christina 127, 132–133, 385
- *Maude* 132–133, 385
Rossetti, Dante Gabriel 132
Rossetti, William Michael 132
Rostek, Joanna 42
Roth, Philip 14, 67, 71, 75, 301–302, 309–314, 338, 345, 395–399
- *The Anatomy Lesson* 314, 395
- *The Counterlife* 14, 396
- *The Facts* 345, 396
- *The Ghost Writer* 309–314, 382, 395
- *Portnoy's Complaint* 312

- *Zuckerman Unbound* 312, 314, 395
Rowling, J. K. 128
- *Harry Potter* 335
Rowson, Susanna 129
- *The Inquisitor* 129
- *Trials of the Human Heart* 129
Roxburgh, Stephen 74
Royal Literary Fund 105, 154
Rubin, Edgar 5
rule 11, 23–24, 27, 30, 78, 96, 154–155, 167, 244, 256, 259, 269, 289, 294, 332, 369
Rushdie, Salman 67, 402
Russia *or* Russian 58, 97, 250, 342–343
Ruth, Jennifer 104
Ryan, Susan 106

S. (Abrams and Dorst novel) 301, 368
The Sacred Fount (James novel) 178
Sage, Liz 256
Said, Edward 66, 377, 383
- *The World, the Text, and the Critic* 377
The Sale of Authors (Campbell dialogue) 35
Salmon, Richard 99, 104, 106, 135
Sandemose, Aksel 354
Sapper (Herman Cyril McNeile) 235
sarcasm 124, 268, 273, 317
Sartor Resartus (Carlyle novel) 38, 99, 120–121, 385
satire 35, 106, 109, 139, 141, 144–145, 211, 229, 256, 275, 283, 286, 301, 335, 381
- authorship satire 35, 100
Satyricon (Petronius) 286–287
Sayers, Dorothy 20, 255, 332, 390–391
- *Strong Poison* 332, 390
Scamp (Camberton novel) 233, 250–253, 392
Scandinavia 354
scepticism 111, 127, 207, 213, 228, 260, 280, 285, 287, 301, 305, 339, 373
Schindler's Ark (Kenneally) 70
Schmid, Wolf 58
Scholes, Robert 286
school 41, 177, 205, 208–209, 262, 266, 283, 315, 334
- Frankfurt School 41, 69
- girls' school 128, 302
- *The Little School* (fictional play) 327
- prep school 286

– public school 20, 215
– summer school 370
Schreiner, Olive 259
Schweighauser, Philipp 79
Schweik, Robert 144
Scoop (Waugh novel) 214, 217, 222, 227, 391
Scott, Sir Walter 89, 141, 162
Scottish 128, 153, 162
screen 365, 375
– aesthetic screen 67
screenplay 287, 333
scribe 29
script 27, 79, 351, 358, 383
Sebald, W. G. 370
– *The Emigrants* 370
The Secret Life of Emily Dickinson (Charyn novel) 8
Secret Lives (Benson novel) 246–247, 256, 390
"Secret Window, Secret Garden" (King story) 319, 329, 396
secularisation 36, 89
segmentation 161, 235, 340
segmentivity 118
segregation 234, 250, 275
self *or* selfhood, *see also* authorship, consciousness, creation, expression, formation, loss, parody, performance, portrait, presentation, production, publishing, reflection, writing 10, 24, 29, 32, 37, 53, 56, 101, 120, 136, 147, 162, 173, 183–184, 186, 188, 192, 199, 228, 244, 248, 288–291, 299, 303, 313, 322, 344, 352, 357, 360, 363, 366, 376
– authorial self 4–5, 14, 28, 40, 47, 49, 68, 81, 137, 184, 187, 228
– autobiographical self 122
– creative self 12, 349, 363
– self-analysis 35, 197
– self-authoring *or* self-authorisation 107. 131, 146, 259, 322–323, 329
– self-centredness 354, 371
– self-construction 47, 49, 245
– self-defence 239, 288
– self-delusion 264–265, 360
– self-denial 133, 313
– self-description 49, 213
– self-destruction 118, 121, 135, 350
– self-determination 167, 322

– self-discovery 37, 229
– self-doubt 105, 132, 316, 372
– self-exploitation 34, 46, 121, 309, 359
– self-fashioning 32, 167, 196, 229, 317, 349
– self-fulfilling prophecy 51, 101
– *Self-Help* (Moore collection) 314, 396, 314
– self-image 216, 230, 314
– self-invention 174, 341
– self-irony 290, 382
– self-justification 182, 230, 372, 378
– self-knowledge 288–289, 305
– self-making 137, 150, 307
– self-pity 124, 233
– self-projection 174, 378
– self-promotion 133, 218
– self-realisation 11, 40, 80–81, 150–151, 313
– self-reference *or* self-referentiality 1, 290, 301, 354
– self-reflexiveness 50, 214, 256, 258, 334, 351, 354, 370
– self-sacrifice 145, 206
– self-satisfaction 210, 230
– self-torture 199, 202
– self-understanding 15, 76, 377, 379
– self-will 371, 382
– shadow self 51, 290, 314
Sentimental Education (Flaubert novel) 44, 81
sequel 123, 190, 333
Sergeant, Howard 272
Seven Men (Beerbohm) 188–192
sex *or* sexuality, *see also* act, identity, pleasure, revolution 9, 36, 71, 75, 93, 121, 128, 156, 181, 198, 201, 206, 225–226, 233, 242, 269–270, 272–273, 286–287, 292, 304, 324–325, 342, 359
– heterosexuality 88, 242
– homosexuality 269, 286
– sexual abuse *or* harassment 75, 272
– sexual frustration 198, 242
– sexual orientation 72, 268
Shakespeare, William 19, 32, 37, 74, 108, 144, 182, 219, 223, 269–270, 289, 366–370
– *Hamlet* 19, 66, 289, 367
– *Julius Caesar* 32
– *Macbeth* 334
– *Pericles* 32
Shapiro, James 368

Sharp, Becky (Thackeray character)   145
Sharp, William   128
Shaynor (character in Kipling's "Wireless")   186–187, 191
She (Rider Haggard novel)   320, 325
Sheldon, Paul (character in King's *Misery*)   319–328
Sheldon, Sidney   320
Sheldon v. Metro-Goldwyn Pictures   187
Shelley, Mary   37–39
– *Frankenstein*   37–39, 328, 366
Shelley, Percy Bysshe   24, 201, 366
The Shining (King novel)   319–320, 327, 395
Shirley: Young Bookseller (Baxter novel)   257
Sickert, Walter   188
Sidney, Philip   67
sign   55, 88, 198, 208, 355, 377
– *Gang Signs & Prayer* (Stormzy album)   33
signal   6, 49, 58, 75, 77–78, 176, 186, 203, 214, 243, 290, 331, 355, 406
signature   94, 121, 136, 271, 296, 298
Sillitoe, Alan   240
Simenon, Georges   7, 9
– *Maigret's Memoirs*   7
sincerity   45, 63, 70, 75, 92, 108, 111, 118, 168, 216, 239, 290, 382
– new sincerity   71, 300–301, 347, 356, 360, 382
singularity   2, 32, 40, 44, 300
Sinykin, Dan   362–363
Siskin, Clifford   34
sitcom   128
Sitwell, Edith and Osbert   243
Six Characters in Search of an Author (Pirandello play)   3
Skelton, John   128
slave *or* slavery, *see also* narrative, trade   35, 57, 79, 102, 158, 184, 325, 353
Small World (Lodge novel)   297
Smith, Dodie   273, 392
– *I Capture the Castle*   273, 392
Smith, Sigismund (character in Braddon's *The Doctor's Wife*)   149–150
Smith, Stevie   233, 245–250, 253, 256–257, 390
– *Novel on Yellow Paper*   233, 245–250, 253, 256–257, 274, 390

Smith, Winston (character in Orwell's *Nineteen Eighty-Four*)   239
Smith, Zadie   49
Snow (Banville novel)   24
Snow Falling (romance novel)   332
Snow, C. P.   296
Soames, Enoch (character in Beerbohm's "Enoch Soames")   188–189
socialism   134, 136–137, 237, 249
society *passim*
– bourgeois society   106, 380
– high society   106, 217
– industrial society   125
– literary society   224
– mass society   216, 381
– Poetry Society   272
– provincial society   262–263
– Society of Authors   101, 127
– *Women and a New Society* (study)   260
sociology   2–3, 19–21, 90
Socrates   55–56, 62
sonnet   24, 32, 37, 90, 94–95, 124, 132, 182, 269
The Sorrows of Satan (Corelli novel)   170, 388
soul   11, 36, 135, 184–185, 187, 202, 218, 220, 223, 290, 292–293, 311, 336, 359–360, 364
– *Hidden Souls* (fictional novel)   218–219, 221–223
Southey, Robert   136
space   2–3, 11, 30, 44, 234, 244, 247–248, 256, 291, 301, 304–305, 308, 310, 321, 327, 361, 363, 368, 376
– literary space   20, 23, 234
– negative space   376
– relational space   3, 80, 406
Spark, Muriel   8, 250, 259, 271–274, 279–280, 282–285, 289, 299, 374, 392–393, 395–397, 399
– *The Ballad of Peckham Rye*   273
– *The Comforters*   8, 250, 282–285, 299, 374, 393
– *The Girls of Slender Means*   271–273, 393
– "The Portobello Road"   279, 393
speaker   55–56, 134
Spear, Hilda   288–289
The Spectator   33

speech, *see also* act, freedom, theory   279, 308
- dialogic speech   61
- direct speech   371
- speech balloon   294
- speech mark   248
- speech type   61, 115
Spencer, Sharon   258
spirit   37, 87, 129, 144–147, 168–169, 205, 228–229, 250, 315
- spirituality   96, 107, 205–206, 208, 228, 243, 295, 310–312, 339
- spiritualism   187, 228
Spitzweg, Carl   34
- *The Poor Poet*   34
"The Spotted Dog" (Trollope tale)   158
stage   3, 81, 107, 110, 113, 204, 207, 284
- stage-directions   358, 367
- stage-manager   115
- staging   31, 45, 94, 192, 220, 223, 249, 253, 264, 297, 350, 359, 380–381, 383
stagnation   172, 197, 216, 244
standard   10, 12, 37, 55, 57, 113, 147, 171, 173, 179, 196, 214, 226, 234, 243, 333, 358, 368–369
- double standard   113
- standardisation   234, 239, 247
Stanford, Derek   272
Stannard, Martin   272
Stanzel, Franz K.   56, 60–62
Staples, Nathan (character in Kennedy's *Everything You Need*)   357
state   48, 69, 99, 189, 197, 236, 239, 239, 266, 286, 315, 325
- state of being   37
- state of mind   27
St Aubyn, Edward   301, 401
- *Lost for Words*   301, 401
Steele, Danielle   323
Steele, Richard   33
Stein, Gertrude   245, 390–391
- *The Autobiography of Alice B. Toklas*   245, 390
Stephen, Leslie   142
Stephens, Fitzjames   111
stereotype   130–131, 140, 246, 260, 265, 276, 310, 366, 370
- gender stereotype   14, 130, 260
Stet (Athill memoir)   260

Stevens, Wallace   247
Stevenson, Robert Louis   48, 160–161, 174, 202
- *The Strange Case of Dr. Jekyll and Mr. Hyde*   191, 328
Stone, Denis (character in Huxley's *Crome Yellow*)   214–218
Stormer, Mrs. (character in James's "Greville Fane")   140
Stormzy [Michael Ebenezer Kwadjo Omari Owuo Jr.]   33
- *Gang Signs & Prayer*   33
story, *see also* world, *passim*
- *Best Seller: The Story of a Young Man* [...] (Youmans novel)   210, 214, 224–226, 390
- detective story   283, 332
- "The Finest Story in the World" (Kipling story)   184, 186–187, 220, 387
- ghost story   182, 190, 279, 379, 383
- horror story   203, 327
- life-story   143, 210, 324, 374, 376
- *Lisey's Story* (King novel)   319
- *A Shabby Genteel Story* (Thackeray)   110
- short story   13, 139, 140, 154–155, 157, 164, 192, 204, 213, 251–252, 261, 265, 302, 304, 310, 315, 319, 336–337, 381, 364
- storyline   332
- *Story of a Modern Woman* (Dixon novel)   162, 388
- storyteller *or* -telling   8–9, 28, 40, 67, 86, 95, 118, 143–144, 283, 300, 319–320, 374
- "The Storyteller" (Benjamin essay)   40
- *The Story-Teller* (Highsmith novel)   333
St Paul's (magazine)   155
Strahan, Alexander   155
The Strand (magazine)   246
The Strange Case of Dr. Jekyll and Mr. Hyde (Stevenson novel)   191, 328
The Stranger (Camus novel)   334
Streicher, Julius   310
The String of Pearls (novel)   25
Strong Poison (Sayers novel)   332, 390
structuralism   9, 22, 41, 55–56, 72, 377
structure, *see also* infrastructure   4, 72, 125, 117, 206–207, 209, 243, 281, 305, 372, 376, 378
- social structure   81, 304, 380, 382

A Struggle for Fame (Riddell novel)   128–129, 387
style   25, 41, 65–66, 79, 117–118, 129, 141, 143–144, 168, 176, 192, 200, 202, 214, 217, 223, 229, 239, 242, 262, 265, 283, 285–286, 302, 308, 314, 319, 338, 347, 377
– lifestyle   218, 353
Styron, William   70, 395
– *The Confessions of Nat Turner*   70
subject, *see also* formation   32, 38–39, 44–46, 49–51, 59, 79, 87, 107, 120, 123, 183, 188, 293–294, 319, 352, 360, 376–377, 379, 382
subjectivity   4, 37–41, 49, 70, 107, 115–116, 125, 211, 289, 373, 376
success *passim*
sublime   79, 349
Sudowrite   47
Sue, Eugène   95
Summertime (Coetzee 'autrebiography')   345, 400
supernatural   189, 191, 202, 205, 219, 222–224, 291, 298, 321, 329
surrealism   245, 365
survival   91, 113, 159, 169, 202, 320, 363
suspense   117, 317, 319, 331–332, 335, 337, 339–340, 345
A Suspension of Mercy (Highsmith novel)   333, 394
Sutherland, John   109, 129, 153, 157, 334
Swancourt, Elfride (character in Hardy's *The Hand of Ethelberta*)   140–142, 150
Sweden *or* Swedish   97, 342–343
Swift, Jonathan   33–34, 169, 221
– *The Battle of the Books*   33, 221
– *Gulliver's Travels*   169
Swinburne, Algernon Charles   128, 249
Swiss *or* Switzerland   183, 296
Sybil (Disraeli novel)   112
Sykes (character in Gissing's *New Grub Street*)   165–166
symbol, *see also* authority, capital, form, order, value   32, 36, 44, 47–48, 64, 86, 99, 110, 121, 123, 136, 149–150, 160, 191, 196–197, 199, 202–203, 205–206, 208, 213, 237–238, 243, 266–267, 273, 294, 304, 328, 352, 362, 377–378
– symbolism   203, 209, 211

– French Symbolism   209
Symonds, Emily Morse   153, 170–171, 388
Symonds, John Addington   177
sympathy   48, 107, 149, 157, 261, 290, 321, 325, 329, 333–334, 362
synthesis   39, 86, 96, 99, 116, 136, 240, 370
system, *see also* novel, theory   3, 10, 23, 25, 37, 80, 102, 110, 112–113, 135, 149, 168, 179, 256, 273, 384
– class system   145, 237
– value system   92, 191, 334
– Wang System   5 (word processor)   327

Tabor, Eliza   173, 376
– *Diary of a Novelist*   173, 386
tale   33, 40, 43, 128, 139–140, 154–155, 158–159, 172, 174–179, 181–182, 184–186, 189, 191–192, 195–196, 199, 201–202, 228, 283, 306, 320, 328, 334, 374
– *The Canterbury Tales* (Chaucer)   32
– cautionary tale   87, 186
– *An Editor's Tales* (Trollope)   139, 153–159, 172, 386
– fairy tale   226, 279, 308, 362–363
– frame tale   383
– *Jack of Spades: A Tale of Suspense* (Oates novel)   335
– *A Tale of Two Cities* (Dickens novel)   57
talent   25, 88, 90–93, 107, 131, 143, 147, 151, 153, 155, 157, 192, 198, 203, 215, 229, 237, 240, 250, 272, 336, 366
The Talented Mr Ripley (Highsmith novel)   333
taste   13, 119, 160, 167, 171, 204, 208, 214, 230, 234, 236, 248–250, 255, 265, 276, 302, 322, 380–381
Taylor, Charles   12
Taylor, Elizabeth   259, 262–265, 274, 392–393
– *Angel*   263–265, 393
– *A View of the Harbour*   262–264, 392
Taylor, Lucian (character in Machen's *The Hill of Dreams*)   199–203, 209
technique   64, 175, 178, 203, 244, 258, 287, 301–302, 307, 309, 316, 350, 354, 371, 382
– distancing technique   284, 286
– literary technique   41, 79, 314
– narrative technique   146, 175, 211, 275, 300

technology   47, 187–188, 222–223, 250, 301, 349–350
television *or* TV   285–286, 332, 338, 344, 365–366
– MTV   353
– reality television   353
Tempestuous Petticoat (Leighton memoir)   264
Tennyson, Alfred   272
tension   15, 24, 50, 72, 104, 109, 117–119, 131, 173, 182, 223, 246, 275
testimony   4, 10, 79, 347
text, *see also* hypotext, intertextuality, paratext, peritext, type *passim*
– co-text   355
– Frankentext   38
– literary text   2, 22, 46, 69, 72, 78–79,
– master text   33
– material text   64, 123
– narrative text   1, 4–5, 13, 42, 48, 51, 63, 115, 300, 378
– printed text   249, 326
– subtext   311
– textuality   11–12, 31, 46, 291, 377
– *The World, the Text, and the Critic* (Said book)   377
Thackeray, William Makepeace   38, 60, 68, 74, 85, 102–111, 113–115, 125, 137–140, 145, 154, 159, 199, 202, 214, 223, 246
– *The Adventures of Philip*   110
– "The Fashionable Authoress"   138, 385
– *The History of Pendennis*   74, 85, 102–110, 112, 118, 138–139, 163, 199, 202, 213–215, 222, 385
– *The Newcomes*   110
– *Vanity Fair*   115, 145
Thackeray Ritchie, Anne   142
– *Miss Angel*   142
theatre   25, 100, 358, 363
theory   8, 10–11, 17, 20, 23, 27, 37, 47, 72, 80, 83, 315, 333, 377, 383
– actor-network theory   21
– autotheory   355
– discourse theory   39
– genetic theory   207
– Hegelian theory   41
– literary theory   20, 50, 56, 72, 297, 378
– Marxist theory   41

– moral theory   114
– narrative theory   2, 4, 41, 51–53, 71
– optional-narrator theory   59
– political theory   266
– postcolonial theory   44
– poststructuralist theory
– psychoanalytic literary theory   19
– reader response theory   19, 65, 322, 377
– rhetorical theory   54
– social theory   113
– speech act theory   80
– structuralist theory   55
– systems theory   3, 21, 39
– *Theory of the Novel* (Lukács)   38
Thirkell, Angela   257, 390–393
Thompson, Hunter S.   70, 242
Those Barren Leaves (Huxley novel)   207, 216, 390
The Three Clerks (Trollope novel)   139
thriller, *see also* plot, trope, writer   10, 24, 331, 338
– authorship thriller   334–335, 381
– meta-thriller   338
– political thriller   345
– psychological thriller   333, 340, 344
– romance thriller   340, 379
Tillotson, Kathleen   53, 61
Tit-Bits (magazine)   166
title, *see also* page   3, 12, 23–24, 47, 49, 94–95, 101, 103, 142, 155, 162, 164, 178, 181, 188, 196, 198, 204, 209–210, 213, 216, 223, 230, 238, 247, 265, 269, 271, 274, 284, 287, 289, 292–293, 303, 308, 311–312, 315, 332, 334, 347, 349, 357, 361, 368, 370, 375, 377, 385
– subtitle   136, 214, 345
Titolo, Matthew   104
TLS (*Times Literary Supplement*)   74, 210, 237, 261
Tokarczuk, Olga   41–42, 61
token   51, 78, 266, 360
Tolkien, J. R. R.   283, 391–392
Tolstoy, Leo   67, 306, 312–313
The Tommyknockers (King novel)   319
Tom Singleton (Follett Synge novel)   334, 387
Tonio Kröger (Mann novel)   42, 389
topos   34, 94, 226

Torquato Tasso (Goethe play)   3
Torrance, Jack (character in King's *The Shining*)   319, 327
totality   116, 351
To the Lighthouse (Woolf novel)   116, 257
trade, *see also* publishing, union   11, 13, 15, 30, 46, 83, 100–102, 105–106, 154, 162, 164–165, 199, 225, 241, 275
– book trade   15, 25, 87
– *The Case of Authors by Profession or Trade, Stated* (Ralph pamphlet)   34
– slave trade   79
tragedy   122–123, 148, 158, 168, 230, 265, 368–369
– *The Tragedy of Arthur* (Phillips novel)   366–370, 400
transformation   2, 4, 6–7, 10, 15, 22, 34–35, 37, 50, 53, 77–78, 81, 85, 90, 109, 125, 134, 143, 157, 159, 170, 188, 204, 218, 221–223, 242, 255, 289, 306–307, 309, 311, 320, 329, 351, 357, 375, 406
Transit (Cusk novel)   370–371, 373–374, 401
Tree of Codes (Foer)   301, 368
The Tremor of Forgery (Highsmith novel)   328, 332–334, 394
Tressell, Robert   238
– *The Ragged Trousered Philanthropists*   238
trial   173, 203, 234, 299
– *Trials of the Human Heart* (Rowson novel)   129
Trilling, Lionel   209, 313
Trollope, Anthony   11, 13, 83, 101–102, 117, 127, 139–141, 145–146, 153–160, 166, 172, 179, 350, 380, 386
– "The Adventures of Fred Pickering"   154, 166, 386
– *Autobiography*   101, 139, 155, 158–159, 350
– *The Belton Estate*   179
– *An Editor's Tales*   139, 153–159, 172, 386
– *He Knew He Was Right*   139
– "Josephine de Montmorenci"   139, 156, 159
– *Lady Anna*   141
– "Mary Gresley"   139, 155–156
– "Mrs. Brumby"   139, 157, 159
– "The Panjandrum"   157, 159
– *Ralph the Heir*   141
– "The Spotted Dog"   158

– *The Three Clerks*   139
– "The Turkish Bath"   155, 159
– *The Way We Live Now*   139, 145, 386
trope   32, 78, 85, 116, 149, 198, 209–211, 238, 280, 301, 331, 350
– horror trope   320, 328
– thriller trope   345
Tropic of Cancer (Miller novel)   13, 241–243, 247, 253, 273, 390
Trotter, David   43, 188
Trouble at Willow Gables (Larkin novella)   128
Trout, Kilgore (Vonnegut character)   1
truth   28, 40, 63, 67, 70–71, 86, 110–111, 115–116, 131, 134, 148, 168, 185, 200–201, 205, 243, 280, 285, 287, 289–291, 295, 340–345, 347, 368–369, 372, 375, 382
– *The Truth about an Author* (Bennett autobiography)   198
Tunisia   333
"The Turkish Bath" (Trollope tale)   155, 159
The Turn of the Screw (James tale)   118, 177
Twain, Mark   354
Twitter   339
type, *see also* stereotype   22, 27–28, 41, 50–51, 53–54, 60, 68, 78, 102, 129, 137, 172, 217–218, 234, 237–238, 249, 259, 264–265, 281, 345, 360, 363, 371, 381
– ideal type   51
– personality type   19
– speech type   61, 115
– text type   211
Typee (Melville novel)   121
typeface   326
typescript   229, 326–328
typewriter *or* -writing   244, 246, 248, 256, 266, 269, 271, 273–274, 282–284, 315, 326–328, 333–334
– *The Type-Writer Girl* (Allen novel)   128, 388
– *Typewriter in the Sky* (Hubbard novel)   284, 391
typing   246, 248–249, 267, 273–274, 298
– Typing Ghost   285
typography   11, 162, 326, 370
typology   21, 30, 51, 60

Ulysses (Joyce novel)   58, 65, 116, 197, 211, 292
"Umney's Last Case" (King story)   319

The Undiscovered Country (Mitchell novel) 285–287, 394
The Unfortunates (Johnson novel) 285
union 173, 205, 218, 221, 292
– Literary Union 105
– trade union 219
US 70, 118, 241, 252, 300–301, 320, 323, 332–333, 344, 354, 365
unity 65–66, 190, 203, 290–291, 294
universalism 20, 131, 188, 294–295, 374
universality 67, 69, 293, 355–356, 365, 376
universe 43, 170, 215, 326, 334
university 215, 283, 295, 310, 334, 368
Unknown (magazine) 284
The Unnamable (Beckett novel) 241
unreliability, *see also* narrative, narration 38, 54, 118, 159, 176, 178, 290, 296, 344
Updike, John 338, 345, 394–395, 397
UR (King story) 319
The Uses of Literacy (Hoggart) 249
Utilitarianism (Mill) 147
utopia 137, 188, 215–216
– *Utopia* (More) 32
utterance 39, 61, 69, 165, 245

value, *see also* literature, system 1–2, 7, 13–14, 24–25, 28, 30, 45, 47, 51, 53, 59, 63, 76–77, 91–92, 99, 104, 110, 115, 117, 120, 127, 137, 150–151, 176, 182, 191, 202–203, 205, 213, 225, 236, 240, 242, 258–260, 263, 274, 276, 279, 285, 290, 298–299, 322, 324, 347–348, 358–360, 363, 369, 373–375, 381, 383, 406
– aesthetic value 30, 45, 104, 160, 381
– commercial value 47, 225, 276
– cultural value 45, 137, 153, 370, 374, 382
– economic value 30, 45, 360, 370, 347, 381
– literary value 149, 161, 165, 210, 328
– market value 90, 104, 271
– monetary *or* pecuniary value 142, 165
– symbolic value 276, 282, 331, 362
Vanity Fair (Thackeray novel) 115, 145
Variety (magazine) 226
Vawdrey, Clare (character in James's "The Private Life") 183
Venice 196
– *Death in Venice* (Mann novel) 196, 389

Verity (Hoover novel) 340–342, 345, 401
Verre, Roland (character in Phillips's *The Tragedy of Arthur*) 367
verse, *see also* novel 132–134, 186, 195, 199, 215
– alliterative verse 24
– blank verse 367
Viala, Alain 20
Victorian, *see also* age, Britain, compromise, literature 2–3, 11, 14, 44, 47, 56, 100–102, 105–108, 110–114, 127–129, 131, 133–135, 137, 140–141, 146–151, 153, 158–160, 167–168, 170–172, 184, 191, 195–196, 202, 234, 240, 248, 262–263, 265, 280, 321, 325, 380, 382, 385
Vidal, Gore 8
– *Myra Breckinridge* 286
view, *see* point of view
– *A View of the Harbour* (Taylor novel) 262–264, 392
Vile Bodies (Waugh novel) 43, 70, 207, 214, 216–217, 223, 248, 381, 390
Villanueva, Jane Gloriana 332
Vincent, Norah 8
– *Adeline* 8
violence 107, 111, 208, 283, 292, 322, 327, 344, 364
– *Stendhal: and Some Thoughts on Violence* (fictional book) 227
Virago Press 73
Virgil (Publius Virgilius Maro) 31–32, 145
– *The Death of Virgil* (Broch novel) 8, 391
virtue 70, 93, 102, 106, 146–147, 196, 312, 371
visibility, *see also* invisibility 10, 12, 22, 25, 43–44, 49, 70–71, 74, 119, 259, 284, 317, 324, 348, 366, 370, 376, 379
– hypervisibility 12, 50, 71, 349, 355
vocation 12, 132–136, 150, 154, 162, 198, 200, 222, 312, 315
voice 40, 42, 50, 55, 59–62, 69, 86, 91, 111, 115, 157, 162, 177, 185, 195, 217, 222–223, 247–249, 259, 268, 283, 285, 287, 291–292, 306, 339, 342, 348, 351
– authorial voice 62–63, 67, 262
– narrative voice 62–63, 116, 259, 271, 383
Vollmann, William T. 353

volume, *see also* novel   90, 108, 142, 155, 162, 164, 188, 195, 214, 244, 248, 252, 309, 340, 364, 370, 373
Vonnegut, Kurt   1, 394–395, 397

Wallace, David Foster   316
Walpole, Hugh   235
Walsh, Richard   59
war   41, 173, 191, 207–208, 217, 249, 251–252, 265, 272, 335, 362
– Civil War   325
– Cold War   70
– culture war   276
– First World War *or* Great War   41, 191, 207–208, 213, 229
– Second World War   41, 217, 229, 252, 255, 262, 264, 271, 286, 381
– Six-Day War   334
– Vietnam war   315
Ward, Mrs. Humphrey (Mary Augusta)   248
Warhol, Andy   381
"Waring" (Browning poem)   227
Warner, Sylvia Townsend   220
– *Lolly Willowes*   220
Wattpad   348–349
Watts, Jasper (character in Youmans's *Best Seller*)   224–225
Waugh, Evelyn   43, 207, 214, 216–218, 222–223, 228, 248, 261, 275, 283, 286, 381, 390–391, 393
– *Brideshead Revisited*   286
– *Scoop*   214, 217, 222, 391
– *Vile Bodies*   43, 70, 207, 214, 216–217, 223, 248, 381, 390
Waugh, Patricia   244, 249, 279–280, 284
The Way We Live Now (Trollope novel)   139, 145, 386
wealth   90, 99, 103, 105, 113–114, 135, 140, 144, 146, 150, 165–167, 195, 222, 322, 364, 371
Weber, Max   51, 248, 295, 381
website   25, 49, 339, 355
Weimann, Robert   28, 85, 196, 211, 275, 381
Wells, H. G.   164, 389
The Westminster Review   100, 136
Whalley, Thomas Sedgewick   128
– *The Fatal Kiss*   128

Wharton, Edith   139, 388
What Maisie Knew (James novel)   118
What's Become of Waring (Powell novel)   227–228
Whelpdale (character in Gissing's *New Grub Street*)   165–166, 168
Whipple, Edwin Percy   119–120
– *Lectures on Subjects Connected with Literature and Life*   120
Whistler, James Abbott McNeill   188
Whitehead, Colson   331
– *Zone One*   331
White-Jacket (Melville novel)   121
Whitman, Walt   350
Wide Sargasso Sea (Rhys novel)   341
Widdowson, Peter   144
Wieland (Brockden Brown novel)   38
Wilde, Oscar   43, 75, 173–174, 188, 202–203, 387
– *The Picture of Dorian Gray*   43, 174, 188, 191
Wild Swans (Chang novel)   350
Wilkes, Annie (character in King's *Misery*)   320–328
Williamson, Margaux   358–359
"William Wilson" (Poe story)   190
Willson, Andrew   104
Will You Please Be Quiet, Please? (Carver)   306, 394
The Windmill (magazine)   261
Winner Take Nothing (Hemingway)   24
"The Winners" (Kipling poem)   236
Winterson, Jeanette   301
– *The PowerBook*   301
"Wireless" (Kipling story)   186–187, 201, 220, 389
wisdom   9, 40, 42, 51, 75, 86, 96, 117, 131, 166
Wishes Limited (Darlington novel)   218–224, 227, 231, 389
Withermore, George (character in James's "The Real Right Thing")   182–183
witness, *see also* literature   1, 10, 44, 70–71, 79, 178, 222, 348, 356, 373, 376, 382
Wodehouse, P. G.   217, 222–223, 256, 389
– *The Little Nugget*   256, 389
– *Piccadilly Jim*   256, 389
Wolfe, Tom   70

woman, see also artist, author, character, novelist, poet, writer, writing   14, 67, 73–74, 93, 111, 127–141, 146–148, 155, 157, 163, 167, 171, 175, 179, 181, 184–186, 201–202, 209, 213–214, 224–225, 233, 237, 239, 242, 246–247, 249, 251–252, 255–262, 264–275, 279, 283, 302–305, 310, 312, 320–321, 327, 335, 344, 358, 375
- *The Clever Woman of the Family* (Yonge novel)   128, 386
- *Dream of Fair to Middling Women* (Beckett novel)   240–241, 390
- fallen woman   135
- *The French Lieutenant's Woman* (Fowles novel)   280
- "How to Be an Other Woman" (Moore story)   314
- *The Indian Woman* (Gardner novel)   265
- *The Madwoman in the Attic* (Gilbert and Gubar study)   131
- Married Women's Property Act   167
- New Woman   167, 171
- *The Story of a Modern Woman* (Dixon novel)   162, 388
- *Woman* (magazine)   128
- *The Woman in White* (Collins novel)   118
- "The Woman Novelist" (Gardner story)   265–267, 274, 392
- woman of letters   10, 13, 100, 129, 260
- woman question   133
- *Women and a New Society* (Luetkens study)   260
- *Women and Work* (Williams study)   260
- *Women's Two Roles* (Klein/Myrdal study)   260
Woolf, Virginia   43, 116, 157, 245, 257, 259, 390
- *Adeline: A Novel of Virginia Woolf* (Vincent novel)   8
- "Mr. Bennett and Mrs. Brown"   157
- *A Room of One's Own*   257, 266
- *To the Lighthouse*   116, 257
- *Who's Afraid of Virginia Woolf* (Albee play)   307
word   8, 38, 58, 60–61, 64, 66, 68–69, 76–77, 91–92, 110, 112–114, 122, 130, 138–139, 158, 161, 164–165, 171, 179, 183, 187, 200, 209, 216, 219–220, 237, 242–243, 246–249, 251, 262, 267, 271–272, 280, 288, 291–294, 296–297, 303–304, 308, 315, 328, 334, 336, 347, 352, 354, 359, 362, 367–369, 371–372
- foreword   288
- keyword   113, 122, 140
- *Lost for Words* (St Aubyn novel)   301
- password   205
- spoken word   328
- word processing *or* processor   47, 319, 324, 327
- "Word Processor of the Gods" (King story)   319
- "A Word to the Reader" (Bulwer)   102
Wordsworth, William   37, 106, 136, 272, 349, 385
- *The Prelude*   37, 106, 136, 385
- "Resolution and Independence"   272
work, see also class passim
- boundary work   49, 75, 113, 323, 347, 356, 379, 383–384
- brain-work   271
- gospel of work   111, 195
- *A Heartbreaking Work of Staggering Genius* (Eggers novel)   12, 350–356, 398
- *A Life's Work* (Cusk novel)   375
- office work   246–247
- overwork   163
- *Women and Work* (Williams study)   260
- work ethic   196
- work in progress   123, 139, 177
- work of art   176, 183, 358–359, 365
- work of fiction   2, 5, 8–9, 54, 66, 213, 345, 374, 379
- work of literature   27, 31, 38, 67, 78–79, 383
- work of writing   34, 124
workshop   29, 306, 341, 347
world, see also history, war   5, 7, 9, 15, 20, 22, 32–33, 38–39, 49, 55, 57, 62, 66–70, 73–75, 77–78, 80, 86–87, 89, 92–93, 95–96, 99–100, 107, 111–112, 115, 117–118, 123–124, 127, 139, 151, 154–155, 162–163, 165–169, 174, 185, 199–200, 204, 215–217, 227, 234, 239, 244, 248, 251, 257, 262, 264–266, 269, 279–280, 289, 291, 293–295, 297, 302–303, 307, 315, 317, 320, 321–322, 326, 329, 332, 344–345, 351, 356, 358, 365, 370, 374, 377, 381, 383

- actual *or* real world   22, 55, 57, 60, 66–67, 72–73, 76, 81, 262, 264, 306, 356, 379, 383–384
- *The Blazing World* (Cavendish novel)   32, 129
- book world   46, 170, 235, 257
- *Brave New World* (Huxley novel)   216
- capitalist world   85, 353
- counterworld   380
- *Down the Road, Worlds Away* (Khan collection)   73
- economic world   48, 159
- fictional world   39, 55, 60, 178, 263, 280, 283, 374
- "The Finest Story in the World" (Kipling story)   184, 186–187, 220, 387
- literary world *or* world of literature   13, 22, 32, 90, 105, 139, 170, 175, 233, 235, 246–247, 253, 258, 260, 265, 271, 303, 305–306, 324, 338
- modern world   96, 236–237, 265, 282, 292, 294–295, 299, 349, 363
- money-world   239
- narrated world   9, 85, 95, 115, 117
- possible world   8
- publishing world *or* world of publishing   15, 87, 100, 127, 161, 214, 218, 225, 227, 229, 234, 248, 250, 352, 370
- *The Real World* (MTV show)   353
- *Small World* (Lodge novel)   297
- social world   109, 117, 229, 307
- storyworld   4, 67, 117, 285
- underworld   294, 365
- worldedness   66
- worldliness   66, 107, 136, 263, 377, 383
- worldmaking   40, 280, 349
- *The World of Chance* (Howells novel)   161, 226, 387
- world of ideas   89
- world of writing   247
- *The World, the Text, and the Critic* (Said book)   377
- worldview   116, 125, 344, 373

"The Wreck of the *Deutschland*" (Hopkins poem)   272

Wright, Jane (character in Spark's *The Girls of Slender Means*)   271–274

writer, *see also* author, detective, protagonist, typewriter *passim*
- creative writer   326, 349
- female writer   128–129, 131, 250, 256, 258
- crime writer   256
- fiction writer   371
- fictional writer   184, 188, 332, 367
- ghost-writer   29, 335, 342–343, 345
- *The Ghost Writer* (film)   335
- *The Ghost Writer* (Roth novel)   309–314, 382, 395
- "How to Become a Writer" (Moore story)   314–316, 396
- male writer   196, 242, 261
- mystery writer   332
- newspaper writer   107
- novel writer   63, 248
- *On Becoming a Writer* (Brittain)
- professional writer   105, 114, 130, 145, 162
- romance writer   320, 332, 340
- singer-songwriter   45
- thriller writer   331
- travel writer   218, 227
- woman writer   14, 62, 73, 127, 129–130, 137–141, 147, 150, 157, 171, 245–246, 249, 255–259, 261–266, 268, 270, 273–276, 279, 360–361, 381
- writeress   138
- writer-narrator   48, 241, 308, 355
- *A Writer of Books* (Paston novel)   153, 161, 170–171, 388
- *Writers & Lovers* (King novel)   12, 172, 356, 360–362, 302
- writer's block   164, 298, 336–337
- writers' colony   357, 361, 363
- writers' conference   374

writing, *see also* act, handwriting, work, world *passim*
- autobiographical writing   131, 382
- autofictional writing   276
- automatic writing   187, 216, 220
- collaborative writing   322
- confessional writing   32, 72, 360
- creative writing   3, 22, 25–26, 36, 219, 246, 267, 306, 315, 338–339, 341, 347, 370, 373
- fiction writing   307
- fine writing   226, 233, 243

- hack writing   34
- imaginative writing   262
- life-writing   79
- literary writing   36, 45, 174, 196, 241, 250, 263, 266, 299, 343, 362
- 'manly' writing   275
- middlebrow writing   162, 255, 257, 276
- novel-writing   101–102, 140, 156, 199, 210, 239
- *On Writing* (King memoir)   321, 327
- rewriting   186–187, 377
- scene of writing   21
- self-rewriting   245
- self-unwriting   245, 253
- self-writing   53, 245, 253
- serial writing   327
- subsistence writing   162
- un-writing   377
- 'womanly' writing   275
- women's writing   247, 250, 256, 264
- writing machine   193, 242
- writing on the body   200
- *Writing the Reader* (Birke study)   2
- writing to the moment   337
Wulf, Anna (character in Lessing's *The Golden Notebook*)   258

Yanagihara, Hanya   348
The Year of Magical Thinking (Didion memoir)   355
"Yellow" (Beckett story)   240
The Yellow Book (magazine)   180, 188
Yonge, Charlotte   128, 386
- *The Clever Woman of the Family*   128, 386
Youmans, N. O. [Allen Clarke Marple]   210, 214, 224–226, 390
- *Best Seller*   210, 214, 224–226, 390
The Young Authoress (Hendriks novel)   130, 133, 257, 385
Youth (Coetzee 'autrebiography')   345, 398
Youth (Conrad novel)   42
Yule family (characters in Gissing's *New Grub Street*)   163, 167–170

zeitgeist   242, 260, 286
Zen   294
Zola, Émile   165–166, 168
Zone One (Whitehead novel)   331
Zuckerman, Nathan (character in Roth novels)   309–314, 395
Zuckerman Unbound (Roth novel)   312, 314, 395

www.ingramcontent.com/pod-product-compliance
Lightning Source LLC
Chambersburg PA
CBHW051533230426
43669CB00015B/2581